D1106276

THE ANNALS OF AMERICA

THE ANNALS OF AMERICA

Volume 19

1969 - 1973

Détente and Domestic Crisis

ENCYCLOPÆDIA BRITANNICA, INC.

Chicago London Toronto Geneva Sydney Tokyo Manila Johannesburg Seoul

Printed in the U.S.A.
Library of Congress Catalog Card Number: 76-547

The editors wish to express their gratitude for permission to reprint material from the following sources:

The American Medical Association for Selection 79. Reprinted by permission of the *Journal* of the American Medical Association.

The American Ordnance Association for Selection 13. Reprinted from the July-August 1969 issue of *Ordnance* magazine by permission of the Editors. Copyright © 1969, American Ordnance Association, Washington, D.C.

Atheneum Publishers for Selection 69. Adapted from *The Plundered Past* by Karl E. Meyer. Copyright © 1973 by Karl E. Meyer. Reprinted by permission of Atheneum Publishers. First appeared in *The New Yorker*.

Beacon Press for Selection 46. Copyright © 1972 by the Vietnam Veterans Against the War, Inc. Reprinted by permission of Beacon Press.

Business Week for Selection 85. Copyright © 1973 by *Business Week*.

Buttenheim Publishing Corporation for Selection 54. Reprinted from the September and October 1971 issues, *American City* magazine. Copyright © Buttenheim Publishing Corporation, 1971.

The Chicago Sun-Times for Selection 18. Reprinted with permission from the *Chicago Sun-Times*.

The Chicago Tribune for Selection 86. Reprinted courtesy of the *Chicago Tribune*.

Council on Foreign Affairs for Selection 84. Excerpted by permission from *Foreign Affairs*, October 1973. Copyright © by Council on Foreign Relations, Inc.

Cowles Communications, Inc. for Selection 52. Copyright © Cowles Communications, Inc. 1971.

Forbes Magazine for Selection 42. Reprinted by permission of *Forbes Magazine*.

Fred R. Harris for Selection 71. Copyright © 1973 by Fred R. Harris.

McClatchey Broadcasting, Sacramento, California, for Selection 9. Reprinted from "A Conversation with Chief Justice Earl Warren."

National Affairs, Inc., for Selection 49. *The Public Interest*, No. 25 (Fall 1971), pp. 14-21. Copyright © by National Affairs, Inc., 1971.

The National Catholic Educational Association for Selection 31. Reprinted by permission.

National Parks and Conservation Magazine for Selection 55. Also for Selection 57. Reprinted by permission from

PICTURE CREDITS

The photographs on pages 49 through 52 are from the National Aeronautics and Space Administration.

The photograph on page 225, bottom, is by Nick Lawrence.

All other photographs are from United Press International.

Contents

1970

1970 - 1973

1971

Introduction

Whether the period immediately after 1968 will be noted by future historians as a temporary aberration or a time of transition bearing the omens of permanent change cannot as yet be determined. But at least it is clear that for the first time in this century (not forgetting the Great Depression and the New Deal), the coming of a new administration to Washington inaugurated a really decisive, although gradual, shift in emphasis in nearly all phases of what is commonly termed "the American way of life." (See Selections 1, 2, and 3.)

The Nixon administration itself wrought many changes, and perhaps the most notable of these were the achievements in foreign policy carried out largely through the agency of Henry Kissinger. Carried into office by his promise to end the Vietnam War, President Nixon not only waged the war for four more years, but widened it considerably. But American participation was finally ended when a shaky truce was signed in January 1973. More spectacular and positive results were gained by the President in his overtures toward the People's Republic of China and the Soviet Union. Détente with the two large communist powers suggested the possible ending of the Cold War and a solution to international tensions. But while the United States drew closer to Russia and China, relations with Western Europe and Japan became strained. This breach was due primarily to two factors: economic competition and America's alleged "go-it-alone" attitude in conducting foreign policy. The Middle East proved perhaps the most difficult issue of all, for the October 1973 war left the Arab nations in a strong bargaining position, and their use of oil as an economic lever to attain political goals threatened to undermine the economies of Western Europe, Japan, and the United States. (See Selections 14, 16, 21, 22, 39, 61, 63, 66, 70, 75, and 84.)

Whatever the accomplishments of the Nixon-Kissinger foreign policy, they were overshadowed in the public mind by what seemed a series of unrelieved crises within the nation itself. Prominent during 1969 and 1970 was the antiwar protest, a carryover from the presidency of Lyndon Johnson. But even as the war continued and expanded, the intensity of the protest waned; and finally with the signing of the 1973 truce, it collapsed altogether. And not only did the protests subside, but the whole flamboyant youth movement of the 1960s disintegrated. The riots on the campuses ended, and college students gave at least the appearance of being no longer deeply concerned with society's ills. Or perhaps they simply turned inward to more immediate goals and pleasures. (See Selections 3, 4, 5, 6, 20, 33, 34, 46, 47, 52, and 63.)

In spite of the ongoing war, what bothered Americans the most in the early 1970s was the state of the economy. The rate of inflation, unparalled since the Korean War, continued to climb at a startling pace through the end of 1973. Federal attempts to halt the trend by imposing wage and price controls were of no avail. The only segment of society to benefit demonstrably from inflation was agriculture. Farmers received unprecedented prices for their products, and for the first time in living memory, agricultural surpluses disappeared. (See Selections 51 and 83.)

In 1973 the already inflation-ridden economy was burdened by another woe in the form of a fuel shortage, or, as it was popularly called, an "energy crisis." This situation, abetted by the Arab oil embargo, promoted further inflation and threatened an economic downturn in 1974. The promise of an end to the fuel shortage early in 1974 did not mean the crisis was past, for the factors that had brought it about persisted. And the demands by the Arab nations for huge price increases for oil exports assured a continuance of inflation. (See Selections 71, 72, 85, and 86.)

Not only did inflation increase the cost of every commodity, it also mitigated against solving the variety of domestic problems that had become so prominent during the previous decade: health care, housing, mass transportation, urban decay, education, jobs for minorities, technical and scientific research, the environment, and so on. Federal programs aimed at dealing with these problems were insufficiently funded or vetoed, often in an effort to stem the very inflation that worsened them. (See Selections 7, 17, 18, 19, 24, 26, 29, 31, 35, 36, 37, 41, 48, 49, and 50.)

The foremost crisis, of course, was that of government itself. The complex of events subsumed under the name Watergate did not much impinge on the public consciousness in 1972, an election year. But in 1973, the web of "White House horrors," as former Attorney General John Mitchell called them, began to unravel. As the trials, convictions, confessions, denials, and congressional investigations followed one upon another throughout the year, public confidence in the Nixon administration fell to an all-time low. But it was not only the administration that fell in esteem. Watergate became the occasion for the American people to manifest a great—and perhaps longstanding, though heretofore concealed—lack of confidence in the workings of the whole political system. What probably most depressed public confidence was the suspicion that the traditional problem-solving mechanisms of government were no longer operable. (See Selections 32, 40, 44, 45, 59, 60, 76, 77, 78, 81, 82, and 87.)

With the optimism of the past becoming restrained and dissatisfaction prominent, American society in the early 1970s became markedly more conservative. It was true that many of the liberal causes and activities of the previous decade persisted: civil rights, the "new morality," women's liberation, and varieties of social protest. But they had lost their early vigor, and a reaction set in against them on many fronts. Such a reaction was probably as inevitable as the "return to normalcy" after World War I. And the new decade, with its new crises and intensification of old problems, manifested little inclination to be innovative and radical. Probably nothing symbolized the new mood better than the "nostalgia craze," the wistful longing for more serene and less complicated times. (See Selections 6, 9, 23, 27, 28, 29, 30, 40, 44, 53, 54, 56, 67, 68, 73, 79, and 80.)

Chronology: 1969-1973

1969

Jan. 3. Congress convenes and the House votes to reseat New York Representative Adam Clayton Powell, Jr., though it strips him of seniority and levies a heavy fine.

Jan. 6. In an unprecedented action, a challenge is lodged against the vote of a North Carolina presidential elector during the formal congressional count of the electoral vote. The elector had been pledged to Nixon but has voted for Wallace. The challenge and its rejection mark the beginning of a debate on reform of the electoral system that continues through the year.

Jan. 7. Sirhan B. Sirhan, charged with the murder of Sen. Robert F. Kennedy, goes on trial in Los Angeles. **April 17.** He is found guilty and on May 21, despite a plea from Sen. Edward Kennedy, is sentenced to death. He remains in jail pending appeal.

Jan. 20. President Nixon is inaugurated amid heavy security precautions because of threats of disruption by various radical and antiwar groups.

January-February. Massive leakage from offshore oil-drilling installations near Santa Barbara, California, causes widespread property damage, water pollution, and wildlife destruction. Leaks recur throughout the year here and elsewhere, adding fuel to a growing debate on pollution and conservation.

Feb. 8. After 148 years the *Saturday Evening Post* publishes its last issue.

Feb. 24. Mariner 6 unmanned space probe is launched toward Mars equipped with television camera for close photographic study of the planet. An identical Mariner 7 is launched a month later. Each passes about 2,130 miles above Mars, Mariner 6 on July 31 and Mariner 7 on August 5, and together they transmit 198 pictures of the Martian surface. **May 15-16.** Soviet space probes Venera 5 and 6 reach Venus and enter its atmosphere. Before the instruments fail they report temperatures of about 800° F. and an extremely dense atmosphere of carbon dioxide.

March 10. James Earl Ray pleads guilty to the murder of Rev. Martin Luther King, Jr., and is sentenced to 99 years in prison.

March 13. Nuclear nonproliferation

treaty, designed to prevent the spread of nuclear weapons to nations other than those already possessing them, is ratified by the Senate.

March 20. Federal grand jury in Chicago indicts 8 persons for violating the anti-riot provision of the 1968 Civil Rights Bill, which prohibits crossing a state line with the intent to incite or participate in a riot. They are also charged with conspiring to violate the law. Charges stem from the disturbances at the Democratic National Convention in 1968. **Sept. 24.** The trial of the "Chicago 8" (later 7) begins and is marked throughout by noisy demonstrations inside and outside the courtroom.

March 28. Former President and General of the Army Dwight D. Eisenhower dies at Walter Reed Hospital in Washington, D.C. After a state funeral attended by high-ranking dignitaries from around the world, he is buried in his boyhood home, Abilene, Kansas.

April 3. Latest figures show that the American combat death toll in the Vietnam War has passed that of the Korean War. By the end of the year more than 40,000 American troops have died in South Vietnam since 1961.

April 4. Houston surgeons implant an artificial heart in a patient. It functions for three days, until replaced by a transplanted human heart.

April 16. Michigan legislature bans the sale of DDT. As public awareness of the dangers of unrestricted use of pesticides grows, several states follow suit. **Nov. 20.** Department of Agriculture announces a step-by-step phaseout that by 1971 would reduce DDT use by about 90 percent.

April 29. Congressional hearing discloses a $2.1 billion cost overrun on the C-5A jet transport being built for the Air Force by Lockheed Aircraft Corporation. Investigation soon widens to include many other defense projects with similar huge deficits.

May 4. *Life* magazine discloses financial transactions between Supreme Court Justice Abe Fortas and a financier recently convicted of violating securities laws. **May 15.** After widespread criticism Fortas resigns, the first justice to do so under fire.

May 10. U.S. and South Vietnamese forces launch ten-day assault on "Hamburger Hill" in the A Shau Valley. One of the bloodiest battles of the war, it draws heavy criticism at home, since the hill has little strategic value. **May 28.** U.S. forces abandon the hill.

May 21. President Nixon names District of Columbia Court of Appeals Judge Warren Burger as chief justice of the Supreme Court. He is confirmed by the Senate on June 9.

May-July. At the President's request New York Gov. Nelson Rockefeller undertakes a series of fact-finding tours of Central and South America. His visits are marked by violent anti-American demonstrations and harsh repressive measures in several countries.

June 2. Talks begin between the U.S. and Japan on the status of the Ryukyu Islands, including Okinawa, held by the U.S. since World War II. **Nov. 21.** President Nixon and Premier Sato announce jointly that the islands will be returned to Japan in 1972.

June 6. District of Columbia Court of Appeals rules illegal a 1967 order from Gen. Lewis B. Hershey, head of Selective Service, instructing local draft boards to reclassify antiwar and antidraft demonstrators. **June 14.** Hershey announces that he will not notify local boards of the ruling. **Oct. 10.** It is announced that Hershey will be replaced as head of Selective Service in 1970.

June 8. President Nixon announces the withdrawal of 25,000 troops from Vietnam, to be completed by August 31. Calling the move a first step, he promises further reductions if the other side scales down combat operations. Subsequent withdrawals are announced on September 16 (35,000) and December 15 (50,000).

June 14. Physicist at the University of Maryland reports detecting gravity waves, a phenomenon predicted by Einstein's general theory of relativity.

June 17. New York Mayor John V. Lindsay loses to conservative "law and order" candidate in Republican primary. **Nov. 4.** As the nominee of the Liberal Party and his own Independent Party, he wins reelection over the major party candidates.

July 1. The Army and the Air Force announce that Social Security numbers will replace the serial numbers used for identification since 1918. The Navy and the Marine Corps plan to follow suit in 1972.

July 8. Charles Evers, brother of slain civil rights worker Medgar Evers, becomes mayor of Fayette, Mississippi. He is the first Negro to be elected mayor of a biracial Mississippi city since Reconstruction.

July 11. The 1968 conviction of Dr. Benjamin Spock for conspiracy to counsel draft evasion is overturned by the Boston Court of Appeals. The conviction of one of his codefendants is also overturned, and the others are granted retrial.

July 20. Four days after liftoff from Cape Kennedy in the Apollo 11 spacecraft, astronaut Neil Armstrong becomes the first man to set foot on a celestial body. Near the lunar landing module *Eagle's* landing site on the moon's Mare Tranquilitatis, Armstrong and Edwin Aldrin set up scientific experiments and collect samples of moon material and then rejoin Michael Collins in the orbiting command ship. **July 24.** Apollo 11 splashes down in the Pacific 950 miles southwest of Hawaii. The astronauts are greeted by President Nixon aboard the carrier *Hornet* and begin an 18-day quarantine period to guard against the possibility of harmful microorganisms from the moon. **Nov. 14-24.** Apollo 12 astronauts successfully complete second lunar landing mission. The landing module *Intrepid* is piloted to the surface about 600 feet from the 1967 Surveyor 3 moon probe.

Aug. 6. After months of congressional and public debate the Senate narrowly votes down military appropriations bill amendments that would block construction of an antiballistic missile system requested by the President. Bill with ABM provision passes the Senate in September and the House in November.

Aug. 8. President Nixon proposes a reorganization of the nation's welfare system. His "family assistance system" would guarantee a minimum income of $1,600 yearly for a family of four and would provide employment and job-training incentives.

Aug. 15-17. Woodstock Music and Art Fair, a three-day rock concert, is held near Bethel, New York. An estimated 400,000 people attend and despite crowded conditions, lack of facilities, and heavy rains, there is no violence and only a small number of arrests, mostly for drug possession. Marijuana is so widespread that no attempt is made to stem its use.

Aug. 17. Dr. Philip Blaiberg of Capetown, South Africa, who has been the longest surviving of the more than 100 heart-transplant patients since 1967, dies after living more than 19 months with a donated heart.

Aug. 18. President Nixon names Clement Haynsworth to the Supreme Court. Opposition to the appointment grows steadily, first because of Haynsworth's record on civil rights and later because of his failure to disqualify himself in several cases heard by his Court of Appeals in which he had a financial interest. **Nov. 21.** The appointment is voted down by the Senate.

Sept. 3. Ho Chi Minh, president of North Vietnam, dies in Hanoi.

Sept. 10. State of Alaska receives bids totaling more than $900 million for leases to oil lands on its North Slope. **Sept. 14.** Oil tanker *S.S. Manhattan* completes Northwest Passage, becoming the first commercial ship to do so and proving the feasibility of using the route for transporting oil from the North Slope field to eastern Canada and U.S.

Sept. 16. Bikini atoll in the Pacific Ocean, site of 23 nuclear test explosions during 1946-1958, is declared safe for habitation by the Atomic Energy Commission.

Sept. 27. In a game marking the centennial of collegiate football Rutgers defeats Princeton 27-0. Rutgers had also won the 1869 game, 6 to 4.

Oct. 15. First National Moratorium Day observances draw large crowds to antiwar demonstrations across the country. Many Senators and congressmen participate and in Washington Mrs. Martin Luther King, Jr., leads 45,000 people in a march from the Washington Monument to the White House. **Nov. 15.** More than 250,000 people gather in Washington for the second Moratorium Day, eclipsing the figure for the 1963 March on Washington. In San Francisco the largest crowd in the city's history protests the Vietnam War, and similar demonstrations take place in most other cities. President Nixon pointedly ignores the day's activities, which despite official warnings, are relatively free of violence.

Oct. 16. New York Mets, perennially of the National League cellar, top an almost incredible late season pennant rush by winning the World Series in 5 games.

Oct. 18. Secretary of Health, Education, and Welfare Robert H. Finch orders the removal of cyclamate artificial sweeteners from the market by early 1970. Experimental evidence has linked cyclamates to cancer in animals. **Oct. 22.** Food and Drug Administration announces plans to review several other food additives, including the widely used monosodium glutamate, which has produced brain damage in experimental mice.

Oct. 29. Supreme Court rules unanimously that school segregation must end immediately, thus rejecting the 1955 "all deliberate speed" formula. The ruling follows months of controversy over the administrations's ambiguous position on enforcing desegregation in the South.

Nov. 13. Speaking in Des Moines, Iowa, Vice President Agnew delivers scathing attack on network television news coverage and commentary, calling it biased, provincial, and unrepresentative. **Nov. 20.** In Montgomery, Alabama, Agnew broadens his criticisms to include the press, particularly the *New York Times* and the *Washington Post.*

Nov. 16. Report is published charging a U.S. infantry unit with killing from 450 to 567 unarmed men, women, and children in the South Vietnamese village of Songmy in March 1968. A sergeant and a lieutenant face court-martial charges of assault and murder. Army investigation into the incident continues.

Nov. 17. Preliminary meetings for the strategic arms limitation talks (SALT) between the U.S. and U.S.S.R. open in Helsinki, Finland.

Nov. 20. Group of American Indians representing more than 20 tribes occupies and claims Alcatraz Island in San Francisco Bay. Former prison site has been abandoned by the government and the Indians demand title to it under an old Sioux treaty. They plan to erect an Indian cultural and educational center.

Nov. 25. President Nixon renounces use of bacteriological agents in warfare and orders the destruction of stocks of such weapons. First strike use of certain chemical agents is also renounced, though others, including tear gas and chemical defoliants widely used in Vietnam, are retained.

Nov. 26. Following passage by Congress of enabling legislation, President Nixon issues executive order establishing a lottery system for choosing men to be drafted into the armed forces. First lottery drawing since 1942 is held on December 1.

Dec. 17. Secretary of the Air Force announces the closing of "Project Bluebook," a 21-year investigation into unidentified flying objects. Study of more than 12,000 UFO sightings has revealed no evidence that they are "flying saucers" of extraterrestial origin, although a small number of the sightings remain unexplained.

During the year several traditionally all-male colleges, including Yale, Bowdoin, and Colgate, have begun admitting small numbers of women students.

Census Bureau estimates the population of the country at the end of the year to be 204,334,344.

1970

Jan. 1. President Nixon signs National Environmental Policy Act, establishing three-member advisory council on environmental quality.

Jan. 5. Public schools in Mississippi are integrated under watchful eye of federal marshalls and Justice Department deputies. Many white parents picket the schools, while others enroll their children in newly chartered private schools. **Jan. 13.** Tax-exemption privileges for segregated private schools in Mississippi are ordered stopped by Supreme Court. **Jan. 14.** Supreme Court orders desegregation deadline of February 1, 1970, for public schools in Alabama, Florida, Georgia, Louisiana, Mississippi, and Texas.

Jan. 6. As part of a plan to control narcotics traffic, Nixon administration announces agreement with France to halt heroin production at Marseilles. Negotiations begin with Turkey to curb cultivation of opium poppy.

Jan. 18. Attorney General John Mitchell announces federal grants of $236 million to states and cities under the Law Enforcement Assistance Administration to combat crime.

Jan. 19. President Nixon nominates G. Harold Carswell to Supreme Court. **April 8.** Nomination is defeated by Senate in 51 to 45 vote, making Carswell second Southern judge in a row to be refused confirmation.

Feb. 25. Supreme Court rules that its one-man, one-vote rule must apply in elections for local officials.

March 1. Voluntary ratings for movies are changed by the Motion Picture Association of America. The new classifications are "G" for general patronage, "GP" for parental guidance recommended, "R" for restricted to young people accompanied by an adult, and "X" for adults (over 17 years) only. In 1972 "GP," which has proved confusing, is changed to "PG."

March 10. Senate passes bill banning cigaret advertising on radio and television after January 1, 1971.

March 31. Supreme Court rules that juvenile defendants have same rights as adults to be judged innocent unless guilt is proved beyond a reasonable doubt.

April 2. Governor Francis Sargent of Massachusetts signs bill providing that servicemen from that state can refuse to engage in armed hostilities in absence of a declaration of war by Congress.

April 13. Reduction of oxygen supply and power on Apollo 13 space craft forces cancellation of planned moon landing. Space ship returns to earth on April 17.

April 14. President Nixon nominates Judge Harry A. Blackmun of Minnesota to be an associate justice of the Supreme Court. **May 12.** Senate confirms Blackmun's nomination.

April 22. Rallies are held in all parts of the nation in observance of Earth Day, to focus on environmental problems.

April 30. In televised address to the nation, President Nixon announces U. S. invasion of Cambodia to clear out North Vietnamese sanctuaries. In subsequent days there are massive antiwar protests, particularly on college campuses. Most notable disturbance takes place May 4 at Kent State University in Ohio, where four students are killed and 11 wounded by National Guardsmen firing M-1 rifles. **May 9.** Antiwar protest brings nearly 100,000 demonstrators to Washington, D. C. Student strikes and protests continue throughout nation.

May 8. Seven Black Panthers who have been indicted for their part in a December 1969 shootout with Chicago police are freed when all criminal charges against them are dropped. Two Panther officials, Fred Hampton and Mark Clark, had been killed in the police raid on Black Panther apartment. **Aug. 24, 1971.** Illinois States Attorney Edward V. Hanrahan and 13 other law enforcement officers are indicted on charges of conspiring to obstruct justice in connection with the raid. **Nov. 1.** Charges are dropped after judge rules that prosecution has failed to prove conspiracy to conceal evidence.

May 10. Walter P. Reuther, president of United Auto Workers, is killed in crash of private plane near Pellston, Michigan.

May 14. Two black youths are shot and killed by police at Jackson State College in Mississippi.

May 19-23. Ten thousand persons take part in 110-mile "march against repression" from Perry, Georgia, to Atlanta. March is sponsored by Southern Christian Leadership Conference and NAACP.

May 23. Permission is granted to International Telephone and Telegraph by insurance commissioners of Connecticut to acquire Hartford Insurance Company, in largest corporate merger in U. S. history.

June 1. New York University scientists announce they have produced in a laboratory the first man-made part of the human cell structure, the lysosome.

June 16. Kenneth Gibson defeats Hugh Addonizio in run-off election to become first black mayor of Newark, New Jersey.

June 29. All U. S. ground troops are withdrawn from Cambodia. **June 30.** Senate approves Cooper-Church amendment to limit U. S. military involvement in Cambodia. **July 9.** House rejects this curb on presidential authority.

June-July. Series of terrorist bombings takes place at several locations in the U. S. **July 23.** Thirteen members of Weathermen faction of Students for a Democratic Society are indicted in Detroit on charges of conspiracy to commit bombings on a nationwide scale.

July 29. President Nixon signs Washington, D. C. Crime Control Act, containing such controversial provisions as authority for "no-knock" searches; pre-trial detention; and broadened use of wiretapping by police.

Aug. 12. President Nixon signs Postal Reform Bill establishing U. S. postal system as independent government agency.

Aug. 24. Massachusetts Governor Francis Sargent signs nation's first no-fault auto insurance law.

Aug. 26. Thousands of women in several cities take part in rallies to demonstrate for "Women's Strike for Equality," in first such nationwide protest since the suffrage movement.

Sept. 3. Vince Lombardi, one of America's most successful football coaches, dies of cancer in Washington, D. C.

Sept. 26. Report of President's Commission on Campus Unrest is released. Focusing on responsibility for shootings at Kent State and Jackson State, its findings are criticized by administration.

Sept. 28. Egyptian leader Gamal Abdel Nasser dies suddenly following an Arab summit conference which has settled at least temporarily a series of Middle East crises between Jordan, Syria, and the Arab commandos. Concurrently, President Nixon is touring the Mediterranean to demonstrate U. S. concern with problems of the region.

Sept. 30. Report of President's Commission on Obscenity and Pornography is released amidst controversy over its findings that urge a repeal of all bans on the sale of pornographic materials to consenting adults on basis that exposure to such material is not a source of misconduct. President Nixon calls findings "morally bankrupt."

Oct. 8-27. Nobel Prizes are awarded to Julius Axelrod of the National Institute of Mental Health for physiology and to Paul Samuelson of the Massachusetts Institute of Technology for economics. Agronomist Norman Borlaug wins Nobel Peace Prize.

Oct. 10-24. United Nations celebrates its 25th anniversary in a protracted commemorative session.

Oct. 16. Grand jury at Ravenna, Ohio, indicts 25 persons on charges stemming from shootings at Kent State University on May 4. Those indicted are faculty members, students, former students, and one nonstudent. No National Guardsmen are indicted.

Nov. 3. Midterm elections, following a bitter campaign, produce mixed results. Democrats gain 11 governorships and keep control of Congress.

Nov. 14. Southern Airways DC-9 jet crashes, killing 75 persons, including all 44 members of Marshall University football team and their coaches.

Nov. 25. Secretary of the Interior Walter Hickel is dismissed from the Cabinet. Originally opposed by conservationists, during his tenure he has made many proconservation decisions. Firing is believed to be linked with outspoken letter of protest he had written to President Nixon following shootings at Kent State University.

Dec. 3. Senate votes to kill funds for controversial Boeing Supersonic Transport jet plane, a project strongly opposed by environmentalists.

1970 census shows U. S. population of 204,765,770, of which 73.5 percent live in places of 2500 or more. For first time suburban population is greater than urban or rural. Western and southern states have grown fastest; population shifts to these states make necessary reapportionment of House of Representive seats in 14 states. California has become most populous state, and now has 43 seats to New York's 39. Claims of undercounts are made, especially by minority groups. Census Bureau announces in 1973 that more than five million persons were not counted in 1970.

1970 - 1971

March 13, 1970. Senate passes bill extending Voting Rights Act, with an amendment lowering voting age to 18. Latter provision is upheld by Supreme Court, but is to apply only to federal elections. Resultant confusion compels Congress to pass, on March 21, 1971, the 26th Amendment, qualifying 18-year-olds to vote in all elections. Within two months and seven days the amendment is ratified by the states.

Nov. 12, 1970. Trial of Lt. William L. Calley, Jr., charged with slaying South Vietnamese civilians at My Lai, begins. He is found guilty on March 28, 1971, and is sentenced to life imprisonment. Following public outcry over sentence, it is reduced to 20 years. Many Americans consider Calley a scapegoat for a crime in which many others participated.

1970 - 1972

Aug. 7, 1970. California Superior Court Judge Harold J. Haley and three of his kidnappers are killed when police block commandeered van outside Marin County City Hall of Justice in San Rafael. Kidnappers are San Quentin convicts. **August 15.** Charges are filed against black activist Angela Davis for supplying guns used in shootout. Having gone into hiding, Miss Davis is not apprehended until October 13. In trial ending June 4, 1972, she is acquitted by all white jury.

1970 - 1973

January 5, 1970. Joseph Yablonski, his wife, and a daughter are found murdered in Clarksville, Pennsylvania. On December 9, 1969, Yablonski had lost a bitterly contested election for presidency of United Mine Workers to W. A. "Tony" Boyle. Three men are eventually indicted and convicted of the crime, and in September 1973 Boyle himself is arrested in connection with case. Boyle had resigned his post on December 19, 1972, after being sentenced to five-year prison term for misusing union funds and after also having been decisively defeated in new election supervised by Department of Labor.

1971

Jan. 15. William Ruckelshaus, administrator of the Environmental Protection Agency, promises to issue cancellation notices for all uses of DDT.

Jan. 18. Senator George S. McGovern of South Dakota opens his campaign for 1972 Democratic presidential nomination.

Jan. 18. George C. Wallace is inaugurated as governor of Alabama for second time. He announces that he will run for presidency of the U. S. in 1972 "if it becomes necessary."

Jan. 22. President Nixon's State of the Union message outlines federal revenue sharing proposals, announces proposed reduction in number of cabinet departments, and calls for "New American Revolution" to turn power back to the people.

Jan. 25. Supreme Court rules that Civil Rights Act of 1964 forbids different hiring policies for men and women.

Jan. 26. Charles Manson and three other defendants are found guilty of first degree murder in killing of actress Sharon Tate and three other persons. Verdict ends the longest trial in California history. **March 29.** Jury recommends death penalty.

Feb. 5. Two astronauts, Alan Shepard and Edgar Mitchell, land lunar module on the moon from Apollo 14 space craft. They are third U. S. team to walk on the moon.

Feb. 8. South Vietnamese troops, with U. S. air, artillery, and logistical support, invade Laos to attack North Vietnamese supply lines.

Feb. 19. Democratic National Committee approves reform plan for the selection of delegates to 1972 national convention to ensure greater participation by women, minorities, and youth.

March 2. Supreme Court rules that poor people should not be jailed prior to trial solely because they cannot afford to pay fines.

March 8. Joe Frazier wins 15-round decision over Muhammad Ali to become undisputed heavyweight boxing champion.

March 15. U. S. discontinues ban on travel to People's Republic of China. **April 14.** President Nixon relaxes 20-year trade embargo with China. Announcement coincides with visit to China of U. S. table tennis team accompanied by American newsmen.

April 7. New York City opens nation's first legalized, off-track betting system.

April 19-24. Hundreds of thousands of persons stage antiwar protests in Washington, D. C., and San Francisco, sponsored by Vietnam Veterans Against the War. **April 23.** As part of protest, 700 veterens throw away their medals and ribbons in front of the Capitol.

April 20. Supreme Court rules that busing to dismantle segregated dual school system is constitutional.

April 28. Captain Samuel L. Gravely, Jr. is nominated to the rank of rear admiral. He is first black to become an admiral in history of U. S. Navy.

May 1. Amtrak, new passenger rail service operated by a quasi-governmental agency, begins service. The 182-train rail system links more than 300 cities. This represents a cut in passenger service of about 50 percent from previous private operations.

May 3-5. More than 7000 persons are detained by police in mass arrests of antiwar protesters and innocent bystanders at Washington, D. C.

June 11. A 19-month occupation of Alcatraz Island ends when federal marshalls remove 15 American Indians from former prison site in San Francisco Bay.

June 13. *New York Times* begins publication of Pentagon Papers, a collection of documents and articles derived from a study made during administration of President Lyndon Johnson concerning U. S. involvement in Vietnam. **June 15.** Justice Department obtains a temporary court order barring further publication, on the basis that papers are classified defense material. This is said to be first instance of prior restraint on the press in U. S. history. Publication of papers is continued by other newspapers, and President Nixon offers the complete text of 47 volumes to Congress. **June 30.** Supreme Court upholds newspapers in their right to publish material. **July 1.** *Times* and *Washington Post* resume publication of documents.

July 15. President Nixon announces he will visit People's Republic of China early in 1972. Visit has been arranged during Henry Kissinger's secret trip to Peking, July 9-11, to meet with Chou En-Lai.

July 31 - Aug. 2. Two U. S. astronauts, David Scott and James Irvin, drive 460 pound electric car on the moon as part of Apollo 15 mission.

Aug. 2. U.S. announces it will support entry of People's Republic of China into United Nations. Administration affirms resistance to any move to deprive Nationalist China (Taiwan) of its U. N. seat, but when PRC is admitted on October 25, Taiwan is expelled.

Aug. 2. Legislation providing $250-million loan guarantee to Lockheed Aircraft Corporation to prevent bankruptcy is passed by Congress and sent to President for signature.

Aug. 15. President Nixon announces 90-day freeze on wages, prices, and rents, in first of several phases of inflation control that, by end of 1973, produce mixed results in stabilizing the economy. Convertibility of dollar into gold is also ended, thus freeing dollar for devaluation against other world currencies.

Aug. 23. Sixteen months of negotiations end with U.S., Britain, France, and Soviet Union reaching accord on Berlin that guarantees unimpeded access of all parties to the city.

Sept. 4. Alaska Airlines 727 jet crashes into mountain in Tongass National Forest west of Juneau, killing all 111 passengers, in worst single air disaster in U. S. aviation history.

Sept. 13. Fifteen hundred state troopers, prison guards, and sheriff's deputies stage assault at Attica Correctional Facility in New York, to put down inmate rebellion and obtain release of hostages. Forty-one persons, including 31 prisoners and nine guards and civilian workers, are killed in assault. Attica incident is described as most serious prison uprising in the nation both in its extent and its outcome.

Sept. 16. *Look* magazine, founded in 1937 by Gardner Cowles, announces it will suspend publication with October 19 issue.

Sept. 17. Associate Justice Hugo Black, 34-year veteran of Supreme Court, resigns for reasons of health. He dies eight days later after suffering a stroke. **Sept. 23.** Associate Justice John Marshall Harlan resigns from Supreme Court because of ill health. He dies on December 29. To fill two vacancies, President Nixon appoints Lewis F. Powell, Jr., of Virginia and Assistant U.S. Attorney General William H. Rehnquist. Both appointments are confirmed by Senate in December.

Sept. 26. President Nixon meets Emperor Hirohito of Japan in Anchorage, Alaska, during latter's stopover on flight to Europe.

Oct. 3. Tennis champion Billie Jean King becomes first woman athlete to earn more than $100,000 in a year.

Oct. 14 - Nov. 2. Nobel Prizes are awarded to Earl W. Sutherland of Vanderbilt University, for physiology and to Simon Kuznets of Harvard University for economics.

Nov. 2. Frank L. Rizzo, former police commissioner of Philadelphia, is elected mayor of city on tough "law and order" platform.

Nov. 13. U. S. interplanetary probe Mariner 9 goes into orbit around Mars, having traveled 247 million miles since its launching on May 30.

Dec. 3. War breaks out between India and Pakistan as Indian troops invade East Pakistan to aid Bengali rebels. War ends on December 16 with India and Bengali secessionists victorious. Bengalis proclaim founding of new state of Bangladesh. During conflict U. S. and China side with Pakistan, while Soviet Union supports India. Although feigning neutrality, both U. S. and U.S.S.R. have naval forces in the vicinity.

Dec. 4. General Motors announces recall of 6,682,000 cars and trucks to secure their V-8 engines against mount breakage, in largest vehicle recall in history of auto industry.

Dec. 6. Mrs. Romana Banuelos is confirmed by Senate as Treasurer of the U. S. She is first Mexican-American to be appointed to such a high position in federal government.

Dec. 17 - 18. Finance ministers and central bank governors of Group 10 industrial nations announce agreement on currency realignment, including 8.57 percent devaluation of the dollar.

Dec. 18. Rev. Jesse Jackson announces in Chicago the formation of new black organization to work for political and economic development, named People United to Save Humanity (PUSH).

Dec. 18. President Nixon signs Alaska Native Land Settlement Act, granting total of $962.5 million, 40 million acres of land, and mineral rights to the Indians and Eskimos of Alaska. Secretary of the Interior is authorized to designate 80 million acres for conservation and recreational purposes. Act also sets aside 800-mile corridor from Prudhoe Bay south to Valdez for proposed oil pipeline.

1971 - 1972

Aug. 24, 1971. Illinois State's Attorney Edward V. Hanrahan and 13 other law enforcement officers are indicted in Chicago on charges of conspiring to obstruct justice in connection with a police raid on a Black Panther apartment on December 4, 1969. Two Panther officials, Fred Hampton and Mark Clark, were killed in the raid. The trial takes place in the autumn of 1972; at its close on November 1, the charges against the defendants are dropped after the judge rules that the prosecution has failed to prove a conspiracy to conceal evidence.

1971 - 1973

June 2, 1971. Juan V. Corona is arraigned at Yuba City, California, on charges of murdering 24 persons. **Jan. 28, 1973.** He is found guilty and sentenced to 25 life terms in prison.

Aug. 16, 1971. Dr. Daniel Ellsberg, who has originally released Pentagon Papers to newspapers, pleads not guilty to charges of illegal use of classified documents. After first trial is declared mistrial in December 1972, a second begins in January 1973. By late spring case is heavily involved with Watergate scandal when White House authorized burglary of Ellsberg's psychiatrist's office is revealed. It is also learned that trial judge William M. Byrne has, during trial, been offered the post of FBI director by presidential domestic affairs advisor John Erlichman. **May 11.** Judge Byrne dismisses all charges against Ellsberg and codefendant Anthony Russo and rules out any retrial on the charges.

Sept. 21, 1971. Senate gives final approval to bill to end military conscription effective June 1973. **Jan. 27, 1973.** Secretary of Defense Melvin Laird announces that draft is ending six months early.

1972

January. *Washington Post* columnist Jack Anderson publishes secret Nixon administration papers dealing with the formulation of policy on the India-Pakistan crisis of 1971. The papers show the administration to have sided secretly with Pakistan in its losing effort to quell the Bengali rebellion. Anderson's ostensible purpose in publishing the material is announced as forcing a showdown with the government over its system of classifying documents.

January. Edmund S. Muskie, Hubert H. Humphrey, George C. Wallace, Shirley Chisholm, Vance Hartke, and Henry M. Jackson, all Democrats, announce their intention of seeking the 1972 presidential nomination of their party. George S. McGovern, John V. Lindsay, and Eugene McCarthy have previously announced similar intentions.

Feb. 1. Federal Aviation Administration orders all scheduled airlines to begin screening passengers and baggage to prevent hijackings and sabotage.

Feb. 3 - 13. Winter Olympics are held at Sapporo, Japan, the first time the games have been held in Asia. The Soviet Union leads in the final standings with 8 gold, 5 silver, and 3 bronze medals. The U. S. ranks fifth with 3 gold, 2 silver, and 3 bronze medals.

Feb. 11. McGraw-Hill publishers and *Life* magazine both concede that Clifford Irving biography of millionaire Howard Hughes is a fraud and cancel plans for publication. Swiss government has already issued warrants for arrest of Irving and his wife, Edith, on charges of fraud, after a $650,000 check from McGraw-Hill intended for Hughes was cashed by Mrs. Irving, using an alias. Mrs. Irving is tried, convicted, and serves a short U.S. prison sentence in addition to a $10,000 fine before being extradicted to Switzerland to face additional charges. Irving is also convicted on fraud charges and sentenced to two and one-half years in prison.

Feb. 15. John Mitchell resigns post as Attorney General to head President Nixon's re-election campaign. Richard Kleindienst is named to succeed him at Justice Department.

Feb. 18. California Supreme Court rules that death penalty is unconstitutional.

Feb. 21 - 28. President Nixon, other administration officials, and newsmen visit People's Republic of China. Nixon meets with Chairman Mao Tse-tung and Premier Chou En-lai to discuss problems between the two nations. Joint communique issued at Shanghai on eve of Nixon's departure indicates agreement on need for further contacts and suggests eventual withdrawal of U. S. troops from Taiwan.

Feb. 29. *Washington Post* columnist Jack Anderson discloses International Telephone and Telegraph Company memo composed by chief ITT lobbyist Dita Beard linking settlement of a federal antitrust action against company to a $400,000 contribution to the Republican National Committee for the 1972 convention at San Diego. Events unfolding from this news lead Republicans to transfer convention to Miami Beach.

March 2. The 570-pound unmanned space ship, Pioneer 10, is launched from Cape Kennedy to make a planetary probe of Jupiter. It is scheduled to arrive in vicinity of the planet in December 1973.

March 6. Death toll reaches 107 in a flood that began February 26 in Lofan County, West Virginia, when a makeshift dam made of coal mine wastes gave way.

March 7. Senator Edmund S. Muskie wins New Hampshire primary election, with Senator George S. McGovern a close second. President Nixon defeats his Republican opposition, Representatives Paul N. McCloskey and John M. Ashbrook, easily.

March 10 - 12. About 3300 delegates and 5000 observers attend first National Black Political Convention, held at Gary, Indiana.

March 17. President Nixon sends message to Congress urging passage of bill to deny courts power to order busing of school children to achieve integration. Issue plays important role in 1972 political campaigns.

March 20 - 22. Jack Anderson of *Washington Post* makes public series of memos showing effort by International Telephone and Telegraph Company to influence U. S. policy toward Chile. Purpose is to undermine government of Marxist President Salvador Allende. **Sept. 11, 1973.** Allende is overthrown by military coup and is killed or commits suicide.

March 21. Supreme Court strikes down lengthy residency requirements for voting in state and local elections, ruling that 30 days is ample time for new arrivals to register and vote.

March 22. Senate approves Equal Rights Amendment and sends it to states for ratification.

April 2. Charlie Chaplin, veteran movie comedian, returns to U. S. after absence of 20 years to appear at Academy Awards presentation.

April 13. First major league baseball players' strike, lasting 13 days, ends as agreement is reached on issue of the players' pension fund. Strike causes delay in opening of season.

April 16. Two giant pandas, gifts from People's Republic of China to the U. S., arrive at Washington Zoo.

April 20. Longest confirmation hearings in Senate history come to an end. At issue has been nomination of Richard Kleindienst to be Attorney General. He is confirmed, but most of testimony has centered around ITT antitrust settlement and $400,000 contribution to Republican National Committee from ITT.

April 24. Supreme Court rules that federal courts have common-law powers to curb environmental pollution, in absence of statutory law.

April 27. Senator Edmund Muskie withdraws from presidential primary race after finishing fifth in a field of six Democratic candidates in Pennsylvania primary.

May 2. J. Edgar Hoover, first and only director of FBI since 1924, dies in Washington, D. C., at age of 77.

May 8. President Nixon announces that he has ordered mining of Haiphong and other North Vietnamese harbors. Air war is also intensified.

May 15. While campaigning at Laurel, Maryland, Governor George C. Wallace is shot and seriously wounded in assassination attempt by one Arthur Bremer of Milwaukee. Hospitalized and left paralyzed from the waist down, Wallace is forced to withdraw from 1972 presidential race.

May 22. Supreme Court rules that juries need not return unanimous verdicts to convict defendants in state criminal court cases.

May 22 - 29. President Nixon visits Soviet Union and holds talks with Premier Kosygin and party leader Leonid Brezhnev. On May 26 they sign Strategic Arms Limitation Treaty, and President delivers nationally televised address to the Russian people.

June 10. Flash flood devastates much of Rapid City, South Dakota, leaving 226 dead and millions of dollars in property damage.

June 12. Air Force General John D. Lavelle acknowledges that in March he has been relieved of his command and demoted for ordering unauthorized bombing missions over North Vietnam between November 1971 and March 1972.

June 17. With its 3225th performance, the musical *Fiddler on the Roof* becomes longest running Broadway production, surpassing old record held by *Life With Father* since 1947.

June 17. Five men are arrested at 2 A.M. in headquarters of Democratic National Committee in Watergate office complex in Washington, D. C. Those held by police are Bernard Barker, James W. McCord, Frank Sturgis, Eugenio R. Martinez, and Virgilio R. Gonzales. Out of this thwarted bugging and burglary attempt will grow most complex and far-reaching political scandal in American history. (See "Watergate Chronology.")

June 29. Supreme Court, in a five to four decision, rules that death penalty as usually enforced in U. S. is a violation of the 8th Amendment. In another ruling court asserts that newsmen have no right to refuse to testify before grand juries about information they obtain in confidence.

June. Hurricane Agnes sweeps from Gulf of Mexico into Eastern seaboard states, causing severe flooding, extensive loss of life, and enormous property damage. Greatest destruction is in Pennsylvania, but New York, Maryland, Virginia, and Florida are also very hard hit.

July 1. John Mitchell resigns as President Nixon's campaign manager and is replaced by former Minnesota congressman Clark MacGregor.

July 8. President Nixon announces that U. S. and Soviet Union have concluded three-year agreement for sale of more than 400 million bushels of American wheat, corn, and other grain.

July 10 - 13. Democratic Party holds its national convention in Miami Beach. George McGovern wins presidential nomination, with Senator Thomas Eagleton of Missouri as his running mate. By early August disclosures that Eagleton has several times been hospitalized for mental depression force his resignation from ticket. He is replaced on August 8 by R. Sargent Shriver.

July 14. Jean M. Westwood is selected as national chairman of Democratic Party. She is first woman to head a major political party.

Aug. 21 - 23. Republican National Convention at Miami Beach nominates Richard Nixon for President and Spiro Agnew for Vice-President.

Aug. 27 - Sept. 11. Summer Olympics are held at Munich, Germany. Soviet Union dominates games, winning 50 gold, 27 silver, and 22 bronze medals; U.S. is second with 33 gold, 30 silver, and 31 bronze medals. Most notable individual winner is American swimmer Mark Spitz, who wins seven gold medals in striking comeback from his performance at Mexico City's Olympics in 1968. Games are brutally interrupted on September 5, when 17 persons, including 11 members of Israeli team, are shot to death by Arab militants claiming to be members of guerilla organization called "Black September." **Sept. 8.** Israeli jet bombers carry out reprisal attacks against Arab bases in Syria and Lebanon.

Sept. 1. Bobby Fischer becomes world chess champion by defeating Boris Spassky of Soviet Union in contest at Reykjavik, Iceland.

Oct. 12 - 26. Nobel Prizes are awarded to John Bardeen of University of Illinois, Leon Cooper of Brown University, and John R. Schreiffer of University of Pennsylvania for physics; to Christian B. Anfinsen of the National Institute of Arthritis, Metabolism and Digestive Diseases and to Stanford Moore and William H. Stein of Rockefeller University, for chemistry; to Gerald M. Edelman of Rockefeller University, for medicine; and to Kenneth Arrow of Harvard University, for economics.

Nov. 7. President Nixon wins election over George S. McGovern in greatest Democratic defeat in U.S. history, carrying 49 states; McGovern wins only Massachusetts and District of Columbia. Electoral vote is 521 to 17; popular vote 47,165,000 to 29,168,000. Democrats gain two seats in Senate, retain majority in House of Representatives, and gain one governorship, making count 31 Democratic governors to 19 Republican.

Nov. 16. The Rev. Theodore M. Hesburgh, president of Notre Dame University, is asked by President Nixon to resign his position as chairman of the National Commission on Civil Rights.

Dec. 7 - 19. Apollo moon program is brought to successful completion with flight of Apollo 17. Astronauts Eugene Cernan and Harrison Schmitt accomplish three-day exploration of lunar surface.

Dec. 9. *Life* magazine, founded by Henry Luce in 1936, announces it will cease publication with December 29 issue.

Dec. 18. Massive bombing of North Vietnam is resumed following breakdown in Paris peace negotiations. Raids are halted on December 30.

Dec. 26. Former President Harry S. Truman dies in Kansas City, Missouri, at age of 88.

1973

Jan. 11. President Nixon ends mandatory wage and price controls, thus beginning Phase 3 of his efforts to combat inflation. Standards imposed under Phase 2 are to be self-administered.

Jan. 22. Former President Lyndon B.

Johnson dies at his ranch in Johnson City, Texas, at age of 64.

Jan. 22. Supreme Court rules that a state may not prevent a woman from having an abortion during first six months of pregnancy.

Jan. 27. Cease-fire agreement to end war in Vietnam is signed in Paris. Agreement, worked out by Henry Kissenger and Le Duc Tho, has already been initialed by them on January 23 and announced to nation in a televised address by President Nixon the same evening. **Jan. 28.** Cease-fire goes into effect.

Jan. 27. University of California at Los Angeles basketball team, under coach John Wooden, breaks intercollegiate record for consecutive wins by defeating Notre Dame University 82 to 63. UCLA goes on to win its seventh consecutive NCAA championship on March 26, in team's 75th consecutive victory.

Jan. 29. President Nixon submtis $269 billion budget for fiscal 1974, with increase in defense spending and cutbacks in domestic program. Some 112 programs, especially anti-poverty efforts, are to be reduced or abolished.

Feb. 2. Among 30 new cardinals nominated by Pope Paul VI are three Americans, Archbishop Humberto Medeiros of Boston, Archbishop Timothy Manning of Los Angeles, and Archbishop Luis Aponte Martinez of San Juan, Puerto Rico.

Feb. 5. Nixon administration reports to Congress that impoundment of allocated funds for domestic programs totals $8.7 billion. In controversy over impoundment that continues for several months, administration wins most of the cases that are taken to court to get funds released.

Feb. 12. Release of U.S., Viet Cong, and North and South Vietnamese prisoners of war begins. All prisoners are to be released within 60 days of January 27 truce agreement.

Feb. 12. Secretary of the Treasury George Schultz announces a 10 percent devaluation of the dollar. This is second devaluation in 14 months. Move, while lowering value of dollar in relation to foreign currencies, improves U.S. balance of trade, helping to eliminate huge deficits that have occurred during first Nixon administration. 1972 deficit had been $6.9 billion, while by late 1973 there is substantial trade surplus.

Feb. 15. U.S. and Cuba sign agreement to curb hijacking of aircraft and ocean-going vessels between the two countries. Agreement does not signal a thaw in U.S.-Cuba relationships, however.

Feb. 18. *New York Times* reveals that 2500 year old Greek vase acquired by Metropolitan Museum of Art in New York has been stolen and smuggled out of Italy. **May 7.** Italian authorities charge seven men with illegal excavation and felony in connection with theft. This occurrence is but one in a rash of reports about smuggled art objects and looted archaeological sites.

Feb. 19. Federal Judge Otto Kerner is convicted of 17 counts of conspiracy, fraud, perjury, bribery, and income tax evasion in connection with purchase and sale of race track stock during his terms as governor of Illinois.

Feb. 21. Government of Laos and Pathet Lao rebels sign agreement to end 20-year war in Laos and establish coalition government. U.S. officials immediately seek release of prisoners of war.

Feb. 27. Two hundred members of American Indian Movement seize village of Wounded Knee, South Dakota. After many weeks of intermittent hostilities, negotiation, charges, and counter charges involving various Indian factions, Bureau of Indian Affairs, FBI, and U.S. military, settlement is reached on May 5. Occupation ends three days later.

March 4. Supreme Court rules that school districts can finance their schools through local property taxes, in spite of disparities in relative affluence of different districts.

March 27. Highlight of Academy Award presentations is giving of the best actor award to Marlon Brando for his part in *The Godfather*. In Brando's absence actress Sacheen Littlefeather announces Brando's refusal of the award and reads his prepared speech denouncing treatment of American Indians by filmmakers and by public at large.

April 1 - 7. Nationwide housewives' meat boycott protests rise in meat prices. At end of boycott prices remain at previous levels despite 50 to 80 percent sales drop during week.

April 2. Equity Funding Corporation of America, a leader in insurance and mutual funds, is accused of engaging in largest fraud in U.S. history involving tens of thousands of false insurance policies, forged bonds, and nonexistent assets. **April 5.** Equity files a bankruptcy petition.

April 5. Nomination of L. Patrick Gray III to become permanent director of FBI is withdrawn at his request because of his involvement in Watergate scandal.

April 23. Henry Kissinger gives address entitled "The Year of Europe" to Associated Press luncheon. Speech proposes new relationship between U.S. and Western Europe, including promulgation of new "Atlantic Charter."

April 30. In nationally televised address on Watergate affair, President Nixon announces resignations of his two chief advisors, H. R. Haldeman and John D. Erlichman, as well as of John Dean, White House lawyer, and Attorney General Richard Kleindienst. President says he accepts responsibility for Watergate affair but has not been personally involved in espionage or coverup.

May 14. Skylab I is launched to stay in orbit for 28 days to produce information on man's ability to live in space under weightless conditions. Because of damage done to Skylab, plus three other delays totalling eleven days, three-man crew for orbiting laboratory is not launched in their Apollo space ship to rendezvous with Skylab until May 25. Docking takes place on May 26, and crew makes what repairs are possible and begins its experiments on 28th. **July 28.** Second Skylab crew is launched for 59-day stay orbiting in space and successfully completes its mission in September.

May 23. Elliot L. Richardson is confirmed by Senate as Attorney General, based on assurances he has given of a full investigation of Watergate affair. He has named Harvard Law School professor, Archibald Cox, to be an independent special prosecutor within Justice Department.

May 29. Thomas Bradley defeats Sam Yorty to become first black mayor of Los Angeles, California.

June 7. Clarence M. Kelley, police chief of Kansas City, Missouri, is named director of the F.B.I. He is confirmed on June 27th.

June 8. U.S.S.R. and two U.S. companies sign preliminary agreement on a 25-year $10 billion project to bring natural gas from Siberia to western U.S.

June 9. Secretariat becomes first horse to win Triple Crown (Kentucky Derby, Preakness, and Belmont Stakes) since Citation in 1948.

June 13. President Nixon announces 60-day price freeze in preparation for Phase 4 of his inflation control plan. Phase 3 has been almost totally unsuccessful in stemming rise in prices.

June 16. Soviet Communist Party leader Leonid I. Brezhnev arrives in U.S. for talks with President Nixon. On June 22 he addresses American businessmen, calling for increased Soviet-U.S. trade; and on June 24 he makes nationally televised speech to American people.

June 21. Supreme Court redefines obscenity by giving new series of guidelines to enable states to ban works offensive to local standards, thus reversing a 15-year trend of relaxing controls on pornography.

June 29. President Nixon and Congress agree to end all U.S. military operations in Cambodia on August 15, unless Congress approves an extension. This compromise is reached after much opposition is voiced to administration's bombing in Cambodia during the year.

July 3. *International Wheat Journal* announces that 1973-74 demand for wheat will exceed supply, largely because of increased demands of India, West Africa, Bangladesh, Pakistan, and U.S.S.R.

July 16. Senate Armed Services Committee begins to investigate charges that Air Force has been secretly bombing Cambodia since 1969, a year before U.S. invasion of that country, and that reports of bombing have been falsified for "political reasons." A Pentagon spokesman confirms that raids have been carried out since March 1969 under orders from President Nixon and Secretary of Defense Melvin Laird.

July 18. Phase 4 economic controls are announced by President Nixon. Price controls under new system will be selective, rather than comprehensive. Price freeze announced June 13 will end on August 12.

Aug. 3. Attorney General Elliot Richardson announces that Justice Department is reopening investigation into May 1970 Kent State University shootings.

Aug. 3. Trial of the "Gainesville 8," charged with conspiring to disrupt 1972 Republican Convention, begins in Florida. Seven defendants are members of Vietnam Veterans Against the War. All are acquitted on August 31.

Aug. 6. Vice-President Agnew announces that he is under investigation by federal grand jury in Maryland for possible violations of the law in connection with alleged kickbacks from contractors and architects during his term as governor. Investigation and promulgation of criminal charges by Justice Department lead to Agnew's resignation on October 10. He also pleads "no contest" in a federal court to charges of tax evasion. He is fined $10,000 and sentenced to three years probation. **October 12.** President Nixon nominates House Minority leader Gerald Ford of Michigan, to be the new Vice-President.

Aug. 7. In Houston, Texas, killing of Dean Allan Corll, allegedly by teenager Elmer Wayne Henley, leads to discovery of one of largest mass-murder incidents in American history. Henley and another teenager admit cooperating with Corll in homosexual-torture slayings of at least 27 boys. In subsequent days many of the bodies are found buried in vicinity of Houston.

Aug. 22. President Nixon announces the resignation of William P. Rogers as Secretary of State and nominates Henry A. Kissinger to replace him.

Sept. 5. Congress passes and President Nixon signs bill eliminating TV "blackouts" of professional football home games, provided the game is sold out.

Sept. 20. Tennis champion Billie Jean King decisively defeats Bobby Riggs at Houston's Astrodome in $100,000, winner-take-all match that is touted as symbolic contest between woman's liberation and male chauvinism.

Sept. 29. Atlanta Braves right fielder, Hank Aaron, hits his 713th home run, leaving him one home run short of Babe Ruth's record.

Oct. 6. War breaks out in Middle East as Syria and Egypt attack Israel in Golan Heights area and in Sinai desert, respectively. **Oct. 25.** U.S. puts its military forces world-wide on standby alert citing concern that Soviet Union may unilaterally send troops to enforce a cease-fire, and incidentally to save Egyptian 3rd Army which has been trapped by Israelis at Suez City. Soviets relent, and the next day a cease-fire goes into effect.

Oct. 16. Maynard Jackson wins runoff election in Atlanta, Georgia, to become first black mayor of a major southern city.

Oct. 16 - 23. Secretary of State Henry A. Kissinger and Le Duc Tho of North Vietnam are awarded Nobel Prize for peace for achieving Vietnam truce in January. Tho subsequently refuses to accept award because fighting still goes on in Indochina. Other Americans winning Nobel Prizes are Professor Wasily Leontief, director of Harvard University's Economic Research Center, for economics, and Dr. Ivar Giaever of the General Electric Company, for physics.

Oct. 20. President Nixon dismisses special Watergate prosecutor, Archibald Cox; Elliot Richardson resigns as Attorney General; and deputy Attorney General William Ruckelshaus is fired for refusing to fire Cox. (See Watergate Chronology) **Nov. 1.** President Nixon appoints Senator William B. Saxbe of Ohio to be Attorney General and former president of the American Bar Association Leon Jaworski of Texas to be special prosecutor.

Oct. 28. Supreme Court Justice William O. Douglas attains longest tenure in the history of the court, 34 years and 196 days.

Nov. 7. Both houses of Congress vote to override presidential veto of 1973 war powers act limiting the authority of the President to commit American forces to foreign conflicts.

Nov. 12-13. Congress approves bill authorizing construction of Alaskan oil pipeline.

Nov. 13. The U.S. and six European nations agree to end March 1968 "two-tier" gold pact, thus allowing gold to find its own price level on the open market.

Nov. 16. Skylab 3 astronauts are launched at Cape Canaveral for 84-day mission aboard the orbiting Skylab space station.

Nov. 25. In a nationally televised address, President Nixon announces a series of orders to offset expected fuel shortage. These include: a 15 percent cut in gasoline delivered to service stations; closing of service stations on Sundays: allocation of heating oil; cutback of jet fuel supplies for air transport; reduced outdoor lighting; and a proposed 50-mile-per-hour speed limit. The measures are to be voluntary until followed up by congressional action.

Dec. 4. William E. Simon, deputy secretary of the treasury, is appointed by President Nixon to be nation's new "energy czar."

Dec. 11. Governor Nelson A. Rockefeller of New York resigns his office. He is succeeded by Lt. Governor Malcolm Wilson.

Dec. 16. O. J. Simpson, Buffalo Bills halfback, becomes first football player to rush for more than 2000 yards in one season.

Dec. 21. Peace conference between Israel and the Arab states opens at Geneva, Switzerland. U.S. Secretary of State Henry Kissinger has provided much of the impetus to arrange talks.

Dec. 23. Persian Gulf oil-producing nations, at meeting in Teheran, announce they will double price per barrel of oil effective January 1, 1974.

Dec. 28. U.S. dollar reaches its highest level on world money markets since February. This renewed confidence in the dollar owes much to European fears of recession because of oil boycott.

A Watergate Chronology

1972

June 17. James W. McCord, Bernard Barker, Frank Sturgis, Virgilio R. Gonzalez, and Eugenio R. Martinez are arrested during a break-in at Democratic National Headquarters in Watergate office complex in Washington, D. C.

June 19. McCord is fired as chief security officer of Committee to Re-elect the President (CRP).

June 28. G. Gordon Liddy is discharged from his job as lawyer for crp because he refuses to answer FBI questions about break-in.

July 1. John N. Mitchell resigns as President Nixon's campaign manager.

July 14. Hugh W. Sloan resigns as treasurer of CRP.

Aug. 28. Attorney General Richard Kleindienst promises thorough investigation of the case.

Aug. 29. President Nixon announces that no one in the administration is involved in the affair.

Aug. 31. News stories tie G. Gordon Liddy and E. Howard Hunt to the break-in.

Sept. 2. John N. Mitchell denies any knowledge of bugging of Democratic National Headquarters.

Sept. 11. Bernard Barker admits his role in the break-in.

Sept. 13. Report of House Banking and Currency Committee states that Maurice Stans, former Secretary of Commerce, has approved a transfer of $100,000 in campaign funds through Mexico City to conceal identity of donors.

Sept. 15. The five men arrested in the break-in, plus Liddy and Hunt, are indicted by a federal grand jury on charges of political espionage.

Oct. 5. News reports allege that former FBI agent Alfred C. Baldwin III has delivered records of eavesdropping on Democrats to CRP prior to June 17.

Oct. 10. News articles report massive political sabotage and espionage directed by White House officials, including Donald H. Segretti and Ken W. Clauson.

Oct. 15. News reports suggest that Segretti was hired by White House aides Dwight Chapin, and Gordon Strachan and that he was paid by Herbert Kalmbach, the President's lawyer.

Oct. 22. Justice Department reveals that Jeb Stuart Magruder of CRP authorized funds for bugging Democratic headquarters.

Oct. 25. H. R. Haldeman, President's chief advisor, is revealed as one official who approved payment for political espionage from campaign funds.

Oct. 29. News stories state that Dwight Chapin admits having hired Segretti.

Nov. 7. Nixon-Agnew ticket re-elected in landslide.

1973

Jan. 8. Trial of seven Watergate defendants begins.

Jan. 11. E. Howard Hunt pleads guilty to his part in break-in.

Jan. 11. Senator Sam Ervin, Jr., Democrat of North Carolina, agrees to head a Senate investigation of Watergate.

Jan. 15. Bernard Barker, Frank Sturgis, Eugenio Martinez, and Virgilio Gonzalez plead guilty to Watergate break-in.

Jan. 30. G. Gordon Liddy and James McCord are convicted of all charges against them.

Feb. 7. Senate votes to set up a committee to investigate Watergate affair and campaign practices.

March 23. Federal Judge John J. Sirica reveals that letter from James McCord charges that others were involved in Watergate, there had been perjury at the trial, and defendants had been pressured to plead guilty. G. Gordon Liddy is sentenced to 6 to 20 years in prison.

March 25. McCord, in testimony before Senate committee counsel, is reported to have said White House lawyer John Dean and Jeb Stuart Magruder both knew of bugging of Democratic headquarters.

April 17. President Nixon announces that there are major new developments in Watergate case and says new White House investigation is under way.

April 19. Attorney General Kleindienst removes himself from investigation because of his close relationship with persons involved. Dean announces he will not be a scapegoat in the case.

April 20. John Mitchell tells reporters of attending a meeting where wiretapping was discussed but says he did not approve plans.

April 23. White House denies that President Nixon knew about bugging in advance.

April 26. Magruder resigns as Assistant Secretary of Commerce. Acting FBI director L. Patrick Gray is reported to have burned documents taken from E. Howard Hunt's White House safe at request of John Dean.

April 27. Gray resigns as acting director of FBI. In Los Angeles Judge William Byrne in Pentagon papers case reveals that Liddy and Hunt had burglarized office of Daniel Ellsberg's psychiatrist.

April 30. In televised address to the nation President Nixon announces resignations of Attorney General Kleindienst, White House officials H. R. Haldeman and John Erlichman, and firing of John Dean.

May 2. Judge Byrne discloses that, during Pentagon papers case, he has been offered directorship of FBI by presidential aide John Erlichman. *New York Times* reports there is evidence that White House and members of the re-election committee conspired to cover up any federal investigation of Watergate. Justice Department files criminal charge against CRP for failing to report $200,000 campaign contribution from Robert L. Vesco while latter was under investigation by Securities and Exchange Commission for looting $224 million from mutual funds.

May 4. Donald Segretti is indicted by Florida grand jury on charges of illegal campaign practices.

May 7. Attorney General-designate Elliot Richardson promises to name a new federal prosecutor to investigate Watergate affair.

May 9. James McCord reports that he was pressured to blame Watergate break-in on Central Intelligence Agency. CIA Director James Schlesinger admits that agency was insufficiently cautious in providing materials for Watergate conspirators. Egil Krogh resigns as undersecretary of transportation, having admitted involvement in planning burglary at Daniel Ellsberg's psychiatrist's office.

May 10. Former Attorney General Mitchell and former Secretary of Commerce Stans are indicted for perjury and obstruction of justice by a federal grand jury in New York.

May 14. U. S. District Court in Washington takes possession of papers John Dean says he removed from his White House office before his resignation.

May 17. Senate committee hearings on Watergate begin.

May 18. Elliot Richardson says he will appoint Harvard Law School professor Archibald Cox special prosecutor for Watergate case. James McCord testifies he was offered executive clemency by a former White House aide.

May 22. President Nixon releases statement conceding that some of his aides had concealed aspects of Watergate affair for national security reasons.

May 23. Elliot Richardson is confirmed by Senate as Attorney General.

May 29. President Nixon says he will not offer either oral or written testimony to the Senate committee or to a federal grand jury.

June 4. White House report acknowledges that President Nixon conferred with John Dean several times earlier in the year on Watergate investigation.

June 5. Senate committee turns down request by Archibald Cox to postpone its public hearings until federal case is resolved.

June 14. Jeb Stuart Magruder testifies that he, John Mitchell, and other campaign and White House officials authorized wiretapping of Democratic National Headquarters. He also alleges that

White House aides fabricated coverup to protect President's re-election chances.

June 20. Re-election finance committee is found guilty on three counts of concealing $200,000 cash contributions from Robert Vesco.

June 25-29. John W. Dean III testifies before Senate Watergate committee, directly implicating President in coverup. On June 27 he reveals the existence of a White House "enemies list."

July 7. President Nixon officially notifies Senate committee that he will not testify or give committee access to his papers.

July 10-12. John Mitchell testifies that he withheld information on Watergate from President Nixon.

July 16. Former Presidential aide Alexander P. Butterfield, in testimony before the Senate committee, reveals that conversations in the President's offices have been taped since 1971.

July 23. President Nixon rejects Senate committee request for White House tapes. He also denies them to Special Prosecutor Cox. Committee issues subpoenas.

July 24-27. John Erlichman testifies before Senate committee, denying substance of John Dean's testimony.

July 30-Aug. 1. H. R. Haldeman testifies before Senate committee, denying Dean's testimony and revealing that he has recently listened to tapes of meetings involving Dean.

Aug. 1. Senate committee makes public 1972 memo by former White House special counsel Charles Colson warning that President Nixon would be linked to controversial settlement of ITT antitrust suit.

Aug. 7. Senate committee hearings recess until September 17.

Aug. 9. Senate committee files suit to obtain Watergate tapes.

Aug. 15. President Nixon, in televised speech, urges nation to put Watergate behind it.

Aug. 22. President Nixon holds first press conference in five months and answers questions on Watergate.

Aug. 29. Judge John Sirica orders President Nixon to surrender tapes to him for private examination and evaluation.

Aug. 30. President announces that he will appeal Judge Sirica's ruling.

Sept. 4. Four former Nixon aides, John Erlichman, Egil Krogh, Jr., David R. Young, and G. Gordon Liddy are indicted in Los Angeles on charges growing out of burglary of office of Daniel Ellsberg's psychiatrist.

Sept. 19. Former White House special counsel Charles Colson invokes Fifth Amendment in refusing to answer questions before Senate committee.

Sept. 24-25. E. Howard Hunt testifies before Senate committee on his involvement in political espionage and sabotage.

Oct. 13. U. S. Court of Appeals, in 5 to 2 ruling, holds that President Nixon must turn over tapes to Judge Sirica.

Oct. 20. President Nixon dismisses Special Prosecutor Archibald Cox and assistant Attorney General William Ruckelshaus. Attorney General Elliot Richardson immediately resigns.

Oct. 23. Several resolutions of impeachment are introduced in House of Representatives. In surprise move, President complies with Judge Sirica's order and agrees to turn over tapes.

Oct. 26. In nationally televised press conference on Middle East crisis, President Nixon attacks press and television for "outrageous, vicious, distorted, . . . frantic, hysterical reporting."

Oct. 31. White House reveals that two of nine tapes to be turned over to Judge Sirica were never made.

Nov. 1. President Nixon appoints Senator William Saxbe of Ohio to be Attorney General. Former president of American Bar Association Leon Jaworski is appointed to be new special prosecutor.

Nov. 9-16. President Nixon undertakes series of meeting with Republican members of Congress to counteract decline in public confidence in his leadership.

Nov. 9. Six of the seven original Watergate defendants are given final prison sentences by Judge Sirica.

Nov. 17-20. President Nixon makes round of personal appearances in the South to counter effect of Watergate.

Nov. 21. President Nixon's secretary, Rose Mary Woods, states in testimony before Judge Sirica that she accidentally erased 18-minute portion of June 20, 1972, tape containing conversation between the President and aide H. R. Haldeman.

Dec. 8. President Nixon discloses data on his personal finances, including income tax returns for 1969-1972. They show that he paid total of $1,670 in taxes for years 1970-1971 on total income of more than $400,000.

1969

1.

Epilogue: The Legacy of 1968

"There comes a time when an honorable man simply has to raise the flag," remarked Senator Eugene McCarthy to Allard Lowenstein when the latter asked him to run against President Johnson in the 1968 primaries. Thus 1968 became McCarthy's year, although in the end the victory would go to Richard Nixon. The months between the March New Hampshire primary and the November election were filled with domestic turbulence: Lyndon Johnson withdrew from the presidential race; Martin Luther King, Jr., was assassinated, whereupon racial violence broke out in many cities; Robert F. Kennedy was assassinated; and, as if to culminate the violence, the Democratic Convention in Chicago was demolished by the confrontation between police and protesters. The overriding issues of the year were the Vietnam war and the mounting protest against it. Senator McCarthy, particularly after Kennedy's death, epitomized the issue of protest. But when the Democratic regulars selected a politically "safe" candidate, Hubert H. Humphrey, the dissidents throughout America had nowhere to turn. They were faced with a three-way contest featuring Republican Nixon, independent George C. Wallace, and Vice-President Humphrey. Nixon won the election by the smallest margin of any President since Woodrow Wilson in 1912. His accession to the presidency was to mark a decisive turning point in American politics, although it was not immediately evident; and because the war did not end in his first term, the politics of protest, mounted so vehemently in 1968, persisted with waning influence until 1971. The following two selections depict two of the main currents that would linger on for the next few years: the antiwar feeling and the division within the country over the war and other social problems. The first selection is a portion of the conclusions of the Walker Report, Rights in Conflict, *issued by the National Commission on the Causes and Prevention of Violence in December, 1968. The second is taken from Nixon's victory statement following the November 5 election.*

Sources: *Rights in Conflict:* A Report Submitted by Daniel Walker, Director of the Chicago Study Team, to the National Commission on the Causes and Prevention of Violence, New York, 1968, pp. 1–11.

New York Times, November 7, 1968.

I. THE WALKER REPORT

During the week of the Democratic National Convention, the Chicago police were the targets of mounting provocation by both word and act. It took the form of obscene epithets, and of rocks, sticks, bathroom tiles and even human feces hurled at police by demonstrators. Some of these acts had been planned; others were spontaneous or were themselves provoked by police action. Furthermore, the police had been put on edge by widely published threats of attempts to disrupt both the city and the Convention.

That was the nature of the provocation. The nature of the response was unrestrained and indiscriminate police violence on many occasions, particularly at night.

That violence was made all the more shocking by the fact that it was often inflicted upon persons who had broken no law, disobeyed no order, made no threat. These included peaceful demonstrators, onlookers, and large numbers of residents who were simply passing through, or happened to live in, the areas where confrontations were occurring.

Newsmen and photographers were singled out for assault, and their equipment deliberately damaged. Fundamental police training was ignored; and officers, when on the scene, were often unable to control their men. As one police officer put it: "What happened didn't have anything to do with police work."

The violence reached its culmination on Wednesday night.

A report prepared by an inspector from the Los Angeles Police Department, present as an official observer, while generally praising the police restraint he had observed in the parks during the week, said this about the events that night:

> There is no question but that many officers acted without restraint and exerted force beyond that necessary under the circumstances. The leadership at the point of conflict did little to prevent such conduct and the direct control of officers by first line supervisors was virtually non-existent.

He is referring to the police-crowd confrontation in front of the Conrad Hilton Hotel. Most Americans know about it, having seen the 17-minute sequence played and replayed on their television screens.

But most Americans do not know that the confrontation was followed by even more brutal incidents in the Loop side streets. Or that it had been preceded by comparable instances of indiscriminate police attacks on the North Side a few nights earlier when demonstrators were cleared from Lincoln Park and pushed into the streets and alleys of Old Town.

How did it start? With the emergence long before convention week of three factors which figured significantly in the outbreak of violence. These were: threats to the city; the city's response; and the conditioning of Chicago police to expect that violence against demonstrators, as against rioters, would be condoned by city officials.

The threats to the city were varied. Provocative and inflammatory statements, made in connection with activities planned for convention week, were published and widely disseminated. There were also intelligence reports from informants.

Some of this information was absurd, like the reported plan to contaminate the city's water supply with LSD. But some were serious; and both were strengthened by the authorities' lack of any mechanism for distinguishing one from the other.

The second factor—the city's response—matched, in numbers and logistics at least, the demonstrators' threats.

The city, fearful that the "leaders" would not be able to control their followers, attempted to discourage an inundation of demonstrators by not granting permits for marches and rallies and by making it quite clear that the "law" would be enforced.

Government—federal, state and local—moved to defend itself from the threats, both imaginary and real. The preparations were detailed and far ranging: from stationing firemen at each alarm box within a six block radius of the Amphitheatre to staging U.S. Army armored personnel carriers in Soldier Field under Secret Service control. Six thousand Regular Army troops in full field gear, equipped with rifles, flame throwers, and bazookas were airlifted to Chicago on Monday, August 26. About 6,000 Illinois National Guard troops had already been activated to assist the 12,000 member Chicago Police Force.

Of course, the Secret Service could never afford to ignore threats of assassination of Presidential candidates. Neither could the city, against the background of riots in 1967 and 1968, ignore the ever-present threat of ghetto riots, possibly sparked by large numbers of demonstrators, during convention week.

The third factor emerged in the city's position regarding the riots following the death of Dr. Martin Luther King and the April 27th peace march to the Civic Center in Chicago.

The police were generally credited with restraint in handling the first riots—but Mayor Daley rebuked the Superintendent of Police. While it was later modified, his widely disseminated "shoot to kill arsonists and shoot to maim looters" order undoubtedly had an effect.

The effect on police became apparent several weeks later, when they attacked demonstrators, bystanders and media representatives at a Civic Center peace march. There were published criticisms—but the city's response was to ignore the police violence.

That was the background. On August 18, 1968, the advance contingent of demonstrators arrived in Chicago and established their base, as planned, in Lincoln Park on the city's Near North Side. Throughout the week, they were joined by others—some from the Chicago area, some from states as far away as New York and California. On the weekend before the convention began, there were about 2,000 demonstrators in Lincoln Park; the crowd grew to about 10,000 by Wednesday.

There were, of course, the hippies—the long hair and love beads, the calculated unwashedness, the flagrant banners, the open lovemaking and disdain for the constraints of conventional society. In dramatic effect, both visual and vocal, these dominated a crowd whose members actually differed widely in physical appearance, in motivation, in political affiliation, in philosophy. The crowd included Yippies come to "do their thing," youngsters working for a political candidate, professional people with dissenting political views, anarchists and determined revolutionaries, motorcycle gangs, black activists, young thugs, police and Secret Service undercover agents. There were demonstrators waving the Viet Cong flag and the red flag of revolution and there were the simply curious who came to watch and, in many cases, became willing or unwilling participants.

To characterize the crowd, then, as entirely hippy-Yippie, entirely "New Left," entirely anarchist, or entirely youthful political dissenters is both wrong and dangerous. The stereotyping that did occur helps to explain the emotional reaction of both police and public during and after the violence that occurred.

Despite the presence of some revolutionaries, the vast majority of the demonstrators were intent on expressing by peaceful means their dissent either from society generally or from the administration's policies in Vietnam.

Most of those intending to join the major protest demonstrations scheduled during convention week did not plan to enter the Amphitheatre and disrupt the proceedings of the Democratic Convention, did not plan aggressive acts of physical provocation against the authorities, and did not plan to use rallies of demonstrators to stage an assault against any person, institution, or place of business. But while it is clear that most of the protesters in Chicago had no intention of initiating violence, this is not to say that they did not expect it to develop.

It was the clearing of the demonstrators from Lincoln Park that led directly to the violence: symbolically, it expressed the city's opposition to the protesters; literally, it forced the protesters into confrontation with police in Old Town and the adjacent residential neighborhoods.

The Old Town area near Lincoln Park was a scene of police ferocity exceeding that shown on television on Wednesday night. From Sunday night through Tuesday night, incidents of intense and indiscriminate violence occurred in the streets after police had swept the park clear of demonstrators.

Demonstrators attacked too. And they posed difficult problems for police as they persisted in marching through the streets, blocking traffic and intersections. But it was the police who forced them out of the park and into the neighborhood. And on the part of the police there was enough wild club swinging, enough cries of hatred, enough gratuitous beating to make the conclusion inescapable that individual policemen, and lots of them, committed violent acts far in excess of the requisite force for crowd dispersal or arrest. . . .

There is some explanation for the media-directed violence. Camera crews on at least two occasions did stage violence and fake injuries. Demonstrators did sometimes step up their activities for the benefit of TV cameras. Newsmen and photographers' blinding lights did get in the way of police clearing streets, sweeping the park and dispersing demonstrators. Newsmen did, on occasion, disobey legitimate police orders to "move" or "clear the streets." News reporting of events did seem to the police to be anti-Chicago and anti-police.

But was the response appropriate to the provocation?

Out of 300 newsmen assigned to cover the parks and streets of Chicago during convention week, more than 60 (about 20 percent) were involved in incidents resulting in injury to themselves, damage to their equipment, or their arrest. Sixty-three newsmen were physically attacked by police; in 13 of these instances, photographic or recording equipment was intentionally damaged.

The violence did not end with either demonstrators or newsmen on the North Side on Sunday, Monday and Tuesday. It continued in Grant Park on Wednesday. It occurred on Michigan Avenue in front of the Conrad Hilton Hotel, as already described. A high-ranking Chicago police commander admits that on that occasion the police "got out of control." This same commander appears in one of the most vivid scenes of the entire week, trying desperately to keep individual policemen from beating demonstrators as he screams, "For Christ's sake, stop it!"

Thereafter, the violence continued on Michigan Avenue and on the side streets running into Chicago's Loop. A federal official describes how it began:

> I heard a 10-1 call [policeman in trouble] on either my radio or one of the other hand sets carried by men with me and then heard 'Car 100—sweep.' With a roar of motors, squads, vans and three-wheelers came from east, west and north into the block north of Jackson. The crowd scattered. A big group ran west on Jackson, with a group of blue shirted policemen in pursuit, beating at them with clubs. Some of the crowd would jump into doorways and the police would rout them out. The action was very tough. In my judgment, unnecessarily so. The police were hitting with a vengeance and quite obviously with relish....

What followed was a club-swinging melee. Police ranged the streets striking anyone they could catch. To be sure, demonstrators threw things at policemen and at police cars; but the weight of violence was overwhelmingly on the side of the police. A few examples will give the flavor of that night in Chicago:

"At the corner of Congress Plaza and Michigan," states a doctor, "was gathered a group of people, numbering between thirty and forty. They were trapped against a railing [along a ramp leading down from Michigan Avenue to an underground parking garage] by several policemen on motorcycles. The police charged the people on motorcycles and struck about a dozen of them, knocking several of them down. About twenty standing there jumped over the railing. On the other side of the railing was a three-to-four-foot drop. None of the people who were struck by the motorcycles appeared to be seriously injured. However, several of them were limping as if they had been run over on their feet."

A UPI reporter witnessed these attacks, too. He relates in his statement that one officer, "with a smile on his face and a fanatical look in his eyes, was standing on a three-wheel cycle, shouting, 'Wahoo, wahoo,' and trying to run down people on the sidewalk." The reporter says he was chased thirty feet by the cycle.

A priest who was in the crowd says he saw a "boy, about fourteen or fifteen, white, standing on top of an automobile yelling something which was unidentifiable. Suddenly a policeman pulled him down from the car and beat him to the ground by striking him three or four times with a nightstick. Other police joined in . . . and they eventually shoved him to a police van.

"A well-dressed woman saw this incident and spoke angrily to a nearby police captain. As she spoke, another policeman came up from behind her and sprayed something in her face with an aerosol can. He then clubbed her to the ground. He and two other policemen then dragged her along the ground to the same paddy wagon and threw her in."

"I ran west on Jackson," a witness states. "West of Wabash, a line of police stretching across both sidewalks and the street charged after a small group I was in. Many people were clubbed and maced as they ran. Some weren't demonstrators at all, but were just pedestrians who didn't know how to react to the charging officers yelling 'Police!' "

"A wave of police charged down Jackson," another witness relates. "Fleeing demonstrators were beaten indiscriminately and a temporary, makeshift first-aid station was set up on the corner of State and Jackson. Two men lay in pools of blood, their heads severely cut by clubs. A minister moved amongst the crowd, quieting them, brushing aside curious onlookers, and finally asked a policeman to call an ambulance, which he agreed to do. . . ."

An Assistant U.S. Attorney later reported that "the demonstrators were running as fast as they could but were unable to get out of the way because of the crowds in front of them. I observed the police striking numerous individuals, perhaps 20 to 30. I saw three fall down and then overrun by the police. I observed two demonstrators who had multiple cuts on their heads. We assisted one who was in shock into a passer-by's car."

Police violence was a fact of convention week. Were the policemen who committed it a minority? It appears certain that they were—but one which has imposed some of the consequences of its actions on the majority, and certainly on their commanders. There has been no public condemnation of these violators of sound police procedures and common decency by either their commanding officers or city officials. Nor (at the time this Report is being completed—almost three months after the convention) has any disciplinary action been taken against most of them. That some policemen lost control of themselves under exceedingly provocative circumstances can perhaps be understood; but not condoned. If no action is taken against them, the effect can only be to discourage the majority of policemen who acted responsibly, and further weaken the bond between police and community.

Although the crowds were finally dispelled on the nights of violence in Chicago, the problems they represent have not been. Surely this is not the last time that a violent dissenting group will clash head-on with those whose duty it is to enforce the law. And the next time the whole world will still be watching.

II. RICHARD M. NIXON
BRING US TOGETHER

LADIES AND GENTLEMEN, I didn't realize so many of you would stay up so late. I want to express my grateful appreciation to all of those in this room, but more than that, through the medium of television and radio, to the thousands, and I understand, millions, across the country who worked for our cause. . . .

I, as you probably have heard, have received a very gracious message from the Vice-President congratulating me for winning the election. I have also had a telephone conversation with him, and I thought I might share with you and also our television audience some of the thoughts that I expressed to him in that telephone conversation.

I congratulated him for his gallant and courageous fight against great odds. I admire a fighter, and he proved himself to be one. He never gave up and he gave us a good fight.

I also told him that as he finished this campaign, that I know exactly how he felt. I know how it feels to lose a close one. Having lost a close one eight years ago, and having won a close one this year, I can say this—winning is a lot more fun.

But I would like to express to him and also to the thousands who worked for him—because he, like myself, had a great corps of volunteer workers, many young people as well as others—a bit of philosophy that has guided me through the years of defeat toward this victory.

It is this: a great victory is never won without defeat. It is always won without fear. What is important is that a man or a woman engage in battle, be in the arena, participate, and I hope that all of those who supported Mr. Humphrey will continue their interest in politics. They will perhaps be in the other party; we may even be contesting again. Who knows? But the important thing is that our process in this country works better when we have devoted, dedicated people giving their all in battle for a cause that they believe in.

And I would urge particularly the young people who supported him and lost not to be discouraged, but to continue their interest and to go on to other areas of public service. . . .

And I've also received a very gracious wire from President Johnson, from Austin, Texas, in which he congratulated me and indicated his desire to be of assistance in the next administration.

I, in turn, pledge again to him my assistance and cooperation in the interim period between now and the inauguration in any activity that may be helpful in bringing the peace to the world that we all want.

And I look forward in the next administration to have a relationship with former President Johnson such as President Eisenhower had with him. Those who have served in this high office, only those who have served in this office, can know the tremendous burdens and they have so much to offer in their years of what will be called retirement.

And then one final thought that I would like to leave with regard to the character of the new administration. I saw many signs of this campaign, some of them were not friendly, some of them were very friendly. But the one that touched me the most was one I saw in Deshler, Ohio, at the end of a long day of whistle-stopping.

A little town. I suppose five times the population was there in the dusk. It was almost impossible to see, but a teen-ager held up a sign: "Bring us together."

And that will be the great objective of this administration at the outset, to bring the American people together. This will be an open administration, open to new ideas, open to men and women of both parties, open to the critics as well as those who support us. We want to bridge the generation gap. We want to bridge the gap between the races. We want to bring America together. And I am confident that this task is one that we can undertake, and one in which we will be successful.

We must realize that today's Establishment is the new George III. Whether it will continue to adhere to his tactics, we do not know. If it does, the redress, honored in tradition, is also revolution.

WILLIAM O. DOUGLAS, Associate Justice of the U. S. Supreme Court, in *Points of Rebellion,* 1970

2.

RICHARD M. NIXON: First Inaugural Address

The tenor of President Nixon's first term had been suggested in an interview he gave in 1967: "I've always thought this country could run itself domestically without a President. All you need is a competent Cabinet to run the country at home. You need a President for foreign policy; no secretary of state is really important; the President makes foreign policy." Nixon was a minority President, winning the 1968 election by a razor-thin margin, with 43.5 percent of the popular vote. This was no popular mandate, and thus Nixon, with only his "plan to end the war" carrying him in over the opposition, took office on January 20, 1969, on a note of conciliation and harmony. The members of his administration, scarcely known to the public at large, were considered basically managers and organizers, not reformers. The new Vice-President, Spiro Agnew, almost totally unknown to the public in July 1968, soon established a reputation as the most vocal spokesman of the new administration. In line with his own view of the presidency, Nixon chose for his closest adviser, Dr. Henry Kissinger from Harvard University.

Source: *Department of State Bulletin*, February 10, 1969.

SENATOR DIRKSEN, Mr. Chief Justice, Mr. Vice-President, President Johnson, Vice-President Humphrey, my fellow Americans—and my fellow citizens of the world community:

I ask you to share with me today the majesty of this moment. In the orderly transfer of power, we celebrate the unity that keeps us free.

Each moment in history is a fleeting time, precious and unique. But some stand out as moments of beginning, in which courses are set that shape decades or centuries.

This can be such a moment.

Forces now are converging that make possible, for the first time, the hope that many of man's deepest aspirations can at last be realized. The spiraling pace of change allows us to contemplate, within our own lifetime, advances that once would have taken centuries.

In throwing wide the horizons of space, we have discovered new horizons on earth.

For the first time, because the people of the world want peace and the leaders of the world are afraid of war, the times are on the side of peace.

Eight years from now America will celebrate its 200th anniversary as a nation. Within the lifetime of most people now living, mankind will celebrate that great new year which comes only once in a thousand years—the beginning of the third millennium.

What kind of a nation we will be, what kind of a world we will live in, whether we shape the future in the image of our hopes, is ours to determine by our actions and our choices.

The greatest honor history can bestow is the title of peacemaker. This honor now beckons America—the chance to help lead the world at last out of the valley of turmoil and onto that high ground of peace that man has dreamed of since the dawn of civilization.

If we succeed, generations to come will say of us now living that we mastered our moment, that we helped make the world safe for mankind.

This is our summons to greatness.

I believe the American people are ready to answer this call.

The second third of this century has been a time of proud achievement. We have made enormous strides in science and industry and agriculture. We have shared our wealth more broadly than ever. We have learned at last to manage a modern economy to assure its continued growth.

We have given freedom new reach. We have begun to make its promise real for black as well as for white.

We see the hope of tomorrow in the youth of today. I know America's youth. I believe in them. We can be proud that they are better educated, more committed, more passionately driven by conscience than any generation in our history.

No people has ever been so close to the achievement of a just and abundant society or so possessed of the will to achieve it. And because our strengths are so great, we can afford to appraise our weaknesses with candor and to approach them with hope.

Standing in this same place a third of a century ago, Franklin Delano Roosevelt addressed a nation ravaged by depression and gripped in fear. He could say in surveying the Nation's troubles: "They concern, thank God, only material things."

Our crisis today is in reverse.

We find ourselves rich in goods but ragged in spirit, reaching with magnificent precision for the moon but falling into raucous discord on earth.

We are caught in war, wanting peace. We are torn by division, wanting unity. We see around us empty lives wanting fulfillment. We see tasks that need doing waiting for hands to do them.

To a crisis of the spirit, we need an answer of the spirit.

And to find that answer, we need only look within ourselves.

When we listen to "the better angels of our nature," we find that they celebrate the simple things, the basic things—such as goodness, decency, love, kindness.

Greatness comes in simple trappings.

The simple things are the ones most needed today if we are to surmount what divides us and cement what unites us.

To lower our voices would be a simple thing.

In these difficult years, America has suffered from a fever of words; from inflated rhetoric that promises more than it can deliver; from angry rhetoric that fans discontents into hatreds; from bombastic rhetoric that postures instead of persuading.

We cannot learn from one another until we stop shouting at one another—until we speak quietly enough so that our words can be heard as well as our voices.

For its part, government will listen. We will strive to listen in new ways—to the voices of quiet anguish, the voices that speak without words, the voices of the heart—to the injured voices, the anxious voices, the voices that have despaired of being heard.

Those who have been left out, we will try to bring in.

Those left behind, we will help to catch up.

For all of our people, we will set as our goal the decent order that makes progress possible and our lives secure.

As we reach toward our hopes, our task is to build on what has gone before —not turning away from the old but turning toward the new.

In this past third of a century, government has passed more laws, spent more money, initiated more programs, than in all our previous history.

In pursuing our goals of full employment, better housing, excellence in education; in rebuilding our cities and improving our rural areas; in protecting our environment and enhancing the quality of life—in all these and more, we will and must press urgently forward.

We shall plan now for the day when our wealth can be transferred from the destruction of war abroad to the urgent needs of our people at home.

The American dream does not come to those who fall asleep.

But we are approaching the limits of what government alone can do.

Our greatest need now is to reach beyond government, to enlist the legions of the concerned and the committed.

What has to be done has to be done by government and people together or it will not be done at all. The lesson of past agony is that without the people we can do nothing, with the people we can do everything.

To match the magnitude of our tasks, we need the energies of our people—enlisted not only in grand enterprises but, more importantly, in those small, splendid efforts that make headlines in the neighborhood newspaper instead of the national journal.

With these, we can build a great cathedral of the spirit—each of us raising it one stone at a time as he reaches out to his neighbor, helping, caring, doing.

I do not offer a life of uninspiring ease. I do not call for a life of grim sacrifice. I ask you to join in a high adventure—one as rich as humanity itself and exciting as the times we live in.

The essence of freedom is that each of us shares in the shaping of his own destiny.

Until he has been part of a cause larger than himself, no man is truly whole.

The way to fulfillment is in the use of our talents. We achieve nobility in the spirit that inspires that use.

As we measure what can be done, we shall promise only what we know we can produce; but as we chart our goals, we shall be lifted by our dreams.

No man can be fully free while his neighbor is not. To go forward at all is to go forward together.

This means black and white together as one nation, not two. The laws have caught up with our conscience. What remains is to give life to what is in the law: to insure at last that as all are born equal in dignity before God, all are born equal in dignity before man.

As we learn to go forward together at home, let us also seek to go forward together with all mankind.

Let us take as our goal: Where peace is unknown, make it welcome; where peace is fragile, make it strong; where peace is temporary, make it permanent.

After a period of confrontation, we are entering an era of negotiation.

Let all nations know that during this administration our lines of communication will be open.

We seek an open world—open to ideas, open to the exchange of goods and people—a world in which no people, great or small, will live in angry isolation.

We cannot expect to make everyone our friend, but we can try to make no one our enemy.

Those who would be our adversaries, we invite to a peaceful competition—not in conquering territory or extending dominion but in enriching the life of man.

As we explore the reaches of space, let us go to the new worlds together—not as new worlds to be conquered but as a new adventure to be shared.

With those who are willing to join, let us cooperate to reduce the burden of arms, to strengthen the structure of peace, to lift up the poor and the hungry.

But to all those who would be tempted by weakness, let us leave no doubt that we will be as strong as we need to be for as long as we need to be.

Over the past 20 years, since I first came to this Capital as a freshman Congressman, I have visited most of the nations of the world. I have come to know the leaders of the world, and the great forces, the hatreds, the fears, that divide the world.

I know that peace does not come through wishing for it—that there is no substitute for days and even years of patient and prolonged diplomacy.

I also know the people of the world.

I have seen the hunger of a homeless child, the pain of a man wounded in battle, the grief of a mother who has lost her son. I know these have no ideology, no race.

I know America. I know the heart of America is good.

I speak from my own heart, and the heart of my country, the deep concern we have for those who suffer and those who sorrow.

I have taken an oath today in the presence of God and my countrymen to uphold and defend the Constitution of the United States. To that oath I now add this sacred commitment: I shall consecrate my Office, my energies, and all the wisdom I can summon to the cause of peace among nations.

Let this message be heard by strong and weak alike:

The peace we seek—the peace we seek to win—is not victory over any other people but the peace that comes "with healing in its wings"; with compassion for those who have suffered; with understanding for those who have opposed us; with the opportunity for all the peoples of this earth to choose their own destiny.

Only a few short weeks ago we shared the glory of man's first sight of the world as God sees it, as a single sphere reflecting light in the darkness.

As the Apollo astronauts flew over the moon's gray surface on Christmas Eve, they spoke to us of the beauty of earth—and in that voice so clear across the lunar distance, we heard them invoke God's blessing on its goodness.

In that moment, their view from the moon moved poet Archibald MacLeish to write:

> To see the earth as it truly is, small and blue and beautiful in that eternal silence where it floats, is to see ourselves as riders on the earth together, brothers on that bright loveliness in the eternal cold—brothers who know now they are truly brothers.

In that moment of surpassing technological triumph, men turned their thoughts toward home and humanity—seeing in that far perspective that man's destiny on earth is not divisible; telling us that however far we reach into the cosmos, our destiny lies not in the stars but on earth itself, in our own hands, in our own hearts.

We have endured a long night of the American spirit. But as our eyes catch the dimness of the first rays of dawn, let us not curse the remaining dark. Let us gather the light.

Our destiny offers not the cup of despair but the chalice of opportunity. So let us seize it not in fear but in gladness—and "riders on the earth together," let us go forward, firm in our faith, steadfast in our purpose, cautious of the dangers, but sustained by our confidence in the will of God and the promise of man.

3.

George Wald: A Generation Unsure It Has a Future

Although gaining its main impetus from the antiwar sentiment, the student protest movement of the late 1960s eventually embraced a wider range of issues: the draft, the power of the Pentagon, ecology, the ever-present threat of nuclear war, civil rights, poverty, and the problem of national priorities. On March 4, 1969, Professor George Wald of Harvard University delivered an address that pointed out the rationale of many of the complaints being made against "establishment" values. Wald, recipient of the Nobel Prize for medicine in 1968, gave the speech to a gathering of more than 1000 students and faculty at Kresge Auditorium on the Massachusetts Institute of Technology campus. Portions of Dr. Wald's speech are reprinted here.

Source: *Vital Speeches*, April 15, 1969.

All of you know that in the last couple of years there has been student unrest breaking at times into violence in many parts of the world: in England, Germany, Italy, Spain, Mexico and needless to say, in many parts of this country. There has been a great deal of discussion as to what it all means. Perfectly clearly it means something different in Mexico from what it does in France, and something different in France from what it does in Tokyo, and something different in Tokyo from what it does in this country. Yet unless we are to assume that students have gone crazy all over the world, or that they have just decided that it's the thing to do, there must be some common meaning.

I don't need to go so far afield to look for that meaning. I am a teacher, and at Harvard, I have a class of about 350 students—men and women—most of them freshmen and sophomores. Over these past few years I have felt increasingly that something is terribly wrong—and this year ever so much more than last. Something has gone sour, in teaching and in learning. It's almost as though there were a widespread feeling that education has become irrelevant.

A lecture is much more of a dialogue than many of you probably appreciate. As you lecture, you keep watching the faces; and information keeps coming back to you all the time. I began to feel, particularly this year, that I was missing much of what was coming back. I tried asking the students, but they didn't or couldn't help me very much.

But I think I know what's the matter, even a little better than they do. I think that this whole generation of students is beset with a profound uneasiness. I don't think that they have yet quite defined its source. I think I understand the reasons for their uneasiness even better than they do. What is more, I share their uneasiness.

What's bothering those students? Some of them tell you it's the Vietnam War. I think the Vietnam War is the most shameful episode in the whole of American history. The concept of War Crimes is an American invention. We've committed many War Crimes in Vietnam; but I'll tell you something interesting about that. We were committing War Crimes in World War II, even before Nuremburg trials were held and the principle of war crimes started. The saturation bombing of German cities was a War Crime and if we had lost the war, some of our leaders might have had to answer for it.

I've gone through all of that history lately, and I find that there's a gimmick in it. It isn't written out, but I think we established it by precedent. That gimmick is that if one can allege that one is repelling or retaliating for an aggression —after that everything goes. And you see we are living in a world in which all wars are wars of defense. All War Departments are now Defense Departments. This is all part of the double talk of our time. The aggressor is always on the other side. And I suppose this is why our ex-Secretary of State, Dean Rusk—a man in whom repetition takes the place of reason, and stubbornness takes the place of character—went to such pains to insist, as he still insists, that in Vietnam we are repelling an aggression. And if that's what we are doing—so runs the doctrine —anything goes. If the concept of war crimes is ever to mean anything, they will have to be defined as categories of acts, regardless of provocation. But that isn't so now.

I think we've lost that war, as a lot of other people think, too. The Vietnamese have a secret weapon. Its their willingness to die, beyond our willingness to kill. In effect they've been saying, you can kill us, but you'll have to kill a lot of us, you may have to kill all of us. And thank heavens, we are not yet ready to do that.

Yet we have come a long way—far enough to sicken many Americans, far enough even to sicken our fighting men. Far enough so that our national symbols have gone sour. How many of you can sing about the "the rockets' red glare, bombs bursting in air" without thinking, those are our bombs and our rockets bursting over South Vietnamese villages? When those words were written, we were a people struggling for freedom against oppression. Now we are supporting real or thinly disguised military dictatorships all over the world, helping them to control and repress peoples all over the world, helping them to control and repress peoples struggling for their freedom. . . .

But that Vietnam War, shameful and terrible as it is, seems to me only an immediate incident in a much larger and more stubborn situation. . . .

I say the Vietnam War is just an immediate incident, because so long as we keep that big army, it will always find things to do. If the Vietnam War stopped tomorrow, with that big a military establishment, the chances are that we would be in another such adventure abroad or at home before you knew it.

As for the draft: Don't reform the draft—get rid of it.

A peacetime draft is the most un-American thing I know. All the time I was growing up I was told about oppressive Central European countries and Russia, where young men were forced into the army; and I was told what they did about it. They chopped off a finger, or shot off a couple of toes; or better still, if they could manage it, they came to this country. And we understood that, and sympathized, and were glad to welcome them.

Now by present estimates four to six thousand Americans of draft age have left this country for Canada, another two or three thousand have gone to Europe, and it looks as though many more are preparing to emigrate. . . .

But there is something ever so much bigger and more important than the draft. The bigger thing, of course, is what ex-President Eisenhower warned us of, calling it the military-industrial complex. I am sad to say that we must begin to think of it now as the military-industrial-labor union complex. What happened under the plea of the Cold War was not alone that we built up the first big peacetime army in our history, but we institutionalized it. We built, I suppose, the biggest government building in our history to run it, and we institutionalized it.

I don't think we can live with the present military establishment and its $80-100 billion a year budget, and keep America anything like we have known it in the past. It is corrupting the life of the whole country. It is buying up everything in sight: industries, banks, investors, universities; and lately it seems also to have bought up the labor unions. . . .

We are told that the United States and Russia between them have by now stockpiles in nuclear weapons approximately the explosive power of 15 tons of TNT for every man, woman and child on earth. And now it is suggested that we must make more. All very regretable, of course; but those are "the facts of life." We really would like to disarm; but our new Secretary of Defense has made the ingenious proposal that one must be practical. Now is the time to greatly increase our nuclear armaments so that we can disarm from a position of strength.

I think all of you know there is no adequate defense against massive nuclear attack. It is both easier and cheaper to circumvent any known nuclear defense system than to provide it. It's all pretty crazy. At the very moment we talk of deploying ABM's, we are also building the MIRV, the weapon to circumvent ABM's.

So far as I know, with everything working as well as can be hoped and all foreseeable precautions taken, the most conservative estimates of Americans killed in a major nuclear attack run to about 50 millions. We have become callous to gruesome statistics and this seems at first to be only another gruesome statistic. You think, Bang!—and next morning, if you're still there, you read in the newspapers that 50 million people were killed.

But that isn't the way it happens. When we killed close to 200,000 people with those first little, old-fashioned uranium bombs that we dropped on Hiroshima and Nagasaki, about the same number of persons was maimed, blinded, burned, poisoned and otherwise doomed. A lot of them took a long time to die.

That's the way it would be. Not a bang, and a certain number of corpses to bury; but a nation filled with millions of helpless, maimed, tortured and doomed survivors huddled with their families in shelters, with guns ready to fight off their neighbors, trying to get some uncontaminated food and water.

A few months ago Sen. Richard Russell of Georgia ended a speech in the Senate with the words: "If we have to start over again with another Adam and Eve, I want them to be Americans; and I want them on this continent and not in Europe." That was a United States senator holding a patriotic speech. Well, here is a Nobel Laureate who thinks that those words are criminally insane.

How real is the threat of full-scale nuclear war? I have my own very inexpert idea, but realizing how little I know and fearful that I may be a little paranoid on this subject, I take every opportunity to ask reputed experts. I asked that question of a very distinguished professor of government at Harvard about a month ago. I asked him what sort of odds he would lay on the possibility of full-scale nuclear war within the foreseeable future. "Oh," he said comfortably, "I think I can give you a pretty good answer to that question. I estimate the probability of full-scale nuclear war, provided that the situation remains about as it is now, at two percent per year." Anybody can do the simple calculation that shows that two percent per year means that the chance of having that full-scale nuclear war, by 1990 is about one in three, and by 2000 it is about 50-50.

I think I know what is bothering the students. I think that what we are up against is a generation that is by no means sure that it has a future.

I am growing old, and my future so to speak is already behind me. But there are those students of mine who are in my mind always; there are my children, two of them now seven and nine, whose future is infinitely more precious to me than my own. So it isn't just their generation; it's mine too. We're all in it together.

Are we to have a chance to live? We don't ask for prosperity, or security; only for a reasonable chance to live, to work out our destiny in peace and decency. Not to go down in history as the apocalyptic generation.

4.

John N. Mitchell: What Kind of World Do You Want?

John Mitchell served as Attorney General during President Nixon's first term, until early 1972, when he resigned to assume charge of the President's re-election campaign. During these three years he was the most influential member of the administration, concerning himself not only with the work of the Justice Department, but also with the whole range of foreign and domestic policy. As Attorney General, he was regarded as a staunch "law and order" advocate, favoring wiretapping, capital punishment, "no-knock" searches, and other liberalized police procedures. One of the primary concerns of his office from 1969 to 1971 was the pervasive campus unrest, sometimes erupting into violence, that was triggered by the antiwar protest. On May 1, 1969, Attorney General Mitchell addressed himself to this issue in a Law Day speech delivered to the Detroit Bar Association. Portions of his remarks are reprinted here.

Source: *Congressional Record*, 91 Cong., 1 Session, May 13, 1969.

CAMPUS DISORDERS are basically a local problem to be solved at the local level and not by the federal government. But as Attorney General—as the senior law enforcement officer in the nation—I believe that I have the responsibility to

John N. Mitchell, attorney general during President Nixon's first term, pursued militants and revolutionaries and claimed full constitutional power to use eavesdropping and wiretapping.

comment on national problems which affect the administration of justice even though my legal jurisdiction may be limited.

I also come to you tonight as a fellow citizen, as a parent with two children recently graduated from college and as a grandfather concerned about the future.

An eminent Nobel laureate said last month in Boston: "What we are up against is a generation that is by no means sure it has a future." I disagree with that assessment.

I suggest that this generation has the most promising future world of any generation of Americans.

But I must pose to them the query of Mr. Justice Holmes:

"Behind every scheme to make the world over lies the question, what kind of world do you want?"

What kind of world do our students want? Do our university officials want? Do our teachers want? Do our citizens want? And I must remind you that when we talk about our students we are not talking about an alien people—we are talking about our own sons and daughters and about the type of nation we are making for them to inherit.

Let me quote briefly to you a capsulized dispatch issued by the Associated Press at 10:15 A.M. EST on April 24:

> Washington—Student militants seize buildings at American University and George Washington University.
>
> Ithaca—Cornell University faculty members agree to demands of students who seized college buildings armed with guns.
>
> Kent, Ohio—Kent college students create physical disturbances.
>
> New Orleans—Southern University students lower the American flag.
>
> Cambridge—Harvard professor resigns in the wake of police-student clash.
>
> Princeton—Sixty students block doorways to a research facility.
>
> New York—One hundred-fifty students and faculty stage a sit-in at Fordham University.
>
> College Park, Maryland—University of Maryland protestors attempt to block entry to a science center.
>
> New York—Two Brooklyn high schools forced to close after three days of student unrest.

That is one day of what kind of world some of our students have. In the current academic year, there have been demonstrations on over 200 college campuses throughout the nation. This has resulted in more than 2300 arrests and property damage in excess of an estimated $2.2 million.

Since January 1, 1969, the protest movement has escalated its tactics. For example, in the State of California:

At San Francisco State a bomb permanently blinded one student and a second bomb was discovered before it exploded.

At Pomona College in Claremont, a secretary was blinded in one eye and lost two fingers when a bomb exploded as she was removing it from a college mailbox.

At the University of California in Santa Barbara, a custodian at the Faculty Club died from burns when he picked up a firebomb.

At Berkeley, in the last eight months, there have been four arsons and two bombings, and $1.1 million in property damage.

This Administration has tried to be patient in the hope that students, faculty, and local officials, working together, would put an end to this chaos.

But the time has come for an end to patience. The time has come for us to demand, in the strongest possible terms, that university officials, local law enforcement agencies and local courts apply the law.

I call for an end to minority tyranny on the nation's campuses and for the immediate reestablishment of civil peace and the protection of individual rights.

If arrests must be made, then arrests there should be. If violators must be prosecuted, then prosecutions there should be.

It is no admission of defeat, as some may claim, to use reasonable physical force to eliminate physical force. The price of civil tranquillity cannot be paid by submission to violence and terror. . . .

To date, we have had disturbances on more than 200 campuses—about nine percent of the colleges in the country. In only a small number of such disturbances was there any severe physical violence and bloodshed reported. The total arrest rate, of 2300, is less than four-tenths of one percent of all of our students.

While accurate statistics are not available, it is believed that less than two percent of our students have engaged actively in any disruptions causing physical or property damage. . . .

A decade ago we saw the "silent generation" going quietly from the university to earning a living. Today, we have the "involved generation" who are interested in the problems of our society. They are active in civil rights, in poverty, in hunger, in education for the poor, in job retraining, and in partisan politics. I welcome this generation's demand that the university not be an extraterritorial community removed from society, but that it and its members deeply involve themselves with the problems of the day.

But if they are to assume a role as adult activists in a community, they must also assume the obligations that go with adult citizenship. And one of the primary obligations upon which we exist is a simple maxim, carved above an entrance of the Justice Department in Washington, which says:

"Law alone can give us freedom. Where law ends, tyranny begins."

Campus militants, directing their efforts at destruction and intimidation, are nothing but tyrants. But there are others who share the blame by failing to act—university administrators must take firm and immediate action to protect the rights of faculty members to teach and of other students to learn. Faculty members should stop negotiating under the blackmail threat of violence. Apathetic students should stand up for the rights of those who wish to pursue civility and scholarship in the academic community. To the extent that they remain neutral or refuse to act, they are all accessories to the tyranny we are now witnessing.

The genesis of our current student problems is thought to lie in our encouragement of lawful dissent.

The right to express disagreement with the acts of constituted authority is one of our fundamental freedoms. The First Amendment expressly protects "the freedom of speech" and "of the press" and "the right of the people peaceably to assemble, and petition the Government for a redress of grievance." ...

But there are definite limits beyond which these First Amendment guarantees may not be carried.

The Supreme Court has flatly rejected the argument "that people who want to propagandize protests or views have a constitutional right to do so whenever and however they please." ...

In any honest discussion on student protests, one must meet the claim that civil disobedience is an accepted tradition in American society.

This is especially true among our student population who claim that their seizures of university buildings and imprisonment of university officials are legitimate acts of civil disobedience similar to their participation in the civil rights protests.

I disagree. First: traditionally, civil disobedience has involved an issue of universal or fundamental morality—such as the equality of the races. No such issue has been involved in the current student protests.

Second: organized disobedience in the civil rights movement has rarely involved violence or bloodshed. It has concentrated, rather, on non-violence and on symbolic action which offered no substantial deprivation of rights to anyone else. One can hardly equate a sit-in at a bus terminal with throwing a student out of a second-story window.

Third: in this country, the historical key to civil disobedience has been its amenability to arrest and prosecution. Indeed, it has always been considered, as Thoreau told Emerson, that the moral righteousness of breaking a law was in the punishment that the law meted out.

Today's militants also reject that concept. They physically resist arrest and they are unwilling to submit the merits of their cause to any tribunal other than their own self-determination.

Having defined the problem, I feel obligated to offer a few suggestions on what can and should be done to resolve it.

My jurisdiction, as you well know, is limited to the application of federal law. Our concept has always been that, unless we in the federal government have a clear mandate, we permit the states and the municipalities to deal with law enforcement problems. The clearest mandate we have, so far, is the anti-riot provisions of the 1968 Civil Rights Act. It prohibits persons from crossing state lines with intent to incite riots.

We have substantial information confirming the widely accepted belief that several major university disturbances have been incited by members of a small core of professional militants who make it their tragic occupation to convert peaceable student dissatisfaction into violence and confrontation.

These circumstances can only lead to the conclusion that this hard core is bent on the destruction of our universities and not on their improvement.

You can be assured that these violence-prone militants will be prosecuted to the full extent of our federal laws.

We are also collecting a great deal of information about student disorders and those who cause them.

We are offering this information to state and local law enforcement officials operating in jurisdictions where campus disorders may occur.

No society, including an academic society, can survive without basic agreement by a great majority of its members as to the fundamental precepts upon which it operates.

The first precept for any academic community must be to outlaw terror.

The second premise is that students, faculty and administration officials should all participate, in some measure, in the decision-making process. What this means, at a minimum, is that university administrators must offer a serious forum for responsible student criticism—and more than that, it must be clear to the students that their grievances will be honestly considered and will not be lightly dismissed under the procedural ruse of an artificial dialogue.

Third: universities must prepare for prospective violence. It is no longer acceptable for a university administration to claim, after the events of this year, that they were taken unaware or that they acted in panic and that their mistakes can be blamed on the alacrity with which the demonstration developed.

Here, too, the entire university community should be consulted since it is the censure or approbation of a majority of this community which will determine the course of student violence.

If, as has been done at some universities, the majority overwhelmingly rejects minority violence, the militants are left isolated except for brute physical power. Since the entire concept of confrontation is to attract the sympathy of the majority—and sometimes the sympathies may be forthcoming because of inappropriate reactions—this major avenue of support for violent demonstrators should be substantially diminished.

In any event, the university administrator should, in anticipation of the outbreak of a disturbance, consult with local law enforcement officials on the methods of handling various disturbances. Preparation and coordination by these parties may well eliminate the disturbance and will assure the timely application of any required counter-force.

Fourth: if all else fails and a disturbance does occur, university officials should consider applying immediately to a court for an injunction. This tactic has proved fairly successful in the past. It takes the university out of the law enforcement business, where it does not belong, and replaces it with the court which is better suited for this purpose.

Let me be specific: University officials are not law enforcement experts or judges. When a violent outbreak occurs, they should not take it upon themselves to decide how long the violence should endure and what rights should be trampled upon until local government is called in. For minor demonstrations, which involve no serious disruptions, the university should have the viability to decide for itself what the best solution may be.

But when people may be injured, when personal property may be destroyed, and when chaos begins, the university official only aids lawlessness by procrastination and negotiation. The university is not an extraterritorial community and its officials have the obligation to protect the rights of the peaceful students on its campus by use of the established local law enforcement agencies and the courts.

5.

Jesse B. Ritter: A Breakdown of Law and Order

The most violent combination of student protest and police reaction during 1969 occurred in Berkeley, California. In May there were disturbances growing out of the closing of a "people's park," established by hippies on University of California property. On May 22 protesting students and others conducted a march through Berkeley. In response, local law enforcement agencies and state National Guardsmen made mass arrests totaling 480 persons. During the disturbance, shotguns, riot gas, and helicopters were used against protesters, bystanders, and, somewhat indiscriminately, on the university campus. The author of this selection, a teacher at San Francisco State College, was on the scene when all this took place. He gave a full description of the day's events in an article entitled "Nightmare for the Innocent in a California Jail."

Source: *Life*, August 15, 1969.

When I moved my family to San Francisco last year to teach in the English department at San Francisco State College, I did so with misgivings. I knew that the educational atmosphere in California was far from tranquil—Governor Reagan was waging virtual war against student protesters, and the political polarization between the left and the right could only be described in terms of paranoia. Through the year, my fears were confirmed as I witnessed student and faculty strikes, bombings, brawls, police assaults, mass arrests. But none of those events—brutal as they were—prepared me for the nightmare that followed my recent chance arrest this spring in Berkeley. Overnight that experience, which can be verified by many reliable witnesses, turned a father of five, veteran of the Korean war and law-abiding citizen into a bitter man.

On Thursday morning, May 22, I left San Francisco State College with four other teachers to drive to Berkeley. We were beginning work on an environmental art project one of the teachers was directing. We planned to borrow a sailboat from a couple I knew in Berkeley and dump a small amount of nontoxic dye in the bay water at strategic points to observe the action of the currents.

We arrived in Berkeley about noon. After a pleasant lunch and a trip to buy supplies for the sail we walked toward Shattuck on Addison Street. There we were to meet my friend's wife, Nora.

The city of Berkeley was then in something like a state of siege because of the People's Park issue. On the streets, under the command of Alameda County Sheriff Frank Madigan, was a vast force of National Guard troops, county sheriffs, San Francisco Tactical Squad units. Madigan had authorized use of shotguns against demonstrators. One man had already been killed, and many others wounded. Demonstrators, workers and onlookers trapped in a plaza on the University of California campus had been sprayed from a helicopter with a virulent form of tear gas currently being used in Vietnam. To protest, approximately 2,000 students had now begun a spontaneous march from the university campus through downtown Berkeley.

We could see a concentration of National Guard troops, policemen and citizens several blocks east of us. I described what Nora looked like to the others and we stopped at the southwest corner of Shattuck and Addison to scan the crowd for her. We decided not to go any farther because we saw soldiers, police and people both to the east and south of us. The National Guard troops nearest us were climbing into trucks and moving out. Small groups of people on each corner of the intersection watched the troops; others walked casually on the sidewalks.

Berkeley policemen and Alameda County deputies began moving our way. An officer leading four or five others approached our group of 12 to 15 people and said, "Let's move out; clear the area!" Everyone on our corner obediently started walking away. Suddenly, a Berkeley policeman ran in front of us, spread his arms and shouted, "Stay where you are!" Behind us, two other policemen kept repeating, "Keep moving, clear out of here!" We said we were leaving, and at this point a Berkeley police sergeant approached and began pointing to various people in our group, saying, "Get that one, that one, that one."

An officer snapped handcuffs on me and joined me with the cuffs to a protesting youngster. I asked if we were under arrest and the officer said yes—we were charged with blocking traffic. We were not allowed to talk to the policemen after that. The sergeant who had us arrested taunted us, using obscenities and accusing us of being revolutionaries, rock-throwers and hippies. Those not fingered by the sergeant continued down the street and were not apprehended. While we were being herded into the paddy wagon, however, officers continued to arrest people at random—mostly young people, and particularly those with long hair, mustaches, sideburns. Three of the teachers with me were arrested; our fifth companion was not, and he immediately began calling friends and relatives to arrange our release.

Nineteen of us—17 men and two women—were packed into a paddy wagon. I was never able to identify myself or state my business; indeed, the policemen threatened anyone who talked at all. We sat in the wagon for about 20 minutes, then it backed up the street a block, where we were transferred to a large bus. We were all being taken to "Santa Rita," a place I had never heard of . . . .

During the 45-minute ride our feelings were reinforced that it had been an indiscriminate bust. Aboard were students with books and notepads who had been on their way to and from classes at the university. There was a U.S. mailman (with long hair), still carrying his bag of mail, and a resident psychiatrist who had stepped outside his hospital for a short walk during a 30-minute break. Others included several young divinity students and five medical observers—young men in white smocks with red crosses—who had accompanied the student march down Shattuck Avenue. The police blew it, I thought. They went too far this time. Most of us will be released when we get to wherever we're going.

The bus stopped inside the Santa Rita Rehabilitation Center and Prison Farm, an institution run by Alameda County. Prison guards who work under the jurisdiction of County Sheriff Madigan now took charge of us. We heard repeated orders through the frosted bus windows: "Unload single file and march. Anybody talks and he'll get a club up the butt!" As we filed off the bus the sight that greeted us was from a World War II movie—shabby wooden barracks, barbed-wire fences, rickety watch towers and rows of men lying face down in an asphalt-paved compound. We were marched into the compound and ordered to lie prone in rows. Those who looked around or stumbled or didn't move fast enough were prodded and hit with clubs. Frequently, men were dragged out of the marching lines and forced to kneel while being struck. The guards shouted and screamed, often giving conflicting commands and clubbing those unable to obey them. Our chief source of terror was not so much the beatings as the wild hysteria that had seized many of the guards. They walked up and down our rows of flattened men, striking upraised hands with clubs, striking us on the soles of our feet with clubs to make us lie in even rows. We were told we would be shot if we tried to escape. We were cursed continuously; we were called dope users, revolutionaries, filthy long-hairs. We would, they shouted, be taught such a lesson that we would never again cause trouble. All of us were identified as political troublemakers. No attempt was made to distinguish us by age, nature of charges or physical condition. Periodically we were ordered to turn our heads to the left or right. I experienced severe leg cramps and sharp twinges of pain from an arthritic elbow. From time to time we were forced to close up ranks by crawling across the asphalt, which was covered with sharp gravel. Those accused of speaking or looking around or moving slightly were dragged out and forced to kneel with their hands behind them in a separate group. Some remained kneeling for hours. There were some 300 men on the ground. . . .

After a few of us asked to use the rest rooms (and were abused for it), guards began allowing small groups to go. At times, the guards said, "You'll have to wait another half hour." One kid near me identified himself as a diabetic in the rest room and was cruelly beaten.

This savage parody of prison discipline had an obvious psychology behind it. Humiliate the prisoners totally from the beginning so they will obey orders and accept punishment without resistance. Of course, we weren't prisoners—*we were simply being held for booking!*

During the time I was lying in the compound, from approximately 4 until 8:30 P.M., new arrestees were brought in and forced to lie in rows. It was cold when the sun went down, and men around me were shivering. At 8 we were allowed to stand and exercise in place for a few minutes. We then lay back down on our faces. They had taken our names when we were first arrested, and about every 20 minutes a guard would call out some names in alphabetical order. At 8:30 my name was called along with seven others, and we were taken into an adjoining barracks for booking.

Here we experienced new refinements. We were forced to sit in single file on the floor, knees together, while a squat, dark-haired guard waving a blackjack shouted that if we didn't do exactly as he said he would beat us until we couldn't walk. He had us face the wall, spread our legs and place our hands high on the wall. We then turned and threw our jackets, belts and the contents of our pockets into a pile. During this procedure, the squat guard struck prisoners in the back, stomach, face and legs with his fist or the blackjack. He struck me four times with the blackjack during the booking process —either for not having my heels tightly together or for not clasping my hands in front of me. He assaulted one of us—a very young boy with long hair—by slugging him with his fist and then grabbing the boy's hair and slamming his face into the wall. Later, in the barracks, we saw that the boy's left eye had swollen badly and he could barely open his jaw.

After the booking and fingerprinting, we again had to sit on the floor with legs drawn up, heels together. We were then lined up and marched to Barracks B across the street. The guard in charge treated us firmly but decently, telling us that while we were in the barracks we could get together and talk, plan our bail procedures and wait our turn to use the telephone. He repeated what other guards had told us in the compound—that the regular prisoners were outraged at us because we were troublemakers, because we were responsible for the regular inmates' missing movies and other privileges. The inmates would beat us terribly, and the guards couldn't prevent it. We would be turned over to "hardened criminals and sex perverts."

At about 11:30, four lawyers from the People's Park Defense Committee appeared in the barracks. They told us they were trying to arrange bail procedures for as many people as possible, but they lacked funds and organizations for rapid release. We filled out forms giving information about our families and personal legal arrangements. We later were told that many of these forms were destroyed by prison guards who claimed they were "messages." At no time during our detention did anyone in my barracks have an opportunity to make a telephone call to relatives or lawyers.

During the night we were taunted and threatened by different prison guards. We left in small groups all through the night to have photos taken—I went in a group at 2:45 A.M. Few of us slept.

At 4:30 A.M., the door crashed open and three guards moved among the bunks rousting out people with curses, threats and blows. We were going to eat, they said, and we would eat what we took or it would be "shoved in your faces." Under continual threats, we were marched to the mess hall. Breakfast was Corn Chex and milk (no sugar), half-cooked prunes, white bread and artificial marmalade. We sat packed at the tables, ordered not to move or talk. Five men were dragged from their seats and forced to kneel before an empty table for such things as "looking around," "talking" or "moving." They were not allowed to eat. One boy was forced to lean his head on a post while the guards beat on the post. His nose began bleeding. Guards would prod him, pull him off the post and strike him, or kick his feet back farther until he was leaning at a severe angle to the post, his head and neck bearing the full weight of his body. After about 15 minutes of quivering spasmodically, the boy collapsed to the floor. Two guards dragged him over to the empty table and made him kneel, still twitching, with the others. After we finished eating, we were forced to kneel on the floor in columns of two and wait for about 15 minutes before being marched back to the barracks.

At 6 A.M. a new guard, a small man with reddish-blond hair on his neck, came into the barracks, yelling, "I had a good night's sleep and I feel like KILLING!" He announced that he was now in total control of us and said he needed a "boss" in the barracks. He grabbed my bunkmate, Professor Gary Oberbillig, by the shirt and dragged him out to the center of the floor. "Get out here," he said.

"You're big; you want to take me? Come on, let's go outside. Want to go outside?" He then instructed Oberbillig that he, Oberbillig, was the "barracks boss" and was to "beat the——! out of anybody who don't do right!"

At 7:30 a guard came in and read off a list of names. We lined up and marched outside into the street, where several other guards spent approximately 30 minutes giving us military marching commands, making those who did not execute the commands smartly do calisthenics. (Ironically, not one of them was able to give an accurate "about-face" command, and our ragged "about-face" maneuvers enraged them.) We marched at double-time, forced to yell "WE LOVE THE BLUE MEANIES!"

The guards were proud of this idea: I overheard one tell another, "Say, we've gotta do that Blue Meanies bit some more." We marched to what appeared to be the receiving center of the prison, where we were put in open-screen cells already occupied by new arrestees. It was here that we learned we would be released soon. While we waited in the cells, several men were dragged out and beaten in our presence and told that they were on the way to further beatings and a stay in the "quiet room."

My three companions and I were finally processed for release on bail by 8:30 A.M., Friday, May 23, nearly 18 hours after our arrest. All released prisoners had to catch rides out of the main gate, a distance of a half mile, with outgoing bail bondsmen.

The first thing I learned facedown on the Santa Rita asphalt was that I could make it without begging or breaking. This felt good; it was enough strength to counter the fears engendered by the heavy blue-black guards' shoes slowly crunching by my eyes six inches away. *But to be put to these tests in America!*

At a press conference, Alameda County Sheriff Frank Madigan admitted there had been "irregularities" at Santa Rita on that Thursday. He put the responsibility on his guards. Many of the deputies assigned there, he said, are young Vietnam war veterans and "they have a feeling that these people should be treated like Vietcong."

On July 2 Madigan suspended 10 of his officers at Santa Rita for "violating civil service and/or departmental rules" in handling the mass arrests. The officers, all of whom were told they had the right to appeal (only four chose to do so), included the commander, his two immediate assistants and a sergeant. By July 9, charges against all the people who had been arrested—a total of 480—had been dropped by the court.

Still, several hundred young men and women came out of Santa Rita believing there is no middle ground anymore—nowhere to stand to reconcile the growing polarities of our political lives. I am haunted by the bitterness brought forth by such assaults on our humaneness and human rights. When in the history of man have prisons and guards ever rooted out the ideas in which men really believe?

6.

Jane Goodsell: "Psychodelerium Tremens"

The much touted generation gap that flourished in the late 1960s manifested itself among the young in a variety of ways: long hair, casual and colorful dress, living in actual or feigned poverty, adherence to some form of the drug culture, rock music, and other forms of protest against the "over thirty" crowd. Nowhere was the youth culture more flamboyant than in its transformation of the American language to suit its purposes. The new jargon had many sources, but derived primarily from the black ghettoes of America. The new colloquialisms served to dismay and confuse the older generation. Gradually, however, many of the new expressions were absorbed into the popular usage and gained wide currency as they were heard on radio or television and printed in newspapers and magazines. The following poem by Jane Goodsell, sister of the late Senator Richard Neuberger, conjures up the jarring difference between the terminologies of past and present.

Source: *Congressional Record*, 91 Cong., 1 Session, April 18, 1969.

Remember when hippie meant big in
the hips,
And a trip involved travel in cars,
planes, and ships?
When pot was a vessel for cooking
things in,
And hooked was what Grandmother's
rug might have been?
When fix was a verb that meant mend
or repair,
And be-in meant simply existing
somewhere?
When neat meant well organized, tidy
and clean,
And grass was a ground-cover, normally
green?
When lights and not people were
switched on and off,
And the pill might have been what you
took for a cough?
When camp meant to quarter outdoors
in a tent,
And pop was what the weasel
went?
When groovy meant furrowed with
channels and hollows,
And birds were winged creatures, like
robins and swallows?
When fuzz was a substance that's fluffy
like lint,
And bread came from bakeries, not
from the mint?
When square meant a 90-degree angled
form,
And cool was a temperature not quite
warm?
When roll meant a bun, and rock was a
stone,
And hang-up was something you did to
a phone?
When chicken meant poultry, and bag
meant a sack,
And junk, trashy cast-offs and old
bric-a-brac?

When jam was preserves that you
spread on your bread,
And crazy meant balmy, not right in the
head?
When cat was a feline, a kitten grown
up,
And tea was a liquid you drank from a
cup?
When swinger was someone who swings
in a swing,
And pad was a soft sort of cushiony
thing?
When way out meant distant and far,
far away,
And a man couldn't sue you for calling
him gay?
When dig meant to shovel and spade in
the dirt,
And put-on was what you would do with
a shirt?
When tough described meat too
unyielding to chew,
And making a scene was a rude thing to
do?
Words once so sensible, sober, and
serious,
Are making the freak scene like
psychodelirious.
It's groovy, man, groovy, but English it's
not,
Methinks that the language has gone
straight to pot.

7.

WALTER J. MCNERNEY: Improving Medical Care

Early in 1963, President Kennedy submitted his proposal for financing hospital and medical care for the aged to Congress. Two and one-half years later the Medicare bill, providing such financing through the Social Security system, passed and was signed by President Johnson. This legislation alleviated some of the burden of costly health care for a segment of the population. But it was also partially responsible for more crowded conditions in hospitals and spiraling increases in medical costs over the next few years. Even short hospital stays could severely deplete a family's financial resources, and long illnesses calling for special treatment could be borne only by the more affluent. Shortages of doctors and of hospital space, combined with expensive medicines and treatment, simply priced most Americans out of the health market. The solution to the problem seemed to be some form of national health insurance, such as was in use among all the other industrialized nations. But fears concerning federal interference in health care moved the medical profession and the hospital associations to lobby against all attempts to establish such a program. This interview with Walter J. McNerney, head of the Blue Cross Association, reveals some of the problems connected with national health care and suggests proposals of reform.

Source: *U. S. News & World Report*, March 24, 1969.

Q. Are many Americans going without medical care because costs are so high?

A. Too many are. There is significance in American mortality and morbidity rates as compared with those in other countries. There are 15 countries with a lower infant-mortality rate than the U.S. And our country ranks something like twentieth in the world in longevity.

With particular reference to the death rate among children, it's pretty clear that we have a problem. The infant-mortality rate among the poor in this country is about twice that of the well-to-do. The death rate among the black poor is likely to be three times the national average.

When one looks behind these figures —and others—and sees that the poor get much less prenatal and postnatal care, worse nutrition, worse housing, and less preventive and rehabilitative care than the average citizen, then one has to suspect strongly that costs are a major problem to certain segments of our population. Fifty percent of the poor are not immunized against common childhood ailments. Sixty-four percent do not see a dentist. And 45 percent of the female poor who have babies do not get prenatal care.

Q. Is the answer increased spending?

A. I think the problem is less *how much* we are spending on health care, and more *how* we are spending this money.

In other words, while we are doing some things well—such as through our expenditures on research, education and treatment of certain acute illnesses—there are some things we are not doing well. For example, preventive care—needed to keep people from getting sick, whether through personal health services or environmental services such as air and stream purification—is inadequate. And the productivity, or efficiency, of some aspects of our health-care system is too low.

Q. Why is medical efficiency so low?

A. The major productivity problem is that while we as a nation have changed significantly, both in terms of living conditions and in terms of medical science, we are still, in too many sections, using the health-care apparatus that we had in the 1930s and 1940s.

Today we are more urbanized, and the pressures of urban living are different from those of a rural economy—resulting in different demand and delivery problems. Medical science has vastly proliferated the numbers and variety of health services that need to be provided. To meet these and other changes, we need a reorganization of our health services.

Q. How would you change the system?

A. In broad terms, we need to bring all major health services together on what might be termed "health campuses." Further, the various services involved must be more closely co-ordinated—for example, doctors' offices, hospitals, extended-care facilities, public-health programs and home-care programs. Also, the physician must become better integrated in the total range of services.

Today, agencies and services are so fragmented it is difficult for the patient to know how to enter and then use the system intelligently. And, obviously, co-ordination problems arise which have cost implications.

In some depressed areas, where ability to travel is limited or knowledge of health services is minimal, there is often a lack of services—compounding the matter of fragmentation.

Q. Should these health centers be developed with government funds, or private money?

A. It will take both. It will take government help to build expensive hospital beds—or, better still, to modernize those beds. It will take significant government help to build or modernize some of the allied facilities and those for education and research. The help will be in the form of grants and loans.

On the other hand, a fair amount of private funds, primarily through prepayment and insurance, can be involved in paying for the services that are provided in these facilities and for assuming some of the capital expenditures that will be required.

To keep these costs as low as possible, however, meaningful control and incentive mechanisms must be applied. For example, planning of physical facilities must be done carefully to avoid costly duplication and needless overspending. There should be some effective system of area-wide planning to fit health facilities to the needs of the community.

Q. Are changes needed in health insurance?

A. We are going to have to provide more comprehensive health care by having prepayment and insurance pay for a broader range of benefits.

At present, prepayment and insurance pay for only one third of the medical-care dollar. This should be increased to 85 or 90 percent as soon as possible, for the cost of even one large health-care item—such as drugs or a hospital stay—can handicap a family severely.

The scope of benefits widely available should be extended very quickly to include such out-of-hospital costs as dental care, prescribed drugs, home care, and particularly preventive care, so that nobody is left in grave danger as far as financing his family's medical care is concerned.

The broadening of benefits would also serve to help reduce the use of our most expensive service—that is, the hospital.

For example, preadmission testing, now in effect in 22 Blue Cross-plan areas, makes it possible for a patient to get his X-ray and lab tests in the outpatient department of the hospital several days or weeks before he's admitted, without spending needless time in a hospital bed.

Potential savings from this kind of testing in one State have been estimated as high as 7.5 million dollars. For convalescing patients, home care, now in effect in 17 Blue Cross plans, costs as little as $10 a day—a fraction of the cost of a hospital stay.

Q. Would you expand federal, or private, insurance?

A. The broadening must be done in both sectors—public and private.

In the private sector, labor and management must recognize that as high a priority must be placed on comprehensive health benefits as on such things as more take-home pay, reduced work-weeks, longer vacations and other fringe benefits. Not only do broad benefits have incentive value, but the payoff of a healthy working population with minimal medical indigency and dependence on tax sources is potentially great.

In the automotive industry, for example, we already find that such things as outpatient psychiatric care, treatment in nursing homes and other extended-care facilities, and prescription drugs are now part of their standard health-insurance contracts. This is an encouraging trend.

In the public sector, the Government should help provide benefits for those who cannot afford them. It will become less and less defensible for the Government to ignore the needs of the poor.

Q. How would you reach those poor people? Would you simply extend the Government's system of medicare to include people of all ages, instead of just the elderly?

A. It would be well to leave medicare focused primarily on the aged, as it is now. In addition, the totally and permanently disabled could be brought into medicare regardless of age—as well as State retirees.

To make medical care more available to the poor who are outside any of the above categories, we should strengthen considerably our medicaid program. Several points come to mind:

The Federal Government could increase its aid to the States under the medicaid program from the present 55 to 83 percent up to 70 to 90 percent, if necessary. A major problem to date has been the inability of States to provide adequate matching funds. State tax resources are considerably less than federal, and increasingly the problem of the poor is becoming a national—as opposed to a local—problem.

I would do away with the current undignified and needlessly complicated system of need determination, which is too subjective and too subject to inequitable interpretation by States and localities. Instead, let a person declare his income on a short form to the Internal Revenue Service.

Presumably, all welfare-cash beneficiaries would not be working and would receive 100 percent help. For those who work, if their income is below a certain figure—they would get something less than 100 percent help. Persons in lower income categories might get 50 percent, others 25 percent, and those above a certain income level would get no help at all.

But these income levels should be reexamined periodically, over all. Federal guidelines should be promulgated as a condition of participation in federal aid—for example, who should be eligible, what evaluative data are to be kept, and the actuarial value of minimum benefits.

Also, the Federal Government should require that the income limits be relatively uniform among the States—taking into account the different costs of living in different areas.

This would be a simpler, more flexible system. If the nation's economy should improve, that could be taken into account. It would reduce demands on already burdened local tax revenues needed for many social purposes like education. It would avoid the regressive aspects of a uniform payroll tax.

Further, the States participating in this plan could purchase their medical care through private carriers which would be responsible for performance under clearly stipulated conditions.

Q. Do you believe in compulsory, tax-paid health insurance for everybody?

A. The States should have some elbow room to work out their own plans. If a State wanted to, it could use a plan like Governor Rockefeller's in New York—which in its original form involved a payroll tax shared jointly by the employer and employe in support of a minimum-benefit package for the working population, and the use of private carriers to administer the benefits. Those on welfare rolls would still need direct government assistance.

Q. Do you have any estimate of what such a program would cost—in taxpayers' money?

A. No, I don't. It has been estimated that it would cost about $250 a year per person to render comprehensive health services under today's health system. The cost of either program would depend, in the last analysis, upon what benefits were included, who was included, and so on.

Q. Speaking of costs, what has caused this sudden jump in hospital and doctor costs?

A. On the hospital side, it is important to note that labor costs account for about

70 percent of the average hospital's budget.

For a long time, wages paid hospital employes were far below the wage standards in most industries for workers of comparable skills. But in recent years, nurses and other hospital employes have begun demanding wages comparable to those paid other workers. In some places, hospital employes have gone on strike; in other places, they have made strong demands. All this, plus the fact that hospital employes were placed under the federal minimum-wage law in 1966, have caused labor costs to accelerate.

So a large amount of the recent rise in hospital costs represents hospital labor catching up on wages.

Q. Have hospital workers now caught up, or is this rapid rise to go on in the future?

A. I would say that the pay of the average hospital employe is still behind that for comparable skills in the community. Therefore, we can look for two or three years more of an exceptional rise. Then it should start to moderate.

Other factors in rising hospital costs include expensive new equipment, new services and the public's rising demand for these services, as well as expensive laboratory tests.

There can also be no doubt that overuse is a factor that is contributing to high hospital bills. In the absence of broad benefits and well co-ordinated allied services, the hospital can become the site of care which can be rendered more economically elsewhere.

Q. How about doctors? Are they making fortunes, as many people believe?

A. The average doctor nets perhaps something like $33,000 a year, according to recent figures. Of course, there are some doctors who make considerably more than that. But I don't think the average income of doctors is too high, considering the cost and long years of their education and their relatively short productive working lives. Whether the doctor is able to be fully productive in today's system is another matter. . . .

Q. You have also said that certain segments of the population are not getting the care that they should. Do you foresee a big increase in the number of people getting medical care or in the extent of medical care that they get?

A. Yes—and it should be recognized that this care is viewed as a right rather than a privilege. Health care for everyone must be regarded as a necessary and vital element of our society.

Apart from the moral issues involved, good health makes good economic sense, as I suggested earlier. It has been estimated, for example, that 10 percent of the nation's income growth over the past 50 years has been due to the declining death rate, resulting in a larger labor force.

It is also estimated that every dollar spent on research into arthritis or rheumatism gives us a potential return of $39 by keeping a person out of bed and having him at work as a taxpayer rather than a drag on our economy. Similar examples could be cited for other debilitating diseases.

It is foolish to pay to keep a lot of sick, unproductive people on welfare when, by the judicious expenditure of little or no more money, we can keep these same people on their feet as working and contributing members of society.

8.

Open Letter to the U. S. Voter on Oil Taxes

The percentage depletion allowance for gas and oil were first written into the tax laws in 1926. The law, sparing oil companies, investors, and royalty owners the burden of paying any taxes on 27.5 percent of their total income, was justified on the basis of the high risks involved in oil and gas exploration. During the 1960s, as so-called tax loopholes became an issue of public controversy, the depletion allowance was widely criticized as an expensive and unnecessary bit of governmental favoritism for one industry. The industry, on the other hand, defended the allowance as both equitable and necessary, since as more oil is pumped, by just so much is the actual wealth of the industry depleted, since the oil is irreplaceable. In a tax reform bill passed late in 1969, however, the allowance was reduced to 22 percent over the strong objections of the oil industry. But it was a popular legislative move in the face of a growing national tax revolt. The following defense of the depletion allowance was published by the oil industry early in 1969.

Source: *Oil and Gas Journal*, April 28, 1969.

PERCENTAGE DEPLETION has been on the federal law books for 43 years. And for 36 of these years, it has been vociferously attacked as an unfair "loophole" for avoiding taxes. It's happening again.

The attackers have been highly placed: Former presidents, cabinet members, lawmakers, college professors. As well as unwashed radicals, uninformed housewives, and entertainers who make poor jokes.

Congress through it all has refused to junk the provision or even modify it.

Why have the attacks by so-called tax reformers failed? Several reasons.

Opponents haven't advanced a single new argument that wasn't thoroughly considered prior to passage of the 1926 measure. The Congress consistently has decided that benefits outweigh costs.

Depletion also is tied closely to the basic concepts of our constitution. These are: Never tax capital. Tax only the income from capital. Taxing away capital is likened to killing the goose that lays the golden eggs.

Why then do the attacks persist?

Taxes are pinching everyone. They always go up. Never down. The bureaucratic taxer-spenders as well as tax-burdened companies and individuals are eager to shut off tax avoidance to ease the pinch. It's easy to level an emotional diatribe against depletion and then hoot down any reasoned explanation of the complex issue.

That's why we must examine the issue constantly.

Percentage depletion has two objects: Recover the producer's capital. And give him an incentive to drill more wells, find more oil.

How does it work?

Stripped of its emotional setting, percentage depletion is simply a deduction available to oil and gas producers—and producers of more than 100 other minerals—in figuring their taxes on income from wells.

The producer may deduct 27.5% from the gross annual income of a lease or property. This is tax free. The figure, however, may not exceed 50% of the net income of the lease. This limitation actually prevents most producers from taking the full deduction. In practice, it averages only 23% and in many cases is much less than that.

This policy recognizes that oil in the ground is part of the producer's capital. It is like real estate. But this capital is used up—or depleted—by operation of an oil or gas well. The rate of deduction when determined 43 years ago, was estimated as equal the capital value of oil in the ground. It's now probably less, and a higher rate would be more equitable.

Opponents, however, favor stripping depletion back until it assures the producer he will recover his actual investment or costs in a lease. After this amount is recovered over a period of time, deductions would end. The producer's income taxes would increase. Thus cost depletion would serve a function similar to depreciation.

This overlooks the unique position of oil as capital in the ground. It also ignores the unusual risks involved in finding replacement petroleum. Depletion encourages the producer to hunt new reserves—depreciation doesn't.

Say, for an example, an oil man recovered only his lease costs deductions. He has no assurance he can take this fund, drill a single well and come up with any oil or gas. The odds are he will drill nine dry holes for every producing well. And what's more, he'll drill 46 marginal wells to every one that nets out a profit. Depreciation funds would melt quickly under these odds. But depletion funds from one good well give a producer the financial staying power to keep drilling.

What would happen if percentage depletion were ended? It would drastically curtail the hunt for oil and gas. Our reserves would dwindle even more. Why? Because operators would become more selective and cautious in their drilling plans. They'd drill only the better prospects, shun the costly and high-risk ones.

Many producers would sell out and take advantage of the more favorable tax rates on capital gains from oil in the ground. They would thus escape the high regular rates on production. The buyer, in turn, would set up to deplete at 100% of his cost. So, it's difficult to see how the government could reap a tax bonanza from this change.

Consumers of petroleum products would suffer, too. The cost of crude oil and natural gas would rise. This inevitably would be translated into higher product prices.

Why then disturb a policy that promises to cause such an upheaval when the benefits are so uncertain?

But the critics cry: "Some companies pay no income tax at all. That's unfair."

Let's examine this one carefully. It comes up every time taxes are mentioned. It's becoming cause celebre among oil-industry critics.

In the first place, any producer who

completely escapes income taxes doesn't do so with percentage depletion alone. The "50%-of-net income" limitation prevents that. So, he must use the benefits of other deductions—most likely the expensing of intangible drilling costs and write-offs for dry holes.

By way of explanation, drilling costs come in two kinds. Tangible drilling costs, such as cost of tanks, equipment, and structures, are depreciated over the years. No argument here. Intangible costs, such as expense for wages, fuel, repairs, and all services, may be recovered the same way or as an operating expense in the year incurred. Most oil men elect to expense the intangibles. This allows them to get their money back more quickly to use in further operations. Expensing of intangibles does reduce the net income of the lease, even may create a loss. All this reduces the total subject to income tax. There are a few facts, however, to keep in mind. The producer can deduct intangible expenses only once. They tend to reduce benefits percentage depletion. And the producer, in order to have intangible deductions, must keep on drilling. This is exactly what the tax policies are designed to do—keep oil men drilling.

WHAT ELSE DO CRITICS find wrong about percentage depletion? What do they suggest? Here are a few, and the answers to them.

Depletion allows companies to offset income from other sources, escape more taxes.

Percentage depletion cannot reduce taxable income from any source except the one lease or property on which it is computed. Oil companies aren't escaping taxes even if the bite of the income tax is lighter on them. It may surprise many to know that the total tax burden of the petroleum industry actually is heavier than average. In 1966, oil paid $2.5 billion in direct taxes. This $2.5 billion amounted to 5.1% of gross revenue from all operations. The direct tax burden for all U.S. business corporations was only about 4.5% of gross revenue. This is about 10% less than the tax burden of petroleum. That plays hob with the contention that oil companies don't pay taxes.

Oil profits are exorbitant. Too many oil millionaires are created by percentage depletion.

The average profit of 99 oil companies in 1968 was equal to a 12.9% return on net worth. This is below the 13.1% return on net worth earned by 2,250 manufacturing companies. There's certainly nothing exorbitant about this. Percentage depletion hasn't made oil millionaires. Oil fortunes rise from the combination in an individual of ability, stubbornness, and luck in finding oil. Success in finding oil is the key—not percentage depletion.

Oil producers don't use tax savings to look for more oil and gas.

The figures show differently. Statistics indicate oil producers would pay $1.3 billion more annually in taxes if present policies were ended. In the last 10 years, they have spent this—plus an average $3.1 billion more on exploration and development.

The depletion rate of 27.5% is too high. Cut it to 20, 15, or 10%.

This is begging the question. A lower rate won't satisfy the critics. They'd be back at the next session to whittle away at the lower rate. As we've noted, the present rate probably already is too low to achieve an adequate return of capital. If it were lower, percentage depletion also would lose effectiveness as an exploration incentive. It would give oil men too little money to finance new drilling. Outside investors would fear other cuts. Uncertainty of their return piled on the normal risk of exploration would cool them on oil ventures. Exploration needs to be made more attractive to risk capital—not less.

Eliminate all deductions and grant an outright federal subsidy to encourage exploration.

Can you imagine what kind of drilling program would emerge if it depended on annual appropriations from Congress? What a boondoggle this opens up! The drilling decision-makers would be bureaucrats who are subject to political pressure and not fitted by training or position to take risks involved. Where would the savings be in this approach?

THERE ARE OTHER arguments. None really new. All have been refuted time and time again. The fact they are being taken seriously is the big surprise.

It is especially surprising in view of the present low state of petroleum exploration. That's the new circumstance in the whole fight.

Our reserves of oil and gas are dwindling at a time they should be rising twice as fast. Spending on exploration should be doubled. Oil and gas now furnish 75% of our nation's energy. We're using petroleum at such a clip that consumption is expected to double by 1980.

Tampering with any policy that encourages exploration for petroleum is courting disaster. The facts speak just as clearly and loudly as ever against changing either the rate or principle of percentage depletion. Congress will serve the nation best by again refusing to change this policy.

If the American people were aware of the full impact of giveaways to the rich, and if they were to receive the same publicity that is given the puny dole afforded fatherless children, the public outcry would compel speedy and drastic reform. Unlike programs for the poor, which are subjected (quite rightly) to never-ending scrutiny, the tax breaks and payoffs to the affluent are seldom discussed. . . .Once established, these handouts tend to perpetuate themselves and to expand, helping the rich get richer.

SENATOR GEORGE MCGOVERN, "Let's Stop Handouts to the Rich," 1969

9.

EARL WARREN: Interview on Justice in America

Earl Warren served as the 15th Chief Justice of the Supreme Court from 1953 until his retirement on June 23, 1969. Existing during a time of dramatic social and economic change, the "Warren Court" was one of the most controversial ones in American history. Warren's most famous ruling, Brown v. Board of Education, *outlawed school segregation and ushered in an era of racial conflict. Equally controversial were the decisions concerning individual rights versus police power, of which* Miranda v. Arizona *in 1965, on protection against self-incrimination, is probably most well-known. In 1962 the "one-man, one-vote" decision,* Baker v. Carr, *by Justice Brennan, led to the reapportioning of many state legislatures and the redrawing of district lines to gain more equitable representation. A few weeks before leaving the Court, Chief Justice Warren gave an interview, reprinted here in part, to Mr. Morrie Landsberg of the McClatchey Newspapers in Sacramento, California. The interview was broadcast on June 25, 1969, over West Coast stations.*

Source: *A Conversation With Chief Justice Earl Warren*, McClatchey Broadcasting, Sacramento, California, n.d.

Q. Mr. Chief Justice, from your days as Attorney General of California, you have consistently complained about the lack of support given law enforcement authorities. How serious do you consider the problem today?

A. If anything, I consider it more serious today than it was then because the police today have a tremendous problem, greater than it was even in the days when I was District Attorney and an Attorney General when we had the bootlegging, the rum running, the hijacking and all of those things. It was a very lawless era, but nothing like it is today. The police have a tremendous problem today and they are entitled to all the support that the public can give them; I mean support when they do right, not when they do wrong; support when they follow the rules of jurisprudence and not when they violate them. But today we see crimes committed on the streets in the presence of a great many people and the police are not able to find a witness who is willing to come and testify. We read of other crimes committed in the presence of a great many people and no witness—no one will even inform the police that a crime has been committed. That is not upholding the law. The police are entitled to respect and assistance because most of them are good people and are carrying a terrific burden, and they are entitled to the support of the public at all times.

Q. Mr. Chief Justice, the late Chief Justice Felix Frankfurter said in 1946, if I may quote, "It is hostile to a democratic system to involve the judiciary in the politics of the people." Have you ever felt that the Supreme Court's jurisdiction should be limited?

A. Well, it is very much limited and always has been and, of course, judges when they take the bench are supposed to detach themselves from politics. I don't mean become disinterested because every American citizen should be interested in politics, but a judge should detach himself from active politics and it has been my experience that most judges with whom I have ever come in contact have obeyed that rule.

Q. Did you feel in the early phase that the court was going it alone in protecting civil rights and liberties?

A. Well, there was a long time, from the 1870's until 15 years or so ago, that Congress passed no laws affecting the civil liberties of the people. That was not entirely the fault of the Congress because the court itself had, in those early years, put some limitations upon the acts of Congress. But because there were no laws passed during that time and because problems involving civil rights were developing, the only refuge people had was in the courts, and the only law that the court could apply was the broad principles of the Constitution and that made a very, very difficult situation for the courts and we were very much alone at that time. But since that time, Congress has passed a number of civil rights laws which encompass a great many of the civil rights and I am sure that will mean the work of the courts will be easier now than it has been in the past.

Q. Were you at times impatient that state and federal officials were not responsive enough in the desegregation matter?

A. In some parts of the country, yes. One couldn't help being impatient when he would see the orders of the court flaunted and just not obeyed in any sense of the word, and where illegal things were changed in form, but not in substance and carried on. Of course, one feels frustrated at that, but there are so many things that have happened to encourage one who has been in this field that I think on the whole, much progress has been made.

Q. I know the court doesn't try to run a popularity poll, but do you feel there has been a general acceptance by the public of recent decisions on such matters as desegregation and civil liberties?

A. That is very difficult for me to say, but I think in the main, the people of this country recognize that the great American ideal is that everyone shall be entitled to equal protection under the laws and while they might disagree with the application of it in something that irritates them particularly, still they have the consciousness that it is not only the law, but that it is right. I think in that sense the American people are in favor of the overall objectives of the Fourteenth Amendment of the Constitution of the United States which guarantees those rights.

Q. How does the black separation movement fit in with what is being achieved or what people are trying to achieve in civil liberties?

A. Well, of course the separation movement is the opposite of equal protection. You see, this is the very thing that was stricken down in the desegregation cases. The old separate, but equal doctrine which existed for a period of some 50 years, or so we thought, had been abolished, but the idea of having separate institutions now and separate governments, and so forth, is the antithesis of equal protection under the laws.

Q. Do you see it creating some problems for this country?

A. Oh yes, of course it does. These problems are great that we are going through; well, I don't have the answers for them. I do believe that in the long run the principles of our Constitution will prevail because they're of the experience of the ages and Americans are reasonable people and on sober second thought they invariably decide the thing not only in the right way, but in a humane way too. So, I think we are on the way to progress even though we abhor many of the things that exist at the present time.

Q. Do you think the militants are trying to push us too far, too fast?

A. Well, militancy is always too fast, but the militancy is taking so many different forms these days it is impossible to discuss it in any brief interview.

Q. Would you say, Mr. Chief Justice, that American justice has been completely desegregated?

A. Oh no, by no means! There aren't 20% of the school children in the South that are in desegregated schools. The same situation exists in some of our northern cities. The black people do not have work opportunities that white people have. They're still having problems in voting in some parts of the country, and no we just haven't put all of our force behind giving people equal rights and that, to me, would be the answer to many of our problems. When the American people, as a whole, recognize that we have, in the past, been wrong in depriving certain minorities of their constitutional rights and when we make the decision to see that they will, in the future, have these rights, then I think we're on the way to solving most of our domestic problems.

Q. What would you list, Mr. Chief Justice, as the Supreme Court's most important decision in your 16 years here? Was it the school desegregation or reapportionment?

A. I think the reapportionment, not only of State legislatures, but of representative government in this country is perhaps the most important issue we have had before the Supreme Court. If everyone in this country has an opportunity to participate in his government on equal terms with everyone else, and can share in electing representatives who will be truly representative of the entire community and not some special interest, then most of these problems that we are now confronted with would be solved through the political process rather than through the courts.

Q. Would this apply mostly to the South?

A. I remember the first case we had, the Baker vs. Carr case, came from one of our northern states and that the legislature in that state had been the same for over 60 years in spite of all the territorial changes. The group that was in power kept the legislature apportioned just exactly as it was over 60 years before, although the State Constitution said that the representation should be equal, but they paid no attention to it. The courts, prior to Baker vs. Carr, said that it was the business of legislatures and not of courts. This court held that the question of whether a person was having equal protection of the laws was a judicial question and we had the right to decide it and we held that the legislatures must give equal representation to everyone. That was where the expression "one man one vote" came into being and, of course, it just isn't state legislatures, but it has been expanded to the Congress and expanded also to local government. If it's right on one level of government, of course, it's right on all levels of government, and in that sense, I think, the case which all the other reapportionment cases followed is perhaps the most important case that we have had since I have been on the court.

Q. In another area, you said awhile back that pornography was the court's most difficult area. Why is that?

A. It's the most difficult area for the simple reason that we have to balance two constitutional rights with each other. Of course, the state and national governments have a right to have a decent society and have the right to make the laws and regulations that will keep it a decent society. On the other hand, we have the First Amendment which says Congress shall pass no laws abridging the right of speech and the press and religion, and so forth, and the question is how far can people go under the First Amendment which gives them freedom of speech without offending the right of the government to maintain a decent society, and when you have those two things coming together, you find it very difficult to write a verbal definition of what obscenity is. I know that in many communities in the past, they have had boards of censorship and the experience that was had under them was atrocious. I recall that in one southern city, the censorship board—board of censorship—ruled that a motion picture which showed little colored children and little white children playing in a school yard was obscene. I remember, also, another instance when in Chicago the police board of censorship, in spite of all that goes on in that great city, held that Walt Disney's picture of a vanishing prairie which showed a mother buffalo giving birth to her little one in a snow storm was obscene. Many other instances of things of that kind show how far boards of censorship will go in determining what is obscene and what is not obscene. When it comes to writing a definition, it is very difficult to do it. The court has done its best, but the people on both sides of the question will stretch it just as far as they can and make tremendous problems.

Q. Do you think that the people who peddle pornography sometimes have gone too far?

A. Oh my goodness yes! Some of the things that go through the mail, some of the things that are sent to my home are just unspeakable and under no decision of this court are they justified, but still nobody seems to do anything about it.

Q. Is it up to the postal authorities or is it a weakness in the law?

A. Well, I don't like to point the finger at anybody, but it is a question of law enforcement and those who say that the Supreme Court has put its approval on obscenity are just not aware of the facts because the court has not done that. The court has specifically said that obscenity is not protected under the free speech clause of the Constitution. The only question involved is what is obscenity, and I haven't seen anyone who has been able to write the definition for obscenity that juries can follow that has been fairly satisfactory.

Q. Is one of the problems the fact that antipornography laws vary from state to state?

A. I am not so sure that's true. I think the states are rather uniform in what they are doing these days, but it's a difficult phase of the law to enforce. Policemen don't like to do it, prosecutors don't like to prosecute them, judges don't like to determine what is obscene and what isn't obscene, and there is just a general inclination for everybody to do nothing and blame somebody else.

Q. Mr. Chief Justice, if we can get into the field of politics, looking back, would you rather have been President?

A. Well, I never was infected, really, with the fever to be President. I was in a few primary elections and I was perfectly willing to be nominated if there was any chance to be nominated, but I never felt that there was any real chance of my being nominated. It was only an outside chance and had I been nominated, of course, I would like to have been elected and served as President, but I never felt the loss of it.

Q. Mr. Chief Justice, do you believe the Bill of Rights would be ratified if it came to a vote today?

A. I think probably that there would be a great debate over some of them because we have never taught our youngsters in the schools, or today are we teaching them in most of our colleges where the Bill of Rights came from, why it is there, and what its purpose is in society. There are a lot of thoughtless people who feel that we don't need any more Fifth Amendment, and we don't need protection as to free speech and freedom of the press and freedom of religion, but I do believe that on sober second thought after a great debate, the American people are wise enough to retain those rights which have made this country the greatest in the world.

Q. Do you believe there is not enough foundation in the basics of what the Bill of Rights stands for?

A. Well, I would teach more of it in the public schools and I'd teach more of it in the universities and I'd teach more of it in the law schools than they do. I also think our Bar Associations should interest themselves more than they have in the past in discussions as to the merits of the Bill of Rights.

Q. You believe there is not enough foundation in the basics of what the Bill of Rights stands for?

A. That is right. People don't understand what they are, they're just a group of words to a lot of people until they affect their particular interest and then, of course, they are interested. I remember one time talking to a newspaper man when we had the loyalty oath fight at the university, if you remember that many years ago. I was Governor then and Chairman of the Board of Regents at the University of California and I was of the opinion that it was not only a destructive thing, but it was a silly thing, this oath, because it wasn't provided by statute. Anybody could take it and then laugh at having taken it, and the only people who would refuse to take it would be people who couldn't in conscience take an oath of that kind. All of them having taken the oath to support and defend the Constitution of the United States, none of them objected to that, it was just this test oath that they objected to; and I talked to a newspaper man one time who was quite hostile at the position I took in opposition to the loyalty oath. I said to him, "Well, let me ask you a question: Now, suppose the Congress was to pass a law saying that before you could use the mails that you would take the test oath to the effect that you were not a communist, that you would not write anything communistic in your newspaper before you put it in the mail. What would you think of that?" And he said, "Well, you know what I would think of that." And I said, "I believe I do, but what would you think of it?" "Well," he said, "I would be against it." I said, "Why?" He said, "Well the first thing you know if we did that, there would be some bureaucrat in Washington telling us that what we were writing was communistic and they would be censoring what we were writing." I said, "You just made the case for these professors at the university because they felt that if they took a test oath like that, there would be somebody in Sacramento that would be looking into their work and saying to them, what you're saying is communistic or subversive in some other respect and, therefore, you must not teach it." And he said, "Oh well, it's much ado about nothing, let's forget it."

Q. You said in 1947, by the way, that our form of government is on trial today. To what extent would you say that our government is on trial?

A. I think that all free governments are on trial and perhaps always will be. You know we had, I say we, but the world had many democracies before the birth of Christ and around the Mediterranean Sea and very few of them lasted very long for the simple reason that the people became tired of governing themselves. They relaxed, they took no interest in their government, they let other interests step in, and they fell prey to some kind of authoritarian government. The only one that lasted was Rome, and it lasted for 1,000 years because Romans were proud of their citizenship, they participated in it and were thoroughly willing to govern themselves, but the rest of them all died. Our country is young by historical standards; it won't be 200 years old until about seven years from now, and in history, that is a very short time and we are still learning day by day how to govern ourselves. If we ever lose the impetus to do that, if we ever become lackadaisical and leave it to somebody else to govern us, if we ever forget the Bill of Rights which came to us in a hard way over the centuries of Anglo-Saxon law, then we're in danger. And we are on trial, always, and we are on trial before the world to see what we can do with this government of ours. The better we make it the more contented our people are, the more equal life is for people in this country, the more assuredly it will be sustained indefinitely.

Q. Mr. Chief Justice, what are some of the forces which challenge a free society today?

A. I think that perhaps the most important force is the force of apathy. When the people are not interested in their government, when they're not willing to participate in it and do the things for the general welfare that our institutions complicate, we are really in danger then. And that, I think, stems from the fact that so many people are unaware of the historical background of our institutions, how they came into being, why they came into being, and so forth. I have no fear at all of our future as long as people are interested in government. No matter how they disagree, as long as they are interested in government and will have the great debate in order to get things established, I have no concern about the future at all. American people in the aggregate are wise and they're good and they will decide things in the right way if we can get everybody interested in the affairs of government.

Q. Have you ever felt that we were headed toward totalitarianism in this country?

A. Well, there have been some things that if permitted to be extended would tend toward totalitarianism, but I don't think that we are in any immediate danger of going into totalitarianism. However, erosion is a terrible thing, you know, and government can erode just by a succession of little things that happen just like a hillside. Those are the things that put us in danger, because when the erosion becomes noticeable, the weakness has developed and then it is very difficult to restore the virility of the government. But we have a great, growing, virile country and there is no reason why anybody should become discouraged or become discouraged because we are not progressing, nor should they become apathetic because we progressed as far as we have because we still have a lot of problems and we must be after them all the time. The free way of life is not the easiest way of life to live by a long ways. If we are going to be free, we have to work for it and it's been said in the past, and I'm sure it's true, that every generation must re-establish its own freedoms and I believe that, because otherwise one generation could erode the freedoms that the others have built up until the next generation couldn't restore them.

Q. What do you say, Mr. Chief Justice, to critics who say that the court, by its decisions, has dealt a death blow to state's rights?

A. Oh, on the contrary, I think that the Supreme Court has established state's rights. What does reapportionment do, but establish state's rights? It establishes in the states the power to govern themselves and most of the problems that we have today in our big cities, for instance, we find they are there because the states have done nothing about them. And the reason they couldn't do anything about them was because most of their legislatures were controlled by interests that were not interested in the preservation of our cities. Now that they are freed from those restrictions, I am sure that the states will do something about cities and won't just look to the Federal government to have everything done for them. Most of this concentration of power that you find in the government, Federal government, comes from the fact that the states have not themselves done their job and they look to the Federal government, therefore, to do it for them. Once the Federal government does it for them, of course, it has to build up a big bureaucracy in order to administer these programs; so, I think in all respects, I can't think of anything that this court has done to destroy state's rights. Now, of course, the term state's rights is abused very, very greatly. I suppose in some parts of the country when we compel the desegregation of schools that we are interferring with state's rights. We are not interferring with the rights of the people in those states because we're guaranteeing to the people the right to have those rights on an equal basis. But as far as I can see, this court has not, in any sense, entrenched upon the Tenth Amendment, which reserves to the states and to the people the rights that are not delegated to the Federal government in the Constitution.

Q. There are some going around the country now saying we are really a federation of sovereign states. Is that the way you see history, Mr. Chief Justice?

A. Again, they use terms in ways that are not realistic. The states are not sovereign because the sovereignty is in the United States government. We have a supremacy clause in the Constitution which says that the laws of the United States are supreme and that makes the sovereignty, but the sovereignty in our country is really in the people through their representative form of government, both in the Federal government and the State government. There was never any indication in the Constitutional Convention that the states were sovereign, that's a word that has been added to it. They have autonomy to a great extent and they have just as much autonomy now as they had then, and probably more, but they never were sovereign after the Constitution of the United States was adopted. They were under the Articles of Confederation, but when the Constitution of the United States was adopted, the sovereignty was in the United States of America through the people.

Q. Mr. Chief Justice, you once said there should be compulsory retirement for all public officials, but didn't specify any age. Do you have any further views on this now?

A. I still believe that compulsory retirement is a good thing because in my opinion the strength of our institutions depends on infusing new blood into them all the time and I don't like to see people stay in public office too long. But I do want to see the compulsory retirement in all branches of the government, not just in the judiciary. That, I would be opposed to. I have been opposed to it all along because people who don't like the decisions of the Supreme Court are very free to say yes, we ought to have compulsory retirement, but they don't want to apply it to themselves. In the Congress they have chairmen of committees who are 80 odd, and one of them recently into the 90's, and those men are all powerful. I think if we are to have compulsory retirement in the courts, we ought to have it in the Congress as well, and I'm in favor of having it in both.

Q. Do you have any suggestions for a retirement age?

A. Oh, I don't have any definite age. I suppose 70 or 75, somewhere in that range. I'm over either of them now, you know.

Q. You're 70????

A. 78.

Q. Mr. Chief Justice, what are your future plans? Will you write memoirs or teach or concern yourself with the administration of justice?

A. One thing I will do is to keep busy. That, I must do. I have been busy all my life and I have been in the public service now, counting my time in the Army, 52 years in August, without a day out of the public service. They have been vigorous years too, every one of them, and I couldn't stand to be idle. I'm not leaving just to go fishing or something of that kind, but there's so many things that can be done, there are so many causes in the world today, that one need never lack one that he can really work on.

Q. Mr. Chief Justice, what was your reaction to the clamor by your critics for your impeachment?

A. Oh, they have a right to do that. I believe that criticism is a proper function in government. No one should be above criticism and while one would rather be praised, I guess, than blamed, I have never had any ill feelings for anyone who criticized the court or even who suggested my impeachment. Although, they knew that there were no grounds for it and it wasn't possible, but they have a right to do it and I have never had any feelings against it.

Q. Do you think there is a better understanding of the court today than there was, let's say, five years ago or ten years ago?

A. No, I can't say, because we have no measuring stick. You see, the court is in a position where it cannot fight back. It never can answer its critics and when all the public hears is one side, one never can tell what lodges in their minds and what they think.

Q. The statement has been made that the

court, under your leadership, made laws instead of interpreting the Constitution. What do you say to that?

A. Well, I think that no one could honestly say that the court makes no law. It doesn't make it consciously, it doesn't do it by intending to usurp the role of Congress, but because of the very nature of our job, when Congress says that everyone is entitled to the equal protection of the laws and it enacts no legislation on a given subject, and we have a case in this court in that area, we are left to interpreting the constitutional section one way or the other. We make law. It couldn't be otherwise, but we don't do it for the purpose of usurping Congress' function because Congress can do as it did in the last few years in the civil rights area, pass some very important civil rights acts and those acts have made our work immeasurably easier because all we have to do now is say what did Congress mean when it said this, and it said that, and it said something else. Before Congress had said nothing and we had to decide whether it came within that broad language of the Constitution, that everyone is entitled to due process of law and to the equal protection of the laws. Now, normally when we interpret congressional statute, if we misinterpret it, it is of no great significance because Congress within a few days can enact a new law to state exactly what they do mean, but when you come to dealing with constitutional questions, then, of course, it's different. Congress can't overrule our opinions on the Constitution. But sure, we have to make law. When two litigants come into court, one says the Act of Congress means this, the other one says the Act of Congress means the opposite of that, and we say the Act of Congress means something—either one of the two or something in between. We are making law, aren't we? Not because we want to invoke our power as against the Congress, but we have to interpret it and whatever way we interpret it we are making some law. But to recognize that as to statutes, if Congress doesn't believe that we interpreted their law properly they can change it overnight if they wish to do it.

Q. Someone once said, Mr. Chief Justice, that the Warren court, as he put it, will rank in history as the court of the people. Is that the way you'd like the court to be remembered?

A. I would like the court throughout its history to be remembered as the court of the people. No one can say how the opinions of any particular court or any particular era will stand the test of time. All one can do is to do his best to make his opinions conform to the Constitution and laws of the United States and then hope that they'll both be so considered in the future.

10.

Neil A. Armstrong, Edwin E. Aldrin, and Michael Collins: The Moon Landing

In May 1961 President Kennedy announced that the U. S. would land a man on the moon before the end of the decade. The commitment required funneling the bulk of American space exploration funds into this one project, eventuating in an estimated expense of approximately $24 billion. The goal was finally attained in the mission of Apollo 11, from July 16 to 24, 1969, providing the most striking television spectacular of the decade for a world-wide audience. The three astronauts were Neil A. Armstrong, Edwin E. Aldrin, Jr., and Michael Collins. The lunar module, nicknamed "Eagle," landed on the moon's surface on July 20, and Armstrong descended the ladder, uttering the now famous sentence: "That's one small step for a man, one giant leap for mankind." Armstrong and Aldrin spent 21 hours and 37 minutes on the moon before launching the module back into orbit and docking with the command ship "Columbia." Several weeks later, on September 16, the three astronauts addressed a joint session of Congress to tell about their experiences on the Apollo mission.

Source: *Congressional Record*, 91 Cong., 1 Session, September 16, 1969.

COL. EDWIN E. ALDRIN

Distinguished ladies and gentlemen, it is with a great sense of pride as an American and with humility as a human being that I say to you today what no men have been privileged to say before: "We walked on the moon." But the footprints at Tranquility base belong to more than the crew of Apollo 11. They were put there by hundreds of thousands of people across this country, people in government, industry and universities, the teams and crews that preceded us, all who strived throughout the years with Mercury, Gemini and Apollo.

Those footprints belong to the American people and you, their representatives, who accept it and support it, the inevitable challenge of the moon. And, since we came in peace for all mankind those footprints belong also to all people of the world. As the moon shines impartially on all those looking up from our spinning earth so do we hope the benefits of space exploration will be spread equally with a harmonizing influence to all mankind.

Scientific exploration implies investigating the unknown. The result can never be wholly anticipated. Charles Lindbergh said, "Scientific accomplishment is a path, not an end; a path leading to and disappearing in mystery."

Our steps in space have been a symbol of this country's way of life as we open our doors and windows to the world to view our successes and failures and as we share with all nations our discovery. The Saturn, Columbia, and Eagle and the Extravehicular Mobility Unit have proved to Neil, Mike and me that this nation can produce equipment of the highest quality and dependability. This should give all of us hope and inspiration to overcome some of the more difficult problems here on earth. The Apollo lesson is that national goals can be met where there is a strong enough will to do so.

The first step on the moon was a step toward our sister planets and ultimately toward the stars. "A small step for a man," was a statement of a fact, "a giant leap for mankind," is a hope for the future.

What this country does with the lessons of Apollo apply to domestic problems, and what we do in further space exploration programs will determine just how giant a leap we have taken. Thank you.

LIEUT. COL. MICHAEL COLLINS

MR. PRESIDENT, members of Congress, and distinguished guests:

One of the many things I have very much enjoyed about working for the space agency, and for the Air Force, is that they have always given me free rein, even to the extent of addressing this most august assemblage without coaching, without putting any words in my mouth. Therefore, my brief remarks are simply those of a free citizen living in a free country and expressing thoughts that are purely my own.

Many years before there was a space program my father had a favorite quotation: "He who would bring back the wealth of the Indies must take the wealth of the Indies with him." This we have done. We have taken to the moon the wealth of this nation, the vision of its political leaders, the intelligence of its scientists, the dedication of its engineers, the careful craftsmanship of its workers and the enthusiastic support of its people. We have brought back rocks and I think it's a fair trade. For just as the Rosetta Stone revealed the language of ancient Egypt, so may these rocks unlock the mystery of the origin of the moon, of our earth, and even of our solar system.

During the flight of Apollo 11, in the constant sunlight between the earth and the moon, it was necessary for us to control the temperature of our space craft by a slow rotation not unlike that of a chicken on a barbeque spit. As we turned, the earth and the moon alternately appeared in our windows. We had our choice. We could look toward the moon, toward Mars, toward our future in space—toward the new Indies—or we could look back toward the earth, our home, with its problems spawned over more than a millennium of human occupancy.

We looked both ways. We saw both, and I think that is what our nation must do.

We can ignore neither the wealth of the Indies nor the realities of the immediate needs of our cities, our citizens, or our civics. We cannot launch our planetary probes from a springboard of poverty, discrimination or unrest. But neither can we wait until each and every terrestrial problem has been solved. Such logic two hundred years ago would have prevented expansion westward past the Appalachian Mountains, for assuredly the Eastern Seaboard was beset by problems of great urgency then, as it is today.

Man has always gone where he has been able to go. It's that simple. We will continue pushing back his frontier, no matter how far it may carry him from his homeland.

Some day in the not-too-distant future, when I listen to an earthling step out onto the surface of Mars or some other planet, just as I listened to Neil step out onto the surface of the moon, I hope I hear him say: "I come from the United States of America!"

NEIL A. ARMSTRONG

We landed on the Sea of Tranquility, in the cool of the early lunar morning, when the long shadows would aid our perception.

The sun was only ten degrees above the horizon, while the earth turned through nearly a full day during our stay, the sun at Tranquility Base rose barely eleven degrees—a small fraction of the month-long lunar day. There was a peculiar sensation of the duality of time—the swift rush of events that characterizes all our lives—and the ponderous parade which makes the aging of the universe.

Both kinds of time were evident—the first by the routine events of the flight—whose planning and execution were detailed to fractions of a second—the latter by rocks round us, unchanged throughout the history of man—whose three-billion-year-old secrets made them the treasures we sought.

The plaque on the "Eagle" which summarized our hopes bears this message:

Here men from the planet earth first set foot upon the moon July 1969 A.D.

We came in peace for all mankind whose nineteen hundred and sixty-nine years had constituted the majority of the age of Pisces—a twelfth of the great year that is measured by the thousand generations the precession of the earth's axis requires to scribe a giant circle in the heavens.

In the next twenty centuries, the age of Aquarius of the great year, the age for which our young people have such high hopes, humanity may begin to understand its most baffling mystery—where are we going? The earth is, in fact, traveling many thousands of miles per hour in the direction of the constellation Hercules—to some unknown destination in the cosmos. Man must understand his universe in order to understand his destiny.

Mystery, however, is a very necessary ingredient in our lives.

Mystery creates wonder and wonder is the basis for man's desire to understand. Who knows what mysteries will be solved in our lifetime, and what new riddles will become the challenge of the new generations? Science has not mastered prophesy. We predict too much for next year yet far too little for the next ten. Responding to challenge is one of democracy's great strengths. Our successes in space lead us to hope that this strength can be used in the next decade in the solution of many of our planet's problems.

Several weeks ago I enjoyed the warmth of reflection on the true meaning of the spirit of Apollo.

I stood in the highlands of this nation, near the Continental Divide, introducing to my sons the wonders of nature, and pleasures of looking for deer and elk.

In their enthusiasm for the view they frequently stumbled on the rocky trails. But when they looked only to their footing, they did not see the elk. To those of you who have advocated looking high we owe our sincere gratitude, for you have granted us the opportunity to see some of the grandest views of the Creator.

To those of you who have been our honest critics, we also thank, for you have reminded us that we dare not forget to watch the trail. We carried on Apollo 11 two flags of this Union that had flown over the Capitol, one over the House of Representatives, one over the Senate.

It is our privilege to return them now

in these halls which exemplify man's highest purpose—to serve one's fellow man.

We thank you, on behalf of all the men of Apollo, for giving us the privilege of joining you in serving—for all mankind.

11.

Proclamation of the Delano Grape Workers

The Delano, California, grape pickers' strike began in September 1965 under the joint sponsorship of the Agricultural Workers' Organizing Committee, a Filipino group, and the National Farm Workers' Union, a Mexican-American organization led by Cesar Chavez. California agriculture is a multibillion-dollar business involving many powerful interests, most of whom were arrayed against the strikers and their quest for union recognition. In the fourth year of the strike, the unions made a bid for nationwide support through a boycott of table grapes. The proclamation printed below was issued by the grape workers for International Boycott Day, May 10, 1969. Finally, after five years, the strike was settled on terms favorable to the unions, in the summer of 1970. But the troubles of Cesar Chavez and his followers were far from over, for they were soon confronted by the International Brotherhood of Teamsters who also claimed jurisdiction over the California field workers. In the spring of 1973, when the union contracts came up for renewal, many growers signed with the Teamsters instead of with Chavez' United Farm Workers. Chavez had the backing of the AFL-CIO, but the Teamsters, favored by the growers, posed a real threat to the survival of the UFW.

Source: *El Malcriado*, April 15, 1969.

WE, THE STRIKING GRAPE WORKERS of California, join on this International Boycott Day with the consumers across the continent in planning the steps that lie ahead on the road to our liberation. As we plan, we recall the footsteps that brought us to this day and the events of this day. The historic road of our pilgrimage to Sacramento later branched out, spreading like the unpruned vines in struck fields, until it led us to willing exile in cities across this land. There, far from the earth we tilled for generations, we have cultivated the strange soil of public understanding, sowing the seed of our truth and our cause in the minds and hearts of men.

We have been farm workers for hundreds of years and pioneers for seven. Mexicans, Filipinos, Africans, and others, our ancestors were among those who founded this land and tamed its natural wilderness. But we are still pilgrims on this land, and we are pioneers who blaze a trail out of the wilderness of hunger and deprivation that we have suffered even as our ancestors did. We are conscious today of the significance of our present quest. If this road we chart leads to the rights and reforms we demand, if it leads to just wages, humane working conditions, protection from the misuse of pesticides, and to the fundamental right of collective bargaining, if it changes the social order that relegates us to the bottom reaches of society, then in our wake will follow thousands of American farm workers. Our example will make them free. But if our road does not bring us to victory and social change, it will not be because our direction is mistaken or our resolve too weak, but only because our bodies are mortal and our journey hard. For we are in the midst of a great social movement, and we will not stop struggling 'til we die, or win!

We have been farm workers for hundreds of years and strikers for four. It was four years ago that we threw down our plowshares and pruning hooks. These Biblical symbols of peace and tranquillity to us represent too many lifetimes of unprotesting submission to a degrading social system that allows us no dignity, no comfort, no peace. We mean to have our peace, and to win it without violence, for it is violence we would overcome—the subtle spiritual and mental violence of oppression, the violence subhuman toil does to the human body. So we went and stood tall outside the vineyards where we had stooped for years. But the tailors of national labor legislation had left us naked. Thus exposed, our picket lines were crippled by injunctions and harassed by growers; our strike was broken by imported scabs; our overtures to our employers were ignored. Yet we knew the day must come when they would talk to us, *as equals.*

We have been farm workers for hundreds of years and boycotters for two. We did not choose the grape boycott, but we *had* chosen to leave our peonage, poverty, and despair behind. Though our first bid for freedom, the strike, was weakened, we would not turn back. The boycott was the only way forward the growers left to us. We called upon our fellow men and were answered by consumers who said—as all men of conscience must—that they would no longer allow their tables to be subsidized by our sweat and our sorrow: they shunned the grapes, fruit of our affliction.

We marched alone at the beginning, but today we count men of all creeds, nationalities, and occupations in our number. Between us and the justice we seek now stand the large and powerful grocers who, in continuing to buy table grapes, betray the boycott their own customers have built. These stores treat their patrons' demands to remove the grapes the same way the growers treat our demands for union recognition—by ignoring them. The consumers who rally behind our cause are responding as we do to such treatment—with a boycott! They pledge to withhold their patronage from stores that handle grapes during the boycott, just as we withhold our labor from the growers until our dispute is resolved.

Grapes must remain an unenjoyed luxury for all as long as the barest human needs and basic human rights are still luxuries for farm workers. The grapes grow sweet and heavy on the vines, but they will have to wait while we reach out first for our freedom. The time is ripe for our liberation.

Astronaut Edwin E. Aldrin, Jr., walking near the lunar module during the Apollo 11 mission

THE MOON AND BEYOND

In May 1961 President Kennedy committed the U.S. space program to the goal of putting a man on the moon before the end of the decade. This commitment resulted in the funneling of most space exploration funds into the Apollo program, but the effort was a success. Manned by Neil Armstrong, Edwin Aldrin, Jr., and Michael Collins, Apollo 11 was launched on July 16, 1969. Having landed their lunar vehicle, Armstrong and Aldrin descended to the moon's surface on July 20 for a stay of 20 hours and 36 minutes. This achievement was witnessed, via television and radio, by hundreds of millions of people in all parts of the world. The next four years saw five more successful moon landings. (Apollo 13, in April 1970, suffered a mishap and returned to earth without completing its mission.) Apollo 17, the final lunar landing mission, took place in December 1972. The end of the Apollo program was concurrent with a general decline in the funding of space programs in the early 1970s, after a decade of enormous expenditure and great technological effort. Nevertheless, in May 1972, President Nixon announced that the United States and the Soviet Union would participate in a joint manned flight in July 1975.

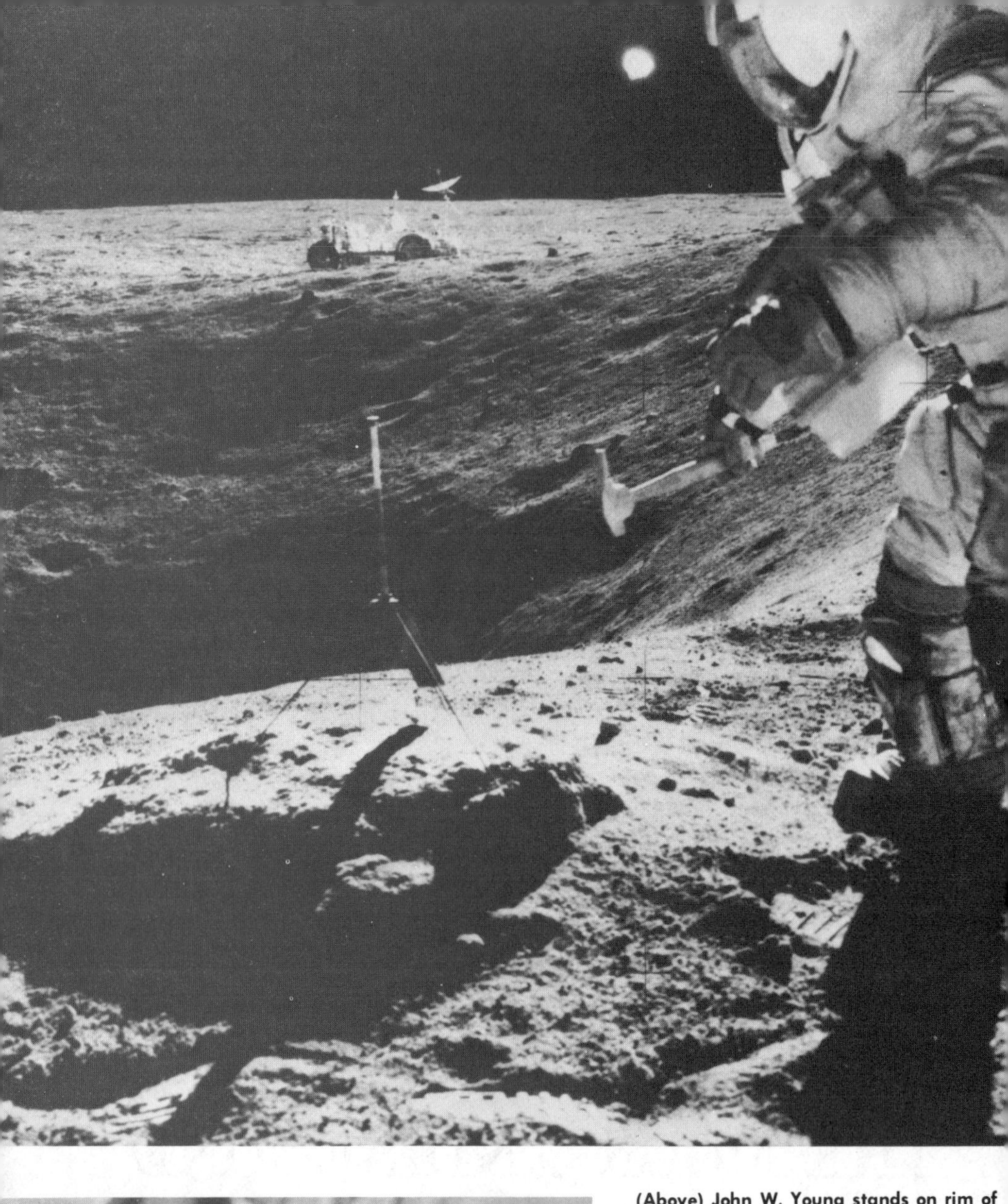

(Above) John W. Young stands on rim of Plum crater during the Apollo 16 mission; (left) Apollo 17 astronauts Cernan and Evans drift weightlessly in the spacecraft.

The final mission of the lunar landing series, Apollo, was billed as perhaps man's last opportunity to walk on the moon in this century. Manned by astronauts Eugene Cernan, Ronald Evans, and Harrison Schmitt, the flight of Apollo 17 lasted from December 7 to 19, 1972. With the moon landings successfully behind it, the United States went on with more diversified aspects of space exploration, notably manned satellites and unmanned interplanetary probes.

The next major venture of the Jational Aeronautics and Space ‹dministration was the Skylab nanned earth satellite program. 'he orbiting laboratory was aunched on May 14, 1973; and luring the year three separate rews of three men were sent up to endezvous with it. In-flight damage to the Skylab itself, as well as ther delays, kept the first crew rom joining the satellite in their ‹pollo spaceship until May 25, for 28-day stay. The second Skylab rew was launched on July 28 for a 59-day stay; and on November 16 he Skylab 3 astronauts went up for n unprecedented 84-day tour orbiting the earth. All missions were uccessful, despite recurring difiiculties with the Skylab equipnent. The purpose of the program vas to demonstrate man's ability o live in space for extended periods of time, and to make asronomical and other scientific obervations.

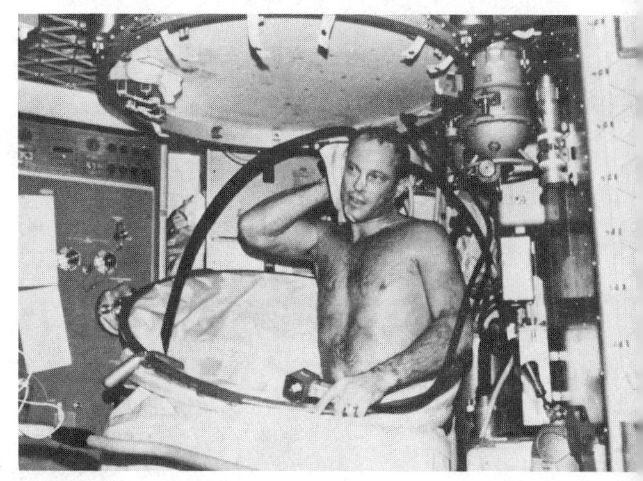

Top) The Skylab space station in orbit; center) Skylab pilot Jack Lousma taking a bath in the orbital workshop; (bottom ight) Owen K. Garriott, Skylab 3 scientist, een during extravehicular activity; (bottom left) Garriott preparing a meal board Skylab 3

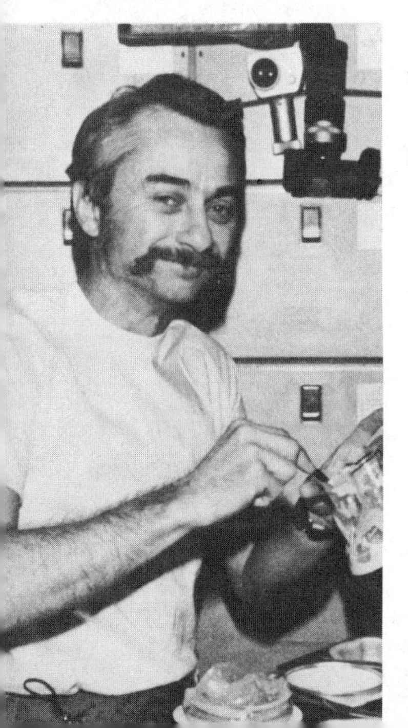

Unmanned spaceships continued to gather information about the solar system, with interplanetary probes in the Pioneer, Mariner, and Explorer programs. The Mariner Spacecraft sent back data from Mars, while several of the Pioneer craft orbited the sun. Pioneer 10, launched on March 2, 1972, passed close to Jupiter in December 1973, sent back information on this largest of planets, then passed on out of the solar system into deep space.

(Above) The Skylab 3 crew photographed the comet Kohoutek; (below) the gigantic volcanic mountain, Nix Olympia, on Mars as photographed from Mariner 9 in January 1973

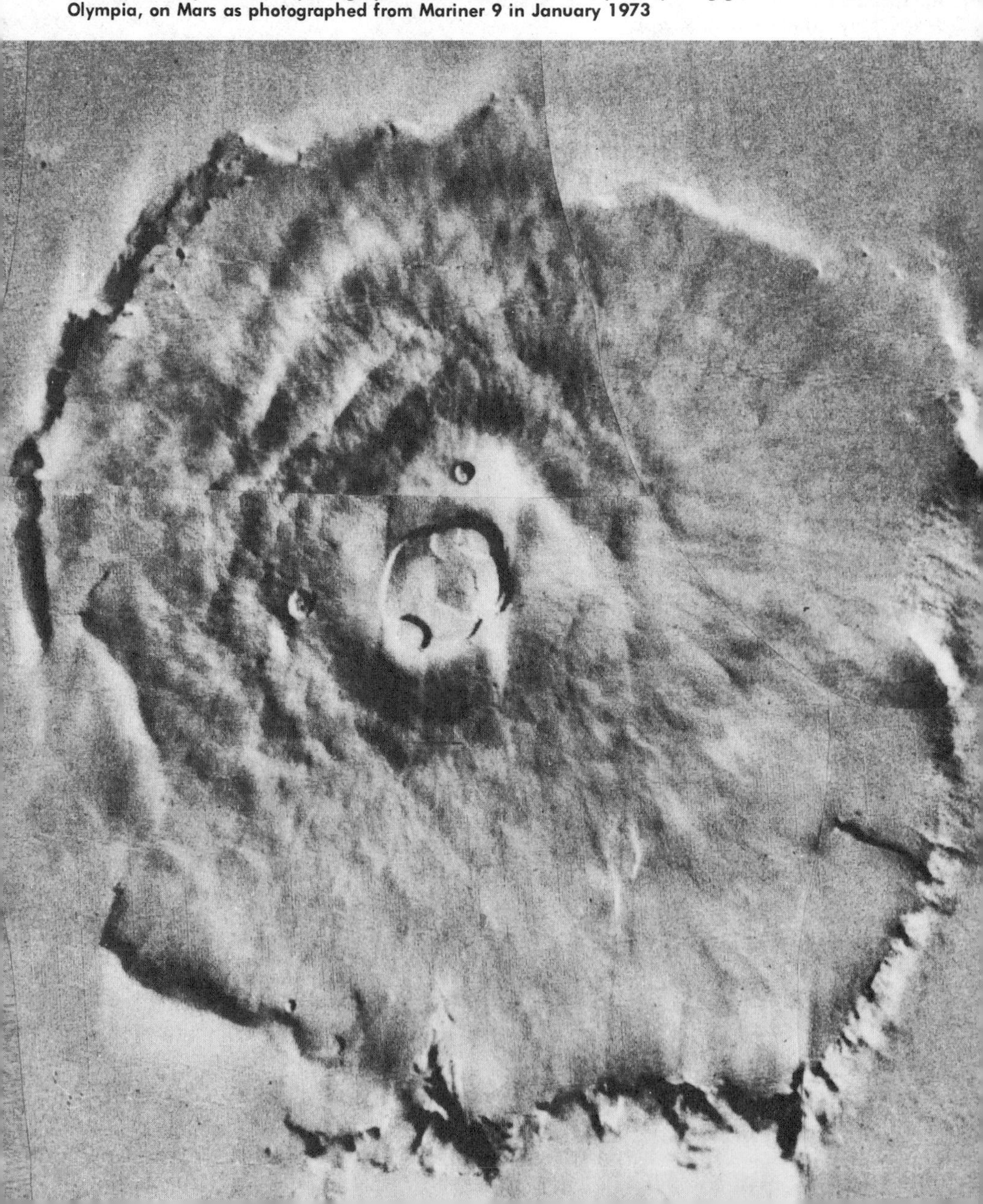

12.

JOSEPH L. RAUH, JR.: Fraud and Violence in a Union Election

The campaign and December 1969 election of a United Mine Workers president inaugurated a series of events that would take several years to unravel. In the election itself, challenger Joseph A. Yablonski was defeated by incumbent, W. A. "Tony" Boyle. On about December 31, Yablonski, his wife, and daughter were murdered in their Clarksville, Pennsylvania, home. The bodies were discovered on January 5, 1970. Eventually three men were indicted, tried, and convicted for the crime. And in September 1973, Boyle himself was arrested in connection with the murders. Failing an attempt at suicide by poison, he was held in custody for trial. He had already resigned his post as union president on December 19, 1972, after being sentenced to prison for a five year term for misusing union funds. He had also been decisively defeated in a new union election supervised by the Department of Labor. This letter of July 9, 1969, from Washington, D. C., lawyer, Joseph L. Rauh, Jr., to Secretary of Labor George Schultz, details some of the tactics used against Yablonski in his 1969 campaign for the union presidency.

Source: *Congressional Record*, 91 Cong., 1 Session, July 15, 1969.

DEAR MR. SECRETARY: Joseph A. Yablonski, candidate for President of the United Mine Workers of America, and H. Elmer Brown, candidate for Vice-President thereof, hereby request an immediate and continuing investigation, pursuant to Section 601 of the Labor-Management Reporting and Disclosure Act of 1959, of the illegal activities of the officers of the Union seeking to prevent the nomination of Mr. Yablonski and Mr. Brown for those offices. If the investigation is to be effective, it must commence immediately and encompass substantially all of the districts and local unions, and especially must include monitoring of local union nomination meetings through Government observers.

The Constitution of the United Mine Workers was amended in 1964 to require nominations by 50 local unions (previously it had been 5) in order for a candidate to have his name placed on the official United Mine Workers ballot. Pursuant to the Mine Workers Constitution, nominations are to be made during the period from July 9 to August 9, 1969, and there is a requirement that all local union members be given one week's notice of the nominating meeting. Since the nominating process starts today, Mr. Yablonski and Mr. Brown urgently request immediate investigatory action by the Department of Labor.

We set forth below the massive efforts being made by the incumbents, W. A. ("Tony") Boyle, President, George J. Titler, Vice-President, and John Owens, Secretary-Treasurer, all of whom are candidates for reelection, to prevent Mr.

Yablonski and Mr. Brown from meeting the new requirement of 50 local union nominations. Before describing the specific illegal acts of the incumbent officers and those working with them, we refer, as background, to some of the methods used by the incumbents to maintain absolute control of the union.

The Labor Department brought suit in 1964 (Civil Action No. 3071-64) in the United States District Court for the District of Columbia against the widespread and now almost universal practice of placing United Mine Worker districts into trusteeship and directing the affairs of local unions through appointed district officers. The Labor Department suit against the United Mine Workers and the appointed district officials seeks to outlaw certain trusteeships and return the districts to democratic control. This suit has been delayed for five years by the incumbents (i.e. Boyle, Titler, Owens), but the facts of their overwhelming power through trusteeships are well known to the Department. The presidents and secretary-treasurers of 19 of the 23 Mine Worker districts in the United States are appointed by Mr. Boyle; the International Executive Board members from 15 of these 23 districts are chosen by Mr. Boyle and ratified without discussion or opposition by the Mine Workers Convention. In addition to the power exercised through this trusteeship process, the records of the Labor Department are replete with nonrepayable loans made by the International Union to the districts, thus making the control through the power of appointment absolute through the power of the purse. It is against this background of the increase from five to 50 locals for nomination, widespread trusteeships, and loans to districts, that the Department must consider the facts set forth below of the incumbents' illegal activities to prevent the nomination of Mr. Yablonski and Mr. Brown.

1. Immediately following Mr. Yablonski's public announcement of his candidacy for President (May 29, 1969), he addressed a letter to Mr. Boyle asking that the Union mail campaign literature at his own expense to the members of the Union in compliance with Section 401(c) of LMRDA. Despite the express terms of Section 401(c) requiring unions to make such mailings, Mr. Boyle in flagrant violation of law rejected even this modest request. On June 23, 1969. District Judge Corcoran ordered the incumbents to mail Mr. Yablonski's literature in compliance with Section 401(c) (Civil Action No. 1662-69). Despite Judge Corcoran's order, an attorney for the United Mine Workers deliberately sought to sabotage the mailing.

2. One week after Mr. Yablonski's announcement of his candidacy (i.e., on June 6, 1969), Mr Boyle removed him from his office as acting director of Labor's Non-Partisan League and threatened him with further reprisals. These reprisals are now the subject of Mr. Yablonski's second suit in the District Court here (Civil Action No. 1799-69).

3. On June 28, 1969, Mr. Yablonski appeared before a group of local union leaders in Springfield, Illinois seeking support for his nomination. While the meeting was breaking up, an as yet unknown assailant knocked Mr. Yablonski unconscious. According to Mr. Yablonski and his doctor, the blow was from the rear and of a professional nature. This matter is under Department of Justice investigation.

4. On the following day, June 29, 1969, a rally of Mr. Yablonski's supporters at Shenandoah, Pa., attended by Mr. Brown because of Mr. Yablonski's injury, was

broken up by paid officials of the United Mine Workers. These officials imported into the area more than 50 hired goons who intimidated persons seeking entrance to the meeting, prevented speakers from being heard, forced others to leave, and caused concellation of the meeting. The full story is reported in the Shenandoah Evening Herald of June 30, 1969. This matter is also under Department of Justice investigation.

5. Supporters of Mr. Yablonski have been systematically approached and directed to support Mr. Boyle. When they refused to do so, they have been threatened with later reprisal. Among those so approached are Victor Pezzoni, Pete Sabo and Eli Matovich.

6. A variation of the threats in the last paragraph was made to Jack Peters, Secretary-Treasurer of Local Union 1787, of which Mr. Yablonski is President. One week after Peters refused to succumb to pressure to support Mr. Boyle, Al Lamo, International Auditor, went to Peters' home and demanded the books of his local union under threat of charges against him.

7. Local union officials who were supporting Mr. Yablonski were offered jobs on the United Mine Workers payroll to persuade them to disavow Mr. Yablonski's candidacy and to go for Mr. Boyle. Among the men so approached are Andrew F. Surma, Joe Sitos, Victor Pezzoni, and Nick Devince.

8. In District 5 where Yablonski will obviously get many local union nominations because he is the democratically elected International Executive Board member and former President of the District, all local unions having 20 members or less were disbanded by letter dated June 27, 1969. This effort to deny him nominations is a clear violation of the Constitution of the United Mine Workers. Even worse, this discriminatory dechartering of small locals was done *only* in the area where Yablonski is strong and not in other districts. This action is in strange contrast to the recognition at recent Mine Workers Conventions of local unions of far less than 20 which were regularly seated. In one case at least, a local with only one member was seated.

9. On June 23, 1969, the charter of Local Union 247, Minenk, Illinois, was revoked at the direction of the International Union. This local, in which there was strong support for Mr. Yablonski, had been in continuous operation even though the mine was closed down in March, 1951. Now, 18 years later, for no reason except that there is an election coming up and opponents of the incumbents are seeking nominations, the charter has been revoked.

10. On Sunday, July 6, 1969, Local 7113 was having its regular meeting. Despite the fact that this was prior to the time for nominations and despite the fact that no notice had been given that nominations would be made at the meeting, financial secretary John Aiello assumed the chairmanship of the meeting, nominated Mr. Boyle, ruled out of order a nomination of Mr. Yablonski, closed the nominations and declared Mr. Boyle nominated. Aiello is a paid employee in District 17, a trusteed district.

11. The same illegal conduct was scheduled for Local Union 2339 the previous day. Five District and International representatives attended the meeting for the purpose of obtaining a similar surprise nomination for Mr. Boyle and blocking off one for Mr. Yablonski. Luckily, Mr. Yablonski himself attended this meeting and the surprise nomination did not occur.

12. On July 2, 1969, in an obvious attempt to repeat the action at Local 7113

and the intended action at Local 2339, Mr. Budzanoski, President of District 5 and one of those who has threatened Mr. Yablonski's supporters, addressed a letter to all recording secretaries in District 5 asking for the date, time and place of the local union meetings at which nominations are to be held. He demanded an immediate response in a self-addressed return envelope and said he had "certain responsibilities" in connection with the nominations. Like Springfield (par. 3), Shenandoah (par. 4), Local 7113 (par. 10), and Local 2339 (par. 11), Mr. Budzanoski's letter portends continuous unlawful activities at nomination meetings.

13. United Mine Workers funds are being illegally used in connection with the nominating process. We have already referred to job offers, but that is only the beginning. To break up the Shenandoah rally (par. 4), $20.00 a person was paid to goons. On June 25, 1969, $10.00 a car load was paid for persons to attend a rally at which Boyle, Titler and Owens were present.

14. An anonymous and libelous sheet about Mr. Yablonski, which has been circulated throughout the Union, was prepared by Mr. Justin McCarthy, editor of the United Mine Workers Journal, and other employees of the Union, all at Union expense.

15. For years the Mine Workers Journal has been a public joke for its efforts to keep the incumbents before the Union membership. Some editions have had more pictures of Mr. Boyle than pages. Recognizing this, Mr. Yablonski, immediately upon the announcement of his candidacy, asked for equal space. Not only was this rejected by Mr. Boyle, but in both of the issues since Mr. Yablonski's announcement, there has been no single reference to Mr. Yablonski and Mr. Boyle has been prominently and favorably displayed. In the June 15th edition, a very prominent picture of him with John L. Lewis was captioned with Mr. Boyle as Lewis's "protege." In the July 1st issue, Mr. Boyle is shown in five pictures and repeatedly given credit for alleged achievements of the Union.

16. At an International Executive Board meeting in February 1969, Mr. Boyle told the presidents of various districts to request a loan from the Washington office in order to finance his reelection campaign. The district presidents at this meeting were Budzanoski, Younker, Philpott, Pass and Kelly. We have made a complaint to the Department of Justice about specific conversions of these loans into Mr. Boyle's election funds.

17. The incumbents have access to and have utilized the list of officers of the local unions of the United Mine Workers. Despite this fact, when counsel for Mr. Yablonski asked for a copy of the list, counsel for the United Mine Workers refused to turn same over to him.

What we have set out above is only the part of the iceberg above the water line. The terror inside a union where a candidate for President is knocked unconscious and where a rally for that candidate is broken up by goons is even greater when it comes to the individual members. The reign of terror makes it hard to get the facts. Many have told Mr. Yablonski and others the same stories as those listed above, but they also talk about their pensions, and their jobs, and their families, and they say that they cannot speak out. What we have presented here is only a small part of the total illegal activities of the incumbents. But it is enough to know that every local union is threatened with unlawful activities up to, during, and after nomination meetings.

There can be no question from what

has been set out above that the incumbents are engaged in massive violations of the Landrum-Griffin Act in order to save their posts in the Union. It is thus clear that the Labor Department will have to take action under Title IV of the Act. The time to get the evidence is while the action is on, during the nominating period starting today. We ask the Department to move now.

13.

J. B. COLWELL: A Vindication of the Military-Industrial Relationship

In his Farewell Address to the nation in 1961, President Eisenhower had warned of the power of the military-industrial complex in our society. His words, coming at a time when the Cold War was still being forcefully waged, went nearly unheeded. But within the decade, as protests against American involvement in Southeast Asia mounted, the whole war-making apparatus of the nation was called into question. The draft was reviled for its inequities and for sending unwilling soldiers to fight an undeclared war. The size of the Pentagon budget, and the waste inherent in it, were criticized. And the allegation was frequently made that the United States needed a wartime economy to flourish. In October 1967, a large antiwar march descended on the Pentagon; draft-card burnings became commonplace; and many young men fled the country to avoid military service. To counter some of this adverse sentiment Vice-Admiral J. B. Colwell, Deputy Chief of Naval Operations, gave the following address to the New York chapter of the American Ordnance Association on April 10, 1969.

THE UNITED STATES TODAY has a very large military-establishment. It is sizable in manpower, numbering over two million men. It is sizable in real property holdings, both here and abroad. It has a sizable inventory of aircraft, vehicles, and ships.

The cost of maintaining this force also is sizable. This year some 60 percent of our governmental budget or 12 percent of our gross national product will be spent in support of our defense establishment. Without debating the adequacy of this outlay, past and current, it is an obvious fact that military preparedness is an expensive business.

This military force is built upon and sustained by the largest industrial economy the world has ever known. To defend our nation in today's environment, we must have the most advanced, most effective weapons which can be produced, and we must have them in sufficient numbers. There is no second-place prize in a military contest.

It is our industrial technology and production capacity which make it possible to put such weapons into the hands of our troops. The resulting military force safeguards our economy. Our economy, thus secure, maintains for our society the world's highest standard of living with its rights to life, liberty, and the pursuit of happiness.

This, simply stated, is the military-industrial relationship which exists in our country.

Certainly there is a so-called "military-industrial complex" in this country! Our military forces could not exist without it, and, in the international environment in which we find ourselves, our country could not long exist without the means to achieve military security.

There are those, however, who would have us believe that the military and industry operate in an entirely different manner from the normal manufacturer-consumer relationships which are accepted in other sectors of our economy.

The country has been warned of an insidious Military-Industrial Complex, controlled by an oligarchy of military and industrial leaders. The necessary teamwork between industrial management and members of the Defense Department is alleged by some to represent a form of conspiracy, generated not in the nation's interest but for the purpose of personal power and immense profit.

The existence of this complex, we are warned, will lead to the ruination of our economy, the reduction of our democracy to a garrison state, and, finally, to our destruction through irrational war.

I am not so naive as to forget that there are historical incidents of illegal activities and collusion in the past, nor to deny that there are people in the military and in business today who would turn a dishonest dollar. But I would emphatically deny that such activity is widespread, and I submit that the possibility of activity so extensive as to approach a conspiracy is indeed remote.

Let me develop the strange kind of logic which leads to an erroneous conclusion about the military-industrial relationship. It begins with the establishment of demand which, in this supposed case, is generated by an aberration in the desires of the military leader whose mind is fixed on war and who demands all the things with which to wage war. It is never satisfied with the capability or quality of the weapons in the arsenal and is constantly striving for more and better arms.

Industry, so the story goes, always interested in a good market, responds to fill this demand. Going further, industry applies the professional hard sell, playing on the fears and egos of the anxious and easily convinced military.

By elaborate advertising and lavish entertainment, the fable continues, industry generates artificial demands for useless weapons. Once this cycle is established, the military and industry join forces and control this process for their mutual advantage. The middlemen are the retired military officers employed by the defense contractors.

How is it that such business can be carried on despite governmental controls and congressional checks? How can it be done right under the noses of a suspicious press and public? Again, the explanation is the military mind.

However, this time the critics have transformed the character of this mind. It is no longer slow and easily persuaded. The point is now made that military opinions and advice prevail because the military has produced an unending supply of distinguished, capable articulate, and effective leaders.

Their skill, energy, and dedication make them dominant in almost every government or civic organization they may inhabit, from high position to the local PTA. They are able to dazzle the Congress by their intricate budgetary footwork.

The public at large is supposedly hoodwinked by a vast public-relations campaign (referred to in the complex as propaganda) and by what might be called the military-industrial auxiliary. This includes all those who have ever served in the military and a number of organizations and persons who are just sympathetic.

They lobby for the complex, supplement the propaganda with periodicals extolling the merits of a strong defense posture, and generally subvert the population by encouraging youth to enlist, making patriotic speeches, and organizing Fourth of July parades.

However, this is *not* the way it works in real life. You know it, I know it, and I think the great American public knows it.

Let us look at the structure which militates against the feared unholy alliance. In the first place, each service has a limited budget which it will not knowingly waste on unneeded weapons or inflated prices.

Secondly, anyone remotely familiar with Government contracting procedures knows that the restraints, checks, audits, and requirements make it extremely difficult for any collusion to take place. Also, the contractors are competing among themselves.

One might ask a contractor who has just lost a major contract-formulation/contract-definition bid, after having spent millions of his own money, what his opinion is of the military-industrial complex!

What about those retired senior officers who are employed by industry? The real reasons are very evident. It is good common sense for a company engaged in building weapons to hire individuals conversant with the operational employment of those weapons. Oil companies employ petroleum engineers, drug firms employ physicians, defense firms hire military professionals. To do otherwise would result in less effective designs and a less capable military arsenal.

If there were such a thing as a highly polished smoothly functioning military-industrial complex working for the mutual benefit of both parties, would our shipbuilding industry be in the shape it is in today? Would 58 percent of U.S. naval combatant ships be 20 years old or older? Would our aging and overworked fleet be on the verge of obsolescence?

Consider these figures: in 1963, the gross national product was just under $600 billion—the Navy shipbuilding account was $2.8 billion; in 1966 the GNP had risen to $750 billion but Navy ship construction had dropped to $2 billion; in 1969, with a near $900 billion GNP, the amount allocated to building new men of war had dwindled to $1.2 billion.

I ask you, what has happened to the smoothly effective operation of the military-industrial complex?

And then there is the charge of militarization of American society. I would submit that in a society which permits citizens dressed as Vietcong to march on Easter Sunday, overemphasis on the military virtues of loyalty, patriotism, duty, discipline, and service to country is hardly the problem. If the culture is so geared to the military, if the military is so respected, admired, powerful, and influential, why is retention of officers and men one of our most serious problems?

No, I think that those who are so concerned with this danger not only have overlooked our long history, they have closed their eyes to the present opposition to the draft, dissension over the Vietnam war, and disillusionment with structured power.

Of all of the fallacious arguments, the one which personally distresses me most is the allegation that the military man essentially wants war. The charge is leveled from time to time that the leaders of the complex deliberately plan wars because war justifies the existence of the establishment; that war provides experience for the military novice, challenges for the professional, and the field to exercise, prove, and perfect the industrial products. Thus war is not only welcomed but actively sought.

Well, what of these charges? What about this mythical beast?

First let me say that there is no such thing as the military mind. Military men as a group have similar inclinations, feelings, and general codes, but to assume that they think differently from any other segment of our society is ridiculous. They are products of the same schools, live in the same neighborhoods, read the same literature, and are exposed to the same pressures of domestic life as are other Americans. And as Americans they differ among themselves in their thinking just as do their neighbors.

In point of fact, the military man historically has opposed reckless, aggressive, belligerent action. He may argue that the danger of war requires more armament, but he will never argue that increased armament makes war desirable. He dreads war.

Concerning the professional associations, it is a significant point that these organizations serve a vital purpose in bringing together professionals who are engaged in a serious, expensive business critical to our national survival. Such liaison has been vastly beneficial in maintaining our defense.

I have attempted to show that fear of a massive military partnership with industry is without basis in fact. Such a thing does not now, nor did it ever, exist. Under our form of government, under the leadership of wise men imbued with an abiding love of country, it will not come to pass.

We cannot return to a simpler time when the problems of world leadership and the complexities of technological warfare did not rest upon our shoulders. The threat which we face is real, and we must have a modern strong military establishment in order to defend ourselves.

I view the military-industrial complex, if we choose to use that term, as an essential element of our national survival. An occasional self-serving individual there may be, for infallibility is a scarce commodity. But patriotism is in rich supply, and our loyalty and integrity are not for sale.

It is not politically hard for me to vote against, say, a new aircraft carrier. But if the shipyard were in my state and five thousand people were waiting for the work, I would be examining very closely, and perhaps less critically, all those reasons why the carrier might be essential to national security.

SENATOR PHILIP HART of Michigan

14.

Debate on the Safeguard Antiballistic Missile

President Nixon's toughest legislative battle in 1969 consisted in getting approval for the Safeguard antiballistic missile program from Congress, especially from the Senate where opposition was strong. He wanted Safeguard both as a test of his ability to deal with Congress and to achieve bargaining power with the Russians in the forthcoming Strategic Arms Limitation Talks. After months of debate, lobbying, and pressure, the Senate vote finally came on August 6. Crippling amendments to the bill were defeated narrowly, and the measure passed the Senate. Three months later it passed the House. In contrast to the previous ABM system, known as Sentinel, Safeguard was to be concentrated in missile silos and command control centers, and would be, when operative, oriented primarily toward the Soviet Union. On July 15, three weeks before the Senate vote, a debate on the merits of the system was aired over nationwide television on the David Frost Show. Participants were former Secretary of State Dean Acheson and Senator Charles Percy of Illinois. Portions of their remarks are reprinted here.

Source: *Congressional Record*, 91 Cong., 1 Session, July 23, 1969.

Frost: Welcome back. And will you welcome now—we're privileged to welcome, on my left—Senator Percy just pointed out he ought to be on the right—but Senator—will you welcome on my left the Honorable Dean Acheson, and on my right Senator Charles Percy.

And initially at the beginning we want to try to do something that's rarely done on television and open this, in a sense, first of all as a debate, and then open it wider. And first of all, particularly in view of the audience's views, and so on. I want to turn, if I may, to you, Mr. Acheson, and ask you if you could outline for us first of all what you regard as the imperative reasons why this country should have ABM.

Dean Acheson: I'll do my best. I've been involved in this nuclear business since the end of the war. Over twenty years, and every once in a while we come to what I think is a corner, a crisis, a turning point in the—in the development of our relations with the other super-state, which is the other great nuclear state, the Soviet Union.

And it seems to me we've reached one of them now. We started off with a great attempt on the part of our government to turn this whole nuclear matter over to international control. This was the first big effort that we made with our allies on the other side of the ocean. First of all in '46 when we presented the Baruch plan, and then in '51, when I presented the disarmament plan in Paris.

But the Russians turned them all down. In fact, Vishinsky said that my proposal kept him awake all night because he laughed so hard. Well, it didn't seem to me that was quite the right response to this effort. But at any rate, we did our best to have international control, and failed.

So we started protecting ourselves, developing our nuclear power, and they were already doing this also. And we have come, to put it very briefly, over the twenty intervening years, to a point where each of us is armed to the extent that Mr. Churchill said created the delicate balance of terror. By which he means that we were both in a position to prevent the other person from making a first move, because it would be what is called doomsday if that happened. The retaliatory power would be so great that once the other person shot, the riposte would kill everybody. This was the balance of terror.

Every once in a while, in this development, a new weapon is introduced. This has to be met. We now have on each side the old manned bombers. They're still in operation and still carry their bombs, and they are provided against by the other side.

The next development was land based missiles, in which the Russians had the lead. We rapidly caught up with them and passed them. And we are now, roughly speaking, approximately equal.

Then we developed the nuclear submarine, the Polaris, and they developed one. And again we had this balance of terror.

Now a new weapon has been introduced into the balance. And that is the SS-9, which is a very large, long range, intercontinental ballistic missile, developed by the Russians, with three warheads which are discharged in space, separate, and each one goes to a target. Each one is not separately aimed, but the whole weapon is directed so that when they divide, each one will go to a predetermined target. And these are so developed that each warhead, if directed toward one of our land based missiles, would, we think, destroy it.

Now there will be a difference probably between the Senator and his advisor, and me and mine, as to the efficiency of these Russian weapons. That is part of the argument that we will have here tonight.

To meet that there has been developed on both sides an anti-ballistic missile. The purpose of this is to meet an incoming missile in space and destroy it in space before it lands. This is to prevent the great destruction which the weapon causes when it hits either a city, or another missile, and the fallout which occurs if it attempts to destroy one of the silos on the ground and throws up a great deal of nuclear charged dust.

Now Russians have these deployed all around Moscow. We are now, under the President's proposal, developing anti-ballistic missiles to deploy around the sites where the Minute Men, our land based missiles are buried.

Now the debate between the Senator and me will be around several issues. One is, is the Russian SS-9 a real danger? We claim it's a serious one. I think his attitude will be that it is not as serious as we think. Or that the Minute Men do not need as much protection as we think they need.

Another issue will be: does the ABM do what it is claimed to be able to do? That is, meet these SS-9s as they come, and destroy them. Another issue will be: are there other ways of meeting this than the one that we propose, or the President proposes? Are they cheaper? Are they better? We say there are none as good. The Senator will doubtless believe that there are some equally good, or even better. That's another issue.

And finally there is an issue as to whether our deploying these weapons will inhibit in any way the furtherance of discussions with the Russians for the purpose of stopping further development of nuclear weapons, or if possible, disarming.

Now on some of these issues obviously I've had experience and am able to make some contribution of my own. On others I'm a layman and don't understand the nuclear scientific issues as well as people who are trained in that discipline, and therefore I have to make a judgment on the basis of what I am told.

Let me therefore start out by saying a word or two about a matter on which I've had a good deal of experience, which is: does this interfere with our negotiations with the Russians?

I believe that it does not. I've had a good deal of negotiation with the Russians. They are not delicate, shy people. They are not frightened by what the other people do. They, themselves, have developed an anti-ballistic missile. They know its function, its purpose. They are quite aware of the fact that this is inherently a defensive weapon. It is to meet something which is aimed at you, as far as we devise it, and destroy that thing. Therefore they are not going to be any less willing to talk, they're going to be more willing to talk if they believe that we are stronger and there's something worth bargaining about. . . .

Percy: Well I think so too. And I think really what Secretary Acheson has said, where he's given us the historical background of what we've done as the defense—that we've built defenses against the bombers, and against the missiles, is really why we're having this great debate. Because what we've done over a period of years because of this tremendous presumed threat from the Soviet Union, have spent billions and billions and billions of dollars building DEW lines, building NIKE sites. I suppose the cost goes thirty, forty, fifty billion dollars, and much of it is now covered by the Arctic snow, and the wastes, and abandoned. Because it simply didn't develop that way. The world didn't turn out the way those defenses were planned for.

And I just wonder today how different this nation might be, and how different life might be here, if we had not had to spend those billions and billions of dollars in the defense establishment.

I don't for a moment presume that the Department of Defense is anything other than utterly patriotic, and zealous in their attempt to guard us against every conceivable type of threat to us. In fact, they are able to plan, and they have on the books, planning two major wars and one minor war, carrying them on simultaneously, and being able to carry them out any place on earth, against any conceivable kind of threat. And I suppose this is their job.

But it's our job in the Congress to set the priorities. To finally and ultimately decide what is more important. And I have come to the conclusion that the threat is greater from within this country, if we don't do the right things and have the right national priorities, than it is from outside.

Now I don't for a moment, David, presume that we do not have to have a credible deterrent. We must have. No possible enemy of ours should ever feel we'll be weak. And we must be strong. From this standpoint I think, however, we have tremendous strength.

And two points are very important to have a credible deterrent. First you must have the power to strike. And second, you must have the will to use that power if you're ever struck against. I can't imagine the Russians, or anyone, as so naive as to believe we do not have the power. We have incredible power. And I hope they wouldn't be so naive as to assume we wouldn't have the guts and the will to use it if we were ever attacked.

That's all I think we need. It's sufficiency. And President Nixon used that word. How many times do we have to prove our ability to destroy the whole world? And how many times as we escalate this nuclear arms race now, do we have to? How many pounds, tons, megatons of firepower do we have to have to destroy every human being on earth?

I think we have enough. And I think the time to draw the line is now. And the ABM is a very good place to draw that line.

Actually I'd have to go back. I felt the Sentinel ABM was the time to draw the line. A few of us fought against it, you remember, when President Johnson was in office. We said it was not a good design, it would escalate the nuclear arms race, it would cost far more than they told us it would cost, and it was not a credible defense of our cities.

We've been proven right, oddly enough. The President has now said the very same things. And where are all the people who before were defending the Sentinel system? Not one of them has stood up since the President said it isn't right for this country, it will escalate, it will cost too much, it's not worth it, and you can't really defend the cities, it's not a credible defense of the cities.

Now we have a new name for it, the Safeguard. We have a way of taking these old systems that President Eisenhower—the NIKE-Zeus and the NIKE-X—said we shouldn't go ahead with; and President Kennedy said we shouldn't go ahead—and now we've bundled it into a new sort of package, with the sex appeal of the Sentinel name first, and then that didn't work, and now the Safeguard.

But it's the same old package. And it's the same old weak design, I think. In fact, the Safeguard is even weaker. It was designed for area defense, the defense of our cities, and now we've abandoned that thought. We've moved it back to the bases, to get them out of the cities where people will protest about being saved from a nuclear war by dragging nuclear bombs right into their neighborhood and back yard, and we're tucking them away out in South (sic) Dakota and Montana.

The odd thing is that the design of, say, the eye of the system, the MSR, the missile site radar, a huge structure, costing a hundred and sixty-five million dollars for each installation—the eye is the most vulnerable part of it. It was designed for an entirely different job, area defense. And now we don't need that design for point defense of the silos. And yet we're going to quickly rush into production and deploy a design that today is very weak. And any technician would admit that they don't even need to use the SS-9s that Dean Acheson mentioned. They can knock that out with the SS-11, which is only a megaton. And they take one-eighth of their existing supply of those, never touch the SS-9s and knock out every single one of the MSRs that we build.

Once you knock out the eye of the system, what good are the Sprints, and the Spartans, and the computers? What good's all the programming? And why wouldn't they use that less costly means of knocking out the heart of the system?

This is the defect of it, it's a weak design. It costs much more, too, than the 6.8 billion we've been told. I'd give you all the tea in China that it would not be built for less than twenty billion—that's Nationalist China—be built for less, less than twenty billion dollars. And I do feel when we're on the brink of negotiations, and we will begin negotiations, I feel confident, with the Soviet Union early in August, why, just as we're about to see whether we can't, both of us, find a mutuality of interest in stopping this madness of piling bombs, on bombs, on bombs, increasing the terror, which does not increase my sense of security and safety.

Why don't we sit down sensibly and rationally, and see, as Secretary Rogers said and President Nixon, whether we both can't go out of the ABM business? In fact, they have said, if they want to go out of the business, we'll go out of the business. And why not just first determine, while we're going ahead and redesigning the eye of the system, the MSR, see whether or not the Soviet Union wouldn't find a mutuality of interest in de-escalating the nuclear arms race?

So for these reasons I think a delay in the deployment of this system would be very wise. It serves our interest, it serves the interest of world peace. I think we'll be more secure that way, rather than rushing into an ABM system which they will retaliate against by increasing their offensive weapons. And they can build those a lot cheaper and faster than we can build this, the most complex, intricate electronic and mechanical system ever devised by mankind—and we have no idea whether it will work. In fact, Secretary Acheson said it may not work. And if it's not workable, at least when we're through with all of this—and he means maybe six to twenty billion dollars —we at least would have the satisfaction of knowing that it's not workable.

That's a pretty expensive thing to try to experiment with, when I can take twenty billion dollars as a Senator, and find a great many places to nation-build here at home with that money, and offer the promise of America to more people, and stop this tremendous flow of rampant inflation, which is distorting every priority we have in this country, and picking the pockets of every single American family.

We have spent a trillion four hundred billion dollars—isn't that the figure?—for defense since World War II, and we are not secure.

REPRESENTATIVE ABNER MIKVA of Illinois, 1969

15.

Firearms and Violence

The National Commission on the Causes and Prevention of Violence, with Milton S. Eisenhower as chairman, was formed on June 10, 1968, five days after the assassination of Senator Robert F. Kennedy. Consisting originally of seven task forces to study every phase of the problem of violence, an eighth, investigative, task force was soon added to look into the disorders at the Chicago Democratic Convention, civil strife in Cleveland, and campus unrest. During the balance of the year the commission held public hearings and undertook investigations in a variety of areas. In 1969 it began issuing reports and recommendations. The task force report on firearms was released on July 28, 1969. Its recommendations are reprinted here.

Source: *Firearms and Violence in American Life,* A Staff Report Submitted to the National Commission on the Causes and Prevention of Violence, Washington, D. C., n.d.

ONE OUT OF EVERY TWO HUNDRED deaths in this country results from the criminal or accidental use of firearms. About the same number of deaths are the result of firearms suicides. Thousands more are wounded each year, and untold others are threatened by someone holding a gun.

An overwhelming majority of the guns in this country are used responsibly. The handgun is the principal weapon of gun misuse, accounting for more than three fourths of all criminal gun violence. Although handguns constitute only about one fourth of all guns in civilian hands in the United States, the number of such guns is formidable—24 million. This amounts to an average of 40 handguns for every 100 households. And the rate is increasing because handgun sales have risen dramatically in the last decade.

It can surprise no one that high rates of gun violence are connected with high rates of handgun ownership. When the number of handguns increases, gun violence increases, and where there are fewer guns, there is less gun violence.

If there were fewer handguns in this country, the knife and other weapons might replace the gun as instruments of violence. Even so, deaths and injuries would be reduced because a gun attack is five times as deadly as an attack with another weapon.

The stockpile of handguns in this country is a legacy of traditional American attitudes toward firearms and decades of lax firearms control. Yet, the handgun in the house generally creates more danger than safety. The use of handguns for target shooting can be accommodated without such a stockpile of guns, and the handgun is unimportant as a hunting weapon. At the same time, civil disorder, racial tension, and fear of crime are turning our nation into an armed camp and have increased the role of firearms in violence. The vicious circle of Americans arming themselves to protect against other armed Americans must be broken. Finding effective and appropriate methods of reducing gun violence must be recognized as a national problem.

We have concluded that the only sure way to reduce gun violence is to reduce sharply the number of handguns in civilian hands in this country. We recognize this will be a massive and expensive task. But, the price is one that we should be prepared to pay.

Rifles and shotguns are a different story. These hunting and sport shooting weapons are an important part of the life of the nation. Their use in crime, by comparison with handguns, is limited.

Many countries distinguish between handguns and long guns in their firearms laws. Yet, no other country has ever attempted to control handguns with over 24 million such guns already in circulation. The success of any such undertaking must depend upon public understanding and support.

We submit the following recommendations with regard to public education, research, and legislation.

PUBLIC EDUCATION

PUBLIC EDUCATION PROGRAMS to inform Americans fully about the role of firearms in accidents, crime, and other forms of violence; a publicity campaign to reduce the number of loaded guns in American homes.

As symbols of our frontier tradition, toys for our children, and props for our movies and television, firearms are so commonplace to Americans that we seldom pause to reflect on their impact on our lives. Our casual attitude toward firearms may be shaken temporarily when tragedy strikes close to home or when the nation as a whole is aroused by a sensational act of gun violence. But Americans do not know the whole story of gun misuse in this country.

An information program is necessary to secure broad public support for meaningful firearms legislation and to encourage the safe and responsible use of firearms. Only after we know the risks to ourselves, our families, and our friends can we appreciate the need for legislation and for voluntary measures to eliminate the loaded gun from the home. If a citizen elects to own a firearm, he must understand the duties and responsibilities of such ownership and the safest methods of handling and storing firearms in his home or business. In addition to reappraising his own attitude toward keeping firearms in his home, each American must also appreciate how the security of our society is affected by millions of guns in millions of homes.

We urge in particular that the National Rifle Association and other private organizations devoted to hunting and sport shooting be enlisted with interested citizens and the media to assist in pointing out the dangers of loaded firearms in the home and the need for meaningful firearms legislation.

RESEARCH

RESEARCH TO HASTEN the development of an effective nonlethal weapon and improved methods of firearms detection; further research on strategies to reduce firearms misuse.

Scientific and technical research is needed to develop an effective nonlethal weapon or ammunition that would incapacitate but not kill an attacker. Replacing existing police and home defense weapons with nonlethal weapons would not interfere with self-protection, but would eliminate many fatal firearms incidents. Private industry, the government, and foundations charged with allocating funds for scientific research should be encouraged to join forces in developing nonlethal weapons.

Scientific research is also needed to develop methods of tracing and detecting firearms so that law enforcement officers can obtain a higher degree of compliance with existing and future firearms laws. No effective means of tracing firearms or ammunition is on the horizon, but electromagnetic, X-ray, chemical, and sensing devices using radioactive materials might allow the development of feasible firearms detection devices.

Research on the relationship between firearms and violence, and on methods of reducing gun violence, is necessary and should receive continuing private and governmental support. At the same time, we cannot use the excuse of incomplete knowledge to postpone dealing with problems which demand immediate attention.

LEGISLATION

EFFORTS TO OBTAIN uniform state firearms laws through voluntary action of the states have proven unsuccessful. We recommend a federal law establishing minimum federal standards for state firearms control systems. Within three years each state would enact a firearms control system meeting the federal standards or a federally administered system based on these standards will be established within that state. Federal guidelines to maximize consistency in interpreting the federal standards should be issued, although each state would be able to adjust its system to meet the federal standards in light of local conditions. Any state failing to enact a firearms law meeting federal standards would be subject to the establishment of a federal firearms control system within its borders.

HANDGUNS

A federal standard of restrictive licensing to confine handguns to persons who need them and to substantially reduce the number of handguns now in civilian hands in this country.

We recommend a national standard of restrictive handgun licensing to reduce substantially the 24 million handguns now in civilian hands in this country and thereby reduce the toll of gun violence. This handgun licensing system should be national in scope because the problem is national, and because a nonexistent or ineffective control system in one state makes it difficult for neighboring states to control gun violence. Yet, different states have different cultural patterns and crime problems, and handgun laws must vary somewhat in accordance with these differences. We recommend, therefore, that federal legislation establish minimum standards for handguns and allow the states some flexibility in adapting these standards to local conditions.

Under state administered restrictive licensing systems, applicants would have to establish both their eligibility to possess and a particular need for a handgun and pass a test designed to determine whether they know how to use and safely store a handgun.

The objective of this state administered national system would be to reduce the number of privately owned handguns in this country to a necessary minimum. All those who are not issued licenses and who must give up their handguns would be duly compensated.

Federal law should prescribe the following minimum standards for state handgun laws:

1. All handgun owners and purchasers

of handgun ammunition must be licensed. Licenses may be issued only to those who establish a need for such a firearm. Although need would be determined separately by each state, federal guidelines can encourage consistency. For instance, police officers, security guards, and some retail merchants should qualify for handgun licenses. Normal household protection would not constitute sufficient need. Under such guidelines, the number of legally held handguns would be reduced to about 10 percent or less of the present 24 million.

2. Handgun licenses will be denied to persons convicted of or under indictment for crimes of violence, fugitives, narcotics addicts, mental incompetents and defectives, and minors under 21.

3. A safety test will be required before issuance of a license.

4. Firearms dealers will be regulated to insure that they sell handguns or ammunition only to persons with licenses. Dealers and individuals intending to sell or transfer handguns will be required to submit reports on all such transactions and wait 20 days before delivering the gun to the transferee; during this period, the state will verify that it is the license holder who intends to acquire a handgun. No such report will be required for sales of ammunition. Pawnshops will be prohibited from dealing in handguns or ammunition.

5. The license program will be administered by a state agency without discrimination as to race, sex, or religion.

6. Licensed handgun owners will be required to supply information on each handgun they own and to notify police promptly if a handgun is stolen or lost. A system of periodic auditing of licensed handgun owners to insure that they still own the handguns licensed to them will be administered by a state agency.

7. A federally financed program to purchase handguns from private citizens and to grant amnesty to persons who relinquish illegally owned handguns will be administered by a state agency.

LONG GUNS

A federal standard of permissive licensing to allow all persons except a small segment of prohibited persons legally to own and use long guns.

We recommend a federal law establishing as a minimum national standard a long gun owner's identification card system in each state similar to the systems now in effect in Illinois and New Jersey, and a system to record any sale or transfer of a long gun.

Identification card: Except for persons under indictment for or convicted of a crime of violence, fugitives, narcotics addicts, and mental incompetents and defectives, all persons would be eligible for a long gun identification card. Persons under 18 would be allowed to use long guns under adult supervision. The state administering agency will issue to each qualified applicant a card, similar to a military identification card, showing his name, address, description, photograph, fingerprint, and social security number.

Transfer notice: We do not recommend registration of all existing long guns. The principal value of a registration system would be to guard against the future flow of firearms from legitimate to illegitimate owners. This objective might be achieved, at lesser cost, by a system of transfer notice. Under such a system, every dealer and individual who transfers a firearm to another person would be required to fill out a form, printed on a computer punchcard, giving the date of the transfer, the type, serial number, and model of the gun, his and the transferee's name, address, and social security and identification card numbers. Blank copies of such forms could be obtained in banks, post offices, state and local governmental offices, and other locations. The transfer would be confirmed by a postcard notice requesting the new owner to verify his ownership. Owners who wish to register long guns could do so at any time by filling out a transfer notice card.

Federal law should prescribe the following minimum standards for state long gun laws:

1. All long gun owners and purchasers of long gun ammunition must have an identification card. Cards will be issued to all applicants except those prohibited from owning any firearm—persons under indictment for or convicted of a crime of violence, fugitives, mental incompetents and defectives, narcotics addicts, and minors under 18.

2. Serially numbered identification cards, similar to military identification cards, showing name, address, personal description, photograph, thumbprint, and social security number will be issued on filing of the proper application to all qualified persons regardless of need.

3. A written test that could be administered by mail, based upon a manufacturer's safety booklet attached to each gun sold, will be required.

4. Long gun owners and firearms dealers will be required to sell or transfer long guns or long gun ammunition only to persons with identification cards. Dealers and individuals intending a sale or transfer of a long gun will be required to submit a report of the transactions. No such report will be required for sales of ammunition. Pawnshops will be prohibited from dealing in long guns or ammunition.

5. The identification card program will be administered by a state agency without discrimination as to race, sex, or religion.

General provisions: A federal firearms agency; limit domestic manufacture to guns suited for sporting purposes; strict enforcement and amendment of the Gun Control Act of 1968; gun turn-in campaigns; shooting clubs for storage of sporting handguns; revision of FBI crime reports; customs declaration for all firearms.

In order to obtain the maximum benefits from the foregoing handgun and long gun proposals, we also recommend:

1. Establishment of a federal firearms agency to accumulate and store firearms information obtained by state and local firearms agencies and to act as a clearing house of firearms information for federal, state, and local law enforcement agencies. The director of this agency might also be empowered to supervise state firearms system to insure fair administration that does not discriminate on the basis of race or other unlawful grounds. A federal review system could also be provided to allow aggrieved parties recourse through the federal courts, on either their own initiative or that of the U.S. Department of Justice.

2. The Gun Control Act of 1968 bans imports of guns that are not suited for sporting purposes. This ban should be extended to firearms of domestic manufacture, excepting only the manufacture of handguns for use by law enforcement agencies and licensed owners.

3. Federal firearms laws should be amended to eliminate the possibility of firearms dealers transferring to nonresidents by renting guns with a high security deposit that is subsequently forfeited. In addition, licensed federal firearms dealers should be strictly policed to

eliminate all but legitimate dealers. Licensed dealers should be required to maintain security procedures to minimize theft of firearms, particularly during civil disorders.

4. Public and private campaigns should be fostered in states and cities to encourage persons to turn in unwanted guns. Such turn-ins could be coordinated with occasional amnesty days when illegally owned handguns could be turned in without penalty.

5. Public and private shooting clubs should be allowed to store handguns suitable for sporting purposes and to permit target shooters to use them on the premises.

6. The FBI should revise its crime reporting system to obtain a statistical breakdown of crimes involving firearms by type of weapon—handgun, rifle, or shotgun.

7. Customs regulations should be amended to require written declaration of each firearm brought into this country from abroad and impounding of such firearms until legality of ownership is established.

16.

Exchange of Letters between Richard M. Nixon and Ho Chi Minh

President Nixon's first four years in office were dominated by the Vietnam war. Shortly after taking office he made the decision to withdraw American forces unilaterally from Southeast Asia, but to do it gradually so there would be no onus of an American defeat there. His withdrawal policy, though not enunciated then, was part of the "Nixon Doctrine" stated during his visit to Guam in July 1969. The timing of the withdrawal was vague from the beginning, and it was kept so by the uncertain conditions prevailing in Vietnam. Nixon hoped that once Ho Chi Minh perceived that the President was in fact withdrawing American combat troops, the North Vietnamese would become less intransigent at the Paris peace talks. To further his plan, Nixon corresponded directly with Ho on July 15, 1969, and received a reply on August 25. Nixon regarded Ho's reply as a rejection of his peace initiative. In any case, Ho died three days later, on August 28, and the war went on as before. The text of the two letters was not released to the public until November 3 when Nixon made a televised address to the nation announcing the "Vietnamization" program.

Source: *Department of State Bulletin*, November 24, 1969.

PRESIDENT NIXON'S LETTER

July 15, 1969

Dear Mr. President:

I realize that it is difficult to communicate meaningfully across the gulf of four years of war. But precisely because of this gulf, I wanted to take this opportunity to reaffirm in all solemnity my desire to work for a just peace. I deeply believe that the war in Vietnam has gone on too long and delay in bringing it to an end can benefit no one—least of all the people of Vietnam. My speech on May 14 laid out a proposal which I believe is fair to all parties. Other proposals have been made which attempt to give the people of South Vietnam an opportunity to choose their own future. These proposals take into account the reasonable conditions of all sides. But we stand ready to discuss other programs as well, specifically the 10-point program of the NLF.

As I have said repeatedly, there is nothing to be gained by waiting. Delay can only increase the dangers and multiply the suffering.

The time has come to move forward at the conference table toward an early resolution of this tragic war. You will find us forthcoming and open-minded in a common effort to bring the blessings of peace to the brave people of Vietnam. Let history record that at this critical juncture, both sides turned their face toward peace rather than toward conflict and war.

PRESIDENT HO'S LETTER

Hanoi, 25 August 1969
(Received in Paris August 30)

To His Excellency
RICHARD MILHOUS NIXON
President of the United States
Washington

Mr. President,

I have the honor to acknowledge receipt of your letters.

The war of aggression of the United States against our people, violating our fundamental national rights, still continues in South Vietnam. The United States continues to intensify military operations, the B-52 bombings and the use of toxic chemical products multiply the crimes against the Vietnamese people. The longer the war goes on, the more it accumulates the mourning and burdens of the American people. I am extremely indignant at the losses and destructions caused by the American troops to our people and our country. I am also deeply touched at the rising toll of death of young Americans who have fallen in Vietnam by reason of the policy of American governing circles.

Our Vietnamese people are deeply devoted to peace, a real peace with independence and real freedom. They are determined to fight to the end, without fearing the sacrifices and difficulties in order to defend their country and their sacred national rights. The overall solution in 10 points of the National Liberation Front of South Vietnam and of the Provisional Revolutionary Government of the Republic of South Vietnam is a logical and reasonable basis for the settlement of the Vietnamese problem. It has earned the sympathy and support of the peoples of the world.

In your letter you have expressed the desire to act for a just peace. For this the United States must cease the war of aggression and withdraw their troops from South Vietnam, respect the right of the population of the South and of the Vietnamese nation to dispose of themselves, without foreign influence. This is the correct manner of solving the Vietnamese problem in conformity with the national rights of the Vietnamese people, the interests of the United States and the hopes for peace of the peoples of the world. This is the path that will allow the United States to get out of the war with honor.

With good will on both sides we might arrive at common efforts in view of finding a correct solution of the Vietnamese problem.

17.

Poverty and the Welfare System

In 1969 President Nixon proposed to Congress a revision of the welfare system based on a concept of a minimum income for all U. S. families. In order to provide an income of at least $1600 per year for a family of four, it was estimated that the federal cost would amount to $4 billion a year, with payments supplemented by state funds. Congress did not pass the proposed legislation, and the nation's welfare system remained as inequitable as before. The populous, industrial states where payments were relatively high became even more overburdened as welfare rolls increased. From August 14 to 16, 1969, Congressman Henry Reuss of Wisconsin conducted a series of public hearings in Milwaukee, covering a variety of social issues such as housing, consumerism, tax reform, war, and youth. The first day's hearing dealt with poverty and the welfare system. The purpose of the hearings was to elicit the opinions of those most closely connected with the matter of welfare to find out ways in which it could be reformed.

Source: *Congressional Record*, 91 Cong., 1 Session, September 4, 1969.

PANEL WITNESSES

Robert Lampman, University of Wisconsin, Poverty Institute

Joseph Baldwin, Milwaukee County Department of Public Welfare

Gary Evans, Social Policy and Action Committee, Southeast Wisconsin Chapter, National Association of Social Workers

Monroe Swan, Director, Northside Concentrated Employment Program

Donald Sykes, Director, Community Relations, Milwaukee Social Development Commission

Ted Uribe, Chairman, Spanish Welfare Rights Organization

Lona Bhiele, Chairman, State Welfare Rights Organization

Supervisor William O'Donnell, Chairman, Milwaukee Country Welfare Board

Mr. Lampman: The question of priority is, I'm sure, very much in people's minds these days. One claim for priority or greater attention is the matter of poverty.

The poverty problem, which was called to our national attention by President Johnson, has been moved somewhat toward resolution in recent years. We have been seeing a smaller number of people in poverty year by year, particularly in recent years, and I would think it terribly important that we continue steps to accelerate that rather good movement toward a smaller number of our population being found below the poverty income line.

At present there are about 11 percent of the nation's population found below the line. Another way of thinking of the size of the problem that remains, is that the amount of money in total that separates the poor from the poverty income line is about $10 billion.

I would emphasize that the welfare system is only one of many ways we have for dealing with the poverty question. We also help people who are poor through other income maintenance. For example, social security and unemployment compensation do give some benefits to the very poor person. We also have, of course, the Veterans Administration and quite a number of other programs that do contribute income in one form or another to very poor persons.

Also, we're concerned with the poor in our educational systems and our health systems.

To return to the welfare system, there has been great agitation and great concern about the national welfare system which includes the federal government's participation, the state governments' participation, and the local governments' participation. Both the administrators on the one hand, and the funders, as well as the recipients of welfare, have been very critical in recent years concerning what has been a pretty static system over the period since 1935 when the Social Security Act was passed.

The numbers of beneficiaries have been increasing in recent years, and the questions of whether our state and local governments can finance their share of the welfare system have been very primary questions.

I would like to call attention to the effort that President Nixon suggests we make in revising the welfare system on the one hand, and introducing a new system of payments to poor persons in the form of a family assistance system.

My own view is that this is a constructive step, that it deserves very careful consideration, and that it should be viewed for what it is: a great innovation, a great pioneering step into a new kind of income maintenance system for this country.

Mr. Baldwin: On July 1, 1969, the Milwaukee County Board of Supervisors adopted the following resolution:

"Whereas, 15 to 30 percent of the nation's people have incomes below established poverty levels, and federal, state and local programs of public assistance have been unable to reduce these figures; and

"Whereas, these public assistance programs have developed unevenly as to coverage and benefits, primarily as a result of state and county limited taxing ability; now, therefore,

"Be it resolved, That

"1. The Federal Government take over complete administration and financing of these public assistance programs:

"2. Nationwide minimum standards for public assistance eligibility related to the cost of living in various regions of the country, be adopted."

Milwaukee County, like most of its fellow counties in the United States has never been remiss in helping the poor. Up until 1935, the county cared for the Aged and Disabled through its County Home and its Poor Relief program, but then the problems became too great and the Federal Government had to enter the picture with Old Age and Survivors Insurance.

Milwaukee County has not been remiss in coming to the aid of families and children, but again the load is getting too great and help from the Federal Government is again called for. The population of Milwaukee County ranks it among the first 15 in size in the United States, thus permitting its classification as an urban center with all the accompanying social upheavals.

Problems now confronting County Supervisors are not of the Supervisors' making. These problems come from migration, from both inside and outside the

State of Wisconsin, from automation which dries up the number of unskilled labor needs, from the rise in the number of broken and incomplete families and from continually rising inflation.

These problems cannot be solved by Milwaukee County or any other county. Although the county has tried to do so by carrying on its property tax rolls more than 40 percent of the cost of welfare and income maintenance programs, it has now reached the limit of its taxing powers and cannot continue to carry this proportion of the burden.

The Milwaukee County Supervisors have therefore proposed that the federal government take over completely both the financing and the administration of the public assistance programs: Old Age, Blind and Disabled Assistance, together with Aid to Families of Dependent Children, and General Assistance.

There might be some who would consider such a transfer as weakening the role of county government. To them let me call attention to the fact that in at least 30 of the 54 tax spending jurisdictions in the United States, the state or its counterpart has already relieved local communities of the responsibility for public assistance program. Fully aware of the fiscal problems of state government, Milwaukee's position for itself and for the remaining states where counties are still bearing the burden is "Let's go the whole way this time."

Round table discussions taking place at the National Association of Counties Conference recently held in Portland, Oregon emphasized the role of counties in performing social services. Actually, the ability to perform these social services would be enhanced by the removal of the burden of financing and administering large scale income maintenance programs. Among the social services with which American counties are now involved are housing, foster and institutional care, training and rehabilitation, transportation, health and the control of environment.

There may be some who will say that vesting the responsibility for public assistance with the federal government would make the programs impersonal and irresponsive. After many years of work in this field, I have come to the conclusion that these programs should be administered on an impersonal basis. As it is now, leeway exists among the states, leeway among the counties within the states and leeway exists within each of the counties with respect to the amount of assistance that a caseworker may authorize for a given family. This phenomenon is responsible for a continuous battle between caseworker and client with respect to the amount and kind of assistance that can be authorized.

Milwaukee County's resolution proposes a uniform payment throughout the United States, adjusted regionally perhaps to reflect difference in the cost of living, but promptly and impersonally administered by federal officials, probably those of the Social Security Administration.

The amounts involved should be just high enough so that individuals in need could rely on their own efforts to make up any deficits which their situations may require.

Such a program would put the burden of supporting an income maintenance program on the level of government which has the tax base which could finance it, provides for the impersonal administering of assistance payments in regular, clearly understood amounts, thus requiring a greater reliance upon the individuals's own efforts if a deficit exists and finally permits the local county government which is nearest to the people and their problems to concentrate on educational, social and health services designed to bring about total community improvement.

Mr. Evans: The present welfare system produces second, third, and fourth generations of welfare families. In most cases the real causes of this cycle of poverty are built into the system. Public welfare has many aspects which strip individuals of their dignity and pride. This is rarely the fault of the welfare administrators or the welfare workers. It is usually the structure within which we have to operate that is to blame.

Welfare recipients are constantly reminded that they are different from and inferior to other parents and children. Eventually many come to believe this. This is especially damaging to the children who receive aid under the present welfare system. It is practically impossible for the children not to feel different from their classmates. Children of welfare recipients stand in separate lines when renting their school books. Instead of paying for lunch in the cafeteria, they have a pass with which to pay for lunch. Other school fees are paid in the same manner, separating those on welfare from those who are not on welfare. These kinds of degrading and embarrassing experiences are probably the reason only three percent of ADC families throughout the state are receiving school fees.

Mr. Reuss: ADC being Aid for Dependent Children, the program which I believe President Nixon said was going to disappear into an across the board welfare program.

Mr. Evans: Right.

Clothing is another sore spot for the children whose parents are receiving welfare. In a nation that is becoming more and more clothes conscious, most children who are receiving welfare have little more than one change of clothing. This again separates them from the others in their school system.

Most of the incidents mentioned thus far are embarrassing and degrading. There are other aspects of the present welfare system that are more damaging. One of these is the lack of an adequate food budget.

According to a study by the Department of Agriculture in 1967, a family of four needed at least $100 a month as a minimum subsistance allowance.

In Wisconsin a family of four receives $78 a month. It must also be kept in mind the cost of living has increased over 14 percent since that study was conducted. The $78 has remained the same.

Some children are under-nourished to the point of suffering mental retardation as a result of this. Many others are working below their potential or experience more health problems than the rest of the population.

The present system is also very effective at destroying a youngster's incentive to work. For example, when a 16 year old boy, whose mother receives ADC get a job, he's allowed to keep only $50 a month. Anything over that amount is deducted from his mother's welfare grant. In order for the family to maintain their present level of functioning, the boy must contribute the amount over $50 to his mother. So regardless of how many hours a week he works, or what his hourly wage is, he receives approximately 31 cents an hour. This could hardly be incentive for him to continue working.

These are just some of the weaknesses

that are built into our present welfare program.

Mr. Swan: In speaking of poverty and our welfare system I think we all recognize that a good deal of time and energy has been put into the question of how to better the welfare system. I think the real problem is that too much thought, too much planning and too much program has been put into the system.

The system has always been directed at the symptoms of the problem. I think it is time now that we gave some thought to the causes rather than treating the symptoms.

I think consideration of a welfare system in some way could be compared to a system of war, or war program. I think that war is undesirable and that ways and means should be sought to eliminate a war or the causes that bring it about.

So I think when we think in terms of a welfare system, we should stop looking at the symptoms and start looking at the causes, trying to bring about solutions to the causes.

We look at problems of our society, we look at our economic system, we look at the discrimination that exists in this country—all of which causes people to be in poverty, people to suffer from unemployment, people to be denied decent housing. This causes people to be alienated from society, to be prohibited from entering the mainstream of American society.

And of course poverty has produced our welfare system, a system that only solves and salves a symptom of a problem.

I think that's putting too much emphasis and energy in the wrong direction.

I say we should look at our economic system and see what our interests are. Whether we will continue to have a good deal too much interest about property maintenance, about efficiency production, or whether we will in turn give some consideration to the human element of our society.

Mr. Sykes: At the risk of sounding like an amateur sociologist, I would just like to make a brief point and that is that deprivation is relative and that we must be very conscious of it. That means to me that when I look at most changes in societies that have been a result of the way people have perceived their injustices and perceived their wrongs, I come to the conclusion that there are probably a number of reasons why people are poor. Two very simple classifications are the temporarily poor and others who may end up on welfare because the family is killed in an accident and they weren't properly insured. Due to accidents or death or something very often people are temporarily in poverty.

I think there is a large segment of this society that is systematically reduced to a state of poverty in a very systematic non-accidental way. Here I am not only talking about blacks and Latins and other minority groups, but many whites as well. Primarily in the minority groups there is a systematic force operating that reduces them to poverty. When I think about the welfare system and the new scheme proposed by our present administration in Washington, I am amazed because I get the feeling that everybody thinks that this is going to be a panacea to deal with the issue.

My feeling is that these welfare systems and any other maintenance system provides a base, maybe beneficial to people who are temporarily poor, but it will not deal with the issue of those people who have been restricted to a level of poverty. I think that it is not a panacea and very

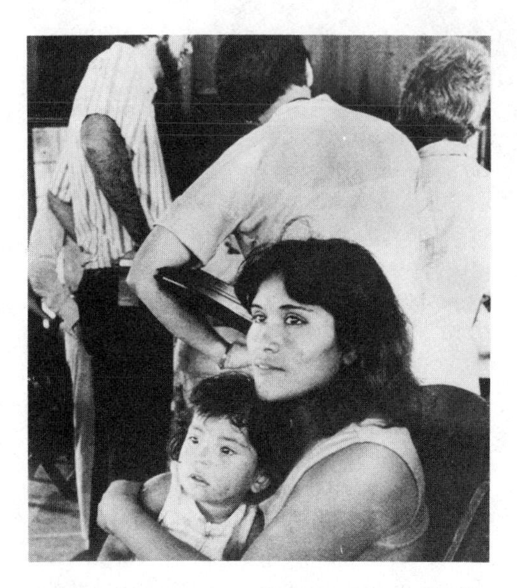

A migrant worker mother waits for medical attention for her child.

often what I see happening is the concentration on these kinds of program as we eliminate those people who have been systematically exploited from participating in the mainstream of American society.

Mr. Uribe: Man has the right to be clothed and educated. This is a modern truth in America in 1969. My group is an organization of Spanish speaking welfare recipients who are struggling to assert themselves as first class citizens. In our country the welfare recipients have the right to lead a more decent and civilized existence. The goal of my group is to label Spanish speaking welfare recipients, and to help deal with the apathy which often accompanies their condition.

Poor people, black people, Mexican-Americans, Puerto Ricans, poor whites, people who are caught in a cycle of poor education, poor paying jobs, substandard housing find this condition transmitted from father to son.

There are many creative alternatives to give the poor a break. A definite legal requirement for civil service jobs, high skilled job training, high skill language training, for non-English speaking people, and asking the government and private industry to create new jobs are just a few. We need a reconsideration of priorities on national, state, county and city levels.

Lona Bhiele: I want to talk about the hypocrites in politics, the ones who are playing God over the poor people, people who go around cutting welfare, condemning mothers with children, pushing them to go to work instead of making stronger laws to bring back the deserting father. They are so happy sitting in the State Assembly making decisions. They are increasing their salaries and making decreases in our checks. Just recently, I think it was in the (State) Senate, they decided they couldn't live on $15 a day away from home. This included $7 a day for their room and restaurant meals. At one time they were paying $5, I believe, for one man to eat supper while the welfare recipient, depending on the size of the family, had to make do with about two dollars a day for a family of four or five.

Also, they say they are helping the taxpayers by cutting away our checks by doing away with Aid for Dependent Children.

This sounds funny but really some of the welfare recipients are trying to help the taxpayer in the long run realize that these so-called politicians are really trying to cheat them out of their money. When they take families off of welfare and put them in another category, taxes go up no matter how pretty they make it sound by getting people off welfare and making them go to work.

Many, I'm speaking for mothers now

because that's where I'm most familiar, would be able to go to work. I don't know how this garnishment law is going to effect us, but I can tell you right now we'll be facing garnishment if we do go to work for bills our husbands left us with. Other mothers have many emotional and physical problems which are not seen by the public, who may think the mother is perfectly healthy or the children are perfectly healthy. Many children are suffering from emotional problems, too.

Many mothers have tried to go to work and found that their children were getting emotionally upset and getting into problems with the law. You have many children in poor families who are in trouble with the school and this is due to a lack of a proper diet. Children can't concentrate if their tummies aren't full with an adequate breakfast. Some families usually eat a lot of starches.

Try to remember that the so-called lush benefits you're being told you are paying for welfare recipients aren't all going to welfare recipients, no matter what category they are in. Much of it is going to the top man, the administration, the legislators. I feel that they shouldn't have the power to vote for their own increases in salaries. This should be left up to the people. If President Nixon was really concerned about the poor, he wouldn't take an entourage of cooks and people to make a full course American meal over in Rumania.

Figure how much of that came out of your pocket. It wasn't a recipient going over to Rumania to put on the dog.

Mr. O'Donnell: There is no national purpose or goal on much of the legislation that has passed both nationally and in the states. Most of the legislation, if it is passed, is begrudgingly passed and it's done on a basis that the poor are here and we'll take care of it but begrudge it.

We should take the same attitude toward welfare that the Congress and the American public have taken toward the commitment to the space program. This is a national commitment of billions of dollars and everybody is very enthusiastic about spending it and reaching the goal. Maybe it is good and maybe it's bad, that's hard to know. But if we could apply the same thing to our problems with the poor and poverty in the cities, then maybe we could accomplish something. I think this is what is needed.

There is need for public relations to tell why people get on general assistance or ADC. What do you do with a single man or single woman that unfortunately has turned into an alcoholic? These people are still human beings and you have to take care of them.

I don't think that any of the legislation that has passed in the area of the poverty program and public welfare is actually passed with any enthusiasm at all.

I think it is passed begrudgingly. I think people feel this. If we can go out and make our national purpose and our national goals to eradicate some of these problems, I think we could reach it in a period of a year. But we are never going to reach it with half of our society begrudging these people bread and butter.

18.

Jesse Jackson: Letter from Jail on Black Economic Opportunity

From 1966 until 1971 the Reverend Jesse Jackson headed Operation Breadbasket, a branch of the Southern Christian Leadership Conference. The Chicago-based organization directed its activities at economic problems plaguing urban black people: jobs, housing, and consumer fraud. After the death of Martin Luther King, Jr., Jackson was recognized as one of the abler national spokesmen for blacks, and his efforts broadened to include most of the issues with which urbanites are concerned. In the fall of 1971, because of a disagreement with SCLC's national officers over the organization-sponsored "Black Expo" in Chicago, Jackson was relieved of his position as director of Operation Breadbasket. He immediately formed his own organization, People United to Save Humanity, or PUSH, to continue the same work he had done while with Breadbasket. In September 1969, while still with SCLC, Jackson was jailed in Chicago for refusing to leave a construction site where he had led pickets in support of the Coalition for United Community Action, a group seeking to pressure the building trades unions to hire and train black workers. Before his release, Jackson wrote the following statement, "Why We're in Jail," as an open letter to the public.

Source: *Chicago Sun-Times*, September 11, 1969.

We are seeking meaningful participation in the American economy ... not just a minimum wage but a livable wage.

It is significant that a period of despair and hopelessness, characterized by the slogan, "Burn, baby, burn," has been transformed into a period of hope with new possibilities characterized by the slogan, "Build, baby, build; earn while you learn."

We do not seek to take white jobs. But neither do we intend to allow whites to keep black jobs while we are passively quiet and docile. There will be no more rest and tranquillity until our just pleas are heeded. Many of the whites are employed upon the prerogatives of discrimination and exclusionary procedures.

We realize that our protest creates a counterprotest. We seek jobs. The whites seek to maintain their jobs. It is understandable that they would want to remain employed. It should be just as understandable that we seek jobs which offer security, protection, opportunity, food, clothing, shelter, education, and the necessities of life. Both groups are frightened that they may be deprived of these necessities.

White insecurity is expressed by an exclusion of the out-group and a ratio of trained workers to jobs that allows the law of supply and demand to enable them to bargain for higher wages. Black insecurity is expressed by direct challenge to the in-group's exclusive hold upon public policy. Blacks are saying we need to declare a state of emergency because of unemployment and underemployment. We need to create a crisis to deal with the emergency. We need training programs.

We'll march, protest, break injunctions, boycott, and use other forms of creative protest in order to be heard, recognized, respected, and allowed to participate.

Ironically, both groups are right. But each group is hardly able to see beyond achieving security for itself. Both think that the elimination of each other is the solution. The real solution is the expansion of the economy to the extent that it can absorb or employ both whites and blacks.

Every American deserves a job or an income. A government is responsible for the welfare of its people or it forces its people to say farewell to it. People develop disloyalty and disinterest in a government that will not rise to the occasion of providing basic opportunities for its people to survive.

Chicago, the scene of historic labor battles and organization, where the eight-hour day was initiated, can be the scene of another creative adjustment in men's search for liberation beyond the throes of poverty, ignorance, and disease.

The labor fight we are engaged in now threatens to further divide the poor black and just recently removed poor white into greater racial polarity, with intensified racial antagonisms. Each group develops programs of race glorification or chauvinism, locking up their jobs, schools, sons, daughters, families, and churches.

This division of the races and the pending fight between the poor must be avoided. This horizontal fight between the have-nots must shift into a vertical fight—if there is to be a fight—between the have-nots and the haves.

These fights between poor blacks and poor whites will inevitably occur if our economy maintains its present collision course. Everyone has a stake in this not occurring. But as long as there is surplus on one hand and starvation on the other, this gap will create tension in our nation.

Our economy has the economic elasticity and capacity. Hopefully it will develop the moral capacity to adjust its priorities and make the dream of full employment a reality.

In the sixties, the burning issue was whether blacks would be allowed to ride the buses and where they would sit. In the seventies, the issues have shifted. Now the issues are whether black people will be allowed to drive that bus, whether the masses of black people will have the money to pay the fare, whether blacks have their rightful place as executives and directors of the bus company and the union it deals with.

VERNON JORDAN, Executive Director of the National Urban League, in a speech to the AFL-CIO convention on November 22, 1971

19.

EDWARD W. BROOKE: The Philadelphia Plan

Early efforts of the Nixon Administration in the area of civil rights centered on the problem of equal employment. The most difficult target singled out by the Department of Labor was the construction industry, comprising several tightly-knit trade unions with membership restricted so as to favor high wages and seniority. On September 23, 1969, Secretary of Labor George Schultz ordered put into effect the "Philadelphia Plan," setting forth specific hiring goals for contractors working on federal construction in the Philadelphia area. The goal of the plan envisioned that by 1973 at least 26 percent of the membership of the building trades unions would consist of minority group workers. The plan was strongly opposed by both Congress and the unions. On October 27 Senator Edward Brooke of Massachusetts, the only black member of the U. S. Senate, read the following statement in favor of the Philadelphia Plan before the Senate Judiciary Committee.

Source: *Congressional Record*, 91 Cong., 1st Session, October 27, 1969.

THE PHILADELPHIA PLAN, as you know, was designed to implement the intent of Executive Order 11246, promulgated by President Johnson on September 24, 1965. Under this order, all Federal government contracts and federally-assisted construction contracts were required to contain specific language obligating the contractor and his subcontractors not to discriminate in employment because of race, color, religion, sex or national origin.

This was no new concept in American jurisprudence. Evidence of this intent is clear in the Constitution, which talks not only about the general principles of Justice, the Blessings of Liberty, and the General Welfare, but which also speaks specifically of freedom of religion, due process of law, equal protection, and the privileges and immunities of all citizens. It is clear in the various civil rights acts passed since 1957, which provide protection specifically against discrimination in accommodations, voting, and employment. It is embodied in the National Labor Relations Act which forbids discrimination by labor unions and employers, and in the regulations issued by the Department of Labor pertaining to applicants, trainees and apprentices. The Government of the United States *does not condone* discrimination on the basis of external factors unrelated to individual capabilities.

Since 1965, however, we have learned that simple prohibition of discrimination is not enough. Overt acts of discrimination not only are becoming less common; they were never the heart of the problem to begin with.

The real problem of discrimination in America is what the Civil Rights Commission has referred to as "systematic discrimination," but what I prefer to call "systemic" or "intrinsic" discrimination. Discrimination against minorities, particularly in the employment field, is built into the very structure of American society. Three black children in *four* in America attends an essentially segregated school from the day he enters kindergarten. Negro children, on an average, complete little more than 10 years of school, as compared to 11.5 for white children. Their schools are for the most part of poorer quality—they are older and lack the facilities enjoyed by students in predominantly white institutions. Funds for job training equipment, for laboratory facilities, for typewriters and teaching aids, simply are not available in many of the schools attended by blacks. A Negro student is more likely than his white counterpart to find his formal education irrelevant to his surroundings. It goes without saying that it does not, in far too many cases, prepare him to compete for jobs or for higher educational opportunities. These circumstances are changing, to be sure, but for the vast majority of non-white youngsters in America they are still a tragic fact of life.

The policy of assigning minority employees to "traditional" jobs or departments is also an informal, systemic barrier to full opportunity in employment. This has been true throughout our society: Negroes have been clerks and custodians, nurses aides but not nurses, teachers in black schools but not in white ones, security guards but never supervisors. These conditions are slowly changing, but even now a past history of discrimination on the part of some employers deters many qualified minority persons from applying for positions.

These are the kinds of situations which the Philadelphia Plan is designed to overcome. Prohibition of discrimination is not enough; positive action is necessary.

In considering what kind of positive action might be employed without hurting present employees or dealing with them unfairly, the drafters of the Philadelphia Plan have come up with a simple yet effective formula. Present employees will not be affected at all by the plan; their jobs will be as secure as they have always been. The Plan does, however, seek to establish a formula for hiring minority members on future jobs. It has been determined by the Department of Labor that each construction craft should have approximately 7.5 percent new job openings annually due to death, disability, retirement, and loss of workers for any other reason. Operating solely on the basis of these anticipated new job openings, the Office of Federal Contract Compliance, working in conjunction with the Federal contracting agency, will devise a set of criteria for minority employment for each contract. These standards will be clearly spelled out in the bids and each contractor who desires to bid on the government contract in question will be obligated to include in his proposal a statement of his goals for attaining these standards. Once the contract is awarded, checks will be conducted to determine whether the employer is in fact living up to his obligation.

I favor this approach for two basic reasons. First, because, as I have stated above, I believe that *positive* efforts to eliminate discrimination are essential. But secondly, I appreciate the fact that there is no question of the Federal government dictating to the states, the cities, or the local contractors. There are, in fact, no Federal standards involved. There is simply a statement of Federal intent, embodied in Executive Order 11246, with the mechanics to be worked out on the local level, taking into account local factors such as: the current extent of minority group participation in the particular trade; the availability of minority group persons for employment in such trade; the need for training programs in the area; and the impact of the program upon the existing labor force. Even then, after all these criteria have been taken into account, the contractor and subcontractors are still allowed leeway in meeting the minority employment targets, and need only demonstrate that they have made a good faith effort to do so.

Mr. Chairman, nothing could be fairer, or more equitable, or ultimately more beneficial for all concerned. The spirit of the law has for too long been ignored in the field of equal employment opportunity. I welcome the promulgation of the Philadelphia Plan, I applaud the Administration's unequivocal support of it, and I hope to see similar plans worked out to achieve similar results in Boston and other communities all across the country. Only in this way can we truly make America a land of opportunity for all our people.

20.

FRANK H. MENTZ: Open Letter to Congress on Vietnam

Contravening the high expectations of most Americans in 1968 concerning a reasonably near end to the Vietnam war, the war went on in 1969 with as much ferocity and as many American casualties as ever. These facts served to increase opposition to the war and to broaden the base of protest. Many who had originally favored the venture, even strong proponents of it, became disillusioned; and some felt that the Administration could not or would not end the conflict. If this were true, Congress was the only agency that could intervene to stop it. The following appeal for congressional action was sent to Congress by Frank H. Mentz of Sheridan, Arkansas. Mentz was the father of a U. S. Marine who had died of a disease contracted in Vietnam.

Source: *Congressional Record*, 91 Cong., 1 Session, September 26, 1969.

WE WISH TO EXPRESS our sincere thanks to the Congress of the United States for their continuing inactivity in regard to their Constitutional responsibilities regarding the Vietnam war.

Because of your inactivity towards stopping our participation in this useless and senseless war, we have lost our only son, and only child, to a Vietnam contracted disease.

In fact, because I am an only son of an only son, the senseless death of our son will eliminate our family name for all time.

Yes, we know we are not the only ones who have lost a loved one in this nonsensical war—and that makes it even more senseless.

How, Gentlemen, can you justify the loss of over 45,000 young American boys' lives in that hell-on-earth for what we have gotten in return, or ever hope to get in return? In fact, Gentlemen, how can you possibly sleep at night when you know that you have been able all along to stop this useless slaughter, if by no other means, than to stop the flow of money to the Armed Forces.

If I understand our Constitution correctly, *no* President of the United States has the right to commit anywhere near the number of troops being used in Vietnam combat, on foreign soil, without first obtaining the full sanction of the U.S. Congress. Yet you have stood by and let three successive Presidents do just exactly that.

And, Gentlemen, for every week you continue to sit on your hands, another 200-300 or more American boys die over there—and for what.

If this were a war where our National Security was at stake, I, and I'm sure most of the other parents, wives, and children, who have lost a loved one, would accept the inevitable possibility that such a thing could and must happen to some of us.

But to lose one to a war that has no more connection to our national security than this one has—only an imbecile would believe that it was necessary. In fact, it's nothing short of criminal on your part that you sit idly by and let this national disgrace continue.

I know that in all probability, if this letter is ever read to you, it will continue to fall on deaf ears—as all pleas to date have—because I am just another of those poor saps of a good American citizen who continue to believe in this country. But for the memory of my son, I had to try to save some other boy like him. It won't bring my son back, but I can now better live with myself because I tried.

I wonder just how many of *you* have lost a son to the Vietnam fiasco? Maybe, God forbid, if enough of you did, you would do what your oath of office expects of you.

In God's name, Gentlemen, bring our boys home—not in 1970 or 1971—but now.

The plain truth is that the day is coming when no single nation, however powerful, can undertake by itself to keep the peace outside its own borders.

ROBERT S. MCNAMARA, former Secretary of Defense

21.

Richard M. Nixon: The Pursuit of Peace in Vietnam

Within the first month after taking office, President Nixon had decided that the only way to deal with the Vietnam war was through unilateral withdrawal of American combat troops. But such a policy was predicated upon some reciprocal action by the North Vietnamese government. An exchange of letters between the President and Ho Chi Minh in the summer of 1969 seemed to indicate that North Vietnamese attitudes were intransigent. Nevertheless the President and his advisors pressed ahead with plans for the withdrawal of American forces, but not in such a way as to leave South Vietnam vulnerable to an immediate Communist takeover. In a television address to the nation on November 3, the President explained his policy to the public. The heart of it was the "Vietnamization plan" whereby the American withdrawal would be paced to allow for a strengthening of the South Vietnamese forces. Portions of Mr. Nixon's address are reprinted here.

Source: *Department of State Bulletin*, November 24, 1969.

Good evening, my fellow Americans: Tonight I want to talk to you on a subject of deep concern to all Americans and to many people in all parts of the world—the war in Vietnam.

I believe that one of the reasons for the deep division about Vietnam is that many Americans have lost confidence in what their Government has told them about our policy. The American people cannot and should not be asked to support a policy which involves the overriding issues of war and peace unless they know the truth about that policy.

Tonight, therefore, I would like to answer some of the questions that I know are on the minds of many of you listening to me. . . .

Let me begin by describing the situation I found when I was inaugurated on January 20.

—The war had been going on for four years.

—31,000 Americans had been killed in action.

—The training program for the South Vietnamese was behind schedule.

—540,000 Americans were in Vietnam, with no plans to reduce the number.

—No progress had been made at the negotiations in Paris and the United States had not put forth a comprehensive peace proposal.

—The war was causing deep division at home and criticism from many of our friends, as well as our enemies, abroad.

In view of these circumstances there were some who urged that I end the war at once by ordering the immediate withdrawal of all American forces.

From a political standpoint this would have been a popular and easy course to follow. After all, we became involved in the war while my predecessor was in office. I could blame the defeat which would be the result of my action on him and come out as the peacemaker. Some put it to me quite bluntly: This was the only way to avoid allowing Johnson's war to become Nixon's war.

But I had a greater obligation than to think only of the years of my administration and the next election. I had to think of the effect of my decision on the next generation and on the future of peace and freedom in America and in the world.

Let us all understand that the question before us is not whether some Americans are for peace and some Americans are against peace. The question at issue is not whether Johnson's war becomes Nixon's war.

The great question is: How can we win America's peace? . . .

In order to end a war fought on many fronts, I initiated a pursuit for peace on many fronts.

In a television speech on May 14, in a speech before the United Nations, and on a number of other occasions, I set forth our peace proposals in great detail.

—We have offered the complete withdrawal of all outside forces within one year.

—We have proposed a cease-fire under international supervision.

—We have offered free elections under international supervision, with the Communists participating in the organization and conduct of the elections as an organized political force. The Saigon Government has pledged to accept the result of the elections.

We have not put forth our proposals on a take-it-or-leave-it basis. We have indicated that we are willing to discuss the proposals that have been put forth by the other side. We have declared that anything is negotiable, except the right of the people of South Vietnam to determine their own future. At the Paris peace conference, Ambassador Lodge has demonstrated our flexibility and good faith in 40 public meetings.

Hanoi has refused even to discuss our proposals. They demand our unconditional acceptance of their terms, which are that we withdraw all American forces immediately and unconditionally and that we overthrow the Government of South Vietnam as we leave.

We have not limited our peace initiatives to public forums and public statements. I recognized in January that a long and bitter war like this usually cannot be settled in a public forum. That is why, in addition to the public statements and negotiations, I have explored every possible private avenue that might lead to a settlement. . . .

But the effect of all the public, private, and secret negotiations which have been undertaken since the bombing halt a year ago and since this administration came into office on January 20 can be summed up in one sentence: No progress whatever has been made except agreement on the shape of the bargaining table.

Now, who is at fault?

It has become clear that the obstacle in negotiating an end to the war is not the President of the United States. It is not the South Vietnamese Government.

The obstacle is the other side's absolute refusal to show the least willingness to join us in seeking a just peace. It will not do so while it is convinced that all it has to do is to wait for our next concession, and our next concession after that one, until it gets everything it wants.

There can now be no longer any question that progress in negotiation depends only on Hanoi's deciding to negotiate, to negotiate seriously.

I realize that this report on our efforts on the diplomatic front is discouraging to the American people, but the American people are entitled to know the truth—the bad news as well as the good news—where the lives of our young men are involved.

Now let me turn, however, to a more encouraging report on another front.

At the time we launched our search for peace, I recognized we might not succeed in bringing an end to the war through negotiation.

I therefore put into effect another plan to bring peace—a plan which will bring the war to an end regardless of what happens on the negotiating front. It is in line with a major shift in U.S. foreign policy which I described in my press conference at Guam on July 25.

Let me briefly explain what has been described as the Nixon doctrine—a policy which not only will help end the war in Vietnam but which is an essential element of our program to prevent future Vietnams.

We Americans are a do-it-yourself people. We are an impatient people. Instead of teaching someone else to do a job, we like to do it ourselves. And this trait has been carried over into our foreign policy.

In Korea and again in Vietnam, the United States furnished most of the money, most of the arms, and most of the men to help the people of those countries defend their freedom against Communist aggression.

Before any American troops were committed to Vietnam, a leader of another Asian country expressed this opinion to me when I was traveling in Asia as a private citizen. He said: "When you are trying to assist another nation defend its freedom, U.S. policy should be to help them fight the war, but not to fight the war for them."

Well, in accordance with this wise counsel, I laid down in Guam three principles as guidelines for future American policy toward Asia:

—First, the United States will keep all of its treaty commitments.

—Second, we shall provide a shield if a nuclear power threatens the freedom of a nation allied with us or of a nation whose survival we consider vital to our security.

—Third, in cases involving other types of aggression, we shall furnish military and economic assistance when requested in accordance with our treaty commitments. But we shall look to the nation directly threatened to assume the primary responsibility of providing the manpower for its defense.

After I announced this policy, I found that the leaders of the Philippines, Thailand, Vietnam, South Korea, and other nations which might be threatened by Communist aggression welcomed this new direction in American foreign policy.

The defense of freedom is everybody's business—not just America's business. And it is particularly the responsibility of the people whose freedom is threatened. In the previous administration we Americanized the war in Vietnam. In this administration we are Vietnamizing the search for peace.

The policy of the previous administration not only resulted in our assuming the primary responsibility for fighting the war but, even more significantly, did not adequately stress the goal of strengthening the South Vietnamese so that they could defend themselves when we left.

The Vietnamization plan was launched following Secretary [of Defense Melvin R.] Laird's visit to Vietnam in March. Under the plan, I ordered first a substantial increase in the training and equipment of South Vietnamese forces.

In July, on my visit to Vietnam, I changed General Abrams' orders so that they were consistent with the objectives of our new policies. Under the new orders, the primary mission of our troops is to enable the South Vietnamese forces to assume the full responsibility for the security of South Vietnam.

Our air operations have been reduced by over 20 percent.

And now we have begun to see the results of this long-overdue change in American policy in Vietnam:

—After five years of Americans going into Vietnam, we are finally bringing American men home. By December 15, over 60,000 men will have been withdrawn from South Vietnam, including 20 percent of all of our combat forces.

—The South Vietnamese have continued to gain in strength. As a result, they have been able to take over combat responsibilities from our American troops.

Two other significant developments have occurred since this administration took office:

—Enemy infiltration, infiltration which is essential if they are to launch a major attack, over the last three months is less than 20 percent of what it was over the same period last year.

—Most important, United States casualties have declined during the last two months to the lowest point in three years.

Let me now turn to our program for the future.

We have adopted a plan which we have worked out in cooperation with the South Vietnamese for the complete withdrawal of all U.S. combat ground forces and their replacement by South Vietnamese forces on an orderly scheduled timetable. This withdrawal will be made from strength and not from weakness. As South Vietnamese forces become stronger, the rate of American withdrawal can become greater.

I have not and do not intend to announce the timetable for our program. There are obvious reasons for this decision, which I am sure you will understand. As I have indicated on several occasions, the rate of withdrawal will depend on developments on three fronts.

One of these is the progress which can be, or might be, made in the Paris talks. An announcement of a fixed timetable for our withdrawal would completely remove any incentive for the enemy to negotiate an agreement. They would simply wait until our forces had withdrawn and then move in.

The other two factors on which we will base our withdrawal decisions are the level of enemy activity and the progress of the training program of the South Vietnamese forces. I am glad to be able to report tonight progress on both of these fronts has been greater than we anticipated when we started the program in June for withdrawal. As a result, our timetable for withdrawal is more optimistic now than when we made our first estimates in June.

This clearly demonstrates why it is not wise to be frozen in on a fixed timetable. We must retain the flexibility to base each withdrawal decision on the situation as it is at that time rather than on estimates that are no longer valid.

Along with this optimistic estimate, I must in all candor leave one note of caution: If the level of enemy activity significantly increases, we might have to adjust our timetable accordingly.

However, I want the record to be completely clear on one point.

At the time of the bombing halt just a year ago, there was some confusion as to whether there was an understanding on the part of the enemy that if we stopped the bombing of North Vietnam, they would stop the shelling of cities in South Vietnam. I want to be sure that there is no misunderstanding on the part of the enemy with regard to our withdrawal program.

We have noted the reduced level of infiltration, the reduction of our casualties, and are basing our withdrawal decisions partially on those factors.

If the level of infiltration or our casualties increase while we are trying to scale down the fighting, it will be the result of a conscious decision by the enemy.

Hanoi could make no greater mistake than to assume that an increase in violence will be to its advantage. If I conclude that increased enemy action jeopardizes our remaining forces in Vietnam, I shall not hesitate to take strong and effective measures to deal with that situation.

This is not a threat. This is a statement of policy which as Commander in Chief of our Armed Forces I am making in meeting my responsibility for the protection of American fighting men wherever they may be.

My fellow Americans, I am sure you can recognize from what I have said that we really only have two choices open to us if we want to end this war:

—I can order an immediate, precipitate withdrawal of all Americans from Vietnam without regard to the effects of that action.

—Or we can persist in our search for a just peace, through a negotiated settlement if possible or through continued implementation of our plan for Vietnamization if necessary—a plan in which we will withdraw all of our forces from Vietnam on a schedule in accordance with our program, as the South Vietnamese become strong enough to defend their own freedom.

I have chosen this second course. It is not the easy way. It is the right way. It is a plan which will end the war and serve the cause of peace, not just in Vietnam but in the Pacific and in the world.

In speaking of the consequences of a precipitate withdrawal, I mentioned that our allies would lose confidence in America.

Far more dangerous, we would lose confidence in ourselves. Oh, the immediate reaction would be a sense of relief that our men were coming home. But as we saw the consequences of what we had done, inevitable remorse and divisive recrimination would sear our spirit as a people.

We have faced other crises in our history and have become stronger by rejecting the easy way out and taking the right way in meeting our challenges. Our greatness as a nation has been our capacity to do what had to be done when we knew our course was right.

I recognize that some of my fellow citizens disagree with the plan for peace I have chosen. Honest and patriotic Americans have reached different conclusions as to how peace should be achieved.

In San Francisco a few weeks ago I saw demonstrators carrying signs reading: "Lose in Vietnam, bring the boys home."

Well, one of the strengths of our free society is that any American has a right to reach that conclusion and to advocate that point of view. But as President of the United States, I would be untrue to my oath of office if I allowed the policy of this nation to be dictated by the minority who hold that point of view and who try to impose it on the nation by mounting demonstrations in the street.

For almost 200 years, the policy of this nation has been made under our Constitution by those leaders in the Congress and in the White House elected by all of the people. If a vocal minority, however fervent its cause, prevails over reason and the will of the majority, this nation has no future as a free society.

And now I would like to address a word, if I may, to the young people of this nation who are particularly concerned—and I understand why they are concerned—about this war.

I respect your idealism.

I share your concern for peace.

I want peace as much as you do.

There are powerful personal reasons I want to end this war. This week I will have to sign 83 letters to mothers, fathers, wives, and loved ones of men who have given their lives for America in Vietnam. It is very little satisfaction to me that this is only one-third as many letters as I signed the first week in office. There is nothing I want more than to see the day come when I do not have to write any of those letters.

—I want to end the war to save the lives of those brave young men in Vietnam.

—But I want to end it in a way which will increase the chance that their younger brothers and their sons will not have to fight in some future Vietnam someplace in the world.

—And I want to end the war for another reason. I want to end it so that the energy and dedication of you, our young people, now too often directed into bitter hatred against those responsible for the war, can be turned to the great challenges of peace: a better life for all Americans, a better life for all people on this earth.

I have chosen a plan for peace. I believe it will succeed.

If it does succeed, what the critics say now won't matter. If it does not succeed, anything I say then won't matter.

Taken together, the military-industrial team, which protects our national interest against foreign enemies, constitutes at the same time a vital national resource that contributes on an ever-increasing scale to solutions for many of our domestic ills.

Air Force Association Statement of Policy, 1969

22.

William P. Rogers: Strategic Arms Limitation Talks

In 1968 both the Soviet Union and the United States began the building of limited antiballistic missile sites. At the same time, both nations expressed willingness to discuss limiting nuclear arsenals and the new defensive systems. When President Nixon took office in 1969 he determined to go ahead with Strategic Arms Limitation Talks (SALT) between the two powers. To negotiate from what he considered a position of strength, he prevailed upon Congress to pass a new ABM program. The SALT talks themselves began at Helsinki, Finland, on November 17 and continued for about 130 intermittent meetings there and in Vienna, Austria. Progress in the conferences seemed negligible, but when Nixon visited Moscow in 1972, a two-part arms agreement was signed limiting the ABM and ICBM potential of both nations. In the speech from which the following selection is taken, Secretary of State William P. Rogers outlined what the U. S. hoped to achieve in the SALT conferences. The address was made before a meeting of Diplomatic and Consular Officers Retired, on November 13, 1969, four days before the SALT negotiations began.

Source: *Department of State Bulletin*, December 1, 1969.

Next Monday in Helsinki the United States and the Soviet Union will open preliminary talks leading to what could be the most critical negotiations on disarmament ever undertaken. The two most powerful nations on earth will be seeking a way to curb what to date has been an unending competition in the strategic arms race.

The Government of the United States will enter these negotiations with serious purpose and with the hope that we can achieve balanced understandings that will benefit the cause of world peace and security. Yet we begin these negotiations knowing that they are likely to be long and complicated and with the full realization that they may not succeed.

While I will not be able to discuss specific proposals tonight, I thought it might be helpful to outline the general approach of our Government in these talks. . . .

The present situation—in which both the United States and the Soviet Union could effectively destroy the other regardless of which struck first—radically weakens the rationale for continuing the arms race.

Competitive accumulation of more sophisticated weapons would not add to the basic security of either side. Militarily, it probably would produce little or no net advantage. Economically, it would divert resources needed elsewhere. Politically, it would perpetuate the tensions and fears that are the social fallout of the nuclear arms race.

So a capacity for mutual destruction leads to a mutual interest in putting a stop to the strategic nuclear arms race.

Nonetheless, technology advances remorselessly. It offers new opportunities to both sides to add to their offensive and defensive strategic systems. Both sides find it difficult to reject these opportunities in an atmosphere of rivalry and in the absence of a verifiable agreement. It raises temptations to seek strategic advantages. Yet, now such advantages cannot be hidden for long, and both sides will certainly take whatever countermeasures are necessary to preserve their retaliatory capability.

This is the situation in which the two sides now find themselves. Where national security interests may have operated in the past to stimulate the strategic arms race, those same national security interests may now operate to stop or slow down the race. The question to be faced in the strategic arms talks is whether societies with the advanced intellect to develop these awesome weapons of mass destruction have the combined wisdom to control and curtail them.

In point of fact, we have already had some successes in preliminary limitations:

—We have a treaty banning military activities in Antarctica.

—We have a treaty banning the orbiting of weapons of mass destruction in outer space and prohibiting the establishment of military installations on the moon or other celestial bodies.

—We have reached agreement with the Soviet Union on the text of a treaty forbidding the emplacement of weapons of mass destruction on the ocean floors, about to be considered at the United Nations General Assembly.

These are agreements not to arm environments previously inaccessible to weapons. Manifestly, there are fewer obstacles to such agreements than there are to agreements controlling weapons already deployed or under development.

But even in already "contaminated" environments there have been two important control agreements:

—We have negotiated and ratified a Test Ban Treaty prohibiting the testing of nuclear weapons in the atmosphere, under water, and in outer space.

—We have negotiated, and are prepared at any time to ratify simultaneously with the Soviet Union, a Nuclear Nonproliferation Treaty.

It should be pointed out, though, that the main objective of a Nuclear Nonproliferation Treaty is to prevent nonnuclear powers from acquiring atomic weapons. The treaty does not restrain any of the present nuclear powers from further development of their capabilities. The nonnuclear countries therefore tend to look upon the treaty essentially as a self-denying ordinance.

Accordingly, during the negotiations they insisted upon assurances that the nuclear powers would seriously pursue strategic arms negotiations. We concurred and incorporated a paragraph in the treaty which would require us to do so. I mention this to underscore two points:

—First, that the disarmament agreements previously concluded have widely been regarded as confidence-building preliminary steps which hopefully might lead to more meaningful agreements on strategic arms.

—Second, when the United States and the Soviet Union ratify the NPT, they will agree to undertake negotiations in good faith for a cessation of the nuclear arms race.

However, given the complexity of the strategic situation, the vital national interests involved, and the traditional impulses to seek protection in military strength, it is easy to be cynical about the prospects for the talks into which we are about to enter.

Nonetheless, some basis for hope exists.

First is the fact that the talks are being held at all. The diplomatic exchanges leading up to these talks were responsible in nature. And the talks themselves will require discussion of military matters by both sides in which the veil of secrecy will have to be, if not lifted, at least refashioned. These factors lead us to the hope that the talks are being entered into seriously.

Second is the matter of timing. Previous disparity in nuclear strength has been succeeded by the situation of sufficiency, of which I have already spoken. And because this condition will continue for the foreseeable future, the time, then, seems to be propitious for considering how to curb the race in which neither side in all likelihood can gain meaningful advantage.

Third is a mutuality of interest. Under present circumstances an equitable limitation on strategic nuclear weapons would strengthen the national security of both sides. If this is mutually perceived—if both sides conduct these talks in the light of that perception—the talks may accomplish an historic breakthrough in the pattern of confrontation that has characterized the postwar world. . . .

The United States approaches the talks as an opportunity to rest our security on what I would call a balanced strategy.

In pursuit of this balanced strategy of security we will enter the Helsinki talks with three objectives:

—To enhance international security by maintaining a stable U.S.-Soviet strategic relationship through limitations on the deployment of strategic armaments.

—To halt the upward spiral of strategic arms and avoid the tensions, uncertainties, and costs of an unrestrained continuation of the strategic arms race.

—To reduce the risk of an outbreak of nuclear war through a dialogue about issues arising from the strategic situation. . . .

But there are also other stakes in these talks that come closer to home. On both sides of this strategic race there are urgent needs for resources to meet pressing domestic needs. Strategic weapons cannot solve the problems of how we live at home or how we live in the world in this last third of the 20th century. The Soviet Union, which devotes a much larger proportion of its national resources to armaments than do we, must see this as well.

Who knows the rewards if we succeed in diverting the energy, time, and attention—the manpower and brainpower—devoted to ever more sophisticated weapons to other and more worthwhile purposes? . . .

To that end this Government approaches the strategic arms limitations talks in sober and serious determination to do our full part to bring a halt to this unproductive and costly competition in strategic nuclear armaments.

23.

Spiro T. Agnew: The Television News Medium

When Spiro Agnew was selected by Richard Nixon in July 1968 to be his vice-presidential running mate, he was "stunned," as he later admitted. The effect on the Republican Party and the nation was similar. "Spiro Who?" was the question often repeated in the press. But as Vice-President, Agnew quickly lifted himself out of anonymity and emerged as one of the most controversial of politicians. In June 1969, finding the routine tasks of office rather unproductive, he decided to begin speaking out on the issues that divided the nation: civil rights, campus unrest, and the news media, to name a few. With his knack for coining a phrase and his willingness to say what he thought, he quickly became the most sought-after speaker for Republican fund-raising dinners. On November 13, 1969, he addressed the Midwest Republican Conference at Des Moines, giving one of the more explosive speeches of his career. In delivering the speech, Agnew was acting with the specific approval and encouragement of the White House, where the idea for it had originated with one of the President's speech writers. On November 20 the Vice-President followed up his attack on television news coverage with a speech denouncing liberal newspapers, specifically the New York Times *and the* Washington Post. *The pattern of direct and indirect attack on the news media was to continue throughout President Nixon's Administration. The text of Agnew's Des Moines address is reprinted here.*

Source: *Congressional Record*, 91 Cong., 1 Session, November 13, 1969.

Tonight I want to discuss the importance of the television news medium to the American people. No nation depends more on the intelligent judgment of its citizens. No medium has a more profound influence over public opinion. Nowhere in our system are there fewer checks on vast power. So, nowhere should there be more conscientious responsibility exercised than by the news media. The question is, Are we demanding enough of our television news presentations? And are the men of this medium demanding enough of themselves?

Monday night a week ago, President Nixon delivered the most important address of his Administration, one of the most important of our decade. His subject was Vietnam. His hope was to rally the American people to see the conflict through to a lasting and just peace in the Pacific. For 32 minutes, he reasoned with a nation that has suffered almost a third of a million casualties in the longest war in its history.

When the President completed his address—an address, incidentally, that he spent weeks in the preparation of—his words and policies were subjected to instant analysis and querulous criticism. The audience of 70 million Americans gathered to hear the President of the United States was inherited by a small band of network commentators and self-appointed analysts, the majority of whom expressed in one way or another their hostility to what he had to say.

It was obvious that their minds were made up in advance. Those who recall the fumbling and groping that followed President Johnson's dramatic disclosure of his intention not to seek another term have seen these men in a genuine state of nonpreparedness. This was not it.

One commentator twice contradicted the President's statement about the exchange of correspondence with Ho Chi Minh. Another challenged the President's abilities as a politician. A third asserted that the President was following a Pentagon line. Others, by the expression on their faces, the tone of their questions and the sarcasm of their responses, made clear their sharp disapproval.

To guarantee in advance that the President's plea for national unity would be challenged, one network trotted out Averell Harriman for the occasion. Throughout the President's message, he waited in the wings. When the President concluded, Mr. Harriman recited perfectly. He attacked the Thieu Government as unrepresentative; he criticized the President's speech for various deficiencies; he twice issued a call to the Senate Foreign Relations Committee to debate Vietnam once again; he stated his belief that the Vietcong or North Vietnamese did not really want military takeover of South Vietnam; and he told a little anecdote about a "very, very responsible" fellow he had met in the North Vietnamese delegation.

All in all, Mr. Harriman offered a broad range of gratuitous advice challenging and contradicting the policies outlined by the President of the United States. Where the President had issued a call for unity, Mr. Harriman was encouraging the country not to listen to him.

A word about Mr. Harriman. For 10 months he was America's chief negotiator at the Paris peace talks—a period in which the United States swapped some of the greatest military concessions in the history of warfare for an enemy agreement on the shape of the bargaining table. Like Coleridge's Ancient Mariner, Mr. Harriman seems to be under some heavy compulsion to justify his failure to anyone who will listen. And the networks have shown themselves willing to give him all the air time he desires.

Now every American has a right to disagree with the President of the United States and to express publicly that disagreement. But the President of the United States has a right to communicate directly with the people who elected him, and the people of this country have the right to make up their own minds and form their own opinions about a Presidential address without having a President's words and thoughts characterized through the prejudices of hostile critics before they can even be digested.

When Winston Churchill rallied public opinion to stay the course against Hitler's Germany, he didn't have to contend with a gaggle of commentators raising doubts about whether he was reading public opinion right, or whether Britain had the stamina to see the war through.

When President Kennedy rallied the nation in the Cuban missile crisis, his address to the people was not chewed over by a roundtable of critics who disparaged the course of action he'd asked America to follow.

The purpose of my remarks tonight is to focus your attention on this little group of men who not only enjoy a right of instant rebuttal to every Presidential address, but, more importantly, wield a free hand in selecting, presenting and interpreting the great issues in our nation.

First, let's define that power. At least 40 million Americans every night, it's estimated, watch the network news. Seven million of them view A.B.C., the remainder being divided between N.B.C. and C.B.S.

According to Harris polls and other studies, for millions of Americans the networks are the sole source of national and world news. In Will Roger's observation, what you knew was what you read in the newspaper. Today for growing millions of Americans, it's what they see and hear on their television sets.

Now how is this network news determined? A small group of men, numbering perhaps no more than a dozen anchormen, commentators and executive producers, settle upon the 20 minutes or so of film and commentary that's to reach the public. This selection is made from the 90 to 180 minutes that may be available. Their powers of choice are broad.

They decide what 40 to 50 million Americans will learn of the day's events in the nation and in the world.

We cannot measure this power and influence by the traditional democratic standards, for these men can create national issues overnight.

They can make or break by their coverage and commentary a moratorium on the war.

They can elevate men from obscurity to national prominence within a week. They can reward some politicians with national exposure and ignore others.

For millions of Americans the network reporter who covers a continuing issue—like the ABM or civil rights—becomes, in effect, the presiding judge in a national trial by jury.

It must be recognized that the networks have made important contributions to the national knowledge—for news, documentaries and specials. They have often used their power constructively and creatively to awaken the public conscience to critical problems. The networks made hunger and black lung disease national issues overnight. The TV networks have done what no other medium could have done in terms of dramatizing the horrors of war. The networks have tackled our most difficult social problems with a directness and an immediacy that's the gift of their medium. They focus the nation's attention on its environmental abuses—on pollution in the Great Lakes and the threatened ecology of the Everglades.

But it was also the networks that elevated Stokely Carmichael and George Lincoln Rockwell from obscurity to national prominence.

Nor is their power confined to the substantive. A raised eyebrow, an inflection of the voice, a caustic remark dropped in the middle of a broadcast can raise doubts in a million minds about the veracity of a public official or the wisdom of a Government policy.

One Federal Communications Commissioner considers the powers of the networks equal to that of local state and Federal Governments all combined. Certainly it represents a concentration of power over American public opinion unknown in history.

Now what do Americans know of the men who wield this power? Of the men who produce and direct the network news, the nation knows practically nothing. Of the commentators, most Americans know little other than that they reflect an urbane and assured presence seemingly well-informed on every important matter.

We do know that to a man these commentators and producers live and work in the geographical and intellectual confines of Washington, D. C., or New York

City, the latter of which James Reston terms the most unrepresentative community in the entire United States.

Both communities bask in their own provincialism, their own parochialism.

We can deduce that these men read the same newspapers. They draw their political and social views from the same sources. Worse, they talk constantly to one another, thereby providing artificial reinforcement to their shared viewpoints.

Do they allow their biases to influence the selection and presentation of the news? David Brinkley states objectivity is impossible to normal human behavior. Rather, he says, we should strive for fairness.

Another anchorman on a network news show contends, and I quote: "You can't expunge all your private convictions just because you sit in a seat like this and a camera starts to stare at you. I think your program has to reflect what your basic feelings are. I'll plead guilty to that."

Less than a week before the 1968 election, this same commentator charged that President Nixon's campaign commitments were no more durable than campaign balloons. He claimed that, were it not for the fear of hostile reaction, Richard Nixon would be giving in to, and I quote him exactly, "his natural instinct to smash the enemy with a club or go after him with a meat axe."

Had this slander been made by one political candidate about another, it would have been dismissed by most commentators as a partisan attack. But this attack emanated from the privileged sanctuary of a network studio and therefore had the apparent dignity of an objective statement.

The American people would rightly not tolerate this concentration of power in Government.

Is it not fair and relevant to question its concentration in the hands of a tiny, enclosed fraternity of privileged men elected by no one and enjoying a monopoly sanctioned and licensed by Government?

The views of the majority of this fraternity do not—and I repeat, not—represent the views of America.

That is why such a great gulf existed between how the nation received the President's address and how the networks reviewed it.

Not only did the country receive the President's address more warmly than the networks, but so also did the Congress of the United States.

Yesterday, the President was notified that 300 individual Congressmen and 50 Senators of both parties had endorsed his efforts for peace.

As with other American institutions, perhaps it is time that the networks were made more responsive to the views of the nation and more responsible to the people they serve.

Now I want to make myself perfectly clear. I'm not asking for Government censorship or any other kind of censorship. I'm asking whether a form of censorship already exists when the news that 40 million Americans receive each night is determined by a handful of men responsible only to their corporate employers and is filtered through a handful of commentators who admit to their own set of biases.

The questions I'm raising here tonight should have been raised by others long ago. They should have been raised by those Americans who have traditionally considered the preservation of freedom of speech and freedom of the press their special provinces of responsibility. . . .

Normality has become the nemesis of the network news. Now the upshot of all thiscontroversy is that a narrow and distorted picture of America often emerges from the televised news. . . .

Perhaps the place to start looking for a credibility gap is not in the offices of the Government in Washington but in the studios of the networks in New York.

Television may have destroyed the old stereotypes, but has it not created new ones in their places?

What has this passionate pursuit of controversy done to the politics of progress through local compromise essential to the functioning of a democratic society?

The members of Congress or the Senate who follow their principles and philosophy quietly in a spirit of compromise are unknown to many Americans, while the loudest and most extreme dissenters on every issue are known to every man in the street.

How many marches and demonstrations would we have if the marchers did not know that the ever-faithful TV cameras would be there to record their antics for the next news show?

We've heard demands that Senators and Congressmen and judges make known all their financial connections so that the public will know who and what influences their decisions and their votes. Strong arguments can be made for that view.

But when a single commentator or producer, night after night, determines for millions of people how much of each side of a great issue they are going to see and hear, should he not first disclose his personal views on the issue as well?

In this search for excitement and controversy, has more than equal time gone to the minority of Americans who specialize in attacking the United States—its institutions and its citizens?

Tonight I've raised questions. I've made no attempt to suggest the answers. The answers must come from the media men. They are challenged to turn their critical powers on themselves, to direct their energy, their talent and their conviction toward improving the quality and objectivity of news presentation.

They are challenged to structure their own civic ethics to relate to the great responsibilities they hold.

And the people of America are challenged, too, challenged to press for responsible news presentations. The people can let the networks know that they want their news straight and objective. The people can register their complaints on bias through mail to the networks and phone calls to local stations. This is one case where the people must defend themselves; where the citizen, not the Government, must be the reformer; where the consumer can be the most effective crusader.

By way of conclusion, let me say that every elected leader in the United States depends on these men of the media. Whether what I've said to you tonight will be heard and seen at all by the nation is not my decision, it's not your decision, it's their decision.

In tomorrow's edition of The Des Moines Register, you'll be able to read a news story detailing what I've said tonight. Editorial comment will be reserved for the editorial page, where it belongs.

Should not the same wall of separation exist between news and comment on the nation's networks?

Now, my friends, we'd never trust such power, as I've described, over public opinion in the hands of an elected Government. It's time we questioned it in the hands of a small and unelected elite.

The great networks have dominated America's airwaves for decades. The people are entitled to a full accounting of their stewardship.

1970

24.

Santa Barbara Declaration of Environmental Rights

During January and February 1969 a massive oil leakage from the Union Oil Company's off-shore drilling installations near Santa Barbara, California, caused widespread property damage, water pollution, and destruction of fish and wildlife. This occurrence was but one of numerous oil spills in various parts of the world, either from drilling leaks or from damaged oil tankers. As a result of the Santa Barbara disaster, the federal government introduced strict regulations governing oil exploration. To call the attention of Congress to the problem, a group of citizens in Santa Barbara drew up the following "Declaration of Environmental Rights."

Source: *Congressional Record*, 91 Cong., 2 Session, January 20, 1970.

ALL MEN HAVE THE RIGHT to an environment capable of sustaining life and promoting happiness. If the accumulated actions of the past become destructive of this right, men now living have the further right to repudiate the past for the benefit of the future. And it is manifest that centuries of careless neglect of the environment have brought mankind to a final crossroads. The quality of our lives is eroded and our very existence threatened by our abuse of the natural world.

Moved by an environmental disaster in the Santa Barbara Channel to think and act in national and world terms, we submit these charges:

We have littered the land with refuse.

We have encroached upon our heritage of open space and wildland.

We have stripped the forest and the grasses and reduced the soil to fruitless dust.

We have contaminated the air we breathe for life.

We have befouled the lakes and rivers and oceans along with their shorelines.

We have exterminated entire species of birds and animals and brought others close to extermination.

We have made much of the physical world ugly and loud, depriving man of the beauty and quiet that feeds his spirit.

Recognizing that the ultimate remedy

Oil-soaked beaches and boat hulls along the 28 miles of coastline at Santa Barbara, California, 1969

for these fundamental problems is found in man's mind, not his machines, we call on societies and their governments to recognize and implement the following principles:

We need an ecological consciousness that recognizes man as member, not master, of the community of living things sharing his environment.

We must extend ethics beyond social relations to govern man's contact with all life forms and with the environment itself.

We need a renewed idea of community which will shape urban environments that serve the full range of human needs.

We must find the courage to take upon ourselves as individuals responsibility for the welfare of the whole environment, treating our own back yards as if they were the world and the world as if it were our back yard.

We must develop the vision to see that in regard to the natural world private and corporate ownership should be so limited as to preserve the interest of society and the integrity of the environment.

We need greater awareness of our enormous powers, the fragility of the earth, and the consequent responsibility of men and governments for its preservation.

We must redefine "progress" toward an emphasis on long-term quality rather than immediate quantity.

We, therefore, resolve to act. We propose a revolution in conduct toward an environment which is rising in revolt against us. Granted that ideas and institutions long established are not easily changed; yet today is the first day of the rest of our life on this planet. We will begin anew.

25.

Theodore H. White: Direct Elections—An Invitation to National Chaos

The one phase of election reform that has proved to be the hardiest perennial for a century and a half is what to do about the electoral college. It is an issue that has perpetually failed of resolution, probably because it would take a constitutional amendment to effect any basic change. An amendment to abolish the electoral college was introduced into the Senate in 1949 but did not pass. In recent years, after the unusually close elections of 1960 and 1968, there has been a revival of agitation to change the Constitution so that presidents would be elected by popular vote. In an article published early in 1970, Theodore H. White marshalled arguments against getting rid of the electoral college. Mr. White, a journalist and keen observer of American politics, has written books on the presidential campaigns since 1960, the most recent of which was The Making of the President, 1972.

Source: *Life*, January 30, 1970.

Last September, in a triumph of noble purpose over common sense, the House passed and has sent to the Senate a proposal to abolish the Federal System.

It is not called that, of course. Put forth as an amendment to the Constitution, the new scheme offers a supposedly better way of electing Presidents. Advanced with the delusive rhetoric of *vox populi, vox Dei,* it not only wipes out the obsolete Electoral College but abolishes the sovereign states as voting units. In the name of The People, it proposes that a giant plebiscite pour all 70,000,000 American votes into a single pool whose winner—whether by 5,000 or 5,000,000—is hailed as National Chief.

American elections are a naked transaction in power—a cruel, brawling yearlong adventure swept by profound passion and prejudice. Quite naturally, therefore, Constitution and tradition have tried to limit the sweep of passions, packaging the raw votes within each state, weighting each state's electoral vote proportionately to population, letting each make its own rules and police its own polls.

The new theory holds that an instantaneous direct cascade of votes offers citizens a more responsible choice of leadership—and it is only when one tests high-minded theory against reality that it becomes nightmare.

Since the essence of the proposal is a change in the way votes are counted, the first test must be a hard look at vote-counting as it actually operates. Over most of the United States votes are cast and counted honestly. No one anymore can steal an election that is not close to begin with, and in the past generation vote fraud has diminished dramatically.

Still, anyone who trusts the precise count in Gary, Ind.; Cook County, Ill.; Duval County, Texas; Suffolk County,

Mass.; or in half a dozen border and Southern states is out of touch with political reality. Under the present electoral system, however, crooks in such areas are limited to toying with the electoral vote of one state only; and then only when margins are exceptionally tight. Even then, when the dial riggers, ballot stuffers, late counters and recounters are stimulated to play election-night poker with the results, their art is balanced by crooks of the other party playing the same game.

John F. Kennedy won in 1960 by the tissue-thin margin of 118,550—less than 1/5 of one percent of the national total — in an election stained with outright fraud in at least three states. No one challenged his victory, however, because the big national decision had been made by electoral votes of honest-count states, sealed off from contamination by fraud elsewhere—and because scandal could as well be charged to Republicans as to Democrats. But if, henceforth, all the raw votes from Hawaii to Maine are funneled into one vast pool, and popular results are as close as 1960 and 1968, the pressure to cheat or call recounts must penetrate everywhere—for any vote stolen anywhere in the Union pressures politicians thousands of miles away to balance or protest it. Twice in the past decade, the new proposal would have brought America to chaos.

—To enforce honest vote-counting in all the nation's 170,000 precincts, national policing becomes necessary. So, too, do uniform federal laws on voter qualifications. New laws, for example, wlll have to forbid any state from increasing its share of the total by enfranchising youngsters of 18 (as Kentucky and Georgia do now) while most others limit voting to those over 21. Residence requirements, too, must be made uniform in all states. The centralization required breaches all American tradition.

—Reality forces candidates today to plan campaigns on many levels, choosing groups and regions to which they must appeal, importantly educating themselves on local issues in states they seek to carry.

But if states are abolished as voting units, TV becomes absolutely dominant. Campaign strategy changes from delicately assembling a winning coalition of states and becomes a media effort to capture the largest share of the national "vote market." Instead of courting regional party leaders by compromise, candidates will rely on media masters. Issues will be shaped in national TV studios, and the heaviest swat will go to the candidate who raises the most money to buy the best time and most "creative" TV talent.

—The most ominous domestic reality today is race confrontation. Black votes count today because blacks vote chiefly in big-city states where they make the margin of difference. No candidate seeking New York's 43 electoral votes, Pennsylvania's 29, Illinois' 26 can avoid courting the black vote that may swing those states. If states are abolished as voting units, the chief political leverage of Negroes is also abolished. Whenever a race issue has been settled by plebiscite—from California's Proposition 14 (on Open Housing) in 1964 to New York's Police Review Board in 1966—the plebiscite vote has put the blacks down. Yet a paradox of the new rhetoric is that Southern conservatives, who have most to gain by the new proposal, oppose it, while Northern liberals, who have most to lose, support it because it is hallowed in the name of The People.

What is wrong in the old system is not state-by-state voting. What is wrong is the anachronistic Electoral College and the mischief anonymous "electors" can perpetrate in the wake of a close election. Even more dangerous is the provision that lets the House, if no candidate has an electoral majority, choose the President by the undemocratic unit rule—one state, one vote. These dangers can be eliminated simply by an amendment which abolishes the Electoral College but retains the electoral vote by each state and which, next, provides that in an election where there is no electoral majority, senators and congressmen, individually voting in joint session and hearing the voices of the people in their districts, will elect a President.

What is right about the old system is the sense of identity it gives Americans. As they march to the polls, Bay Staters should feel Massachusetts is speaking; Hoosiers should feel Indiana is speaking; blacks and other minorities should feel their votes count; so, too, should Southerners from Tidewater to the Gulf. The Federal System has worked superbly for almost two centuries. It can and should be speedily improved. But to reduce Americans to faceless digits on an enormous tote board, in a plebiscite swept by demagoguery, manipulated by TV, at the mercy of crooked counters—this is an absurdity for which goodwill and noble theory are no justification.

26.

RICHARD J. DALEY: Urban Housing Needs

During the 1960s the urban housing market deteriorated rapidly for several reasons: increasing interest rates, higher construction costs, scarcity of materials, and the propensity of contractors to build homes in the more affluent suburbs instead of in the cities. The situation was especially noticeable in older cities such as New York, Detroit, Cleveland, Chicago, and Milwaukee where older buildings have not been kept in good repair, and vacant, often burnt-out structures have not been torn down and replaced. By 1973 the interest rates were so high and shortages increasing so rapidly that the housing industry was on the verge of collapse. A housing crisis in the cities meant of course that those hardest hit were low- and middle-income families who could not afford the high mortgage rates in the inflated economy. Early in 1970 the House Banking and Currency Committee, under chairman Wright Patman, held hearings to investigate additional sources of mortgage funds at reasonable rates for city dwellers. On February 4 Mayor Richard Daley of Chicago testified before the committee on the housing problems of his city. Portions of his testimony are reprinted here.

Source: *Congressional Record*, 91 Cong., 2 Session, February 5, 1970.

THE GOAL OF THE CITY is to provide a decent home for each and every citizen. At one time, this major task was left entirely in private hands, to the builder, the real estate broker, and the manager of property, and private social agencies.

The city and the Federal Government have stepped into this area because private industry failed to meet the needs, particularly for those in the lower economic brackets. The city basically has obligations under health and housing codes for the protection of its citizens. There is no authority or responsibility spelled out in the charters of cities or anywhere else making it the responsibility of the city to provide housing for its citizens.

The cities have accepted this responsibility because someone must—not only in the field of housing but in the broad social field. Now the city is held responsible for these services but without the financial resources and facilities to adequately provide them.

Unfortunately, in the past, the thrust of private enterprise and for that matter, the policy of the national government, has served to produce housing outside of the central city. This has been recognized by the Congress which has sought to fill the gap by the passage of many measures directed to the housing needs of low and moderate income families in the cities.

Although efforts to make the FHA more flexible in financing housing in the inner city have had some effect, there still is much the agency can do.

Despite all these efforts, we have not been able to meet the needs of low and moderate families in the cities and today we find that even middle income families have been priced out of the market throughout the Nation.

Since financing for housing is supplied almost solely through the mortgage market, when money becomes tight, the housing market shows the greatest sensitivity. New home production is usually contingent upon the availability of long-term mortgage-secured loans to finance ultimate purchasers. If this financing is not available, it will have a drastic effect on the amount of building.

In recent years, real estate has become even more dependent on increasing amounts of credit per transaction. Changes in credit conditions may be transmitted to the mortgage market in several ways; the capacity and willingness of commercial banks to advance short-term construction credit to builders, interim credit to other real estate lenders, and permanent mortgage credit to buyers. Further, as yields on other types of competitive market investments become more attractive, they tend to divert the flow of funds from housing. In addition the policies established by the Federal Reserve Banks and the Federal Open Market Committee, which is used to influence the general availability and cost of credit have a direct effect on the availability of credit and interest-rate levels throughout the economy.

All the recent actions of these agencies in tightening credit and slowing down the economy to halt inflation is rapidly creating a crisis condition in the housing market.

Oddly enough, our efforts to improve housing conditions—with the active support of the National Government—have only served to worsen the situation. All of us are agreed that in our affluent society there is no justification for slums or substandard housing. The city of Chicago, like other cities, has many programs underway to reduce and eliminate these substandard conditions. For example, in the past 10 years the Building Department working through the courts has demolished more than 8,000 buildings which have been found to be in a hazardous condition. Ten years ago the city budget for this program was $5,000. Today it is $1,200,000 and that doesn't include federal financing.

We have a strict code enforcement program which often leads to court action and the vacation of the buildings because the landlords are unwilling or unable to comply with the health and safety standards.

In Chicago, we also have established a receivership program to take over properties where landlords have refused to comply with building and health ordinances. In hundreds of instances the Chicago Dwellings Association, a quasi-public not-for-profit organization, has been appointed receiver by the courts to take over such buildings. Where possible the C.D.A. rehabilitates the buildings and provides safe housing for the tenants. However, in hundreds of instances, the C.D.A. has found the buildings so deteriorated that rehabilitation is unfeasible. The courts then order the buildings vacated. At the present time, the courts are reluctant to order a building vacated, despite its deteriorated condition, because there are insufficient vacant apartments for the tenants.

In addition we have the normal attrition caused by fire and obsolescence, as well as relocation made necessary by the construction of such essential facilities as schools, police and fire stations, hospitals, public works and other community facilities.

The housing programs arise directly from the insistent demands by our citizens and the Department of Housing and Urban Development that slums be eliminated and housing standards be strictly enforced. But, as essential as these programs are—and they must be carried on—they, nevertheless, contribute directly to a reduction in the housing supply.

Frankly, the cities are caught in a dilemma. Our citizens and the Federal Agencies rightly demand we tear down every substandard home. At the same time, the same Federal Agencies say we cannot tear down bad buildings until we relocate the tenants in standard housing. Meanwhile, they say they cannot tear down bad buildings until we relocate the tenants in standard housing. Meanwhile, they say they cannot provide the resources to build relocation housing or new housing. This situation has been further aggravated by an intolerably tight credit situation.

Let us face facts. To demand that cities improve housing while denying them the resources to supply new housing is a basic contradiction—and places the cities in an untenable situation.

The city of Chicago, like many other cities, has taken advantage of every possible program to increase the supply of housing, especially for the low and moderate income groups. The Chicago Housing Authority now has almost 38,000 public housing apartments and they are all occupied. By the end of 1970, the CHA will have completed construction of almost 2,500 more apartments and homes. Recently the city obtained from the Federal Government authority to build three thousand more units—1500 for families and 1500 for elderly citizens.

May I point out that in 1969 alone, more than 1,000 new units were made available, and of these, 58 percent were three-, four- and five-bedroom apartments to meet the needs of large families. Under our new policy, all public housing homes are built on scattered lots and are three stories or less in height.

At the present time there are 7,000 families and 12,000 elderly citizens on the waiting list.

We sought and were granted in 1969 eight hundred additional units for our leased housing program which uses the private housing market. At the present time the CHA has more than 2,100 leased units in private housing. Shortly we will have 400 more leased units—for a total of 2,500.

The Chicago Dwellings Association, which I mentioned before, has an intensive rehabilitation program on the west side. More than one thousand dwelling units are under contract now to be modernized. Many of these units are in abandoned buildings and so we are adding to the housing supply.

In its efforts to supply housing for low- and moderate-income families, the city made a major breakthrough when an agreement was reached with the Chicago building trades, industry, and the Government for the construction of modular or prefabricated homes. We built more than 200 three- and four-bedroom modular homes. For example, a three-bedroom modular townhouse, including stove and refrigerator, offering comparable facilities to those of a conventionally constructed home and approved by the building code, building trade and FHA, was sold for $15,000 excluding land cost. These were not subsidized homes but were built by private contractors, constructed and assembled by building trade members at union wages. As a result of our experiences, we are now launching a program which we hope will see the construction of hundreds more of these homes.

In another breakthrough in the construction industry, we have seen negotiations involving the building trades union, contractors, members of minority groups, and the city resulting in agreement which will open the doors of opportunity for minority workers in the building trades. This was a voluntary agreement. It promises great hope for the future.

The Department of Urban Renewal, over the past decade, has provided and cleared sites for 7,833 homes and apartments. Most of these were for moderate- and low-income families.

In 1970 we anticipate construction starts on 6,000 homes and apartments for low- and moderate-income families in fifteen urban renewal project areas. Final planning for these areas and arrangements for land disposition procedures will be completed by the end of the year. Of course, much depends on the availability of mortgage money to developers and to home buyers.

I have not included in this recitation the thousands of apartments and homes built by private developers for middle and high income families.

The fact is that despite all our efforts, we were unable to meet our housing needs even before the recent Federal tight money policy.

The sharp increase in interest rates has served to aggravate the housing shortage. Under present conditions, money must be made available if we are to meet our current needs—let alone reach our national housing goal.

I am in full agreement with your chairman when he states: "Among the things which are obviously needed is the channeling of large blocks of funds into housing from the sources which until now have remained relatively untapped."

H.R. 15402 will require private pension funds to invest in federally-insured or guaranteed mortgages on low or moderate income housing in both urban and rural areas. It also will make available the assets of the Federal Reserve for the purchase of residential mortgages, especially mortgages for low- and moderate-income families.

The bill will do much to meet the imperative need for adequate financing essential to increase the supply of new housing. This is a priority of the highest order and it follows that those who need housing desperately should not be made the victims of anti-inflationary policies. I strongly urge the passage of the bill which will make mandatory the use of pension funds as an investment in the welfare and well-being of our citizens.

What is also needed urgently is an increase in Federal assistance for all the programs directed toward filling the housing needs of our low-income families. Congress has heard of these needs from the U.S. Conference of Mayors, the National League of Cities, the Urban Coalition and other groups vitally interested in the rebuilding of our cities.

There are many new programs which can be launched but they too are dependent upon a policy which seeks to encourage and stimulate housing. I would like to mention a few.

Since most of the Nation's major cities desperately need to augment their housing inventories, especially for low- and moderate-income families, and have virtually no vacant land on which to build, some new program approaches are needed to provide the land or space required.

One possibility would be to assist and encourage cities to make residential use of land in space now being occupied by obsolete, abandoned, and uneconomic industrial and commercial uses, which may not be located in blighted areas. For example, almost every city of any size in the Nation, has large open land areas which contain railroad yards and rail storage facilities which are obsolete and uneconomic. The uses of such railroad rights-of-way for new housing offer an immediate opportunity of increasing the supply of decent shelter in many of the existing inner-city neighborhoods with little or no displacement of residents. Existing law should be changed or new laws enacted which would provide grants to study the potential of alternative uses of existing railroad property. Also a new program should authorize acquisition of railroad rights-of-way by cities for residential use and provide a subsidy so that the land may be used for housing.

Another possibility is the use of air rights developments over expressways, railroads and in some instances, waterways, which cut through many of the nation's inner-city neighborhoods. The utilization of platforms over such rights-of-way could substantially expand the supply of housing without the upheaval caused by relocation.

Federal grants should be provided to local governments to cover the cost of preparation of air rights sites, design and construction of foundations, platforms and other facilities. Considerable progress has been made in eliminating the pollution problem accompanying the use of air rights over expressways. Federal grants should be provided to expedite this research because of its great potential.

Throughout city neighborhoods are strips of land, sometimes vacant or occupied by obsolete factories or loft buildings, junk yards and lumber yards. More often than not areas of this kind cannot qualify under the general eligibility standards set forth under the renewal program. A new and improved redevelopment program could make considerable amounts of desperately needed housing available with an absolute minimum of relocation. Further, such redevelopment programs would serve to eliminate a blighting element in many of our city neighborhoods.

While conventional wisdom dictates that we accept as sacrosanct existing parks and open space, there is no question that needs and conditions have changed and are changing. Certainly we should not reduce—we should add to the supply of park and open space land, especially in our major metropolitan areas, but the way such land is currently being used is open to serious question. The possibility of using existing parks and open space for residential or institutional purposes in cases where equal amounts or more can be subsequently cleared or made available in trade should be explored in detail. Federal funds should be available to test the feasi bility of such land trades including the development of appropriated legal safeguards to guarantee adequate replacement.

There is no question that these kinds of programs call for great outlays of money and to some could be considered as contributing to inflation. But there can be no priority that is more important than to give every family an opportunity to live in a decent home. The existence of any slum in a society of affluence is intolerable.

27.

Memorandum on the Proposed Equal Rights Amendment

The women's liberation movement had achieved enough momentum by 1970 to push for an Equal Rights Amendment to the Constitution to outlaw legal discriminations against women. In March 1970 the Citizens' Advisory Council on the Status of Women drew up a lengthy memorandum, reprinted here in part, detailing the need for and nature of such an amendment. The amendment was, in itself, not a new idea: an equal rights amendment had been bottled up in congressional committees for 47 years. On August 10, 1970, the amendment finally passed the House, but the final version as it went to the states for ratification did not emerge from Congress until March 22, 1972. Needing the approval of 38 states within seven years, the Equal Rights Amendment was quickly ratified by more than two dozen state legislatures. But then the momentum flagged, and opposition to the amendment was mobilized in several states. Some states even voided their previous ratification.

Source: *Congressional Record*, 91 Cong., 2 Session, March 26, 1970.

THIS PAPER WAS PRESENTED to the Council by its study group on equal legal rights: Sarah Jane Cunningham, Chairman; Virginia R. Allan, Lorraine L. Blair, Rachel E. Scott, Irene Wischer, Mary Eastwood, Technical Staff.

The proposed equal rights amendment to the U.S. Constitution would provide that "Equality of rights under the law shall not be denied or abridged by the United States or by any State on account of sex," and would authorize the Congress and the States to enforce the amendment by appropriate legislation.

The purpose of the proposed amendment would be to provide constitutional protection against laws and official practices that treat men and women differently. At the present time, the extent to which women may invoke the protection of the Constitution against laws which discriminate on the basis of sex is unclear. The equal rights amendment would insure equal rights under the law for men and women and would secure the right of all persons to equal treatment under the laws and official practices without differentiation based on sex. . . .

The Citizens' Advisory Council on the Status of Women, at its meeting February 7, 1970, endorsed the Equal Rights Amendment, adopting the following resolution:

The Citizens' Advisory Council on the Status of Women endorses the proposed Equal Rights Amendment to the United States Constitution and recommends that the Interdepartmental Committee on the Status of Women urge the President to immediately request the passage of the proposed Equal Rights Amendment by the Congress of the United States.

The Council's recommendation was transmitted to the President on February 13, 1970.

Resolutions proposing an equal rights amendment have been introduced in every Congress since 1923. Hearings were held by the House and Senate Judiciary Committees in 1948 and 1956, respectively. The amendment has been repeatedly reported favorably by the Senate Judiciary Committee, most recently in 1964 (S. Rept. No. 1558, 88th Cong., 2d Sess.), and has twice passed the Senate, in 1950 and 1953.

Both times it was passed, however, with the so-called "Hayden rider," which provided that the equal rights amendment "shall not be construed to impair any rights, benefits, or exemptions now or hereafter conferred by law, upon persons of the female sex." Both times the rider accomplished its purpose of killing the proposed amendment since as the Senate Judiciary Committee has noted, the rider's "qualification is not acceptable to women who want equal rights under the law. It is under the guise of so-called 'rights' or 'benefits' that women have been treated unequally and denied opportunities which are available to men." (S. Rept. No. 1558, *supra*)

Since the proposed equal rights amendment has failed to pass Congress for the past 47 years, it may appear to be a loser, although admittedly it took women more than 50 years to secure the adoption of the 19th amendment. However, a revival of the feminist movement has occurred during the past four years and it is greatly increasing in momentum, especially among younger women. Thus the demand for equal rights and support for the amendment is becoming more widespread, with a corresponding increase in likelihood of early adoption of the amendment.

A number of studies have been made in recent years by the President's Commission on the Status of Women, the Citizens' Advisory Council on the Status of Women, and State commissions on the status of women concerning the various types of laws which distinguish on the basis of sex. Opposition to the equal rights amendment in the past has been based in part on "fear of the unknown," *i.e.*, lack of information concerning the types of laws which distinguish on the basis of sex and would therefore be affected by the amendment. Further delay in approving the amendment thus need not await any further study of the kinds of laws that discriminate on the basis of sex.

These studies have shown that numerous distinctions based on sex still exist in the law. For example:

1. State laws placing special restrictions on women with respect to hours of work and weightlifting on the job;

2. State laws prohibiting women from working in certain occupations;

3. Laws and practices operating to exclude women from State colleges and universities (including higher standards required for women applicants to institutions of higher learning and in the administration of scholarship programs);

4. Discrimination in employment by State and local governments;

5. Dual pay schedules for men and women public school teachers;

6. State laws providing for alimony to be awarded, under certain circumstances, to ex-wives but not to ex-husbands;

7. State laws placing special restrictions on the legal capacity of married women or on their right to establish a legal domicile;

8. State laws that require married women but not married men to go through a formal procedure and obtain court approval before they may engage in an independent business;

9. Social Security and other social benefits legislation which give greater benefits to one sex than to the other;

10. Discriminatory preferences, based on sex, in child custody cases;

11. State laws providing that the father is the natural guardian of the minor children;

12. Different ages for males and females in (a) child labor laws, (b) age for marriage, (c) cutoff of the right to parental support, and (d) juvenile court jurisdiction;

13. Exclusion of women from the requirements of the Military Selective Service Act of 1967;

14. Special sex-based exemptions for women in selection of State juries;

15. Heavier criminal penalties for female offenders than for male offenders committing the same crime.

Although it is possible that these and other discriminations might eventually be corrected by legislation, legislative remedies are *not* adequate substitutes for fundamental constitutional protection against discrimination. Any class of persons (i.e., women) which cannot successfully invoke the protection of the Constitution against discriminatory treatment is by definition comprised of "second class citizens" and is inferior in the eyes of law.

The Fourteenth Amendment to the U.S. Constitution provides that no State shall "deprive any person of life, liberty, or property, without due process of law; nor deny to any person within its jurisdiction the equal protection of the laws." The Federal government is similarly restricted from interfering with these individual rights, under the "due process clause" of the Fifth Amendment.

During the past century, women have been largely unsuccessful in seeking judicial relief from sex discrimination in cases challenging the constitutionality of discriminatory laws under these provisions. As the Committee on Civil and Political Rights, President's Commission on the Status of Women, noted in its 1963 Report,

"In no 14th amendment case alleging discrimination on account of sex has the United States Supreme Court held that a law classifying persons on the basis of sex is unreasonable and therefore unconstitutional. . . ."

It is, of course, possible that the 5th and 14th amendments will in the future be interpreted by the courts as prohibiting all sex distinctions in the law. Nothing in the proposed equal rights amendment would preclude this from occurring; the amendment would in no way cut back, modify, or qualify any protection against discrimination based on sex which may be afforded by the 5th and 14th amendments. As pointed out in Story, *Commentaries on the Constitution of the United States* (5th Edit. 1938, 1939):

The securities of individual rights, it has often been observed, cannot be too frequently declared, not in too many forms of words; nor is it possible to guard too vigilantly against the encroachments of power, nor to watch with too lively a suspicion the propensity of persons in authority to break through the "cobweb chains of paper constitution." . . .

Conceding, therefore, that if correctly construed, and applied according to their true intent and meaning, other constitutional provisions, State and national, might afford ample security for individual rights, we may nevertheless pardon the anxiety for further prohibitions, and concede that, even if wholly needless, the repetition of such securities may well be excused so long as the slightest doubt of their having been already sufficiently declared shall anywhere be found to exist.

The proposed amendment would secure the right of all persons to equal treatment under the law without any distinction as to sex. If the protection against sex discrimination provided by the equal rights amendment should prove to be duplicative of protections afforded by enlightened interpretations of the 5th and 14th amendments, no harm would be done.

Supporters of the equal rights amendment believe that the potential of the 14th amendment is too unclear and that women's constitutional rights to equality are too insecure to rely exclusively on the possibility of getting more enlightened court decisions under that amendment. . . .

Following is a five-point analysis of the impact the equal rights amendment will have on the various types of Federal and State laws which distinguish on the basis of sex:

1. *Strike the Words of Sex Identification and Apply the Law to Both Sexes.*

Where the law confers a benefit, privilege or obligation of citizenship, such would be extended to the other sex, i.e. the effect of the amendment would be to strike the words of sex identification. Thus, such laws would not be rendered unconstitutional but would be extended to apply to both sexes by operation of the amendment, in the same way that laws pertaining to voting were extended to Negroes and women under the 15th and 19th amendments.

Examples of such laws include: laws which permit alimony to be awarded under certain circumstances to wives but not to husbands; social security and other social benefits legislation which give greater benefits to one sex than the other; exclusion of women from the requirements of the Military Selective Service Act of 1967 (i.e., women would be equally subject to military conscription).

Any expression of preference in the law for the mother in child custody cases would be extended to both parents (as against claims of third parties). Children are entitled to support from *both* parents under the existing laws of most States. Child support laws would be affected only if they discriminate on the basis of sex. The amendment would not prohibit the requiring of one parent to provide financial support for children who are in the custody of the other.

2. *Laws Rendered Unconstitutional by the Amendment.*

Where a law restricts or denies opportunities of women or men, as the case may be, the effect of the equal rights amendment would be to render such laws unconstitutional.

Examples are: the exclusion of women

from State universities or other public schools; State laws placing special restrictions on the hours of work for women or the weights women may lift on the job; laws prohibiting women from working in certain occupations, such as bartenders; laws placing special restrictions on the legal capacity of married women, such as making contracts or establishing a legal domicile.

3. *Removal of Age Distinctions Based on Sex.*

Some laws which apply to both sexes make an age distinction by sex and thereby discriminate as to persons between the ages specified for males and females. Under the foregoing analysis, the ages specified in such laws would be equalized by the amendment by extending the benefits, privileges or opportunities under the law to both sexes. This would mean that as to some such laws, the *lower* age would apply to both sexes. For example: a lower minimum age for marriage for women would apply to both sexes; a lower age for boys under child labor laws would apply to girls as well. In other words, the *privileges* of marrying or working would be *extended* and the sex discrimination removed.

As to other laws, the *higher* age would apply to both sexes. For example: a higher cut-off age for the right to paternal support for boys would apply to girls as well; a higher age for girls for juvenile court jurisdiction would apply also to boys. In these cases, the *benefits* of paternal support or juvenile court jurisdiction would be *extended* to both sexes.

Thus, the test in determining whether these laws are to be equalized by applying the lower age or by applying the higher age to both sexes is as follows:

If the age limitation restricts individual liberty and freedom the lower age applies; if the age limitation confers a right, benefit or privilege to the individuals concerned and does not limit individual freedom, the higher age applies.

4. *Laws Which Could Not Possibly Apply to Both Sexes Because of the Difference in Reproductive Capacity.*

Laws which, as a practical matter, can apply to only one sex no matter how they are phrased, such as laws providing maternity benefits and laws prohibiting rape, would not be affected by the amendment. The extension of these laws to both sexes would be purely academic, since such laws would not apply differently if they were phrased in terms of both sexes. In these situations, the terminology of sex identification is of no consequence.

5. *Separation of the Sexes.*

Separation of the sexes by law would be forbidden under the amendment except in situations where the separation is shown to be necessary because of an overriding and compelling public interest and does not deny individual rights and liberties.

For example, in our present culture the recognition of the right to privacy would justify separate restroom facilities in public buildings.

As shown above, the amendment would not change the substance of existing laws, except that those which restrict and deny opportunities to women would be rendered unconstitutional under the standard of point two of the analysis. In all other cases, the laws presently on the books would simply be equalized, and this includes the entire body of family law. Moreover, the amendment in no way would restrict the State legislature or the Congress in enacting legislation on any subject, since its only purpose and effect is to prohibit any distinction based on sex classification.

28.

ABRAHAM RIBICOFF: School Segregation in the North

Many Southern leaders were hopeful that with the arrival of a new administration in the White House school desegregation would be rolled back, or at least moderated. The failure to accomplish this led some members of the Nixon Administration and some Southerners to call attention to the rigid segregation that prevailed in many urban school districts outside the South, a segregation that was based on neighborhood housing patterns. On January 27, 1970, Senator John Stennis of Mississippi proposed amendments to the Civil Rights Act of 1964 and the Elementary and Secondary Education Act of 1966. These amendments would forbid integration or segregation as well as zoning or school transfers for either purpose unless requested by parents. They would also require federal guidelines to be applied uniformly to all regions of the country. Stennis was joined in this move by Senator Abraham Ribicoff of Connecticut, who, in a speech in the Senate on February 9, accused the Northern states of hypocrisy in their handling of segregation in the schools. Portions of Ribicoff's speech are reprinted below.

Source: *Congressional Record*, 91 Cong., 2 Session, February 18, 1970.

THE SENATOR FROM MISSISSIPPI [John Stennis, Democrat] has argued that if segregation is wrong in the public schools of the South, it is wrong in the public schools of all other states.

On this statement the Senator from Mississippi is correct. Therefore, I will support the Senator from Mississippi in his . . . amendment designed to apply the guidelines for desegregation uniformly across the whole nation.

The North is guilty of monumental hypocrisy in its treatment of the black man. Without question, Northern communities have been as systematic and as consistent as Southern communities in denying the black man and his children the opportunities that exist for white people.

The plain fact is that racism is rampant throughout the country. It knows no geographical boundary and has known none since the great migration of rural blacks after World War II. . . .

Perhaps we in the North needed the mirror held up to us by the Senator from Mississippi in order to see the truth. If Senator John Stennis of Mississippi wants to make honest men of the Northern "liberals," I think we should help him. But first we must be honest with ourselves.

Our problem is not only the dual systems of education which exist 16 years after the Supreme Court struck them down in 1954. The more fundamental problem is the dual society that exists in every metropolitan area—the black society of the central city and the white society of the suburb.

Massive school segregation does not exist because we have segregated our schools but because we have segregated our society and our neighborhoods. That is the source of the inequality, the tension and the hatred that disfigure our nation.

The truth is that we cannot separate what has happened in the central cities from what has happened in the suburbs. Black migrants to the cities were trapped in poverty because the whites who fled to the suburbs took the jobs with them and then closed the door on the black man. The implications of this are obvious.

We cannot solve our urban crisis unless we include the suburbs in the solution. We can talk all we want about rebuilding the "ghetto," better housing, tax incentives for job development and massive funds for education. Hopefully, we may even do this. But improving the "ghetto" is not enough.

One reason is that it fails to offer to the black man something we have heard much about in this chamber recently: freedom of choice. The black man must have the freedom to choose where he wants to live, where he wants to work and where he wants to send his child to school.

If he wants to remain in a central city, he should be helped. But a man should not be condemned to a "ghetto" when opportunity exists elsewhere.

The second reason why improving the "ghetto" is not enough is because the opportunity—the jobs and the housing—are in the suburbs.

According to the Suburban Action Institute, a nonprofit agency located in White Plains, N.Y., 80 percent of the new jobs created in large metropolitan areas during the past two decades are located in the suburbs. Yet the black and the poor remain in the central city, either unable to take advantage of them or able to take advantage of them only at great personal inconvenience. . . .

How much more sensible, both in terms of economic growth and simple humanity, it would be to open up our suburbs to the black and the poor so that they live near their places of employment.

Many will argue that the blacks no longer want integration—and whenever a black man says this, you can almost hear the sigh of relief in the suburbs. Many Negroes may not want integration —but many will—and our responsibility is to provide access to that opportunity.

The suburbs are the new America. That is where the private economy is moving. That is where our growing population will be housed. We cannot exclude millions of Americans from that growth because of the color of their skin or the size of their income.

How shall we proceed? In the first place, we should encourage private industry to take a major leadership role. They have as much at stake as anyone.

Suburban Action Institute estimated that a year ago the unfilled suburban jobs across the country totaled 250,000. These could have provided work for many unemployed or underemployed central-city residents. But where were they to live?

American industry could make an enormous contribution. First, it could hire men and women from the central city to work in its new suburban plants. Second, it could use its taxpaying potential to obtain from the suburbs low-income housing for those central-city workers it is hiring. . . .

There is also a role for the Federal Government. We can develop a more useful concept of "impacted" aid to schools. We can provide special funds for those suburbs, towns and school districts that provide housing and employment for blacks from the central city. . . .

The Federal Government should also

review its urban policy and all its urban programs to learn whether they are all aimed at rebuilding the "ghetto" or whether they contain any incentives to include the suburbs in the solution of our urban problems. If not, we should devise new programs.

The Federal Government also should refuse to locate federal facilities in suburban communities until guarantees are received that housing will be provided for low-income people who work for that Government agency. . . .

We seem to have lost sight of the fact that the purpose of education is to help the child. Let us start talking about education that way and concentrate on building the system around the needs of children—not forcing children to meet the needs of the system.

29.

Daniel P. Moynihan: Benign Neglect

Harvard professor Daniel Moynihan, a Democrat, came to the new Nixon Administration as sort of a "house liberal," in contrast to the many conservatives who were appointed advisers to the President. Moynihan became a Cabinet-level adviser on domestic affairs, especially problems of poverty, welfare, housing, race, and the cities. His chief task proved to be dissuading the President from dismantling the programs of previous Democratic administrations, and further, to implement innovative programs of his own in the pressing area of welfare reform. Although Moynihan had excellent liberal credentials, in the face of the militancy and often seeming anarchy of the civil rights and antiwar movements of the late 1960s, his liberalism began to coincide increasingly with moderate Republicanism on a number of social issues. This trend is illustrated by a widely reprinted memorandum on the status of the Negroes that Moynihan sent to President Nixon early in 1970.

As the new year begins, it occurs to me that you might find useful a general assessment of the position of Negroes at the end of the first year of your Administration, and of the decade in which their position has been the central domestic political issue.

In quantitative terms, which are reliable, the American Negro is making extraordinary progress. In political terms, somewhat less reliable, this would also appear to be true. In each case, however, there would seem to be countercurrents that pose a serious threat to the welfare of the blacks and the stability of the society, white and black.

The nineteen-sixties saw the great breakthrough for blacks. A third (32 percent) of all families of Negro and other races earned $8,000 or more in 1968 compared, in constant dollars, with 15 percent in 1960.

The South is still a problem. Slightly more than half (52 percent) of the Negro population lived in the South in 1969. There, only 19 percent of families of Negro and other races earned over $8,000.

Young Negro families are achieving parity with young white families. Outside the South, young husband-wife Negro families have 99 percent of the income of whites! For families headed by a male age 25 to 34, the proportion was 87 percent. Thus, it may be this ancient gap is finally closing.

Income reflects employment, and this changed dramatically in the nineteen-sixties. Blacks continued to have twice the unemployment rates of whites, but these were down for both groups. In 1969, the rate of married men of Negro and other races was only 2.5 percent. Teen-agers, on the other hand, continued their appalling rates: 24.4 percent in 1969.

Black occupations improved dramatically. The number of professional and technical employees doubled in the period 1960-68. This was two and a half times the increase for whites. In 1969, Negro and other races provided 10 percent of the other-than-college teachers. This is roughly their proportion of the population (11 percent).

In 1968, 19 percent of Negro children 3 and 4 years old were enrolled in school, compared to 15 percent of white children. Forty-five percent of Negroes 18 and 19 years old were in school, almost the equal of the white proportion of 51 percent. Negro college enrollment rose 85 percent between 1964 and 1968, by which time there were 434,000 Negro college students. (The total full-time university population of Great Britain is 200,000.)

Educational achievement should not be exaggerated. Only 16 percent of Negro high school seniors have verbal test scores at or above grade level. But blacks are staying in school.

This problem does not get better, it gets worse. In 1969, the proportion of husband-wife families of Negro and other races declined once again, this time to 68.7 percent. The illegitimacy ratio rose once again, this time to 29.4 percent of all live births. (The white ratio rose more sharply, but was still only 4.9 percent.)

Increasingly, the problem of Negro poverty is the problem of the female-headed family. In 1968, 56 percent of Negro families with income under $3,000 were female-headed. In 1968, for the first time, the number of poor Negro children in female-headed families (2,241,000) was greater than the number in male-headed families (1,947,000).

The incidence of antisocial behavior among young black males continues to be extraordinarily high. Apart from white racial attitudes, this is the biggest problem black Americans face, and in part it helps shape white racial attitudes. Black Americans injure one another. Because blacks live in de facto segregated neighborhoods and go to de facto segregated schools, the socially stable elements of the black population cannot escape the socially pathological ones. Routinely, their children get caught up in the antisocial patterns of the others.

You are familiar with the problem of crime. Let me draw your attention to another phenomenon, exactly parallel, and originating exactly the same social circumstances: Fire. Unless I mistake the trends, we are heading for a genuinely serious fire problem in American cities. In New York, for example, between 1956 and 1969 the over-all fire alarm rate more than tripled, from 69,000 alarms to 240,000. These alarms are concentrated in slum neighborhoods, primarily black. In 1968, one slum area had an alarm rate per square mile 13 times that of the city as a whole. In another, the number of alarms has, on an average, increased 44 percent per year for seven years.

Many of these fires are the result of population density. But a great many are more or less deliberately set. (Thus, on Monday, welfare protestors set two fires in the New York State Capitol.) Fires are in fact a "leading indicator" of social pathology for a neighborhood. They come first. Crime, and the rest, follows. The psychiatric interpretation of fire-setting is complex, but it relates to the types of personalities which slums produce. (A point of possible interest: Fires in the black slums peak in July and August. The urban riots of 1964-1968 could be thought of as epidemic conditions of an endemic situation.)

With no real evidence, I would nonetheless suggest that a great deal of the crime, the fire-setting, the rampant school violence and other such phenomena in the black community have become quasi-politicized. Hatred—revenge—against whites is now an acceptable excuse for doing what might have been done anyway. This is bad news for any society, especially when it takes forms which the Black Panthers seem to have adopted.

This social alienation among the black lower classes is matched and probably enhanced, by a virulent form of anti-white feeling among portions of the large and prosperous black middle class. It would be difficult to overestimate the degree to which young, well-educated blacks detest white America.

As you have candidly acknowledged, the relation of the Administration to the black population is a problem. I think it ought also to be acknowledged that we are a long way from solving it. During the past year, intense efforts have been made by the Administration to develop programs that will be of help to the blacks. I dare say, as much or more time and attention goes into this effort in this Administration than any in history. But little has come of it. There has been a great deal of political ineptness in some departments, and you have been the loser.

I don't know what you can do about this. Perhaps nothing. But I do have four suggestions.

First. Sometime early in the year, I would gather together the Administration officials who are most involved with these matters and talk out the subject a bit. There really is a need for a more coherent Administration approach to a number of issues. (Which I can list for you, if you like.)

Second. The time may have come when the issue of race could benefit from a period of "benign neglect." The subject has been too much talked about. The forum has been too much taken over to hysterics, paranoids and boodlers on all sides. We may need a period in which Negro progress continues and racial rhetoric fades. The Administration can help bring this about by paying close attention to such progress—as we are doing—while seeking to avoid situations in which extremists of either race are given opportunities for martyrdom, heroics, histrionics or whatever. Greater attention to Indians, Mexican-Americans and Puerto Ricans would be useful. A tendency to ignore provocations from groups such as the Black Panthers might also be useful. (The Panthers were apparently almost defunct until the Chicago police raided one of their headquarters and transformed them into culture heroes for the white—and black—middle class. You perhaps did not note on the society page of yesterday's Times that Mrs. Leonard Bernstein gave a cocktail party on Wednesday to raise money for the Panthers. Mrs. W. Vincent Astor was among the guests. Mrs. Peter Duchin, "the rich blonde wife of the orchestra leader," was thrilled. "I've never met a Panther," she said. "This is a first for me.")

Third. We really ought to be getting on with research on crime. We just don't know enough. It is a year now since the Administration came to office committed to doing something about crime in the streets. But frankly, in that year I don't see that we have advanced either our understanding of the problem, or that of the public at large. (This of course may only reveal my ignorance of what is going on.)

At the risk of indiscretion, may I put it that lawyers are not professionally well equipped to do much to prevent crime. Lawyers are not managers, and they are not researchers. The logistics, the ecology, the strategy and tactics of reducing the incidence of certain types of behavior in large urban populations simply are not things lawyers think about often.

We are never going to "learn" about crime in a laboratory sense. But we almost certainly could profit from limited, carefully done studies. I don't think these will be done unless you express a personal interest.

Fourth. There is a silent black majority as well as a white one. It is mostly working class, as against lower middle class. It is politically moderate (on issues other than racial equality) and shares most of the concerns of its white counterpart. This group has been generally ignored by the Government and the media. The more recognition we can give to it, the better off we shall all be. (I would take it, for example that Ambassador [Jerome H.] Holland is a natural leader of this segment of the black community. There are others like him.)

I have nothing but utter contempt for the double hypocrital standard of Northerners who look at the South and point the finger and say, "Why don't those Southerners do something about their race problems?"

President Nixon, at Birmingham, Alabama, May 25, 1971

30.

Resolution Against Busing to Achieve Integration

From 1969 through the election campaign of 1972 busing of school children for purposes of integration remained a highly emotional issue that found vehement opposition among both black and white citizens. The Nixon Administration remained decidedly cool to busing for racial balance, but in April 1971 the Supreme Court ruled, in Swann v. Charlotte-Mecklenburg Board of Education, that desegregation must be achieved even if the methods be "administratively awkward, inconvenient, or even bizarre," and allowed that busing was an acceptable means. The Administration pressed for a moratorium on busing, and Congress, in July 1972, passed a bill to accomplish this end. There was even talk of a constitutional amendment to outlaw busing. The Supreme Court, in four separate rulings during 1972, decided that a moratorium on busing did not apply to court orders written to correct unlawful segregation. Out of all the legal and judicial uncertainty over the issue, there grew a public mood of hostility and defiance toward busing and in favor of local control of the public schools in both the North and South. One resolution against busing was adopted by the Georgia Jaycees on February 22, 1970, and is reprinted here.

Source: *Congressional Record*, 91 Cong. 2 Session, April 7, 1970.

WHEREAS, THE FEDERAL JUDICIARY has recently set forth the concept that a mathematical racial balance of faculty and students must be maintained in the public school systems; and

Whereas, this concept will force school systems to classify and locate people according to their race in order to achieve a mythical racial balance; and

Whereas, it is strongly felt that the busing of children to areas in which they do not live for the purpose of obtaining a mathematical racial balance is a denial of individual dignity, worth and equality, and is a denial of the constitutional rights of these children to the freedom of choice of attending a school in close proximity to their homes; and

Whereas, we believe that the implementation of a mathematical racial balance of teachers and pupils will be utterly chaotic and will prevent the continued growth of quality education; and

Whereas, school children and teachers, by federal courts' orders, are being regimented and moved about like pawns on a chessboard to achieve an unlawful objective in direct contradiction to the position taken by the United States Congress and the President of the United States.

Now, therefore, The Georgia Jaycees does unanimously oppose the busing and transferring of school children and teachers for the purpose of accomplishing a mathematical racial balance of faculty and students in the public school systems and deplore the absolute disregard of the Federal Judiciary in creating a chaotic condition by requiring mass transfers of teachers to the detriment of a quality education being obtained by innocent children.

Be it further resolved that the Georgia Jaycees favors an unitary school system accomplished by the children having a freedom of choice of attending schools in close proximity to their homes without regard to achieving mathematical balances based on race, creed or color.

Be it further resolved that the Georgia Jaycees does urge the President of the United States, the United States Congress, and the Supreme Court of the United States to take necessary actions and steps to seek a reversal of this concept as set forth in a decision of the Fifth Circuit Appeals Court of the United States and that copies of this Resolution be forwarded to them requesting their immediate attention and action in order to avoid the continued disruption and a complete breakdown of the public education system.

Be it still further resolved, that we, as Georgia Jaycees, individually and collectively, encourage and endorse a Jaycee "People to People" effort designed to inform and alert the Citizenry of America of this great threat to our public schools, asking that individuals and groups call upon their elected officials to defeat and reverse the disastrous edicts and directives under which our schools are presently governed.

31.

Francesco Cordasco: Survival of the Catholic Urban School

In 1969 the enrollment of Roman Catholic primary and secondary schools in the United States stood at 5,573,810. By 1973 the figure had dropped by nearly two million, to 3,789,007. This sharp decline in attendance was owing to several factors, including a more casual attitude toward religion; resentment to changes in the church since Vatican II; the exodus of many white families from cities to suburbs; shortages of funds and faculty, and the consequent closing of many schools. In an address to the National Catholic Education Association convention in Atlantic City, New Jersey, in April 1970, Professor Francesco Cordasco of Montclair College surveyed the problems facing Catholic city schools. Portions of his remarks are reprinted here.

Source: *Proceedings* of the 67th Annual Convention of the National Catholic Education Association

If there is agreement on anything in American Catholic education, it is in the grim statistical data which delineate a symptomatology of decline in enrollments and the closing of schools. Catholic school enrollment has dropped 500,000 in two years; in June 1969, some 301 Catholic elementary and secondary schools closed throughout the nation, and some 111 more began phasing out grades and consolidating classes. In 1968, school closings numbered 445 with the heaviest attrition in the elementary sector; the school mortality pattern in American Catholic education was inexorably progressive: in 1966-67, 50 elementary schools closed; in 1967-68, 152; and in 1968-69, 225. The National Catholic Education Association has predicted that some 200 schools will close in 1969-70. According to Msgr. James C. Donohue, director, Division of Elementary and Secondary Education, U.S. Catholic Conference, "Enrollment in Catholic elementary and secondary schools has dropped from 5.6 million in the 1964-65 school year to an estimated 4.86 million in the current school year (1969-70)—a decline of three quarters of a million students in only five years." And Msgr. Donohue couples with his notice of the declination of enrollments the severe financial straits in which Catholic schools currently find themselves, and the adverse fiscal burdens which the loss of children from the Catholic schools impose on the public schools.

The reason is obvious. When children leave a Catholic school which has closed or been forced to cut back its operations for financial reasons, they do not vanish. They go to school somewhere, and "Somewhere else" means the local public school.

The dollars and cents implication for public schools are clear. The more former students of Catholic schools enroll in public schools, the more public schools will be obliged to provide additional teachers, classrooms, equipment, and materials—and this is at precisely the time when they are increasingly hard pressed for funds. Indeed, the conclusion seems inescapable that the the condition of public education is worsened by the financial crisis in non-public education.

The available figures demonstrate that this is no fantasy. For instance, it is estimated that taxpayers in the Detroit area have paid some $90 million over the past four years to accommodate in public schools some 50,000 former Catholic school students who have been forced out of Catholic schools which have closed, consolidated, or curtailed classes. This is, furthermore, a continuing expense, since these students will continue to be a drain on the taxpayers' pocketbook for as long as they remain in public schools.

There can be no retreat before the appalling attrition in Catholic school enrollments; and there can be no denial of the fiscal burdens which have rendered, in a period of inflationary havoc. Catholic schools are no less immune to the rigid and iron laws of economics. But Catholic leadership has failed to examine the total context out of which the declining enrollments have emerged.

In my judgment, Catholic educators, in their emphasis on the search for financial support, have made a twofold tragic error. First, they have attributed to the need for money, the grave and imperiled condition of Catholic schools; and second, they have failed to discern that the struggle for public support for Catholic schools can no longer be argued in the rhetoric and language which characterized the 1950's and early 1960's. And this is not to minimize the struggle of those earlier years, or to suggest that the history of public support for private schools in America has been fully written. It is as yet an unfolding story, but the enactment of the Elementary and Secondary Education Act in 1965, with its provisions for Federal support to private schools, has unequivocally established the principle of support.

A survey conducted by the American Jewish Congress showed that bills to provide direct state aid to parochial and other private schools were considered by 20 state legislatures in 1969, with passage achieved in three of the legislatures, but with "a continuing effort by religious groups to win public funds for parochial schools." Whatever form public support of private schools assumes, it is, in my judgment, inevitable; and the intricacies of the pattern it assumes will be formulated within the ensuing few years. The questions which should concern Catholic educators are those which ask: What is the quality of our schools? Whom are we (and whom should we be) educating? What are our responsibilities to the new poor in the cities in which our schools have been traditionally located? Have we a philosophic commitment and a set of clearly defined objectives which justify Catholic schools? What is to be done about the declination in religious vocations and the staffing of parish schools? . . .

The contemporary urban educational scene is one of confusion, bitterness, a worsening reality which persists despite massive federal aid and a plethora of ambitiously experimental constructs: the answers to a multitude of problems are not easy, but as Daniel P. Moynihan (who is an exemplar both of ethnicity and social class) sardonically observes, it may be that the problems have not been correctly defined.

As the decade closed the New York City Master Plan was to declare: "The plain fact is that no one yet knows how to make a ghetto school work."

This statement in itself is a considerable advance, even though the problem is still poorly stated by describing the slum school as a "ghetto" school.

(The plain fact is that nobody knows how to make a real ghetto school—that is, one made up of European Jewish students—not work. The ghetto schools of Europe were where Nobel physicists first learned calculus. One of the most profound misstatements of the situation of the black in urban America—or, for that matter, that of the Irish, Italian and other agricultural immigrants who arrived in the cities in circumstances comparable to those of the blacks—has been to state it in terms of the Jewish experience.)

Nonetheless, the illusion of knowledge faded with the New York City Master Plan, and this at least is the beginning of problem solving.

Characteristically, Moynihan will have infuriated some people, but with typical perspicacity, he has cut down to the root of the matter. If education is to be effective (Moynihan is saying) in urban schools (which have traditionally been the schools of the minority poor), then it must reflect the lifestyles, the mores, and the needs of its constituency; in sum, it must be both of and by the community. The public schoolmen have not yet comprehended this elemental dynamic: the complexity of the struggle for the control of public schools cannot be understood unless one sees the struggle in ethnic and community terms with all of the intricacies of a socio-economic tableau in which new destinies and power are being forged.

But the Catholic schools do understand the dynamic; both their genesis and experience confirm the fact. For the Catholic urban schools, the problem has a different dimension. As community schools, the problems of community relevancy and participation would (in my view) be quickly resolved for urban Catholic schools. An Irish, Italian, or Polish Catholic slum school which has kept intact its ethnic wellsprings and community anchorages can be equally as well a black or Hispanic Catholic slum school with the strength which ethnicity and community afford. For Catholic schoolmen, the problem quite simply is: "Will we undertake to educate the black and Hispanic poor who are the new constituencies of our urban parishes?" And the answer to this question must be forthright and honest; on it hinges the survival of the urban Catholic school.

It is not an easy question. And it cannot be dismissed by noting that the black urban poor are, in the main, non-Catholic: for, if this imposes the need to define Catholic endeavour in apostolic terms, it cannot obscure the relatively modest efforts of American Catholicism in behalf of Black Americans. But what of the Hispanic poor, traditionally Catholic, and the mission of the Catholic urban school? How are we to explain our essentially unsubstantial efforts in their behalf? Has the urban parish school retreated so far from its twin dynamics of ethnicity and community that the Hispanic poor are invisible in its midst?

It is the urban *demos* which Catholic schoolmen must redefine once again. With this done, other problems will be easily resolved. If we keep in mind that it is to the urban citadels of the poor that Father McCluskey is referring in his apostrophe to the Catholic school, his words have a poignant eloquence:

"Have the Catholic schools in America been a failure or a success? The first answer is a retort: Has any human institution been an unqualified failure or success? One could as easily ask: Is any marriage an unqualified failure or success? Perhaps in all fairness, we should let each generation return its own answer. In general, however, it can be readily said that in many important ways, as shall be seen, the Catholic school has been and is an outstanding success. Frankly, where it may have fallen short of its demanding ideal, a portion of the blame can be laid at the door of government whose policies on support have made the burden of financing the Catholic schools such a heavy one. In any event, the Catholic school has tried to keep troth with the transcendent character of its Master's mission."

I have prepared a seven-point check list of recommendations for Catholic schools, and they are skeletally appended: in my text I have intruded on most of them, and they might be considered an inventory for survival. No one of them is listed without a full awareness of the difficulties imposed and the uncertainties to be encountered. Yet, in my considered judgment, they point the way to a renaissance of Christian effort in behalf of children: For Catholic schools there can be no retreat from the urban centers and the contexts of socio-economic deprivation; Catholic schoolmen must define as their major constituency the urban poor; ethnicity and community must provide the animus which gives meaning and dimension to educational programs, governance, and participation; Catholic schools must draw support from all Catholic institutions (health services, *etc.*) to assure all needed service for the child and his family; the declination in religious vocations must be reversed, and the dominant administrative and teaching cadres of Catholic schools must be the religious; liaison between suburban and urban Catholic schools must be established with a major assumption of fiscal support borne by affluent suburban parishes, with a continuing exchange of staff, students, and an eclectic sharing of facilities; Catholic colleges and universities must be continuously involved in educational experimentation within Catholic schools and must become the major resource for innovation and advisement.

32.

Mortimer Caplin et al.: Privacy of Income Tax Returns

On April 11, 1970, the chairman of the Democratic National Committee, Lawrence O'Brien, charged the Nixon Administration with gaining access to federal income tax returns of individuals in violation of laws governing the confidentiality of such returns. O'Brien's charge was based on a legal opinion he had received from two former commissioners of the Internal Revenue Service, Mortimer Caplin and Sheldon Cohen, and from Mitchell Rogovin, former Assistant Attorney General. The legal opinion, in the form of a letter to Mr. O'Brien, is reprinted here. In 1973, as investigations into the Watergate affair proceeded, evidence was presented that administration officials had, in fact, sought ways to use the Internal Revenue Service to embarass critics and political opponents.

Source: *Congressional Record*, 91 Cong., 2 Session, April 16, 1970.

Dear Mr. O'Brien:

It has been reported that an aide to the President currently has access to federal income tax returns upon his written request. You have asked for a legal opinion on whether this reported arrangement with the Internal Revenue Service comports with existing law and regulations. It is our legal opinion that such access is not in conformity with existing law and regulations relating to disclosures of tax returns.

Section 6103 of the Internal Revenue Code sets up the statutory procedures necessary to insure that tax returns and the confidential information appearing thereon are not made available to people who have no legitimate interest in the return. First enacted in 1910, this central provision of our present law provides that returns will be open for inspection "only upon order of the President and under rules and regulations prescribed by the Secretary or his delegate and approved by the President." The inviolate nature of tax information is fundamental to our tax system, not only in the name of privacy, but also to insure increased and more accurate taxpayer compliance. As to the latter, more accurate reporting on income tax returns appears to bear a close relationship to the degree of confidence in which the information is held by the Internal Revenue Service.

The regulations promulgated under section 6103 provide in detail, the manner and circumstances under which tax returns may be legally inspected by the public, state tax officials, Treasury officials, Executive Department officials, U.S. Attorneys and Department of Justice attorneys, Executive Branch agencies, and Congressional Committees. Specific requirements for inspection of federal income tax returns have been prescribed in the regulations to intentionally make it burdensome to secure inspection of such returns. This is in order to maintain the confidentiality of such returns except in unusual circumstances, melding the legitimate needs of government with the right to privacy of the individual. For example, with respect to inspection of returns by executive departments' officials other than the Treasury Department, the request must be in writing, it must be made by the head of the Agency requesting the opportunity to inspect the return, the request must relate to a matter officially before the Agency head, it must specify the taxpayer's name and address, the kind of tax reported, the taxable period covered, the reason why inspection is requested, and the name and official designation of the person by whom inspection is to be made.

The federal official in the news report is Special Counsel to the President and as such, he is an employee of the Executive Office of the President. Reg. Sec. 301.6103 (a)-1(f) covers access to tax returns by such an employee. Under this regulation, the President would be the only Executive Branch official with the authority to request the Commissioner to make tax returns available to employees of the Executive Office of the President. Such a Presidential request would presumably have to comply with the various requirements of the regulations detailed above.

It has been suggested that since the employee in question acts as agent for the President in matters of investigation, no written request by the President is required. We are unaware of any theory of law which would support such an argument. Indeed, this type of argument has been specifically rejected by the very language of the regulation.

The criminal sanction relating to the disclosure of confidential tax information is found in section 7213 of the Code. It makes it a misdemeanor for any federal employee to divulge tax information except as provided by law.

If tax returns are made available in a manner not in conformity with section 6103 of the Code and the regulations, it would appear that such divulgence of tax information is not as provided by law.

Cambodia is one country where we can say with complete assurance that our hands are clean and our hearts are pure.

Secretary of State William P. Rogers, in testimony before the Senate Foreign Relations Committee, April 1970.

33.

RICHARD M. NIXON: The Cambodia Invasion

An incursion into Cambodia to destroy enemy sanctuaries and to disrupt supply lines had been discussed for several years, but never had such an operation seemed so feasible as in the spring of 1970. The existence of the sanctuaries posed a real threat to President Nixon's Vietnamization program and to the withdrawal of American troops. The sudden overthrow of Cambodian Prince Norodom Sihanouk by General Lon Nol in March 1970 made the situation even more inviting. For Lon Nol took an extremely anti-Communist stance by ordering all Viet Cong and North Vietnamese troops out of the country. The debate within the Nixon Administration over a Cambodian incursion was henceforth argued not so much from the military standpoint as for its possible effect on the American public. The generals in Saigon and in the Pentagon urged an invasion using American forces. Other presidential advisers, more fearful of the domestic reaction, were hesitant, suggesting that only South Vietnamese troops be used. But by late April the President had decided to go all the way and use the full force of American as well as South Vietnamese troops. On the evening of April 30 he made a nationally televised address to the nation announcing the invasion and the reasons for it.

Source: *Department of State Bulletin*, May 18, 1970: "The Cambodia Strike: Defensive Action for Peace."

GOOD EVENING, MY FELLOW AMERICANS. Ten days ago, in my report to the Nation on Vietnam, I announced a decision to withdraw an additional 150,000 Americans from Vietnam over the next year. I said then that I was making that decision despite our concern over increased enemy activity in Laos, in Cambodia, and in South Vietnam.

At that time, I warned that if I concluded that increased enemy activity in any of these areas endangered the lives of Americans remaining in Vietnam, I would not hesitate to take strong and effective measures to deal with that situation.

Despite that warning, North Vietnam has increased its military aggression in all these areas, and particularly in Cambodia.

After full consultation with the National Security Council, Ambassador Bunker, General Abrams, and my other advisers, I have concluded that the actions of the enemy in the last 10 days clearly endanger the lives of Americans who are in Vietnam now and would constitute an unacceptable risk to those who will be there after withdrawal of another 150,000.

To protect our men who are in Vietnam and to guarantee the continued success of our withdrawal and Vietnamization programs, I have concluded that the time has come for action.

Tonight I shall describe the actions of

the enemy, the actions I have ordered to deal with that situation, and the reasons for my decision.

Cambodia, a small country of seven million people, has been a neutral nation since the Geneva agreement of 1954—an agreement, incidentally, which was signed by the Government of North Vietnam.

American policy since then has been to scrupulously respect the neutrality of the Cambodian people. We have maintained a skeleton diplomatic mission of fewer than 15 in Cambodia's capital, and that only since last August. For the previous four years, from 1965 to 1969, we did not have any diplomatic mission whatever in Cambodia. And for the past five years, we have provided no military assistance whatever and no economic assistance to Cambodia.

North Vietnam, however, has not respected that neutrality.

For the past five years, as indicated on this map that you see here, North Vietnam has occupied military sanctuaries all along the Cambodian frontier with South Vietnam. Some of these extend up to 20 miles into Cambodia. The sanctuaries are in red, and as you note, they are on both sides of the border. They are used for hit-and-run attacks on American and South Vietnamese forces in South Vietnam.

These Communist-occupied territories contain major base camps, training sites, logistics facilities, weapons and ammunition factories, airstrips, and prisoner of war compounds.

For five years neither the United States nor South Vietnam has moved against these enemy sanctuaries, because we did not wish to violate the territory of a neutral nation. Even after the Vietnamese Communists began to expand these sanctuaries four weeks ago, we counseled patience to our South Vietnamese allies and imposed restraints on our own commanders.

In contrast to our policy, the enemy in the past two weeks has stepped up his guerrilla actions, and he is concentrating his main forces in these sanctuaries that you see on this map, where they are building up to launch massive attacks on our forces and those of South Vietnam.

North Vietnam in the last two weeks has stripped away all pretense of respecting the sovereignty or the neutrality of Cambodia. Thousands of their soldiers are invading the country from the sanctuaries; they are encircling the Capital of Phnom Penh. Coming from these sanctuaries, as you see here, they have moved into Cambodia and are encircling the Capital.

Cambodia, as a result of this, has sent out a call to the United States, to a number of other nations, for assistance. Because if this enemy effort succeeds, Cambodia would become a vast enemy staging area and a springboard for attacks on South Vietnam along 600 miles of frontier, a refuge where enemy troops could return from combat without fear of retaliation.

North Vietnamese men and supplies could then be poured into that country, jeopardizing not only the lives of our own men but the people of South Vietnam as well.

Now, confronted with this situation, we have three options.

First, we can do nothing. Well, the ultimate result of that course of action is clear. Unless we indulge in wishful thinking, the lives of Americans remaining in Vietnam after our next withdrawal of 150,000 would be gravely threatened.

Let us go to the map again. Here is South Vietnam. Here is North Vietnam. North Vietnam already occupies this part of Laos. If North Vietnam also occupied this whole band in Cambodia, or the entire country, it would mean that South Vietnam was completely outflanked and the forces of Americans in this area, as well as the South Vietnamese, would be in an untenable military position.

Our second choice is to provide massive military assistance to Cambodia itself. Now, unfortunately, while we deeply sympathize with the plight of seven million Cambodians, whose country is being invaded, massive amounts of military assistance could not be rapidly and effectively utilized by the small Cambodian Army against the immediate threat.

With other nations, we shall do our best to provide the small arms and other equipment which the Cambodian Army of 40,000 needs and can use for its defense. But the aid we will provide will be limited to the purpose of enabling Cambodia to defend its neutrality and not for the purpose of making it an active belligerent on one side or the other.

Our third choice is to go to the heart of the trouble. That means cleaning out major North Vietnamese and Viet Cong occupied territories—these santuaries which serve as bases for attacks on both Cambodia and American and South Vietnamese forces in South Vietnam. Some of these, incidentally, are as close to Saigon as Baltimore is to Washington.

Now, faced with these three options, this is the decision I have made.

In cooperation with the armed forces of South Vietnam, attacks are being launched this week to clean out major enemy sanctuaries on the Cambodian-Vietnam border.

A major responsibility for the ground operations is being assumed by South Vietnamese forces. For example, the attacks in several areas, including the Parrot's Beak that I referred to a moment ago, are exclusively South Vietnamese ground operations under South Vietnamese command, with the United States providing air and logistical support.

There is one area, however, immediately above Parrot's Beak, where I have concluded that a combined American and South Vietnamese operation is necessary.

Tonight American and South Vietnamese units will attack the headquarters for the entire Communist military operation in South Vietnam. This key control center has been occupied by the North Vietnamese and Viet Cong for five years in blatant violation of Cambodia's neutrality.

This is not an invasion of Cambodia. The areas in which these attacks will be launched are completely occupied and controlled by North Vietnamese forces. Our purpose is not to occupy the areas. Once enemy forces are driven out of these sanctuaries and once their military supplies are destroyed, we will withdraw.

These actions are in no way directed at the security interests of any nation. Any government that chooses to use these actions as a pretext for harming relations with the United States will be doing so on its own responsibility and on its own initiative, and we will draw the appropriate conclusions.

Now, let me give you the reasons for my decision.

A majority of the American people, a majority of you listening to me, are for the withdrawal of our forces from Vietnam. The action I have taken tonight is indispensable for the continuing success of that withdrawal program.

A majority of the American people want to end this war rather than to have it drag on interminably. The action I have taken tonight will serve that purpose.

Two American infantrymen watch a third enter an underground bunker in Cambodia in search of guerrillas.

A majority of the American people want to keep the casualties of our brave men in Vietnam at an absolute minimum. The action I take tonight is essential if we are to accomplish that goal.

We take this action not for the purpose of expanding the war into Cambodia, but for the purpose of ending the war in Vietnam and winning the just peace we all desire. We have made and we will continue to make every possible effort to end this war through negotiation at the conference table rather than through more fighting on the battlefield.

Let us look again at the record. We have stopped the bombing of North Vietnam. We have cut air operations by over 20 percent. We have announced withdrawal of over 250,000 of our men. We have offered to withdraw all of our men if they will withdraw theirs. We have offered to negotiate all issues with only one condition—and that is that the future of South Vietnam be determined not by North Vietnam, not by the United States, but by the people of South Vietnam themselves.

The answer of the enemy has been intransigence at the conference table, belligerence in Hanoi, massive military aggression in Laos and Cambodia, and stepped-up attacks in South Vietnam designed to increase American casualties.

This attitude has become intolerable. We will not react to this threat to American lives merely by plaintive diplomatic protests. If we did, the credibility of the United States would be destroyed in every area of the world where only the power of the United States deters aggression.

Tonight I again warn the North Vietnamese that if they continue to escalate the fighting when the United States is withdrawing its forces, I shall meet my responsibility as Commander in Chief of our Armed Forces to take the action I consider necessary to defend the security of our American men.

The action that I have announced tonight puts the leaders of North Vietnam on notice that we will be patient in working for peace, we will be conciliatory at the conference table, but we will not be humiliated. We will not be defeated. We will not allow American men by the thousands to be killed by an enemy from privileged sanctuaries.

The time came long ago to end this war through peaceful negotiations. We stand ready for those negotiations. We have made major efforts, many of which must remain secret. I say tonight that all the offers and approaches made previously remain on the conference table whenever Hanoi is ready to negotiate seriously.

But if the enemy response to our most conciliatory offers for peaceful negotiation continues to be to increase its attacks and humiliate and defeat us, we shall react accordingly.

My fellow Americans, we live in an age of anarchy, both abroad and at home. We see mindless attacks on all the great institutions which have been created by free civilizations in the last 500 years. Even here in the United States, great universities are being systematically destroyed. Small nations all over the world find themselves under attack from within and from without.

If, when the chips are down, the world's most powerful nation, the United States of America, acts like a pitiful, helpless giant, the forces of totalitarianism and anarchy will threaten free nations and free institutions throughout the world.

It is not our power but our will and character that is being tested tonight. The question all Americans must ask and answer tonight is this: Does the richest and strongest nation in the history of the world have the character to meet a direct challenge by a group which rejects every effort to win a just peace, ignores our warning, tramples on solemn agreements, violates the neutrality of an unarmed people, and uses our prisoners as hostages?

If we fail to meet this challenge, all other nations will be on notice that despite its overwhelming power the United States, when a real crisis comes, will be found wanting.

During my campaign for the Presidency, I pledged to bring Americans home from Vietnam. They are coming home.

I promised to end this war. I shall keep that promise.

I promised to win a just peace. I shall keep that promise.

We shall avoid a wider war. But we are also determined to put an end to this war. . . .

I have rejected all political considerations in making this decision.

Whether my party gains in November is nothing compared to the lives of 400,000 brave Americans fighting for our country and for the cause of peace and freedom in Vietnam. Whether I may be a one-term President is insignificant compared to whether by our failure to act in this crisis the United States proves itself to be unworthy to lead the forces of freedom in this critical period in world history. I would rather be a one-term President and do what I believe is right than to be a two-term President at the cost of seeing America become a second-rate power and to see this nation accept the first defeat in its proud 190-year history.

34.

Kent State—May 4, 1970

No action of President Nixon's first term aroused such vehement response as the Cambodian invasion. Although the public at large seemed to support the venture, the President's April 30 speech proved to be the catalyst that revived the flagging antiwar movement on campuses across the nation. The student disturbances were unprecedented in their ferocity. At Kent State University in Ohio the reaction culminated in a riot on May 2 in which the ROTC building was burned down. The governor declared martial law and sent National Guard troops onto the campus. As the demonstrations continued on Monday, May 4, guardsmen suddenly opened fire, killing four students and wounding eleven. The killings stunned the nation and gave greater impetus to a previously planned mass demonstration in Washington, D.C., on May 9. By May 10, 448 colleges and universities were on strike or closed. Official investigations as to exactly what had happened at Kent State were inconclusive, although the case was reopened by the Justice Department in 1973 for further study. The following selection reprints the conclusions and recommendations of the Report of the President's Commission on Campus Unrest. *The commission, under former Pennsylvania governor William Scranton, issued its report on September 26, 1970.*

Source: *The Report of the President's Commission on Campus Unrest*, Washington, D.C., 1970.

CONCLUSION

KENT STATE WAS A NATIONAL TRAGEDY. It was not, however, a unique tragedy. Only the magnitude of the student disorder and the extent of student deaths and injuries set it apart from similar occurrences on numerous other American campuses during the past few years. We must learn from the particular horror of Kent State and insure that it is never repeated.

The conduct of many students and nonstudent protestors at Kent State on the first four days of May 1970 was plainly intolerable. We have said in our report, and we repeat: Violence by students on or off the campus can never be justified by any grievance, philosophy, or political idea. There can be no sanctuary or immunity from prosecution on the campus. Criminal acts by students must be treated as such wherever they occur and whatever their purpose. Those who wrought havoc on the town of Kent, those who burned the ROTC building, those who attacked and stoned National Guardsmen, and all those who urged them on and applauded their deeds share the responsibility for the deaths and injuries of May 4.

The widespread student opposition to the Cambodian action and their general resentment of the National Guardsmen's presence on the campus cannot justify the violent and irresponsible actions of many students during the long weekend.

The Cambodian invasion defined a watershed in the attitude of Kent students toward American policy in the Indochina war.

Kent State had experienced no major turmoil during the preceding year, and no disturbances comparable in scope to the events of May had ever occurred on the campus. Some students thought the Cambodian action was an unacceptable contradiction of the announced policy of gradual withdrawal from Vietnam, or that the action constituted invasion of a neutral country, or that it would prolong rather than shorten the war. Opposition to the war appears to have been the principal issue around which students rallied during the first two days of May.

Thereafter, the presence of the National Guard on campus was the focus of discontent. The Guard's presence appears to have been the main attraction and the main issue for most students who came to the May 4 rally. For students deeply opposed to the war, the Guard was a living symbol of the military system they opposed. For other students, the Guard was an outsider on their campus, prohibiting all their rallies, even peaceful ones, ordering them about, and tear gassing them when they refused to obey.

The May 4 rally began as a peaceful assembly on the Commons—the traditional site of student assemblies. Even if the Guard had authority to prohibit a peaceful gathering—a question that is at least debatable—the decision to disperse the noon rally was a serious error. The timing and manner of the dispersal were disastrous. Many students were legitimately in the area as they went to and from class. The rally was held during the crowded noontime luncheon period. The rally was peaceful, and there was no apparent impending violence. Only when the Guard attempted to disperse the rally did some students react violently.

Under these circumstances, the Guard's decision to march through the crowd for hundreds of yards up and down a hill was highly questionable. The crowd simply swirled around them and reformed again after they had passed. The Guard found itself on a football practice field far removed from its supply base and running out of tear gas. Guardsmen had been subjected to harassment and assault, were hot and tired, and felt dangerously vulnerable by the time they returned to the top of Blanket Hill.

When they confronted the students, it was only too easy for a single shot to trigger a general fusillade.

Many students considered the Guard's march from the ROTC ruins across the Commons up Blanket Hill, down to the football practice field, and back to Blanket Hill as a kind of charade. Tear gas canisters were tossed back and forth to the cheers of the crowd, many of whom acted as if they were watching a game.

Lt. Alexander D. Stevenson, a platoon leader of Troop G, described the crowd in these words:

> At the time of the firing, the crowd was acting like this whole thing was a circus. The crowd must have thought that the National Guard was harmless. They were having fun with the Guard. The circus was in town.

The actions of some students were violent and criminal and those of some others were dangerous, reckless, and irresponsible. The indiscriminate firing of rifles into a crowd of students and the deaths that followed were unnecessary, unwarranted, and inexcusable.

The National Guardsmen on the Kent State campus were armed with loaded M-1 rifles, high-velocity weapons with a horizontal range of almost two miles. As they confronted the students, all that stood between a guardsman and firing was the flick of a thumb on the safety mechanism, and the pull of an index finger on the trigger. When firing began, the toll taken by these lethal weapons was disastrous.

The Guard fired amidst great turmoil and confusion, engendered in part by their own activities. But the guardsmen should not have been able to kill so easily in the first place. The general issuance of loaded weapons to law enforcement officers engaged in controlling disorders is never justified except in the case of armed resistance that trained sniper teams are unable to handle. This was not the case at Kent State, yet each guardsman carried a loaded M-1 rifle.

This lesson is not new. The National Advisory Commission on Civil Disorders and the guidelines of the Department of the Army set it out explicitly.

No one would have died at Kent State if this lesson had been learned by the Ohio National Guard.

Even if the guardsmen faced danger, it was not a danger that called for lethal force. The 61 shots by 28 guardsmen certainly cannot be justified. Apparently, no order to fire was given, and there was inadequate fire control discipline on Blanket Hill. The Kent State tragedy must mark the last time that, as a matter of course, loaded rifles are issued to guardsmen confronting student demonstrators.

Our entire report attempts to define the lessons of Kent State, lessons that the Guard, police, students, faculty, administrators, government at all levels, and the American people must learn—and begin, at once, to act upon. We commend it to their attention.

RECOMMENDATIONS

Far more important than the particular recommendations of this Commission are the underlying themes that are common to all:

— Most student protestors are neither violent nor extremist. But a small minority of politically extreme students and faculty members and a small group of dedicated agitators are bent on destruction of the university through violence in order to gain their own political ends. Perpetrators of violence must be identified, removed from the university as swiftly as possible, and prosecuted vigorously by the appropriate agencies of law enforcement.

— Dissent and peaceful protest are a valued part of this nation's way of governing itself. Violence and disorder are the antithesis of democratic processes and cannot be tolerated either on the nation's campuses or anywhere else.

— The roots of student activism lie in unresolved conflicts in our national life, but the many defects of the universities have also fueled campus unrest. Universities have not adequately prepared themselves to respond to disruption. They have been without suitable plans, rules, or sanctions. Some administrators and faculty members have responded irresolutely. Frequently, announced sanctions have not been applied. Even more frequently, the lack of appropriate organization within the university has rendered its response ineffective. The university's own house must be placed in order.

— Too many students have acted irresponsibly and even dangerously in pursuing their stated goals and expressing their dissent. Too many law enforcement officers have responded with unwarranted harshness and force in seeking to control disorder.

— Actions—and inactions—of government at all levels have contributed to campus unrest. The words of some political leaders have helped to inflame it. Law enforcement officers have too often reacted ineptly or overreacted. At times, their response has degenerated into uncontrolled violence.

— The nation has been slow to resolve the issues of war and race, which exacerbate divisions within American society and which have contributed to the escalation of student protest and disorder.

— All of us must act to prevent violence, to create understanding, and to reduce the bitterness and hostility that divide both the campus and the country. We must establish respect for the processes of law and tolerance for the exercise of dissent on our campuses and in the nation.

We advance our recommendations not as cure-alls but as rational and responsive steps that should be taken. We summarize here our major recommendations, addressed to those who have the power to carry them out.

For the President

We urge that the President exercise his reconciling moral leadership as the first step to prevent violence and create understanding. It is imperative that the President bring us together before more lives are lost and more property destroyed and more universities disrupted.

We recommend that the President seek to convince public officials and protestors alike that divisive and insulting rhetoric is dangerous. In the current political campaign and throughout the years ahead, the President should insist that no one play irresponsible politics with the issue of "campus unrest."

We recommend that the President take the lead in explaining to the American people the underlying causes of campus unrest and the urgency of our present situation. We recommend that he articulate and emphasize those values all Americans hold in common. At the same time we urge him to point out the importance of diversity and coexistence to the nation's health.

To this end, nothing is more important than an end to the war in Indochina. Disaffected students see the war as a symbol of moral crisis in the nation which, in their eyes, deprives even law of its legitimacy. Their dramatic reaction to the Cambodian invasion was a measure of the intensity of their moral recoil.

We urge the President to renew the national commitment to full social justice, and to be aware of increasing charges of repression. We recommend that he take steps to see to it that the words and deeds of government do not encourage belief in those charges.

We recommend that the President lend his personal support and assistance to American universities to accomplish the changes and reforms suggested in this report.

We recommend that the President take steps to assure that he be continuously informed of the views of students and blacks, important constituencies in this nation.

We recommend that the President call a series of national meetings designed to foster understanding among those who are now divided. He should meet with the governors of the states, with university leaders, with law enforcement officers, and with black and student leaders. Each participant in these meetings should be urged to bring with him practical suggestions for restoring trust and responsibility among those whom he represents, and commit himself to continue this process of national reconciliation in frequent meetings throughout the school year.

For Government

We strongly urge public officials at all levels of government to recognize that their public statements can either heal or divide. Harsh and bitter rhetoric can set citizen against citizen, exacerbate tension, and encourage violence.

Just as the President must offer reconciling leadership to reunite the nation, so all government officials—at all levels—must work to bring our hostile factions together.

Like the President, the governors of the states should hold meetings and develop contacts throughout the school year to further the cause of reconciliation. Like the President, other federal, state, and local officials must be sensitive to the charge of repression and fashion their words and deeds in a manner designed to refute it.

We urge state and local officials to make plans for handling campus disorders in full cooperation with one another and with the universities. We urge the states to establish guidelines setting forth more precisely the circumstances that justify ordering the Guard to intervene in a campus disorder.

We recommend that the federal government review all its current policies affecting students and universities to assure that neither the policies nor administration of them threatens the independence or quality of American higher education. At the same time government should increase its financial support of higher education.

We urge public officials to reject demands that entire universities be punished because of the ideas or excesses of some members and to honor their responsibility to help preserve academic freedom.

We recommend that the Department of Defense establish alternatives to ROTC so that officer education is available to students whose universities choose to terminate on-campus ROTC programs.

We recommend greatly increased financial aid for black colleges and universities. All agencies of government that support such institutions should massively increase their grants to enable these colleges to overcome past shortcomings.

We support the continuing efforts of formerly all-white universities to recruit black, Mexican-American, Puerto Rican, and other minority students, and we urge that adequate government-sponsored student aid be made available to them. We recommend that in the process of becoming more representative of the society at large, universities make the adjustments necessary to permit those from minority backgrounds to take maximum advantage of their university experience.

Bombing and arson pose an increasing threat to lives and property on campus. We urge prompt enactment of strict controls over the sale, transfer, and possession of explosive materials. Such statutes are needed at both the federal and the state level.

For Law Enforcement

We have deep sympathy for peace officers—local and state police, National Guardsmen, and campus security officers—who must deal with all types of campus disorder. Much depends on their judgment, courage, and professionalism.

We commend those thousands of law enforcement officers who have endured taunts and assaults without reacting violently and whose careful conduct has prevented violence and saved lives.

At the same time, we recognize that

there have been dangerous and sometimes fatal instances of unnecessary harshness and illegal violence by law enforcement officers.

We therefore urge that peace officers be trained and equipped to deal with campus disorders firmly, justly, and humanely. They must avoid both uncontrolled and excessive response.

Too frequently, local police forces have been undermanned, improperly equipped, poorly trained, and unprepared for campus disturbances. We therefore urge police forces, especially those in smaller communities, to improve their capacity to respond to civil disorders.

We recommend the development of joint contingency plans among law enforcement agencies. They should specify which law enforcement official is to be in command when several forces are operating together.

Sending civil authorities on to a college campus armed as if for war—armed only to kill—has brought tragedy in the past. If this practice is not changed, tragedy will come again. Shoulder weapons (except for tear gas launchers) are very rarely needed on the college campus; they should not be used except as emergency equipment in the face of sniper fire or armed resistance.

We recommend that National Guardsmen receive much more training in controlling civil disturbances. During the last three years, the Guard has played almost no role in Southeast Asia but has been called to intervene in civil disorders at home more than 200 times.

We urge that the National Guard be issued special protection equipment appropriate for use in controlling civil disorders. We urge that it have sufficient tactical capability and nonlethal weaponry so that it will use deadly force only as the absolute last resort.

For the University

Every university must improve its capability for responding effectively to disorder. Students, faculty, and trustees must support these efforts. Universities must pull themselves together.

The university should be an open forum where speakers of every point of view can be heard. The area of permitted speech and conduct should be at least as broad as that protected by the First Amendment.

The university should promulgate a code making clear the limits of permissible conduct and announce in advance what measures it is willing to employ in response to impermissible conduct. It should strengthen its disciplinary process. It should assess the capabilities of its security force and determine what role, if any, that force should play in responding to disorder.

When criminal violence occurs on the campus, university officials should promptly call for the assistance of law enforcement agencies.

When faced with disruptive but nonviolent conduct, the university should be prepared to respond initially with internal measures. It must clearly understand the options available to it and be prepared to move from one to another if it is reasonably obvious that an earlier tactic has failed.

Faculty members who engage in or lead disruptive conduct have no place in the university community.

The university, and particularly the faculty, must recognize that the expansion of higher education and the emergence of the new youth culture have changed the makeup and concerns of today's student population. The university should adapt itself to these new conditions. We urge that the university make its teaching programs, degree structure, and transfer and leave policies more flexible and more varied in order to enhance the quality and voluntariness of university study.

We call upon all members of the university to reaffirm that the proper functions of the university are teaching and learning, research and scholarship. An academic community best serves itself, the country, and every principle to which it is devoted by concentrating on these tasks.

Academic institutions must be free—free from outside interference, and free from internal intimidation. Far too many people who should know better—both within university communities and outside them—have forgotten this first principle of academic freedom. The pursuit of knowledge cannot continue without the free exchange of ideas.

Obviously, all members of the academic community, as individuals, should be free to participate actively in whatever campaigns or causes they choose. But universities as institutions must remain politically neutral except in those rare cases in which their own integrity, educational purpose, or preservation is at stake.

One of the most valid criticisms of many universities is that their faculties have become so involved in outside research that their commitment to teaching seems compromised. We urge universities and faculty members to reduce their outside service commitments. We recognize that alternative sources of university funding will have to be developed to take the place of the money attached to these outside commitments. Realistically, this will mean more unrestricted government aid to higher education.

Large universities should take steps to decentralize or reorganize to make possible a more human scale.

University governance systems should be reformed to increase participation of students and faculty in the formulation of university policies that affect them. But universities cannot be run on a one man, one vote basis with participation of all members on all issues.

Universities must become true communities whose members share a sense of respect, tolerance, and responsibility for one another.

For Students

Students must accept the responsibility of presenting their ideas in a reasonable and persuasive manner. They must recognize that they are citizens of a nation which was founded on tolerance and diversity, and they must become more understanding of those with whom they differ.

Students must protect the right of all speakers to be heard even when they disagree with the point of view expressed. Heckling speakers is not only bad manners but is inimical to all the values that a university stands for.

Students must face the fact that giving moral support to those who are planning violent action is morally despicable.

Students should be reminded that language that offends will seldom persuade. Their words have sometimes been as offensive to many Americans as the words of some public officials have been to them.

Students should not expect their own views, even if held with great moral intensity, automatically and immediately to determine national policy. The rhetorical commitment to democracy by students must be matched by an awareness of the central role of majority rule in a democratic society and by an equal commitment to techniques of persuasion within the political process.

The Commission has been impressed and moved by the idealism and commitment of American youth. But this extraordinary commitment brings with it extraordinary obligations: to learn from our nation's past experience, to recognize the humanity of those with whom they disagree, and to maintain their respect for the rule of law. The fight for change and justice is the good fight; to drop out or strike out at the first sign of failure is to insure that change will never come.

This Commission is only too aware of America's shortcomings. Yet we are also a nation of enduring strength. Millions of Americans—generations past and present—have given their vision, their energy, and their patient labor to make us a more just nation and a more humane people. We who seek to change America today build on their accomplishments and enjoy the freedoms they won for us. It is a considerable inheritance; we must not squander or destroy it.

35.

BEN EAST: Is It Taps for Wild Alaska?

Atlantic Richfield Oil Company, in cooperation with Humble Oil, sank an oil well on Alaska's North Slope near Prudhoe Bay in the fall of 1967. By September 1968 they had confirmed the presence of a large oil reservoir in the area, and other oil companies with leases also drilled exploratory wells. On September 10, 1969, the state of Alaska auctioned off leases to 450,858 acres of potential oil land for more than $900 million, the largest sale of federal and state lands in history. To get the oil to the rest of the United States, a pipeline running 800 miles from Prudhoe Bay south to Valdez was projected. Unfortunately for the oil companies, the idea for the pipeline came along at the same time that environmental consciousness was increasing across the nation. Construction of the pipeline was delayed for years as the environmentalists battled the oil companies in the courts and in the Interior Department. Finally, in November 1973, the pipeline bill passed Congress and was signed by the President. Determination to get the line built had been markedly enhanced by the oil shortage that developed during 1973. The main concern of those who opposed construction of the pipeline was potential damage to the wildlife and tundra of the North Slope, as well as fears of massive oil spills. In the article from which the following selection is taken, Ben East, senior field editor of Outdoor Life, *described the threat to the ecology of Alaska posed by the new oil fields.*

Source: *Outdoor Life*, May 1970.

"IT IS LITERALLY NOW OR NEVER."

The man who said that, last January 1, was President Richard M. Nixon, and he was talking about the urgent and alarming need to halt pollution of the air and water of this country.

"The 1970s," the President continued, "absolutely must be the years when America pays its debt to the past by reclaiming the purity of its air, its waters, and our living environment."

Coming from the White House, that harsh warning carried great weight, but it was not new. It echoed what worried conservationists have been saying with increasing frequency in recent years about our headlong haste to ruin resources that cannot be replaced.

At this moment the nation's top example of impending ruination is in Alaska.

The Great Land, Alaskans call their state. It is a splendid land, more than twice the size of Texas, with vast areas of primitive mountain and tundra, lake and river and forest. Its bears and wolves, moose and caribou, Dall sheep and goats, wolverines and beavers, ptarmigan, waterfowl, and salmon have had things mostly to themselves since before the dawn of history.

That long and idyllic era, it is now plain, is fast coming to an end. The bell began to toll for wild Alaska in June 1968 when a drilling rig struck oil on the barren tundra beside the Artic Ocean some 200 miles east of Point Barrow. The exact location was at Prudhoe Bay on the coastal rim of Alaska's North Slope, the broad shelf that lies betwen the Brooks Range and the polar sea.

That desolate region is locked in ice through the darkness of the winter night, melting on the surface in summer to create soggy muskeg and shallow ponds. A few feet down, under the thin layer of earth and sphagnum moss, lies permafrost (ice and frozen mud that never thaw) as thick as 1000 feet.

That drilling operation tapped what may be the biggest oil field on the North American continent, and it touched off a wild free-swinging oil boom that almost matches Alaska's Klondike gold rush of 70-odd years ago. It is bringing a mixed bag of consequences.

A huge tract of wilderness has been opened up; camps, roads, and airfields are being built; and air traffic is rocketing. A winter ice road, called the Hickel Highway in honor of the state's former governor (Walter J. Hickel, now Secretary of the Interior), has been cut through the wilderness as far as Sagwon, 150 miles from the arctic coast. The road was hardly more than opened when thaws last spring converted it into an unusable trail of mud. But as 1970 came in, Governor Keith Miller announced plans for an all-year gravel road to the oilfields, to be completed by year's end.

When winter closed in last October, 3000 to 5000 men were living in camps scattered over the North Slope, pressing the search for oil.

The most dramatic result of the strike was a sale of leases last September that poured $900 million into Alaska's state treasury. Governor Miller could hardly be blamed for calling the boom "a rendezvous with destiny."

Probably a majority of Alaskans agreed with him. It's only natural that they should look on the oil strike as a financial windfall of staggering size.

On top of that, while many residents of the state are deeply concerned about protecting their unspoiled outdoors, others resent the interest shown in Alaska's wildlife and wilderness by people outside. Alaska's game and fish and scenery are Alaska's business, they argue. But sportsmen and conservationists throughout the U.S. do not agree. To them Alaska is a place unique, and their view is that anything that menaces this uniqueness should be resisted.

When a colonel of the U.S. Army Corps of Engineers was quoted as saying, in connection with the oil boom, "The 55-gallon oil drum is the new state flower of Alaska," a lot of people thought things were being carried too far.

As happy as the oil industry, other business interests, and promoters were about the new bonanza, others—residents and nonresidents alike—saw another side to the coin of oil riches and were worried.

The influx of oil workers, the exploration and drilling, and the construction of camps and roads and airfields would change everything. Caribou, grizzlies, polar bears, walrus and seals, foxes, wolves, bird life, and fish would face new pressures and a drastically altered environment. Could they survive? Oil development is notorious for its lack of concern about fish and game.

"The boom is going to mean standing room only," said one sportsman, "and standing room for people is rough on bears and caribou herds."

A scientist from the Arctic Research Laboratory added: "In a crash program, conservation seldom has a chance."

What are the forecasts of Alaska's own wildlife authorities? I asked that question of Wallace Noerenberg, acting commissioner of the Department of Fish and Game. First of all, he told me, he foresees beneficial results in the form of access to what are now almost inaccessible fish-and-game populations.

That opening up of roadless and remote country, however, is the very thing that many conservationists are worried about. All too often, easy access into such areas via roads and airfields means a nosedive in the quality of hunting and fishing.

"Grizzly and wolf populations on the North Slope may become susceptible to heavy hunting pressure," Noerenberg went on, "and additional restrictions will be needed. Some have already been enacted. And of course the oilfield development will change the wilderness character of the land.

"The greatest potential threat to game," Noerenberg went on, "may come from the system of pipelines needed to collect the oil from the wells. We conclude that these feeder lines, carrying hot oil, will have to be elevated above ground, to avoid problems connected with burying such lines in permafrost. They could prevent the free movement of caribou. Reindeer are notoriously poor jumpers; an ice fence three or four feet high will contain them. Feeder lines of this same height might also restrict caribou movement."

The area that will be laced by these lines includes the calving grounds and migration routes of caribou herds numbering many thousands.

When I asked Noerenberg about damage to streams from gravel removal, he replied, "Gravel for road, airport, and oil-pad construction has come primarily from streambeds nearest the sites. At this time, construction is near the coastline, in an area where little or no fish spawning takes place. By precluding gravel removal from active stream channels and by further field investigations to define spawning areas, we feel that conflicts can be minimized."

He does not, however, say how rules are to be enforced. Up to now they have not been. And *Outdoor Life* was told that the Alaska Department of Natural Resources (entirely separate from the Department of Fish and Game) has issued "free use" gravel permits to the oil companies, allowing them to take unlimited amounts from unspecified streams, wherever they need it, at no cost.

In view of what has already happened, Noerenberg's statement sounds surprisingly mild. But in fairness to him it must be remembered that no one connected with the Alaska Fish and Game Department today is really free to express an opinion on this subject. . . .

Regardless of what Alaska officials and the oil industry may claim, the area is being torn up and its fish-and-game resources are being seriously damaged.

Take, for example, the Sagavanirktok River near Prudhoe Bay, commonly called the Sag. It had a heavy spawning run of arctic char, and an excellent population of grayling where tributaries flow in. Huge quantities of gravel have recently been dug from its downstream channels, and no one can say what the effects will be.

Other rivers with good fish populations, such as the Kuparuk and Kavik, have fared little better. Last summer one channel of the Kuparuk was closed off by a dike, and a drilling rig operated in midstream.

Up to now, so little research has been done that in some instances Alaska fishery biologists are not even sure which North Slope rivers serve as spawning streams. So it will be a long time before the effects of the gravel dredging, pollution, siltation, and blocking of channels can be evaluated.

A graphic eyewitness description of what is happening to fish and game and the tundra environment itself was supplied to *Outdoor Life* by Wilbur Mills, a freelance photographer from the Seattle area who spent the summers of 1968 and 1969 on the North Slope.

"Gravel removal from coastal beaches has turned them to mud," Mills says. "River channels have been silted and blocked, spawning grounds of migratory fish destroyed. Countless miles of vehicle tracks and trails left by oil-exploration crews crisscross the tundra, causing thawing and erosion of the frozen soil. I have seen ruts deep enough to hide a man.

"Garbage and debris have been left to rot in a climate in which it takes 50 years for a tin can to turn to dust. Often, raw human sewage marked the garbage dumps left behind on the ice of lakes that were used for winter camps.

"In July of 1968," says Mills, "I found debris strewn around an old camp at Lobo Lake in the Sheenjek River valley. Along a seven-mile stretch of beach that I explored I found 49 derelict oil drums. The U.S. Fish and Wildlife Service told me that the company responsible had agreed to remove the trash, but when I went back in August of 1969 it was still there.

"Peters and Schrader lakes, at the foot of the high mountains of the Brooks Range, provide excellent aircraft access to both the mountains and the arctic foothills. This is a beautiful scenic area, but the accumulation of trash blights it. I could not hike 100 yards along the shore of either lake without encountering barrels, cans, wooden crates and planks, canvas, steel pipe, and aircraft remains.

"On occasion oil has been pumped into sump ponds and burned, and there were days last summer when a black, smokey haze covered large areas of the coastal plain.

"Grizzlies have been shot and trapped when garbage dumps lured them into camps. Wolves have been killed illegally from aircraft, and both bears and wolves are chased by helicopters and light planes for 'sport.' Caribou have been seen hopelessly tangled in seismic wire, countless miles of which have been left behind by oil-exploration crews."

In February 1969 there appeared what may prove the gravest danger of all. That's when plans were announced for the building of the Trans Alaska Pipeline

System, now commonly called TAPS, a 48-inch-diameter line running 800 miles across the state from Prudhoe Bay to the ice-free (and earthquake-prone) port of Valdez on the south coast.

A state legislator called the announcement "the most electrifying news Alaska has had since statehood." Conservation forces found it electrifying in a different sense. They saw in it a threat of frightening proportions.

The pipeline—crossing southward over the North Slope, passing through the Brooks Range probably by way of Anaktuvuk Pass, and continuing south through some of the most-rugged wilderness and best game lands in the state — would traverse areas with big populations of caribou, moose, Dall sheep, grizzly and black bears, bison, goats, wolves, and wolverines. The greatest hazard would be to some 400,000 North Slope caribou whose migration routes it would cross, to moose and bison, to grizzlies that would be killed at garbage dumps, and to Dall sheep from increased hunting pressure.

As for the impact on sportfishing, an official Fish and Game Department report, not made public, lists 36 rivers and streams along the proposed route that have excellent fishing for salmon, char, grayling, trout, sheefish, and other species and also serve as migration routes for major spawning runs. The list includes such rivers as the Sag and Koyukuk, plus tributaries of the Tanana and Copper rivers and many streams flowing into Valdez Bay.

"The schedule for completion of the pipeline does not allow reasonable time to assess the impact on sportfish," the report says.

The Sport Fishing Institute in Washington seconded this complaint. The pipeline route crosses or parallels more than 120 rivers and streams, the institute pointed out. What about erosion, silting, sedimentation? No one could say.

When I asked Noerenberg what impact he thought the line would have on hunting and fishing, he showed less concern about the pipeline itself than about the threat of oil pollution from big tankers operating at its southern terminal at Valdez.

"The stipulations agreed on by TAPS pertaining to construction will insure adequate protection for streams and rivers," he told me. "Unless the line should rupture, causing a catastrophic pollution incident, we do not believe any fish or game populations will be adversely affected.

"It is potential problems resulting from oil loading, ballast treatment, and possible tanker accidents on the Valdez Arm of Prince William Sound that are our most serious consideration," he continued. "The pipeline production guarantees almost continuous tanker operation, and a tanker accident anywhere in the sound would jeopardize the spawning area of 50 percent of the salmon stocks there. This area also contains sea otters and nesting and wintering waterfowl. A major spill might affect the nesting area of the dusky Canada goose in the Copper River Delta as well as the extensive razor-clam beaches near Cordova."

Worries about tanker operations are even stronger among commercial fishermen and conservationists. When tanker traffic at Valdez reaches its peak, the ships are expected to haul one million barrels of oil a day. The risk of accident is real, and one wreck could wipe out an entire salmon cycle. Many of the salmon there are "intertidal" spawners—that is, they don't ascend streams to reproduce.

Equally menacing is the chance that

tankers may deliberately discharge oil-polluted ballast into Prince William Sound.

And conservationists do not share Noerenberg's optimism about the consequences of the pipeline itself. The line poses the danger of oil spills that would dwarf the infamous spill at Santa Barbara, California.

Much of the pipeline's route lies across permafrost, frozen mud that slides when thawed. Oil heated to 140 degrees to 170 degrees would flow through the four-foot pipe at the rate of 500,000 gallons per mile. Scientists estimate that such a pipe, buried in that material and heated to that temperature, will ultimately thaw the permafrost to a depth as great as 50 feet, and that the thawed mud will flow like a fast-moving glacier.

"There is no assurance that the line will stay in place once it's laid," the Wildlife Management Institute warned, "or that it will not rupture and spill great quantities of oil across the landscape and into the streams."

It is a reasonable warning. The 500,000 gallons in each mile of TAPS is about twice the total amount involved at Santa Barbara.

The U.S. Geological Survey shares the concern of the conservationists. At the conclusion of detailed studies, the agency bluntly warned that a hot-oil pipeline buried in permafrost would be likely to endanger both the environment and the security of the line itself.

One construction firm has proposed suspending the line from towers, placing it high enough above ground that it would cause no melting and would allow wildlife to pass under it. But up to the time this article was written, there had been no official reaction to that suggestion.

Another consideration is the unavoidable damage to Alaska's wilderness in an area where scars are very slow to heal. Almost anywhere else in the U.S., scars on the land except for such atrocious wounds as the unreclaimed aftermath of strip mining—repair themselves within a few years. The opposite is true in the Alaska oil country and in the Brooks Range.

The layer of soil that covers the permafrost is thin and fragile. Foot trails erode swiftly into gullies, and a dog tied to a stake for a few days can cause the ground surface within the animal's walking range to drop a foot. Because of this condition and the extremely slow growth of all plant life, scars endure for decades. And in the cold climate, litter disappears slowly, if ever. . . .

Advocates of the pipeline scoff at the idea that a single narrow right-of-way across Alaska, even one that's 800 miles long, can do any serious damage. They overlook the roads, camps, airfields, and stream crossings, the cutting of timber and dredging of gravel, the pumping stations and rubbish dumps, the heedless behavior of construction crews. . . .

Authority to approve the project rests with Secretary of the Interior Walter J. Hickel, subject to an O.K. from the two Interior committees of Congress. When the oil companies asked for the necessary permit to build the pipeline, Hickel moved promptly to seek a green light from the committees. He got it last January, and on a visit to Alaska about that time he predicted that construction of the line would begin this spring.

In the meantime, TAPS was acting as if the permit were a foregone conclusion. Oil interests are accustomed to getting their way when they deal with government. The pipeline firm went ahead with road construction, cleared right-of-way, and ordered millions of dollars worth of pipe.

Hickel had promised all along that no permit would be issued until adequate safeguards to prevent environmental damage were assured. Just how that goal can be accomplished is still a matter for debate, but up to the time this article was written the Secretary of the Interior, considered by many observers a partisan of the oil interests, had surprised his critics by sticking to his guns. His delay in issuing the permit had caused TAPS to reject all bids for the laying of the pipeline from Valdez north to the Yukon River.

An oil-industry spokesman commented, "Everybody knew it was going to happen if Interior kept bringing up new stipulations and delaying a right-of-way permit, but no one quite believed it could happen. It did."

Predictions about the pipeline are hazardous at this point, but it seems likely now that construction will not begin before late summer. However, no one expects the project to be blocked for long. And no one can yet say what its consequences will be for wild Alaska. While conservationists in and out of the state look on, the fate of wildlife and wilderness is being decided by people who have little concern for either.

36.

Gladwyn Hill: After Earth Day

Earth Day, as it was observed on April 22, 1970, was originally conceived of as a college campus "teach-in" comparable to the May antiwar teach-ins of the late 1960s. The idea was first suggested by Senator Gaylord Nelson of Wisconsin who, along with Representative Paul McCloskey of California, served as honorary co-chairmen of the Environmental Teach-in organized in January 1970 at Washington, D.C. The outcome on April 22 far exceeded the expectations of the original planners. More than 2000 colleges, 10,000 grade and high schools, hundreds of communities, and several state legislatures joined in a massive display of concern over environmental problems. One estimate said that at least 20 million Americans participated in Earth Day. The impact of the day was weighed several weeks later by Gladwyn Hill, environmental correspondent for the New York Times.

Source: *National Wildlife*, August-September, 1970.

Psychologists have long recognized a phenomenon called "the self-fulfilling prophecy." It has nothing to do with extra-sensory perception or witchcraft. It simply means that the more talk there is about something—be it a potential riot or the success of a fund drive—the more likely it is to actually happen because people's thoughts and actions are subconsciously attuned to accomplishing what is talked about.

This explains the extraordinary intensity of public interest in environmental reform that reached a crescendo in the April 22 observance of Earth Day—an event such as the world had never seen before. For the first time in history virtually an entire nation, including Congress, paused in its workaday activities to contemplate the deterioration of its physical surroundings and life-patterns.

"Can the enthusiasm of Earth Day be sustained?" Although this question has been asked a million times, it is the wrong question. It tends to put Earth Day in the role of *cause* rather than *effect*.

The exact extent of Earth Day activities probably will never be known. Environmental Action, the Washington-based group of young people which promoted the event, now estimates that at least 20 million people participated in 4,000 campus and community programs that ran the gamut from picking up litter to praying. . . .

But neither the numbers nor the activities were as important as the fact that virtually everyone in the country *heard* about the observances, and were compelled to give the subject some thought. And equally significant is the fact that neither thoughts nor actions were of a one-day nature, but were part of a perceptible continuum.

When we consider the varied things that have happened since April 22, it is evident that while they reflect the preoccupations of Earth Day, few can be traced exclusively to it. Their origins in most cases lie farther back in time and deeper in motivation.

There is intense ferment on college campuses, in public schools, among citizen groups and in conservation organizations. Political activism is the new battle cry as newly-formed coalitions are exerting immediate influence on legislation regarding water pollution pesticides, and the SST. There are ever-widening areas of impact:

—Politicians: There is new environmental sensitivity among politicians and government agencies. Congress and state legislatures have more measures before them than anyone can count.

—Industrialists: A thunderous impact has hit industry, business and finance—from technical pollution controls to radically changed concepts of corporate responsibility.

—Educators: There are profound stirrings in the professional realm of education, from curricular innovations to the mounting of long-range public television informational campaigns.

—Lawyers: There is new impetus in the field of law toward modernizing it into a prime implement of environmental reform.

—Theologians: Even conservative quarters in theology have been jolted into reassessment of the Judeo-Christian ethic's seeming over-glorification of man over his physical surroundings.

From an age when the extermination of wolves was, per se, a virtue, we have moved into an era when the wearing of a real animal skin is becoming unfashionable.

How much of all this is sound and how much of it is substantial?

Anything as big as the environmental crisis and the environmental revolution is bound to involve both the sham and the real—as history itself does.

There is an immense amount of lip service, of political opportunism, of official trimming and tacking. There are still few effective Federal and state measures against such elementary evils as air and water pollution. But no one who attended the May 22 General Motors stockholders' meeting in Detroit could doubt that a new value-system is descending upon American industry. The reformers lost the vote-skirmish, but their thesis remained virtually unchallenged: A new dimension of public well-being, physical and aesthetic, has to be built into the profit-making structure.

As people examine the significance of the environmental upheaval, they almost inevitably end up like the blind men examining the elephant, drawing different conclusions from disparate parts. The whole is almost too big to conceive.

That is why we now have some people talking about litter in the streets, while others are talking about the nogrowth economy; why the success of a bond issue in the state of Washington will be taken as evidence that "environment" is triumphing, while the mutterings of some super-patriots that ecology is communistic will be chronicled as "emergent backlash."

Obviously the peak of involvement and excitement that came on Earth Day cannot be sustained through the year. But to suggest conversely—with the American propensity for casting things in alternative extremes—that concern might vanish, is to categorize the life-and-death problems of environment with crab-grass or pornography. The only way people can escape facing up to environmental problems is for the world to stop and let them off.

The immensity of it all means there are many questions that may not be resolved soon. For example: How do we mesh anti-pollution efforts with equally important aspects of environment such as race relations, civil rights and poverty? It will be no use to have clean air if the breathers are stifled by rancor and inequity; neither will it be any use to solve sociological problems if, as solutions are achieved, everyone is gasping his last.

Where, then, do we go from here?

One thing that Earth Day helped make clear is that the environmental crisis involves a vast array of problems, all of which need attention. The task is staggering, but there are some historic guidelines for coming to grips with it.

World War II, if we reflect, presented a similar complexity. It took riflemen in Belgium and fliers in New Guinea, farmers in North Dakota and aluminum-savers in Florida, and the actions of many others, to consummate the effort. The critical ingredients were a consensus on the objective, a scale of priorities, a mass effort, and coordination at many levels.

Earth Day was an expression of consensus—if not on precise objectives, at least on the existence of the problem. In 1965 only 17 percent of a national opinion sampling put air and water pollution among the nation's topmost problems. But in a Gallup survey shortly after Earth Day 53 percent ranked pollution alleviation second only to crime abatement.

Pollution of course is only one facet of the environmental problem. But in the public preoccupation with it, there is implicit sensing of valid priorities. Air pollution might kill us sooner than anything else.

At the same time, there is rapidly mounting recognition that the worldwide "population bomb," although a delayed-action threat, could work unimaginable havoc, and equally needs immediate attention. And it's starting to get it.

Plainly, environmental reform is too big, ramified and long-range to be organized with the neatness and facility of a war effort. But the scope of the problem does not excuse inaction. We simply have to begin attacking all facets of pollution and population problems while at the same time proceeding with plans for wise land use.

Ideally, in the opinion of some, the

President of the United States might proclaim a "national emergency" on the environmental front and mobilize a wartime-type complex of corrective efforts. This might yet happen in certain instances—if, for instance, cities continue to fumble with air pollution controls until there is a sudden series of lethal smog episodes.

Most likely the main impetus for environmental reform will continue to come from the citizenry, and it will be up to them, painstakingly and laboriously, to develop remedies for present problems and make plans for wise use of our resources in the future. In this regard, the "old line" conservation organizations, and the environmental media will have a critical new role in bringing some order to the current mixture of concern, spelling out the priorities in which they have dealt for so long.

Countless people are going around today, vaguely aware of the problems, asking "What can *I* do?" This interest will never disappear as long as environmental problems are so omnipresent. But neither will it do any good until it is channelled and guided.

The "self-fulfilling prophecy" is a misnomer if anyone thinks it exempts him from doing anything.

37.

ROBERT A. CAMPBELL: Federal Funding of Medical Research

To combat inflation, the Nixon Administration recommended budget cuts in a whole array of domestic programs, including medical and other scientific research and education. Many medical research programs had to be cut back, forcing lay-offs of staff and a reassessment of priorities. Some institutions were forced to apply for private financing as they were caught in a squeeze between federal fund cutoffs and their own greatly increased budgets. The financial plight of the medical schools threatened to aggravate the already severe shortage of physicians precisely at the time medical education needed to expand to meet the burgeoning health crisis. In 1970 there were 102 medical schools in the U.S., with new admissions of about 11,000 students. During the year, the American Medical Association revealed a program to train more than 50,000 by 1985 so the nation could attain a ratio of 175 doctors to every 100,000 population; but the federal budget cuts threatened to make this goal unreachable. In this letter to Senator Mark Hatfield, Dr. Robert Campbell of the University of Oregon Medical School argued the case for increased federal funding to stave off serious cutbacks in education and research.

Source: *Congressional Record*, 91 Cong., 2 Session, July 7, 1970.

DEAR SENATOR HATFIELD:

Along with many of my colleagues in medicine and medical science, I am increasingly perplexed by the paradoxical and erratic federal policies governing the course and development of our health resources.

It is abundantly clear to most everyone

who has pondered our health problem that a sustained, balanced building and staffing program is essential. Increased above our present rate of growth, more new medical schools are an absolute necessity if we are ever to catch up with our expanding population. Moreover, if we are to significantly improve the quality of the care as well, a further bulge and another growth slope must be introduced. In addition our presently established schools need expanded facilities to train additional physicians, medical scientists, nurses, and other professional people in related paramedical specialties.

When we contemplate the above needs in the light of the fact that we currently have 1600 vacancies in academic medicine and 600 vacancies in academic dentistry, it is obvious that our first and foremost effort must be directed to an increase in our life blood, capital goods, namely our training facilities and trained people to man them. Not only are we badly in need of this added intellectual capital, but we must have progressively better capital, consistent with increasing technologic, diagnostic and therapeutic complexities of our time. The doctor product we send out to the community must not be poorly informed, thus, in the face of the present information explosion in medicine, there is a greater necessity to have faculty who can understand, collate, integrate and disseminate the kinds of information, and provide the training experience necessary to make the physician of tomorrow. Most people would agree that an improperly trained physician is almost as bad as no physician at all.

Despite the above considerations and the need to expand our medical facilities, graduate training programs, post-doctoral medical fellowship stipends and the medical research grants to sustain our institution are being withdrawn. Several federally supported training programs for graduate students at our medical school are in jeopardy and will be amputated unless a transfusion of some kind is soon undertaken. The present outlook would lead one to believe that the present graduate student program, which is the life blood of the basic biomedical atmosphere at the University of Oregon Medical School, will be cut to about one-half or one-third in a year or two. This will mean that support for some faculty salaries made possible by these training grants will no longer be available. This will mean that much basic biomedical research will perforce grind to a stop. Therefore we will not be turning out many professional leaders and scholars in the fields of bacteriology, physiology, biochemistry, anatomy or pharmacology. I am reminded of our physiological laboratory experiments, the object of which was to determine how much blood loss our dogs could tolerate before they went into shock.

Curtailment of medical research grants continue and the burners and lights are going out in the laboratories. Loyal and experienced workers of long standing are being let go for lack of funds. The principle investigator, losing a grant, frequently loses part of his salary support as well. Where does this teacher-researcher-scholar get his support? Hard-earned tenure is no protection if the state legislature, unwilling to go into debt, is unable to provide a salary floor. Curtailment of medical research grants has another adverse effect. Overhead, which is a part of every biomedical research grant, is being lost. These overhead funds often provide salary support for the members of the teaching faculty of our biomedical institutions. It can be seen that teaching and training are intimately related to research programs.

Thus they both are damaged further. These mechanisms are at work in Oregon.

Now let us take up the postdoctoral clinical fellowships. These serve a multiple function. Most importantly, the fellow of today is the academician of tomorrow. Further, they allow the clinician, with his fellows, to organize and properly analyze the body of information about problem patients being treated so that better approaches can be developed. It allows the director of the program to devise and develop new tests clinically not yet available, thus better serving the patients with serious and difficult management problems. These programs are a remarkable stimulus to thinking, for the faculty member in charge, but as well for the fellows, residents, interns and students with whom they are in continuous contact. If these post-doctoral fellowship programs are not maintained, it is very likely that some of the faculty will have to leave this institution. Why? Because, while faculty members must give direct service to the ill patients on the wards and in the clinics, his function primarily is to be a teacher of fellows, residents, interns and students in amplifying and enriching their professional experiences. If the fellows are not available, some faculty would be so barraged with day to day patient care problems they could neither teach, study, write or do clinical research.

With declining tax receipts in Oregon, and Oregon being a relatively poor state, even tenured professors are in no position to feel secure. Oregon is a "soft-money school," that is to say much of our money comes from the outside, and many faculty members' salaries are derived from these sources. Oregon's vigorous faculty has constantly generated income from outside the state through hard work in maintaining its competitive position.

As money contracts, and the work-load expands with our increasing population, each faculty member must do more and more. If clinical faculty members leave because they are "under the stretch," and their research programs are cut, this just makes it increasingly difficult for those remaining behind to have "esprit de corps" and a reasonable morale.

This hits the faculty in many other ways. Travel to national scientific meetings is abrogated. Some of our faculty members were unable to attend medical meetings in the field of their interest this year. Our summer research college and medical student programs are contracting. In the past these programs have helped get the students through and broadened their experience. Student loans have been curtailed.

Direct financial transfusions to our medical and dental schools are needed now. We have talented administrative and faculty people who know their schools, their state, local and intramural biomedical problems well. They know how, where and when assistance can best be directed during these difficult times. Prolonged "study" or the setting up of commissions "to review the problem" or setting up of new bureaucratic programs to treat the symptoms rather than the cause will only cause further delay, dislocation and deterioration. In my opinion, the Deans of our medical and dental institutions should be provided with *direct emergency funds* to maintain viability of these cherished resources. In truth, only they know the minimum required to prevent a major health catastrophe in the next two years.

National Guardsman standing watch during a May Day rally in New Haven, Connecticut, in 1970

VARIETIES OF VIOLENCE

Whether there has been more violence in ne United States in recent years than ever efore is highly debatable. What is certain that there has been a heightened awareess on the public's part of the many forms nat violence takes. Television has given us "you-are-there" perspective on studentolice confrontation, civil rights demonstraons, airplane hijackings, political assassiations, battles in Southeast Asia and the Aiddle East, and, on occasion, crime in the treets. So all-pervasive has the daily diet of ne unexpected and bizarre become that nany Americans are ready to conclude that nese are the worst of times. But in fact, the nanifold forms of social violence, that seemed to abound on every side from 1966 to 1971, had diminished drastically by the end of 1973. The civil rights movement became quiescent; public marches in behalf of various causes became fewer; domestic hijacking of aircraft virtually ceased (under the strict surveillance of airport inspections); and the campuses became quiet. Perhaps most important of all, the United States was no longer fighting in Vietnam. Americans faced an increasing number of domestic problems, such as inflation, the energy shortage, and the crisis of government. But they were not issues that could be solved by protest marches, civil rights demonstrations, or confrontation.

The most noticeable form of social violence from 1969 to 1971 was a carryover from the previous three years: student protest against the Vietnam war. For some months it seemed that the uproar in Chicago during the 1968 Democratic Convention might have turned aside the willingness to protest. Then too, there was a wait-and-see attitude toward the new President, who was given a chance to end the war, as he had promised. But by the fall of 1969 massive protest was under way again. And with the widening of the war into Cambodia in April 1970, violence reached a new pitch on the campuses. The culmination was the shooting at Kent State University in Ohio. The Kent State affair seemed to mark a turning point in the whole politics of protest, for it became clear that the administration would pursue the war relentlessly in spite of any amount of public outcry. Even before the Vietnam truce was signed in January 1973, the whole student movement had pretty well disintegrated.

(Above) An Arab "Black September" guerrilla in a makeshift face mask on the balcony of the Israeli Olympic squad's headquarters on September 5, 1972, before the squad was murdered; (below) National Guardsmen fire a tear gas barrage into a crowd of demonstrators at Kent State University on May 4, 1970.

Above) A hijacked BOAC jetliner is blown up by Arab guerrillas at Dawson's Field, Jordan, in September 1970; three hijacked planes were destroyed after the passengers were allowed to debark; (below) a bullet-ridden building at Jackson State College in Mississippi; two youths were killed during demonstrations on May 15, 1970.

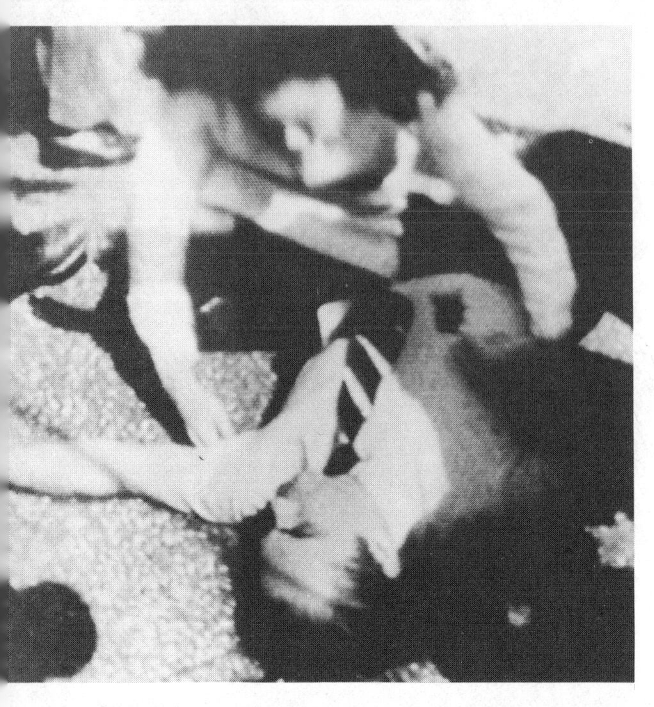

If protest and confrontation were on the decline, more persona forms of violence were not. Airline hijackings became frequent, and were usually motivated by economic or political blackmail. Some of the most sensational form of political violence were perpe trated by Arab guerrilla groups in Europe and the Middle East. The world was stunned in Septembe 1972 by the murders of 17 mem bers of the Israeli squad committe at the Olympic Games in Munich b a Palestinian commando group "Black September." 1972 also saw the machine-gunning of 28 person by Japanese terrorists at the air port in Tel Aviv, Israel. In the United States, Governor Georg Wallace, campaigning for the Democratic presidential nomina tion, was shot during a pre-primar rally at a Laurel, Maryland, shop ping center.

(Above) George Wallace's wife, Cornelia, leans over him moments after he was shot at Laurel, Marylan (below) cult leader Charles Manson at Los Angeles jail following his indictment for the murders of Sharon Ta and six others in 1969

38.

Jean-Jacques Servan-Schreiber: The Multinational Challenge of the Seventies

From 1955 to 1970 American business investment abroad increased from $49 billion to more than $65 billion, with the heaviest concentration in Canada and Western Europe. Much of this investment was in manufacturing, including the requisition of factories, distribution centers, and office buildings from which both foreign and U. S. markets were served. Thus many of our large corporations were no longer "American" as such. Auto, drug, oil, computer, and chemical firms became so heavily involved in foreign markets that they lost their national character. And some of the corporations are richer and more powerful than many nation-states. The influence and power of American investment in Europe was described by French journalist Jean-Jacques Servan-Schreiber in his 1967 book, The American Challenge, *in which he warned Europe of becoming an economic appendage of the United States. In 1970 he entered politics and won a seat in the French national assembly in the June election. A month later, while visiting in the U. S., he testified on the problem posed by multinational corporations before the Joint Economic Committee of Congress, Subcommittee on Foreign Economic Policy. Portions of his statement are reprinted here.*

Source: *Congressional Record*, 91 Cong. 2 Session, July 31, 1970.

I APPEAR BEFORE YOU as a fellow parliamentarian, recently elected by the legendary region of Lorraine, the land of the Cross of Lorraine—for me a joyous cross to bear. I also appear as one dedicated to the ideal of an integrated and unified Europe.

In 1967, while I was still a journalist and publisher, I wrote a book: *The American Challenge.* The Communists criticized it as a hymn to American capitalism. Others saw it as an anti-American call to arms. In truth, I tried to express both admiration for your economic dynamisms and anxiety lest its vitality and our passivity engulf the European way of life. Today I would like to comment on how we are all affected by this challenge, which has become multinational, and by various other challenges that we are facing in common. . . .

Like church and state, economic and political power must be separated as much as possible if each is to fulfill its mission. This was the essence of Luther's reform philosophy. It holds a vital message for us today. The best judges in matters of investment and profitability are generally the entrepreneurs, not the state. Public ownership of means of production has been irrevocably discredited by the experience of the Communist East. Private industry must be allowed to perform to the full its function as a factor of material progress. Politics has another and more crucial role: to consecrate itself to the service of man—the worker—rather than to the efficiency of production—the corporation.

The ferociousness of competition among business enterprises is a locomotive of innovation, development and enrichment. It must be given full play. But the main goal of politics is to prevent this ferociousness from hurting man himself. If those who lord over industry are also to be those who by their influence dictate the direction of political life, then we will inescapably fall into the most bitter and dangerous social upheavals. The separation of economic and political power is, therefore, a primary task for the future.

The great British economist, John Maynard Keynes, wrote in the '30s that "the essence of capitalism is the preponderance of the role of money in society, and the love of money by the individual." It is this that we must extirpate from our social system with human generosity and solidarity. This reformist objective is a worthy and urgent mission for the '70s.

The intensified conduct of business across national borders has augmented the benefits and the miseries of the capitalist system. The development of corporated activity on a global scale by firms such as IBM, Ford, Siemens, Fiat, Phillips and Lofoarge make for more efficient productivity and a wholesome cross-fertilization of intelligence, talent and of creativity. Consequently, it is a force for social wellbeing. But, because of the worldwide empires which they are carving out for themselves, the multinational corporations are also able to create a new jungle. Widely spread out in their component parts and commanded from geographically remote bases, they account to no single national authority. And since international law is feeble, or non-existent, they are free of international authority as well. Fraudulent or undisciplined organizations, often operating with funds invested by unsuspecting people of modest means, enjoy far-ranging immunity from any meaningful form of regulation or supervision, unless you consider Panama or Liechtenstein acceptable legal systems.

Profit-making activities which draw undue advantage from tax havens, holding company privileges, the weaknesses and contradictions of international tax enforcement and other loopholes without any redeeming economic function, rob society of much of the material abundance created by the market economy and the dynamism of legitimate multinational business. That portion of the available wealth which should go into collective investment for the benefit of all (health, education, housing, transportation, etc.) is too often diverted into hands where it is not needed and where it does not belong.

Some of us see models in the institutions which you have developed during the momentous days of the "New Deal": the Security and Exchange Commission, for example. But we are also afraid of the awesome size and vigor of your business institutions, and we must take steps in our own defense.

Consider the fact that the real value of American investments in the European Common Market currently stands at close to 40 billion dollars. American subsidiaries control 95 percent of the total production of integrated circuits, 80 percent of electronic calculators and 30 percent of automobiles. Because the process of integration on the Continent is so slow, and so heavily obstructed by nationalistic considerations (my own country being a principal offender), it is difficult to develop a coordinated policy vis-a-vis the multinational corporation. The European countries vie with each other for a larger share of these investments, occasionally offering generous subsidies and tax concessions. When General Motors was denied the privilege to build a plant in Alsace, it was immediately welcomed across the border, to use German workers and supply the French market under the preferred tariff structure of the European Economic Community.

Our capital markets are also dominated by American-controlled institutions. Indeed, the banking centers of London, Frankfurt and Zurich seem to be at the mercy of the Eurodollar. And it is an extraordinary paradox that the savings of Europeans are used to finance the acquisition of local industries by U.S. companies. In 1959, for example, American borrowings in Europe stood around 500 million dollars; in 1967 it reached 2.6 billion dollars. During the same period the proportion of U.S.-generated funds to finance investments in Europe fell from 25 percent to 16 percent.

I mean to be neither nationalistic nor Chauvinistic in pointing out the drama of this situation and the patterns which it announces for the future. American investments are welcomed in Europe. They stimulate the efficiency and energy of our own economies. But we cannot help being disturbed by the form of the invasion in certain sectors. Our industries are still too unsophisticated to stand up against the multinational American giants in face-to-face competition. This is demonstrated by the fact that European companies which venture into the U.S. market with operating subsidiaries are hardly able to hold their heads above water.

Penetration into a foreign country, which is a natural by-product of the multinational phenomenon, cannot go without a commensurate sense of social responsibility. The multinational corporations must show greater sensitivity than they have to conditions prevailing in the host country. What is good for General Motors may be good for America, but not necessarily for Belgium or Holland. They must respond to our need for industrial decentralization; they must realize that we too have differences of a type which exists between West Virginia and Massachusetts. And I, for one, intend to do more for Lorraine on the sensitive banks of the Rhine. Unashamedly, I propose to campaign for a greater share of American and European investments in a region which boasts all of the resources and the scientific and technical skills that any multinational corporation may require. So, as you see, I am not against multinational corporations. On the contrary, I regard them as new tools of progress. In fact, a very fine one, McGraw-Hill, has been for more than three years a partner in my enterprises in France.

Happily, the world is no longer as polarized as it used to be. Strong centrifugal forces are at work both in the East and in the West. Russia, no less than America, is learning the limitations of military might and developing dangerous internal cracks. The empire over which it presides is discovering the inevitable link between economic progress and human freedom. This is the tender sword which will open the East.

In the last few years the Eastern countries have given evidence of their desire to become integrated into the world economy. They deserve to be met halfway. Today, the national leaders of Communist countries scarcely disguise their admiration, even envy, of Western production and marketing efficiency. For Europe, this affords opportunities which are at once economically attractive and helpful in strengthening the fragile fabric of peace.

Communist planners are groping for new techniques to improve the competitive position of their economies and the standard of living of their people. The dynamic character of production in Western Europe, Japan and the United States has become the main object of their envy. Under these new conditions, international co-operation becomes imperative. If the Eastern countries wish to participate in the feast of industrial development, they can no longer afford the luxury of splendid isolation and the suppression of creative freedom. This process must be helped along, for it can help to reopen the East.

The economic experience of the last two decades has proven the indivisibility of technical progress. Men living apart on their own side of the ideological fence cannot generate as ample and varied a range of goods and ideas as can be produced by the entire world pursuing innovation and freely exchanging its benefits. If the gap in industrial development is to be narrowed, East-West intercourse must extend beyond the mere exchange of commodities. The domain of technology and management must be given primary attention, along with broadly based business co-operation across the borders of geography and politics.

As Europeans, we view the East in light of the economic and cultural indivisibility of the Continent, rather than its ideological cleavage. While the longing for civil and intellectual liberties in the Communist societies still remains unfulfilled, a manifestation of national identity and a rejection of the dogmas of the past is clearly in evidence. Indeed, the Gaullist notion of "Europe des Patries" has touched a more responsive nerve in the Eastern than in the Western part of the Continent.

It is becoming increasingly clear that in the '70s Europe will have a much more important economic and moral role to play than in the two previous decades; a very special role, since our old Continent, at least that part of it which lies to the West, no longer aspires to the dream of world empire. It has learned from bitter experience that military conquest brings no rewards. Within this experience lies a lesson which can help *you*.

A major task at the other end of the Atlantic is the construction of a federalized Europe, one which is larger, more self-sufficient, socially more just and democratically more compatible. In this you can help *us*.

Priority must be given to East-West reconciliation, the road toward which objective passes through active co-existence, economic and industrial co-operation and broader exchange of products, ideas and men. This is an enterprise which we shall tackle *together*.

By far the greatest challenge is the passion of youth, admirable in its motivation, dangerous in its frustration. The quest of the young for dignity, sincerity and truth in our generation is one of the two great sources of human energy. The other source is industry. Both are highly progressive and liberating forces. If we allow them to remain as they are today, on a collision course, the future will be dark. If we forge their alliance by reform, then we will have met the challenge of our generation.

39.

J. WILLIAM FULBRIGHT: Old Myths and New Realities in the Middle East

Following the Six Day War of 1967, the Middle East remained in a state of armed truce, with occasional hostilities and raids committed by both sides. The Arab-Israeli standoff was further complicated by the activities of Palestinian commandos whose loyalty was to a cause, not to a nation. These commando actions were not limited to Palestine, but included terrorist bombings and airplane hijackings in many countries. Jordan's King Hussein seemed in danger of losing his kingdom should a full scale war break out between his army and the commandos. It was in this crisis atmosphere that the United States offered a peace initiative, known as the Rogers peace plan, devised in 1969 and accepted in principle by Russia, Israel, Jordan, and the United Arab Republic in 1970. A cease-fire was declared in the Suez Canal region on August 7 and remained in effect while negotiations got under way. On August 24, the day before negotiations began in New York, J. William Fulbright, chairman of the Senate Foreign Relations Committee, spoke in Congress on the issues dividing the Arabs and Israel. Portions of his speech are reprinted here.

Source: *Congressional Record*, 91 Cong. 2 Session, August 24, 1970.

THE MYTHS THAT SHAPE EVENTS in the Middle East are the oldest myths of all.

Some derive from religion. The contested land is a "holy" land; more than a place for raising crops and building cities, it is "sacred soil" for three great religions. Jerusalem contains both the Wall of the Temple, which is sacred to Jews, and the Dome of the Rock, which is sacred to Muslims. Neither can hold exclusive title to the city without also owning the other faith's shrine. Now, as in the days of the Crusades, religion exacerbates the issue, because, now as then, the behavior of the belligerents is more affected by the zeal with which they hold their beliefs than by the humane ethics taught by their respective religions. Now, as in the past, it is hard to strike a bargain over sacred soil.

Then there are the myths of mutual victimization. Perhaps I should say the half-myths, because both Jews and Arabs have victimized each other, though surely not with the deliberate and malign intent that each attributes to the other.

The Jews are obsessed with the fear of a repetition of the Nazi holocaust, and the Arabs do nothing to allay this fear with extravagant talk about "holy wars" and about throwing the Jews into the sea. These threats have understandably alarmed the Israelis in much the same way that Khrushchev's talk of "burying" us agitated Americans a decade ago. As I shall point out in detail later on, President Nasser and King Hussein have both, in effect, repudiated such draconian threats, but the Israelis seem not to have noticed the disavowals. . . .

As survivors of genocide, they can hardly be expected to distinguish with perfect clarity between Nazi crimes and Arab rhetoric. All they know is that they came to Palestine in peace, settlers in an underpopulated land, but have been allowed no peace; they have fought three wars they never wished to fight and still their enemies remain implacable, refusing even to talk to them, contesting—until recently—their right to survive as a state. Nonetheless, the Arab-Nazi analogy is a faulty one; it clouds the distinction between the myth and reality of Arab intent—whatever these may be.

The Arabs, for their part, perceive Zionism as a new form of western imperialism. Having lived on the land of Palestine for thousands of years, they can have little sympathy for the historic sentiments of the Jewish diaspora. It is, I should think, impossible for them to put themselves in the place of the Jews, whose cultural attachment to their ancient homeland sustained them through centuries of dispersal and persecution. The Arabs are on a different wave length: while the Jews prayed for Palestine—"next year in Jerusalem," they said in their prayer—the Arabs inhabited the land. They could not see the Jews as the Jews saw themselves: as refugees from genocide seeking safe haven. What did this have to do with the Arabs? They had done the Jews no harm and could see no reason why they should compensate the Jews for the crimes of Europeans. In fact, to Arab eyes, the Jews were Europeans, armed with European skills and technology, coming on the heels of other Europeans to drive them from their homes and steal away their lands.

In its way Zionism has seemed to the Arabs even more threatening than the old European imperialism. The British and French after all were only establishing colonies and, bad as that was, colonies come and go. But the Jews were establishing a homeland, and homelands do not come and go. On the contrary, once established, they are likely to expand. The Jewish state actively encourages immigration from all over the world, creating for Arabs the specter of a Jewish drive for lebensraum, which could only mean the annexation of even more Arab lands. Some elements within Israel and the world Zionist movement openly proclaim the need of a policy of expansion, which must give rise to a fear among Arabs not unlike that felt by the Jews when the Arabs talk of throwing them into the sea. To the Arabs, in short, Zionism is not a program of deliverance for a persecuted race but a foreign conquest bolstered by strong ties between the conquering people and the most powerful governments of the West.

As if the Arab-Israeli problem were not enough, the great powers have made their own special contribution to the mythology of the Middle East by infusing the crisis with the hocus pocus of geopolitics. The Middle East, in geopolitical terms, is something far more abstract than an oil-rich desert contested by feuding Semitic peoples. Beyond that, it is the "gateway to the East," the "hinge of NATO," and the crucial cockpit of the historic Russian drive toward warm water. By sending planes and missiles to Egypt the Russians are not merely bolstering a shaky client; to the X-ray eye of the geopolitician, they are embarked upon a drive to convert the Mediterranean into a Soviet lake. The concept is admittedly vague: would the Russians close the Mediterranean to foreign shipping? Prohibit fishing? Use it as a vacation resort? No one really knows what a Russian mare nostrum would be like, but the concept serves the purpose of its users: It scares people; it imputes the "vital interests" of the great powers to a regional conflict, converting it into a battleground of the cold war. In this frame of reference one even suspects the Russians of an insidious design in wishing to reopen the Suez Canal—something which used to be considered a good thing, before the geopoliticians came along.

The vital interests of the great powers are, in fact, involved in the Middle East—primarily because those powers have chosen to become involved. The ultimate danger is that the Arab-Israeli conflict could draw the superpowers and the world into a nuclear war—and that certainly is a matter of vital interest—but the danger is not inherent in the local situation, nor is it predestined by fate. It has come about because the great powers have surrendered much of their own freedom of action to the bellicose whims of their respective clients. There is of course one way—in case anyone still cares—in which the great powers are obligated to intervene: as members of the United Nations Security Council charged by the Charter with the responsibility to "decide what measures shall be taken" in response to a "threat to the peace, breach of the peace or act of aggression." Instead, the Soviet Union and the United States have played the role of cobelligerents to their respective clients, arming, and financing them, committing their own prestige to the issue and, in so doing, converting a local conflict into a potential world conflict. All that can be said in mitigation is that both great powers have shown a certain prudence by holding back at times on the arms supplied to the warring parties.

Finally there is the myth of militarism, and that affects all of the parties. Each clings to the notion that another round may settle things—although three wars have settled nothing—or that some new weapons system will stabilize the balance of power—as if either side would accept the other's notion of what it takes to establish a proper balance.

Since the June war of 1967 the Egyptians have acquired vast arsenals of Soviet weapons, including air support and advanced ground-to-air missiles, and they have launched a "war of attrition." What has it gotten them? The Israelis have been compelled to stop their deep penetration air raids but they still hold the Sinai; until the cease fire they were bombing Egyptian installations on the west bank of the Canal around the clock; and they have every prospect of acquiring additional Phantom and Skyhawk jets from the United States so as to reestablish their version of the balance of power. Nor has any of this new Egyptian hardware wrung any political concessions from the Israelis: Prime Minister Meir explicitly rejects the borders of 1967 and, instead of offering concessions, Foreign Minister Eban contributes pithy ironics about recognizing the right of the United Arab Republic to exist.

The Israelis, for their part, have hardly profited from their military successes. They have gained territory and they have established their military superiority, but they have failed to gain what they most want: security. In 1967 they felt desperately insecure along the Gaza Strip frontier; today they feel desperately insecure along the Suez Canal, so much so that they and their friends abroad seem almost to have forgotten that it is not their own but Egyptian territory that they are defending so tenaciously. One begins to understand the spheres-of-influence psychology, which causes a nation to believe that it can have no security at all until it has robbed its neighbors of all semblance of security.

Surrounded by hostile neighbors, holding down occupied lands inhabited by a million Arabs, plagued by fedayeen attacks and oppressed by the costs of armaments, Israel is a desperately insecure nation. That is clear, but it is anything but clear that her present policy of relying on military superiority is ever going to alter the situation. If the Suez frontier does not provide security, what boundary would? And even if the United States provides all the Phantom jets the Israelis want and the electronic jamming gear which may neutralize the SAM-2 and SAM-3 missiles, it is unlikely that Israel will gain more than a respite; the Russians will soon enough come up with something else. . . .

Because the conflict is a threat to the outside world, it cannot be left solely to the humors of the belligerents. I have never fully understood why some of our statesmen feel that it would be a heinous crime for external parties to impose a solution. Under the United Nations Charter the Security Council has full authority —possibly even the obligation—to impose a settlement upon warring parties who fail to make peace on their own. . . .

I think it would be a fine thing—a useful step forward for civilization—if, in the absence of a voluntary settlement by the parties, the United Nations were to impose a peaceful settlement in the Middle East. It would be an equally fine thing if the United Nations could impose a settlement in Southeast Asia.

There are four major perspectives on the Middle East conflict and need of a fifth. The needed one, as I have suggested, is that of the world community through its duly constituted organ, the United Nations. The development of such a perspective and its translation into action will require changes and adjustments in the long frozen perspectives of Arabs and Israelis, Russians and Americans. There are at present some hopeful signs of possible change, brought forth by Secretary Roger's constructive initiative. In this slightly improved atmosphere it may be well to review the prevailing perspectives of those involved in the Middle East, with a view to detecting misconceptions, desirable directions of change, and opportunities for future agreement.

Starting with Israel, it is less than adequate to say that Israel is concerned with her survival. Surrounded and outnumbered by seemingly implacable foes, the Israelis are obsessed—as anyone else in their position would be—with the fear of being destroyed. This fear is based on salient facts but it is reinforced by fear itself, and by a 2,000 years' history which planted the fear of extermination deeply in Jewish minds. The result, I suspect, is a tendency on the part of the Israelis to exaggerate their own vulnerability, to credit their adversaries with more relentless hostility than in fact they may harbor, and to dismiss tentative gestures of conciliation as hypocritical tricks.

It is noteworthy, in this connection, that, when President Nasser responded favorably to Secretary Rogers' peace proposal, the initial reaction of the Israelis and of some Americans was that Nasser was setting a trap in which Israel would be forced either to stop bombing the west bank of the Suez Canal or risk alienating the United States. Quite possibly that was President Nasser's motive—no outsider really knows—but how can there ever be progress toward peace if neither side is ever willing to take the other's word for anything, if each insists upon crediting the other with the most fraudulent and devious possible motives, and if each bases its policy on its own suspicions rather than the other's behavior?

Would Israel, and Israel's friends in the United States, have liked it better if President Nasser had rejected the American proposal? Would they have thought better of him for it? Would they have commended him for candor and courage?

Chronic suspicion is ultimately unrewarding: it is the kind of outlook which causes myths to displace realities in the minds of statesmen who pride themselves on realism and hardheadedness. It has distorted American perceptions of China and the Soviet Union, and it has distorted the Israeli view of Arab intentions and capacities. When suspicion governs policy, it becomes impossible for adversaries to communicate or negotiate because neither side is receptive to even the bare possibility that the other may be telling the truth when he makes a conciliatory gesture, or that he may be amenable to compromise.

The Israeli conviction of Arab hostility is by no means invention, but there is a touch of paranoia about it—just as there is in our own attitude toward communism—and the worst of it is that the prophecy is self-fulfilling. It is a truism of modern psychology that we influence the behavior of others by our own expectations of how they are going to behave. The critical question for Israel is whether it is willing to risk taking the Arabs at their word when they offer to live in peace—as they have done in effect by accepting the Security Council resolution of November 1967—and, in taking this risk, helping to influence Arab behavior in the direction of compromise and peace. This is not to say that Israel can or should gamble her survival on the hope of Arab good will; Israel has the unchallengeable right to survive as a state and, as I shall indicate later, I would be willing to support a significant new commitment by the United States to assure Israel's survival. Nonetheless, I think it is incumbent upon Israel at this juncture to credit President Nasser with good faith when he says that he is willing to live in peace. A change in Israeli expectations might well bring about a change in Egyptian behavior. . . .

Israeli policy since the Six Day War has been characterized by a lack of flexibility and foresight. The establishment of Israeli settlements on the occupied west bank of the Jordan River and in the Sinai, as well as on the Golan Heights, can only be interpreted as steps toward foreclosing the return of these territories to their previous Arab owners. The insistence upon the nonnegotiability of the status of Jerusalem and upon the retention of certain other occupied territories—notably the Golan Heights, the Gaza Strip and Sharm el Sheikh—lends unfortunate credence to President Nasser's pessimistic assertion, in accepting Secretary Rogers' peace proposal, that, "While we inform the United States that we have accepted its proposals, we also tell them that our real belief is that whatever is taken by force cannot be returned except for force."

Equally distressing—although not entirely unprovoked—is the Israeli view of the United Nations as what Mr. Eban calls a packed court whose recommendations may be ignored. The insistence upon the nonnegotiability of Israel's annexation of Arab East Jerusalem is in open contempt of the United Nations General Assembly, which censured that unilateral act by a vote of 99 to 0.

I speak critically of Israeli policy in part because of my belief that Israel, as the momentary victor, has both an obligation and an interest in a policy of magnanimity. . . .

The Arabs, too, must face up to certain

realities: that Israel has come to stay; that it is demagogic nonsense to talk—as some of the Palestinian guerrillas still do—of driving the Jews into the sea; that in any case the Arab States can have no realistic hope of doing that because they themselves cannot defeat Israel, the Russians are not likely to do it for them, and the United States would almost certainly intervene to save Israel from destruction. Once these facts are recognized—as in large measure they have been recognized by the governments of Egypt and Jordan—the Arab countries will be able to free themselves from their morbid preoccupation with past defeats, from futile dreams of revenge, and from the oppressive burden of armaments which slows their development and makes them dependent upon foreign powers.

While Egypt and Jordan are still widely credited with the desire to destroy Israel, both in fact have repudiated any such ambition and have done so explicitly and repeatedly. They did it in the first instance by accepting the United Nations Resolution of November 22, 1967, which required them to give up positions to which they had held tenaciously for 20 years. By accepting that resolution, Egypt and Jordan committed themselves to terminate their belligerency against Israel; to acknowledge Israel's sovereignty, territorial integrity and right to live in peace within secure and recognized boundaries; and to respect Israel's right to freedom of navigation through the Suez Canal and the Strait of Tiran.

Having accepted these provisions of the resolution—which in fact meet all of Israel's stated and legitimate aspirations—the Egyptians and Jordanians now emphasize the other provisions of the resolution of 1967; the withdrawal of Israel from occupied territories; a just settlement of the refugee problem; and the inadmissibility of the acquisition of territory by war.

The last is a general principle which goes beyond the special interest of the Arab States. Its vindication—even in one instance—would represent a long step forward toward the establishment of the rule of law in international relations. That would serve everybody's interests—everybody, that is, who wishes to survive the nuclear age and who still has some hope that the United Nations can be developed into an effective peacekeeping organization. It is natural enough for Israel to resist the honor of being the first modern military victor to be obliged to abide by the principles and specifications of the United Nations Charter, especially when the great powers who dominate the Security Council have set such a wretched example. Be that as it may, the principle involved is too important to be cast away because of the hypocrisy or self-interest of its proponents. . . .

The status of the Palestinians and the question of the occupied territories are the critical issues for peace in the Middle East. The two issues are closely related because many Palestinian Arabs are haunted by the fear that there are no bounds to Israel's territorial aspirations—a fear which feeds upon classic Zionist ideology as well as upon the declarations of military-minded Israelis who press the claim for "strategic" frontiers. A declaration by the Israeli Government of willingness to restore all of the occupied territories as part of a general peace settlement would go far to alleviate Arab fears of Zionist expansionism. Such a statement would meet the Egyptian-Jordanian condition for peace and would also improve the chances for a settlement in Palestine.

In the Arab perspective the central issues are the occupied territories and the Palestinians. In the Israeli perspective the issue is the survival and security of the Jewish state. The United Nations Resolution of 1967 recognizes the legitimacy of both parties' concerns. The question now is whether the two sides, and their great power mentors, are ready to proceed through the renewed mediation of Dr. Jarring toward the translation of general principles into specific agreements. . . .

Central and indispensable to a peace settlement based on the Security Council Resolution of November 1967 would be the guarantee of the entire settlement by the United Nations. Such a guarantee would properly take the form of a specific commitment by the United Nations Security Council to enforce the peace and all of its specifications, including the "secure and recognized boundaries" of both Israel and her Arab neighbors and the neutralized status of designated border zones. The agreement should also specify strict limitations on the sale or provision of arms to Middle Eastern states by outside powers. As permanent members of the Security Council, the United States, the Soviet Union, the United Kingdom and France would have major responsibility for enforcement of the peace terms, but that obligation would fall upon them not in their capacity as "great powers" but as members of the Security Council, which is entrusted by article 24 of the Charter with "primary responsibility for the maintenance of international peace and security."

It might also be appropriate and desirable for the Security Council's guarantee to be ratified formally by the legislative bodies of the signatory states. Such action would represent a mark of the seriousness attached to this new commitment by members of the Security Council, although it might not be regarded as juridically essential since, by ratifying the Charter in the first place, every member of the United Nations is already committed, under article 25, to "accept and carry out the decisions of the Security Council." It would do no harm, however, by formal parliamentary act, to remind the members of this frequently forgotten obligation.

For reasons of varying merit Israel has indicated on numerous occasions a lack of confidence in the United Nations. In order to accommodate this attitude and provide Israel with an added assurance of security, I, for one, would be willing to supplement a United Nations guarantee with a bilateral treaty—not an Executive agreement but a treaty consented to by the Senate—under which the United States would guarantee the territory and independence of Israel within the borders of 1967. This guarantee should neither add to, nor detract from, nor in any way alter the multilateral guarantee of the United Nations—which would obligate us, as a member of the Security Council, to defend the "secure and recognized boundaries" of both Israel and her Arab neighbors. The supplementary, bilateral arrangement with Israel would obligate the United States to use force if necessary, in accordance with its constitutional processes, to assist Israel against any violation of its 1967 borders which it could not repel itself, but the agreement would also obligate Israel, firmly and unequivocally, never to violate those borders herself.

I conceive of an American treaty of guarantee with Israel as an instrument which would come into effect after—and only after—the multilateral guarantee of the United Nations had been agreed upon and ratified by all parties. The bilateral treaty with Israel would represent no more than a repetition of, and an additional assurance of, our intent to honor the multilateral guarantee of the United Nations. Essentially the bilateral arrangement would serve as an accommodation to the fact of Israel's mistrust of the United Nations. It would repeat a commitment which every member of the Security Council, including the Soviet Union, would also have made through their multilateral guarantee of the borders of all of the states concerned.

40.

THEODORE M. HESBURGH: Civil Rights Enforcement

The Rev. Theodore M. Hesburgh, president of Notre Dame University, had been a member of the United States Civil Rights Commission since its inception in 1958, and in 1969 was appointed to be its chairman by President Nixon. But his relationship with the new administration was not a happy one, owing to the commission's persistent criticisms of federal policies on race relations. In October 1970, on the occasion of the commission's issuing a report on civil rights enforcement by the government, Father Hesburgh made the following statement assailing administration policies. Immediately following the 1972 election he was asked to resign his post on the commission. The commission was left without a permanent chairman until December 1973, when President Nixon announced the appointment of Arthur S. Flemming, former president of Ohio Wesleyan University, to fill the vacancy.

THE REPORT WE ARE RELEASING this morning, "The Federal Civil Rights Enforcement Effort," is one of the most important documents the commission has issued in its 13-year history. What the commission has attempted to do in this report is identify with precision the current status of civil rights enforcement activities of virtually every federal department and agency having civil rights responsibilities.

This report, in a very real sense, is addressed not only to the President and Congress, but to the American people, who have the right to know whether the laws that govern us are working.

Our examination of various laws, executive orders, and judicial decisions has disclosed that there is indeed an impressive array of civil rights guarantees that provide protection against discrimination in virtually every aspect of life—in education, employment, housing, voting, administration of justice, access to places of public accommodation, and participation in the benefits of federally assisted programs. There is, however, a gap between what these guarantees have promised and what has actually been delivered.

We are a result oriented nation. We judge the effectiveness of institutions on the basis of the results they achieve. By this yardstick, progress in ending inequity by the application of law has been disappointing. In many areas in which civil rights laws afford pervasive legal protection—employment, housing, education—discrimination persists and the goal of equal opportunity is far from achievement.

The commission has examined the Federal civil rights enforcement effort and found it wanting. Each civil rights law that has been passed, each executive order that has been issued, and each court decision favorable to the cause of civil rights, has been viewed as another step along the road to full equality for all Americans.

But perhaps what has been lost sight of is that these legal mandates in and of themselves cannot bring about a truly open society, that they must be implemented—and it is at this point that we have found a major breakdown.

It is important to recognize that despite the shortcomings pointed out in this report, the civil rights laws have by no means been a total failure. In many areas—voting, education, hospital services, public accommodations—these laws have contributed substantially to ending discrimination. But despite the progress made possible by the various civil rights laws and policies, discrimination is still with us.

I want to stress two important points about the report. First, while the report necessarily discusses the programs and activities of particular departments and agencies, the purpose is not to single out any of them for blame—or, for that matter, for praise. The commission's concern in this report is with the system of Federal civil rights enforcement and our purpose is to identify the problems which are systemic and to seek systemic changes.

Second, while the report deals primarily with the current civil rights posture of the Federal Government, it should be understood that the inadequacies described have roots that lie deep in the past. These inadequacies did not originate in the current Administration, nor was there any substantial period in the past when civil rights enforcement was at a uniformly high level of effectiveness.

The commission's study has revealed a number of weaknesses and inadequacies in civil rights enforcement that are common to most agencies, regardless of the programs they administer or the civil rights laws they enforce.

It is these inadequacies that are of principal concern. They cannot be corrected through actions of individual departments and agencies, but only through more basic, systemic changes involving the entire Federal bureaucracy. These are some of the major weaknesses the commission has found in the Federal civil rights enforcement effort.

First, the commission has found that no agency has been provided with sufficient staff and other resources to carry out its civil rights responsibilities with maximum effectiveness. In most departments and agencies, the chief civil rights officer is of relatively low rank and reports to someone other than the head of the agency. This necessarily impedes the efforts of civil rights officials to assure that civil rights needs and goals are accorded an appropriately high priority among agency activities.

There are other impediments, systemic to the Federal civil rights enforcement effort, which would prevent agencies from fully carrying out their civil rights responsibilities even if staff and status were at a sufficiently high level.

Most agencies have failed to state the goals of their civil rights programs with sufficient specificity to enable them adequately to shape their civil rights policies and procedures. Other agencies, while they have stated civil rights goals, have stated them narrowly—often merely tracking the language of the civil rights laws which they administer.

Lacking civil rights goals of sufficient breadth and specificity, the inevitable result often is that agencies fail to establish systematic compliance priorities and strategies. They concentrate their efforts on processing individual complaints, rather than attacking institutional patterns of discrimination and inequity.

In many agencies, civil rights and substantive programs are carried out in isolation from one another. Civil rights officials often are excluded from the decision-making process governing the operation of substantive programs and many of these programs tend to perpetuate racial and ethnic inequity. In some agencies, civil rights responsibility is assigned to program officials, many of whom lack civil rights training and are unsympathetic with civil rights goals.

One of the major weaknesses in the Federal civil rights enforcement effort has been the passive role that many agencies have adopted in carrying out their civil rights responsibilities. In some cases, agencies have been content to rely on assurances of nondiscrimination and make no effort to determine for themselves whether these assurances are in fact being honored. A number of agencies rely on the receipts of complaints as the principle or sole indicator of civil rights compliance.

Another major weakness has been the failure to make sufficient use of the sanctions available to enforce civil rights laws. In the contract compliance program, for example, the sanctions of contract termination and debarment never have been used.

Under Title VI, many of the agencies that administer programs subject to that law never have imposed the sanction of fund termination, the principal weapon available to enforce nondiscrimination requirements. Instead, agencies have placed undue emphasis on obtaining voluntary compliance, permitting delays and interminable negotiations.

Further, the Government has not instituted a sufficient number of lawsuits to make litigation a viable alternative to the imposition of administrative sanctions. As a result, the credibility of the Government's total civil rights effort has been seriously undermined.

There also has been a failure to provide over-all coordination and direction to the entire Federal civil rights enforcement effort. This, in the commission's view, has been the most serious flaw in the admininistration of the Federal civil rights program.

The commission believes that the President's recent reorganization of the White House and his executive office presents a unique opportunity for establishing the kind of systematic coordination and direction of Federal civil rights enforcement that is so badly needed.

Under the reorganization plan, the President has created a Council on Domestic Affairs, chaired by the President and including as members the Vice-President and the heads of all Cabinet departments except the Departments of State, Defense, and the Post Office.

The Domestic Affairs Council has the potential of structuring and institutionalizing many important civil rights functions that previously were performed on an ad hoc basis by the President's personal staff. We believe it is important for the President to establish a permanent civil rights subcommittee of the council to assure systematic direction and coordination of civil rights goals, policies, and priorities. The commission has made this its first recommendation in considering ways of strengthening the Federal Government's total civil rights effort.

The President has also reorganized another of his principal staff arms—the Bureau of the Budget. The President has established the Office of Management and Budget to replace the old Bureau of the Budget and has directed that its duties will focus on such matters as program evaluation and coordination. Thus while the Council on Domestic Affairs is concerned with what policies are established, the concern of O.M.B. is with how these policies should be carried out and how well they are carried out.

The commission believes that the Office of Management and Budget can play a significant role in assuring that civil rights laws and policies are carried out with maximum effectiveness. The commission recommends establishment of a division of civil rights within the Office of Management and Budget to work closely with the civil rights subcommittee of the Council on Domestic Affairs and to provide civil rights guidance and direction to budget examiners and other office units within O.M.B.

The commission also recommends that the various office units of O.M.B. be directed to rights considerations in their dealings with Federal departments and agencies.

The commission realizes that achievement of civil rights goals and the full exercise of equal rights by minority group members will involve more than adjustments in civil rights machinery. Many of the weaknesses we have identified also reflect more deep-seated problems—problems of hostile bureaucracies that view civil rights as a threat to their prerogatives and programs, and problems of inadequate or misordered national priorities.

These problems can be resolved only through dedication and effort on the part of Government officials, private civil rights organizations, and the American people, alike. The commission concludes in its report:

In the final analysis, achievement of civil rights goals depends on the quality of leadership exercised by the President in moving the nation toward racial justice. The commission is convinced that his example of courageous moral leadership can inspire the necessary will and determination, not only of the Federal officials who serve under his direction, but of the American people as well.

We feel that the matters raised in this report have grave implications. As a nation firmly rooted in the rule of law, we are firmly committed to the principle that laws must be enforced.

Failure to implement those court degrees, executive orders, and legislation relating to civil rights, weaken the fabric of the nation. Those who look to the law as an impartial arbiter of right and wrong and find that some laws are implemented while others are not despair of the fairness of the system.

This cannot be allowed to happen. What we have proposed is nothing more than that use be made of existing laws to assure all Americans equal opportunity.

41.

A. J. CERVANTES: Revenue Sharing in the Cities

On October 13, 1969, in a message to Congress, President Nixon stated: "We intend to begin a decade of government reform such as this nation has not witnessed in half a century. . . That is the watchword of this administration: Reform." The slogan soon coined to specify the nature of this reform was "New Federalism," which suggested turning power back to the states and localities for the solving of their own problems. One facet of the reform program had been announced two months earlier, on August 13, in a message calling for legislation to provide federal revenue sharing for state and local governments. The places most in need of funds were, of course, the cities, where a great part of the population and a preponderance of the problems were to be found. Municipal financing had worsened dramatically in the 1960s to the point where some cities were on the verge of bankruptcy. On October 13, 1970, Mayor A. J. Cervantes of St. Louis, Missouri, spoke before the Federal Agency Review Workshop at Annapolis, Maryland, delineating the problems of a city administration and how money should be allocated to meet the urban crisis. Portions of his speech are reprinted here.

Source: *Vital Speeches*, November 15, 1970.

GENTLEMEN: It may sound like a bit of banter and playful needling for a Mayor of one of the older, larger cities to initiate our discussion by stating: "I have dreamed of the day when I would have the chief administrators of the federal grant program before me so that I could tell them exactly what I as a Mayor think of their whole system of categorical grants."

I know some Mayors who are so exasperated with the whole federal grant system that they would give up their own spleen and their cities' "maximum feasible participation" programs to have the opportunity to meet in one room with you chief administrators of the Departments of Labor, Justice, Commerce, Defense, Agriculture, Transportation, HEW, HUD and OMB to tell you that as far as the core cities and their poverty peoples are concerned the grant system itself hasn't worked, isn't working, and can't possibly work.

These Mayors would tell you that the whole system of categorical grants "is over-regulated, under-supported, divisive, wasteful, frustrating, completely beyond the federal bureaucracy's capacities, substantially ineffective, in the long run subversive of the very federal system that gave it birth, and that the whole system must be radically altered from a revenue grant system to a revenue sharing system."

I think, gentlemen, that you will agree with me that that would be quite a statement.

But it is not my temperate intention to make such a statement.

Furthermore, I need not make such a critical statement.

For, as I will document in a moment, this statement has already been implicitly made by our President, Mr. Richard Nixon, and by the conservative Republican Mr. Edward Banfield in his Model Cities Task Force Report released by the White House just two weeks ago.

I recognize that I am before some of the most intelligent, committed, and capable administrators of which this country can boast.

You and your agencies' representatives have always treated St. Louis with a consideration and generosity far beyond the call of duty.

I wish to take this occasion to thank you and your representatives for all the creative assistance that you have afforded St. Louis and other cities, such as St. Louis, now in the throes of the urban crisis.

I know that the reason why we are here today is to address ourselves to the question of federal grant reform.

The particular categorical grant reform under consideration is that of revenue sharing.

My simple role is merely to give some informal observations on federal-city relationships as seen from the office of a Mayor.

My point of departure are the words of President Nixon and Professor Banfield in submitting why, and I quote the Banfield Task Force's principal recommendation, "most federal aid should go to the cities by way of revenue-sharing rather than by categorical grants-in-aid."

Fourteen months ago today, on August 13, 1969, President Nixon announced to Congress that he was submitting legislation providing "without federal strings" Federal Revenue Sharing with State and local governments.

Mr. Nixon first pointed out that "Revenues of the Federal government have increased ninety-fold in thirty-six years."

"Under our current budget structure," continued Mr. Nixon, "Federal revenues are likely to increase faster than the national economy. At the local level, the reverse is true. . . . The result is a 'fiscal mismatch' with potential Federal surpluses and local deficits."

My head swims and my mouth waters when I try to conjure with the concept of a ninety-fold increase of federal revenues in 36 years.

How does near-bankrupt St. Louis react to this?

Despite the fact that in the past 36 years St. Louis, as other older core cities, has become a concentration center of high cost citizens, its revenue increase has not been 9000 percent but 600 percent (from $18 to $109 millions).

In St. Louis we are averaging a yearly revenue increase of only 1.3 percent with a yearly cost increase of over 5 percent.

Income - 1.3 percent increase.

Outgo - 5.1 percent increase.

Clearly something had to give in St. Louis. Poorer city services, streets not fixed, one-third of the housing stock in serious disrepair, housing code enforcement lapsing, inadequate money to pay for policemen, firemen, teachers, city workers; peak taxation and peak deficits —the whole urban crisis bag—with bankruptcy not far down the fiscal pike.

I have just returned from the International Conference of Mayors in West Berlin.

While attending the conference I was the guest of West Berlin's Mayor Klaus Schuetz.

The other evening I remarked to Mayor Schuetz how amazed I was that the cities of Europe so recently in war bombed ruins were now beautifully rebuilt. European cities that I saw do not have the core rot slums that infect American cities.

Mayor Schuetz with a shrug of his shoulders uttered two words that speak volumes: "Marshall Plan."

A Marshall Plan for ravaged European cities but no Marshall Plan for ravaged American cities.

Here likewise is a type of "fiscal mismatch."

You notice that I have not said that the federal government has not supplied the St. Louis community with money.

It has.

Lots of it.

According to the computer print-outs of the Federal Information Exchange System, in Fiscal Year '68 it was $1.7 billion.

In Fiscal Year '69, $1.5 billion.

During the first half of this past Fiscal Year it was $571 million.

But as with the general national spending priorities so with the federal spending pattern in St. Louis. Two-thirds of the federal spending in St. Louis is for military and defense-related expenditures. $1.2 billion or 66 percent of the $1.8 billion spent by the federal government in the City of St. Louis in '68 are listed under "Department of Defense" expenditures.

Of course I am proud of what St. Louis industries are doing for national defense.

But I am sure that you sympathize with me when I sigh a bit when I hear those billions of dollars of Phantom Jets roar over City Hall on the way to Vietnam. I quietly think of what it would mean to our city if only $1 billion of this investment could be put into St. Louis housing.

$1,000,000,000!

A billion dollars would build 50,000 $20,000 homes!

And that too is a fiscal mismatch. There were not 50,000 homes built in St. Louis last year but only 7 throughout the whole of the city.

But the "fiscal mismatch" argument of federal-city relationship is of itself no argument whatsover in favor of the revenue sharing plan.

And neither the President nor the Banfield Report says that it is.

All that the "fiscal mismatch" argument indicates is that the cities deserve more money from the federal government in order to fulfill their tasks.

Just because you put one gallon of gas in a Cadillac car for a five-gallon trip is no argument against the Cadillac because the gas investment brings the Cadillac far short of its goal.

Pour a greater gas investment into the same car and it will get you where you want to go.

And here we come to the cutting edge of the President's and the Professor's capital argument.

Their argument is, and I agree, that the more fiscal gas that the United States pours into this categorical grant vehicle the more clearly we see that the vehicle itself is defective.

The system itself is incapable of getting us where we want to go.

It's not the drivers of the vehicle—you administrators.

It's not the amount of gas—the amount of money that is poured into the system.

It is the categorical grant system itself which must be replaced by a new model called "Revenue Sharing."

Let us take several examples from my home town.

a. Education

Consider Title I of the Elementary and Secondary Education Act.

It was certainly programmed for the right goal. It was set to alleviate the educational distress primarily of the disadvantaged. That was the target goal.

It was juiced up with a billion dollars worth of gas.

But the system itself proved incapable of reaching its goal of assisting primarily the poor.

In the Office of Education's 268 page report analyzing Title I, the average Title I expenditure per participant in rich districts was $226 as compared to $107 in poor districts.

In the St. Louis Metropolitan area these appalling disparities mean that if a child is a resident of Clayton, an affluent suburb, almost $1,500 will be invested in his education.

If he is resident of the City of St. Louis one-half of $1,500 will be expended.

If he is a resident of Kinloch less than one-fourth of the Clayton $1,500 will be expended.

And, I submit, the life's chances of each child varies accordingly.

The present federal grant system did not, as Congress and its administrators intended, lessen this inequality of opportunity. It had the opposite effect. It heightened the inequality.

We recognize that the impeding intervening variable is the State Government through which most grants to the cities, as those of the Office of Education, must pass—or be rerouted or blocked. The system as it is established cannot reach its goal.

b. Housing-Highways

Or take the cases of the federal mortgage and the federal highway grants.

These programs are heralded as having been eminently successful.

And they were.

Except for the older central cities of our metropolitan areas.

These programs have ringed the expanding black neck of the central city with a lily white lasso and stabbed the heart of the central city with severing concrete knives.

Just how long will it take Secretary Romney and his Assistant Secretary Jackson, for all of their uniquely wonderful work, to bind up the federally inflicted wounds of a divided society with the alleviating ointment of suburban open housing?

c. School Lunch Program

The following is a statistic that I simply cannot understand. It concerns the federal school lunch program. I don't understand it because I happen to know that the Department of Agriculture and the Office of Education have done everything possible to assist St. Louis in a very special way.

But the statistic is this. Throughout the State of Missouri 60 percent of the children are receiving hot lunches. In the affluent St. Louis County it is only 40 percent. But in the City of St. Louis where poverty is concentrated it is only 20 percent of the pupils who are receiving hot lunches.

During this past year there were over 30,000 children from aid to dependent children families in our St. Louis schools. Less than half received free lunches. (cf. *St. Louis Globe Democrat*, 3/2/70)

The grant system as now devised has not been able to provide preferential and compensatory mass service primarily for the no-income and low-income citizen even when it is so programmed.

d. The Laws Delay

It is inevitable that a system as incredibly complex and run by individuals who are neither immediately present nor immediately involved should be characterized by delay and uncertainty.

St. Louis has been waiting for thirty-five years, through a whole succession of congressional delays, to see the completion of the Jefferson National Expansion Memorial.

Not all of our grants take this long to come through. But considering the number of steps and forms and processes that must be traversed before a grant-in-aid can be delivered to a city, it is a wonder that they don't take this long.

Year after year in our summer programs, for instance, we do not know until June how much money will be available for our various programs. Without these special federally assisted programs I know the city would literally go up in flames. But it would be a relief if we could plan not by crisis but by orderly process.

I look forward to the time when under a revenue sharing formula that considers not only population and tax effort but likewise need, the cities will know exactly how much grant money will be coming to them. I have much greater confidence in the speed and efficiency of a computer working in the basement of the Treasury Department in getting our St. Louis grants delivered than I have in my own efforts at walking with my hat in one hand and a tin cup in the other from door to door in the Congressional and Department hallways. . . .

Gentlemen, I have nothing but the highest respect for the ability and commitment of federal administrators.

But I say that under the present system of grants where you are congressionally charged with the ultimate responsibility and try to run everything from Washington for a hundred thousand different neighborhoods throughout a pluralistic country such catastrophic misunderstandings, seemingly contradictory directives, and riot-provoking discontinuities of promises and expectations are inevitable.

I agree with President Nixon and Professor Banfield—the system simply must be changed.

The federal grant system of its very nature deprives the local executive of his authority and effectiveness in whatever area it extends its assistance. . . .

What President Nixon infers when he states that there has been a decline of authority of local executives "as grants have become tied to functional bureaucracies" and what Banfield spells out is that under the present system of grants you administrators in Washington are constrained to keep the controls over the programs and that you can't possibly hand over the authority to the Mayor or to anyone else.

You are the administrators and for all the euphemisms that are used with us Mayors we know you are the prime administrators.

You have the money to pay the piper and you call the tunes you see fit.

Your priorities are your priorities—and not necessarily the Mayor's.

Your application forms, your management devices, your multifarious reporting systems, your multiple audit systems are yours—a hundred strong and by no means standardized even in your own Departments.

This is all built into the present system. "*Better that all should suffer rather than that one should go astray.*"

More than that.

Your far-flung Department may detect the mishandling of let us say OEO or HUD monies in New York or Berkeley and all but immediately the St. Louis

CAP administration is penalized with a dozen more "safeguards" though year after year the St. Louis Human Development Corporation has handled a $17 million program with disadvantaged persons and has not been guilty of misplacing a cent.

Gentlemen, the United States can not have it both ways.

Either Washington will be the prime administrators of the programs or the United States will adopt a system of revenue sharing whereby the authority can be handed back to the local communities.

42.

ROYAL LITTLE: Interview on the Conglomerates

Although the term "conglomerate" did not come into general use until 1964-65, such business mergers had been on the increase since 1950. Whereas the older form of corporate mergers had involved companies in the same, or related, lines of business, the conglomerates were the products of merging diverse forms of enterprise. The number and size of the conglomerates that were put together in the 1960s prompted one writer to describe them as "the most vivid industrial feature of the decade," and possibly "the dominant form of American business in the last third of the century." This optimism was somewhat misplaced. The most flourishing years for the conglomerates were from 1960 to 1969, after which many of them found themselves in deep financial trouble; and some of the multibillion dollar enterprises collapsed. After the drastic stock market decline of 1970, the future of the conglomerates seemed quite uncertain. Later in the year, Royal Little, the founder of Textron and one of the earliest "conglomerators," was interviewed by Forbes *magazine senior editor James Cook on the prospects for the conglomerates.*

Source: *Forbes*, December 15, 1970: "As They See It."

Do you still believe in the basic concept? Or do you think that companies are better off these days sticking to one or two lines of business?

"I'm as convinced as I was originally," Little replied between munches of a light lunch in his modest office in Providence, R.I. "When they are conservatively run, unrelated businesses are all excellent means of managing capital."

Forbes picked up the distinction. For the conglomerates that were not conservatively run, what do you think really went wrong?

"A combination of things. Some companies have not been able to properly control the managements of their divisions, so that divisions have sometimes gotten into trouble without the managements realizing there was trouble coming. In a well-run diversified company, you must have very close financial control, but most important, you must have highly skilled divisional managements given autonomy to run the divisions without too much home office interference. My experience shows that excessive home office interference drives the really competent executive to look for other opportunities.

"A large diversified company is only as good as its component parts. The money is made at the divisional level. The most important thing in any business is the quality of management—right on down."

Listening to Little talk thus, we began to see what had probably been the basic mistake made by many of the latter-day conglomerators: They had begun to think of their businesses in terms of mere numbers, forgetting that the numbers are only shorthand for what is going on in the real world, at the "divisional level," as Little would probably put it. Intoxicated by numbers, they began to think that they could expand there indefinitely; that they could ignore problems in the real world of sales, of engineering, of personnel.

Little went on to point out that his original concept had been a good deal more conservative and realistic, though less dramatic, than later variations on it. He had not been looking for supergrowth. In shifting his assets from textiles to totally unrelated businesses, Little explained, he was simply looking for a better return on his invested capital.

"We had three basic concepts. We chose a course which we felt would avoid: 1) the cycles involved in being 100 percent in any one industry, 2) any problems with the Justice Department and the Federal Trade Commission, since we planned never to buy businesses that were allied in any way and 3) the pressure that aggressive management is always under to overexpand its capacity.

"We had noticed that many of the cycles industries went through were caused by management itself—through the overexpansion of capacity. So we decided that instead of overexpanding, our available capital would be used to purchase other businesses that perhaps had a growth potential. Those three concepts were what led us to diversify, and I feel they still hold good today."

As Little went on to explain how many of the later conglomerators went wrong, the same theme recurred: too much attention to numbers, not enough to underlying values, to underlying realities, to management.

"Many companies that followed our lead had high-multiple stocks that made it very easy for them to acquire, on an attractive basis, other businesses. Textron's multiple ran about eight times earnings, so in most cases it couldn't afford to use stock in the early days to make acquisitions. But if you look at the record, I think you'll find that many of the companies that had high multiples have been the ones that ended up getting into trouble. Because they had a negotiable security—one that may have been overpriced when later evaluated in relation to future market conditions—they grew too fast."

Litton Industries, we suggested, Whittaker Corp., companies of this sort. We reminded Little that the later conglomerators didn't think they were going too fast. They tended to think rather that Little's idea had outgrown its originator, and they carried it much further. But the imitators made a major mistake: In adopting Textron's form *they had neglected to adopt its* content.

"Basically," Little explained, "we started off with the idea of acquiring the leading or second-best company in relatively small fields, rather than companies in huge industries where the competition—General Electric or General Motors, say—was particularly difficult for the small participants. If you look at Textron's present portfolio, you'll find pretty close to 12 divisions which illustrate that basic theory—Gorham silverware, Bostitch staplers, Homelite chain saws, Speidel watchbands, etc. In the long run, I believe, companies of that sort will have fewer cyclical problems, particularly where they make consumer products."

These were already good companies, we remarked.

"Yes," Little replied, "but I would say that Textron at least has been able to assist management in their different fields to get the capital to expand their activities and to become more important factors in their particular industries. When we acquired it, Homelite was doing approximately half the volume of its leading competitor. Today it's doing over twice the volume of that former leading competitor. That was in part because Textron could supply it with capital for the building of new low-cost plants in the South."

We said that in our experience many conglomerates, even where they bought good companies, went wrong in the end because they failed to keep the managements they thought they had acquired. Either that or they failed to motivate the managers as well as they had been motivated when on their own. How did Textron handle that problem?

"By tying our cost-incentive bonuses to the return on capital. Under the old type of incentive, where bonuses were paid on some percentage of earnings, the smart manager would get more and more capital, regardless of whether it increased his average return on equity, because he would get some portion of any increased earnings, even though he might reduce the overall return on capital 30 percent or 40 percent. Under the form of incentive that we adopted, the manager is in exactly the same spot as the stockholder. He's got to analyze the effect of any investment on his bonus, which means that, if he recommends an investment that's going to drop the rate of return on his division, he's going to seriously question whether it's advisable to do it. On the other hand, under that system, you have to provide for the unusual development expenses that may be necessary for new products, by permitting them to be capitalized and written off over, say, three to five years.

We said that a lot of conglomerate companies overstated their earnings to impress the stock market. Wasn't there the same temptation on the divisional level?

"In the companies I've been involved with, the managements have been very careful not to do anything of that sort. The incentive compensation is determined by the outside public accountants, and, of course, the home office scrutinizes the accounting procedures to be sure that the management isn't taking advantage of accounting procedures to get themselves bigger bonuses."

As we listened to Little, we couldn't help thinking again and again that here was a rare businessman: He never got carried away by his success; unlike so many of the later conglomerators, he recognized the strength of his idea but also its limitations.

At 74, Royal Little is still very much worth listening to. He is slim and arrow-straight. His hands are a bit gnarled now and his hair has receded, but his eyes are still bright, his manner youthful and enthusiastic.

We asked him whether he agreed that recent federal policy had finally blown the whistle on any further large-scale conglomeration.

"I don't think so. I don't think the Justice Department is interested in stopping smaller diversified companies—like Amtel of which I'm chairman of the board. We started that about five years ago as a relatively small operation with two divisions, and we're already up to, I think, $125 million in sales, and I think 12 divisions. I see no reason why a company like Amtel should have any trouble from the Justice Department so long as we stick to the principle of not buying competing operations or trying to integrate forward or backward. It's only when you get up over a billion dollars that I think the Government's going to take a careful look at any big acquisitions."

How about changes in accounting methods? Are not they a big deterrent? After all, even Textron became devoted to pooling-of-interest accounting in the late Sixties.

"Everyone used pooling of interest on voting stock for acquisitions because it avoided an enormous goodwill item on the balance sheet. I think the new accounting rules are ridiculous because, in effect, they are saying that on a tax-free exchange you have to build up a goodwill item and create an asset which cannot be written off with any advantage. From an operating point of view, that's a ridiculous theory. I realize it was probably brought about by some of the abuses in the past, but I still feel it's an incorrect concept.

"I wonder whether the accountants thought up this idea in order to preserve a lot of the clients they were losing through merger. I'm sure the accountants would deny it, but I'm sure one of the reasons they thought up this plan was to preserve the status quo and stop their clients from swapping their accounting firms by the merger route."

We asked: What opportunities for acquisition remain? Haven't the most likely prospects been pretty much picked over?

"I think the reason that there were so many acquisitions in the last few years was that, first, the multiples of many of the common stocks of the acquiring companies were high; second, the seller knew he was peaking out in his earnings and it was a good time to sell. The combination of those things created an atmosphere where many businesses decided the time had come to sell and get some diversification of investment.

"At the present time, you've got the reverse condition: Unless forced to by some tax problem, the owners of good businesses will not sell because their earnings are down. In periods of recession, the owners of good businesses just wait until the next recovery before they discuss sale. On the other hand, the acquiring companies have such low multiples that they don't want to use stock for acquisitions, and, of course, with tight money, most of the financial institutions won't let their clients borrow money to make acquisitions for cash.

"So what is happening today is that good businesses or good divisions are being sold by companies that have indigestion—that need the cash to pay off their debts—to companies that have the credit and cash to pick up reasonably good bargains."

1970 - 1973

43.

An All-Volunteer Army

On March 27, 1969, President Nixon created an advisory commission to develop a plan for eliminating military conscription and to plan for all-volunteer armed services. Chairman of the commission was Thomas Gates, who had served as Secretary of Defense from 1959 to 1961 under President Eisenhower. The Gates Commission report, issued early in 1970, called for just such a volunteer military force as the President envisioned and inveighed against peacetime conscription, or the draft, as it was usually called. In September 1971 the Senate gave final approval to a bill ending the draft, effective June 1973. Under the authority of the law, Secretary of Defense Melvin Laird actually proclaimed an end to the draft on January 27, 1973, six months ahead of schedule. But establishing a volunteer army and making it work proved to be two different things, as the first year of its operation demonstrated. In an interview published in August 1973, entitled "Toward a Professional Army," Lt. General Bernard W. Rogers, Deputy Chief of Staff for Personnel, Dept. of the Army, analyzed the problems of maintaining an all-volunteer force. The selections reprinted here comprise the conclusions of the Gates Commission Report of February 21, 1970, and the interview with General Rogers.

Sources: *Congressional Record*, 91 Cong., 2 Session, February 24, 1970.

Soldiers: Official U. S. Army Magazine, August 1973.

THE GATES COMMISSION REPORT

SINCE THE FOUNDING of the Republic, a primary task of the Government of the United States has been to provide for the common defense of a society established to secure the blessings of liberty and justice. Without endangering the nation's security, the means of defense should support the aims of the society.

The armed forces today play an honorable and important part in promoting the naion's security, as they have since our freedoms were won on the battlefield at Yorktown. A fundamental consideration that has guided this commission is the need to maintain and improve the effectiveness, dignity and status of the armed forces so they may continue to play their proper role.

The commission has not attempted to judge the size of the armed forces the nation requires. Instead, it has accepted a range of estimates made for planning purposes which anticipate maintaining a total force in the future somewhere between two million and three million men.

We unanimously believe that the nation's interests will be better served by an all-volunteer force, supported by an effective stand-by draft, than by a mixed force of volunteers and conscripts: that steps should be taken promptly to move in this direction, and that the first indispensable step is to remove the present inequity in the pay of men serving their first term in the armed forces.

The United States has relied throughout history on a voluntary armed force except during major wars and since 1948. A return to an all-volunteer force will strengthen our freedoms, remove an inequity now imposed on the expression of the patriotism that has never been lacking among our youth, promote efficiency of the armed forces and enhance their dignity. It is the system for maintaining standing forces that minimize Government interference with the freedom of the individual to determine his own life in accord with his values.

The commission bases its judgments on long-range considerations of what method of recruiting manpower will strengthen our society's foundations. The commission's members have reached agreement on their recommendations only as the result of prolonged study and searching debate, and in spite of initial division.

We are, of course, fully aware of the current and frequently emotional public debate on national priorities, foreign policy, and the military, but are agreed that such issues stand apart from the question of when and how to end conscription.

To judge the feasibility of an all-volunteer force, it is important to grasp the dimensions of the recruitment problem in the next decade.

If conscription is continued, a stable midrange force of 2.5 million men (slightly smaller than pre-Vietnam) will require 440,000 new enlisted men per year. To maintain a fully voluntary stable force of the same effective strength, taking into account lower personnel turnover, we estimate that not more than 325,000 men will have to be enlisted annually.

In recent years, about 500,000 men a year have volunteered only because of the threat of the draft, the best estimates are that at least half—250,000 men—are "true volunteers." Such men would have volunteered even if there had been no draft, and they did volunteer in spite of an entry pay that is roughly 60 percent of the amount that men of their age, education, and training could earn in civilian life.

The often ignored fact, therefore, is that our present armed forces are made up predominantly of volunteers. All of those men who have more than four years of service—8 percent of the total—are true volunteers; and so are at least a third of those with fewer than four years of service.

The return to voluntary means of raising and maintaining our armed forces should be seen in this perspective. With true volunteers now providing some 250,000 enlisted men annually, a fully volunteer force of 2.5 million men can be achieved by improving pay and conditions of service sufficiently to induce approximately 75,000 additional young men to enlist each year from the 1.5 million men who will annually turn 19 and who will meet the physical, moral and mental requirements.

A voluntary force of 3 million men would require 400,000 enlistments each year, or 150,000 additional volunteers from the 1.5 million eligible 19-year-olds. Smaller forces would require fewer than 75,000 additional volunteers annually. Reasonable improvements in pay and benefits in the early years of service should increase the number of volunteers by these amounts.

INTERVIEW WITH LT. GENERAL ROGERS

Soldiers: How is the All-Volunteer Army shaping up in terms of enlistments?

LtG. Rogers: Between July 1972 and this past May our goal was 165,100 non-prior service male enlistees. We have fallen short of this goal by 9,800—enlisting 155,300 non-prior service males. However, the months of February-May are historically poor recruiting months, and we hope to reverse this trend in the good recruiting months June through September.

Soldiers: Were the volunteers of the quality desired?

LtG. Rogers: Of course, that answer depends upon one's definition of quality. In the final analysis, one should judge quality by a man's overall performance on the job. One measure of quality for an enlistee we have been using—and it may not be the best measure—is whether he is a high school graduate. Since February 1 we have limited our recruitment of non-high school graduates to 30 percent of our total enlistment objectives and are receiving encouraging reports concerning quality from training center commanders. Another measure we have been using is the mental category of the enlistee as determined by his results on the Armed Forces Qualification Test (AFQT). Here again we have been meeting or exceeding our objectives for the percentages by various mental categories.

Incidentally, I don't wish to give the impression that we have anything against non-high school graduates; far from it. The great majority of them are fine young men and will serve well. But the fact remains, our experience has shown that from the standpoint only of disciplinary problems being created by graduates versus non-graduates, a disproportionate share is created by the non-graduates.

Soldiers: Industry is also recruiting high school graduates. Will we be able to recruit them in sufficient numbers to maintain an All-Volunteer Army?

LtG. Rogers: I think we will get our share and probably continue to get them in the numbers we have in the past. I would like to point out, however, that we are taking a close look at finding a better means of measuring quality than solely by the standards of being a graduate or being in a certain mental category as related to AFQT results.

Frankly, it is still too early to state positively that we will be able to enlist soldiers of the quality we need in the quantity required to man our structure. However, we are moving along a relatively uncharted course. As you know, since World War II we have only had one 15-month period—1947-1948—when we didn't rely on the draft. The conditions and circumstances which existed within our society then, as well as among the youth of that society, were different from those today. Thus we have no previous experience upon which to base a prediction.

Soldiers: Some Army officials have suggested that four-year enlistments—especially where some skills require lengthy training periods—would result in better manpower utilization and reduced recruiting costs. Are four-year enlistments going to become the standard?

LtG. Rogers: I don't see that happening soon except in the skills for which an enlistment bonus is paid. If we looked at it purely from a cost effectiveness standpoint, four years is the way we would go with all enlistments. However, you also have a psychological factor working here. Looking at it from the perspective of an 18- or 19-year old, four years represents a big chunk of his life. It seems like a whole lifetime to some of them. I think it's best that we have less than four years to offer so the man can enlist for a shorter period and see how he likes the Army.

Soldiers: You began paying a $1,500 bonus for combat enlistments in June 1972. The bonus was increased to $2,500 during this past May and June. Did the $1,500 fail to attract enough qualified volunteers for the combat arms?

LtG. Rogers: We did fail to meet our combat arms enlistment objectives by 30 percent during that one-year period.

Let's look at the entire bonus picture. Congress authorized payment of $3,000 for enlistment in the combat elements. Department of Defense then authorized us to run a one-year test, paying $1,500. Combat arms enlistments averaged only 300 per month before we began offering certain enlistment options and then later paying the bonus. With the bonus, four-year enlistments increased from five percent to 15 percent. In addition, the number going into combat arms as a result of the bonus and some enlistment options increased to about 3,000 per month. But westillcameup30 percent short overall.

We also had shortfalls in some of our hard skill MOSs, so with OSDs approval we increased the bonus to $2,500 and included volunteers in those combat-related hard skills, particularly in the missile and electronics fields. This increased bonus package is being conducted as a two-month test ending in June.

Soldiers: Did the bigger one attract more volunteers?

LtG. Rogers: It is not attracting more overall enlistments, but it is proving that such a bonus can change the distribution pattern of enlistees by increasing enlistments in the hard skills I mentioned and causing them to enlist for four years. We are happy about that.

Soldiers: Critics of the All-Volunteer Army concept suggest that blacks, other minority groups and the poor will be attracted to the Army in large numbers, resulting in an Army largely composed of minorities and the poor.

LtG. Rogers: Present trends suggest that their fears are unfounded. Let's take that one apart, however.

We don't ask what an enlistee's father earns. We don't care. It makes no difference whether a man's father earns $25,000 a year or whether his folks are on welfare. If a man is qualified, willing to enlist in the Army and perform to the best of his ability, why shouldn't he be able to serve?

As for minority groups, there has been some increase in the number of non-Caucasian enlistments. Minority groups comprise about 18 percent of the overall Army strength. I see no indication of a substantial increase.

Soldiers: Suppose you did have a substantial increase?

LtG. Rogers: I would answer your question with another question: So what if there were?

I know in the eyes of many it would be most tidy if we had, say, 11 percent blacks —that is their approximate percentage of the total population—and, say, two percent other non-Caucasians. That would represent a fairly good cross-section of the American population.

Life just isn't that tidy or precise. Furthermore, if non-Caucasian enlistments did increase significantly and you asked when should we cut them off, I certainly couldn't give you an answer as to when or if, and I know of no one in a position of responsibility who could.

Soldiers: Today's young soldiers are getting married earlier than they did a decade ago. Are we going to expand health care services and build more family housing?

LtG. Rogers: More of our young soldiers do get married earlier. If that trend continues we will have to think about building fewer barracks and more family housing. We must take a very hard and long look at this because here we are talking about projects involving millions of dollars.

Greater health care services may be needed; however, we're thinking in terms of the total environment for the soldier and his family. We would hope to improve all post services: Post Exchanges, in- and out-processing, recreational facilities, commissaries, educational opportunities and the like.

Soldiers: The Qualitative Management Program for enlisted personnel is causing some concern among NCOs. Some question the wisdom of denying reenlistment to NCOs, while increased emphasis is being placed on enlisting greater numbers of younger soldiers.

LtG. Rogers: We don't intend to change the Qualitative Management Program, although we may make some fine-tuning carburetor adjustments as we go along. The Army is going to be smaller but we're still going to do a professional job with fewer people. The NCOs have all got to be professionals.

We have established standards of performance, behavior and attitude. As long as an NCO measures up he need not be concerned. An NCO should know what those standards are and if he is not measuring up he had better be concerned because he may be on the way out. There is no place in the Army for those who believe they have the right to serve for 20 or 30 years irrespective of performance, conduct and attitude. That day has passed, if indeed it ever existed.

We are denying reenlistment to only those persons at the lower end of the performance, conduct and attitude scale. The officer corps has had such a program for many years. In fact, I think you will find that most NCOs are pleased that there exists a system to police their ranks. They want their corps to consist of motivated, well-behaved professionals in every sense of the word.

Soldiers: Some NCOs believe that the up-or-out program is unfair because it forces them to retire irrespective of the fact that they have done good jobs during their many years of service.

LtG. Rogers: The strength of senior NCOs in grades E-8 and E-9 cannot exceed three percent of the total enlisted strength. We have to have cut-off points so the young soldiers coming along can have a fair career progression.

Let's take the case of a master sergeant: The "window" through which he has to pass to be promoted to E-9 is so small that promotion becomes increasingly difficult at that level. It's the same way with a colonel who hasn't been promoted to brigadier general and has to retire after

30 years. There should be no stigma attached to the master sergeant or the colonel. Those grades carry great responsibilities and a person exercises a high degree of authority in those grades. Remember, the window is small.

I'll tell you one thing, though. Going through that window is a humbling experience—especially when you know so many fine persons whom you thought deserved to go through and didn't make it.

Soldiers: What about a person in the middle NCO grades who is doing a fine job but is happy with his present status. Will you retain him?

LtG. Rogers: No, not indefinitely. You see, that person might be happy with his present status, but there is a younger man below him who eventually wants to move up. We won't retain this man indefinitely. You see, that person might be blocking a more aggressive soldier's chances for advancing.

Soldiers: Was the current officer reduction-in-force (RIF) designed to improve leadership?

LtG. Rogers: No. To do that we have a continuing program of identifying and separating those officers who fail to measure up. This RIF is a quantitative one caused by our having more officers than required and permitted.

This RIF is very painful because, among other things, it involves many good officers. We're separating 4,900 officers for two reasons. First, our authorized officer strength is based on a percentage of the overall Army strength. As an example, prior to the Vietnam buildup our officer strength comprised about 11.6 percent of the total Army population. It had reached 14.9 percent by the end of FY 1972. We must get down to 13.7 percent by the end of this fiscal year and this requires that we separate a number of officers. That percentage will continue to decline in the future.

Second, our officer structure has a sizeable hump in it resulting from the requirements for Vietnam. That hump—an overstrength—is generally in Year Groups 1967 to 1970. If we left that hump in place when it reached the promotion window to major, many in the excess year groups could not be promoted and they would then have to be separated under the law. We thought it would be fairer to separate them now while they are young enough to start a second career.

We are also taking other actions to reduce officer strength: During the past 10 years we have brought an average of approximately 28,000 officers to active duty each year. We are only bringing in 8,900 during FY 1974. Of that figure, 3,800 are ROTC officers, and of those, we are obligated to bring in 2,550 who are Distinguished ROTC Graduates or scholarship students. We will also only bring in 350 OCS graduates in FY 74.

Soldiers: What officers will be most affected by the RIF?

LtG. Rogers: The great majority will be from Year Groups 1967-1970.

Soldiers: One of the stated goals of the All-Volunteer Army is to provide the soldier with a satisfying job. Hundreds are being involuntarily reclassified into new MOSs. Won't that have an adverse effect on the overall program?

LtG. Rogers: Yes, for a while. But surplus MOSs are also having an adverse effect. We wound up with large excesses of Vietnam-related MOSs, one example being in the aviation field. It's obvious that we don't need as many aviation personnel as we did during the Vietnam War. On the other hand we can't have people sitting around with nothing to do, nor do they like not being meaningfully employed. We have personnel teams going to CONUS posts and taking a look at surplus MOSs and trying to get the soldiers reclassified and retrained into shortage MOSs. CONUS commanders and CINCUSAREUR have the authority to reclassify soldiers out of overage skills. I think it likely that many reclassified men will find new interest and new challenge in their new MOS. But let there be no doubt about it, MOS imbalance and MOS mismatch comprise one of our big problems at this time.

Soldiers: There are complaints that involuntary reclassification hurts NCOs when they're considered for promotion or QMP board action.

LtG. Rogers: I can understand how they might have that feeling. All I can say is that members of boards do take involuntary and voluntary reclassifications into account. I've observed enough of those boards to know that their members exercise a great degree of judgment in their deliberations.

While we're still on the subject of MOS, let's take a closer look at this MOS mismatch situation. As is often done, if we only compare a man's duty MOS with his primary MOS, one may well find a mismatch. But if one compares the duty MOS with his secondary or alternate MOS, he might also find a match. So one must look closely at the method used in determining MOS mismatch.

Soldiers: Senior NCOs are required to be qualified in at least two skills. Will soldiers of all grades eventually be required to do so?

LtG. Rogers: We certainly encourage all soldiers to learn as many skills as possible, and we have recently implemented a program to require qualification in two skills. However, in the case of a young soldier, it normally takes a few years for him to master his primary skill. We don't believe we can require him to learn another one before he masters the first one.

Soldiers: Will the Army ever reach MOS equilibrium?

LtG. Rogers: By equilibrium I take it that you mean one soldier—no more and no less—for every MOS in every unit. We will never reach that day, because too many things happen that are beyond our control.

First, there is the inability to predict with absolute precision which men with what skills will become future losses and then have new men in training to replace them at just the right time. Then there are continual changes in our structure, in TAs and TOEs, some related to activation/deactivation, of units, to the introduction of new weapons systems, to base closures and the like. So you see, there are several variables in the equation which have their impact. But we can improve our MOS imbalance and mismatch and we are working hard towards that end.

We are also looking at a concept which would reduce the number of MOSs by training the soldier in, say, basic infantry and having his unit train him in such skills as mortar crewman or other specialized training. We are taking a hard look at that one.

Soldiers: Rumors have it that the Women's Army Corps will vanish as a separate corps within another year. Are the rumors true?

LtG. Rogers: The WAC was established as a separate corps by the Congress and only Congress can change the law. I can't say when that will happen, but in my judgment somewhere down the road the WAC will no longer exist as a separate corps.

There are 17,000 members of the Women's Army Corps serving in the Army and that figure will increase to at least 24,000 by 1978. Of the 480-plus enlisted skills, we've opened all but 48 of them to women. WAC officers may now be assigned to approximately 65 percent of the officer skills and we're taking another look because we think we can open up more.

In recent action we've eliminated the word male from our aviation regulations and qualified women may now become pilots.

We've also opened all ROTC programs to women beginning with school year 1973. A young lady can now join the Army ROTC on any college campus that has a unit, providing the host college or university agrees. Now, there are two things that I don't see happening. We won't see women serving in fox-holes in a combat situation, and they won't be assigned to positions in which they cannot maintain their privacy.

We are not going to be rushed into changes just for the sake of change or for cosmetic purposes. We will continue to make changes with respect to the utilization of women when the changes are right for the Army and right for the women, and we'll make them without fanfare.

Soldiers: Many NCOs have expressed concern over the retention of Article 15 records in the soldier's permanent file.

LtG. Rogers: A lot of officers also have the same concern for the soldiers in this regard. However, we're not going to change the policy at this time. It will be reviewed at the end of a year to determine if it should be changed.

I'm sure you understand the reason for the policy. For example, when a man is considered for board action—promotion, retention, schooling, special assignment and the like—all that is generally available is his record to be considered by the board. Let's suppose he's an officer or NCO being considered for promotion. The board looks at his record and those of his contemporaries. If that person has received an Article 15 for misconduct or failure to perform his duties satisfactorily and none of the other individuals being considered has received an Article 15, it just seems unfair to the rest that the one be viewed as having performed equally as well as all the others. And yet that would have to be the board's judgment if the Article 15 is not in the man's file. . . .

Soldiers: A few commanders have expressed a reluctance to give Article 15s, knowing they become a permanent part of the soldier's record.

LtG. Rogers: I am unaware of any decline in the number of Article 15s since the policy was initiated.

Soldiers: What do you see in the future for the all-volunteer Army?

LtG. Rogers: As to size and composition, I can give you a better picture down the road a ways. However, I would expect the volunteer Army to be a professional Army. I would expect it to be professional in terms of the skills and motivation of its members; professional in training, equipment and combat readiness; and comprised of disciplined and dedicated men and women who want to be in the Army, and who find it a proud, challenging and satisfying career. That is the kind of Army we must have—the kind our Nation expects and should require that we have.

1971

44.

JEROME ROSOW: Blue Collar Blues

In December 1971, Secretary of Health, Education, and Welfare Elliot L. Richardson authorized a study of the "institution of work" in America. The occasion of the study was the general observation, both in and out of the government, that there was in the 1960s and afterwards what the Department of Labor called "a gut revolt against work as it is organized in the American economy." The evidences for this conclusion were widespread: growing absenteeism, industrial sabotage, poor morale, and apathy. Some of these symptoms were traced to unrest over inflation, depressing working conditions, inequitable promotion systems, monotony on the job, and general job dissatisfaction. On February 9, 1971, Assistant Secretary of Labor Jerome Rosow addressed the American Management Association annual conference on the subject of economic productivity in relation to the evident failure of the traditional work ethic. Portions of his speech are reprinted here.

Source: *Vital Speeches*, June 1, 1971.

I'D LIKE TO DISCUSS with you today productivity and motivation as they relate to lower-middle-income workers and what you as managers can do to improve the situation.

As many of you know, we have recently spent a great deal of time studying these workers and their problems. What we found bears directly on the topic of this conference and impacts primarily on business and industry. Not that there is no impact on the public sector. But the role of business and industry is so predominant that it is fitting to begin here.

The fact is that millions of workers, who earn between $5 and 10 thousand a year are getting increasingly frustrated. Despite steady labor they cannot attain the quality of life for themselves or their families that is expected to result from conscientious job performance:

—Their paychecks do not cover legitimate basic family needs.

—Their work life is unsatisfactory but they see no way of breaking out.

—Their total life pattern is discouraging.

In short, they are caught in a three-way squeeze: an economic squeeze, a workplace squeeze and a socio-environmental squeeze.

These squeezes involve persons who are members of families where income is above the poverty line but below what is required to meet moderate family budget needs. We estimate that some 20 million families—about 80 million individuals—are in this income range. Many are permanently trapped.

Our pride in the fact that millions of workers share in the Nation's abundance should not diminish concern for those millions of other steady workers who face some very basic problems.

The majority are white, but the group has a disproportionate number of non-whites. Most of the heads of these families are blue collar workers but many are in white collar or service jobs. More are low-skilled than highly skilled, and proportionately more are non-union than union.

These are the people about whom we are concerned: lower-middle income; looking toward and aspiring to a middle class life but achieving at best a low quality substitute.

Let's look at the economic squeeze: This bind results from an imbalance between wages and budget-needs, aggravated by heavy taxes and inflation. In fact, inflation has eaten away most of the wage increases won through collective bargaining since 1965.

Take, for example, the 40-year-old worker. At age 40, a worker is likely to be supporting a wife and two children, one in high school. Ten years earlier he had a wife and one pre-school age child.

According to studies of the Bureau of Labor Statistics, to maintain the same standard of living for his growing family that he and his smaller family used to enjoy, he needs to have increased his real income by about six percent a year.

But average productivity increases run about three percent a year. Over the past decade he has lost position in the economic race.

And promotion opportunities and supplemental earning routes are limited:

—Promotion opportunities are restricted by mobility patterns within firms; lack of information about better jobs in other firms and inadequate educational qualifications.

—Moonlighting is limited by the availability of jobs, the physical stamina of the individual and his willingness to give up leisure time and family activities. Despite these drawbacks at least 15 percent of lower-middle income men moonlight.

—The scarcity of reliable, reasonably priced facilities for day care and after school supervision makes working and earning supplemental income an uphill effort for many wives. Despite a myriad of problems—including inadequate tax deductions for child care—wives in the $5-10 thousand group work more frequently than do other wives. And more than one-half of those who work have school age children. We also have new findings which reveal that men with working wives are more alienated than other workers.

The difficulties of the 40-year-old worker may be compounded later in life when he must pay college costs and/or help support aging parents. At that point, when family budget costs are at their peak, the worker usually has reached a plateau in his job level.

The result is that after years of vigorous, dependable job performance, many find themselves *worse off* economically than when they started their working lives. This is a sad situation—in stark contrast to the American dream and our world of rising expectations. . . .

A pioneering survey of workingmen by

the University of Michigan Survey Research Center found that American workers generally expect that working entitles them to more than a paycheck; that the lack of these extras is a source of worker concern, and that millions of workers—primarily in lower income categories—are *not* in jobs where employers provide such benefits as medical, surgical or hospital insurance; life insurance, retirement, or, for women workers, maternity leave.

The survey found that among all workers:

—28 percent did not receive medical, surgical or hospital insurance coverage

—38 percent are not covered by a life insurance policy

—39 percent are not included in a retirement program

—41 percent of the women workers are not entitled to maternity leave with full reemployment rights

—61 percent did not have employer-sponsored training available.

The three top job-related problems, as ranked by the workers, were health and safety hazards, inadequate fringe benefits and inadequate income.

Job challenge or "interesting work" was rated by workers as *the single most important* aspect of job satisfaction.

Repetitive tasks that restrict personal freedom and limit decision-making are at the root of much of the feelings of alienation. Yet that is the nature of many lower-middle income jobs.

The Michigan survey found that promotion opportunities are strongly related to job satisfaction and mental health. Workers' perceptions of the "fairness" of the promotions at their place of employment had some of the most sizable and most consistent relationships with job satisfaction/mental health measures. On each of the measures, the least favorable scores were those of workers who reported that their employers did not handle promotions fairly.

It can be assumed, because of employers' promotion-patterns for non-supervisory workers, that lack of promotion opportunities are a major source of dissatisfaction among workers in the lower-middle income group. In fact, two out of three workers indicated that they "never" expect to be promoted from their present jobs.

It is not surprising that a preponderance of lower-income workers in the Michigan survey cited unpleasant working conditions as their major job problem: A $5,000 to $10,000 worker is much more vulnerable than the man in a higher-income bracket to boredom and repetition. . . .

Another squeeze is also at work: workers in the lower-middle income bracket are likely to live closely with some of the major environmental problems of the Nation. These combine with certain sociological and personal factors to make home life less than satisfactory:

—Off-the-job hours are likely to be spent in neighborhoods that show signs of urban decay and reduced or reducing city services; where the sense of community has been eroded by freeways and urban renewal and where concentrations of traffic and industry intensify noise and air pollution.

—Crime and fear of crime hits hard at millions of workers, both black and white, who live in the center or near the center of the city. According to the Report of the President's Commission on the Causes of Violence, the violent crime rate doubled between 1958 and 1968. Black workers and their families suffer the effects of crime almost three times more often than whites.

—Lower-middle income workers often

live close to those who receive government aid. A steady worker whose paycheck does not reach far enough; whose worklife is less than optimal, and whose home environment is both drab and frightening, understandably may view with some resentment the use of his tax dollars to help his nonworking neighbor rather than himself out of a squeeze.

—In addition, many lower-middle income workers, quite justifiably, feel that society does not prize the kind of work they perform. Our culture dramatizes diploma-accredited professionals but neglects skilled and unskilled workers who transform ideas into tangible goods and services. The result is that young people look on many of the jobs in the $5,000 to $10,000 bracket as jobs of last resort; fathers hesitate to describe their jobs to their sons and hope to find, if not for themselves, at least for their children, another way to make a living.

In short, at home and at work, these people are living in a mine field. They are overwhelmed with problems and their dissatisfaction is expressed in workplace conduct that impacts negatively on productivity and increases employers costs. The behavior and list of economic penalties are well known to all of us:

—work that is poor in quality and inadequate in quantity

—increased tardiness, absenteeism and work-injuries

—energy-sapping moonlighting

—higher turnover—stimulated by the endless search for a better break

—excessive wage demands in the futile effort to beat inflation

—mounting grievances that can lead to strikes and the complete rupture of production.

The problem is familiar enough to all of us. But what about the solution?

I think that within our highly established and effective labor-management system we can do a number of things in the constructive interest of both workers and industry—if both management and labor squarely face up to the pressures that impinge on the productivity of lower-middle income workers and look for ways to relieve these pressures.

There are certain specific areas that should be examined for solutions:

First, organization of work. Such hackneyed phrases as job enrichment, job ladders, job redesign, and participation, have been cheapened and therefore often discarded. Yet, the fact remains that full-scale enrichment with a real commitment from management has produced remarkable results in the pioneering plants that have tried it.

Second, opportunities for advancement. Building wage and salary plans will not alone alleviate worker dissatisfaction. They must be supported by promotion policies that work at the lower levels of the organization at least as well as they do at middle and top levels. . . .

Fourth, supervisory training. Dissatisfaction with treatment *by* supervisors has been reported as one of the major blue collar complaints. Supervisors are the management in the eyes of the worker, like it or not. How first line supervisors relate to subordinates or handle grievances reflects on management. Industries whose supervisors are not sensitive to the changing expectations of the oncoming generation and its demand to take part in decision-making can look for growing problems in their plants in the 1970s.

Fifth, occupational health and safety. Industry needs to take a close look at this both in terms of worker protection on the job and the adequacy of sickness and accident benefits. . . .

Sixth, employee thrift plans offer a very attractive method for easing the economic squeeze on workers. Under an employee thrift plan, costs can be fixed and benefits can be multiplied both to the firm and to the worker. If employer and employee contribute regularly by payroll deduction formula, the employee begins to accumulate a small and steadily growing account. . . .

Seventh, pension systems need review. About half of the 30 million American workers covered by private pension plans will never draw a penny in benefits. The reason, of course, is that pension benefits are forfeited when workers change jobs before retirement or before earning a nonforfeitable right—a vested pension.

Eighth, working wives can be an asset to both industry and the worker—if certain adjustments are made.

There are two ways that industry can employ women to its greater advantage. One is to increase the number of part-time jobs which are not only more compatible to the life style of working wives with school age children, but may reduce the inferior production caused by full-time work on a repetitive task. The other is to improve or provide child care arrangements. The fact is that in the United States good child care is difficult and makeshift arrangements affect productivity. . . .

When life seems to be a closed-loop system of economic pressure, job dissatisfaction and community problems, then performance as a worker, as a citizen and as a person suffers. Workers who run the daily rat race on a muddy track, and are also-rans, can't be inspired to win.

The employer concerned with morale and motivation as adjuncts to strong profit-results needs to increase his awareness of the interplay between job performance and human expectations. Before an employer can effect real and lasting changes he must know the degree and nature of the problem in his specific workforce.

The nature of the job itself is intertwined with a man, his family, his life, his accomplishment, his status and his outlook on society. This dynamic interaction of the world of work with the life style of the worker is a fact.

Economic rewards, personal job satisfaction and future opportunity are three basic elements that turn people on. Failure and frustration turn them off.

The future productivity of our society and its capacity to make a better world and a better America rests upon our ability to provide a better opportunity for more people. In the final analysis this involves the workplace more than any other single element.

Do you know what I do? I fix seven bolts. Seven bolts! Day in and day out, the same seven bolts. What do I think about? Raquel Welch!

General Motors employee in Tarrytown,
New York, during a 1970 strike

45.

WARREN E. BURGER: Court Reform

Few institutions escaped the general malaise that infected American society in the late 1960s and early 1970s. The criminal justice system was no exception. It came under attack as inequitable, incompetent, and, on occasion, corrupt. The court system was criticized because of overloaded dockets, endless postponements, dishonest or incompetent judges, frequently bad pay, and corruption by the spoils system of politics. After becoming Chief Justice of the U. S. Supreme Court in 1969, Warren E. Burger often addressed public gatherings on the problems of the legal and judicial professions, spelling out definite proposals for change and improvement in the system of civil and criminal law and prison reform. On March 12, 1971, he addressed the National Conference on the Judiciary in Williamsburg, Virginia, on methods of court reform. Part of his speech is reprinted here.

Source: *Vital Speeches*, April 15, 1971

TODAY THE AMERICAN SYSTEM of criminal justice in every phase—the police function, the prosecution and defense, the courts and the correctional machinery—is suffering from a severe case of deferred maintenance. By and large, this is true at the State, local and Federal levels. The failure of our machinery is now a matter of common knowledge, fully documented by innumerable studies and surveys.

As a consequence of this deferred maintenance we see:

First, that the perpetrators of most criminal acts are not detected, arrested and brought to trial;

Second, those who are apprehended and charged are not tried promptly because we allow unconscionable delays that pervert both the right of the defendant and the public to a speedy trial; and

Third, the convicted persons are not punished promptly after conviction because of delay in the appellate process. Finally, even after the end of litigation, those who are sentenced to confinement are not corrected or rehabilitated, and the majority of them return to commit new crimes. The primary responsibility of judges, of course, is for the operation of the judicial machinery but this does not mean we can ignore the police function or the shortcomings of the correctional systems.

At each of these three stages the enforcement, the trial, the correction—the deferred maintenance became apparent when the machinery was forced to carry too heavy a load. This is what happens to any machine whether it is an industrial plant, an automobile or a dishwasher. It can be no comfort to us that this deferred maintenance crisis is shared by others; by cities and in housing, in the field of medical care, in environmental protection, and many other fields. All of these problems are important, but the administration of justice is the adhesive

—the very glue—that keeps the parts of an organized society from flying apart. Man can tolerate many shortcomings of his existence, but a civilized society cannot remain so without an adequate system of justice, and by that I mean justice in its broadest sense.

I have said nothing of civil justice—that is the resolution of cases between private citizens or between citizens and government. This, unhappily, is becoming the stepchild of the law as criminal justice once was. Most people with civil claims, particularly those in the middle economic echelons, who cannot afford the heavy costs of litigation and who cannot qualify for public or government-subsidized legal assistance, are forced to stand by in frustration, and often in want, while they watch the passage of time eat up the value of their case. The public has been quiet and patient, sensing on the one hand the need to improve the quality of criminal justice but also experiencing frustration at the inability to vindicate private claims and rights. . . .

I need not burden this well-informed audience on the subject of the tension and the strains existing between the State and Federal courts in recent years. Because of the existence of those problems and the reasons underlying them I urged last August, at the ABA convention in St. Louis, that the chief justice of each State take the initiative to create an informal *ad hoc* State-Federal judicial council in each State. The purpose, of course, was to have these judges meet together informally to develop cooperation to reduce the tensions that have existed in recent years. I was pleasantly surprised, even astonished, at the speed with which the chief justices responded, for I am now informed that such councils are in actual operation in 32 of the States. Many of these councils have been created by formal order of the State supreme court. I am also informed that once the channels of communication were opened these State and Federal judges found other areas of fruitful cooperation and exchange of ideas. I regard this development of such importance that I wish to express my appreciation to the Conference of State Chief Justices and to Chief Justice Calvert of Texas, its chairman.

In urging the cooperation between the State and Federal judges, and in urging the State judges to call upon the State bar associations and on the American Bar Association, I have no thought whatever that all State court systems or all judges be cast in one mold. Far from this, I have an abiding conviction that the strength of our entire system in this country and the essence of true federalism lies in diversity among the States. It will not impair this diversity, I submit, to work together to develop effective post-conviction remedies for example, or common standards of judicial administration, common standards of professional conduct for lawyers, and, indeed, for judges, or the improvement in the method of selection, the tenure, and compensation of judges.

In terms of methods, machinery, equipment and the flow of papers—and we know the business of courts depends on the flow of papers—most courts have changed very little fundamentally in a hundred years or more. I know of no comprehensive surveys, but spot checks have shown for example that the ancient ledger type of record books, sixteen or eighteen inches wide, twenty-four or twenty-six inches high, and four inches thick are still used in a very large number of courts and these cumbersome books, hazardous to handle, still call for longhand entries concerning cases. I mention this only as one symptom of our tendency to cling to old ways. We know that banks, factories, department stores, hospitals and many government agencies have cast off anachronisms of this kind.

With relatively few exceptions, we still call jurors as in the past. We still herd them into a common room in numbers often double the real need because of obsolete concepts of arranging and managing their use. This process is often complicated by the unregulated arbitrariness of a handful of judges, for example, who demand more jurors than they can possibly use to be allocated each day for their exclusive use. There is almost a total absence of even the most primitive techniques in predicting the need for jurors just as there is a large vacuum in the standards and procedures to coordinate the steps of bringing a case and all of its components—the lawyers, witnesses, experts, jurors and court staff—to the same place at the same time.

Happily, a very distinguished committee of the American Bar Association under the chairmanship of Judge Freedman of the United States Court of Appeals of the third circuit is now launching a comprehensive program of bringing up to date the minimum standards of judicial administration.

Independent of what we do in the courtroom itself, we need careful study to make sure that every case which reaches the courtroom stage is there only after every possibility of settlement has been exhausted. Those parties who impose upon the judicial process and clog its functioning by carrying the cases through jury selection before making a settlement which could have been made earlier should be subject to the risk of a very substantial discretionary cost assessment at the hands of the trial judge who can evaluate these abuses of the system. Someone must remind the bar and the public of the enormous cost of a trial.

As litigation has grown and multiple-judge courts have steadily enlarged, the continued use of the old equipment and old methods has brought about a virtual breakdown in many places and a slowdown everywhere in the efficiency and functioning of courts. The judicial system and all its components have been subjected to the same stresses and strains as hospitals and other enterprises. The difference is that, thirty or forty years ago, doctors and nurses recognized the importance of system and management in order to deliver to the patients adequate medical care, this resulted, as I have pointed out on other occasions, in the development of hospital administrators and today there is no hospital of any size in this country without a trained hospital administrator who is the chief executive officer dealing with the management and efficient utilization of all the resources of the institution. Courts and judges have, with few exceptions, not responded in this way. To some extent, imaginative and resourceful judges and court clerks have moved partially into the vacuum, but the function of a clerk and the function of a court executive are very different, and a court clerk cannot be expected to perform both functions.

From the day I took office, twenty-one months ago, this seemed to me the most pressing need of the courts of this country, and particularly so in my area of responsibility, the Federal courts. The first step I took was to help lay the foundations for a facility to train executives and I requested the American Bar Association to take the leadership in accomplishing this. That association did so with the American judicature society and the institute of judicial administration as cosponsors, together they created the institute of court management at the University of Denver Law School. That institute has now graduated the first group of trainees with an intensive full-time course over a period of six months including actual field training in the various courts. It will train two additional classes this year. This is not a Federal facility and indeed I expect most of its output will go to State court systems.

In the meantime, the Congress has taken one of the most important steps in a generation in the administration of justice by providing for a court executive in each of the eleven Federal circuits. The court executive will work under the direction of the judicial council of each circuit. I need not say, surely, to an audience including so many chief judges and administrative judges, that this will not only relieve judges to perform their basic judicial functions but it will provide a person who will, in time, be able to develop new methods and new processes, which busy judges could not do in the past.

The function of a court executive is something none of us really knows very much about. There are only a handful of court administrators or executives in this country and up to 1970 they are all self-taught. The few who were in being were in the State courts and we called upon them to be members of the teaching faculty for the new Court Management Institute. The concept of court executive or court administrator will have its detractors but I predict they will not be heard for very long. The history books tell us how the admirals reacted when General William Mitchell insisted that an airplane could sink a battleship.

The desperate need for court executive officers does not alter the fact that it will require great patience and industrious homework on the part of judges and chief judges to learn to utilize these officers for their courts.

A great many of the infirmities in our procedures could be cured if judges had broad rulemaking power and exercised that power. The best example of this was given a generation ago in the Federal Rules of Civil Procedure and later in the Criminal and Appellate Procedure Rules. . . .

The combined experience of this country for nearly two hundred years now, with elective judges in most of the States holding office for limited terms and Federal judges who are appointed with tenure, affords a basis for a careful reexamination of the whole method of the selection of judges. This is part of the long range problem, but it deserves some mention. The aggregate of two centuries of experience should be sufficient to give us material for a comprehensive reexamination of the methods of selection and the tenure of State judges. In saying this, I, of course, intend no reflection whatever on those State systems having elected judges with limited terms and the many splendid judges in those States.

The fine quality of judicial work of State judges is in spite of, not because of, the method of selection.

The election of judges for limited terms is a subject on which reasonable men can reasonably have different views. Nevertheless the very nature of the judicial function calls for some comprehensive studies directed to the alternative methods developed in the last generation in some States. Those alternatives tend to preserve the virtues of popular choice of judges and at the same time develop a high degree of professionalism, offering an inducement for competent lawyers to make a career of the Bench.

We know that while there are certain patterns common in the fifty States as to the selection and tenure of judges, there is at the same time a wide disparity in their compensation in such States as New York, California, and Illinois, to mention but three of the large States, the compensation of judges of the higher courts is as much as three times the compensation of their counterparts in some other States of the Union.

As lawyers and judges we know that the function of the courts in a small State is essentially the same as the function of the courts in the larger State. The size of the State has no relationship to the nature of the function, the degree of the responsibility, and the degree of the professional competence called for. It is, therefore, an anomaly for a wide disparity to continue. I do not suggest, by any means, that there need be a rigid, uniform standard of compensation or tenure for all the States. All I suggest is that the judges in the small States are performing essentially the same function as that of their brothers in a large State, and the conditions of their service should not vary excessively. It is not a wholesome or healthy thing for the administration of justice to have the highest court of a geographically large and economically powerful State receive two or three times as much as his counterpart a few hundred miles away. If we want quality justice we must pay for it. . . .

For a long time we have talked of the need for a closer exchange and closer cooperation among the States and between the States and the Federal courts on judicial problems. No States are without grave problems in the administration of justice. The problems vary chiefly in degree from those States with grave troubles to those on the threshold of disaster in their courts. The valuable work of the National College of Trial Judges is just one example of the value of cooperative enterprise.

We now have in this country a great ferment for court improvement. It is a ferment that has been gaining momentum slowly over a long period of time. More recently, this has taken on a new thrust and force under the leadership of the American Bar Association. The time has come, and I submit that it is here and now at this conference, to make the initial decision and bring into being some kind of national clearing house or center to serve all the States and to cooperate with all the agencies seeking to improve justice at every level. The need is great, and the time is now, and I hope this conference will consider creating a working committee to this end—before you adjourn. I know that you will do many important things while you are here, but if you do no more than launch this much-needed service agency for the State courts, your time and attendance here would be justified.

I felt the guys still in Vietnam—nobody here cared about them really—were like an outpost. Everyone in the States had forgotten us, left us to live or die, anything, so long as they weren't involved.

A Vietnam veteran, quoted in *No Victory Parades,* by Murray Polner (1971)

Kathy Harjo, a full-blooded Seminole, and one of the youngest delegates at the 1972 Democratic Convention

MULTIPLE MINORITIES

The 1960s saw the emergence of a powerful civil rights movement among black Americans. The majority of blacks held varying degrees of commitment to nonviolence, but some groups took a militant posture under the slogan, "Black Power." In imitation of, and partly in reaction to, the black rights movement, a great variety of other, hitherto unheard from, minorities began to exert public and political pressure on their own behalf. The so-called "white ethnics," mostly Italian, Polish, Czech, or Irish Americans, formed new organizations and infused new life into old ones. The American Indians, certainly the most deprived group in the nation, began to coalesce for their rights. Mexican-Americans sought not only to remove economic and political obstacles to their well-being, but, like Puerto Ricans, Indians, blacks, and others, also to assert the right to maintain their cultural heritage. That violent confrontations often resulted when the various ethnic groups banded together to claim their rights is not surprising. Discrimination had persisted for decades, and the patterns of legality erected by the white majority to perpetuate its vested interests were firmly entrenched. The majority's fear was, of course, economic: another's gain might be one's own loss.

(Above) Police surround the body of Jerome Johnson, reported to have made an assassination attempt on Joseph Colombo, Sr., at an Italian-American Unity Day rally in New York; Colombo was shot three times in the head, but did not die; (left) Mexican Braceros doing stoop labor in a California strawberry field while their families remain behind in Mexico OPPOSITE PAGE: (Top) Member of the American Indian Movement watches federal agents at Wounded Knee, S.D.; (bottom) many Puerto Ricans who came to the mainland seeking better opportunity found little chance for well-paid employment.

Not all minorities were ethnic. ut even when they were, the oals they sought did not always ave much to do with ethnicity. The oals were usually social recogni-ion, economic justice, and some oice in the political process. Eth-icity often provided a cohesion hat was otherwise lacking. Some-imes the bonds of unity were ormed across ethnic lines, as in he case of migrant workers. In one ase, that of the so-called "hard ats," or blue collar workers, it vas the cohesion of an economic lass. But the hard hats comprised minority more in name than in act. Other minorities united be-ind causes in which ethnicity layed no part. The homosexuals, r "gay liberation movement," imed aggressively at getting rid f a social stigma and odious tereotypes. Their quest was for he right to be what one is without eing penalized for it by job dis-crimination and other sanctions. Probably the most influential and wide-ranging of movements in the ate 1960s was women's liberation. Women as such are not a numeri-cal minority, but certainly many of the controversial views espoused by women's liberation were not held by a majority of Americans, or even by a majority of women. Great strides were made for women in removing educational and job barriers, in getting equal pay for equal work, and in in-creased political representation.

Perhaps the most beneficial aspect of all minority efforts to improve their status was a revived emphasis on individual achievement. One's potential, and how he or she realized it, became more important than one's sex, ethnic background, or racial stock. Hank Aaron, Billie Jean King, Mark Spitz, Lee Trevino, and Larry Csonka deserved recognition for what they did in their respective sports, without reference to any group affiliations. And this became true not only for celebrities. New opportunities also opened for millions in work, school, and society, based on what they could do as persons.

(Above) Members of the Gay Liberation movement call for an end to oppression of homosexuals; (below) tennis champion Billie Jean King is greeted by fans in July 1973 two months before her challenge match with Bobby Riggs, in which she roundly defeated him.

46.

The Winter Soldier Investigation

Some of the most effective and poignant protests against the Vietnam war were mobilized by men who fought in it. Their organization, Vietnam Veterans Against the War, gave an impetus to the movement that could only have been supplied by those who had participated in the conflict and could testify about what they had seen. After the nation had been startled by the revelation of the 1968 My Lai massacre, more attention was devoted, both in the news and in protests, to the phenomenon of atrocities committed by Americans. On January 31, 1971, the VVAW convened what they called the "Winter Soldier Investigation" in Detroit to stage a public inquiry into American war crimes. During three days of hearings more than 100 veterans, plus a few civilians, testified concerning war crimes they had witnessed or participated in. The selection below includes portions of testimony by two of the veterans.

Source: *The Winter Soldier Investigation:* An Inquiry into American War Crimes by the Vietnam Veterans Against the War, Boston, 1972, pp. 28-33;42-45.

SGT. MICHAEL McCUSKER,
1ST MARINE DIVISION

I'M FROM PORTLAND, OREGON. I was in the 1st Marine Division, in I Corps, in 1966 and 1967. I was discharged on 19th October 1967 as a Sergeant E-5. This ragged piece of paper here is a Xeroxed copy of my discharge papers. I was in the 1st Marine Division with the Informational Services Office, which meant that I was an infantry reporter-photographer. I spent all of my time out in the field with the infantry on infantry operations. I went out with damned near every Marine outfit in all of I Corps from 1st Marine Division and 3rd Marine Division units. And so, these things in the field, the torturing of prisoners, the use of scout dogs in this torture, the "Bell Telephone Hour" with the field phones—by seeing all of these units, I discovered that no one unit was any worse than another. That this was standard procedure. That it was almost like watching the same film strip continually, time after time after time. Within every unit there was the same prejudice; there was the same bigotry toward Vietnamese. All Vietnamese.

I just want to mention a few atrocities of a larger scale that I saw. All three of them were ironically with the same battalion—1st Battalion, 5th Marine Regiment, 1st Marine Division. All three atrocities happened in the month of September and October 1966. Now the first one took place around September 6th or 7th, 1966, about ten miles northwest of the province capital of Tam Ky, near the mountains. It was in a pineapple forest and a Marine had just been killed. He had been hit by a sniper and the entire battalion, in revenge, destroyed two entire villages, wiping out everything living, the people (and that was men, women, their children), all their livestock, burning the huts, destroying the paddies, their gardens, their hedgerows, just wiped them out—erased them. They did not exist the moment after the Marines were finished and they might never have existed. . . .

They then rounded up ten villagers, put 'em in a hut (I don't know how they killed them—grenaded them or shot 'em down), and burned the hut. They came back to the company area where it was bivouacked for the night while on a regular routine search and destroy mission. I personally came into contact with this when the squad came back, told their CO, who was a lieutenant, and they hastily set back off again towards that village with the lieutenant. I sort of tagged along in the rear and when I got up there they were distributing these bodies that were charred and burned and I asked what these bodies were. They said, "Oh, we were hit by an ambush. These were the people who ambushed, but we got 'em." Okay, I didn't want to ask them how they killed them because all the bodies were burned as if they'd been roasted on a spit.

There was a tiny little form, that of a child, lying out in the field with straw over its face. It had been clubbed to death. As later was brought out, the Marine that clubbed the child to death didn't really want to look at the child's face so he put straw over it before he clubbed it. The woman survived, somehow, and crawled to a neighbor; the neighbor ran off to the ARVN commanders. The commanders were rather angry, put pressure on the Marine Corps, and these men were tried. However, they got very light sentences—a little slap on the wrist. I don't know exactly how much time they got nor do I know how much time they actually served, but they're on the streets again because I ran into one about two years ago in New York.

The third atrocity was a village called Duc Pho, which was farther northwest of Tam Ky, across the first range of mountains into several valleys. This area was not touched for two years until the Army started taking up operations in that area. Jonathan Shell wrote a very, very graphic two-part story for the *New Yorker* concerning that area, mentioning that nobody had been in there for two years after the Marines had passed through. Nobody had to. There wasn't really much left after we went through. In this one particular village of Duc Pho, another man was killed by a sniper. This involved Bravo Company, 1st Battalion, 5th Marines, and I believe it was the 1st Platoon with the company commander along. Well, the CO pulled us back. We were sweeping across the paddy when this sergeant got hit. He pulled us back and called in for nape, which is napalm, or which the military now likes to refer to as incinder jell, as if it were as harmless as Jello, an after-dinner dessert. But it was napalm.

We walked into the ville after the fires burned down and there was an old man lying on a cot, burned to death with his hands stiff in rigor mortis, reaching for the sky as if in prayer or supplication forgiving us for what we had done. We walked past him and across the hedgerow there was an old woman lying dead curled into the fetal position as if she had been just born. An old man lay beside her. Over the next hedgerow there were 30 dead children. They had been lying out there in this courtyard for us to see them before we got into that village. They were laid out there by survivors, who split into the jungle. Now these kids, 30 of them, none were over fifteen; some of them were babies. Some looked like they had just been sunburned, that was all. Their skins were a very ruddy, ruddy pink or scarlet color. Others were just charred with their guts hanging out. Ironically it was my mother's birthday, 27 October, and I somehow seemed to feel that these were her children.

An officer, a captain, walked up to me and said, "Well, Sgt. McCusker,"—remember I was the reporter—"Do you see what the Viet Cong did to their own people?" And I said, "Captain, I saw our planes drop the napalm." He says, "Well, Sgt. McCusker, you had better write that the Viet Cong did it." I told the captain politely what I thought he should do to himself and I walked off. Now these things happened. Now these were some of the more gruesome things that happened, or more gruesome because of the numbers. But daily things like this happened—a kid shot down in the paddy because, well, it looked like an adult running away. I couldn't see, so we walk up to him, and it's a kid. The philosophy was that anybody running must be a Viet Cong; he must have something to hide or else he would stick around for the Americans, not taking into consideration that he was running from the Americans because they were continually shooting at him. So they shot down anybody who was running.

I was in a helicopter once and I saw this farmer in a cart. Suddenly the farmer in the cart just blew into all sorts of pieces and the helicopter I was in was shaking like the devil. It wasn't hard to put it together because I watched the gunner finish off the rounds. He had extra ammo.

The tortures started in the villages. Prisoners were picked up by the average infantryman, who really didn't have much idea of exactly what intelligence was needed. So, therefore, you're all prisoners. We'll let interrogators take care of it. The method of taking prisoners was that you take the villagers that were left in the village, not those that had run away. You tied them to a tree and got the dog handler to let the dog jump and bite at the person tied to the tree. Or again, with the field telephone, you wired it up to his ears, his nose, his genitals. This was done to women—I've seen it done to women. In Ben Song, which was the province capital, in a prison, this guy was telling me all about why war was hell. He took me down to this dungeon where South Vietnamese troops were pulling fingernails out of an old woman. There was an American captain standing by, rocking on his heels, rather enjoying the show.

I could testify to the systematic destruction of village hospitals, by mortars, by air, by artillery, believing that if these hospitals were destroyed the Viet Cong could not use them for their wounded. I was also on an operation in the Rung Sat area just north of Saigon, which is just mud flats, like the Mississippi delta at high water. It was in April 1966, with the 1st Battalion, 5th Marines again. They were a battalion landing team at that time. We came across a big NLF hospital complex and destroyed it out of hand. Now interestingly enough, in Portland, Oregon, where I was a medic in the student strike, we had an unauthorized hospital tent in what was called the park blocks out in front of the college. The city decided to destroy it because it was an unauthorized hospital. We did have patients in it, but these were unauthorized people too. They were long-hairs. So the cops came in, the tactical squad with their sticks. They bloodied up about 30 of us pretty badly and did a lot more damage to perhaps 50 more. So not only in Vietnam do Americans destroy hospitals. It was graphically pointed out to the people in Portland that they were destroyed, too, by police power—except of course, the hospital was not officially authorized. Nor are Vietnamese hospitals in the villages.

Doctor Margarette, who was in Quang Ngai, can testify to the condition of the provincial hospital in Quang Ngai, the Vietnamese hospital for the province. That hospital is so damned overcrowded that they can't get anything done. People are dying in those wards; they just shove them off the beds and put somebody else on them. One of the reasons that that damn hospital is so crowded is because all the little hospitals within the villages were all destroyed.

Quang Ngai, in that province of Quang Ngai, an entire war of attrition is being put across there. My Lai is in Quang Ngai; My Lai suffered that war of attrition. When Calley and his people went through there, it was not the first time anyone went through My Lai and put the torch to it, nor was it the last time. You can prove it by a Reuters dispatch of October 1969. They were doing it again, and in the villages of the whole Son My province. The entire Quang Ngai area was slated for destruction. The Vietnamese were slated for relocation and forced urbanization—which is what is happening in this country as a matter of fact. So the methods don't differ.

I guess, really, that's the end of my testimony except right now, while I'm speaking, it's happening in all of Southeast Asia; some guys are going through what I did, what all of us did; they are going through it right now. The Vietnamese, Cambodians, and Laotians are dying right now, at this exact moment and they will continue to die tomorrow, maybe even next year.

SGT. JAMIE HENRY,
4TH INFANTRY DIVISION

I'M 23 YEARS OLD. I was drafted on March 8, 1967. ETS'd March 7, 1969. Entered Vietnam August 31, 1967 and returned to the United States in August 1968. I'll be testifying on the murder of innocent civilians, which ultimately culminated in the execution of 19 women and children and the causes behind these murders.

Okay, what I have to say is a direct result of the policy by the United States Army in Vietnam, and what I'm going to detail was reported to the United States Army CID.

On August 8th our company executed a 10-year-old boy. We shot him in the back with a full magazine M-16. Approximately August 16th to August 20th—I'm not sure of the date—a man was taken out of his hootch sleeping, was put into a cave, and he was used for target practice by a lieutenant, the same lieutenant who had ordered the boy killed. Now they used him for target practice with an M-60, an M-16, and a 45. After they had pretty well shot him up with the 60, they backed off aways to see how good a shot they were with a 45 because it's such a lousy pistol. By this time he was dead.

On February 8th—this was after a fire fight and we had lost eight men—on February 8th, we found a man in a spider hole. He was of military age. He spoke no English, of course. We did not have an interrogator, which was one of the problems in the field. He was asked if he were VC and, of course, he kept denying it. "No VC, no VC." He was held down under an APC and he was run over twice—the first time didn't kill him.

About an hour later we moved into a small hamlet, this was in I Corps, it was in a Marine AO. We moved into a small hamlet, 19 women and children were rounded up as VCS (Viet Cong Suspects) and the lieutenant that rounded them up called the captain on the radio and he asked what should be done with them. The captain simply repeated the order that came down from the colonel that morning. The order that came down from the colonel that morning was to kill anything that moves, which you can take anyway you want to take it. When the captain told the lieutenant this, the lieutenant rang off. I got up and I started walking over to the captain thinking that the lieutenant just might do it because I had served in his platoon for a long time. As I started over there, I think the captain panicked—he thought the lieutenant might do it too, and this was a little more atrocious than the other executions that our company had participated in, only because of the numbers. But the captain tried to call him up, tried to get him back on the horn, and he couldn't get a hold of him. As I was walking over to him, I turned, and I looked in the area. I looked toward where the supposed VCS were, and two men were leading a young girl, approximately 19 years old, very pretty, out of a hootch. She had no clothes on so I assumed she had been raped, which was pretty SOP, and she was thrown onto the pile of the 19 women and children, and five men around the circle opened up on full automatic with their M-16s. And that was the end of that.

Now there was a lieutenant who heard this over the radio in our company—he had stayed back with some mortars—he, when we got back to our night location, he was going halfway out of his mind because he had just gotten there, relatively. He was one of these—I don't know, I guess he was naive or something, believed in the old American ideal. He was going nuts. He was going to report it to everybody. After that day he calmed down and the next day he didn't say anything about it. We got in a wretched fire fight the next day and the whole thing was just sort of lost in the intensity of the war.

I don't want to go into the details of these executions because the executions are the direct result of a policy. It's the policy that is important. The executions are secondary because the executions are created by the policy that is, I believe, a conscious policy within the military. Number one, the racism in the military is so rampant. Now you have all heard of the military racism. It's institutionalized; it is policy; it is SOP; you are trained to be a racist. When you go into basic training, you are taught that the Vietnamese are not people. You are taught they are gooks and all you hear is "gook, gook, gook, gook." And once you take the Vietnamese people, or any of the Asian people, because the Asian serviceman in Vietnam is the brunt of the same racism because the GIs over there do not distinguish one Asian from another. They are trained so throughly that all Asians become the brunt of this racism.

You are trained "gook, gook, gook," and once the military has got the idea implanted in your mind that these people are not humans, they are subhuman, it makes it a little bit easier to kill 'em. One barrier is removed, and this is intentional, because obviously, the purpose of the military is to kill people. And if you're not an effective killer, they don't want you. The military doesn't distinguish between North Vietnamese, South Vietnamese, Viet Cong, civilian—all of them are gooks, all of them are considered to be subhuman. None of them are any good, etc. And all of them can be killed and most of them are killed.

Now the second reason for atrocities that occur is because it doesn't take very long for an infantryman in the field to realize that he is fighting for nobody's freedom. You can ask any of the men here. They may have thought they were fighting to protect their mother when they got there, but they sure didn't believe that very long. And this isn't just the grunt. It's the lieutenants, it's the officers in the field. Our captain believed it.

It takes only a few months to be subjugated to the circumstances of Vietnam when you come to the realization that you are not fighting for Ky's freedom; you are not fighting for Thieu's freedom; you are not fighting for your mother's freedom or anybody's freedom. You're just getting your asses shot up and all you want to do is go home.

47.

Trial of Lieutenant William Calley

Probably the bitterest lesson to be brought home to Americans concerning the Vietnam war was the realization that the war was, as one author-psychologist put it, "an atrocity-creating situation." The whole issue of war crimes centered on the famous My Lai massacre of March 1968, and the visible symbol of that affair became army Lt. William L. Calley. In 1970 Calley was charged with slaying civilians at My Lai. His trial, which ran from November 12, 1970 to March 28, 1971, ended in a verdict of guilty. He was sentenced by the court martial to life imprisonment, but there was such a public outcry over the sentence (many felt that Calley was simply a scapegoat) that it was reduced to 20 years. While the public outcry was going on, President Nixon took the unusual step of ordering Calley freed from the stockade and confined to his bachelor apartment under house arrest. Nixon then announced that he would review the case personally. In response to the President's involvement in the case, the prosecutor in the court martial, Captain Aubrey M. Daniel III, wrote a widely published letter to the President criticizing his handling of the matter. The first selection here is Lt. Calley's statement to the court on March 30, just after the verdict had been handed down. The second selection is Captain Daniel's letter to the President.

LIEUTENANT CALLEY:
Statement to the Court

LET ME KNOW if you can't hear me sirs. Your Honor, members of the court, I asked my attorney, George Latimer, and my other attorneys not to go into mitigation in this case. There's a lot of things that aren't appropriate, and I don't think it really matters what type of individual I am.

And I'm not going to stand here and plead for my life or my freedom.

But I would like you to consider a thousand more lives that are going to be lost in Southeast Asia, the thousands more to be imprisoned, not only here in the United States, but in North Vietnam and in hospitals all over the world as amputees.

I've never known a soldier nor did I ever myself ever want to only kill a human being in my entire life. If I have committed a crime, the only crime I've committed is in judgment of my values. Apparently I valued my troops' lives more than I did that of the enemy.

When my troops were getting massacred and mauled by an enemy I couldn't see, I couldn't feel and I couldn't touch—that nobody in the military system ever described them as anything other than Communism.

They didn't give it a race, they didn't give it a sex, they didn't give it an age. They never let me believe it was just a philosophy in a man's mind. That was my enemy out there.

And when it became between me and that enemy, I had to value the lives of my troops—and I feel that was the only crime I have committed.

Yesterday, you stripped me of all my honor. Please, by your actions that you take here today don't strip future soldiers of their honor, I beg of you.

CAPTAIN DANIEL:
Letter to President Nixon

IT IS VERY DIFFICULT FOR ME to know where to begin this letter. As I am unaccustomed to writing letters of protest, I only hope that I can find the words to convey to you my feelings as a United States citizen, and as an attorney, who believes that respect for the law is one of the fundamental bases upon which this nation is founded.

On November 26, 1969, you issued the following statement through your press secretary, Mr. Ronald Ziegler, in referring to the My Lai incident:

> An incident such as that alleged in this case is in direct violation not only of U.S. military policy, but is also abhorrent to the conscience of all the American people.
>
> The secretary of the Army is continuing his investigation. Appropriate action is and will be taken to assure that illegal and immoral conduct as alleged be dealt with in accordance with the strict rules of military justice.
>
> This incident should not be allowed to reflect on the some million and a quarter young Americans who have now returned to the United States after having served in Vietnam with great courage and distinction.

At the time you issued this statement, a general court-martial had been directed for a resolution of the charges which had been brought against Lt. William L. Calley, Jr. for his involvement at My Lai.

On December 8, 1970, you were personally asked to comment on the My Lai incident at a press conference. At that time you made the following statement:

> . . . what appears was certainly a massacre, and under no circumstances was it justified.
>
> One of the goals we are fighting for in Vietnam is to keep the people of South Vietnam from having imposed upon them a government which has atrocity against civilians as one of its policies.
>
> We cannot ever condone or use atrocities against civillians in order to accomplish that goal.

These expressions of what I believed to be your sentiments were truly reflective of my own feelings when I was given the assignment of prosecuting the charges which had been preferred against Lt. Calley. My feelings were generated not by emotionalism or self-righteous indignation but by my knowledge of the evidence in the case, the laws of this nation in which I so strongly believe, and my own conscience.

I knew that I had been given a great responsibility and I only hoped that I would be able to discharge my duties and represent the United States in a manner which would be a credit to the legal profession and our system of justice. I undertook the prosecution of the case without any ulterior motives for personal gain, either financial or political. My only desire was to fulfill my duty as a prosecutor and see that justice was done in accordance with the laws of this nation.

I dedicated myself totally to this end from November of 1969 until the trial was concluded. Throughout the proceedings there was criticism of the prosecution, but I lived with the abiding conviction that once the facts and the law had been presented there would be no doubt in the mind of any reasonable person about the necessity for the prosecution of this case and the ultimate verdict. I was mistaken.

The trial of Lt. Calley was conducted in the finest tradition of our legal system. It was in every respect a fair trial in which every legal right of Lt. Calley was fully protected. It clearly demonstrated that the military justice system which has previously been the subject of much criticism was a fair system.

Throughout the trial, the entire system was under the constant scrutiny of the mass media and the public, and the trial of Lt. Calley was also in a very real sense the trial of the military judicial system. However, there was never an attack lodged by any member of the media concerning the fairness of the trial. There could be no such allegation justifiably made.

I do not believe that there has ever been a trial in which the accused's rights were more fully protected, the conduct of the defense given greater latitude, and the prosecution held to stricter standards. The burden of proof which the government had to meet in this case was not beyond a reasonable doubt but beyond possibility. The very fact that Lt. Calley was an American officer being tried for the deaths of Vietnamese during a combat operation by fellow officers compels this conclusion.

The jury selection, in which customary procedure was altered by providing both the defense and the prosecution with three pre-emptory challenges instead of the usual one, was carefully conducted to ensure the impartiality of those men who were selected.

Six officers, all combat veterans, five having served in Vietnam, were selected. These six men who had served their country well were called upon again to serve their nation as jurors and to sit in judgment of Lt. Calley as prescribed by law.

From the time they took their oaths until they rendered their decision, they performed their duties in the very finest tradition of the American legal system.

If ever a jury followed the letter of the law in applying it to the evidence presented, they did. They are indeed a credit to our system of justice and to the officer corps of the United States Army.

When the verdict was rendered, I was totally shocked and dismayed at the reaction of many people across the nation.

Much of the adverse public reaction I can attribute to people who have acted emotionally and without being aware of the evidence that was presented and perhaps even the laws of this nation regulating the conduct of war.

These people have undoubtedly viewed Lt. Calley's conviction simply as the conviction of an American officer for killing the enemy. Others no doubt out

Lt. William Calley leaves for the stockade in March 1971 after being sentenced to life imprisonment.

of a sense of frustration have seized upon the conviction as a means of protesting the war in Vietnam.

I would prefer to believe that most of the public criticism has come from people who are not aware of the evidence, either because they have not followed the evidence as it was presented or having followed it they have chosen not to believe it.

Certainly, no one wanted to believe what occurred at My Lai, including the officers who sat in judgment of Lt. Calley. To believe, however, that any large percentage of the population could believe the evidence which was presented and approve of the conduct of Lt. Calley would be as shocking to my conscience as the conduct itself since I believe that we are still a civilized nation.

If such be the case, then the war in Vietnam has brutalized us more than I care to believe, and it must cease.

How shocking it is if so many people across this nation have failed to see the moral issue which was involved in the trial of Lt. Calley—that it is unlawful for an American soldier to summarily execute unarmed and unresisting men, women, children and babies.

But how much more appalling it is to see so many of the political leaders of the nation who have failed to see the moral issue or, having seen it, to compromise it for political motives in the face of apparent public displeasure with the verdict.

I would have hoped that all of the leaders of this nation, which is supposed to be the leader within the international community for the protection of the weak and the oppressed regardless of nationality, would have either accepted and supported the enforcement of the laws of this country as reflected by the verdict of the court or not made any statement concerning the verdict until they had had the same opportunity to evaluate the evidence that the members of the jury had.

In view of your previous statements concerning this matter, I have been particularly shocked and dismayed at your decision to intervene in these proceedings in the midst of the public clamor.

Your decision can only have been prompted by the response of a vocal segment of our population who, while no doubt acting in good faith, cannot be aware of the evidence which resulted in Lt. Calley's conviction.

Your intervention has in my opinion, damaged the military judicial system and lessened any respect it may have gained as a result of these proceedings.

You have subjected a judicial system of this country to the criticism that it is subject to political influence when it is a fundamental precept of our judicial system that the legal processes of this country must be kept free from any outside influences.

What will be the impact of your decision upon future trials, particularly those within the military?

Not only has respect for the legal process been weakened and the critics of the military judicial system been given support for their claims of command influence, the image of Lt. Calley, a man convicted of the premeditated murder of at least twenty-one unarmed and unresisting people, as a national hero has been enhanced, while at the same time support has been given to those persons who have so unjustly criticized the six loyal and honorable officers who have done this country a great service by fulfilling their duties as jurors so admirably.

Have you considered those men in making your decisions? The men who since rendering their verdict have found themselves and their families the subject of vicious attacks upon their honor, integrity and loyalty to this nation?

It would seem to me to be more appropriate for you as the President to have said something in their behalf and to remind the nation of the purpose of our legal system and the respect it should command. I would expect that the President of the United States, a man whom I believed should and would provide the moral leadership for this nation, would stand fully behind the law of this land on a moral issue which is so clear and about which there can be no compromise.

For this nation to condone the acts of Lt. Calley is to make us no better than our enemies and make any pleas by this nation for the humane treatment of our own prisoners meaningless.

I truly regret having to have written this letter and wish that no innocent person had died at My Lai on 16 March 1968. But innocent people were killed under circumstances that will always remain abhorrent to my conscience.

While in some respects what took place at My Lai has to be considered to be a tragic day in the history of our nation, how much more tragic would it have been for this country to have taken no action against those who were responsible.

That action was taken, but the greatest tragedy of all will be if political expendiency dictates the compromise of such a fundamental moral principle as the inherent unlawfulness of the murder of innocent persons, making the action and the courage of six honorable men, who served their country so well, meaningless.

Respectfully yours,
Aubrey M. Daniel III

48.

John V. Lindsay: New National Cities

In 1971 the National Urban Coalition's 12-member task force, under the dual chairmanship of Mayor John V. Lindsay of New York and Senator Fred R. Harris of Oklahoma, issued a report entitled The State of the Cities. *The conclusions of the report indicated that conditions in American cities had generally worsened since 1968 when the Kerner Report on urban violence had been published: the races were more polarized; welfare rolls were longer; the housing shortage was critical; public mass transportation was in dire straits; crime rates were up, as was drug addiction; education was nearly bereft of funds; and public institutions were generally undergoing a crisis of confidence. As people moved out of the central cities, the revenue base dropped, and the states were unable and often unwilling to make up for deficits. The only solution seemed to be more reliance on the federal government. The problems were complicated by overlapping jurisdictions and limits to what cities could legally do to solve their dilemmas. The city versus state controversy in New York reached such a pitch that in 1971 a "Committee to Make New York City a State" was formed. Not too far removed from this solution was another that was proposed by Mayor Lindsay in a speech in Indianapolis at a conference on cities of NATO countries, May 26, 1971.*

Source: *New York Times*, June 9, 1971.

It is no longer reasonable to say that under our federal system cities must continue only as supplicants to their states. Cities like Houston and Detroit and Philadelphia are each larger than fifteen of the 50 states. And the budget of my own city is larger than the budget of New York State.

It is time that we rethought the role of these cities in the American governmental system. It is time for us to recognize that they are "national cities," with a unique role to play in our national life and deserving a prominent status in our political structure.

The Federal Government should charter a number of "national cities" with a grant of special powers. Under their charter, national cities could deal directly with Washington on matters of trade, finance and social welfare. They could receive broader federal financial support in order to ensure functions of national responsibility. They could have independent authority on issues of local concern and urban development.

There are parallels in federal law for a national cities charter. In the area of corporate law and finance, the Federal Government has responded to high-priority needs with the creation of federal corporations and nationally chartered banks. The Federal Deposit Insurance Corporation was set up across state and local lines to guarantee bank deposits at a time of economic crisis. T.V.A.—the Tennessee Valley Authority—was established to generate the power for the development of an important region. Amtrak has just moved to operate our declining railroads.

These are different from a "national cities" charter, which would probably require a constitutional amendment to authorize this change in our federal structure. But evolution and change have been the strength of our constitutional system. . . .

Our cities are already corporate entities—but chartered by the states. They perform services for the states, but far more importantly, they fulfill vital federal functions. Their claim to national status is strong and clear. The 25 American cities with over 500,000 population certainly qualify as national cities. Perhaps others would, too.

I know this would confirm the sense of many of us in these great cities that our futures are linked to one another far more than to the governments of our states. We have only recently discovered that Seattle and Baltimore, Atlanta and Milwaukee, San Francisco and Pittsburgh have inherited a common national legacy. Despite state differences—despite a long history of regional competition for national resources, we have learned, as the NATO countries have, that the things that unite us are more important than the things that divide us.

A national cities charter would free these cities from the restraints imposed by unresponsive state governments. It would lift the inequitable burdens and restrictions imposed by state legislatures under the domination of anticity interests. And it would formalize the Federal responsibility for the national scope of urban development.

This is not to suggest that we can "solve" our urban problems by a mere change in structure. The needs of the working man denied marginal security, the jobless veteran, the pressured pensioner, the welfare mother, and the harried commuter in our cities involve the whole range of vital urban services—police, fire, sanitation, health, education, jobs, and recreation. Obviously, a new structure is only a beginning.

This is not to suggest, either, that the three-tiered concept of American federalism is not relevant to the issues of the seventies. It is, and should remain the basic pattern of American government.

But a national cities charter does suggest that after nearly 200 years of the American experience, we have understood the changes that have occurred not only in our own country, but in world civilization.

There are, of course, other fundamental defects in the present structure of our cities. Looking outward to the suburbs, we see the irrationality of present city boundaries as a tax base and a service area. The move toward metropolitan and regional government is spreading. Looking inward, we find that city governments with a million citizens can be remote and unresponsive to their residents. We need a more compact unit of government at the neighborhood level to rebuild a sense of urban community.

Ideally, we might dream of redrawing the map of America so that each national city becomes a metropolitan government which incorporates smaller neighborhood government units. That would be a new metropolitan federalism—with a national, regional and neighborhood government. Some of us have looked longingly at the structure of London for such a model.

But American history, geography and law make that dream unreal for most of our cities. Instead, we will respond to the need for metropolitan and neighborhood government in our own local ways. There will be a mix of structures and arrangements. But we can meet the overriding need for national commitment with a new national cities policy.

Recently, I toured the Brownsville section of my own city with a group of twelve other big-city mayors. Seeing the empty shells of abandoned buildings and the ruins of a once thriving community of 170,000 people, the Mayor of Seattle, Wes Uhlman, said to me: "God, it looks like Dresden after World War II."

I could not help but think that if it were Dresden, it would have long since been rebuilt with substantial American support. Indeed, I have sometimes wondered, if Brownsville had been discovered in Burma, whether our national Government would not have responded far faster and with greater generosity than it has, so far, here at home.

America's $135 billion commitment to foreign aid, including the Marshall Plan, was not only an act of generosity. It also marked the real end of American isolationism. A commitment to a national cities policy would be no less significant—for it would signal the end of America's bias against its own cities.

49.

George Sternlieb: The City as Sandbox

In the generation span from the Great Depression to the early 1970s, the United States changed from an urban to a suburban society. The 1970 census revealed that in this period some 76 million people had fled to the suburbs from the cities, with most of this exodus taking place after World War II. The result for the inner city has been financial and social dislocation of staggering proportions. In the article reprinted here in part, George Sternlieb, professor of urban and regional planning at Rutgers University, assesses the plight some of the older major metropolitan areas in which these population shifts have occurred.

Source: *The Public Interest*, No. 25, Fall 1971.

It is often said that our older central cities are essentially colonies—areas rich in resources which are systematically exploited by the suburban hinterlands. The residents of the latter drive into the city in the morning, use its services all day, and then creep out at night, taking with them much of the city's income and wealth. In one or another variant, this is the vision subscribed to by most city leaders, and they find it a satisfying one. For it implies that the Golden Return is at hand if only the city is given justice. The city's lack of such equity, which creates all its problems, is the result of a shortsighted plot by "outside" interests. Let there be a reallocation of wealth, and all will be well again.

The only problem with this notion is that it is untrue. The size of the constituency which lives outside the cities but still wants to preserve them at any cost grows smaller day by day. It is not exploitation that the core areas must fear; it is indifference and abandonment. The crisis of the cities is a crisis of function. *The major problem of the core areas of our cities is simply their lack of economic value.*

For a long time, the principal role of our inner cities was as a staging area for the floods of immigrants who came from Europe and elsewhere. Cities provided jobs, schools, and an infrastructure which helped earlier groups of immigrants move upward and outward. Although each of these groups left a residue of those who didn't make it, on the whole the city was an extremely successful processing center. Now that these great migrant flows have been reduced to a comparative trickle, the city has lost its *raison d'être.* Formerly the focal point for cheap labor, uniquely amassable there in great volume, it now finds that competition from welfare payments keeps its labor far from cheap and that its traditional jobs have been taken over by Puerto Rico, Formosa, Hong Kong, Singapore, and the like. As its current group of immigrants begins to make it, they too are moving out; but because no new groups are moving in, the city emigrés leave behind a vacuum.

America's major cities are unique in that *they are losing population.* Everywhere else—in Moscow or Buenos Aires or Calcutta—the flow of the agrarian poor off the land to the big city is at its flood stage. We have already gone through that phase; we are now on uncharted territory. To be sure, the Puerto Rican migration may from time to time increase, depending on relative economic conditions, and small pockets of surplus population remain in the south. But for the most part, large-scale immigration to the city is a thing of the past, and much of the migration which does take place bypasses the older population centers for more promising areas.

The absence of replacements for the new emigrés from the city means that some of the first rungs in the nation's traditional ladder of upward mobility have been eliminated. The consequences of this development are already making themselves felt. One of the most common ways for earlier immigrant groups to accumulate capital was as slum landlords. They bought, as they could afford to buy, only the poorest and weakest of structures, which they would rent, at whatever they could get, to their immigrant successors. By trading up the real estate ladder to bigger and better properties, these slumlords became prominent sources of capital for the business-oriented among their own ethnic group. But today, there is no new immigrant group to exploit. Slum tenement ownership has become a dead end, instead of an avenue to wealth —a fact symbolized by the abandoned slum dwelling.

Another way for earlier ethnic groups to move upward and outward was the exploitation of their own countrymen. Members of the immigrant group could rise as brokers between their ethnic labor pool and the external economy. If one wanted to build a sidewalk a generation or two ago, the cheapest labor available was Italian. Because the people who wanted sidewalks built rarely spoke Italian themselves, they dealt with bilingual Italian brokers, who would assemble and supervise the strong backs that were needed for the job. That was the stuff general contractors were made of. Or, to take another case, two generations ago the cheapest needle workers available were non-English-speaking Jews. Their labor was exploited by Jewish sweatshop owners, who served as go-betweens with the department stores of Grand Street.

Of course the needle workers themselves had no chance to become rich; but the go-betweens did.

The need for strong backs and 15-hour-a-day sweated labor has been reduced to almost nothing by the transportation revolution, which has had the effect of homogenizing time and distance. Much of our labor-intensive work is now imported from abroad. Welfare legislation, minimum wages, maximum work hours, and the like have minimized the economic function of the conglomerations of poor-but-willing people in our cities. Similarly, the goad of hunger has been mitigated by the rising level of welfare payments. In Newark a woman with three children lives very badly on welfare payments, but these nevertheless average somewhere around $300 to $350 per month. To live at the same level, a man with a wife and three children would have to make about $5,500 a year. For unskilled labor, that sort of money just isn't available.

Given that the older central cities have lost their capacity to serve as effective staging areas for newcomers, the question inevitably poses itself: What *is* the function of these cities? Permit me to suggest that it has become essentially that of a sandbox.

A sandbox is a place where adults park their children in order to converse, play, or work with a minimum of interference. The adults, having found a distraction for the children, can get on with the serious things of life. There is some reward for the children in all this. The sandbox is given to them as their own turf. Occasionally, fresh sand or toys are put in the sandbox, along with an implicit admonition that these things are furnished to minimize the level of noise and nuisance. If the children do become noisy and distract their parents, fresh toys may be brought. If the occupants of the sandbox choose up sides and start bashing each other over the head, the adults will come running, smack the juniors more or less indiscriminately, calm things down, and then, perhaps, in an act of semi-contrition, bring fresh sand and fresh toys, pat the occupants of the sandbox on the head, and disappear once again into their adult involvements and pursuits.

That is what the city has become—a sandbox. Government programs in the core city have increasingly taken on this cast. A glance at Sar Levitan's *The Great Society's Poor Law* or the Marris and Rein work, or for that matter Tom Wolfe's *Mau-Mauing the Flack Catchers* is enough to make clear the lack of effective flow of much poverty money to its ostensible targets. Instead, this money has been used to create a growing bureaucracy which is sustained by the plight of the poor, the threat of the poor, the misery of the poor, but which yields little in the way of loaves and fishes to the poor. This is the height of sandboxism. When old programs begin to lose their credibility or become unfashionable, they are given new names—therefore, they are new programs. The act of repackaging or relabelling is equated with creativity.

This is not to belittle the importance of government programs. They do have trickle-down effects; they are creating, if not efficiently then certainly in bulk, some measure of leadership, and this leadership is highly cynical about the nature of the faucet from whence all goodies flow and, possibly as a result, is increasingly effective. Perhaps most significantly, these programs have become forms of symbolic action. In their ritualistic aspects they are of particular value. They give psychic satisfaction to the patrons of the poor, convince outsiders—especially the media—that "something is being done," and indicate to the urban poor that some one up there really cares. In a word, these programs are placebos, and they often produce all the authentic, positive results which placebos can have in medical practice. One of the greatest shortcomings of the present administration in Washington is its failure to recognize the salutary placebo-effects of social programs. The failure has been not so much in what it has done, as in what it has called what it has done—not so much in the substance of its programs, as in its rejection of the gamesmanship which does not merely accompany programs but is central to them. . . .

Jobs are leaving the central city. Except for insurance companies, banks, and other institutions which juridically find it difficult to leave, business institutions are virtually deserting the central cities. All major department store chains now do the bulk of their business in the suburbs; the efforts of urban renewal to retain major retail facilities in the core areas have died and are mourned by few. Smaller retailers in secondary urban shopping areas on the "trolley car streets" are also leaving or going out of business. The old mom and pop stores, candy stores, grocery stores on every block, fish stores, neighborhood bakeries, etc., are things of the far past. There has also been a flight of professionals. In the last ten years, Newark has lost half its physicians, and many of those who remain have one foot in the suburbs and are just waiting for their practices to take hold before moving out. As for cultural activities, it is the first-run movie theaters rather than opera houses or symphony halls which have been of especially great economic importance to the vitality of the core city. In Newark, *there is not a single first-run theater left in the entire city of 400,000*, while in the suburbs one of the most desirable pieces of realty available is a site for a movie theater and shopping center. True, the museum and public library still exist downtown, but their wealthy patrons become fewer, galleries must be closed off for lack of money to pay guards, and book acquisition budgets and opening hours must be reduced as the city's budget crisis makes its impact felt.

Meanwhile, the suburbs have achieved critical mass, a scale of population and buying power which permits them to sustain amenities of a type and at a level which once only the central city was capable of sustaining. The shopping center which had at best a single department store branch now has three and soon will have four. The suburban music calendar is evolving from a marginal summer collection of odds and ends to a year-round independent activity. Small suburban hospitals have grown to thousand-bed monsters which can supply all the services and specialists available in the biggest central-city hospitals.

Who is left in the central city? Ride down the Central Avenues and Main Streets of our older cities and you will see that the new tenants are offshoots of the poverty program: pseudo-training programs for the poor, enlarged offices of the Welfare Department, and the like. These are the focal points of the new central-city entrepreneurs, the people who, in the absence of a booming private economy, are trying to make it with government money. The predominance of these public-sector entrepreneurs is an index of the degree to which the central city—its inhabitants' training irrelevant to the needs of the larger society—has become a forgotten back alley in a nation whose principal business still is business.

This process of the "defunctioning" of

the central city would have occurred even if there had not been a problem of race. It would have been considerably slower in that case, and the capacity of society to adjust to it would have been greater, for the pace of change in our central cities has unquestionably been speeded up by racial tensions and fears. But serious though that cost has been, perhaps the greatest cost of the race factor is that it has obscured the real nature of what is going on in the central city. Even if there were no racial difference in our society, there would probably still be as many people on welfare and as many under- or unemployed, and they would still be unwelcome among their more affluent fellow citizens.

What, then, of the future? The first point to be made is that there is no going back in time. The city as we have known it, and the forms of economic and social organization which characterized it, are simply irrecoverable. The folkways of our society have changed; they have also become homogeneous and monolithically dominant as no fashion has ever before been. The thin mist of eloquence emanating from upper-middle-class occupants of high-rise apartments cannot hide the fact that the dominant ethos today is a suburban one. It is as pervasive among minority groups as it is in the society as a whole. Thus, if we define the problems of the city as the gap between the reality of the cities as they exist today and a romanticized fantasy of cities as they used to be—as the economic center of the nation, as the font of civility and graciousness, as the source of everything that warms the hearts of social critics—then those problems are simply unsolvable and always will be unsolvable, at least for many of our older central cities.

Yet there is another way of defining the problems of the cities that does permit some real choice: Are they to become sandboxes entirely, or will we permit them to regain some useful economic function? Shall we optimize the machine, maximize capital investment and capital returns at the cost of human involvement, and then take the largesse so provided and redistribute it in the form of welfare or subsidized, irrelevant, unproductive make-work? Or should we reject the sandbox on the ground that useful, productive work is essential to human well-being, and design our policies to insure that everyone has an opportunity for such work, even if this involves cost to overall economic growth and wealth?

The plight of the inhabitants of our central cities, and the strategy we seem to be adopting to meet that plight, indicate that we are opting for the sandbox. What this will mean for our society in the future we do not fully know; but that the consequences are likely to be cruel and disagreeable has become only too clear.

Most cities by 1980 will be preponderantly black and brown and totally bankrupt.

Fred Harris and John V. Lindsay in *The State of the Cities: Report of the Commission on the Cities in the Seventies (1972)*

50.

ART LINKLETTER: Drug Abuse

The narcotics problem came out of the ghetto and into public consciousness in the late 1960s as the "drug culture," an aspect of the youth movement, or the "counter-culture," as it was frequently called. The use of the hallucinatory drug LSD, promoted by Timothy Leary, and other narcotics soon was widely practiced in the hippie communities, notably in the Haight-Ashbury neighborhood of San Francisco. By the end of the decade drug abuse was described by government officials as an epidemic, and the smoking of marijuana spread far beyond the youth culture. The use of LSD fell off rapidly by 1970, but other "hard" drugs such as "speed" and heroin persisted, education campaigns and stricter laws notwithstanding. One byproduct of growing drug use was an increase in crime, particularly in urban areas. Drug abuse by soldiers in Vietnam was also reported to be very extensive, and many veterans returned home as addicts. In October 1970 Congress passed the toughest drug control law in history, but no great hope was entertained that laws alone could stem the situation. One of the best known spokesmen in the campaign against drugs was television entertainer Art Linkletter, whose daughter had died after using LSD. On September 14, 1971, he spoke to a special United Nations audience in New York on effective ways to deal with the drug menace.

Source: *Vital Speeches*, October 15, 1971.

UNTIL TWO YEARS AGO my life was occupied principally in television and radio in the United States. My specialty was having fun with people. In fact, my best known NBC show for twenty years was called "People Are Funny." My ability to talk with young children was featured on the CBS network five times a week, for twenty-five years.

My professional life as an entertainer kept me on the sunny side of the street, with happy detours to every part of the world visiting my "adopted" children. Over the last thirty years, Mrs. Linkletter and I, acting as "foster parents," have taken care of underprivileged and orphan children in France, Italy, Germany, Greece, China, Japan, The Phillipines, Vietnam, and Peru. Our own five children learned to love their overseas brothers and sisters through visits, letters, and the exchange of presents.

Then, part of my life died in October 1969, when our beautiful daughter Diane was lost in the aftermath of LSD use. She would have been 21 years old that month. She was a victim of the reckless urge to experiment with hallucinogenic chemicals that became the fashionable thing to do among the young people of the world in the mid-sixties. In Hollywood this insane desire to take pills, marijuana and LSD swept through the film colony, and many, many beautiful young sons and daughters of my friends have been ruined because of their teenage yearning to be "part of the crowd."

That is why I am here today.

I am here to tell you something of what I have learned during these past two years.

Most of my generation had fixed ideas about drug addicts and dope that have been radically altered through research and knowledge based on fact—not myth. Until recently, we thought that marijuana was addictive and invariably led to narcotics. We thought all "pushers" were evil criminals sent to school yards to entice small children into becoming dope addicts. We thought that people who took any drugs for excitement and fun, or to forget their problems, were criminals and should be put in jail.

Today, we have learned that excessive users of psychotropic or narcotic drugs are sick people and only incidentally criminals. We have learned that pushers are often our own children searching for status or thrills or extra money. We have found out that you cannot stop drug abuse by making stricter laws, bigger jails, or by hiring more policemen. We have learned that drug abuse is a complex, perplexing subject that can never be simply, miraculously solved by some new drug or by some push-button method. And we have learned that it is not a passing fad that will go away with acid rock music or mod clothes. Drug abuse is on the doorstep of the world to stay. It is no new problem. . . .

Drug abuse is as complex and contradictory as it is damaging. It has been easy in the past to pose a simple cause-effect-solution syndrome. For example, we say, "The person took drugs. The person met with tragedy. Eliminate the drugs, and you have eliminated the possibility of tragedy."

I can report to you from my own tragic experience that such a simplistic model is invalid. There are too many factors at work, too much uncertainty about human behavior and human interaction, to dismiss the drug abuse problem by talking only about the drugs.

The phenomenon of drug abuse touches our hearts, our minds, our courage and our imagination. A simple answer simply will not do. . . .

The American people have been forced to acknowledge the bitter irony of our times. We walk on the moon, yet at least 250,000 of us are heroin addicts. We probe the secrets of the living cell, yet our hospitals are crowded with men and women who cannot throw off alcohol or other drugs. We say that our future is in our young people, yet every year sees increases in the misuse of drugs among the young.

So I am talking today not about what should be done in the rest of the world, but what must be done in all of the world. Not your nation, not my nation, but all our brothers and sisters share the pain and need our help.

It will not be easy to map out a worldwide plan to combat drug abuse. Perhaps it is wisest to begin by taking note of some of the things we should not do, some of the pitfalls we should avoid, as we begin to attack the problem.

First, let no nation speak with arrogance or false wisdom on the subject of drug abuse. Chauvinism and political pride have no place in our deliberations. My country has made this mistake in the past, and our present crisis makes a mockery of our boasts. I am confident that the United States will learn from its own mistaken attempts to prescribe drug abuse cures for the world, and I am equally confident that other nations will exercise good judgment in this regard.

Second, let no nation be guilty of saying that "it's somebody else's responsibility." No nation in the world is free from at least some form of drug abuse and no nation should attempt to excuse itself from the world-wide effort to combat it.

Third, let us avoid secrecy and intrigue in our work. The medical, scientific, academic and law enforcement communities of the world must be allowed to cooperate freely if we are to make any headway. There is nothing to be gained by refusing to share resources and insights with each other. In fact, there is everything to lose.

Fourth, let us refrain from making wrong-headed assumptions about alleged "character flaws" on the part of one people or another. It might be popular in some circles for one country to dismiss another's drug abuse problem as the result of ethnic or cultural deficiencies. Clearly, though, it would be incorrect. If any character is being tested, it is the spirit and strength of the whole human family.

Finally, let us not fall prey to those who would use drug abuse as an excuse to divide the world. Let us resist the fearmongers and the wall-builders. I do not think there is much chance for success in a worldwide campaign of repression, recrimination and revenge. Nor do I think the people of the world would tolerate any attempt to drive wedges between countries or hemispheres.

My fear is that we will again be deceived by the mistaken notion that we have "cures" for drug abuse, and that those "cures" need only be applied around the world with sufficient force, and then the drug abuse problem will disappear. . . .

In my travels throughout the United States of America, in small towns or big cities, I have found that there is unanimous "head nodding" to my warning statements but too often no action. Until you have personally been touched by the degradation and death that follows drug abuse, the inclination is to "let the other fellow do it." The defensive statements from every segment of our society are repudiated by what I like to call "universal" guilt. All of us, in one way or another, are partly responsible for the drug abuse epidemic.

To begin with, we are living in a drug-oriented society. We find people of all ages, and from every walk of life, increasingly turning to chemicals for relief from stress.

As I see it, there are today two separate but related problems involved in heavy drug abuse. There is, first, the hard core narcotic use, and second, there is the related illegal international trade. This we may call the traditional drug problem. One is a dangerous sickness that should be treated . . .the other is a death dealing trade that should be struck down. . . .

Here in the U. S. we have seen in the past decade millions of middle class youngsters turning to pot, acid, uppers and downers to escape from boredom or anxiety, to have a thrilling experience they've heard about or read about, to achieve a sense of belonging, to achieve "understanding" or "insight," or to express independence and sometimes hostility.

The drug abusers cut across all economic, religious, and political lines. They are found in small and large towns. They come from liberal or conservative homes. And they have followed the example and leadership of acid rock stars until taking drugs has become almost a puberty rite in America. Now, heroin and cocaine are becoming their "in" drugs.

Most of these millions of youngsters and Thank God—are only experimenters who will try so called "soft" drugs a few times and then discard them. The next largest group become week-end, recreational smokers or drug users who use pot and pills at parties of their friends. Then we come to the 10 percent who have come to depend on drugs almost daily to get them through their problems and keep them happy. And finally, the smallest hard core group of users, those who have insured the tragedy of drug abuse with the hypodermic needle: injecting amphetamines and heroin.

At this moment in time, the people of the United States are thoroughly aroused over the problem of drug abuse. In a recent Roper poll of public opinion, drugs were voted as the number one problem over war, unemployment, and violence in the streets. . . .

In the last three years, the federal government will have spent a little over a quarter of a billion dollars to develop programs to deal with drugs. Funding for the overall federal program jumped to about $135 million in 1971. Of this latter amount, the United States proposed to apply the funds as follows: $46.6 million for law enforcement and $90 million for treatment, rehabilitation, education and research and other support.

America is aroused. America is doing something about it. But trying to get people to stop taking drugs just because society decrees them illegal is trying to bail the Atlantic with a teacup. . . .

I recommend that the Economic and Social Council and its Commission on Narcotic Drugs begin at once to find answers to basic questions we must face if we are to put an end to drug abuse. These questions have to do not with methods of detection, or techniques for investigation, or codified approaches to human behavior; instead, they are questions about human life.

How do drugs become a part of daily life for millions of people? We know that some people reject drug abuse while others are caught by it. Why does this happen?

What about human goals and aspirations? Is there anything left to accomplish, or have we done everything there is to do? Is drug abuse a substitute for other risks we no longer need to take?

How do dangerous drugs get a death-grip on young people in underdeveloped nations, and in slum neighborhoods of rich nations? If an empty, agonizing life drives people to drugs, how do we change that life?

Why are there so many suicides in the world? Why do so many people arrive at a personal crisis unable to face it, resolve it, overcome it? Why is drug abuse so often a part of the tragic picture?

Is life boring? In the final analysis, do we turn to drugs because life holds so little challenge, so little meaning?

Can we talk to each other anymore? Some have said that communication is easier now than ever before, because of technology. But has technology helped us communicate, or has it merely hastened the flow of empty words over the great gulf that divides us?

These are the kinds of questions that must be answered if we are to do away with the abuse of drugs. I do not pretend that finding the answers is all that we must do, but it is certainly the first thing we must do.

The United Nations, through its agencies will serve all mankind if it begins the dialogue on these compelling questions. Working in this way, you will be going to the heart of the drug abuse crisis, and the results of your labors will enrich the understanding of the specialists in medicine, sociology, education, law enforcement and human development. The fund which has been established would be flexible enough to meet this challenge.

An independent council I head may serve as an example of this point. This national council combines the energies and skills of more than 100 diverse groups, agencies and institutions. It allows its member organizations to share information and resources, and by so doing, develops an interdisciplinary approach to our struggle with drug abuse education and treatment.

The operating philosophy of the council is that no one approach is likely to be sufficient in the face of the staggering complexity of the problem. Therefore, a multidisciplinary approach is required, one in which a sharing of insights and skills is not only necessary, but possible.

I would recommend this operating philosophy to the United Nations, because I believe it holds the most promise for our work: it is based on cooperation and interaction, and its goal is material improvement in the programs we develop to combat drug abuse.

51.

Richard M. Nixon: Wage and Price Controls

The stock market collapse of 1970 and the recession that followed it found the economy with an unemployment rate of six percent by mid-1971 and an inflation that balked at control. It was apparent to most members of the Nixon Administration that slowing down inflation by moving into a recession had not worked. Gradually, from the end of 1970 until August 1971, the President began to change his mind about how to deal with the economy. One of the strongest influences on his thinking during 1971 was his new secretary of the treasury, John Connally, who urged a system of controls as a means to reverse the unfavorable balance of trade and slow inflation. On August 15 the President went on national television to announce his new economic program of wage and price controls, and fiscal and monetary changes. The major portion of his address is reprinted here. The President also recommended to Congress a cut in taxes, including repeal of the seven percent excise on automobiles, and an increase in the personal exemption for 1971 and 1972.

Source: *Vital Speeches*, September 1, 1971: "A New Economic Policy."

Prosperity without war requires action on three fronts. We must create more and better jobs; we must stop the rise in the cost of living; we must protect the dollar from the attacks of international money speculators.

We are going to take that action—not timidly, not halfheartedly and not in piecemeal fashion. We are going to move forward to the new prosperity without war as befits a great people, all together and along a broad front.

The time has come for a new economic policy for the United States. Its targets are unemployment, inflation and international speculation, and this is how we are going to attack those targets:

First, on the subject of jobs. We all know why we have an unemployment problem. Two million workers have been released from the armed forces and defense plants because of our success in winding down the war in Vietnam. Putting those people back to work is one of the challenges of peace, and we have begun to make progress. Our unemployment rate today is below the average of the four peace-time years of the nineteen-sixties, but we can and we must do better than that.

The time has come for American industry, which has produced more jobs at higher real wages than any other industrial system in history, to embark on a bold program of new investment of production for peace. To give that system a powerful new stimulus I shall ask the Congress when it reconvenes after its summer recess to consider as its first priority the enactment of the Job Development Act of 1971.

I will propose to provide the strongest short-term incentive in our history to invest in new machinery and equipment that will create new jobs for Americans: a 10 percent job development credit for one year effective as of today with a five percent credit after Aug. 15,1972.

This tax credit for investment in new equipment will not only generate new jobs. It will raise productivity; it will make our goods more competitive in the years ahead.

Second, I will propose to repeal the seven percent excise tax on automobiles effective today. This will mean a reduction in price of about $200 per car.

I shall insist that the American auto industry pass this tax reduction on to the nearly 8 million customers who are buying automobiles this year. Lower prices will mean that more people will be able to afford new cars, and every additional 100,000 cars sold means 25,000 new jobs.

Third, I propose to speed up the personal-income-tax exemptions scheduled for January 1, 1973, to January 1, 1972, so that taxpayers can deduct an extra $50 for each exemption one year earlier than planned.

This increase in consumer spending power will provide a strong boost to the economy in general and to employment in particular.

The tax reductions I am recommending, together with this broad upturn of the economy, which has taken place in the first half of this year, will move us strongly forward toward a goal this nation has not reached since 1956 fifteen years ago: prosperity with full employment in peacetime.

Looking to the future, I have directed the Secretary of the Treasury to recommend to the Congress in January new tax proposals for stimulating research and development of new industries and new techniques to help provide the 20 million new jobs that America needs for the young people who will be coming into the job market in the next decade.

To offset the loss of revenue from these tax cuts, which directly stimulate new jobs. I have ordered today a $4.7-billion cut in Federal spending.

Tax cuts to stimulate employment must be matched by spending cuts to restrain inflation. To check the rise in the cost of government I have ordered a postponement of pay raises and a five percent cut in Government personnel.

I have ordered a ten percent cut in foreign economic aid. In addition, since the Congress has already delayed action on two of the great initiatives of this Administration. I will ask Congress to amend my proposals to postpone the implementation of revenue sharing for three months and welfare reform for one year.

In this way, I am reordering our budget priorities so as to concentrate more on achieving our goal of full employment.

The second indispensable element of the new prosperity is to stop the rise in the cost of living. One of the cruelest legacies of the artificial prosperity produced by war is inflation. Inflation robs every American, every one of you. The 20 million who are retired and living on fixed incomes—they are particularly hard hit. Homemakers find it harder than ever to balance the family budget. And 80 million American wage earners have been on a treadmill.

For example, in the four war years between 1965 and 1969, your wage increases were completely eaten up by price increases. Your paychecks were higher, but you were no better off. We have made progress against the rise in the cost of living. From the high point of six percent a year in 1969, the rise in consumer prices has been cut to four percent in the first half of 1971. But just as is the case in our fight against unemployment, we can and we must do better than that. The time has come for decisive action—action that will break the vicious circle of spiraling prices and costs.

I am today ordering a freeze on all prices and wages throughout the United States for a period of 90 days.

In addition I call upon corporations to extend the wageprice freeze to all dividends. I have today appointed a Cost-of-Living Council within the Government. I have directed this council to work with leaders of labor and business to set up the proper mechanism for achieving continued price and wage stability after the 90-day freeze is over.

Let me emphasize two characteristics of this action. First, it is temporary. To put the strong vigorous American economy into a permanent straitjacket would lock in unfairness; it would stifle the expansion of our free-enterprise system, and second, while the wage-price freeze will be backed by Government sanctions, if necessary, it will not be accompanied by the establishment of a huge price-control bureaucracy.

I am relying on the voluntary cooperation of all Americans—each one of you: workers, employers, consumers—to make this freeze work. Working together, we will break the back of inflation, and we will do it without the mandatory wage and price controls that crush economic and personal freedom.

The third indispensable element in building the new prosperity is closely related to creating new jobs and halting inflation. We must protect the position of the American dollar as a pillar of monetary stability around the world.

In the past seven years, there's been an average of one international monetary crisis every year. Now who gains from these crises? Not the working man, not the investor, not the real producers of wealth. The gainers are the international money speculators: because they thrive on crises, they help to create them.

In recent weeks, the speculators have been waging an all-out war on the American dollar. The strength of a nation's currency is based on the strength of that nation's economy, and the American economy is by far the strongest in the world.

Accordingly, I have directed the Secretary of the Treasury to take the action necessary to defend the dollar against the speculators.

I directed Secretary Connally to suspend temporarily the convertibility of the dollar into gold or other reserve assets except in amounts and conditions determined to be in the interest of monetary stability and in the best interests of the United States.

Now what is this action—which is very technical—what does it mean to you? Let me lay to rest the bugaboo of what is called "devaluation." If you want to buy a foreign car or take a trip abroad, market conditions may cause your dollar to buy slightly less.

But, if you are among the overwhelming majority of Americans who buy American-made products, in America, your dollar will be worth just as much tomorrow as it is today.

The effect of this action, in other words, will be to stablize the dollar. Now this action will not win us any friends among the international money traders. But our primary concern is with the American workers, and with their competition around the world.

To our friends abroad, including the many responsible members of the international banking community who are dedicated to stability in the flow of trade, I give this assurance: The United States has always been and will contunue to be a forward-looking and trustworthy trading partner.

In full cooperation with the International Monetary fund and those who trade with us, we will press for the necessary reforms to set up an urgently needed new international monetary system. Stability and equal treatment is in everybody's best interest. I am determined that the American dollar must never again be a hostage in the hands of international speculators.

I am taking one further step to protect the dollar, to improve our balance of payments and to increase jobs for Americans. As a temporary measure I am today imposing an additional tax of 10 percent on goods imported into the United States.

This is a better solution for international trade than direct controls on the amount of imports. This import tax is a temporary action. It isn't directed against any other country. It's an action to make certain that American products will not be at a disadvantage because of unfair exchange rates.

When the unfair treatment is ended, the import tax will end as well. As a result of these actions the product of American labor will be more competitive and the unfair edge that some of our foreign competition has will be removed.

This is a major reason why our trade balance has eroded over the past 15 years.

At the end of World War II, the economies of the major industrial nations of Europe and Asia were shattered. To help them get on their feet and to protect their freedom, the United States has provided over the past 25 years $143-billion in foreign aid.

That was the right thing for us to do. Today, largely with our help, they have regained their vitality. They have become our strong competitors, and we welcome their success.

But now that other nations are economically strong, the time has come for them to bear their fair share of the burden of defending freedom around the world. The time has come for exchange rates to be set straight, and for the major nations to compete as equals.

There is no longer any need for the United States to compete with one hand tied behind her back.

The range of actions I have taken and proposed tonight on the job front, on the inflation front, on the monetary front, is the most comprehensive new economic policy to be undertaken in this nation in four decades.

52.

DANIEL ELLSBERG: Interview on the Pentagon Papers

On June 13, 1971, the New York Times *began publishing a collection of hitherto classified documents derived from a study made during the administration of President Johnson concerning American involvement in Vietnam. Collectively these documents were referred to as the "Pentagon papers." On June 15 the Justice Department obtained a restraining order barring the* Times *from publishing any more of the documents, only to have other papers take up the effort. On June 30 the Supreme Court ruled in favor of the* Times *and on July 1 the* Times *and the* Washington Post *resumed printing portions of the Pentagon papers daily. Having lost the fight to bar publication of the documents, the federal government undertook a prosecution of the man who had originally leaked them to the press, Daniel Ellsberg. He was indicted on June 28 by a Los Angeles grand jury on charges of violating the Espionage Act and of stealing government property. The trial of Ellsberg and his alleged co-conspirator, Anthony Russo, Jr., ended in a mistrial in December 1972. A second trial began in January 1973, but by late spring the case had become deeply involved with the Watergate affair. It was revealed that a special White House investigative unit had burglarized the office of Ellsberg's psychiatrist. Trial judge William M. Byrne also told of having been offered the directorship of the Federal Bureau of Investigation by presidential advisor John Erlichman. On May 11, 1973, Judge Byrne dismissed all charges against the defendants and ruled out any new trial on the same charges. In the autumn of 1971 Ellsberg granted an interview to J. Robert Moskin, an editor of* Look, *in which he explained why he had released the Pentagon papers to the public. Parts of the lengthy interview are reprinted here.*

Source: *Look*, October 5, 1971: "Ellsberg Talks."

When you turned yourself in, you said you had made the Pentagon papers public as a responsible American citizen. Really, the essential question we want to talk about is: What is the moral responsibility of the citizen who thinks he sees his government doing evil?

I was in dual position. Like every American, I had a feeling of obligation to the Constitution and to my fellow citizens. At the same time, I was a researcher through most of this period, doing consulting for the Government, and someone whose reflexes in terms of loyalty had been set by 12 to 15 years of service to the Executive Branch—15 years would include the three years with the Marine Corps.

I question the identification of the state or the Government with the Executive Branch or with the President. All the members of the Executive Branch are the creatures of one elected representative of the people, the President. When you look at the entire Executive Branch, you confront this enormous structure of somewhat conflicting institutions in which only one man has been elected by the people. The effects of this are very great.

In the early sixties, before I ever got on the subject of Vietnam, I was granted interagency access at a very high level to study the decision-making process in crises like the Cuban missile crisis, Suez, Skybolt, U-2 and so forth. In fact, the arrangements for that study were set up by Walt Rostow, who was then head of the Policy Planning Council of the State Department.

I was at Rand and was brought to Washington as the sole researcher for what was to be a year's study. That study exposed to me the importance of the President in every one of these crises, the peculiar, very powerful influence of the President's personal judgment and personal preconceptions.

This conflicts with another view of the decision process in Government, which says that the President, although he may look powerful, is given surprisingly little leeway by the bureaucratic agencies under him, in which to influence policy, that he has to fight for influence, to connive, to maneuver, in order to have any impact whatever.

It's a position that's very plausible from within the system. The bureaucrat gets a sense that presidential policy reflects the success of one or another agency in tying his hands. He doesn't have a sense of presidential initiative and power.

The most startling thing to me was to discover how critical the President's role had been, that if his hands were tied at all, it was because he chose to cooperate in having his position forced by one pressure or another. . . .

And something else that I also came to understand: Because the President is a politician up for reelection, a man who expects to have his reputation recorded in history books, and a leader of a party, a man who is concerned with getting a legislative program through Congress, all these political considerations bear on presidential decisions in a way unlike the decision-making of any other bureaucrat. To take the U-2 example, Eisenhower's decision to announce the truth, rather than tell a lie, was undoubtedly influenced by domestic political considerations. In the opinion of his political advisers, to deny he knew of the flight could be damaging in the 1960 elections and sustain the belief that Eisenhower had been a know-nothing President.

The basic problem is we have a system, then, with a lot of people who don't know what it means to be accountable to the public. The Congress is the enemy, just as the press is the enemy. And the public is seen by members of the Executive in general as the great beast, treacherous, ignorant, irrational, not to be respected, either individually or in the mass.

As part of the elite, the bureaucracy, you must have seen things this way to some degree. And then somehow there was a metamorphosis? Or do you still feel this way now?

Not at all. For example, to come right up to the present, the views that seem to me appropriate in understanding the conflict in Vietnam are views that are held not by the elites that have monopolized Executive positions for generations but by the mass of the people speaking through public-opinion polls and through elections—especially polls, by the way, because it still is not evident that the mass of the public cares enough about foreign policy, and even war and peace, to vote on that issue predominantly. I think that's regrettable.

The polls reveal that most people think we should get out of Vietnam and it was a mistake to have gotten in. I share that view. Obviously, the Administration does not, and many of the former officials who were my colleagues do not. It's not all that hard to explain. The people must face the issues in terms of their own sons and of the impact of the war on their lives, considerations that the man in the Administration—whose life is much improved by the condition of war, which swells the Executive and Executive salaries—doesn't have to face.

How did you come out of this bureaucratic point of view toward your present one? Was it related to your going to Vietnam?

We might go into the question of why I went to Vietnam. I went to Vietnam in 1965 in large part because I felt that I had been involved in the policy discussions and the planning that had led to the sending of American soldiers and draftees over to fight a war in Asia and that I should be over there with them and no longer viewing the war from Washington. . . .

What was your reaction to those realities?

That the programs we were pursuing had no chance of succeeding. They were not in any way proceeding as people thought they were back in Washington. Of course, that in itself didn't speak to the question of whether the war was a just one, or whether the aims we were pursuing were right for us to pursue. . . .

What made you ask why, finally?

Coming back to this country. In July of '67, I came back to a country where armed helicopters were flying over my hometown of Detroit. In fact, I wanted to visit my father, who lived on the outskirts of Detroit, and I had to cancel the trip because it was not clear just then that I could get to his house from the airport during the Detroit riot. Earlier, there was the Newark riot.

It wasn't hard to relate this to the inattention to domestic factors that the war was causing. So you immediately became far more aware of the domestic costs of the war, and that forced you to look harder at the question of whether it was really essential for us to be there.

So by mid-'67, I had already reached the opinion that we should get out of the war. Then the next big thing, the crucial thing for me, was contact with the Pentagon study, because that called into question the aims for which we were supposedly intervening over there and imposing these costs both on the Vietnamese and on our own people.

While working on the Pentagon study, it was astonishing, in going through files at the Pentagon, to read the national intelligence estimates from 1950 on. I read all those estimates, probably 40 of them covering a period of almost 20 years, and it was astonishing to discover that, with a few exceptions, they were very realistic, very detailed and skeptical. On the whole, they gave the President quite good predictions of what to expect.

That posed a really enormous puzzle. How did a succession of Presidents bring themselves time after time to increase our involvement, or even to sustain it, when they were being told by the national intelligence estimates that what they were doing would be inadequate to achieve any kind of success and could lead only to getting out in the future or escalating further? Why had Presidents apparently ignored this information?

The simple answer of our interests in avoiding World War III or the total Communistic take-over of Southeast Asia or a great loss of prestige didn't seem to account for these decisions, because the estimates, and even the recommendations made by the bureaucracy, indicated strongly that we would not be able to achieve those interests by what we were doing. So I had to look for other explanations, other interests.

I think that few bureaucrats appreciate, unless they get to fairly high levels—and I was privileged to work at the level of the assistant secretary, as a special assistant to John McNaughton—the peculiar kind of White House influence that goes into policy. The presidential role as a whole is not committed to paper very much, and in particular, the presidential interest in domestic politics does not get on paper because it is a shibboleth that domestic politics ought not to influence foreign policy.

When you use that term "domestic politics" in this way, what are you talking about?

I mean a variety of things, all wrapped up together. I don't mean only the problem of getting elected in the next presidential election, although that's a central aspect to it.

I also mean the problem of getting an entire legislative program through Congress, the degree to which the President pays deference and attention to the desires and prejudices of particular leaders in Congress. It also means his interest in congressional elections that will win him support in Congress, which will help him not only in his presidential campaign but in his legislative program. And it means his relations with the press for all these purposes. And his ability to get appointments through, and it affects the budget. Almost nothing of all this is ever mentioned in official writings. When people talk of the limitations of the Pentagon papers, that's a major limitation.

By the time you got involved in the Pentagon study, you felt we should get out as soon as possible. Was the study set up to prove this, as it has been charged, or was this just your own feeling?

Oh, no, no, no. This was my personal feeling. When they say most people in the study felt that way, it happens to be true, but it ignores the fact that most people in the Pentagon felt that by this time. Most people in the Government who had any experience with Vietnam had by late '67 come to feel that the official optimism that was coming out of the top, from Rusk, from Westmoreland, was quite unjustified. This was even before the Tet offensive, and most of the work on the study was done after the Tet offensive.

So that was one metamorphosis of Daniel Ellsberg, from participating enthusiastically in the Vietnam war to wanting to get out of it as soon as possible. There was another metamorphosis, from participating in the study to participation in its public disclosure.

Right. The study immediately showed policy emerging not simply as an interplay of bureaucrats and agencies, but as a result of deliberate choices by Presidents who had been told that they would probably not succeed.

Remember, I did my work on the '61 volume of the study basically in November and December 1967. That was only one example; it didn't show me a pattern. It just set up some puzzles. Why had Kennedy done this? It wasn't until early '69, a year later, that most of the study actually became available. At that time, to my knowledge, I was the only man at Rand—actually, in the country—who was on Government funds, spending full time doing research drawing lessons from our Vietnam experience.

When I started on the study, I was still recovering from hepatitis that I had caught in Vietnam, and they were very anxious to get me. I was only willing to do it on condition that I would be able to profit from it intellectually by reading the whole study. That was the price I asked for participating as a researcher. So I was given the commitment that I would be able to read this thing ultimately. No other researcher got that commitment on the study. Rand was not given access. I was only given personal access on the basis of this prior agreement. The point then was that I was the only researcher in the country with authorized access to the entire study.

Because of this promise, I was authorized by the Assistant Secretary of Defense to have personal access to the entire study. After all, I didn't steal these documents and I didn't use them for my own profit.

The startling thing that came out of them was how the same sets of alternatives began to appear to each President, and ultimately the choice was neither to go for broke and adopt military recommendations, nor negotiate a settlement to get out. The decisions year after year were to continue the war, although all predictions pointed to a continued stalemate with this kind of approach and thus to prolong the war indefinitely.

That meant that no one President was responsible in the sense that he acted very differently from his counterparts in other Administrations. It came to seem not like Kennedy's war or Johnson's war. It was a pattern of behavior that went far beyond any one individual that held that position.

I think now to a large extent it was an American President's war. It was a war no American President had, let's say, the courage to turn down or to stay out of. From a military point of view, you could say he didn't have the courage to go in to win, but on the other hand, he was assured by intelligence estimates—which checked out pretty well, year by year—that the kinds of things proposed by the military would not win.

The explanation seemed to me contained in the very earliest period—'49 and '50—when we did get involved. There one can see the motivation quite clearly. It was the motivation of the Democratic President not to add the fall of Indochina to the fall of China. The very fact the decision-making looked similar year by year from then on, supported the conjecture that no American President, Republican or Democrat, wanted to be the President who lost the war or who lost Saigon.

Was this a heritage from the McCarthy era in a way?

Yes, that's the way it was seen—as a fear of McCarthyism. No question about it.

When did you get the feeling that the public ought to know what was in the Pentagon papers?

That came late. I got the last of these documents, which covered the earliest period, in August, 1969, as late as that. It was really reading those at the last that impressed me with how much an American war this had been, with the fact that from the earliest period we consciously were aware, especially in North Vietnam, that we were imposing our own interests on the desires of the majority of the Vietnamese people who wanted peace and who in fact wanted a government under Ho Chi Minh.

But we were consciously opposing those desires for reasons that didn't seem very legitimate. It wasn't until I had read those final documents that I began to think that these papers themselves were highly relevant to the current process, even under Nixon, of getting out.

It was in the early fall of '69 that I began to deliver these documents to the Senate Foreign Relations Committee.

Even that was an enormous change for me—to go outside the Executive Branch. It was still within the U.S. Government, but it was a decision for which I expected to go to prison for the rest of my life.

But you felt it was important enough?

Yes, because, you see, the documents themselves had the lesson in them, it seemed to me, that Nixon was the fifth President in succession to be subjected to the same pressures that had led four other Presidents to maintain involvement; that his assurances that he had no intention of staying in Indochina were no more to be believed than other Presidents' assurances; that it was a Vietnamese war, and not ours, and that whatever his feelings were as of '69, the more he got involved, the more sure it was that he would stay involved.

For domestic political reasons?

Yes, that's right. That's the way I saw it. Now, there are other explanations, but they point in the same direction. One is that he was a true believer, like all the others to a greater or lesser degree, and he really felt it was essential that we not get out of the war. That's an alternative explanation, and they're not entirely competing; they can both be true. They go in the same direction.

Another lesson of the study is, to me, that domestic political considerations were so important to the President that mere discussion or argument within the Executive Branch would never affect that policy. The only way to affect it was to change the political calculations by the President, to change the political pressures. You could think of that very easily as a favor to the President. You could say that if the President wants to get out, the only way to make it possible for him is to assure him that he will not be subject to fatal attack and he will not be attacked by the other party if he does get out.

So my first efforts were entirely along the lines of getting Congress and leading Democrats to urge the President, or even require him, to get out, so that the responsibility wouldn't fall entirely on his shoulders.

I sent a letter around to leading Democrats, urging them, in effect, to take the position: it's not your war, Mr. Nixon; it's our war; we made the mistakes; don't you make those same mistakes. Get us out of it. I was communicating with a lot of Democrats, urging them to come out for total withdrawal. They were quite unwilling. So that failed.

At the same time, six of us at Rand who had worked on Vietnam with official access to the documents put out a letter calling for total unilateral withdrawal within a year. But in the President's speech of November 3, he put his stamp so strongly on the policy, making it Nixon's war, that it was clear he would fight any effort to get out faster. From then on, it meant that you couldn't share responsibility with the President; Congress, if it was to get us out of the war, would have to take almost total responsibility.

Now we're getting very much into the question of responsibility. Congress (including the whole set of doves) recoiled from taking on themselves the whole responsibility for what might happen if we got out of Vietnam entirely. So we have a situation where the President is not willing to share the responsibility. The Congress is, I think, by this time ready to share it with the President but unwilling to take full responsibility. And so on both sides, the war goes on.

I think we could have gotten out two years ago if Nixon had been willing to share the risk. I think Nixon's really a true believer in the cold-war premises and does not feel we ought to get out. And this feeling is reinforced by his political reading of what might happen to him if he did.

Anyway, your approach to the Congress didn't work.

It didn't work because Congress did not hold hearings. Frankly, from then on I did try, I won't go into details, but I did try a number of other official channels. I hoped there might be ways of getting the study into the courts. I specifically hoped that some kind of proceedings, not necessarily criminal, but civil suits or injunctions claiming the unconstitutionality of the war, would provide a channel whereby the Pentagon documents could enter public consciousness.

A number of leading lawyers took the attitude that we don't have the kind of documentation that was available to the Nuremberg war-crimes tribunal. I said you shouldn't think it impossible that documents as comprehensive as those available to the Nuremberg war-crimes tribunal would be available. I'd even gone further with some and described the study. In fact, I proposed myself as a possible defendant or witness, if somebody could get a case going, in hopes that the study could be subpoenaed. Nobody rose to that at all.

Is that when you went to the press, to the public directly?

No. Actually, I began to do the next two things simultaneously. I began to think the press might be the only outcome, but with the regrettable feature that doing it through the press—I had gotten some legal advice on this—would be the surest way to get myself in prison for a long time.

Do you expect to go to prison?

Less than I did when this arose. Now that lawyers have been looking at it, the law on the subject is much less clear than I had assumed it was. It is simply not clear at this point that I have broken any law.

You said you did two things simultaneously.

The other was to go back to members of Congress and try them out on an individual basis rather than on a committee basis. I talked to a number of them and had hopes that they would introduce this stuff themselves into the *Congressional Record* or make speeches on it. That, plus the newspapers. So in the end it came out through the newspapers. That was the result of a year-and-a-half process.

By this spring, I had to say that since the fall of '69 when I started this, 9,000 more American men had died and hundreds of thousands of Vietnamese had died. Moreover, two more invasions had occurred, and it looked like the next thing facing us was the heavy bombing of North Vietnam, which would undoubtedly fail to succeed and might be followed by an invasion of North Vietnam. So again the urgency seemed very great.

Maybe we could go back to one thing. You asked, was I ready to stand this prison sentence? Well, if you start mixing with people who are active against the war, soon you begin to meet a lot of people who are on their way to prison for draft resistance or who have been in prison. I found draft resisters very conscientious, reasonable and not fanatics as far as I could see. They just seemed to feel that they could not collaborate in the war, and were prepared to go to prison.

Now, I said to myself, if I were willing, and it always seemed that I should have been willing, to risk my life, my body, again and again in support of the war when I believed it was right for us to be in the war, how could I shrink from being willing to go to prison to resist the war, when I feel the war is against the interest of the country and that stopping it is our vital interest?

And I just didn't have any answer to that. I didn't want to go to prison, but, on the other hand, I was confronted with the situation where there seemed a very evident way to contribute to stopping the war, and, for that matter, to contribute to the strengthening of our democratic processes, which had been weakened by lying and Executive usurpation in the last 20 years. . . .

One person was comparing your act to Martin Luther, in that he went beyond the law of the Establishment, of the Church, and based his actions on individual conscience. In other words, where did you get your authority to do what you did?

In this case, I would say, one doesn't have to go beyond very human institutional documents, the Constitution and the U.N. Charter, which was ratified by the Senate, and the international conventions we ratified, like the Hague Conventions and the Geneva Conventions. The courts have been unwilling to adjudicate these issues, simply because they do not wish to be in conflict with the Executive Branch.

This has supported a growing tendency by Executive officials to believe that, in the service of the President, they are literally outside the law. They, with the President, have begun to think of themselves as beyond all law and to act like an outlaw. We have an outlaw Executive, a scofflaw Executive. Except that a scofflaw suggests parking tickets, and we're talking about mass murder. That's the situation we're in.

That's why I keep insisting upon this point: It is a mistake for an American citizen to believe that our official actions in Vietnam are the result of the normal processes of the state, but rather, I think, they are the result of an Executive Branch that is acting beyond any restraint by the Constitution.

But here are five different people who have been elected to this office and made what you regard as similar decisions. Have they all been duped or have they all been evil or been lied to or what are you saying?

I think you can see it quite simply. Congress, the courts, the press are all put to sleep by the Executive during war. Now, the cold war is seen as having been in effect for the last 20 years. If you give a man such overwhelming power, if you put him in charge of the whole Government, in effect, then he quickly notices that the responsibility for failure is his alone.

We compare a war against 18 million people of South Vietnam and the 19 or 20 million of North Vietnam to the war against Nazi Germany for control of all of Western Europe. When I find a man of the intelligence of Secretary of State Rusk continually talking about Munich and the Rhineland to explain why we are burning Laos down, I am led to guess that the interpretation is one that is very necessary for him, however unrealistic it may be. The reality is that whatever the issues are at stake in Indochina for the United States, they are so far removed from issues we faced in World War II in importance, that they could not possibly justify the fact that we have been led to drop in the last two years more tonnage of bombs on Indochina, mostly in Laos with its three million people, than we dropped in all the theaters in World War II. We dropped a little over two million tons in all the theaters in World War II. Nixon has dropped 2.7 million tons, mostly in

Laos, in his Administration. Nixon. And that's while we're winding down the war.

When you read Speer's memoirs, there are certain passages that are almost unbearable. He took a full share of the responsibility in everything the Hitler regime did, though he says he did not know the Jews were being exterminated. He says very strong measures were taken to achieve secrecy on this, but he says this is not at all an excuse. He could have known, and it was his duty to know. He chose not to know. He says he was like a man following a trail of bloody footsteps in the snow and not realizing a murder was taking place.

Those are sentences I think a McNamara would find extremely difficult to read. It must occur to him that the things he did not know were things that he could and should have discovered. It also occurred to me that I had opposed the bombing, but I stayed within the system. I didn't go out and criticize it outside the system.

You mentioned McNamara. McNamara finally did quit.

McNamara never did quit. McNamara was fired. Shifted out. No official quit over Vietnam in conscience and told the public what he knew.

The Executive demands only one kind of loyalty—loyalty to the boss. And that's what these people value very highly throughout their lives. To get ahead, to earn your salary, to keep your job.

On the Dick Cavett show, you mentioned a Los Angeles Times *clipping about the Green Beret trial for the death of a double agent in Vietnam.*

Well, its a long story, but the specific significance of the Green Beret clipping for me was that it focused me on the role of lying by the Executive, automatically, unreflectively, to conceal murder. It had a very strong effect. I read that and felt I cannot be a part of this system any more. I cannot any more be led to lie because superiors or regulations tell me to. I acted almost immediately. I decided that I would reveal the deception of the Executive Branch, the concealment of murder over the last 20 years, to the Congress.

Was this a solo performance by you?

I really don't want to comment. From the decision-making point of view, yes, I was the man who had the documents and I was the man who decided to reveal them.

Didn't you perform an act of civil disobedience?

That's right. Nonviolent civil disobedience is a way of making a dramatic statement of conscience. In my case, the content of the statement was more important than the nature of the act, but I would be glad if the act itself was an example to some others.

I've seen you quoted as saying that you feel you were a war criminal.

I've often said that. I have wanted to make my former colleagues in the Government and the people who are still in the Government feel that they were accountable to the American public for what they were doing. I began to raise the war-crimes issue quite a bit, to interest people in the subject and to advertise myself as someone who might be available as a witness.

Is the charge against you now that you had the documents, not that you distributed them?

That seems to be it; also, that I converted them to my use, which would seem to mean giving them to a U.S. senator, for instance, and later to the press. That shows how unclear the law is. Can they really win a case that I stole the documents when what they are talking about was giving copies of them—not even the documents, the Defense Department still has my set of those—to a United States senator, Senator Fulbright, not for profit? Funny thing. After all, I gave them to the Senate Foreign Relations Committee a year and half before I gave them to the press. That doesn't strike me as the strongest case in the world for the Government to go in with.

If you are a war criminal, who else is one?

I wanted to raise that question in people's minds. Implicitly, what I was saying was that *even* I am a war criminal. I don't want to give myself airs. It would be pretentious to suggest that I'm a very important war criminal.

It strikes me as a very reasonable idea that people who had high staff or command responsibility connected with our Vietnam policy should be denied the right to serve the public as officials on security policy for some significant period of time, 10 to 20 years. And I would think this applies to me.

Let me mention one other thing. I said that when I came back from Vietnam, I saw newsreels of armed choppers with 50-caliber machine guns over our cities, but also of bombings of ROTC buildings and so forth. That faction of the peace movement repelled me because they were so familiar to me. These are people of the same education and class and background as my colleagues in the Defense Department. They had the same tone of tolerance of violence and intolerance toward other humans. And I suppose it's natural for some of them, as people who are against the war, to exhibit many of the same intellectual and personal characteristics of their fathers who applauded the war.

If you want someone reading this to take a single lesson away from the Pentagon papers, what would you say he should get out of them?

I will say this: Everybody knows the slogan "Power corrupts." But have we believed it? For Americans? We've really paid very little attention to the possibility that something like absolute power for the President of the United States could be enormously corrupting.

Do you realize that there's not a hint in any piece of legislation, to my knowledge, that says the President does not have the legal constitutional right tomorrow to send out all the nuclear forces of the United States to explode their weapons in pursuit of our national interests? There is no limitation that he has to consult Congress or the courts or the public or the press before he does that. Nobody else in the history of the world has had that degree of power. It's a very corrupting thought.

To give a man, unchecked and unmonitored, a command of such power is, virtually, to tempt him, over time, to use it in pursuit of interests of the United States as he alone defines them or even of his personal interest when it comes to protecting his place in history or his personal or party interests in getting reelected.

What doesn't have to happen is that he should be allowed to think that without any challenge. And that's what has come to happen. . . .

Do you believe the motivations of these men were venal or just mistaken?

Oh, I believe they were far more than mistaken. They reflected personal values that are subject to great criticism.

Their "dirty little secret"—as the Victorians put it—is their fascination with power. These are men to whom feelings of power were of great importance. This isn't to say that any human being is immune to such a temptation. But it is clear that these are individuals who were more drawn to power than some other people. When I say that eventually power corrupts, it corrupts precisely by tempting them to pander to that desire for power. To stay in the game. Desires like that—not just for power, but for action, activity, excitement—become an addiction.

Do you expect men to serve in these positions who don't have that desire, that addiction?

No, and that is to say how wise the makers of our Constitution were in designing a governmental structure that would pit power-seeking men in one branch against power-seeking men in another branch and thus to some extent restrain them in the interests of the people. To give all power to any one branch, particularly to any one individual like the President, is just asking for the kinds of policy we have gotten.

Do you want these men who were attracted to power, the Bundys, the Rostows, the McNamaras, punished?

The punishment I want for them is that which I have had to suffer. I want them to be compelled to read every page of the 7,000 pages of the Pentagon documents, to see their own decisions laid end to end in the context of all the other decisions made during that period. Beyond that, I would like them exposed, as I was, to the human physical impact of their decisions on the people of Indochina. I would like them to know what happened as a result of the bombing. I want them to see the footage that never got on television of the wounded children, of the defoliation, of the refugee camps, of the impact of this war on Indochina. And then I want them to decide for themselves what they ought to do.

The aim of any inquiry on the origins of the war—and there should be an investigation—should be to help public understanding and to bring about a change in the policies these men pursued, not to add them to the victims of those policies. There are too many political prisoners already.

What's really needed is not new prisoners but amnesty—amnesty for the people who are in jail right now, simply for opposing the criminal policies of these officials, amnesty for the people of Indochina who might still be sentenced to death by these policies in the future and amnesty for all our own sons who may now be sentenced to risks of killing or dying. Some papers, some facts have now been freed from safes. I'd like to see a lot of prison cells opened too.

Let me ask you one last question. What happens to your own future? What happens to you now?

The odds are in favor of my spending a long time in prison.

53.

Attica, September 1971

During 1971 there were several prison revolts of varying degrees of violence across the nation. At San Quentin in California, three inmates and three guards were killed on August 21 in what was called by prison officials an attempted jail break. One of the slain prisoners was black militant and author George Jackson. In November, inmates of New Jersey's Rahway State Prison seized the warden and five guards and held them until the governor promised to give consideration to prisoner complaints. There were other prison disturbances in Massachusetts, Illinois, Idaho, and Florida. But the worst prison revolt of the year occured at Attica Correctional Facility in New York in September. The rebellion began on September 9 when a strike by members of a work detail turned into a riot. The rioters were confined to one cell block and a yard, but they held more than 30 guards and other employees as hostages. The prisoners issued a list of demands dealing with prison conditions. The state commissioner of corrections, Russell Oswald, accepted most of their demands; but the fact that a guard had been injured in the original outbreak prompted Governor Nelson Rockefeller to decline amnesty. The negotiations moved into a stalemate until September 13, when state authorities ordered state troopers, sheriffs' deputies, and prison guards to storm the cell block and yard. The selection reprinted here consists of several portions of the official report of the New York State Special Commission impaneled to investigate the whole affair. The report was published a year after the events in question took place.

Source: *Attica:* The Official Report of the New York State Special Commission on Attica, New York, 1972, pp. xi-xv, 317-325, 332-340.

PREFACE

FORTY-THREE CITIZENS of New York State died at Attica Correctional Facility between September 9 and 13, 1971. Thirty-nine of that number were killed and more than 80 others were wounded by gunfire during the 15 minutes it took the State Police to retake the prison on September 13. With the exception of Indian massacres in the late 19th century, the State Police assault which ended the four-day prison uprising was the bloodiest one-day encounter between Americans since the Civil War. . . .

The main purpose of the report is to dispel the long-persisting doubts about what actually happened between September 9 and 13, 1971. The Commission is satisfied that the factual statement is accurate and complete.

In addition to fact-finding, we were asked to make judgments about antecedent causes and subsequent occurrences, where objective facts do not necessarily provide answers. While differing interpretations are of course possible about matters as subjective as assessment of responsibility at crucial stages along the way, the Commission is unanimous even on these questions of judgment.

But the facts and the judgments disclose only the tip of the fiery hell that lies below. It is not enough to answer the doubts about the events themselves, or even to fix responsibility for defects of planning and performance. The worrisome reality is that prisons, prisoners, and the problems of both are essentially invisible in the United States. We Americans have made our prisons disappear from sight as if by an act of will. We locate them mostly in places remote from view, and far removed from the homes of the inmates; we emphasize security almost to the exclusion of rehabilitation; and we manage to forget inmates and custodians alike by pretending that the prisoners will not reutrn to our cities and our villages and our farms.

The Attica Correctional Facility in September 1971 was not perceptibly better or worse than the other maximum security prisons which at that time housed nine of every ten adult male offenders in the state system. While conditions at Attica may not have been exactly like those at other prisons in New York State or elsewhere, the problems in that institution at that time are sufficiently representative of the prison universe to justify some generalization. Accordingly, the principal significance of this report may lie in the fact that it documents in considerable detail every aspect of the life and structure of a major prison, based upon more precise information than has ever before been assembled about any single institution. Interviews with the vast majority of inmates, correction officers, and others involved in the daily life of Attica in September 1971 provide a unique opportunity to fix attention upon an entire institution at a particular instant of time. In capturing that moment we have examined state rules and procedures, prison politics, the changing nature of the inmate population, and festering racism—a dangerously volatile mix. That the explosion occurred first at Attica was probably chance. But the elements for replication are all around us. Attica is every prison; and every prison is Attica. . . .

Prison is the end of the criminal justice line—for inmates, for supervisory personnel, and for members of the public who have conveniently forgotten the institutions to which they abandon their most difficult fellow citizens. But official indifference and public forgetfulness is unacceptable. When society places a person behind walls, it cannot put aside its obligation to try to change and help that individual. Chief Justice Warren E. Burger made the point in an address:

> When a sheriff or a marshal takes a man from a courthouse in a prison van and transports him to confinement for two or three or ten years, *this is our act. We* have tolled the bell for him. And whether we like it or not, we have made him our collective responsibility. We are free to do something about him; he is not.

Attica, one of those forgotten institutions, housed more than 2,200 inmates on September 9, 1971. There, as at other institutions, the emphasis was on confinement and security. Despite brave talk about rehabilitation as a prime objective of detention, the shortage of trained personnel and the inadequacy of facilities made rehabilitation an impossible dream. In fact, it is not even clear that it was then, or is now, a real objective of the American prison system.

At Attica there was no meaningful program of education for those who wished to learn and no rehabilitation program for those who were willing to rejoin society as constructive citizens. Idleness was the principal occupation. Most correction officers were not equipped by training to communicate with their inmate charges, and did not consider it their duty to understand or to resolve inmate problems. It is scarcely surprising that the original uprising developed almost spontaneously out of small misunderstandings only indirectly related to the major grievances that smoldered below the surface.

When the uprising was unexpectedly successful in its initial stages, all ingredients of major disaster were present. Mistrust between inmates and their custodians made good-faith negotiation almost impossible, particularly since the roles of negotiators and observers were never defined. When the officials decided that a negotiated settlement was not possible, the inmates were not told—and perhaps would not have believed—that the state officials intended to retake the institution with guns.

The assault itself was not carefully planned to minimize the loss of life: the choice of weapons and ammunition was based upon ready availability, not upon the logic of the specific situation; no safeguards were established to protect against excessive use of force by those who were authorized to fire; no effective control was imposed to prevent firing by those who were not supposed to participate; no adequate arrangements were made for medical care of the severe casualties that should have been anticipated; and no responsible system was established to prevent vengeful reprisals against inmates after the retaking.

Whatever explanation might be advanced for official failure to deal effectively with an emergency of crisis proportions, no excuse can justify the failure of the American public to demand a better system of criminal justice, from arrest, trial, and sentencing to ultimate release from confinement. Chief Justice Burger has spoken of "correction systems that do not correct" and has warned that "our national trait of impatience has distorted our approach to the problems of prisoners and rehabilitation." But, as he has also observed, time is running out, particularly when we *know* better than we do. . . .

THE GOVERNOR'S DECISIONS

Russell Oswald had been chairman of the Board of Parole under Governor Rockefeller's predecessor and the Governor continued him in office. In 1970, the Governor chose Oswald to become the first head of the new Department of Correctional Services. In selecting Oswald the Governor had, in his own words, committed the state to a policy of converting the prisons "from custodial to rehabilitative treatment." The American Prison Association had first adopted that standard a century earlier.

The Governor told the Commission in executive session that "one of the things I regret most is my own lack of preception of the tremendous need which existed" in the corrections area, and that had he been aware of the need, he would have taken steps to reform prison conditions years earlier.

The Governor also told the Commission that his efforts at overhauling the prison system in 1971 were hampered by the state's worst fiscal crisis and that Oswald had warned in May 1971 that prison unrest was increasing "fomented and exacerbated by internal and external revolutionary political activities which were increasingly zeroing in on the criminal element in our society."

The Governor viewed the Attica rebellion as another step in an ominous world trend. As he told the Commission:

> ... one of the most recent and widely used techniques of modern-day revolutionaries has been the taking of political hostages and using the threat to kill them as blackmail to achieve unconditional demands and to gain wide public attention to further their revolutionary ends. I have followed these developments with great interest and considered that, if tolerated, they pose a serious threat to the ability of free government to preserve order and to protect the security of the individual citizen.
>
> Therefore, I firmly believe that a duly elected official sworn to defend the constitution and the laws of the state and the nation would be betraying his trust to the people he serves if he were to sanction or condone such criminal act by negotiating under such circumstances.

In the handling of the Attica uprising, the Governor found that these views conflicted with his belief in delegation of responsibilities to the department heads he had selected. Despite his own convictions against negotiating with the holders of the hostages, the Governor chose not to overrule the man whom he had named and he supported Oswald's decision to attempt a negotiated settlement.

The Governor was in Washington when the uprising began and remained there until Friday, when he returned to his home in Pocantico Hills, New York. He kept in contact with the developments at Attica by telephone, speaking several times a day with Commissioner Oswald, Dr. Hurd, Robert Douglass, and Michael Whiteman. While the Governor sent Hurd, O'Hara, Douglass, and Shapiro (Whiteman's assistant) to Attica, he made it clear that he was not disturbing the chain of command in the negotiations—Oswald was to remain in charge. And Oswald, in fact, made all of the decisions through Sunday afternoon, rejecting in several instances the advice of Robert Douglass. Douglass counseled against admitting Bobby Seale, and against permitting the observers to return to the yard Sunday afternoon (p. 274).

When Oswald informed the Governor that he was prepared to accept the 28 Points, the Governor backed him up with the assurance that he would recommend the legislation contemplated by the Points.

The Governor stood firm, however, on one matter—he told Commissioner Oswald that even if he had the power to grant amnesty, which he and his counsel agreed he did not have—he would not grant it as a matter of principle. The Governor drew a sharp distinction between amnesty, which he considered a "political" objective not negotiable with the holders of hostages, and penal reform promised in the 28 Points, which he testified Oswald "had in mind anyway."

The Governor began to take a more direct role in the handling of the situation on Sunday even before the observers called for his appearance. He had supported Oswald's acceptance of the observers' role, even though, as he explained to the Commission, he was not clear "what their function was, what their responsibilities were, who they were working for, who they represented, how they were selected, how they were organized, who was their head." But when the 28 Points were rejected by the inmates the Governor urged Oswald to dismiss the observers, and to advise the inmates directly that amnesty was nonnegotiable. The Governor explained:

> . . . it seemed to me that we now had passed the last possible vestige of hope that this uprising was going to be settled on the basis of a desire for prison reform. . . .

Then suddenly on Sunday, the Governor was confronted with the request by the observers that he come to Attica to meet with them. The request was relayed first through Robert Douglass, who advised the Governor that amnesty was still the key issue.

By the time the Governor received a telephone call, shortly after noon on Sunday, from Dunne, Wicker, Badillo, and Jones, he had already concluded that a visit would not serve a useful purpose.

As a result of the observers' pleas, the Governor agreed there would be no assault on Sunday, giving the inmates an additional day to accept the Points. But the Governor remained opposed to a trip to Attica.

All the observers, including upstate Republican legislators, joined in the plea for the Governor to meet with them in Attica. Dunne, Wicker, Badillo, and Jones, who telephoned the Governor, had been encouraged by the Governor's staff to serve as observers. Dunne, also a Republican, was the chairman of the State Senate committee dealing with prisons. Why then did the Governor refuse their unanimous plea to come to Attica?

The Governor's reasons were stated in a public statement drafted on Sunday afternoon by Robert Douglass and approved by the Governor over the telephone. It read, in part:

> The key issue at stake, however, is still the demand for total amnesty for any criminal acts which may have occurred. I do not have the constitutional authority to grant such a demand and I would not, even if I had the authority because to do so would undermine the very essence of our free society—the fair and impartial application of the law. In view of the fact that the key issue is total amnesty—in spite of the best efforts of the committee and in spite of Commissioner Oswald's major commitments to the inmates—I do not feel that my physical presence on the site can contribute to a peaceful settlement.

The Governor presented a fuller explanation to the Commission during his interview. He stated that the observers acknowledged that the inmates were still insisting on criminal amnesty as the price of settlement. Their pleas for his visit, the Governor said, all reduced themselves to the proposition that the observers wanted further time. The Governor found this unpersuasive. He pointed out that without coming to Attica he had postponed an assault for 24 hours, and the problem as he saw it was not lack of time to achieve an agreement, but the inmates' continued intransigence on the amnesty issue. In these circumstances, the request by the observers for the Governor's visit appeared to him to be a grasping for straws by men "who did not want to admit defeat."

Moreover, the Governor, with his concern that "revolutionaries" were playing a major role in the Attica uprising, concluded that his visit would be exploited by those "who were not interested in seeing the settlement or seeing a reform," but who wanted to drag this out, preserve the theater for worldwide coverage relating to revolutionary forces."

OSWALD'S PLEAS

THE PLEAS OF THE OBSERVERS for the Governor's appearance at Attica were not without effect upon Commissioner Oswald. He remained reluctant to order the assault.

Following his session with the observers on Sunday evening, Oswald telephoned the Governor. Oswald testified concerning this call:

> I suggested that it would seem that it might be appropriate for someone as warm and understanding as Governor Rockefeller to walk that last mile and come, although I went on to express the view that I didn't feel that it was going to be productive.

General O'Hara joined in recommending that the Governor come. According to Oswald, the Governor asked: " 'Do you feel it will be productive? Will it save lives?' I said, 'I don't believe so.' "

Both Oswald and O'Hara suggested that the Governor could be subject to public criticism if he failed to come. The Governor replied that he was not concerned about his image and that in view of the inmates' insistence on amnesty, he still believed his trip would serve no purpose. . . .

THE COMMISSION'S VIEWS

No one can be sure whether the Governor's presence would have succeeded in producing a settlement that had eluded Oswald and the observers. Present or not, the Governor was unwilling to grant amnesty, the critical inmate demand. Nevertheless, the Governor's decision not to go to Attica has tended to overshadow all other issues as a subject of public debate.

The Commission can readily understand why the Governor was unwilling to go to Attica prior to Commissioner Oswald's request on Sunday evening. The Governor's presence could have undermined Oswald's authority in dealing with the observers and inmates. But when the Governor refused Oswald's request that he come, he was spurning the recommendations of the man on whom he had relied to bring about a peaceful resolution, and departing from his usual policy of giving full support to his appointee.

The Commission does not underestimate the problems that would have faced the Governor had he gone to Attica. The observers stated to the Governor that they were asking only that he meet with them—not with the inmates. But it is probable that the presence of the Governor at Attica would have precipitated a demand by inmates that he enter the yard. The pressure would have been intense, as the Governor's refusal to comply with the request could have been characterized by inmates as indication of bad faith, precluding a peaceful settlement and jeopardizing the lives of the hostages.

Recognizing that the decision was not an easy one for the Governor to make, the Commission nevertheless believes that conditions made it appropriate for the Governor to go to Attica. At the time of the uprising, the Governor realized that the prison system had long been neglected and was in need of major reform. Many of the inmates' grievances were acknowledged to be legitimate by both the Commissioner and the Governor. In such circumstances, where state neglect was a major contributing factor to the uprising, the Commission feels that the Governor should not have committed the state's armed forces against the rebels without first appearing on the scene and satisfying himself that there was no other alternative and that all precautions against excessive force had been taken.

It is possible that, even without a grant of amnesty, the Governor's presence at Attica would have overcome inmate mistrust of the state's commitment to reform, and induced acceptance of the 28

Points. Some inmates have expressed this view to the Commission. But even if a settlement were not achieved, the Commission believes that the presence of the Governor would have had a stabilizing effect on the troopers and correction officers taking part in the assault and rehousing of inmates, many of whom were bitter toward Commissioner Oswald for his negotiations with the inmates, but respectful of the Governor.

Finally, the Commission believes that the Governor should, at the very least, have accepted the "modified proposal" presented to him by his aides late Sunday night—that he offer to go to Attica to negotiate further on the 28 Points if the inmates would first release the hostages and then return to their cells. It is true that the Governor and Commissioner Oswald felt there was little chance of inmate acceptance of this proposal. But, it is equally true that the Governor had nothing to lose by making this proposal, which, if accepted by the inmates, could have brought a peaceful end to the uprising. As General O'Hara testified:

> . . . my feeling was that if the inmates would relase the hostages that there was nothing to be lost by having the Governor come.

By these conclusions the Commission does not mean to suggest that the Governor's failure to appear at Attica was the cause of the deaths and casualties that followed. Full amnesty was the paramount issue at all times and there was no evidence before the Governor that the inmates were prepared to accept less. However, even if one could be certain that the Governor's appearance would not have led to a settlement, the gravity of the situation warranted the Governor's presence before the decision was reached to commence the assault.

In summary, the Commission believes that the Governor should have gone to Attica, not as a matter of duress or because the inmates demanded his presence, but because his responsibilities as the state's chief executive made it appropriate that he be present at the scene of the critical decision involving great risk of loss of life, after Commissioner Oswald had requested him to come. . . .

SUMMARY

When the failure of the negotiations left the state with no alternative but to retake the prison by force, officials from the Governor on down expressed concern that the force employed be only the minimum necessary to restore order. But that concern was not translated into effective restraints, and, in fact, the assault of September 13, 1971, and its aftermath were marred by excesses. Thirty-nine persons were killed by gunfire and 80 others suffered gunshot wounds during the assault. One out of every ten persons in D yard that morning was struck by gunfire and more than a quarter of the hostages died of bullet wounds.

But guns were not the only inflicters of pain at Attica that day; in the aftermath of the assault, hundreds of inmates, stripped of their clothing, were brutalized by correction officers, troopers, and sheriffs' deputies. In addition, the suffering of the wounded was needlessly prolonged by an inexcusable failure to make adequate prior arrangements for medical attention. The authorities' indifference to the lawlessness which followed the crushing of the rebellion continued even after the physical pain subsided and was still evident as the Commission completed its investigation and held public hearings.

The tragedy of September 13 is expressed in the testimony of Dr. John Cudmore, a National Guard surgeon who entered Attica twenty minutes after the shooting stopped:

> As we sit here today in a well-lit, reasonably well-appointed room with suits and ties on, objectively performing an autopsy on this day, yet we cannot get to the absolute horror of the situation. To people, be they black, yellow, orange, spotted, whatever, whatever uniform they wear, that day tore from them the shreds of their humanity. The veneer of civilization was penetrated. . . .

THE ASSAULT

ALTHOUGH HIGH-RANKING state officials from several agencies were on the scene at Attica, the entire planning of the police action to retake the institution was left to the local State Police troop commander. In devising the tactical plan, he could use only the personnel and equipment available to the State Police and did not have the benefit of advice or review by civilian or military authorities.

The decision to employ lethal force was an inevitable consequence of the decision to retake the prison. In view of the known buildup of inmates' defenses and crude, but deadly weaponry, the State Police never considered mounting an assault without firearms. In fact, after the assault, the State Police recovered over 1,400 weapons, including two teargas guns, spears, Molotov cocktails, baseball bats, scissors, knives, razors, wooden and metal bludgeons, and other objects.

The assault planners acknowledged that they did not possess the capability of reaching the hostages in time to save their lives, if the inmates were in fact set upon killing them. Since there could be no certainty of saving the hostages, in reality the first priority in drafting the assault plan was to minimize the risk of injury to the assault forces themselves.

The State Police used the weapons available to them—high-powered rifles with telescopic sights, sidearms, and 12-gauge shotguns. While the rifles and handguns with which the police were equipped were appropriate for their intended use in the assault, the shotguns, loaded with "00" buckshot pellets which would spread at distances exceeding 30 yards and hit unintended targets, created a high risk of injury and death to unresisting inmates and hostages when discharged in or into the prison yard. The State Police did not have in their arsenal an alternative weapon for use against expected close-range threats from armed inmates. To minimize the risk of inmates seizing guns from troopers, the assault forces were forbidden by their commanders to engage in hand-to-hand combat, leaving them with little alternative but to fire their shotguns whenever they apprehended danger from an inmate.

State Police commanders said they were aware of the increasing tension and hostility among their men and gave instructions concerning the excessive use of firepower. However, the tactical plan left the decision on whether to discharge a weapon to the discretion of each individual trooper. No specific safeguards were developed to avoid hitting hostages and unresisting inmates with the spread and overfire from shotgun blasts.

Preassault briefings were given in large groups and there was no procedure for instructing individual troopers concerning the behavior expected of them. Gas masks inhibited verbal communication and no alternative means, such as hand signals, were developed for transmitting fire and cease-fire orders or other instructions once the assault was under way.

The problems of the assault planners were aggravated on the morning of the assault when inmates, as a final act of bravado, brought eight hostages up onto the catwalks, which were to be the assault force's route to D yard. They held knives to the hostages' throats, shouted threats to kill them, and taunted the waiting troopers. As the assault began, inmates inflicted knife wounds upon four of the hostages, although none died of such wounds.

The Governor had ordered that correction officers, because of their emotional involvement, should be excluded from the assault forces. This order never reached the State Police or correctional supervisors in control of the men and, in fact, correction officers joined assault details and discharged weapons in several areas of the prison. Their gunfire killed at least one inmate and one hostage.

In practice, the deficiencies in the assault plan took their toll in death and injury. The faith of the assault planners in the discretion and restraint of individual troopers proved in many cases to be misplaced. Had the majority of the assault force not acted with restraint, the toll of dead and wounded would undoubtedly have been greater. But restraint, unfortunately, was not universal. Individual members of the assault force provided detailed explanations of hostile or threatening inmate activity which, they said, occasioned their fire. However, other accounts and objective evidence—principally photographs—are inconsistent with many of the assault forces' explanations. From an analysis of all the available evidence, the conclusion is inescapable that there was much unnecessary shooting. Troopers shot into tents, trenches, and barricades without looking first. In addition, even where the firing may have been justified—as in the case of a State Police lieutenant assaulted by an inmate in D yard—the use of shotguns loaded with buckshot in the heavily populated spaces of D yard led to the killing and wounding of hostages and of inmates who were not engaged in any hostile activity.

Analysis of the statements and testimony given by the members of the assault force not only leads to the conclusion that there was unnecessary shooting, but also indicates that the statements were in many cases exaggerated, embellished, and even fabricated. The alleged hostile acts of inmates were reconstructed by the men who fired in a degree of detail which was not matched by their descriptions of other occurrences. The acts alleged to have occurred were, in many cases, unsubstantiated by photographs which would have shown them if they had in fact occurred. And at least one trooper admitted to the Commission that the men in his troop encouraged one another to embellish their accounts.

The top-level decision to exclude correction officers from the assault was sound, not only because of doubts about their ability to control their personal feelings, but also because they are not well trained in military maneuvers or in the use of weapons. At Attica, that policy decision was, inexcusably, never translated into direct orders to the men involved.

The troopers' riot-control training is suited primarily to open areas in which rioters can be dispersed by gas and batons. They are ill equipped by training, matériel, and tradition to engage in large-scale missions where gas and batons may not be sufficient and where their normal policy of dispersal is inapplicable. In addition, less than 1/3 of 1 percent of the troopers are black. If the tragedy of Attica is not to be repeated, it is imperative that the New York State Police adopt definable policies and procedures for quelling serious and large-scale disturbances in enclosed areas. Such procedures must include provisions to ensure that the risk of injury to unresisting persons is minimized, if not eliminated. It is also imperative that the State Police become integrated.

The Commission believes that, except for the most extreme emergencies, a police force cannot be said to be prepared to act until every participant armed with a gun and authorized to use it against other citizens is as fully and completely informed of all instructions, objectives, and goals of the mission as is his commander. Even the best-trained trooper cannot function professionally, however, in an emotionally charged atmosphere in which he cannot distinguish between fact and rumor and in which his personal frustrations and prejudices have been allowed free rein. Training for missions such as Attica must instill not only technical expertise, but tolerance as well.

The State Police used only what weapons they had and there were no nonlethal alternatives. Our advanced society surely possesses the technical capability to develop implements of force which are not also implements of death. Research and development of such nonlethal weaponry is in progress. Attica demands urgent efforts to complete the development of such instruments and deploy them to the domestic peace-keeping forces which require them. The Commission recognizes that domestic upheavals, in prisons and elsewhere, will not always be capable of peaceful resolution. But the avoidance of widespread death and injury is within our capacity.

A final word must be added concerning the exaggerated accounts which troopers gave after the assault to justify the discharge of weapons. Those who fired were never made to feel that absolute candor about what happened was expected of them and, in some cases a lack of candor was encouraged.

The Division of State Police, like many established institutions, has developed a tradition in which members find security, take pride, and defend one another vigorously. Division members too frequently allow their colleagues or the agency itself to become their first concern, instead of the public they serve and the laws they enforce. That sense of camaraderie has closed the State Police to outside scrutiny.

TREATMENT OF THE WOUNDED

THE AUTHORITIES were well aware that the assault might result in a large number of gunshot casualties and in fact publicly expressed relief when it was all over that the toll had not been higher. However, they failed to make adequate provision in advance for the evacuation and treatment of the wounded. When the shooting stopped, leaving over 120 inmates and hostages dead or wounded, there were only ten medical personnel inside the walls, and only two of them were doctors. A National Guard unit capable of evacuating casualties and providing a "holding operation" pending definitive medical treatment had been mobilized, but had not yet reached the facility. Doctors at local hospitals, who could have rushed in with the necessary know-how, professional assistants, and equipment to perform emergency surgery, had not yet been asked to come to Attica.

It was not until after 2:00 P.M., some four hours after the shooting stopped, that emergency surgical procedures be-

Attica inmates in the prison yard during a skin search after the insurrection was put down

gan. In the meantime, wounded and dying inmates lay on stretchers in the tiny prison hospital or on the grass outside awaiting treatment, while young National Guardsmen worked feverishly trying to ease their suffering. When the doctors finally did arrive, they were shocked at the conditions prevailing and amazed that they had not been alerted hours prior to the assault. Once there, they performed admirably under the circumstances, and miraculously no one died solely because of the delay in receiving medical attention.

Nevertheless, the agony of the wounded was immeasurably increased by the lack of prompt treatment. Of all of the needless suffering at Attica, this was the most easily avoidable. But no one assumed the responsibility for making the necessary arrangements. The Commission believes that there was no excuse for failure to make arrangements for sufficient doctors, nurses, ambulances, surgical supplies, and drugs, and to develop a swift and efficient procedure for evacuation of casualties from the prison to nearby hospitals, well before the first shot was fired.

REPRISALS

STATE OFFICIALS expected physical reprisals against immates in the aftermath of the rebellion, but did nothing to prevent them. Such reprisals had followed previous prison uprisings and the fear of them was uppermost in the minds of the inmates during the negotiations. A Federal court order consented to by Commissioner Oswald, as well as the 28 Points to which he agreed, contained provisions against reprisals. Once the assault was over, the orderly return of inmates to their cells, without physical and verbal harassment, should have been given priority.

In fact, correction officers and, to a lesser extent, state troopers and sheriffs' deputies, engaged in frequent and systematic acts of retribution against inmates. National Guardsmen and other outside observers, as well as a few troopers and correction officers, confirmed the almost universal inmate descriptions of widespread beatings, proddings, kickings, and verbal abuse of the vilest nature.

Physical reprisals, accompanied by racial and sexual epithets, began as inmates were herded out of D yard to be stripped and searched, continued as the inmates were run through a gauntlet to cells in A block, and did not subside even after they were locked naked three to a cell. Reprisals were especially severe in HBZ, where the suspected leaders of the uprising were taken. There were even some incidents of reprisals on the following days. Eight days after September 13, doctors assigned to make a physical inventory reported finding bruises, lacerations, abrasions, and broken bones among 45 percent of the inmates who had been in D yard.

What has proved most disturbing about the reprisals was the refusal of most persons in authority at Attica that day to acknowledge that they took place or to accept responsibility for them. During the Commission's public hearings, after the occurrence of physical reprisals had been documented by objective eyewitness testimony, Deputy Commissioner Walter Dunbar minimized the extent of the reprisals.

No effective steps were taken on September 13 to see that reprisals did not occur and no satisfactory explanation has been given for that failure. An uprising in which inmates had demanded above all that they be treated as human beings thus ended with their being treated inhumanly. While the Commission can understand the pent-up emotions and frustrations which took hold of correction officers and others producing such behavior, the public has a right to expect that men whose profession it is to uphold order will not permit their emotions to interfere with their responsibilities. Nor are supervisory officials free to look the other way and allow resentment and anger to reign where there is a desperate need for reason and restraint.

AFTERMATH

Official insensitivity extended beyond the hours following the assault, Rumors of atrocities, which had circulated throughout the four days, were reported as fact by high state officials. Without any authoritative verification, they announced that hostages had died of slit throats and that story was published around the world. When autopsies proved those reports to be false, the first reaction of some officials was to search for ways to question or discredit the medical examiners, rather than to face up to their own mistake.

The families of hostages experienced excruciating delays in learning whether their loved ones were dead or alive. Similarly, days passed before all of the dead inmates were identified and their families notified. When attorneys and doctors attempted to enter the prison in the days following the assault to assist the inmates, they were obstructed at every turn by prison authorities who chose to ignore a Federal court order rather than admit them. It was not until a watchdog panel named by presiding Justice Goldman of the Appellate Division entered the institution on Friday, September 17, that a semblance of normalcy returned.

In the months following the uprising, Attica underwent many changes. Some of the reforms demanded by the inmates in D yard were instituted, although the authorities maintained that they did not feel bound by the 28 Points to which Oswald had agreed. While Attica was changing, the pervasive feeling months later was that nothing had really changed. Memories of the horrors of September 13 faded rapidly and inertia reappeared. Although inmates were allowed to organize a liaison committee for the expression of grievances, they were still given no sense of participation in the decisions affecting their lives. In July 1972, they turned again to the politics of confrontation and the specter of another Attica rose again.

54.

The Police Crisis

The maintenance in the United States of domestic tranquility, or "law and order," came under a severe strain in the years after 1963. The police power had to meet the challenges of civil rights demonstrations, race riots, antiwar protests, and sharply rising crime rates. In addition to the press of these situations, and in part because of them, the police as an institution were confronted by ambivalent public attitudes. Some citizens evinced a sharp hostility to policemen, while others demanded greater powers for police departments to stem the increase in crime and disorder. Police departments in some major cities were rocked by scandals relating to corruption and brutality. Policemen themselves organized unions and fraternal societies to improve their status and to afford protection against some of the charges being leveled at them. Basic to the whole issue was the matter of finding qualified policemen, and this depended on adequate funding and up-to-date manpower policies. The National Advisory Commission on Criminal Standards and Goals noted in 1973 that police work has come to be regarded "as a second class occupation open to anyone with no more than a minimal education, average intelligence, and good health." The commission recommended upgrading the requirements by demanding personnel with college degrees and added education for those now on police forces. The question of how to professionalize the police was dealt with in 1971 in a series of interviews with three police chiefs: Jerry V. Wilson of Washington, D. C.; Clarence M. Kelley of Kansas City, Missouri; and John P. Howard of Wauwatosa, Wisconsin. On June 7, 1973, President Nixon appointed Chief Kelley the new permanent director of the Federal Bureau of Investigation, replacing the late J. Edgar Hoover. Portions of the interviews, conducted by Gary M. Chamberlain, associate editor of American City Magazine, *are reprinted here.*

Source: *American City*, September and October 1971: "How to Solve the Police Crisis."

How can we recruit more and better police officers?

Chief Howard: There is not and never has been a shortage of people willing and qualified to be police officers. Every city that pays an adequate salary, uses realistic physical, age and residency standards and makes more than a half-hearted effort can get more qualified applicants than it can ever hire. More departments are doing this every year and filling their ranks. The only discouraging thing I have ever found in recruiting is the large number of well-qualified people I could not hire because there were not enough vacancies.

Chief Wilson: In order to recruit more and better-qualified people into the field of law enforcement, emphasis must be given to providing higher salaries and better promotional and retirement opportunities that are attractive to men of high calibre.

Chief Kelley: This will be realized largely

through attracting college trained personnel. The role in which the police officer is cast in today's society dictates that he must, by necessity, be better trained in the psychological and sociological aspects of life, particularly as they relate to human behavior. We must, of course, have the capacity to pay salaries commensurate with their qualifications.

What police functions would benefit by a regional approach?

Chief Howard: Several functions would benefit from a regional approach—training, recruiting, intelligence, major crime investigation and crime laboratory facilities. However, the basic responsibility for police service belongs with the many small units of government which have proven functional in our American political system. About 70% of the U.S. population is served by small and medium-sized police departments, and the population shift, as revealed by census figures, is *out* of the big cities and into the smaller ones. While it is true that many very small towns cannot furnish adequate police service and could improve service by consolidation of forces with neighboring communities, it also is true that a department can be too big to be responsive to the needs of the citizenry. Comparing the crime problems and levels of police service of big versus small cities one is inclined to doubt the alleged merits of bigness and centralization.

Chief Wilson: Present-day realities are such that police operations on a regional basis are impractical. Interest in local self-value, and the national fear of the development of a "police state," form sufficient barriers to retard any changes that point in this direction.

Chief Kelley: Many metropolitan police operations will be regionalized in the not too distant future. This idea is both economically and administratively sound and can be realized at a great savings to the taxpayers. An outstanding example of regionalization is our own Regional Center for Criminal Justice. Included in the operation is an areawide training academy and laboratory funded by the Northwest Missouri Law Enforcement Assistance Council. I also foresee regionalized computer facilities and regionalized disaster investigative groups. . . .

What are the most pressing police problems? Why?

Chief Kelley: The most pressing problem facing the law enforcement profession today is our financial plight.

The seeming revolt among taxpayers is an indication to me that this problem will become increasingly more critical as municipalities increase their ever-widening search for additional revenue with which to meet the increased financial demands necessary to finance police operations. I believe the ultimate solution to the problem will be realized through federal financial assistance to the law enforcement profession.

Chief Howard: Getting more and better citizen participation in the crime prevention effort. Making police education and training more appropriate to the demands of the job, and improving the quality of training. Restructuring both the organization and the jobs to better utilize the full range of abilities and talents available in the local community.

Chief Wilson: In these days of deep social unrest when our government and social institutions are being challenged as never before, we in the law enforcement field are confronted with the problem of accurately defining our role and responsibilities relative to this phenomena. Our role, if properly defined, can serve as the bridge between social factions and divided ethnic and racial groups, or, if inaccurately defined, we can be the bridge that widens the gap. . . .

Is the current trend toward considering alcholism as a disease a good one? Should drug abuse be considered in the same category?

Chief Wilson: The trend toward treating alcholism and drug use as a medical matter is the proper approach to a problem which the criminal justice system has been unable to rectify.

Chief Kelley: I favor considering alcholism as a disease, but hesitate to consider drug abuse as such. Drug use and abuse is a violation of our statutes. The treatment of these allied problems should stress cure rather than penalty.

Chief Howard: It has been pretty well established that alcohol and drug abuse are public health problems. The police and courts have vital roles in finding and committing the abusers for treatment, and in cutting off the illegal supply of drugs.

What federal police policies do you like? Why?

Chief Wilson: I like the Omnibus Crime Control and Safe Streets Act of 1968—a milestone for this nation. It addresses many of our most pressing criminal justice problems, and it does this on a far-reaching scale. It offers federal funds to help states and local communities toward conducting a massive attack on crime. The Act offers an unparalleled opportunity to strengthen law enforcement.

In addition, the Criminal Justice System in the District of Columbia has been significantly strengthened through the enactment of the "D.C. Crime Bill" by the Congress. The bill authorizes preventive detention of dangerous offenders. A no-knock provision empowers police to enter a house on a search or arrest warrant without knocking only: when there is "probable cause" to believe that prior notice and delay will: (1) "likely" endanger the life or safety of police or other persons; (2) "likely" permit a hunted suspect to escape; and (3) "likely" permit destruction or disposal of evidence. The bill further completely reorganizes the District of Columbia court structure and authorizes an increase in badly needed judges.

Chief Kelley: Many of the federal police programs available to the local law enforcement agencies are necessary to our very existence. I would like to see federal agencies have more latitude in entering and advising local agencies in serious cases, but where no violation of a federal statute is involved. A good example might be our recent bombing incidents where local police agencies have neither the talent, manpower or the resources with which to bring such incidents to a successful conclusion. In addition, we need to organize and establish methods for a more meaningful exchange of information between local agencies and those of the federal law enforcement process.

Chief Howard: My only complaint about federal programs for local law enforcement is that they have not yet been adequately funded to meet the needs. In spite of its slow start, I believe the idea of bloc grants to states under the Omnibus Crime Control Act is the proper approach. The states and cities are responsible for police protection and they should allocate the funds.

Have recent court decisions hampered or helped law enforcement? Which ones and why?

Chief Wilson: Many people believe that recent judicial interpretations of the Constitution and various statues have unduly and inappropriately inhibited the work of the police. Part of this stems from the fact that many of these decisions were made without the needs of law enforcement, and the police policies designed to meet these needs, being effectively presented to the court. If judges are to balance accurately law enforcement needs against human rights, the former must be articulated. This was illustrated in the case of Miranda v. Arizona which prohibited, by a 5-4 decision, the questioning of a suspect in custody unless counsel is present, or the suspect expressly waives his right to counsel. It is still too early to assess the effect of this decision on law enforcement's ability to secure confessions and to solve crimes.

Recent decisions have changed law enforcement and it is difficult to determine their impact on police work. These changes are in order, however, as it should be readily apparent that old police methods and court decisions are becoming more and more ineffective every day. A case in point is Easter v. District of Columbia where it was held that a person could not be taken into custody by the police for public drunkenness absent any violation of law. Obviously this decision frees patrolmen for other duties as well as removing prospective defendents from the court dockets. The impact of recent decisions has changed police work and whether for good or bad only time will tell.

Chief Kelley: While recent Supreme Court decisions have hampered law enforcement, I feel they have also caused us to upgrade the quality of our investigations. They have done a great deal to insure the rights and personal liberties of those persons accused of a criminal offense. However, they have caused some serious setbacks, particularly in the area of search and seizure. The Supreme Court has gone too far in this area. Probably the most controversial decisions in this area were the Shimmel case and, of course, Mapp v. Ohio. These landmark decisions are not typical cases and to apply their provisions to typical cases proves cumbersome indeed.

Chief Howard: The decisions of the last 10 years have forced police to bring better, stronger cases into court. They also have resulted in non-prosecution of countless guilty persons, or prosecution of felons on minor misdemeanor charges. Police have neither the man-power nor the resources to prepare the kind of cases needed to convict all of the persons they detect for the crimes they actually commit. And even if they had, the courts and prosecuters as presently staffed could never handle the increased load.

Is the practice of letting those persons convicted of several crimes serve concurrent sentences for these crimes a good one?

Chief Wilson: This is a matter of the court's discretion.

Chief Kelley: This may be practical from an economic standpoint. I do not believe it serves as a deterrent to future criminal activity.

Chief Howard: The practice may have some merit in individual cases where rehabilitation is likely. I suppose, too, that it has some value in plea bargaining — although this subject is not often discussed publicly. However, I see no justification in letting a man with a long criminal record serve a couple of years for a series of five or six robberies. Society is entitled to have him "off its back" for longer than that. . . .

Do police spend too much time in court? Should they receive pay for off-duty appearances in court?

Chief Wilson: We are now exploring ways and means toward reducing the time our officers spend sitting idly in court awaiting their case to be called. It is our department's practice to pay officers for each second and subsequent appearance in a case while in an offduty status.

Chief Kelley: Our officers spend more time in court than is necessary. An officer is often required to appear in court in connection with cases where his testimony is of little consequence. This holds especially true in such cases as public drunkenness and family disturbances. I realize that such practices are often predicated upon state and local laws. I definitely feel that officers should be paid for off-duty court appearances.

Chief Howard: Police officers do not spend too much time in court. They spend too much time getting to court. The judicial process needs to be speeded. The state, as well as the defendant should be entitled to a speedy trial. Officers should be paid for court appearances. These are an integral part of their work. The fact that a citizen is not paid for court appearances is irrelevant. The citizen is not required to go around looking for people to take into court and to prepare the cases against them. There is no "offduty" appearance of a policeman in court. This is part of his duty.

Should police have more formally recognized discretionary power in processing and charging minor criminal offenders, such as summons in lieu of arrest or a written warning notice in lieu of summons?

Chief Wilson: The decision of whether or not to invoke the criminal process is largely a matter of police judgment. Among the factors accounting for the exercise of discretion are the volume of violations, the limited resources of the police, the over-generalization of legislative enactments defining criminal conduct, the various local pressures defining criminal conduct and the various local pressures reflecting community values and attitudes. A police officer has a wide area of discretion when he is on patrol. In view of this, our department has instituted a citation release program which gives officers formal guidelines for the use of this power.

Chief Kelley: I would say yes. Discretion actually exists and is available to the individual officer, but many hesitate to use this very important power. It is my firm belief that, if it were formally recognized, many more officers would take advantage of this approach.

In regard to the summons in lieu of arrest, I assume you mean in lieu of bond. Our department presently does this. We have a General Ordinance Summons (GOS) issued for many instances involving misdemeanor cases. A signature is accepted on the summons in lieu of bond. Written warning notices are an accepted practice with most departments and prove a very sensible approach in many areas of violation. This department does not have a formal or written warning notice as such, but many officers issue verbal warnings which appear to have some preventive value.

One single factor makes the police lot on the street a difficult one — laws simply have not kept abreast or in step with the developments in human relations. We have reached the point where it is absolutely imperative that we take very aggressive steps toward alleviating this real gap which exists between the law and the times. Policemen must be able to freely engage in dealing with individual problems on an individual basis and avoid handling every situation in a static manner, simply because the law says that is the way it must be done.

We are experiencing turbulent times and archaic legal machinery is one of the catalysts in the upheaval. As we achieve the goal of further and better-educating our law enforcement officers, we are going to safely be able to entrust them with this vast discretionary power. Decision-making has always been an important part of a police officer's life. As his decisions are based upon genuine understanding and an absolute desire to help, then many of our problems will be overcome. If his decision has its origin in misunderstanding, then we shall continue to experience very significant and serious problems in our urban centers.

Chief Howard: States should enact laws recognizing and governing the descretionary powers of police. Wisconsin, as of July 1, 1970, has such laws permitting summons in lieu of arrest, release without bail, and release of minor offenders without charge. The law should explicitly recognize and the public should clearly understand that police do not and cannot enforce "all the laws, everywhere, all the time," and that they should not arrest or summon every violator of every law and ordinance.

55.

ANTHONY W. SMITH: The Corporation and the Profit Motive

Concern for the environment gave at least temporary promise of being the most overriding social issue of the 1970s. The Santa Barbara oil spill of January 1969 served as a vivid catalyst to rally popular support for curbing pollution that derived from America's advanced technology and enormous use of energy resources. By late 1970 the government had set up the Environmental Protection Agency to be responsible for all controls on air, water, solid wastes, pesticides, and radiation hazards, and to police all states, municipalities, and industries on pollution abatement. The only major hinderance to pollution control was the unanswered question of what strict regulations might mean to the economy and to the affluence most Americans had grown used to since World War II. Many industries that stood to be affected by the new controls showed attitudes ranging from reluctance to hostility on the ecology issue. The corporation versus the environment question was dealt with in a speech by the president and general counsel of the National Parks and Conservation Association, Anthony W. Smith, on October 12, 1971, to the Conservation Committee of the Garden Club of America in New York City. A portion of his speech is reprinted here.

Source: *National Parks and Conservation Magazine*, January 1972.

THE MODERN CORPORATION is a fascinating institution. It is different from what it thinks it is. At least since Berle and Means we know that it is run by managers, often effectively self-perpetuating, and yet with dominant stockholders, usually minority stockholders, exerting an ultimate restraint. And most of us have known for a long time that the large corporations are the dominant institutions of our age.

The big public agencies, the commissions, boards, bureaus, grew up in response to the corporation. The history of the New Deal is largely one of that response.

The big labor unions grew up in response to the power of the corporations. This also was a large part of the history of the New Deal. It was the entire history of the old Congress of Industrial Organizations, the former labor federation, with which I served as Assistant General Counsel through almost its entire life. And so I understand the labor relations side of the industrial managerial process.

Because of the power which business managers exert, to say nothing of the personal wealth of which many can dispose, their decisions are of basic public importance. The large private corporations are not private institutions, even though hundreds of thousands of people may use them as savings banks. Their impact on the economy, on the environment, on employment, on the structure of cities, and on the quality of life for everyone, makes them *de facto* public institutions.

It is no longer true, if it ever was, that businessmen, even when thinking only in terms of their own interests, could rely on profitability as an adequate guide to policy. Managers who are also men of social vision, and there are many of them, think of their corporations as units in a productive economy, not merely as money machines. The must learn to think of their enterprises more and more as participating in environmental processes which can be beneficial or malignant to human society, depending on the conduct of the corporations.

I am suggesting that corporation managers must cultivate an ecological conscience, and a humanitarian conscience as well. It is no longer good enough to say that one is not in business for one's health, or for the welfare of society, or for the welfare of the world; the corporations are indeed in business to make money, or they would be out of business, but they are also in business to produce beneficial, not harmful commodities, and to do so by methods which improve, not impair the environment and the community, because the corporations are public institutions.

As the economic and social chaos of our society deepens, more and more public regulation becomes inevitable; inevitable, that is, unless corporation managers can assume a greater share of responsibility for the consequences of the operations of their enterprises. I would argue today for the rapid assumption of such responsibility.

Let us look briefly at some of the major aspects of the environmental crisis; first of all, atmospheric pollution. American factories (and Russian as well) are still belching forth intolerable quantities of poisonous gases and dust. The power plants are doing the same thing.

Much of this pollution can be eliminated, and some of it can be converted to useful byproducts. Regulation is coming, because human beings do not intend to be smothered. Much better than forced regulation would be a strong voluntary movement within industry to police itself.

Take thermal pollution. This has been bad enough with conventional power plants. It is going to be much worse with atomic energy. Even if we get over from fission to fusion, the thermal pollution problem will be grave. For the rivers it means pressures for the storage of water in farm and forest country which will have serious environmental repercussions. The pumped-storage reservoir compounds the problem. The big reservoir, with its deep and hideous drawdowns, may now be a thing of the past for pollution dilution purposes, but the battle against the reservoir for cooling water and pumped storage is just beginning. We are aware of the limitations and complexities of cooling towers, particularly dry towers, and the additional costs they impose on production, but we shall have to get going with them. Regulation will force this course on industry; how much better it would be if industry took the initiative.

Take the energy crisis, which is central to the environmental crisis. Everyone knows that electric power consumption has been skyrocketing far beyond the growth of population. Among the causes is the mismanagement of our cities; the plunge into air-conditioning, with our office buildings otherwise hermetically sealed, has multiplied the energy requirements of the cities; likewise the digging underground for parking spaces; with stress on ventilation and illumination.

We seem to be locked into this trap. We got there because we did not plan ahead. We got there because we think that gadgets can solve all problems. And because people, and specifically entrepreneurs, were pushing air-conditioning without regard for the environmental and economic consequences.

Take water pollution. We have just witnessed one of the most disgraceful retreats ever executed by a powerful government. All of the Federal agencies with responsibility for the prevention or mitigation of water pollution have announced that phosphate detergents are here to stay.

Run back in your memory over this evolution. First we had soap, which was serviceable. Then we had detergents, the first generation, which bubbled, and our creeks and rivers overflowed with bubbles. Then we had phosphate detergents which did not bubble; but they polluted our streams, rivers, and estuaries with a secondary pollution consequent upon the overstimulation of algae by fertilization, the death of the algae, the death of the fish, and so forth.

And so, for this reason and many others, pollution prevention laws were passed and agencies set up and given responsibility for preventing water pollution, pollution by detergents among others. The corporations ran advertisements to the effect that they were working on a new generation of detergents; please be patient, because the new ones might be worse than the old; and apparently, indeed, they were.

The washing machine manufacturers had built their business on detergents; the notion had also spread, aided by advertising, that every man's collar must be spotless when it came back from the laundry. A reasonably good wash job was good enough for our ancestors, who survived: the public health aspect of a spotless collar is questionable; we could still go back to soap. . . .

This means big research and development operations for the corporations. It means absorbing the environmental costs or deferring production. The consumer will be opposed to taking over these costs, whether by price increases or tax increases. The consumer is getting to be better organized. Environmentalists and consumers will be working together.

Take the management of our forests. I was associated with Gifford Pinchot, America's first great forester, when he was Governor of Pennsylvania. I set up a forestry program in the old CIO, because we had trade union members in the timber industry, and because I was always concerned about the forests. Pinchot was my first consulting forester.

We embarked more recently in the

NPCA on an effort to find and describe a few examples of good forestry in the United States; we had a brief shock at the beginning, because we thought we might not find any good examples. We are discovering them gradually, but they are hard to come by.

Most timber harvesting in America is clear cutting, a method which has devastating effects on soil, water-courses, many forms of wildlife, and recreational, environmental, and scenic factors. Clear cutting is faster and cheaper, but it is not silviculture; it is not, as a general thing, good forestry.

Our big corporations are exploiting these practices all over the world. The Indonesian forests for example, virgin tropical stands, are about to be clear-cut by American corporations under contract. Tropical soils wash away, burn up in the heat, bake into rock when forests are clear-cut. This has happened in Vietnam as a result of military defoliation.

I am one of those who thinks that the overseas practices of American timber companies should be brought under regulation within America; else, we shall be a grimly destructive force elsewhere in the world. And the remarkable thing about it is that many of the major companies have good foresters and highly defensible long-range plans for their own holdings. An ecological conscience is clearly at work in some of the companies. . . .

Take the automobiles and the highways. This is a place, as the signs used to say on the churches, for meditation and prayer. How long is it going to take this nation to outlaw the poisonous exhaust from our automobiles? The haze which hangs over the eastern seaboard seems to be almost continuous and permanent. The congestion of traffic in our cities is ludicrous, though tragic.

I realize that some of the automobile manufacturers are working on alternatives to the present type of internal combustion engine; likewise the Environmental Protection Agency. The United Automobile Workers have issued a strong call to get going fast.

Environmentalists are pushing for the dedication of highway trust funds to the formulation of a sound national transportation policy, which might among other things restore commuter passenger rail transportation, reducing the need for enormous jetports, slowing down the proliferation of dual highways everywhere.

Industry, which has the know-how, should be taking the lead in all these efforts. The public relations benefits would be obvious; but that is not the point. The point is that the corporations have an ecological and humanitarian responsibility in these matters; the impact of the corporation on our total society is the impact of public institutions. Can the environmentalists, the consumers, labor, and industry get together to work for a constructive national transportation policy, and indeed an international policy to avoid such fracases as the SST?

Take a side glance at the Trans-Alaska Pipeline. This was going ahead great guns until about a year and a half ago when the environmentalists stopped it in court. We organized the Environmental Coalition for North America on the issue, and that also had something to do with holding things up. The probability is that it will be held up a lot longer; a good bit of money is tied up. The oil industry should have planned ahead.

The proposed line would gravely impair the delicate Arctic tundra, interrupt caribou migration routes; cross a dangerous earthquake zone; require loading to tankers at Valdez, and a dangerous journey down the coast. The alternative route up the Mackenzie River through Canada, south to Edmonton, forking southeast and southwest has not been fully explored.

The Alyeska Consortium plays with palliative notions; what is needed is to cancel the project unless the Canadian route proves economically and environmentally feasible. What is needed is a genuine effort by the oil industry to serve the public interest. . . .

When we talk about the environmental crisis we must talk about measures for its abatement. When we talk about corporate irresponsibility in the environmental field, we should suggest courses which responsible managers might take.

Responsible industrial managers, in my opinion, should be working for effective public regulation of the abuses in their industries. It has always been rather standard practice for management to oppose regulation. But the truth of the matter is that regulation bears upon the irresponsible; the responsible companies which would like to follow sound practices, guided not only by their ecological and humanitarian consciences, but by sound public relations considerations as well, always find themselves undercut by the fast-buck-only people.

In other words, men of conscience in industrial management should be working with the environmentalists, not against them, to devise legislative, economic, and political measures which will help their industries function on an ecological and humanitarian basis.

If the modern corporation were merely a money making machine, such a proposal would be ridiculous; I would be a silly sentimentalist to advance it. But the modern corporation is in fact, willy-nilly, a social institution; it is going to be bound into the ecological and humanitarian mainstream of modern society, whether it wants to be bound or not. It will be bound by public regulation or public ownership unless it undertakes to commit itself to sound social purposes.

The public-interest purposes of the corporations, and the self-interest purposes of the well managed corporations, as contrasted with the more predacious business units, call for a measure of soundly conceived regulation and for public institutions which will help steer industrial processes in benign directions.

The U. S. standard of living is a bourgeois baby blanket for executives who scream in their sleep. No Pleistocene swamp could match the pestilential horror of modern urban sewage. No children of White Western Progress will escape the dues of peoples forced to haul their raw materials.

EMMET GROGAN, in *Ringolevio: A Life Played for Keeps* (1972)

56.

FRANK CHURCH: Farewell to Foreign Aid

As originally conceived, American economic aid to foreign countries in the postwar era was a means to rehabilitate nations devastated by war or to aid underdeveloped countries. But as the years passed, foreign aid became closely tied to Cold War politics: the need to stop Communist aggression and revolutions in underdeveloped areas, as well as the determination to keep other nations neutral. Much foreign aid thus turned into military aid. Countries whose economies had only marginal health were pressed into buying enormous quantities of armaments from both the United States and the U.S.S.R. It was hardly a coincidence that 95 percent of the post-World War II conflicts were fought in the so-called "third world." American aid to underdeveloped countries led on occasion to an American presence, such as the military advisors in Southeast Asia; and the American experience in that part of the world prompted many citizens to re-evaluate foreign aid policies and to urge, as Senator J. William Fulbright did in 1971, abandonment of the whole program. On October 29, 1971, Senator Frank Church of Idaho gave a speech in the Senate urging a complete revamping of the whole foreign aid concept. Portions of his speech are reprinted here.

Source: *Congressional Record*, 92 Cong., 1 Session, October 29, 1971.

WE STAND IN THIS YEAR 1971 at the end of one decade of disillusion, with no good reason to believe that we are not now embarked upon another. Ten years ago, the leaders of the United States—and to a lesser degree the American people—were filled with zeal about their global goals. With supreme confidence both in our power and capacity to make wise and effective use of it, we proclaimed the dawning of a new era in which America would preserve world peace, stem communism and lead the improverished masses of mankind through the magic point of "takeoff" into a "decade of development." To bring these glories to pass—so we allowed ourselves to believe—we had only to recognize the simple, central fact which Professor Walt Rostrow assured us would bring victory in Vietnam and success in all our other foreign enterprises, "the simple fact that we are the greatest power in the world—if we behave like it."

Looking back on the sixties, no one can deny that we were indeed "the greatest power in the world" and that we surely did "behave like it"—if throwing our might and money around is the correct measure of "behaving like it." Nonetheless, we not only failed to accomplish what we set out to accomplish ten years ago; we have been thrown for losses across the board: in the name of preserving peace, we have waged an endless war; in the guise of serving as sentinel for the "free world," we have stood watch while free governments gave way to military dictatorship in country after country, from one end of our vast hegemony to the other. Today, confidence in American leadership abroad is as gravely shaken as is confidence in the American dollar. As for the "decade of development," ten years of American foreign aid spread far and wide, not only has failed to narrow the gap between rich nations and poor; the gap between the small, wealthy elites and the impoverished masses in most underdeveloped lands has also widened.

Against this backdrop of general failure, the Senate is again being asked to authorize yet another year of foreign aid, as usual. For fiscal year 1972, President Nixon has asked for a foreign aid authorization of more than $3.5 billion, as compared with $3.1 billion appropriated last year, which included $500 million added on for Israel. Clearly, the Administration seeks not just to sustain, but to increase, the level of spending.

The annual foreign aid authorization bill, however, is no more than the visible tip of the iceberg. It constitutes only about two-fifths of a total foreign aid program of over $9 billion proposed for this fiscal year by the Executive Branch.

The magnitude of the foreign aid program can be better grasped by projecting its costs over the period of the next five years. Calculating these costs on a conservative basis, estimating on a projection of existing, not hypothetical, spending levels, the staff of the Senate Foreign Relations Committee forecasts that foreign assistance for the five year period, February 1973-1977, will exceed $50 billion! Less than half of the five year total will result from programs authorized in the regular foreign assistance and military credit sales bills. Thirteen billion will be attributable to programs now funded through the Defense Appropriation bill, and the P.I. 480 program will account for an additional $7 billion. . . .

On the basis of our experience over the last decade in dealing with the third world—unquestionably the "disaster area of our foreign policy"—John Kenneth Galbraith suggests four lessons that we should have learned:

First, it now seems clear that the "Marshall Plan syndrome"—the belief that American capital, energy and know-how could not fail to work economic wonders in any country on whom these blessings might be conferred—has turned out to be largely irrelevant and unworkable in the poor countries which lack Europe's pre-existing organizational, administrative and technical capacities.

Second, it is evident now, if it was not before, that in the poor rural societies of the third world the concepts of "communism" and capitalism are of little more than "terminological" significance. The fact that these countries are poor and rural has vastly greater meaning than the fact that such little enterprise as they have may be "socialist" or "free."

Third, in the course of discovering that the inner life and development of the third world lie beyond the reach of external control, we have also discovered that the futile effort to shape another country's development calls into being an enormous, intrusive civilian and military bureaucracy. Whereas colonial power was exercised directly, Professor Galbraith observes, through a simple line of command, our campaign to win the hearts and minds of foreign populations requires "a much more massive table of organization." Indeed, in the course of recent hearings on Brazil in the Western Hemisphere Subcommittee of the Senate Foreign Relations Committee, the fact came out that, relative to population, we have twice as many American officials administering our aid program in Brazil today as the British had in India governing that country before independence.

Finally, Professor Galbraith notes, we have seen how an overseas bureaucracy acquires a life and purpose of its own, only tenuously controlled by the Executive in Washington and effectively beyond the reach of Congress and the American people. Like any bureaucracy —especially a colonial service far removed from its home base—the American aid and military establishment abroad are motivated by one simple unshakable ambition: to survive and perpetuate their species.

Finally, I would suggest a fifth lesson to be drawn from the experience of the sixties: that, even with enormous power and the best of intentions, there are some things we cannot do, things which are beyond our moral and intellectual resources. If we learn nothing else from the experience of the sixties, it will profit us immeasurably to have learned that being richer and stronger than everybody else has not made us wiser. When it comes to wisdom, we are part of the pack; just knowing that will be wisdom enough. . . .

Nonetheless, our Administration persists in the delusion that it can buy influence with aid. So President Nixon seems to believe in his insistence on letting military and economic aid filter through to the government of West Pakistan, even though American arms may be used to carry out the savage suppression of the people of East Pakistan. When the House of Representatives voted in early August to suspend aid to the West Pakistani regime, except for relief assistance in East Pakistan and for East Pakistani refugees in India, President Nixon expressed his disapproval on the gound that an aid cutoff would jeopardize the Pakistani government's ability to create "stability" and would undermine our own ability to "influence the course of events . . ." In terms of the *realpolitik* of which this Administration seems so fond, our continuation of aid "already in the pipeline" to Pakistan is supposed to buy us influence with the ruling generals in Islamabad and help offset the influence of Communist China. The cost of this "influence"—such as it may be—is the loss of our influence with India, which has now concluded a friendship treaty with the Soviet Union. Worse still, as the *New York Times* put it in a recent editorial, our continuing support of the Pakistani government "has put the United States in the position of subsidizing, and thus seeming to condone, crimes against humanity unequaled since Hitler's time."

While experience has shown that our aid programs have little if any relevance either to the deterrence of communism or the encouragement of democracy, they have been effective in certain instances in keeping unpopular regimes in power. They have certainily contributed to that end in the cases of the Greek colonels, the Pakistani generals and the Brazilian junta. All of these regimes are dictatorships, but they are anti-communist and therefore pass our eligibility test for membership in the "free world." A government may torture and terrorize its own population but—from the standpoint of our policy makers—as long as it remains anti-communist, provides "stability," generally supports American foreign policy and is hospitable to American investment, it qualifies, for purposes of aid, as a "free country."

"Stability" is an antiseptic word; it reveals nothing about how individual people live and die. "Stability," as Richard Barnet points out, "is an *antidevelopment* goal in countries where the established institutions perpetuate poverty and the ruling elites show no serious commitment to change. . . ."

The foreign assistance bill, now before us, contains authorizations totaling approximately $1.5 billion in military and economic aid for 42 of the 74 member-states that either opposed our position or abstained on this key vote.

Correspondingly, the bill contains aggregate authorizations of approximately $2.4 billion for 55 member-states that either voted against our position, or abstained, on the second question that admitted the People's Republic to the United Nations and expelled Nationalist China.

If our long-term loans, made in the name of nourishing development abroad, serve neither to deter communism nor strengthen democratic government, and if they do so little to furnish the destitute with a broader measure of social justice wherever they may live, why do we persist in making them? To find the answer to that question, one must begin the search here at home, in the land of the lender.

There is abundant evidence that our foreign aid program is much less philanthropic than we have cared to portray. Indeed, the figures suggest that it is patently self-serving. Former AID Director William Gaud discloses that, as a result of tied loans "ninety-three percent of AID funds are spent directly in the United States. . . . Just last year 4,000 American firms in fifty states received $1.3 billion in AID funds for products supplied as part of the foreign aid program." Similarly, George D. Woods, former President of the World Bank, has observed that "bilateral programs of assistance have had as one of their primary objectives helping the high-income countries themselves; they have looked toward financing export sales, toward tactical support of diplomacy, toward holding military positions thought strategic."

The oft-asserted lament that our foreign aid program lacks a constituency in the United States is just another of those myths we hold dear. Actually, our bilateral aid program is, in effect, the soft-loan window of the Export-Import Bank; it is the source from which foreign governments borrow money on easy terms with which to buy goods and services from within the United States. As such, it enjoys a lively constituency which exerts steady pressure on the government to keep the program going. . . .

I can no longer cast my vote to prolong the bilateral aid program, as it is now administered. I could understand—though perhaps not condone—a foreign aid program that is essentially self-serving. We live, after all, in a selfish world. But the present program is designed primarily to serve private business interests at the expense of the American people. In far too many countries, as in the case of Brazil, we poured in our aid money for one overriding purpose, the stabilization of the economy in order to furnish American capital with a "favorable climate for investment." The search for foreign investment opportunities by the largest American corporations is relentless and irrepressible, as the biggest profits are to be found abroad, where the tax bite can frequently be reduced or averted. Moreover, the risk of loss due to political instability, riot, revolution or expropriation, has been largely lifted from the investor and shifted to the U. S. Government. OPIC, the Overseas Private Investment Corporation, backed by the Federal Government, readily insures American companies against risks abroad for which no comparable insurance is available at home. The multi-million dollar losses incurred by American copper companies, resulting from the nationalization of their holdings by Allende's Marxist regime in Chile, are likely to be borne—not by the companies that eagerly invested there—but by the American taxpayer. Our foreign aid program has become a spreading money tree under which the biggest American businesses find shelter when they invest abroad! Small wonder that the crumbling ghettoes in our cities, along with our declining rural communities, have to beg and scrounge for new capital!

As my service in the State amply demonstrates, I am not a foe of a genuine foreign aid program, having long since acknowledged that any country as advantaged as ours should do what it can to help other people improve their lot. But no longer will I endorse with my vote a foreign aid program which has been twisted into a parody and a farce.

The major preoccupation of the present foreign aid program is the massive disbursement of munitions which we either give away or make available at bargain basement prices. We ply half a hundred foreign governments with our weaponry. Most of the world has become a dumping ground for ships, tanks and planes, which we label as excess to our needs. Easy credit is available at interest rates well below the cost of money to the U. S. Government. The Military Assistance Program has become a preposterous scandal. It should be drastically curtailed, not enlarged.

As for our long-term bilateral loans made in the name of promoting economic development, it is long past time that this function were passed over entirely to the World Bank, the Asian Bank, the Inter-American Development Bank and other multilateral lending agencies, which were set up for this purpose. I am prepared, now and in the future, to support substantial U. S. contributions to these agencies. In this manner, we could set a worthy example of international responsibility and beckon other rich nations to share the load with us.

I would confine our bilateral aid in the future to technical assistance grants, administered, where feasible, by the Peace Corps. It was through technical assistance—the successor to Harry Truman's original Point 4—that the "green revolution" was achieved in Asia and the hand of famine stayed. This aspect of our foreign aid, involving outright grants, not loans, has constituted the worthiest part of the program. On account of it—and in hopes that the objectionable parts would be whittled down and ultimately displaced—I have tarried too long as a supporter and indulged in too much wishful thinking.

Events of the past few weeks on Capital Hill have finally dispelled my illusions. Instead of cutting back on the foreign aid package, Congress is about to enlarge on it. We are in the process of doing the same with the gigantic military budget, approving more money for the Pentagon this year than we spent at the height of our involvement in Vietnam. Incredible, but true!

The acquiescence of Congress to these money demands of the Nixon Administration make it clear that we have no disposition, despite all the pious talk, of changing our spending habits. The "new priorities" promised the American people won't be realized, as long as we refuse to cut our huge foreign and military spending. The long-neglected problems of crime, drugs, poverty and pollution, which afflict so many of our people here at home, will continue to fester and grow.

1972

57.

Peter Harnik: Funmobile Folly

The first snowmobile with commercial possibilities was developed as early as 1936 by Joseph A. Bombardier of Quebec. But it was not until 1959 that the one- or two-passenger vehicles now in general use were manufactured and marketed. During the 1960s the snowmobile became an enormously popular winter recreation machine in many parts of the United States and Canada; and by the end of the 1971-72 winter season there were at least 1.3 million of them in operation. Their use for hunting, fishing, and racing also served to provide a source of income for resort areas that had normally closed up for the season after the summer vacationers and autumn hunters had departed. As the generally unregulated use of snowmobiles became prevalent, it was apparent that they could be a source of numerous safety and ecological hazards that had not been much thought about in the early 1960s. In an article published in January 1972, the editor of Environmental Action, *Peter Harnik, described some of the problems connected with this new form of recreation. Portions of his article are reprinted here.*

Source: *National Parks and Conservation Magazine*, January 1972.

The snowmobile, a hybrid recreational vehicle that combines two skis with the tread of a tank, has virtually completed its invasion of the northland. Although a great deal of hostility and resistance remains among the natives, spokesmen for the machine say they have the situation under control. Nothing short of a massive governmental counterattack, they feel, could dislodge the powerful snowmobile from its control of the northern United States and Canada.

Official chroniclers of the snowmobile's meteoric takeover have attributed the machine's success to its brilliant analysis of the American mentality. They point out that it caters to our infatuation with noise, speed, and the great outdoors. They delight in showing how the machine fills the need for "healthful" activity without demanding any work. They write in tones of hushed admiration about the machine's advertising campaigns showing young girls flying through the air on snowmobiles.

Most important, they say, was the timing of the machine's introduction. The first snowmobile prototypes appeared in the mid-'50s, but the machine did not go into mass production until the early 1960s —just in time to take advantage of the new crop of consumers born during the post-war baby boom.

There are nearly two million snowmobiles in North America, up from less than 100,000 in 1965 and 259 in 1959. Snowmobiling is now a billion-dollar industry.

The snowmobile industry credits the sport with revolutionizing winter in the northern states and in Canada. Industry spokesmen say that tourists, snowmobilers, and vast sums of money have been lured northward, and that the traditional flow of northerners to Florida and other southern spots in winter has been stemmed. . . .

Unfortunately, some of the people who visit summer cabins in the dead of winter do not own them. Complaints of vandalism have increased with sales of snowmobiles. Cabins and shacks that had been unreachable and unprotectable now are at the mercy of snowmobilers, some of whom justify causing damage on grounds of "fun" or, worse, "need"—it is cold in the northern woods in midwinter.

State troopers and state legislators began receiving other, more serious complaints as the snowmobile boom swept the nation. For one thing, litter began to turn up in hitherto pristine places. For another, the number of mangled snowmobilers began to mount.

One hundred and two people were killed in snowmobile accidents last year, and 428 injuries were reported. These figures represent a casualty rate about six times as high as that of automobiles. Many snowmobilers, in fact, were killed by automobiles, but others were crushed by trains, decapitated by fences and wires, and lured to frigid deaths by wide expanses of glistening, thin ice.

The snowmobile industry steadfastly maintains that the machines are safe and that accidents and mishaps are overwhelmingly the fault of reckless, careless operators—"the rotten apples in every bunch." While there is truth to the contention, there is also evidence that the average snowmobile is a fairly shoddy piece of merchandise. Brakes have failed, throttles have been known to freeze in the "open" position, handlebars have bent and broken, and almost every engine has proven dangerously loud and dirty. Furthermore, the design and construction of snowmobile seats has been uniformly inadequate, and frequent spinal and back injuries have occurred even with proper use.

The actual mechanical faults of snowmobiles, however, probably lead to fewer fatalities than do the manufacturers' advertising policies. Like its relatives the all-terrain vehicle and the dune buggy, the snowmobile is promoted as a "go anywhere, do anything" machine. Its image is one of power and adventuresomeness and not one of caution and restraint, either on the part of its drivers or for the benefit of the natural environment.

With names like Stinger, Hurricane, SST 443, Rocket, and Firebird, these machines were not built to appeal to those who wish to use them on quiet, peaceful treks into the wilds. The average snowmobile owner, according to surveys, is a 40-year-old skilled laborer or manager who earns somewhat over $10,000 a year; the average snowmobile driver, according to general observation, is his teenage son.

Snowmobile users have descended heavily upon both public and private lands. Because few snowmobile owners are large enough landholders to suit their explorative urges, and because the machines are prohibited, for the most part, from public roadways, snowmobilers have taken to traversing the countryside with abandon. Their practices have ranged from illegally using national park lands to snipping fences and wires on private land and, in more extreme cases, to terrorizing children at play and racing around and around the properties of "unpopular" neighbors.

State regulatory agencies, although ordinarily reluctant to move aggressively on such problems, have begun to recognize the beginnings of a crisis. The North Dakota State Outdoor Recreation Agency, for instance, issued a statement that said, in part: "The step by [the North Dakota] government to tighten up [snowmobiling] rules has been a direct result of foolhardy snowmobilers who cannot tell what time of night it is, or the difference between public and private property, or have any common sense for the safety of passengers, pedestrians, and the like. A cut fence, trampled crops, dead livestock, and assorted abuses have ruined the hunter-farmer relationship. Snowmobiling is approaching this unreconcilable plateau."

Even if a method of restricting snowmobile operators to responsible persons were to be developed, a number of extremely serious problems with the machines would remain. These problems relate not to questions of health and safety, nor to legal problems, but to a critical area that is much harder to quantify and to analyze: the wintertime ecology. . . .

The most immediate and pressing allegations related to the snowmobile's most publicized shortcoming: noisiness. The machines are noisy enough to annoy nonusers and nearby residents, both indoors and outside. Snowmobiles are so loud as to terrify certain species of wildlife and to affect the metabolic rates and breeding patterns of other species. They are loud enough to drown out the sounds of approaching automobiles and trains. Some of them, in fact, are so loud as to cause varying degrees of hearing loss among their drivers and riders. Dr. Fred Bess, Director of Audiology at Central Michigan University, stated that the winner of the Michigan International 500 Snowmobile Race "reported deafness for two solid weeks following the race."

Among his other findings at the International 500 race, Bess came up with two shockers. The noise level in the spectator area was found to exceed 116 decibels at times. This is equivalent to the sound of a chain saw at work 50 feet away. More astounding, his studies added: "Analysis of the snowmobile engine noise demonstrated that some machines produced intensity levels in excess of 140 dB [decibels] at two-thirds throttle. These levels exceed the threshold of pain." For comparison, the threshold of pain is also exceeded by the roar of a jet engine at less than 50 feet. . . .

The most distressing facet of these allegations and the many others that are being brought to light as research continues is that all of them are the result of the mechanical workings of the snowmobile itself. Even the world's best driver cannot fail to leave tracks in the snow, cannot avoid breaking saplings that are just below the surface of the snow, and cannot control the damage he does to crops.

The charges of environmental injury that are leveled against snowmobiles are very serious. And they do not even include such "sports" as motorized hunting, harassing wildlife, leaving behind debris, and reckless driving—all of which seem to characterize the sport wherever it becomes established.

Snowmobiling has consistently received bad press, and the industry is as defensive as it is rich. To counteract the rising tide of hostility among local populations, outdoorsmen, and conservationists, the industry has encouraged the creation of snowmobile clubs and associations—groups that can serve as self-regulatory police forces on their membership. While these clubs do a reasonably good job, they cannot, of course, make arrests for misdeeds or confiscate snowmobiles from consistently reckless users.

What the clubs *can* do, however, is exert pressure on local citizenry and governments to make more land available to snowmobiles, either through easement agreements or through purchases. In effect, the snowmobile associations have become grassroots pressure groups that push the cause of the snowmobile into the most remote areas. Thus, while little headway is made in curbing environmental and social problems, further gains are made in assuring that the snowmobile is "here to stay."

The snowmobile industry proudly hails its creation as a "revolutionary" vehicle. Although the term is applied with typical Madison Avenue flippancy, it is far truer than the manufacturers might care to believe. The snowmobile, along with its sister all-terrain vehicles, represents a major challenge to the traditional concepts of private property and individual rights.

Put simply, the snowmobile and other off-road vehicles have never had a technological precedent. Therefore, lawmakers, regulatory officials, and the courts never have had to deal with comparable entities in formulating and promulgating policy. Automobiles are sharply limited by size and design to relatively flat and well maintained roadways. Motorboats, of course, are restricted to fairly significant bodies of water, and even there they usually can be controlled. Airplanes, while often a nuisance, are restrained by their need for landing facilities. Snowmobiles, however, given snow, can penetrate virtually any area with relative ease.

Regulatory agencies have been typically slow to face the challenge. In the early days of snowmobiling, public land managers and rural officials apparently hoped the "fad" would somehow disappear by itself. They consoled themselves that the problems were slight by virtue of the small numbers of snowmobilers. Then, when the sport mushroomed in the late 1960s, it was too late. Snowmobile users had become as much a part of "the public" as nonusers in the eyes of the regulators and deserved equal protection under law. The user had, in effect, finessed the nonuser—first by being too inconspicuous to warrant attention and then by becoming too powerful to stop.

Naturally, state legislatures were even slower to react. In fact, with one exception—the almost universal banning of snowmobiles from public roads—state legislation continues to be piecemeal, stopgap, and nonuniform. Politicians tend to be even more hamstrung by divergent public opinion than are administrators.

Even the courts, the traditional guardians of individual rights, have handed down conflicting rulings. In some areas snowmobile bans have been upheld on grounds of public nuisance. In other places snowmobilers who were arrested got off with barely a warning from judges who did not consider the infractions serious enough to warrant attention. And in at least one other case a property owner was denied the right to close his property to snowmobilers on the grounds that he permitted hikers to use the same route in the summertime!

So where do we stand? Until recently, virtually every federal and state land management agency had established different policies on snowmobiles. Some state parks contained specially marked and maintained trails solely for snowmobilers. Others forbade them entirely. Some municipalities and counties banned them during certain nighttime hours. Others encouraged them. The U.S. Forest Service left the decision to the discretion of Forest Supervisors, with a policy position that the use of off-road vehicles was to be considered a legitimate use of the forests—unless it conflicted with other uses. In the Department of the Interior, the Bureau of Land Management exercised virtually no control over off-road vehicles, the Park Service left the decision to Park Superintendents, and the Bureau of Reclamation had "no policy." The Park Service indicated that it was anxious to control snowmobiles quite closely through regulation, while BLM pursued an educational approach by seeking the cooperation of user associations.

Although the Interior Department's policy has recently been unified and consolidated through the work of a task force on off-road vehicles, this small step makes little difference in terms of widespread snowmobile use. The long term effects on the wintertime ecology are still virtually unknown. Wildlife will continue to be harassed. Young saplings will still be injured and become stunted. Nonusers from coast to coast will still be bothered by noise and fumes. Users will continue to receive aural damage and hearing loss. Unnecessary deaths will still occur. And the industry will continue to shovel in the profits.

It would be ridiculous, even in a forum such as this, to advocate a total ban on snowmobiles. The time for that has come—and long gone. The snowmobile is here to stay.

What is not here to stay, however, is the noisy, unsafe snowmobile with its largely unregulated and often reckless driver who crisscrosses terrain without heed to ownership or ecological imperatives. Conservationists *can* fight back against domination by this machine and these abuses. In fact, nonusers and regulators alike have the obligation to force the snowmobile industry and snowmobile users to absorb all the costs of their Fun Machine.

This means the snowmobile noise level should be limited to no more than 72 decibels at a distance of 50 feet, no matter how much that adds to the cost of the machine. This is equivalent to the sound of a vacuum cleaner at 10 feet.

Snowmobiles should be banned from high-density areas, from areas of ecological value and fragility, from areas of historic importance, and from areas that are important to wildlife. They should also be excluded wherever there is inadequate snow cover to protect saplings. And in each case it should be the snowmobiler who must prove that an area can safely be opened up, not vice versa.

Snowmobiling should be limited to daytime use except in emergencies and in cases of real economic hardship.

A luxury tax should also be placed on the machines, with the money slated for research into the damage caused by off-road vehicles.

Most important for effective regulation, snowmobilers must be required to have a license that is mandatorily revoked for a year in the event of any offense.

The snowmobile, with all of its life-saving and death-dealing capabilities, has lived "off the land" for too long. It has amassed some very large debts to the society around it, many of them unknowingly. Nevertheless, it is time to pay all the debts back. It is up to aggrieved nonusers and conservationists to make sure that the debts *are* all paid back and to take steps so that no more are incurred.

58.

The Leisure Boom

By the 1970s tourism had become the world's largest single industry. In the United States all the variations on tourism including camping, boating, hunting, water-skiing, winter sports, fishing, bicycling, and ordinary vacation trips expanded greatly during the 1960s. The money spent by Americans on these and other spare time activities amounted to more than $105 billion by 1972. The following report published in 1972 surveyed the range of activities on which Americans spent their time and money.

Source: Reprinted from *U.S. News & World Report*, April 17, 1972.

A "LEISURE BOOM" that has grown to phenomenal proportions will push 105 billion dollars into the U. S. economy this year.

The money Americans are now spending on spare-time activities exceeds national-defense costs. It is more than the outlay for construction of new homes. It surpasses the total of corporate profits. It is far larger than the aggregate income of U. S. farmers. It tops the over-all value of this country's exports.

And estimates are that the dollar volume of leisure-time expenditures will more than double during the decade of the '70s.

A study by the Economic Unit of "U. S. News & World Report" shows the nature and extent of the boom, its market aspects and its dynamics.

Main factors powering the surge are these:

1. The rapid rise in personal income — totaling an estimated 920 billion dollars in 1972, a gain of almost 50 percent in a five-year period.

2. More free time. For example, over 40 million people now work under conditions of employment entitling them to three-week vacations. A federal law on holidays, which became effective in 1971, provides five three-day week-ends each year. Also, a trend toward a four-day workweek has now become discernible, with about 2,000 companies now following that procedure.

3. Earlier retirement is spurred by improved private-pension plans and higher Social Security benefits.

Where the money goes. Spending for recreational equipment and for admission to sporting events, movies, stage plays, concerts and other cultural attractions adds up to a whopping total of 50 billion dollars.

The most spectacular splurge is in purchases of products used in the pursuit of pleasure or relaxation—from bowling balls to bicycles, from color-television sets to camping vehicles, from cameras to cabin cruisers.

Dollar totals in sales of leisure equipment have increased about 52 percent for the past five years. The rate varies sharply among individual items.

One reason for the spiral in equipment buying is the accelerating desire to "get back to nature." The lure of the great outdoors is proving more magnetic, year after year, statistics show.

For instance, the National Park Service expects a record 212 million visits to its areas this year. The Army's Corps of Engineers, responsible for 8.5 million acres of land and water, anticipates more than 300 million visits to its preserves.

A survey by the Department of the Interior shows that 75 percent of the U.S. population from age nine upward is involved in some form of outdoor recreation.

The mounting interest in camping has triggered a boom of its own. Right now, there are four million camping vehicles in the United States, at a price scale going all the way from $300 trailers to self-propelled, customized "motor homes" costing as much as $25,000.

The recreational-vehicle industry estimates that its sales this year will amount to more than 1.8 billion dollars—of which "motor homes" are expected to account for 720 million dollars. About 72,000 of these will be manufactured in 1972, selling for an average of around $10,000. Four years ago, the annual output of "motor homes" was only 13,200, valued at 114 million dollars.

"Motor homes"—equipped with facilities for sleeping, cooking, eating and bathing—are designed for those who want to camp or tour in luxury.

Less expensive are travel trailers, of which 200,000 are expected to be produced this year, valued at 680 million dollars. Average price: $3,400.

Tent trailers and self-contained truck "campers" are popular. Estimated production total this year is 228,000. Retail value: 415 million dollars.

By 1978, the number of camping vehicles in use in the United States will nearly double, to 7.5 million, if projections are accurate.

The upsurge already is straining facilities in national parks and other scenic areas. In three national parks, the Department of the Interior has begun limiting visitors to wilderness areas.

New ways to get around. The "leisure boom" has given rise to many types of recreation vehicles—snowmobiles, dune buggies, minibikes are examples.

Snowmobiles are proliferating in astonishing numbers. By the end of this year's winter season, 1.3 million were in operation.

The ski-tracked vehicle can carry two persons at speeds up to 50 miles an hour. Average cost is $1,000.

Industry spokesmen forecast sales of 600,000 snowmobiles in 1972. Sales of accessories—such as suits, helmets and sleds that can be towed behind the vehicles—will help to make the sport a billion-dollar business this year, it is predicted.

Skiing is another snow sport on which people are spending lavishly. In 1971, about 4.25 million ski enthusiasts spent 1.3 billion dollars on equipment, lodging, travel, lift tickets and entertainment at winter resorts, according to Ski Industries America.

Unseasonably warm weather in the Northeast—which does about 40 percent of the nation's ski business—held down the number of skiers on the slopes this year, but industry officials remain confident that skiing will be a 2-billion-dollar-a-year leisure activity by 1974.

The comeback of the bicycle continues to delight bike manufacturers. Sales last year were the highest in history—8.5 million units. Industry leaders say the demand for their product is sure to keep growing. The Department of the Interior reports that there are 37 million American bicyclists.

The urge for fun on wheels has led to a minibike vogue. The minibike is a small two-wheeler, usually powered by a four-cycle engine of from two to six horsepower. These machines, which cost from $130 to $400, are especially favored by youngsters.

By the end of 1971, there were more than 2 million minibikes rolling along—10 times as many as in 1965.

Aquatic activities. Water skiing is a pastime that is attracting devotees in rapidly growing numbers. The American Water Ski Association estimated that 11 million people tried the sport at least once in 1971—spending 45 million dollars for skis alone.

Other forms of aquatic activity are generating plenty of business, too. There are 1.5 million surfboard users, about half of whom are true zealots.

It's a sport for the young. The average devotee is 17 years old. Average outlay is $225 a year for equipment, beach fees and travel. Skin diving, too, has upward for a million regulars who spent around 30 million dollars for equipment in 1971.

More people than ever before are playing tennis. The 10.7 million who now enjoy that game buy 50 million dollars' worth of rackets, balls and accessories every year.

A wintertime variation that is catching on is platform tennis, played on a raised court that is only one fourth the size of the regulation tennis court. About 2,000 platforms have been built. The growth rate for players and courts is 25 percent a year, according to Richard C. Squires, one of the leading advocates of the game.

Golf, of course, is an important segment of the leisure-oriented industry. There are 12.25 million golfers and 10,500 courses in the U.S.

When green fees, club-membership costs, prices of golf clubs, rental of electric carts and other expenses are totaled, it adds up to a 3-billion-dollar-a-year activity.

The turn to second homes. One effect of the spreading determination to break away from routine is being felt in the housing market. At this point, about 2 million U.S. families own second homes—used for vacationing—and trade sources say that the number is increasing each year by from 150,000 to 200,000 units. Sales value is currently estimated at more than 2 billion dollars a year—almost 55 percent higher than five years ago. The total is expected to double in the next eight years.

Vacation homes come in all sizes, shapes and degrees of cost. The two most popular architectural styles, according to "Vacation Home & Leisure Living" magazine, are the chalet and the A-frame. The magazine's survey also found that:

—Two thirds of vacation homes being built in the U.S. cost $10,000 or more, exclusive of land costs. Nearly one fourth represent an investment of at least $20,000.

—More than 60 percent have three or more bedrooms; 50 percent have two or more baths; 75 percent have more than 1,000 square feet of living space.

—Among second-home owners, 86 percent have incomes of $10,000 a year or higher; 54 percent exceed the $15,000 mark. More than half are under 40 years of age and four fifths are married.

—More than half of the vacation homes are custom built; 40 percent are manufactured or prefabricated.

—Proximity to water is an important factor. The survey disclosed that 57 percent of vacation-home sites are near a lake, a river or the seashore.

The "vacation condominium"—at seashore and other resort areas—is proving to be appealing to those who prefer apartment-style living.

These homes—rising in formidable numbers—can cost as little as $15,000 or as much as $80,000.

A new boost for the vacation-home market appears to be imminent. The Federal Housing Administration is preparing to insure second-home mortgages. Officials of the Department of Housing and Urban Development say that the insurance may be available as early as next year.

Race for vacation land. Complementing the interest in holiday homes is a flourishing market for vacation land and lots. According to the American Land Development Association, a trade group, there are now 9,000 vacation-land-development firms in the U.S. Last year, the ALDA estimates, the industry sold 650,000 lots, valued at 5.5 billion dollars.

The average vacation lot sells for $9,000 and is only one quarter of an acre in size.

The cost is high because more and more developers are offering special amenities for community use, such as clubhouses, riding stables, tennis courts, marinas, swimming pools, private beaches and ski slopes.

One land expert comments:

"The public is demanding the better life. People don't want a lot on the far corner of some farmer's acreage. They want all the conveniences and they're willing to pay for them."

All levels of government are participating in the land race.

The Federal Government, from 1965 through July 1, 1973, will have provided 1.6 billion dollars for acquisition of recreation lands. Part of the money—channeled through the Land and Water Conservation Fund—is earmarked for State and local governments in a matching-grant program.

Mainly through bond issues, States and localities have raised about 1.8 billion dollars since 1965 for recreational purposes. Some of this ties in with the federal matching funds.

The search for fun. With all their spending on home-area sports and vacation cottages, Americans keep showing increasing mobility.

This year, according to latest estimates of the American Automobile Association, 40 billion dollars will be spent on domestic pleasure travel. This—the second largest component of the leisure budget—includes vacation trips, overnight journeys, and sparetime jaunts of more than 100 miles.

Just getting to and from vacation areas, motorists will drive more than 300 billion miles in the U.S. this year, the AAA estimates. That is 33 percent of the total estimated mileage for privately owned vehicles. The AAA says that 90 percent of all domestic pleasure travel is by automobile. About 85 percent of all such travel is for distances of 300 miles or less.

Travel abroad is attracting more and more Americans. This year, indications are that about 6.3 million U.S. citizens will go to foreign countries on vacation trips.

These travelers are expected to spend 7.5 billion dollars—a 700-million-dollar increase over 1971.

Devaluation of the dollar—which has been cheapened by about 12 percent, on the average, in relation to European currencies—is not expected to deter U.S. tourists from going overseas in record numbers.

A spot check of advance bookings on transatlantic airlines indicates an increase of eight to ten percent over last year's tourist travel. Many travelers cut costs by using "group inclusive" rates, which are appreciably lower than basic individual fares.

Worry about inflation, the political scrambles in a presidential election year, tax burdens and other considerations have little effect, the statistics show, on "escape" spending.

There is impressive evidence that satisfying the leisure-time desires of the people of the U.S. is a growth operation with few parallels.

59.

Erwin Knoll: The Education of Henry Durham

In 1970 Ernest Fitzgerald, Air Force management advisor, testified before a congressional committee that cost overruns on the new C-5A cargo jet would be at least $2 billion. For making these embarrassing revelations, Fitzgerald was fired from his job by the Pentagon. (In 1973, after appeals to the U. S. Civil Service Commission, he was reinstated.) The C-5A was built by Lockheed Aircraft Corporation of Marietta, Georgia. The following selection tells the story of a Lockheed employee who learned from the inside what the problem of cost overruns was all about. The article, consisting mostly of Henry Durham's own statements, was written by Erwin Knoll, Washington editor of the Progressive. *It is reprinted here in part.*

Source: *The Progressive*, January 1972.

Drive west on the highway that cuts through Marietta, past the old town square with its statue of Senator Alexander Stephens Clay, past the sprawling Lockheed plant on Dobbins Air Force Base, where they are building the huge C-5A cargo plane. If you are caught in the traffic crush when a shift lets out, you will find it hard to believe that Lockheed is in trouble—so much trouble that the taxpayers of the United States must keep the company afloat with a $250 million loan guarantee. Lockheed's Marietta payroll is down from 30,000 a couple of years ago to fewer than 20,000 today, but that is still enough to make it the largest industrial employer in Marietta, in Cobb County, in Georgia.

The landscape turns suburban a few miles past the Lockheed plant. You drive along tree-lined streets where comfortable brick ramblers sit on carefully tended lawns—the homes of engineers and computer programmers and middle-management men. The house at 256 Merrydale Drive SW is one of these. The jeep parked in the driveway has an American flag decal and a National Rifle Association emblem affixed to the rear window.

The house, the jeep, the flag decal, and the NRA membership belong to Henry Durham, whose neighbors and former friends have recently proclaimed him Public Enemy Number Two. In Marietta, the top title—Public Enemy Number One—is reserved for Senator William Proxmire, the Wisconsin Democrat who led the unsuccessful Senate effort to block the Lockheed loan guarantee.

The calls have let up lately, though I still get an occasional one in the middle of the night, Henry Durham told me. *Sometimes they call me names, sometimes they just breathe into the telephone and hang up. Uptown I see people I've known for twenty years. They give me a dirty look and turn away. A thing like this sure lets you find out who your friends are. . . .*

The reaction of the church was what hurt us worst. All of a sudden, when this happened, the church just turned cold as a cucumber. They told Nan that they "understood" she didn't want to teach Sunday school any more. Not one member of the church, not one officer, not the preacher, has made any move at all to ease the community pressure against us. Not one word has been said. You would think the preacher would be the first to hold high the banner of integrity, or at least to affirm that a person has the right to say what he thinks. Not a word. . . .

We didn't understand that Billy Graham was a business, too—a big business. We've had to learn a lot about a lot of things. . . .

I was determined to advance to a vice presidency, or as far as I could go. I've always felt that a person should advance within a company in accordance with his determination, effort, skill, and dedication to doing a good job, you know. I worked long, hard hours—an average of ten to twelve hours a day—and then I'd go in on the weekends. Sometimes they paid me for the overtime and sometimes they didn't—I never asked. I went in on Saturdays, and on Sundays, when my wife went to church, I'd go in to Lockheed to catch up on my paperwork and do my planning. Everything had to be perfect. I never left without having organized for the next day.

I neglected my family—I know I did, and I regret it now. When I came home at night the kids would have been fed and Nan would cook another supper for me. Lockheed had priority; Lockheed came first. I can see now how large corporations do that to people. If Lockheed said something was right, you know, it was right. What was good for Lockheed was good for the world, as far as I was concerned.

The education of Henry Durham began in the summer of 1969, when he became a general department manager in the Marietta plant, with jurisdiction over some 250 employees involved in production control operations on the C-5A flight line. The big plane was already in big trouble. More than a half year earlier, A. Ernest Fitzgerald, a civilian cost analyst for the Air Force, had revealed before Senator Proxmire's Joint Economic Committee that costs on Lockheed's C-5A contract would run some $2 billion higher than initial projections. In his new job, Durham began to learn why.

I began to notice serious discrepancies on the airplanes almost immediately—starting with the first one I saw. The production people were making parts requests for which they had no authority; the paperwork showed that the parts had already been installed. Some were small parts, no bigger than your fingernail, some were large and tremendously expensive. Thousands of missing parts—and they really were missing.

At first I thought it was just some kind of clerical error. I didn't want to believe that anything dishonest was going on. I wanted to believe there was just some fantastic unseen problem that was causing this, you know. I had always known that Lockheed had problems in quality control, and I had been fighting those problems for years. But this was something bigger. . . .

When I was sure of my facts, beyond a shadow of a doubt, I went to my superiors and told them about it. I went to see all levels of management—the production manager, the assistant to the director of manufacturing, the director of manufacturing. I went to see all the division managers in production, the people responsible for having the parts installed. At first, they expressed shock and concern, and told me not to worry about it, they would take care of it. Then I began getting adverse, hostile reactions. They would say something like, "You SOB, what do you mean running around talking about missing parts? Why don't you just go mind your own business and let us tend to ours?" That just made me more determined than ever.

All I wanted Lockheed to do was to halt everything, if necessary, and lay all the cards out on the table—admit that there were serious problems, get help, and do something about them. I was worried about the company. I just wanted it to get back on an even keel. Instead, they insisted on going on with the subterfuge.

In the fall of 1969, Durham began compiling and submitting to his superiors written reports and documentary evidence of the chaotic C-5A production process. At about the same time he began to feel the pressure in the plant. People stopped talking to him on the job, and he was excluded from management meetings dealing with production aspects under his jurisdiction.

Finally, they moved me off the flight line. They gave me another job, with equal responsibility, up in the final assembly area. They didn't know it, but I welcomed the opportunity to go up there, because it would give me a chance to check on the upper end of the business, to see if I could find out more about the problem.

I remember when Ship 23 [the twenty-third C-5A to be produced] *came up, the papers showed forty-seven items left to be installed: That was real good, but I knew it wasn't factual. So I got some people who were familiar with production paper to go in there with me and check on what was really going on. There were more than 2,000 missing parts, and I wrote another report.*

Durham had been present on March 2, 1968, when President Lyndon B. Johnson had come to Marietta to help celebrate the "roll-out" of the first C-5A. He recalls the President saying, "You could put an awful lot of hay in there." Apparently, hay storage was about all the plane was good for at that point. Durham has a memo from a former Lockheed colleague who wants to remain anonymous; he wrote: "This ship, which was supposed to be complete in every detail except for scattered engineering changes, came into the test program a virtual skeleton—missing many large structural assemblies and thousands of smaller parts and electronic components. When the ship was 'rolled out' for the inspection of President Johnson and other dignitaries, many portions of the ship had been hastily structured from plywood and paper and were installed strictly for show. A complete 'teardown' of the aircraft took place immediately after the President's inspection."

The President of the United States can be forgiven for failing to recognize a mock airplane, but what about the inspectors—military and civilian—whom the Air Force constantly assigns to the C-5A production lines?

They never talked to me, and I never talked to them. At Lockheed, you're dead if you talk to the Air Force about a Lockheed problem. That's one of the first things you learn. People have been fired for it.

Either the Air Force inspectors were blind, or there was collusion between Lockheed and the

Air Force. I personally don't feel it could have been anything but collusion. They couldn't have missed seeing all this. . . .

By this time, having exhausted all lower levels of management, Durham had taken his case—and an eight-inch stack of documentation—to R. H. Fuhrman, the president of Lockheed-Georgia.

I gave him examples of double-ordering and triple-ordering of parts. I gave him all kinds of proof. He listened mostly, didn't say much. Finally, he said, "Where there's so much smoke there's got to be some fire. We'll look into it." I said to myself, "Man, at last I'm getting somewhere."

Two weeks later I was told my job was to be abolished. I was offered a downgrade and a substantial pay cut.

Instead, he decided to give two weeks' notice and take a layoff, which would enable him to collect severance pay and other fringe benefits. He felt he "just had to get out of that plant for a while." He sent a four-page letter, with accompanying documents, to Daniel J. Haughton, chairman of the board of the Lockheed Aircraft Corporation, the parent company of Lockheed-Georgia.

"Mr. Haughton," Durham wrote, "I know that many statements made by outside sources regarding Lockheed management are true as far as the Georgia company is concerned. However, I do feel that Lockheed management as a whole throughout the corporaration is beyond reproach. I know the Lockheed Corporation had to be built on integrity to be as large as it is and to have enjoyed the respect it has gained through the years."

From Lockheed corporate headquarters at Burbank, California, Haughton replied that he would launch an investigation and advise Durham of the results. Durham is still waiting for further word.

I should have had guts enough to admit that Lockheed just didn't want to do anything about this. The fact is, I wanted to believe in them, you know. All my life I'd heard about Uncle Dan—Uncle Dan this, Uncle Dan that. I really thought the dear old white-haired patriarch of the Lockheed family was going to do something. I found out that he's in on this thing as much as anyone else.

After a couple of months of lay-off—"I stayed home and talked to my children for the first time in a long time"—Durham was invited to come back to work for Lockheed. He refused to return to the Marietta plant and was given a job in Chattanooga, 100 miles away, at a $5,000-a-year cut in pay. The Chattanooga plant, where Lockheed makes ground equipment for the C-5A, is known to Lockheed employees as the "Siberia" of the corporation.

I discovered that things were even worse in Chattanooga than in Marietta. There was horrible waste and mismanagement—absolutely gross. I found tools that were rusting away in the yard, some that had been out there for years. I found them buying material from vendors at exorbitant prices when they had the same material available in Chattanooga—or in Marietta—but they didn't know they had it because they had no inventory controls. I found tons and tons of steel that had rusted beyond recognition. When I tried to clean the place up, we scrapped forty-two tons of ruined metal.

I just couldn't stand it any longer. It was so rotten and so terrible that I finally decided the only thing I could do was to get out and attack the problem in a different way. I hadn't heard from Haughton, I hadn't heard from anybody, so in May, 1971, I decided just to call it quits. . . .

Durham returned to Marietta, where his family had remained during his months in Chattanooga, and embarked on a letter-writing campaign. The Lockheed loan guarantee was pending in Congress, and Durham wrote to every member who might conceivably be interested—eighty-six Senators and Representatives in all—offering to come to Washington at his own expense to provide information that might have a bearing on the Lockheed matter. He received sixteen replies—most of them what he calls "Dear Friend" letters thanking him politely for his communication.

One of my great disappointments was with the chairmen of the House and Senate Armed Services Committees. I wrote to them before the Lockheed bail-out bill had reached the floor, advising them that I had irrefutable evidence of gross mismanagement, waste, and corruption on the C-5A military contract. I implored them to let me come up and show them the evidence before they voted on the bill. I felt certain they would be vitally concerned. Aren't they supposed to be overseeing military spending? I never got a word. To this day I haven't heard a thing from them. I've really thought a lot about that. . . .

I started receiving calls by Sunday noon—about the time people were getting home from church—and they increased in frequency through the day and night. The callers were vicious in almost every case, threatening my life, my family, my children. They were anonymous—some local and some long-distance. They said I was trying to close down Lockheed and jeopardize the livelihood of thousands of people. One caller said, "The only way you're going to Washington is in a box." Another said, "You won't be here when the sun comes up tomorrow morning." Still another told me, "You've got a pretty daughter now, but she won't be pretty long." In some cases it seemed to be an organized telephone attack—people calling to ask, "How much is Senator Proxmire paying you?" I'd just answer, "Thank you, is there anything else?" and hang up.

I took it rather lightly at first, as something that would go away in a few days. But I slept on a sofa down in the den, with a pistol on the coffee table, and every time I heard an unusual noise I went outside to check. I took all the calls myself—I didn't want my wife and children to hear the vulgar language—and about midnight I would take the phone off the hook so we could get some sleep.

By this time, Proxmire had invited Durham to testify before the Joint Economic Committee. As a Congressional witness, he was entitled to Federal protection, and when the abusive calls intensified instead of abating, Durham appealed to Proxmire for help. For more than two months this summer and fall, Federal marshals stood guard over the Durham family 'round the clock. Their presence—and some inquiries made by agents of the FBI about threats at the Lockheed plant—seemed to reduce the pressure. . . .

Durham, accompanied by two marshals, went to Washington on September 29 to testify before the Joint Economic Committee. His testimony was voluminous and detailed, and was accompanied by letters, reports, production forms—even rusted parts and drill bits from the Chattanooga plant. When he finished, Proxmire told him, "I can't tell you how much I admire your courage. Very few people are called upon to show the kind of guts you have. If it weren't for people like you, we'd have a far poorer country.". . .

I always conducted myself the way the company would want me to. For years I was pro-management and anti-union, because that was what the company wanted. Now I realize that there's a union because the company makes it necessary. I've learned that a union member has protection—he can speak out against company practices because he has a contract. A management man has no protection—he can be fired on the spot.

This is one reason why a corporation can bilk

the country out of hundreds of millions of dollars through mismanagement and waste: The people in management who know about these things are too frightened to speak out; to do so would jeopardize their very existence. It's a very strong club the corporation wields—not only over the country but over its own management. It's a very strong lever. . . .

I have become greatly concerned about issues that never bothered me because I thought they were somebody else's problems; now I realize they're everybody's problems—the problems of old people, of poor people. There's something wrong with a society where children born across the tracks can't get enough milk to drink or food to eat and are looked down on by a more fortunate group. There's something wrong with a society whose Government will rescue an outfit like Lockheed and let our environment go down the drain.

My attitude towards the things the company has done has made me look hard at the things my country has done. Until recently I favored the Vietnam war because my Government favored it. If my Government said it was good, it was good. But what my Government did about Lockheed made me start asking questions. I looked at the war and decided—I hope I'm wrong about this—that it has been prolonged to keep our economy going, because so much of our economy depends on the production of military hardware. It's a horrible thing to think that people may have died to maintain production.

I'm beginning to realize some things—even though I'm a Southerner, born in the Bible Belt. We're patriotic in this part of the country, and we've produced many heroes, but I've come to understand that you're just as much of a hero when you see things wrong and do something about them. You're as much a hero to do that as to go out and die in Vietnam. I'm still proud of our country, I just realize we're going to have to do better.

So many things have to be changed in this country, and I'm hoping the young people will do it—not by blowing up toilets but by turning out of office the mossbacks who hold power now. I hope young people will have the courage to do what my generation has been unable to do. I would like to go out and speak to them—to all voting people—about what I have learned. We could have a peaceful revolution in this country that might save the basic qualities of life—instead of turning out more airplanes.

Increasingly, the larger corporations have become the primary custodians of making our entire system work.

HAROLD GENEEN, President of ITT, 1970

60.

The ITT Affair

On February 29, 1972, Washington Post *columnist Jack Anderson reported that the Justice Department had made a favorable settlement of an antitrust suit against International Telephone and Telegraph. The suit had attempted to stop a merger of ITT with the Hartford Insurance Company, a merger that was eventually consummated. Anderson's story was based on a secret memorandum written by ITT lobbyist Dita D. Beard to William R. Merriam, head of ITT's Washington office. The memo, written on June 25, 1971, and published in Anderson's column, seemed to connect a $400,000 pledge to the Republican Party for its 1972 convention (at that time scheduled for San Diego, but later shifted to Miami) to the actions of the Justice Department. The publication of the memo proved to be quite inflammatory, endangering as it did the Senate confirmation of Richard Kleindienst as Attorney General and eventually involving members of the White House staff. The full story of the ITT merger had not been sorted out two years later, but in the summer of 1973 another memo, this one by Charles Colson, special White House counsel, was made public in the press. Written on March 30, 1972, it warned that the Kleindienst confirmation hearings might directly link high administration officials to the controversial antitrust ruling favoring ITT. What seemed to be most suspicious was the fact that nine days after the $400,000 pledge was affirmed to the San Diego Convention Bureau, the antitrust suit was settled. Both of the memos relating to the case are reprinted here. The persons mentioned in the Dita Beard memo are as follows: EJG–Ned Gerrity, public relations man for ITT; John Mitchell–the Attorney General who resigned to become campaign manager for President Nixon in 1972; Ed Reinecke–lieutenant governor of California; Bob Haldeman–chief presidential advisor; Wilson–Bob Wilson, congressman from California's 36th district; Hal–Harold Geneen, president of ITT; Louie–Louis Nunn, governor of Kentucky.*

Sources: Anthony Sampson, *The Sovereign State of ITT*, New York, 1973, page 201.

Facts on File, July 29–August 4, 1973.

THE DITA BEARD MEMO

I JUST HAD A LONG TALK with EJG. I'm so sorry that we got that call from the White House. I thought you and I had agreed very thoroughly that under no circumstances would anyone in this office discuss with anyone our participation in the Convention, including me. Other than permitting John Mitchell, Ed Reinecke, Bob Haldeman and Nixon (besides Wilson, of course) *no one* has known from whom that 400 thousand commitment had come. You can't imagine how many queries I've had from "friends" about this situation and I have in each and every case denied knowledge of any kind. It would be wise for all of us here to continue to do that, regardless of from whom any questions come; White House or whoever. John Mitchell has certainly kept it on the higher level only, we should be able to do the same.

I was afraid the discussion about the three hundred/four hundred thousand commitment would come up soon. If you remember, I suggested that we all stay out of that, other than the fact that I told you I had heard Hal up the original amount.

Now I understand from Ned that both he and you are upset about the decision to make it four hundred in *services*. Believe me, this is not what Hal said. Just after I talked with Ned, Wilson called me, to report on his meeeting with Hal. Hal at no time told Wilson that our donation would be in services ONLY. In fact, quite the contrary. There would be very little cash involved, but certainly some. I am convinced, because of several conversations with Louie re Mitchell, that our noble commitment has gone a long way toward our negotiations on the mergers eventually coming out as Hal wants them. Certainly the President has told Mitchell to see that things are worked out fairly. It is still only McLaren's mickey-mouse we are suffering.

We all know Hal and his big mouth! But this is one time he cannot tell you and Ned one thing and Wilson (and me) another!

I hope, dear Bill, that all of this can be reconciled—between Hal and Wilson—if all of us in this office remain totally ignorant of any commitment ITT has made to anyone. If it gets too much publicity, you can believe our negotiations with Justice will wind up shot down. Mitchell is definitely helping us, but cannot let it be known. Please destroy this, huh?

THE CHARLES COLSON MEMO

ADMITTEDLY IT IS ALL OPINION at this point, but Johnson, MacGregor and I unanimously do not believe that Kleindienst can be confirmed by June 1. Johnson does not feel he can be confirmed at all and on this point I am at least doubtful. I emphasize that this is an opinion and a judgment call. Lots of things could happen. We could get a big break in the case; the media could turn around and become sympathetic to Kleindienst; the Democrats could decide that they are better having him in the job than beating him. Obviously, there are many unforeseen possibilities, but as of now that is our best assessment. I would think that whatever decision we make now should be based on the most knowledgeable and I would add the most detached assessment of our legislative prospects.

Wally Johnson has done a detailed analysis of the various procedural moves that are likely to be made in committee or on the floor. He is not shooting from the hip. He has analyzed it, and a Senate vote, in his judgment, cannot be achieved by June 1; the Democrats will only let it come to a vote if they have votes to reject Kleindienst, which is the least desirable outcome. Neither Johnson, MacGregor or Colson are prepared to predict whether we can hold the votes necessary to confirm him should the nomination in fact get to a vote.

Assuming MacGregor, Johnson and Colson are correct, then setting June 1 as our deadline date merely puts the hard decision off to a time when it will be considerably more volatile politically than it is today. Kleindienst's withdrawal will then be an admission of defeat but it will come two months closer to the election. In June Kleindienst will be a hot issue for the Democratic convention. Confirmation of Kleindienst's replacement will also be vastly more difficult in June than it would be now. Obviously this again is opinion.

Charles W. Colson, former special counsel to President Nixon

The most serious risk for us is being ignored in the analysis you gave us this morning—there is the possibility of serious additional exposure by the continuation of this controversy. Kleindienst is not the target, the President is, but Kleindienst is the best available vehicle for the Democrats to get to the President. Make no mistake, the Democrats want to keep this case alive—whatever happens to Kleindienst—but the battle over Kleindienst elevates the visibility of the I.T.T. matter and, indeed, guarantees that the case will stay alive. It may stay alive in any event and, hence, the key question not addressed in your analysis is whether pendency or withdrawal of the Kleindienst nomination serves to increase the Democrats' desire to continue. That is the hardest call to make but for the following reasons it may be the most important point to make.

Neither Kleindienst, Mitchell nor Mardian know of the potential dangers. I have deliberately not told Kleindienst or Mitchell since both may be recalled as witnesses and Mardian does not understand the problem. Only Fred Fielding, myself and Ehrlichman have fully examined all the documents and/or information that could yet come out. A summary of some of these is attached.

Certain I.T.T. files which were not shredded have been turned over to the S.E.C., there was talk yesterday in the committee of subpoenaing these from I.T.T. These files would undermine Griswold's testimony that he made the decision not to take the appeal to the Supreme Court. Correspondence to Connally and Peterson credits the delay in Justice's filing of the appeal to the Supreme Court in the Grinell case to direct intervention by Peterson and Connally. A memo sent to the Vice-President, addressed, "Dear Ted," from Ned Gerrity tends to contradict John Mitchell's testimony because it outlines Mitchell's agreement to talk to McLaren following Mitchell's meeting with [I.T.T. President Harold S.] Geneen in August 1970.

It would carry some weight in that the memo was written contemporaneous with the meeting. Both Mitchell and Geneen have testified discussed policy only, not this case, and that Mitchell talked to no one else. The memo further states that Ehrlichman assured Geneen that the President had "instructed" the Justice Department with respect to the bigness policy. (It is, of course, appropriate for the President to instruct the Justice Department on policy, but in the context of these hearings, that revelation would lay this case on the President's doorstep.) There is another internal [I.T.T. employe John F.] Ryan to [William] Merriam [I.T.T. representative in Washington] memo, which is not in the hands of the

S.E.C.; it follows the 1970 Agnew meeting and suggests that Kleindienst is the key man to pressure McLaren, implying that the Vice-President would implement this action. We believe that all copies of this have been destroyed.

There is a Klein to Haldeman memo, dated June 30, 1971, which of course precedes the date of the I.T.T. settlement, setting forth the $400,000 arrangement with I.T.T. Copies were addressed to Magruder, Mitchell and [White House aide William] Timmons. This memo put the A.G. [attorney general] on constructive notice at least of the I.T.T. commitment at that time and before the settlement, facts which he has denied under oath. We don't know whether we have recovered all the copies. If known, this would be considerably more damaging than [California Lt. Gov. Ed] Reinecke's statement. Magruder believes it is possible, the A.G. transmitted his copy to Magruder. Magruder doesn't have the copy he received, he only has a Xerox of the copy. In short, despite a search this memo could be lying around anything at 1701.

The Justice Department has thus far resisted a request for their files, although their files were opened to Robert Hammond, one of Turner's deputies and a holdover who is now a practicing Democratic lawyer in Washington. Hammond had access to several memos that could be embarrassing. Whether he kept them or not is unknown, but it is probable that he recalls them. One is a memo of April 1969, from Kleindienst and McLaren to Ehrlichman responding to an Ehrlichman request with respect to the rationale for bringing the case against I.T.T. in the first place. There is a subsequent April 1970, memo from [White House aide Tod] Hullin to McLaren stating that Ehrlichman had discussed his meeting with Geneen with the A.G., and suggesting to McLaren that Mitchell could give McLaren "more specified guidance."

There is another memo of September 1970, from Ehrlichman to the A.G. referring to an "understanding" with Geneen and complaining of McLaren's actions. There is a May 5, 1971, memo from Ehrlichman to the A.G. alluding to discussions between the President and the A.G. as to the "agreed upon ends" in the resolution of the I.T.T. case and asking the A.G. whether Ehrlichman would work directly with McLaren or through Mitchell. There is also a memo to the President in the same time period. We know we have control of all the copies of this, but we don't have control of the original Ehrlichman memo to the A.G. This memo would once again contradict Mitchell's testimony and more importantly directly involve the President. We believe we have absolute security on this file within Justice, provided no copies were made within Justice and provided there are no leaks. We have no idea of the distribution that took place within Justice.

Merriam's testimony will of necessity involve direct contact with Jack Gleason. I can't believe that after Merriam's testimony, Gleason will not be called as a witness.

61.

The Shanghai Communique

Probably the most notable and surprising achievement of President Nixon's first term was his visit to the People's Republic of China in February 1972. The visit had been arranged through the mediation of Henry Kissinger on a secret trip to Peking in July 1971 to meet with Chou En-lai. But there had been hints earlier in the year of a thaw in the relations between the two nations. On March 15, 1971, the President had announced a discontinuation of the travel ban to China, thus enabling the U.S. table tennis team to visit there in April. And on April 14 he relaxed the trade embargo that had been in effect for a quarter of a century. The following selection is the joint U.S.–P. R. C. communique issued at Shanghai on February 27, 1972, at the end of the President's visit.

Source: *Department of State Bulletin*, March 20, 1972.

PRESIDENT RICHARD NIXON of the United States of America visited the People's Republic of China at the invitation of Premier Chou En-lai of the People's Republic of China from February 21 to February 28, 1972. Accompanying the President were Mrs. Nixon, U.S. Secretary of State William Rogers, Assistant to the President Dr. Henry Kissinger, and other American officials.

President Nixon met with Chairman Mao Tse-tung of the Communist Party of China on February 21. The two leaders had a serious and frank exchange of views on Sino-U.S. relations and world affairs.

During the visit, extensive, earnest and frank discussions were held between President Nixon and Premier Chou En-lai on the normalization of relations between the United States of America and the People's Republic of China, as well as on other matters of interest to both sides. In addition, Secretary of State William Rogers and Foreign Minister Chi Peng-fei held talks in the same spirit.

President Nixon and his party visited Peking and viewed cultural, industrial and agricultural sites, and they also toured Hangchow and Shanghai where, continuing discussions with Chinese leaders, they viewed similar places of interest.

The leaders of the People's Republic of China and the United States of America found it beneficial to have this opportunity, after so many years without contact, to present candidly to one another their views on a variety of issues. They reviewed the international situation in which important changes and great upheavals are taking place and expounded their respective positions and attitudes.

The U.S. side stated: Peace in Asia and peace in the world requires efforts both to reduce immediate tensions and to eliminate the basic causes of conflict. The United States will work for a just and secure peace: just, because it fulfills the aspirations of peoples and nations for freedom and progress; secure, because it removes the danger of foreign aggression. The United States supports individual freedom and social progress for all the peoples of the world, free of outside pressure or intervention. The United States believes that the effort to reduce tensions is served by improving communication between countries that have different ideologies so as to lessen the risks of confrontation through accident, miscalculation or misunderstanding. Countries should treat each other with mutual respect and be willing to compete peacefully, letting performance be the ultimate judge. No country should claim infallibility and each country should be prepared to re-examine its own attitudes for the common good. The United States stressed that the peoples of Indochina should be allowed to determine their destiny without outside intervention; its constant primary objective has been a negotiated solution; the eight-point proposal put forward by the Republic of Vietnam and the United States on January 27, 1972, represents a basis for the attainment of that objective; in the absence of a negotiated settlement the United States envisages the ultimate withdrawal of all U.S. forces from the region consistent with the aim of self-determination for each country of Indochina. The United States will maintain its close ties with and support for the Republic of Korea; the United States will support efforts of the Republic of Korea to seek a relaxation of tension and increased communication in the Korean peninsula. The United States places the highest value on its friendly relations with Japan; it will continue to develop the existing close bonds. Consistent with the United Nations Security Council Resolution of December 21, 1971, the United States favors the continuation of the ceasefire between India and Pakistan and the withdrawal of all military forces to within their own territories and to their own sides of the ceasefire line in Jammu and Kashmir; the United States supports the right of the peoples of South Asia to shape their own future in peace, free of military threat, and without having the area become the subject of great power rivalry.

The Chinese side stated: Wherever there is oppression, there is resistance. Countries want independence, nations want liberation and the people want revolution—this has become the irresistible trend of history. All nations, big or small, should be equal; big nations should not bully the small and strong nations should not bully the weak. China will never be a superpower and it opposes hegemony and power politics of any kind. The Chinese side stated that it firmly supports the struggles of all the oppressed people and nations for freedom and liberation and that the people of all countries have the right to choose their social systems according to their own wishes and the right to safeguard the independence, sovereignty and territorial integrity of their own countries and oppose foreign aggression, interference, control and subversion. All foreign troops should be withdrawn to their own countries.

The Chinese side expressed its firm support to the peoples of Vietnam, Laos and Cambodia in their efforts for the attainment of their goal and its firm support to the seven-point proposal of the Provisional Revolutionary Government of the Republic of South Vietnam and the elaboration of February this year on the two key problems in the proposal, and to the Joint Declaration of the Summit Conference of the Indochinese Peoples. It firmly supports the eight-point program for the peaceful unification of Korea put forward by the Government of the Democratic People's Republic of Korea on April 12, 1971, and the stand for the abolition of the "U.N. Commission for the Unification and Rehabilitation of Korea." It firmly opposes the revival and outward expansion of Japanese militarism and firmly supports the Japanese people's desire to build an independent, democratic, peaceful and neutral Japan. It firmly maintains that India and Pakistan should, in accordance with the United Nations resolutions on the India-Pakistan question, immediately withdraw all their forces to their respective territories and to their own sides of the ceasefire line in Jammu and Kashmir and firmly supports the Pakistan Government and people in their struggle to preserve their independence and sovereignty and the people of Jammu and Kashmir in their struggle for the right of self-determination.

There are essential differences between China and the United States in their social systems and foreign policies. However, the two sides agreed that countries, regardless of their social systems, should conduct their relations on the principles of respect for the sovereignty and territorial integrity of all states, nonaggression against other states, noninterference in the internal affairs of other states, equality and mutual benefit, and peaceful coexistence. International disputes should be settled on this basis, without resorting to the use or threat of force. The United States and the People's Republic of China are prepared to apply these principles to their mutual relations.

With these principles of international relations in mind the two sides stated that:

—progress toward the normalization of relations between China and the United States is in the interests of all countries;

—both wish to reduce the danger of international military conflict;

—neither should seek hegemony in the Asia-Pacific region and each is opposed to efforts by any other country or group of countries to establish such hegemony; and

—neither is prepared to negotiate on behalf of any third party or to enter into agreements or understandings with the other directed at other states.

Both sides are of the view that it would be against the interests of the peoples of the world for any major country to collude with another against other countries, or for major countries to divide up the world into spheres of interest.

The two sides reviewed the long-standing serious disputes between China and the United States. The Chinese side reaffirmed its position: The Taiwan question is the crucial question obstructing the normalization of relations between China and the United States; the Government of the People's Republic of China is the sole legal government of China; Taiwan is a province of China which has long been returned to the motherland; the liberation of Taiwan is China's internal affair in which no other country has the right to interfere; and all U.S. forces and military installations must be withdrawn from Taiwan. The Chinese Government firmly opposes any activities which aim at the creation of "one China, one Taiwan," "one China, two governments," "two Chinas," and "independent Taiwan" or advocate that "the status of Taiwan remains to be determined."

The U.S. side declared: The United States acknowledges that all Chinese on either side of the Taiwan Strait maintain there is but one China and that Taiwan is a part of China. The United States Government does not challenge that position. It reaffirms its interest in a peaceful settlement of the Taiwan question by the Chinese themselves. With this prospect in mind, it affirms the ultimate objective of the withdrawal of all U.S. forces and military installations from Taiwan. In the meantime, it will progressively reduce its forces and military installations on Taiwan as the tension in the area diminishes.

The two sides agreed that it is desirable to broaden the understanding between the two peoples. To this end, they discussed specific areas in such fields as science, technology, culture, sports and journalism, in which people-to-people contacts and exchanges would be mutually beneficial. Each side undertakes to facilitate the further development of such contacts and exchanges.

Both sides view bilateral trade as another area from which mutual benefit can be derived, and agreed that economic relations based on equality and mutual benefit are in the interest of the peoples of the two countries. They agree to facilitate the progressive development of trade between their two countries.

The two sides agreed that they will stay in contact through various channels, including the sending of a senior U.S. representative to Peking from time to time for concrete consultations to further the normalization of relations between the two countries and continue to exchange views on issues of common interest.

The two sides expressed the hope that the gains achieved during this visit would open up new prospects for the relations between the two countries. They believe that the normalization of relations between the two countries is not only in the interest of the Chinese and American peoples but also contributes to the relaxation of tension in Asia and the world.

President Nixon, Mrs. Nixon and the American party expressed their appreciation for the gracious hospitality shown them by the Government and people of the People's Republic of China.

62.

Arthur H. Westing and E. W. Pfeiffer: The Cratering of Indochina

No land in history has been so ravaged by war as Indochina, particularly North and South Vietnam. The authors of the article from which this selection is taken surveyed the environmental damage while the U.S. was still involved in the war, and their report was published in May 1972. As it happened, some of the heaviest American bombing of the war took place in December 1972, shortly before a truce agreement was signed. Arthur H. Westing is professor of biology at Windham College, and E. W. Pfeiffer is professor of zoology at the University of Montana.

Source: *Scientific American*, May 1972.

The unprecedented use of herbicides on a massive scale as an instrument of war in Vietnam has prompted several studies of the probable long-term effects of these chemical agents on the land of Indochina. Much less attention has been paid to the effects of the tearing up of the land by bombing and shelling. Yet the released tonnage statistics alone suggest that these effects must be sizable. In the seven-year period from 1965 to 1971 the area of Indochina, a region slightly larger than Texas, was bombarded by a tonnage of munitions amounting to approximately twice the total used by the U.S. in all the theaters of World War II.

During three tours of war zones of Indochina to assess damage done to the environment by herbicides, we became increasingly conscious of the ubiquitous scarring of the landscape by bomb and shell craters. From the air some areas in Vietnam looked like photographs of the moon. How would this cratering of the land affect life and the ecology in Indochina when its people attempted to pick up normal living after the war? It seemed that the physical alteration of the terrain by bombing might have created long-range problems fully as serious as those produced by the defoliation campaign (which had attacked more than five million acres of forest and cropland in Vietnam). In order to initiate investigation of the crater problems, the two of us went to Vietnam for a preliminary study in behalf of the Scientists' Institute for Public Information in August, 1971. From the U.S. Department of Defense we collected the limited information that was available to the public about the expenditures of munitions in Indochina. Then in the field we surveyed bombed areas on the ground and from the air (in helicopters) and interviewed many people, including farmers, lumbermen and other persons who had observed various effects of the bombing on the land, the economy and various occupations.

In the seven years between 1965 and 1971 the U.S. military forces exploded 26 billion pounds (13 million tons) of munitions in Indochina, half from the air and half from weapons on the ground. This staggering weight of ordnance amounts to the energy of 450 Hiroshima nuclear bombs. For the area and people of Indochina as a whole it represents an average of 142 pounds of explosive per acre of land and 584 pounds per person. It means that over the seven-year period the average rate of detonation was 118 pounds per second. These average figures, however, give no indication of the actual concentration; most of the bombardment was concentrated in time (within the years from 1967 on) and in area. Of the 26 billion pounds, 21 billion were exploded within South Vietnam, one billion in North Vietnam and 2.6 billion in southern Laos. The bombardment in South Vietnam represented an overall average of 497 pounds per acre and 1,215 pounds per person; the major part, however, was focused on two regions: the five northern provinces and the region around Saigon.

Craters pock every area of South Vietnam: forests, swamps, fields, paddies, roadsides. Certain areas, notably the "free fire," or "specified strike," zones, show severe cratering. We personally observed large areas that had been subjected to intensive transformation of the landscape in Tay Ninh, Long Khanh, Gia Dinh, Hau Nghia and Binh Duong provinces around Saigon and Quang Ngai, Quang Tin and Quang Nam provinces of the northern part of the country. And of course the concentration of craters is particularly marked in areas such as the demilitarized zone (DMZ) between North Vietnam and South Vietnam and the supply trails in southern Laos.

We were able to visit on foot an area in the Mekong Delta that had been until fairly recently a free-fire zone. The area was near the hamlet of Hoi Son about 30 miles south of My Tho. Farmers were being resettled there on their previously fought-over land because senior officials considered the region fairly secure. (The degree of security became evident during our stay when U.S. aircraft were observed rocketing and strafing only a few miles away.) Several families that had left the area a decade earlier because of fighting were interviewed, and they took us to three craters that they said had been made in 1967. The craters had probably been produced by 500-pound bombs dropped by fighter-bombers. Each crater was about 30 feet in diameter, filled with water, and at the time of our visit was about five feet deep in the center. The entire immediate area had been a rice paddy, but during the years when no cultivation had occurred, the rice had been replaced by a very tall reed, genus *Phragmites*, which surrounded the crater at a distance of 10 to 20 feet. Growing from the rim of the craters and into the reeds was a species of relatively short grass, *Brachiaria*, and a taller grass, *Scirpus*. The farmers were growing seed rice near the craters and were plowing under the reeds and grasses in preparation for planting rice. It was obvious that they could not use the cratered areas for rice cultivation because the water was much too deep. The only apparent solution was to bring in soil from elsewhere, but this was obviously not practical.

We also observed at close hand many craters on the flat terrace lands northwest of Saigon that had previously supported an evergreen hardwood forest. In this area the craters generally contain no water during the dry season, so that their natural history is considerably different from the history of the craters of the Delta region that are permanently filled with water. The craters were very numerous in this area; there was at least one every 100 feet. Each crater was 20 to 40 feet across and five to 20 feet deep. There were many generations of craters from different air strikes. The most recent ones were bare of vegetation but contained some rainwater. (We observed these craters in the wet season.) In the older craters a few sprigs of grass, probably *Imperata*, were sprouting in the center. As the craters age grass grows radially, eventually covering the bottom to meet vines trailing down from the peripheral vegetation. There is some filling of old craters with soil washed down from the sides, but this is limited because old craters almost completely covered with grass were still five to 10 feet deep. They thus became permanent features of the landscape.

From the data available to us on the quantity of munitions expended we calculated tentative estimates of the total area affected by cratering and other damage to the land. For these estimates we had to make some very free and general assumptions. For example, we assume that about half (by weight) of the total amount of munitions employed in Indochina consisted of bombs, shells and other missiles that would produce craters. We assume further that on the average each of the crater-producing missiles was equivalent to a 500-pound bomb and formed a crater 30 feet in diameter and 15 feet deep, displacing 131 cubic yards of earth. (A large proportion of the cratering has been produced by B-52 bomber raids; each of these big planes typically carries 108 500-pound bombs.) We also estimate that the fragments from each crater-producing missile were spread over an area of 1.25 acres.

On the basis of these assumptions (some of which are supported by actual measurements) we estimate that the number of craters produced in Indochina by the bombardments from 1965 to 1971 totaled some 26 million, covering a total area of 423,000 acres and representing a total displacement of about 3.4 billion cubic yards of earth. The area of missile-fragment spread totals 32.6 million acres, if we disregard overlap. Again we note that South Vietnam has borne the brunt of this damage. In the period mentioned (through 1971) South Vietnam is estimated to have received about 21 million craters, covering all together about 345,000 acres, and to have had millions of acres contaminated by missile fragments, even allowing for overlap. The total area of the country is 42.8 million acres.

Let us now examine some specific effects, for the present and for the future, of this massive application of "landscape management" by high explosives. There is evidence from previous wars that the effects will be long-lasting. A decade after the end of World War II the craters of heavily shelled areas on Okinawa were still barren of vegetation and reddened by rusting shell fragments. On Eniwetok craters were clearly in evidence two decades after the war. Four decades after World War I vegetation in the Negev desert of Israel outlined the craters from that war, and even in France's Verdun area many of the World War I craters are still clearly visible and in some cases to this day are devoid of vegetation.

To begin with, we can see that the displacement and scattering of soil and subsoil from the craters in Indochina have given rise to harmful physical consequences. (Over the seven years the displacement of soil by bombardment in Indochina proceeded at a rate of nearly 1,000 cubic yards of soil per minute.) In hilly terrain the tearing up of the soil promotes erosion. In Indochina, where some of the soil is vulnerable to laterization (hardening to a bricklike state), the removal of vegetation and humus may make the area in and around craters permanently barren. At the least it has resulted in colonization of cratered regions by weedy, worthless grasses and shrubs. Furthermore, the deep craters have made many areas almost impassable for travel.

Many of the craters, particularly in the Delta and coastal regions, have penetrated the water table and remain filled with water during much or all of the year. They have thereby probably become breeding grounds for mosquitoes, greatly increasing the hazards of malaria and dengue fever for the population. Reports by military authorities indeed confirm that "malaria has been causing increasing concern in Vietnam" and has spread to previously unafflicted areas.

The impact of cratering on agriculture has been substantial. Farmers in South Vietnam, notably in the Mekong Delta, have been reluctant or unable to attempt to reclaim rice paddies or other farmlands that have been pocked by craters. One of the important deterrents is the presence of unexploded munitions buried in the ground. A number of farmers have been killed by the detonation of such shells or bombs by their plows. Moreover, the ubiquitous missile fragments in the ground cut the hooves of the water buffaloes used as draft animals, causing infection and death of the animals. The unexploded bombs and shells lying about in the soil of Indochina are known to number several hundred thousand. Bombing has also disrupted rice-growing in Indochina by breaking up many of the intricate irrigation systems, and in some areas near the seacoast it has opened the land to encroachment by salt water.

The timber industry of South Vietnam, potentially one of the most important elements in the region's predominantly agricultural economy, has been particularly hard hit by the bombing. It has catastrophically slashed the values of the once prime timberlands northwest and northeast of Saigon, for example. The heavy shelling and bombing have damaged the trees in three ways: outright destruction, riddling of the timber by missile fragments and subsequent weakening of the trees through infection by wood-rotting fungi. . . .

A study by U.S. agents has determined that about 10 percent of the agricultural land of South Vietnam has had to be abandoned because of the destruction wrought by bombardment and other weapons used in this war. It has been a war against the land as much as against armies. Indeed, it appears that one of the main strategies of our military effort has been to disrupt and destroy the social and economic fabric of rural, agricultural Vietnam in order to drive the peasant population into areas under central control and to deprive the guerrilla enemy of a power base.

Only about five to eight percent of the U.S. bombing missions in Indochina have been directed at tactical military targets, that is, in direct support of troops. The rest of the bombing missions are described as "harassing" or "interdiction" attacks. They are also referred to as strategic bombing missions. Whereas the targets of strategic bombing in World War II were the factories, port cities, railroads and so forth of the enemy, in the Indochina war the strategic targets are the land and forests of Indochina because they give cover and sanctuary to the other side. It is important to note here that whereas factories, ports and other man-made sources of production can be rapidly rebuilt, as demonstrated in Europe and Japan, it is doubtful that many of the forests and lands of Indochina can be rehabilitated in the foreseeable future.

From 1966 on the B-52's carried out incessant attacks on a schedule of almost daily missions. From an altitude of 30,000 feet, where they are usually unheard and unseen from the ground, they have been sowing systematic destruction. A typical B-52 mission, comprising seven planes on the average, delivers 756 500-pound bombs in a pattern that saturates an area about half a mile wide and three miles long, that is, nearly 1,000 acres. Thus on a schedule of four or five missions per day of seven sorties each, such as was followed during 1971, the B-52's alone were creating about 100,000 new craters each month. Unfortunately the release of air-war data is now severely restricted.

The cumulative impact of the munitions attack on the land has to be seen to be grasped fully. Reports by military observers speak of the landscape's being "torn as if by an angry giant," and of areas of the green delta land's being pulverized into a "gray porridge." Our brief survey has only suggested some of the grim consequences for the present and future life of the inhabitants of Indochina. Still to be assessed are the effects of the persisting bombardment on the people's habitations, on the animal life and general ecology of the region. The damage caused by the large-scale disorganization of the environment may be felt for centuries.

Meanwhile the steady bombardment and shattering of the land, shielded from the Western world's view and concern by the wide Pacific Ocean and the supposed "winding down" of the war, goes on with no end in sight.

63.

Richard M. Nixon: The Moscow Summit

Coming three months after his trip to China, President Nixon's visit to Moscow from May 22 to 29, 1972, inaugurated a new era of detente with both the major Communist powers and raised hopes internationally that the Cold War was drawing to a close. While in the Soviet Union, the President met with Premier Aleksei N. Kosygin and Communist Party leader Leonid I. Brezhnev to discuss such matters as preventing nuclear war, arms limitation, China-Soviet relations, and increased trade between the U.S. and the U.S.S.R. The most important immediate outcome of the summit meeting was the signing, on May 26, of the strategic arms limitation treaty. On June 1, just after his return from Russia, President Nixon addressed a joint session of Congress in a televised broadcast to the nation detailing the results of his trip. Portions of his speech are reprinted here.

Source: *Department of State Bulletin*, June 26, 1972.

Mr. Speaker, Mr. President, Members of the Congress, our distinguished guests, my fellow Americans: Your welcome in this great Chamber tonight has a very special meaning to Mrs. Nixon and to me. We feel very fortunate to have traveled abroad so often representing the United States of America. But we both agree after each journey that the best part of any trip abroad is coming home to America again.

During the past 13 days we have flown more than 16,000 miles and we visited four countries. Everywhere we went—to Austria, the Soviet Union, Iran, Poland—we could feel the quickening pace of change in old international relationships and the people's genuine desire for friendship for the American people. Everywhere new hopes are rising for a world no longer shadowed by fear and want and war, and as Americans we can be proud that we now have an historic opportunity to play a great role in helping to achieve man's oldest dream: a world in which all nations can enjoy the blessings of peace. . . .

I have not come here this evening to make new announcements in a dramatic setting. This summit has already made its news. It has barely begun, however, to make its mark on our world, and I ask you to join me tonight—while events are fresh, while the iron is hot—in starting to consider how we can help to make that mark what we want it to be.

The foundation has been laid for a new relationship between the two most powerful nations in the world. Now it is up to us, to all of us here in this Chamber, to all of us across America, to join with other nations in building a new house upon that foundation, one that can be a home for the hopes of mankind and a shelter against the storms of conflict.

As a preliminary, therefore, to requesting your concurrence in some of the agreements we reached and your approval of funds to carry out others, and also as a keynote for the unity in which this government and this Nation must go forward from here, I am rendering this immediate report to the Congress on the results of the Moscow summit. . . .

Recognizing the responsibility of the advanced industrial nations to set an example in combating mankind's common enemies, the United States and the Soviet Union have agreed to cooperate in efforts to reduce pollution and enhance environmental quality. We have agreed to work together in the field of medical science and public health, particularly in the conquest of cancer and heart disease.

Recognizing that the quest for useful knowledge transcends differences between ideologies and social systems, we have agreed to expand United States-Soviet cooperation in many areas of science and technology.

We have joined in plans for an exciting new adventure, a new adventure in the cooperative exploration of space, which will begin—subject to congressional approval of funding—with a joint orbital mission of an Apollo vehicle and a Soviet spacecraft in 1975.

By forming habits of cooperation and strengthening institutional ties in areas of peaceful enterprise, these four agreements to which I have referred will create on both sides a steadily growing vested interest in the maintenance of good relations between our two countries.

Expanded United States-Soviet trade will also yield advantages to both of our nations. When the two largest economies in the world start trading with each other on a much larger scale, living standards in both nations will rise and the stake which both have in peace will increase.

Progress in this area is proceeding on schedule. At the summit, we established a Joint Commercial Commission which will complete the negotiations for a comprehensive trade agreement between the United States and the U.S.S.R. And we expect the final terms of such an agreement to be settled, later this year.

Two further accords which were reached last week have a much more direct bearing on the search for peace and security in the world.

One is the agreement between the American and Soviet navies aimed at significantly reducing the chances of dangerous incidents between our ships and aircraft at sea.

And second, and most important, there is the treaty and the related executive agreement which will limit, for the first time, both offensive and defensive strategic nuclear weapons in the arsenals of the United States and the Soviet Union.

Three-fifths of all the people alive in the world today have spent their whole lifetimes under the shadow of a nuclear war which could be touched off by the arms race among the great powers. Last Friday in Moscow we witnessed the beginning of the end of that era which began in 1945. We took the first step toward a new era of mutually agreed restraint and arms limitation between the two principal nuclear powers.

With this step we have enhanced the security of both nations. We have begun to check the wasteful and dangerous spiral of nuclear arms which has dominated relations between our two countries for a generation. We have begun to reduce the level of fear by reducing the causes of fear for our two peoples and for all peoples in the world.

The ABM [antiballistic missile] Treaty will be submitted promptly for the Senate's advice and consent to ratification, and the interim agreement limiting certain offensive weapons will be submitted to both Houses for concurrence—because we can undertake agreements as important as these only on a basis of full partnership between the executive and legislative branches of our government. . . .

In addition to the talks which led to the specific agreements I have listed, I also had full, very frank, and extensive discussions with General Secretary [of the Soviet Communist Party Leonid I.] Brezhnev and his colleagues about several parts of the world where Americans and Soviet interests have come in conflict.

With regard to the reduction of tensions in Europe, we recorded our intention of proceeding later this year with multilateral consultations looking toward a Conference on Security and Cooperation in all of Europe. We have also jointly agreed to move forward with negotiations on mutual and balanced force reductions in central Europe.

The problem of ending the Vietnam war, which engages the hopes of all Americans, was one of the most extensively discussed subjects on our agenda. It would only jeopardize the search for peace if I were to review here all that was said on the subject. I will simply say this: Each side obviously has its own point of view and its own approach to this very difficult issue. But at the same time, both the United States and the Soviet Union share an overriding desire to achieve a more stable peace in the world. I emphasize to you once again that this administration has no higher goal, a goal that I know all of you share, than bringing the Vietnam war to an early and honorable end. We are ending the war in Vietnam, but we shall end it in a way which will not betray our friends, risk the lives of the courageous Americans still serving in Vietnam, break faith with those held prisoners by the enemy, or stain the honor of the United States of America.

Another area where we had very full, frank, and extensive discussions was the Middle East. I reiterated the American people's commitment to the survival of the state of Israel and to a settlement just to all the countries in the area. Both sides stated in the communique their intention to support the Jarring peace mission and other appropriate efforts to achieve this objective.

The final achievement of the Moscow conference was the signing of a landmark declaration entitled Basic Principles of Mutual Relations Between the United States and the U.S.S.R. As these 12 basic principles are put into practice, they can provide a solid framework for the future development of better American-Soviet relations.

They begin with the recognition that two nuclear nations, each of which has the power to destroy humanity, have no alternative but to coexist peacefully because in a nuclear war there would be no winners, only losers.

The basic principles commit both sides to avoid direct military confrontation and to exercise constructive leadership and restraint with respect to smaller conflicts in other parts of the world which could drag the major powers into war.

They disavow any intention to create spheres of influence or to conspire against the interests of any other nation—a point I would underscore by saying once again tonight that America values its ties with all nations, from our oldest allies in Europe and Asia, as I emphasized by my visit to Iran, to our good friends in the Third World, and to our new relationship with the People's Republic of China.

The improvement of relations depends not only, of course, on words but far more on actions. The principles to which we agreed in Moscow are like a roadmap. Now that the map has been laid out, it is up to each country to follow it. The United States intends to adhere to these principles. The leaders of the Soviet Union have indicated a similar intention. . . .

For decades, America has been locked in hostile confrontation with the two great Communist powers, the Soviet Union and the People's Republic of China. We were engaged with the one at many points and almost totally isolated from the other, but our relationships with both had reached a deadly impasse. All three countries were victims of the kind of bondage about which George Washington long ago warned in these words: The nation which indulges toward another an habitual hatred is a slave to its own animosity.

But now in the brief space of four months, these journeys to Peking and to Moscow have begun to free us from perpetual confrontation. We have moved toward better understanding, mutual respect, and point-by-point settlement of differences with both the major Communist powers.

This one series of meetings has not rendered an imperfect world suddenly perfect. There still are deep philosophical differences; there still are parts of the world in which age-old hatreds persist. The threat of war has not been eliminated—it has been reduced. We are making progress toward a world in which leaders of nations will settle their differences by negotiation, not by force, and in which they learn to live with their differences so that their sons will not have to die for those differences.

It was particularly fitting that this trip, aimed at building such a world, should have concluded in Poland.

No country in the world has suffered more from war than Poland has, and no country has more to gain from peace. The faces of the people who gave us such a heartwarming welcome in Warsaw yesterday, and again this morning and this afternoon, told an eloquent story of suffering in the past and of hope for peace in the future. One could see it in their faces. It made me more determined than ever that America must do all in its power to help that hope come true for all people.

As we continue that effort, our unity of purpose and action will be all-important.

For the summits of 1972 have not belonged just to one person or one party or to one branch of our government alone. Rather they are part of a great national journey for peace. Every American can claim a share in the credit for success of that journey so far, and every American has a major stake in its success for the future.

New York Mets pitchers Jerry Koosman and Tom Seaver in a ticker tape parade welcoming home the 1969 World Series winners

SPORTS MARKET

Whether television made sports or sports made television would be a futile argument to engage in. But there was no doubt that the great number of sports telecasts provided some of the best fare the medium had to offer. And the "sports widow," whose husband watched baseball in spring and summer, football in the fall, and basketball and ice hockey in the winter became a stock character for cartoon humor. Not only were the traditional sports watched by millions of viewers, but also golf, tennis, swimming, auto racing, horse racing, track meets, skiing, ice skating, boat races, and such special events as the Summer and Winter Olympics. No game depended for its audience or income on the size of an arena. Television delivered an audience of millions for each event (and its commercials). And during such major spectacles as the World Series or the Super Bowl, no competing program could hope for many viewers. Television brought more than viewers to sports. It turned athletics, even at the collegiate level, into a multimillion dollar business.

(Above) Houston Aero left wing Mark Howe (right rear) watches his father, Gordy Howe, chase the puck; (below) Joe Frazier (l) decisioned Muhammad Ali to retain his heavyweight crown on March 8, 1971.

The rigorous distinction that had long been maintained between amateur and professional athletics was severely eroded by the vast amount of money that began flowing to the professionals. They were not only celebrities in their own right, but they earned salaries in some cases comparable to those paid Hollywood stars. Amateur (high school and college) baseball, football, hockey, and basketball became training grounds for advancement into the pro ranks. If any benefit derived from this kind of "free enterprise" approach to sports, it was at the level of performance. To get the enormous salaries, bonuses, and other gratuities that came with a contract, one had to be able to perform. Every season had its new heroes, and records were broken almost as fast as they were set. And to satisfy the television audiences' apparently insatiable desire to watch sporting events, new professional leagues were set up in hockey, basketball, and football. The season for each sport became longer; there were more pre- and post-season games; and at the amateur levels there were more tournaments.

(Below) O.J. Simpson of the Buffalo Bills became the first to rush for 2000 yards on the ground for one season; (right) Wilt Chamberlain of the Los Angeles Lakers hits for two points.

Olga Korbut, sensational teenage Russian Gymnast, performs in Chicago during a tour of the U.S.

Besides the abundant viewing of domestic sports events available to Americans, an international communications satellite made possible live telecasts of such events as the Winter Olympics at Sapporo, Japan, in February 1972, and the Summer Olympics in Munich, Germany, several months later. Telecasts of such lesser events as skiing in Austria, gymnastics in the Soviet Union, or cricket matches in Ireland were also routine. And major American sportscasts were often relayed overseas.

The American table tennis team leaves China April 17, 1971, after a week-long visit during which they won few games but gained many friends.

64.

GEORGE S. MCGOVERN: Where I Stand

Having announced his candidacy in January 1971 and come successfully through the primaries a year later, Senator George S. McGovern of South Dakota was nominated for the presidency at the Democratic National Convention in Miami on July 12, 1972, with Senator Thomas F. Eagleton of Missouri as his running mate. When Eagleton was forced off the ticket early in August, owing to news stories about his previous hospitalization for nervous exhaustion, he was replaced by R. Sargent Shriver, former director of the Peace Corps. In the November election President Nixon won by a huge landslide over the McGovern-Shriver ticket, obtaining 521 electoral college votes to McGovern's 17. Only Massachusetts and the District of Columbia went for the Democratic challenger. In July 1972, Senator McGovern published a statement defining the issues of the campaign as he saw them. Portions of his statement are reprinted here.

Source: *The Progressive*, July 1972.

THE BIGGEST MISTAKE the Democratic Party could make in this election year would be to underestimate the deep sense of public disgust at government, which scarcely changes regardless of which party is in power. The American people will not be impressed if we just offer to lie a little bit less, if we suggest a slightly stronger commitment to peace, or if we propose to tinker with the system and call it "new priorities." It is bad tactics and bad policy to snuggle up to President Nixon—if, indeed, we can find out where he is or where he might be by November.

Instead of clutching at some mythical and soggy "center"—a place which has meaning only to a few pundits anyway—we must offer change that is substantial enough to affect the lives of ordinary people. The primaries have given us some idea of where the people are. Instead of dragging them back to the status quo, we must stand with them in seeking a truly just and decent society. . . .

We have heard many times that Vietnam will no longer be an issue by the time the fall election approaches. I don't know whether it will be or not. For the sake of the thousands of Vietnamese peasants still dying from American bombing raids, the GIs still dying of booby traps and heroin, the American POWs rotting in the jails of Hanoi, I sincerely hope it will not be an issue. But *Vietnam thinking* surely *will* be an issue, regardless of what happens in Indochina in the next four months. By "Vietnam thinking" I mean wasting our strength on paranoiac defense policies while neglecting the needs of our own people. . . .

I believe the American people are ready to turn away from Vietnam thinking if they are given leadership whose judgment they can respect and whose word they can believe. In place of the madness of Vietnam thinking, I have proposed a rational reordering of our national priorities and redistribution of our resources. I have shown that building a "zero base" defense budget, starting at zero and budgeting only what is realistically needed, would cost no more than $54.8 billion in fiscal 1975 instead of the $87.3 billion that the current level of military spending, allowing for inflation, would cost by then.

The $54.8 billion military budget I have recommended is, first, clearly a vast sum of money and, second, an amount that is more than ample to meet foreseeable threats to our security. In fact, it can accomplish that goal more effectively than present spending levels. It will give us armed forces built on muscle instead of fat; armed forces that are better equipped to defend our own country and our truly vital interests. It is a defense posture with which all Americans can feel both security and confidence that hard-earned tax dollars are not being wasted.

What I propose is that we spend all that is necessary for a prudent national defense, and no more. I propose that we conserve our limited resources:

—By no longer underwriting the appalling waste of money and manpower that has become such a bad habit in our military establishment;

—By rejecting the purchase of weapons which are designed to fight the last war better, with almost no relevance to today's threat;

—By refusing to maintain extra military forces that can have no other purpose than to repeat our experience in Vietnam, a venture which nearly all of us now recognize as a monstrous national blunder;

—By repudiating the false world of old discredited myths, made up of blocs, puppets, and dominoes, facing instead the real world of today and the future, with multiple ideologies and interests. . . .

The recommended force and spending levels of this alternative defense budget should be achieved by fiscal 1975, with proportional reductions beginning in fiscal 1973. This phased approach allows, first, for an appropriate response to possible changes in the threat. Second, the process of phased reductions will allow advance preparations by military planners, to assure that obligations incurred in prior years do not exceed the 1975 recommended ceiling. Third, the recommended timetable will permit fulfillment of the Government's obligation to assist in the conversion of excess military resources into other public and private enterprise. A program to meet accumulated civilian needs, applying both savings from the military sector and general revenues, can occupy a large share of the facilities freed by this budget. Such a program can also guarantee alternative employment to all workers displaced from the defense sector, and reduce economic dependence on superfluous military spending.

The truth is that we are surrounded by research and development needs. They simply have not been backed up with money, or with institutional reforms designed to stimulate innovation. In the private sector some of our major industries—electronics, steel, shipbuilding, and others—are losing out to competition from overseas, in large part because we have lagged behind in developing new products and production techniques.

Let me suggest some of the directions I would pursue:

First, we need to greatly expand funding for real research—for laboratory and feasibility studies, for experimentation and design. And we should be doing that across a broad range of civilian needs—in health, in water pollution control, in waste recycling, in energy conservation, in air traffic control, in noise abatement, in mass transit systems, in population planning, in law enforcement methods, in drug rehabilitation, and in a host of others.

SECOND, we need to find effective methods of stimulating research in the private sector, especially by smaller firms, even if it has purely commercial applications. Considering the enormous influence of technology on our rate of economic growth and on the world trade balance, I see little justification for the long-standing resistance to Federal support for research that might be used exclusively in the private sector.

THIRD, we should search for ways to stimulate and encourage smaller technical enterprise. The bulk of Federal research and development funds go to the biggest corporations. About eighty-five percent goes to companies with more than 5,000 employes each. Yet, independent inventors and small research-based companies have consistently produced far more than their share of important new ideas and innovations. The cyclotron, the Xerox process, Polaroid, automatic transmission, oxygen steelmaking, modern steel hot rolling techniques, titanium, the jet engine, the helicopter—these are a few of the major inventions which have been produced in small laboratories in this country, and the list goes on and on.

Hence, in this context as in others, it makes sense for the Government to pursue a vigorous free enterprise policy—to come down hard on the side of smaller enterprise.

FOURTH, Federal research and development programs should be consolidated in a Cabinet-level Department of Science and Technology. The Department would be actively involved with all other Federal agencies, and also with the states and the cities and with the private sector, in seeking out and funding worthwhile research and development programs. And it would be responsible for all existing R&D efforts, including those conducted by the Department of Defense and the National Aeronautics and Space Administration. . . .Whether geared to peace or war, the Nixon Administration's economic policies have proven to be a failure. For the past three years we have seen the American economy steadily deteriorate, and the President's belated intervention has not dealt effectively either with unemployment or with inflation. We need a Phase III in economic policy, and that is to phase Mr. Nixon out of office and back into private life.

I have presented a series of alternative economic proposals encompassing these main points:

—Immediate Federal investment of $10 billion to create 2.6 million new jobs.

—Inflation insurance—in the form of Government bonds with automatic cost-of-living features—for those living on fixed incomes.

—Exemption of low-wage occupations from controls, and full application of the wage provisions of existing collective bargaining agreements.

—A Senate investigation of price-fixing by industry under cover of the price freeze and selective, rather than general, application of controls to prices and wages.

—An excess-profits tax for windfall profits.

—Interest subsidies for agriculture, education, and housing loans.

—Increases in farm income supports. The corporate invasion of American agriculture can be checked by the elimination of tax loopholes which give corporations and wealthy individuals unfair tax advantages, accompanied by a revision of the antitrust laws to place specific limits on corporate agricultural involvement. Elimination of other loopholes in our Federal tax laws would enable the Federal Government to assume at least a third of the cost of elementary and secondary education. This would reduce reliance on property taxes which are generally unfair but particularly inequitable to agricultural producers, since their property taxes have increased 260 percent in the last twenty years while their real income has been declining. . . .

I propose a minimum income tax so that the rich could not avoid their share of the tax burden no matter what loopholes they used. One possible formula would be a minimum income tax to apply to all those with total incomes in excess of $50,000. The entire income of any person in this range would be subject to payment of taxes at a rate of seventy-five percent of the current statutory rates at the rate that they would have to pay if there were no loopholes. All income regardless of source would be included.

The corporate income tax is gradually being abolished. Because of steady reductions in the taxable base over the past twenty years, the effective corporation income tax rate has been cut in half. I propose that the actual corporation income tax be returned to its 1960 level by the elimination of the special loopholes that have been opened since then.

My reforms of the Federal tax system relating to individual and corporation income taxes and to estate and gift taxes would result in additional revenues of about $18 billion this fiscal year and $28 billion in fiscal 1973. Depending on how these additional revenues were applied they could bring about the reduction or elimination of the local property tax for education; they could be spent on other urgent national needs such as rebuilding our cities, pollution control, adequate nutrition for all; or they could go a long way toward financing my proposed minimum income grant program. . . .

I propose that every man, woman, and child receive from the Federal Government an annual payment. This payment would not vary in accordance with the wealth of the recipient. For those on public assistance, this income grant would replace the welfare system. It has also been suggested that the national income grant could replace certain social security benefits.

It would not be necessary to finance all of the minimum income grant by tax increases. The billions of dollars saved in welfare benefits and the cumbersome administration of the welfare system—a total since it began of $9.6 billion or $1.4 billion in fiscal 1970—could be allocated for this purpose. It should be noted that this procedure would represent a major saving for states and localities which would not be required to finance the welfare system and could use the resulting funds—an estimated $5 billion—to lower property taxes. As a nation, we have the resources to feed the hungry, care for the sick, give work to the jobless, provide decent housing for the homeless, clean up our air and waters, educate all of our children properly. We are simply misusing our strength. And we have allowed our attention to be diverted away from the real concerns of the American people. I can think of no better example of such diversionary tactics than the political panic engendered by the various "antibusing" proposals initiated in Congress and by the Nixon Administration. . . .

Yet with those and other issues unresolved, some act as if the survival of the American way of life turned on whether or not some of our children will be bused to integrated schools. That, I submit, is a sorry spectacle to present to the American people in 1972. The school bus, after all, is not public enemy Number One. Certainly it is an inconvenience to have to ride a bus to school, rather than to have the school within walking distance. No one disputes that. But about sixty-five percent of the school children in this country ride buses and other vehicles to school every day, simply because the school is too far away to walk. Such busing has nothing to do with race. In fact, the school bus has been used for decades as a vehicle to affect the racial makeup of schools. It has been used to bus white children past black schools and black children past white schools, and to keep black and white children apart. . . .We must begin to restore public trust in government. Opinion surveys in recent years have consistently shown that confidence in government has fallen to all-time lows—that many Americans have begun to doubt or disbelieve virtually everything they are told by politicians and public officials, and to believe that government exists not to serve the needs of the people but simply to preserve its own power.

The sources of public suspicion and alienation are not hard to find. Put bluntly, the Government is not believed because it has not been leveling with the American people. The gap between preelection promise and postelection performance has grown to a yawning chasm in recent years, in nearly every area of public concern from war and peace to law and order. Political campaigns have degenerated into contests between polling techniques and advertising agencies, to see who is best at packaging candidates and manipulating public opinion. . . .

An informed electorate is a primary condition of democracy. It follows that the deceptive practices of recent years, while they create a serious political issue, also raise doubts about the survival of self-government in this country. We are embarked on a dangerous trend toward control by a collection of elitists whose interests and inclinations dominate national policy irrespective of the public will, and often at the expense of the public good.

We have no reason to expect popular confidence in government until politicians and public officials begin exhibiting their own confidence in the democratic system and in the American people. The electorate has a preeminent right to know what the Government is doing and why, and to hear the honest judgments of their leaders.

I am doing my best in this election campaign to let the American people know where I stand. If I am elected President, I intend to let the American people know where their Government stands. It is, after all, *their* Government, and I propose to return it to them.

65.

The Press as Watchdog

Freedom of the press, as defined by the First Amendment, was beset by a number of threats during the 1970s. Prominent, of course, were the attacks by administration officials, especially Vice-President Agnew, on television news reporting and the liberal newspapers. Then in the summer of 1971 the issue took a legal twist when the Justice Department attempted to block publication of the Pentagon papers. This was the first occasion of prior restraint on the press in U. S. history, and it was resolved in favor of the newspapers by the Supreme Court. Another phase of the controversy as it developed during 1971-72 concerned investigative reporting, its secret sources, and the so-called "news leak." Some reporters were arrested and jailed for refusing to divulge the sources of their stories, and early in 1973 a series of Supreme Court rulings seemed to put a limit on the extent to which reporters could protect their sources. On October 22, 1972, the radio program "Yale Reports" broadcast a panel discussion on the subject of journalistic privilege. Members of the panel were Alexander Bickel, William Nelson, and Abraham Goldstein of the Yale Law School; and John Fischer, associate editor of Harper's *magazine. Portions of the discussion are reprinted here.*

Source: "Yale Reports," #625, Sunday, October 22, 1972.

Announcer: The concept of freedom of the press is embodied in the First Amendment to the Constitution of the United States in the words, "Congress shall make no law abridging the freedom of speech or of the press."

For the first time in our history, the Supreme Court has fairly effectively denied the existence of this privilege under the First Amendment with decisions in the Branzburg, Caldwell and Pappas cases. Reporters are now in the position of ordinary citizens who have to answer legitimate questions by government agencies engaged in legitimate inquiries.

Will this seriously affect the freedom of the press?. . .

Mr. Bickel: Newspaper reporters, as well as other writers who depend a great deal on gathering information from various sources, have for some time claimed a privilege to withhold information about their confidential sources (the identity of confidential sources chiefly) from government investigative agencies (again, chiefly grand juries investigating some criminal offense and courts in the course of a trial). For the first time in our history this spring, oddly enough, considering this problem has been around for a long time, the Supreme Court in three cases fairly effectively denied the existence of such a privilege under the First Amendment. There are some qualifications in the decision, perhaps, but the privilege as claimed under the First Amendment was denied and newspapermen assimilated, again with some qualifications, to the position of ordinary citizens who have to answer when asked a legitimate question by a government agency engaged in a legitimate inquiry. The average layman might be a little puzzled about the justification that journalists have offered for the claim to a privilege. Jack, what is the justification that a reporter will normally offer for claiming the privilege?

Mr. Fischer: I deplore the decision on two grounds, one personal and one a public policy ground. The personal one is the hardest to defend, but every reporter feels it very keenly because the decision would, in effect, put reporters out of business. A great deal of information that you collect has to be done under terms of confidentiality. Politicians, for example, are very reluctant to speak candidly to a reporter unless they are assured that they will not be quoted directly and that their names will not be disclosed as a source of the information. Every reporter feels that when he learns something in confidence he has to preserve that confidence even at the risk of going to jail. My only asset as a reporter is the confidence that my news sources have that I will preserve any secrecy that they impose on me. The second and more important objection to the decision is that it would deny the public a great deal of information it needs to make intelligent decisions about politics and other matters of public concern because such material would no longer appear in print. The reporter cannot get it unless he is able to assure that he will keep it in confidence.

Mr. Goldstein: If I may, Jack, I'd like to try to put in historical perspective the problem of newsman's privilege. We don't write against a blank slate. As Alex pointed out, these opinions in the Supreme Court were the first opinions (in the line of lower court cases out of which they come) in which the First Amendment claim was importantly raised. We have been living dominantly in these United States without a newsman's privilege since the beginning of the Republic. There have been a relatively small number of states, perhaps 17, that have privilege statutes. Newsmen have been busily accumulating information from confidential sources and not being sent to jail. Indeed, the most celebrated news eras in our history, the great muckraking eras, were ones in which obviously there weren't even the handful of newsman's privilege statutes that we now have. So we've got to line up your assertion with the whole problem of privilege which is essentially an effort on the part of some group, usually a professional group, to separate itself out from the generalized obligation to provide information to public investigative authorities.

When you have the public investigatory authority putting a question, whether it's through a grand jury or through a legislative investigating committee, then our law has always regarded it as very extraordinary for somebody to claim that he has a right to withhold information. I find it a curious thing that the news media who have been most aggressive about demanding freedom of access to public records and public information have resisted the challenge of government authorities which claim that they could withhold information from the news media through doctrines like government privilege and have done a turnabout and been so aggressive in claiming that they should be added to a very narrow category of people who are free to withhold information from legitimate investigatory authorities.

Mr. Bickel: But they are the ones whose claim even colorably, even plausibly, can be placed and has been placed on a Constitutional foundation. With everybody else (lawyers and priests, for instance) the basis of the privilege is common law, statute, which suggests the beginnings of the answer to the question that you posed, a question that's a special one; in this case you have involved an enormous public policy embodied in the First Amendment. Unlike lawyers, unlike priests, where there's public policy involved always, reporters have a Constitutional public policy that they're vindicating; the flow of information to the public which would be appreciably lessened by taking the privilege away from them. At this stage I'm only posing the other side. To require a symmetry between reporters' rights to withhold information and those of the government is to disregard the policy of the First Amendment, the thrust of which is that governmental privacy is hurtful in a way that almost no other privacy in our system is. How far that should go is another issue.

Mr. Fischer: And the theory of the newspaper business traditionally has been that its first duty is to be a watchdog over government. This kind of privilege is essential if it's to be an effective watchdog. I'm not clear whether the privilege of lawyers, priests and doctors is protected by statute. It certainly isn't a Constitutional privilege.

Mr. Goldstein: Alex may have understated the potential Constitutional base for the attorney-client privilege and the priest-penitent privilege, for example. Those are two privileges which are most commonly recognized by the states in the United States. They are virtually universal in the United States. It's because they antedated the Constitution that it may well be that the issue has never really arisen. If one were to address the question of the Constitutional base today, it's substantially arguable that the priest-penitent privilege might have something to do with religion, and the attorney-client privilege might have something to do with the right to counsel and right to effective assistance.

Mr. Bickel: Might; but, for example, the attorney-client privilege, as I understand the common law, does not cover information that comes to counsel of the prospective commission of a crime. The privilege claimed for the newsman does cover that, at least the claim does. If the attorney-client privilege were measured against the Constitution, we would find it difficult to predict what its perimeters would be. It might turn out to be a very much narrower thing than we have on the books now. As for the priest-penitent privilege, that's even more tenuous. The fact is that those are traditional ones that the common law has given us. Any extension other than the newsman's has always been by statute which brings up the point that reporters' privilege can also be done by statute. You have mentioned the existence, Abe, of a variety of some 17 state statutes that are on the books now. There is a bill in Congress that would extend the privilege and this, of course, under the Supreme Court decision remains entirely possible. The Court merely said that the First Amendment does not protect the newspapermen to the extent claimed. It didn't even say it doesn't protect them at all. It said nothing about what kind of protection a state legislature or Congress might wish to extend. They might wish to extend a total one. The statutes of New York and Michigan, for example, extend a very substantial privilege, indeed.

Mr. Fischer: I would not put the journalists' claim quite as strongly as you did. I don't think any newsman ought to accept confidential information about the future commission of a crime. There are a good many kinds of confidential information that he ought not to accept. Presidential press conferences go a great deal too far in trying to keep things off the record. One of the most effective forms of secrecy is to call newspapermen together and say, "I am going to tell you something important on grounds that you never use it."

Mr. Bickel: That's a paradox, too. Why does that protect the people's right to be informed?

Mr. Fischer: It doesn't and I don't think any newsman ought to accept those conditions. Sometimes he should accept a condition that the source will not be disclosed. There are valid reasons (diplomatic reasons, for example) why a President would want to explain a policy but not have it known that he is making that statement himself. . . .

Mr. Goldstein: One problem that affected this issue, or may have, more than is commonly understood and certainly more than we've noted here, is the problem of definition of who a newsman is. This is much more complex than the definition of who an attorney is, the definition of who a priest is. When you are dealing with a well-established profession which has licensing requirements, supervisory processes and sanctioning mechanism one can feel a little easier about defining the class of persons to endow with this kind of power to withhold information from the public. Very early in the discussions of newsman's privilege, particularly in recent times when it surfaced as a First Amendment issue, one of the critical questions was, who is a newsman? Which media are we going to protect? Underground newspapers, campus newspapers, high school newspapers, what are we talking about?

Mr. Bickel: Writers of books who immediately plunged in.

Mr. Goldstein: It raced away. The speed with which the claim to protection escalated may have put a damper on the original inclination to create the privilege.

Mr. Fischer: A good many newsmen or quasi-newsmen make claims that they had no right to under this same rubric. I don't think any newsman has a right to misrepresent facts, and I don't think either the libel law or any law of privilege ought to protect him when he does misrepresent facts, although that has been done in some of these peripheral cases.

Mr. Bickel: Yes, he is protected.

Mr. Fischer: In some cases as a matter of self-protection public officials are now insisting on making their own tapes of an interview since they can't ask for the tapes that the newsman or the television station may have made. This is a reasonable thing under the circumstances. Just as a reporter has an obligation to go to jail before disclosing confidential sources, he has an equally strong obligation to report facts accurately. What is 'accurately' gets to be a difficult question.

Mr. Bickel: Starting with the Sullivan case the law has gone substantially in the direction of protecting a falsehood for reasons which whether they justify it all the way are substantial reasons. In publishing a daily newspaper, if you have to worry every night that everything in it is true, subject to libel laws, there is a lot that you won't publish even though you believe it to be true because litigation is a fearfully expensive and troublesome thing. You give a law like that a wide berth. So there is some justification for the freedom to publish falsehood although there may not be justification for the frequency of its exercise.

Mr. Fischer: My firm recently came into quite a lot of criticism from the press itself in a case of this kind. We published a book about the opium traffic in Southeast Asia, implicating the CIA in at least condoning such traffic. The CIA protested and asked to see proofs of the book. We showed them proofs, saying that we are not granting any right of censorship but if there are any factual errors we want to know before it's published. We found no factual errors and published it as it was originally written, but many journalists criticized us quite sharply for even showing it in advance. It is a reasonable precaution to try to be sure that you are accurate.

Mr. Bickel: So often, despite the sensitivities of newspapers and maybe the oversensitivity that they exhibit, these intractable problems that don't lend themselves too easily to Constitutional adjudiction or to codification by law are handled among sensible men in sensible, informal ways so that at the very least if the whole problem isn't solved, at least it's reduced to a minimal problem and doesn't seem as frightening and as major as it might in its initial aspect.

1973

66.

HENRY KISSINGER: Vietnam Truce

During the autumn of 1972 presidential adviser Henry Kissinger conducted negotiations in Paris with Le Duc Tho of North Vietnam to gain a settlement of the war. On October 26 Kissinger announced that the negotiations had been successful and that "peace was at hand." But it turned out that the bilateral settlement with Hanoi lacked the approval of South Vietnam, and thus peace was stalemated again. In mid-December President Nixon ordered saturation bombing of North Vietnam. By the end of the month the bombing was ordered stopped, and the Paris peace talks were scheduled to resume. On January 15, 1973, the President ordered a halt to all military action against North Vietnam because progress was being made in Paris. On January 23, in a televised address to the nation, Nixon announced that Kissinger and Le Duc Tho had initialed an agreement to end the fighting. Details of the agreement were explained by Dr. Kissinger in a nationally televised news conference on January 24. Portions of the news conference clarifying the main points of the truce are reprinted here. In addition to the agreement, there were several protocols relating to such matters as the return of American prisoners, implementation of an international control commission, cease-fire regulations, institution of a joint military commission, and the removal of mines from Haiphong harbor.

Source: *Department of State Bulletin*, February 12, 1973.

LADIES AND GENTLEMEN: The President last evening presented the outlines of the agreement, and by common agreement between us and the North Vietnamese we have today released the texts. And I am here to explain, to go over briefly, what these texts contain and how we got there, what we have tried to achieve in recent months, and where we expect to go from here.

Let me begin by going through the agreement, which you have read.

The agreement, as you know, is in nine chapters. The first affirms the independence, sovereignty, unity, and territorial integrity, as recognized by the 1954 Geneva agreements on Vietnam, agreements which established two zones divided by a military demarcation line.

Chapter II deals with the cease-fire.

The cease-fire will go into effect at seven o'clock, Washington time, on Saturday night. The principal provisions of chapter II deal with permitted acts during the cease-fire and with what the obligations of the various parties are with respect to the cease-fire.

Chapter II also deals with the withdrawal of American and all other foreign forces from Vietnam within a period of 60 days. And it specifies the forces that have to be withdrawn. These are, in effect, all military personnel and all civilian personnel dealing with combat operations. We are permitted to retain economic advisers, and civilian technicians serving in certain of the military branches.

Chapter II further deals with the provisions for resupply and for the introduction of outside forces. There is a flat prohibition against the introduction of any military force into South Vietnam from outside of South Vietnam, which is to say that whatever forces may be in South Vietnam from outside South Vietnam, specifically North Vietnamese forces, cannot receive reinforcements, replacements, or any other form of augmentation by any means whatsoever. With respect to military equipment, both sides are permitted to replace all existing military equipment on a one-to-one basis under international supervision and control. . . .

Chapter III deals with the return of captured military personnel and foreign civilians, as well as with the question of civilian detainees within South Vietnam.

This, as you know, throughout the negotiations presented enormous difficulties for us. We insisted throughout that the question of American prisoners of war and of American civilians captured throughout Indochina should be separated from the issue of Vietnamese civilian personnel detained, partly because of the enormous difficulty of classifying the Vietnamese civilian personnel by categories of who was detained for reasons of the civil war and who was detained for criminal activities, and secondly, because it was foreseeable that negotiations about the release of civilian detainees would be complex and difficult and because we did not want to have the issue of American personnel mixed up with the issues of civilian personnel in South Vietnam.

This turned out to be one of the thorniest issues, that was settled at some point and kept reappearing throughout the negotiations. It was one of the difficulties we had during the December negotiations.

As you can see from the agreement, the return of American military personnel and captured civilians is separated in terms of obligation, and in terms of the time frame, from the return of Vietnamese civilian personnel.

The return of American personnel and the accounting of missing in action is unconditional and will take place within the same time frame as the American withdrawal.

The issue of Vietnamese civilian personnel will be negotiated between the two Vietnamese parties over a period of three months, and as the agreement says, they will do their utmost to resolve this question within the three-month period.

So I repeat, the issue is separated, both in terms of obligation and in terms of the relevant time frame, from the return of American prisoners, which is unconditional.

We expect that American prisoners will be released at intervals of two weeks or 15 days in roughly equal installments. We have been told that no American prisoners are held in Cambodia. American prisoners held in Laos and North Vietnam will be returned to us in Hanoi. They will be received by American medical evacuation teams and flown on American airplanes from Hanoi to places of our own choice, probably Vientiane.

There will be international supervision of both this provision and of the provision for the missing in action. And all American prisoners will, of course, be released, within 60 days of the signing of the agreement. The signing will take place on January 27 in two installments, the significance of which I will explain to you when I have run through the provisions of the agreement and the associated protocols.

Chapter IV of the agreement deals with the right of the South Vietnamese people to self-determination. Its first provision contains a joint statement by the United States and North Vietnam in which those two countries jointly recognize the South Vietnamese people's right to self-determination, in which those two countries jointly affirm that the South Vietnamese people shall decide for themselves the political system that they shall choose and jointly affirm that no foreign country shall impose any political tendency on the South Vietnamese people.

The other principal provisions of the agreement are that in implementing the South Vietnamese people's right to self-determination, the two South Vietnamese parties will decide, will agree among each other, on free elections, for offices to be decided by the two parties, at a time to be decided by the two parties. These elections will be supervised and organized first by an institution which has the title of National Council for National Reconciliation and Concord, whose members will be equally appointed by the two sides, which will operate on the principle of unanimity, and which will come into being after negotiation between the two parties, who are obligated by this agreement to do their utmost to bring this institution into being within 90 days.

Leaving aside the technical jargon, the significance of this part of the agreement is that the United States has consistently maintained that we would not impose any political solution on the people of South Vietnam. The United States has consistently maintained that we would not impose a coalition government or a disguised coalition government on the people of South Vietnam. . . .

The next chapter deals with the reunification of Vietnam and the relationship between North and South Vietnam. In the many negotiations that I have conducted over recent weeks, not the least arduous was the negotiation conducted with the ladies and gentlemen of the press, who constantly raised issues with respect to sovereignty, the existence of South Vietnam as a political entity, and other matters of this kind. . . .

Chapter VI deals with the international machinery, and we will discuss that when I talk about the associated protocols of the agreement.

Chapter VII deals with Laos and Cambodia. Now, the problem of Laos and Cambodia has two parts. One part concerns those obligations which can be undertaken by the parties signing the agreement—that is to say, the three Vietnamese parties and the United States—those measures that they can take which affect the situation in Laos and Cambodia. A second part of the situation in Laos has to concern the nature of the civil conflict that is taking place within Laos and Cambodia and the solution of which, of course, must involve as well the two Laotian parties and the innumerable Cambodian factions.

Let me talk about the provisions of the agreement with respect to Laos and Cambodia and our firm expectations as to the future in Laos and Cambodia.

The provisions of the agreement with respect to Laos and Cambodia reaffirm, as an obligation to all the parties, the provisions of the 1954 agreement on Cambodia and of the 1962 agreement on Laos, which affirm the neutrality and right to self-determination of those two countries. They are therefore consistent with our basic position with respect also to South Vietnam.

In terms of the immediate conflict, the provisions of the agreement specifically prohibit the use of Laos and Cambodia for military and any other operations against any of the signatories of the Paris agreement or against any other country. In other words, there is a flat prohibition against the use of base areas in Laos and Cambodia.

There is a flat prohibition against the use of Laos and Cambodia for infiltration into Vietnam or, for that matter, into any other country.

Finally, there is a requirement that all foreign troops be withdrawn from Laos and Cambodia, and it is clearly understood that North Vietnamese troops are considered foreign with respect to Laos and Cambodia.

Now, as to the conflict within these countries which could not be formally settled in an agreement which is not signed by the parties of that conflict, let me make this statement, without elaborating it: It is our firm expectation that within a short period of time there will be a formal cease-fire in Laos which in turn will lead to a withdrawal of all foreign forces from Laos and, of course, to the end of the use of Laos as a corridor of infiltration.

Secondly, the situation in Cambodia, as those of you who have studied it will know, is somewhat more complex because there are several parties headquartered in different countries. Therefore, we can say about Cambodia that it is our expectation that a de facto cease-fire will come into being over a period of time relevant to the execution of this agreement.

Our side will take the appropriate measures to indicate that it will not attempt to change the situation by force. We have reason to believe that our position is clearly understood by all concerned parties, and I will not go beyond this in my statement.

Chapter VIII deals with the relationship between the United States and the Democratic Republic of Vietnam.

As I have said in my briefings on October 26 and on December 16 and as the President affirmed on many occasions, the last time in his speech last evening, the United States is seeking a peace that heals. We have had many armistices in Indochina. We want a peace that will last.

And therefore it is our firm intention in our relationship to the Democratic Republic of Vietnam to move from hostility to normalization, and from normalization to conciliation and cooperation. And we believe that under conditions of peace we can contribute throughout Indochina to a realization of the humane aspirations of all the people of Indochina. And we will, in that spirit, perform our traditional role of helping people realize these aspirations in peace.

Chapter IX of the agreement is the usual implementing provision.

67.

LEWIS F. POWELL: *San Antonio School District v. Rodriguez*

School districts in all parts of the nation found themselves increasingly hard pressed for operating funds in the late 1960s and early 1970s. Between 1967 and 1972 the cost of running the schools rose by more than 80 percent. To meet this crisis in education the schools turned more and more toward the state governments for financing, instead of trying to rely on local tax bases, especially the traditional property tax. The governor of Michigan proposed in 1972 that a state income tax be used to supply the revenue. Other states considered lotteries or other means to replace property tax levies. In August 1971 a decision by the California Supreme Court in the case of Serrano v. Priest *seemed to offer new hope to hard-pressed school districts, because the ruling required that the financing of a child's education could no longer depend on the relative affluence of the school district in which he lived. Instead, public schools were to be funded on the basis of the wealth of the state taken as a whole. This ruling obviously mitigated against sole reliance on property taxes for education. Later in 1971, this ruling was applied by the U.S. district court in San Antonio, Texas, in a suit challenging the financing of Texas public schools. The court found that "the state may adopt the financial scheme desired so long as the variations in wealth among the governmentally chosen units do not affect spending for the education of any one child." The case was appealed to the U.S. Supreme Court, which on March 21, 1973, in a 5 to 4 decision, reversed the ruling of the Texas court. The decision of the Supreme Court was rendered by Associate Justice Lewis F. Powell and is reprinted here in part.*

Source: *U.S. Supreme Court Bulletin*, 1972-1973 Term, Vol. I.

THIS SUIT ATTACKING the Texas system of financing public education was initiated by Mexican-American parents whose children attend the elementary and secondary schools in the Edgewood Independent School District, an urban school district in San Antonio, Texas. They brought a class action on behalf of school children throughout the State who are members of minority groups or who are poor and reside in school districts having a low property tax base. Named as defendants were the State Board of Education, the Commissioner of Education, the State Attorney General, and the Bexar County (San Antonio) Board of Trustees. The complaint was filed in the summer of 1968 and a three-judge court was impaneled in January 1969. In December 1971 the panel rendered its judgment in a *per curiam* opinion holding the Texas school finance system unconstitutional under the Equal Protection Clause of the Fourteenth Amendment. The State appealed, and we noted probable jurisdiction to consider the far-reaching constitutional questions presented.406 U.S. 966 (1972). For the reasons stated in this opinion we reverse the decision of the District Court. . . .

Until recent times Texas was a predominantly rural State and its population and property wealth were spread relatively evenly across the State. Sizable differences in the value of assessable property between local school districts became increasingly evident as the State became more industrialized and as rural-to-urban population shifts became more pronounced. The location of commercial and industrial property began to play a significant role in determining the amount of tax resources available to each school district. These growing disparities in population and taxable property between districts were responsible in part for increasingly notable differences in levels of local expenditure for education.

In due time it became apparent to those concerned with financing public education that contributions from the Available School Fund were not sufficient to ameliorate these disparities. Prior to 1939 the Available School Fund contributed money to every school district at a rate of $17.50 per school-age child. Although the amount was increased several times in the early 1940s, the Fund was providing only $46 per student by 1945.

Recognizing the need for increased state funding to help offset disparities in local spending and to meet Texas' changing educational requirements, the state legislature in the late 1940's undertook a thorough evaluation of public education with an eye toward major reform. In 1947 an 18-member committee, composed of educators and legislators, was appointed to explore alternative systems in other States and to propose a funding scheme that would guarantee a minimum or basic educational offering to each child and that would help overcome interdistrict disparities in taxable resources. The Committee's efforts led to the passage of the Gilmer-Aiken bills, named for the Committee's co-chairmen, establishing the Texas Minimum Foundation School Program. Today this Program accounts for approximately half of the total educational expenditures in Texas.

The Program calls for state and local contributions to a fund earmarked specifically for teacher salaries, operating expenses, and transportation costs. The State, supplying funds from its general revenues, finances approximately 80 percent of the Program, and the school districts are responsible—as a unit—for providing the remaining 20 percent. The districts' share, known as the Local Fund Assignment, is apportioned among the school districts under a formula designed to reflect each district's relative taxpaying ability. . . .

The school district in which appellees reside, the Edgewood Independent School District, has been compared throughout this litigation with the Alamo Heights Independent School District. This comparison between the least and most affluent districts in the San Antonio area serves to illustrate the manner in which the dual system of finance operates and to indicate the extent to which substantial disparities exist despite the State's impressive progress in recent years. Edgewood is one of seven public school districts in the metropolitan area. Approximately 22,000 students are enrolled in its 25 elementary and secondary schools. The district is situated in the core-city sector of San Antonio in a residential neighborhood that has little commercial or industrial property. The residents are predominantly of Mexican-American descent: approximately 90 percent of the student population is Mexican-American and over six percent is Negro. The average assessed property value per pupil is $5,960—the lowest in the metropolitan area—and the median family income ($4,686) is also the lowest. At an equalized tax rate of $1.05 per $100 of assessed property—the highest in the metropolitan area—the district contributed $26 to the education of each child for the 1967-1968 school year above its Local Fund Assignment for the Minimum Foundation Program. The Foundation Program contributed $222 per pupil for a state-local total of $248. Federal funds added another $108 for a total of $356 per pupil.

Alamo Heights is the most affluent school district in San Antonio. Its six schools, housing approximately 5,000 students, are situated in a residential community quite unlike the Edgewood District. The school population is predominantly Anglo having only 18 percent Mexican-Americans and less than one percent Negroes. The assessed property value per pupil exceeds $49,000 and the median family income is $8,001. In 1967-1968 the local tax rate of $.85 per $100 of valuation yielded $333 per pupil over and above its contribution to the Foundation Program. Coupled with the $225 provided from that Program, the district was able to supply $558 per student. Supplemented by a $36 per pupil grant from federal sources, Alamo Heights spent $594 per pupil.

Although the 1967-1968 school year figures provide the only complete statistical breakdown for each category of aid, more recent partial statistics indicate that the previously noted trend of increasing state aid has been significant. For the 1970-1971 school year, the Foundation School Program allotment for Edgewood was $356 per pupil, a 62 percent increase over the 1967-1968 school year. Indeed, state aid alone in 1970-1971 equaled Edgewood's entire 1967-1968 school budget from local, state, and federal sources. Alamo Heights enjoyed a similar increase under the Foundation Program, netting $491 per pupil in 1970-1971. . . .

Despite these recent increases, substantial interdistrict disparities in school expenditures found by the District Court to prevail in San Antonio and in varying degrees throughout the State still exist. And it was these disparities, largely attributable to differences in the amounts of money collected through local property taxation, that led the District Court to conclude that Texas' dual system of public school finance violated the Equal Protection Clause. . . .

The District Court's opinion does not reflect the novelty and complexity of the constitutional questions posed by appellees' challenge to Texas' system of school finance. In concluding that strict judicial scrutiny was required, that court relied on decisions dealing with the rights of indigents to equal treatment in the criminal trial and appellate processes, and on cases disapproving wealth restrictions on the right to vote. Those cases, the District Court concluded, established wealth as a suspect classification. Finding that the local property tax system discriminated on the basis of wealth, it regarded those precedents as controlling. It then reasoned, based on decisions of this Court affirming the undeniable importance of education, that there is a fundamental right to education and that, absent some compelling state justification, the Texas system could not stand.

We are unable to agree that this case, which in significant aspects is *sui generis*, may be so neatly fitted into the conventional mosaic of constitutional analysis under the Equal Protection Clause. Indeed, for the several reasons that follow, we find neither the suspect classification nor the fundamental interest analysis persuasive. . . .

The argument here is not that the children in districts having relatively low assessable property values are receiving no public education; rather, it is that they are receiving a poorer quality education than that available to children in districts having more assessable wealth. Apart from the unsettled and disputed question whether the quality of education may be determined by the amount of money expended for it, a sufficient answer to appellees' argument is that at least where wealth is involved the Equal Protection Clause does not require absolute equality or precisely equal advantages. Nor, indeed, in view of the infinite variables affecting the educational process, can any system assure equal quality of education except in the most relative sense. Texas asserts that the Minimum Foundation Program provides an "adequate" education for all children in the State. By providing 12 years of free public school education, and by assuring teachers, books, transportation and operating funds, the Texas Legislature has endeavored to "guarantee, for the welfare of the state as a whole, that all people shall have at least an adequate program of education. This is what is meant by 'A Minimum Foundation Program of Education.'" The State repeatedly asserted in its briefs in this Court that it has fulfilled this desire and that it now assures "every child in every school district an adequate education." No proof was offered at trial persuasively discrediting or refuting the State's assertion. . . .

However described, it is clear that appellees' suit asks this Court to extend its most exacting scrutiny to review a system that allegedly discriminates against a large, diverse, and amorphous class, unified only by the common factor of residence in districts that happen to have less taxable wealth than other districts. The system of alleged discrimination and the class it defines have none of the traditional indicia of suspectness: the class is not saddled with such disabilities, or subjected to such a history of purposeful unequal treatment, or relegated to such a position of political powerlessness as to command extraordinary protection from the majoritarian political process.

We thus conclude that the Texas system does not operate to the peculiar disadvantage of any suspect class. But in recognition of the fact that this Court has never heretofore held that wealth discrimination alone provides an adequate basis for invoking strict scrutiny, appellees have not relied solely on this contention. They also assert that the State's system impermissibly interferes with the exercise of a "fundamental" right and that accordingly the prior decisions of this Court require the application of the strict standard of judicial review. . . . It is this question—whether education is a fundamental right, in the sense that it is among the rights and liberties protected by the Constitution—which has so consumed the attention of courts and commentators in recent years.

Education, of course, is not among the rights afforded explicit protection under our Federal Constitution. Nor do we find any basis for saying it is implicitly so protected. As we have said, the undisputed importance of education will not alone cause this Court to depart from the usual standard for reviewing a State's social and economic legislation. It is appellees' contention, however, that education is distinguishable from other services and benefits provided by the State because it bears a peculiarly close relationship to other rights and liberties accorded protection under the Constitution. Specifically, they insist that education is itself a fundamental personal right because it is essential to the effective exercise of First Amendment freedoms and to intelligent utilization of the right to vote. In asserting a nexus between speech and education, appellees urge that the right to speak is meaningless unless the speaker is capable of articulating his thoughts intelligently and persuasively. The "market-place of ideas" is an empty forum for those lacking basic communicative tools. Likewise, they argue that the corollary right to receive information becomes little more than a hollow privilege when the recipient has not been taught to read, assimilate, and utilize available knowledge.

A similar line of reasoning is pursued with respect to the right to vote. Exercise of the franchise, it is contended, cannot be divorced from the educational foundation of the voter. The electoral process, if reality is to confrom to the democratic ideal, depends on an informed electorate: a voter cannot cast his ballot intelligently unless his reading skills and thought processes have been adequately developed.

We need not dispute any of these propositions. The Court has long afforded zealous protection against unjustifiable governmental interference with the individual's rights to speak and to vote. Yet we have never presumed to possess either the ability or the authority to guarantee to the citizenry the most *effective* speech or the most *informed* electoral choice. That these may be desirable goals of a system of freedom of expression and of a representative form of government is not to be doubted. These are indeed goals to be pursued by a people whose thoughts and beliefs are freed from governmental interference. But they are not values to be implemented by judicial intrusion into otherwise legitimate state activities.

Even if it were conceded that some identifiable quantum of education is a constitutionally protected prerequisite to the meaningful exercise of either right, we have no indication that the present levels of educational expenditure in Texas provide an education that falls short. Whatever merit appellees' argument might have if a State's financing system occasioned an absolute denial of educational opportunities to any of its children, that argument provides no basis for finding an interference with fundamental rights where only relative differences in spending levels are involved and where—as is true in the present case—no charge fairly could be made that the system fails to provide each child with an opportunity to acquire the basic minimal skills necessary for the enjoyment of the rights of speech and of full participation in the political process.

We have carefully considered each of the arguments supportive of the District Court's finding that education is a fundamental right or liberty and have found those arguments unpersuasive. In one further respect we find this a particularly inappropriate case in which to subject state action to strict judicial scrutiny. The present case, in another basic sense, is significantly different from any of the cases in which the Court has applied strict scrutiny to state or federal legislation touching upon constitutionally protected rights. Each of our prior cases involved legislation which "deprived," "infringed," or "interfered" with the free exercise of some such fundamental personal right or liberty.

Every step leading to the establishment of the system Texas utilizes today—including the decisions permitting localities to tax and expend locally, and creating and continuously expanding state aid—was implemented in an effort to *extend* public education and to improve its quality. Of course, every reform that benefits some more than others may be criticized for what it fails to accomplish. But we think it plain that, in substance, the thrust of the Texas system is affirmative and reformatory and, therefore, should be scrutinized under judicial principles sensitive to the nature of the State's efforts and to the rights reserved to the States under the Constitution.

We need not rest our decision, however, solely on the inappropriateness of the strict scrutiny test. A century of Supreme Court adjudication under the Equal Protection Clause affirmatively supports the application of the traditional standard of review, which requires only that the State's system be shown to bear some rational relationship to legitimate state purposes. This case represents far more than a challenge to the manner in which Texas provides for the education of its children. We have here nothing less than a direct attack on the way in which Texas has chosen to raise and disburse state and local tax revenues. We are asked to condemn the State's judgment in conferring on political subdivisions the power to tax local property to supply revenues for local interests. In so doing, appellees would have the Court intrude in an area in which it has traditionally deferred to state legislatures. This Court has often admonished against such interferences with the State's fiscal policies under the Equal Protection Clause:

> The broad discretion as to classification possessed by a legislature in the field of taxation has long been recognized. . . . [T]he passage of time has only served to underscore the wisdom of that recognition of the large area of discretion which is needed by a legislature in formulating sound tax policies. . . . It has . . . been pointed out that in taxation, even more than in other fields, legislatures possess the greatest freedom in classification. Since the members of a legislature necessarily enjoy a familiarity with local conditions which this Court cannot have, the presumption of constitutionality can be overcome only by the most explicit demonstration that a classification is a hostile and oppressive discrimination against particular persons and classes. . . . *Madden v. Kentucky*, 309 U.S. 83, 87-88 (1940).

Thus we stand on familiar ground when we continue to acknowledge that the Justices of this Court lack both the expertise and the familiarity with local problems so necessary to the making of wise decisions with respect to the raising and disposition of public revenues. Yet we are urged to direct the States either to alter drastically the present system or to throw out the property tax altogether in favor of some other form of taxation. No scheme of taxation, whether the tax is imposed on property, income, or purchases of goods and services, has yet been devised which is free of all discriminatory impact. In such a complex arena in which no perfect alternatives exist, the Court does well not to impose too rigorous a standard of scrutiny lest all local fiscal schemes become subjects of criticism under the Equal Protection Clause.

It must be remembered also that every claim arising under the Equal Protection Clause has implications for the relationship between national and state power under our federal system. Questions of federalism are always inherent in the process of determining whether a State's laws are to be accorded the traditional presumption of constitutionality, or are to be subjected instead to rigorous judicial scrutiny. While "[t]he maintenance of the principles of federalism is a foremost consideration in interpreting any of the pertinent provisions under which this Court examines state action," it would be difficult to imagine a case having a greater potential impact on our federal system than the one now before us, in which we are urged to abrogate systems of financing public education presently in existence in virtually every State.

Appellees do not question the propriety of Texas' dedication to local control of education. To the contrary, they attack the school finance system precisely because, in their view, it does not provide the same level of local control and fiscal flexibility in all districts. Appellees suggest that local control could be preserved and promoted under other financing systems that resulted in more equality in educational expenditures. While it is no doubt true that reliance on local property taxation for school revenues provides less freedom of choice with respect to expenditures for some districts than for others, the existence of "some inequality" in the manner in which the State's rationale is achieved is not alone a sufficient basis for striking down the entire system.

Appellees further urge that the Texas system is unconstitutionally arbitrary because it allows the availability of local taxable resources to turn on "happenstance." They see no justification for a system that allows, as they contend, the quality of education to fluctuate on the basis of the fortuitous positioning of the boundary lines of political subdivisions and the location of valuable commercial and industrial property. But any scheme of local taxation—indeed the very existence of identifiable local governmental units—requires the establishment of jurisdictional boundaries that are inevitably arbitrary. It is equally inevitable that some localities are going to be blessed with more taxable assets than others. Nor is local wealth a static quantity. Changes in the level of taxable wealth within any district may result from any number of events, some of which local residents can and do influence. For instance, commercial and industrial enterprises may be encouraged to locate within a district by various actions—public and private.

Moreover, if local taxation for local expenditure is an unconstitutional method of providing for education then it may be an equally impermissible means of providing other necessary services customarily financed largely from local property taxes, including local police and fire protection, public health and hospitals, and public utility facilities of various kinds. We perceive no justification for such a severe denegration of local property taxation and control as would follow from appellees' contentions. It has simply never been within the constitutional prerogative of this Court to nullify statewide measures for financing public services merely because the burdens or benefits thereof fall unevenly depending upon the relative wealth of the political subdivisions in which citizens live.

In sum, to the extent that the Texas system of school finance results in unequal expenditures between children who happen to reside in different districts, we cannot say that such disparities are the product of a system that is so irrational as to be invidiously discriminatory. Texas has acknowledged its shortcomings and has persistently endeavored—not without some success—to ameliorate the differences in levels of expenditures without sacrificing the benefits of local participation. The Texas plan is not the result of hurried, ill-conceived legislation. It certainly is not the product of purposeful discrimination against any group or class. On the contrary, it is rooted in decades of experience in Texas and elsewhere, and in major part is the product of responsible studies by qualified people.

It cannot be questioned that the constitutional judgment reached by the District Court and approved by our dissenting brothers today would occasion in Texas and elsewhere an unprecedented upheaval in public education. Some commentators have concluded that, whatever the contours of the alternative financing programs that might be devised and approved, the result could not avoid being a beneficial one. But, just as there is nothing simple about the constitutional issues involved in these cases, there is nothing simple or certain about predicting the consequences of massive change in the financing and control of public education. Those who have devoted the most thoughtful attention to the practical ramifications of these cases have found no clear or dependable answers and their scholarship reflects no such unqualified confidence in the desirability of completely uprooting the existing system.

The complexity of these problems is demonstrated by the lack of consensus with respect to whether it may be said with any assurance that the poor, the racial minorities, or the children in overburdened core-city school districts would be benefitted by abrogation of traditional modes of financing education. Unless there is to be a substantial increase in state expenditures on education across the board—an event the likelihood of which is open to considerable question—these groups stand to realize gains in terms of increased per pupil expenditures only if they reside in districts that presently spend at relatively low levels, *i. e.*, in those districts that would benefit from the redistribution of existing resources. Yet recent studies have indicated that the poorest families are not invariably clustered in the most impecunious school districts. Nor does it now appear that there is any more than a random chance that racial minorities are concentrated in property-poor districts. Additionally, several research projects have concluded that any financing alternative designed to achieve a greater equality of expenditures is likely to lead to higher taxation and lower educational expenditures in the major urban centers, a result that would exacerbate rather than ameliorate existing conditions in those areas.

These practical considerations, of course, play no role in the adjudication of the constitutional issues presented here. But they serve to highlight the wisdom of the traditional limitations on this Court's function. The consideration and initiation of fundamental reforms with respect to state taxation and education are matters reserved for the legislative processes of the various States, and we do no violence to the values of federalism and separation of powers by staying our hand. We hardly need add that this Court's action today is not to be viewed as placing its judicial imprimatur on the status quo. The need is apparent for reform in tax systems which may well have relied too long and too heavily on the local property tax. And certainly innovative new thinking as to public education, its methods and its funding, is necessary to assure both a higher level of quality and greater uniformity of opportunity. These matters merit the continued attention of the scholars who already have contributed much by their challenges. But the ultimate solutions must come from the lawmakers and from the democratic pressures of those who elect them.

68.

MARLON BRANDO: Unfinished Oscar Speech

At the Academy Awards ceremony in Los Angeles on March 27, 1973, the best actor award went to Marlon Brando for his role as Don Vito Corleone in The Godfather. *But Brando declined to accept the award in order to protest Hollywood's and the nation's treatment of the American Indian. Brando himself did not attend the award ceremonies, but instead, a statement prepared by him was read to the audience by actress Sacheen Littlefeather, an Apache Indian and a member of the Native American Affirmative Image Committee. Miss Littlefeather did not succeed in reading the whole statement because of hostile audience reaction. It is reprinted here in its entirety. Brando's concern for the Indians was significant at the time because the whole nation had been made aware of the 37-day confrontation at Wounded Knee, South Dakota, between militant Indians and federal officials.*

Source: *New York Times*, March 30, 1973.

FOR 200 YEARS we have said to the Indian people who are fighting for their land, their life, their families and their right to be free: "Lay down your arms, my friends, and then we will remain together. Only if you lay down your arms, my friends, can we then talk of peace and come to an agreement which will be good for you."

When they laid down their arms, we murdered them. We lied to them. We cheated them out of their lands. We starved them into signing fraudulent agreements that we called treaties which we never kept. We turned them into beggars on a continent that gave life for as long as life can remember. And by any interpretation of history, however twisted, we did not do right. We were not lawful nor were we just in what we did. For them, we do not have to restore these people, we do not have to live up to some agreements, because it is given to us by virtue of our power to attack the rights of others, to take their property, to take their lives when they are trying to defend their land and liberty, and to make their virtues a crime and our own vices virtues.

But there is one thing which is beyond the reach of this perversity and that is the tremendous verdict of history. And history will surely judge us. But do we care? What kind of moral schizophrenia is it that allows us to shout at the top of our national voice for all the world to hear that we live up to our commitment when every page of history and when all the thirsty, starving, humiliating days and nights of the last 100 years in the lives of the American Indian contradict that voice?

It would seem that the respect for principle and the love of one's neighbor have become dysfunctional in this country of ours, and that all we have done, all that we have succeeded in accomplishing with our power is simply annihilating the hopes of the newborn countries in this world, as well as friends and enemies alike, that we're not humane, and that we do not live up to our agreements.

Perhaps at this moment you are saying to yourself what the hell has all this got to do with the Academy Awards? Why is this woman standing up here, ruining our evening, invading our lives with things that don't concern us, and that we don't care about? Wasting our time and money and intruding in our homes.

I think the answer to those unspoken questions is that the motion picture community has been as responsible as any for degrading the Indian and making a mockery of his character, describing him as savage, hostile and evil. It's hard enough for children to grow up in this world. When Indian children watch television, and they watch films, and when they see their race depicted as they are in films, their minds become injured in ways we can never know.

Recently there have been a few faltering steps to correct this situation, but too faltering and too few, so I, as a member in this profession, do not feel that I can as a citizen of the United States accept an award here tonight. I think awards in this country at this time are inappropriate to be received or given until the condition of the American Indian is drastically altered. If we are not our brother's keeper, at least let us not be his executioner.

I would have been here tonight to speak to you directly, but I felt that perhaps I could be of better use if I went to Wounded Knee to help forestall in whatever way I can the establishment of a peace which would be dishonorable as long as the rivers shall run and the grass shall grow.

I would hope that those who are listening would not look upon this as a rude intrusion, but as an earnest effort to focus attention on an issue that might very well determine whether or not this country has the right to say from this point forward we believe in the inalienable rights of all people to remain free and independent on lands that have supported their life beyond living memory.

Thank you for your kindness and your courtesy to Miss Littlefeather. Thank you and good night.

Racial injustice is as American as apple pie. But so is the struggle against it.

Kenneth Clark, 1973

69.

KARL E. MEYER: The Traffic in Art and Antiquities

In 1972 a 2500-year-old Greek vase was purchased by the Metropolitan Museum of Art in New York for more than $1 million. The vase had allegedly been smuggled out of Italy by an individual who had been known to be involved with stolen art objects. During 1973 several other pieces of ancient art made the news as either stolen or smuggled: a bronze sculpture by Lysippus on sale in Munich; ancient Etruscan art works stolen from a grave site near Cerveteri, Italy; a painting by Tiepollo stolen from a church in Rovetta, Italy; a Roman mosaic stolen from an archaeological site in Syria and sold to the Newark Museum; and several others. In October 1973 the New York Times *revealed the presence in a New York City art gallery of an old, sacred wood carving, the Afo-A-Kom, belonging to a small African principality from which it had been stolen six years before. It, unlike most such purloined art objects, was returned to the Cameroon on December 5. A counterpart of the traffic in stolen art is the ravaging of archaeological sites that are uncovering the remnants of ancient cultures. In a three-part article published in March-April 1973 and later issued as a book, Karl E. Meyer analyzed the issues inherent in such art acquisitions by museums and private collectors. A selection from his work is reprinted here.*

Source: *New Yorker*, March 24 and 31, 1973: "International Art and Antiquities Traffic."

AT A MEETING of the College Art Association in Chicago in 1971, the Stanford University art historian Albert Elsen said that in his opinion "there is no more explosive issue before the art world than that of illegal international traffic in works of art." Since then, there have been scores of articles and speeches about the illicit trade, and about the related matter of museums' acquisition policies. This hitherto sedate topic has in the past month burst onto the front pages, with the *New York Times*' sensational investigation of how and where the Metropolitan Museum of Art obtained a breathtaking calyx krater that it put on display in November. The vase, about twenty-five hundred years old and from the hand of the Greek master Euphronios, had been bought, the museum said, from a Lebanese dealer who had had it for many years. The Italian police took sharp issue with this version of its provenance; they alleged that the krater, and a companion cup by Euphronios, had been looted by grave robbers in 1971 from an Etruscan tomb not far from Rome—allegations that they were prepared to pursue. The whole remarkable affair pointed up for the public the highly clandestine nature of many contemporary art transactions. The art market is a closed world whose denizens seek to keep important information strictly within it. Prices, the names of dealers and customers, the routes of supply—all these matters tend to be cloaked in the chiaroscuro language of the trade. Such secrecy was perhaps justified when the art market was a cozy club consisting of a few thousand people and when its profits were minuscule by comparison with other markets. This is no longer so. Art is big business, and the international market has an annual turnover of at least a billion dollars. Yet, with works of art increasingly regarded as speculative commodities, there is no equivalent in the United States—where most of the money is spent—of a Securities and Exchange Commission, to enforce fair dealing and to protect the public interest.

A collector or a museum may "own" a Rembrandt, but in a larger sense the painting belongs to the world. Since the collective judgment of mankind gives any work of art its value, the collective conscience of mankind should rightly be concerned with its preservation. Those who profit from the rising prices of art cannot justifiably complain about public concern, since it is the public that gives their property its value—a value often realized when bequests or gifts are made to museums. To cite a comparison, a real-estate speculator can earn large profits by wisely buying lots in a developing commercial district, but the value of what he owns derives from community enterprise, and the community has an unchallengeable right to impose limits—such as building codes or zoning laws—on how the owner uses his property. An extension of this principle should apply when what we are dealing with is, in the largest sense, the destruction and theft of the remains of the human past.

This is particularly relevant in the case of antiquities buried in archeological sites. Though an American may "own" an Indian mound or an Italian may "own" an Etruscan tomb, there is a general interest in what either does with his property. (In Italy, this interest is recognized, if often not enforced, by law; in the case of most Indian sites in the United States it is neither recognized nor enforced.) Every archeological site is like a time capsule, containing, in some degree, unique evidence about our past. When such a time capsule is destroyed, either by a looter or by a bulldozer, the loss is total. One cannot grow another Indian mound. And yet the tempo of destruction is currently so great that by the end of the century most remaining important archeological sites may well be plundered or paved over. We face a future in which there may be no past, beyond that which is already known and excavated. Or equally sad, what is left may be so ruinously mutilated as to afford only a forlorn fragment of a vanished legacy.

The art market is not the biggest business in the world, but in the past two decades its growth has outpaced that of almost every other field for risk capital. Even those in the art market are impressed, puzzled, and sometimes a little worried. When there is a tight money market, art prices go up; when there are recessions, political upheavals, or fiscal crises art prices go up; and when there is a boom art prices soar like a balloon exuberantly out of control. A bit of canvas with a few dollars' worth of paint on it—provided that the brush was wielded by a Cézanne or a Renoir—can bring greater capital gains than glamour stocks or a prime building site in downtown New York. . . .

Most evident is the matter of theft. Within the past decade, the stealing of art has been transformed from an amusing nuisance into an international plague. Every day, an important work of art is stolen somewhere, and though some of the thefts are committed by cranks or the simpleminded, most are not. In certain instances, the thieves extort ransom for the stolen art, which then turns up in an abandoned car or a baggage locker. More often, the missing works are sold. Paintings by lesser-known masters can be sold to unsuspecting dealers or collectors; sometimes the works are doctored by restorers so that the risk of discovery is minimal. In other cases, art is stowed in Swiss banks while the owners wait for statutes of limitation on the sale of stolen goods to expire. (In Italy, the wait is ten years.) . . .

In the case of stolen paintings, there is a consolation—albeit a thin one. Very few of them are destroyed; they may vanish for years into clandestine vaults, but they do survive, and so—in the most important cases, at least—do photographic reproductions of them. The illicit looting of archeological sites gets less publicity, but its consequences are more serious, because they include the total loss of unrecorded information. The stimulus of the art market has made ancient sites the targets of an unexampled assault by looters armed with shovels, bulldozers, and even dynamite. Objects taken from a site are often mutilated, and, in any case, their context is obliterated; the looted piece becomes an orphan without pedigree, its very legitimacy open to question. . . .

As a result of both deliberate looting and the expansion of civilization, the material remains of the past are being churned up at an unprecedented rate. Sometimes the spoliation is rooted in greed; at other times its source is indifference. Either way, the consequences are the same. Given the present tempo of destruction, by the end of the century all unexplored major archeological sites may be irrevocably disfigured or ravaged. We are witnessing the equivalent of the burning of the library at Alexandria by the Romans—the catastrophic bonfire in which much of the wisdom of antiquity was consumed. One can see most of the ingredients of such a conflagration in the relentless demolition of pre-Columbian sites here in the Western Hemisphere. The pre-Columbian field is a prime example of what might be called a "growth market" in art. Forty years ago, the market scarcely existed, but today it lures scores of dealers and thousands of collectors. Most of the art comes from three areas—Mexico, Central America, and the Andean republics of South America—and nearly all of it has been smuggled out of the countries of origin. . . .

All this is part of the price paid for the priority given Acquisition—notably, the purchase of star works of art. A more serious cost is the physical destruction of historical evidence—which relates directly to the question of buying suspect goods. In major American museums, the question arises every week. It happens like this: A dealer comes into a curator's office and spreads on the desk marvellous treasures, or photographs of marvellous treasures, that can have been unearthed only in clandestine excavations and clearly have been smuggled from the country of origin. There is a pleasant patter of conversation, an exchange of gossip, as the curator looks—without seeming too eager—at the prizes before him. Are they genuine? On this point, the curator must rely on his educated scrutiny while he listens to the tale told by the dealer. (There is always a tale, and it usually sounds more or less convincing; Norbert Schimmel, a New York collector of great discernment, says that his maxim is "Buy the piece but never the story.") If the curator wants the object, he will next plead for time. He must consult others, the price seems high, the budget is tight this year; these are ritual moves in the courtly saraband while both parties make their hard private calculations.

The pressure to buy can be palpable. An American curator is known by the acquisitions he recommends. (Mr. Hoving's rise at the Metropolitan dates from the museum's purchase, at his urgent plea, of the Bury St. Edmunds cross, in 1963, for a still undisclosed price, from a collector in Switzerland.) The curator in many cases submits his choices to a special committee of museum trustees, whose members esteem enterprise. Price is often not a consideration, at least in the usual sense; rather, it may be a means of giving a special halo of merit to the piece under consideration. If a dealer does not ask a high price for a unique work, the museum may feel that the vender does not believe in his own wares—a feeling that is all the stronger when the origins of the piece are obscure. Still, there will be a problem of scruple, or a fear that a foreign government will cause an unpleasant fuss. The dealer is equal to such doubts. He will suggest that if the museum does not buy the treasure it could vanish into the vitrines of a private collector, or that a rival museum is interested in it. What is the curator's first obligation? Surely it is to see that the public—his public—has access to a supremely interesting piece. Even if it has been smuggled from abroad, the dealer may point out, no American law has been broken, and why should a museum be responsible for another country's failure to enforce its own often absurdly inflexible laws?

So persuasive are these arguments that established American museums, acting in good faith, have wound up subsidizing the wholesale devastation of antiquity. Nowhere can the results be more clearly seen than in Turkey. . . .

"THE MONEY IS THE MESSAGE." This unflattering headline appeared in March, 1971, over a front-page review in the *London Times Literary Supplement* of centennial histories of the Metropolitan Museum and the Boston Museum of Fine Arts. The anonymous author, who was obviously well informed, made some telling points about the deficiencies of great American art museums. He spoke of the unceasing pressure to mount new exhibitions and make new purchases, invariably with the aim of increasing museum attendance. He referred to the "severe trial" imposed on young curators by the need to cultivate rich patrons who might be potential benefactors—an obligation that distracted them from their primary responsibility. . . .

Anyone who takes the trouble to speak with younger museum curators about the *T.L.S.* review will find that it touched a nerve. The same misgivings that led Francis Henry Taylor to resign as Metropolitan director in 1954 cause many younger museum workers to wonder whether their jobs are, in the end, really worthwhile. Statistics are not necessarily a measure of excellence, whether the figure is the price tag on a work of art or the number of people who have passed through museum turnstiles. The truth, as these dissidents see it, is that their institutions have come to reflect all too accurately a national obsession with quantity and a national weakness for the star system.

In this sense, the debate over museum-acquisition policies really comprehends the larger dispute over the values of American life. The museum is a mirror as well as a public gallery, and it may be unrealistic to expect that even such a special institution can evince an outlook at odds with that of the society around it. Yet even if this may be so, there is evidence enough to suggest that American art museums could benefit from a period of pause, from a hiatus for reflection. In concrete terms, this could be achieved by a moratorium on acquisitions. The moratorium idea has occurred to a number of people since the beginning of this year. One of them is Allen Wardwell, curator of primitive art at the Art Institute of Chicago. In its evolution, his outlook has been much like that of other museum workers. When he assumed his post, in 1960, he bought freely, even when he knew that what he was buying was "hot," and on being reproached for buying a Mexican fresco he replied that if the Institute didn't make the acquisition, someone else would, and, moreover, the museum was preserving the fresco. Later, there was a furor over museum acquisition of large-scale monuments, and, like other curators, Wardwell decided that it was justifiable to purchase only smaller, portable objects. But this was no solution. The demand for the smaller figurines and ornaments was so great that it stimulated large-scale destruction of burial sites. Wardwell had come to feel that a more basic answer was required—that it was time for all American museums to declare a two- or three-year moratorium on the acquisition of antiquities. This would provide time for them to think through their own priorities, and it would also encourage antiquity-rich countries to reconsider their laws with the aim of creating a legal market in exportable art. In a paper on the problem, presented in January at a symposium on primitive and pre-Columbian art at Columbia University, Wardwell reached this conclusion: "Fine as many of these antiquities may be as works of art, they are unfortunately tainted by suggestions of dishonesty, corruption, and greed. It is the responsibility of our museums to cooperate with the nations of the world so that these objects may truly fulfill their primary purpose: to express the greatest qualities of man."

One has the sense that the notion of a moratorium is an idea whose time is coming. New works would continue to flow to museums through gifts and bequests, and the money saved on purchases could be used to fulfill currently neglected museum functions. Moreover, new and imaginative loans and swaps could be arranged between museums; an example of this is the spectacular success of the Tutankhamen loan exhibitions in Paris and London in 1967 and 1972. Acquisition, it can be reasonably argued, has reigned long enough. Conservation, Study, Interpretation, and Exhibition—the other purposes named by Mr. Noble in his "Museum Manifesto"—could well be given a larger role in the American art museum. Otherwise, the Muses of Art and History will continue obscenely to consume each other.

70.

Henry Kissinger: The Year of Europe

On April 23, 1973, presidential advisor Henry Kissinger made a major foreign policy address to the annual meeting of the American Newspaper Publishers Association. The background for the speech was the observation on the part of many European and some American leaders that U.S. relationships with Europe had been deteriorating for several years as the U.S. pursued a solitary role in Indochina and sought détente with the U.S.S.R. and China. Fears in the U.S. that the European Economic Community would become a strong competitor in world trade and fears in Europe that the U.S. would tend to go it alone in both defense and commerce had also promoted misunderstanding. But the hopes that Kissinger's speech inspired were not to be realized in 1973. Plans for a projected visit by President Nixon to see European leaders had to be shelved because of the Watergate affair. And in October the new crisis in the Middle East further alienated European nations from the direction of U.S. policy. A portion of Kissinger's speech is reprinted here.

Source: *Department of State Bulletin*, May 14, 1973.

THIS YEAR HAS BEEN CALLED the year of Europe, but not because Europe was less important in 1972 or in 1969. The alliance between the United States and Europe has been the cornerstone of all postwar foreign policy. It provided the political framework for American engagements in Europe and marked the definitive end of U.S. isolationism. It insured the sense of security that allowed Europe to recover from the devastation of the war. It reconciled former enemies. It was the stimulus for an unprecedented endeavor in European unity and the principal means to forge the common policies that safeguarded Western security in an era of prolonged tension and confrontation. Our values, our goals, and our basic interests are most closely identified with those of Europe.

Nineteen seventy-three is the year of Europe because the era that was shaped by decisions of a generation ago is ending. The success of those policies has produced new realities that require new approaches:

—The revival of western Europe is an established fact, as is the historic success of its movement toward economic unification.

—The East-West strategic military balance has shifted from American preponderance to near-equality, bringing with it the necessity for a new understanding of the requirements of our common security.

—Other areas of the world have grown in importance. Japan has emerged as a major power center. In many fields, "Atlantic" solutions to be viable must include Japan.

—We are in a period of relaxation of tensions. But as the rigid divisions of the past two decades diminish, new assertions of national identity and national rivalry emerge.

—Problems have arisen, unforeseen a generation ago, which require new types of cooperative action. Insuring the supply of energy for industrialized nations is an example.

These factors have produced a dramatic transformation of the psychological climate in the West—a change which is the most profound current challenge to Western statesmanship. In Europe, a new generation to whom war and its dislocations are not personal experiences takes stability for granted. But it is less committed to the unity that made peace possible and to the effort required to maintain it. In the United States, decades of global burdens have fostered, and the frustrations of the war in Southeast Asia have accentuated, a reluctance to sustain global involvements on the basis of preponderant American responsibility.

Inevitably this period of transition will have its strains. There have been complaints in America that Europe ignores its wider responsibilities in pursuing economic self-interest too one-sidedly and that Europe is not carrying its fair share of the burden of the common defense. There have been complaints in Europe that America is out to divide Europe economically, or to desert Europe militarily, or to bypass Europe diplomatically. Europeans appeal to the United States to accept their independence and their occasionally severe criticism of us in the name of Atlantic unity while at the same time they ask for a veto on our independent policies—also in the name of Atlantic unity.

Our challenge is whether a unity forged by a common perception of danger can draw new purpose from shared positive aspirations.

If we permit the Atlantic partnership to atrophy, or to erode through neglect, carelessness, or mistrust, we risk what has been achieved and we shall miss our historic opportunity for even greater achievement.

In the forties and fifties the task was economic reconstruction and security against the danger of attack; the West responded with courage and imagination. Today the need is to make the Atlantic relationship as dynamic a force in building a new structure of peace, less geared to crisis and more conscious of opportunities, drawing its inspirations from its goals rather than its fears. The Atlantic nations must join in a fresh act of creation equal to that undertaken by the postwar generation of leaders of Europe and America.

This is why the President is embarking on a personal and direct approach to the leaders of western Europe. In his discussions with the heads of government of Britain, Italy, the Federal Republic of Germany, and France, the Secretary General of NATO, and other European leaders, it is the President's purpose to lay the basis for a new era of creativity in the West.

His approach will be to deal with Atlantic problems comprehensively. The political, military, and economic issues in Atlantic relations are linked by reality, not by our choice nor for the tactical purpose of trading one off against the other. The solutions will not be worthy of the opportunity if left to technicians. They must be addressed at the highest level.

In 1972 the President transformed relations with our adversaries to lighten the burdens of fear and suspicion.

In 1973 we can gain the same sense of historical achievement by reinvigorating shared ideals and common purposes with our friends.

The United States proposes to its Atlantic partners that by the time the President travels to Europe toward the end of the year we will have worked out a new Atlantic charter setting the goals for the future, a blueprint that:

—Builds on the past without becoming its prisoner.

—Deals with the problems our success has created.

—Creates for the Atlantic nations a new relationship in whose progress Japan can share.

We ask our friends in Europe, Canada, and ultimately Japan to join us in this effort.

This is what we mean by the year of Europe.

The problems in Atlantic relationships are real. They have arisen in part because during the fifties and sixties the Atlantic community organized itself in different ways in the many different dimensions of its common enterprise.

—In economic relations the European Community has increasingly stressed its regional personality; the United States at the same time must act as part of, and be responsible for, a wider international trade and monetary system. We must reconcile these two perspectives.

—In our collective defense we are still organized on the principle of unity and integration, but in radically different strategic conditions. The full implications of this change have yet to be faced.

—Diplomacy is the subject of frequent consultations but is essentially being conducted by traditional nation-states. The United States has global interests and responsibilities. Our European allies have regional interests. These are not necessarily in conflict, but in the new era neither are they automatically identical.

In short, we deal with each other regionally and even competitively on an integrated basis in defense, and as nation-states in diplomacy. When the various collective institutions were rudimentary, the potential inconsistency in their modes of operation was not a problem. But after a generation of evolution and with the new weight and strength of our allies, the various parts of the construction are not always in harmony and sometimes obstruct each other.

If we want to foster unity we can no longer ignore these problems. The Atlantic nations must find a solution for the management of their diversity to serve the common objectives which underlie their unity. We can no longer afford to pursue national or regional self-interest without a unifying framework. We cannot hold together if each country or region asserts its autonomy whenever it is to its benefit and invokes unity to curtail the independence of others.

We must strike a new balance between self-interest and the common interest. We must identify interests and positive values beyond security in order to engage once again the commitment of peoples and parliaments. We need a shared view of the world we seek to build. . . .

We have entered a truly remarkable period of East-West diplomacy. The last two years have produced an agreement on Berlin, a treaty between West Germany and the U.S.S.R., a strategic arms limitation agreement, the beginning of negotiations on a European Security Conference and on mutual balanced force reductions, and a series of significant practical bilateral agreements between Western and Eastern countries, including a dramatic change in bilateral relations between the United States and the U.S.S.R. These were not isolated actions, but steps on a course charted in 1969 and carried forward as a collective effort. Our approach to détente stressed that negotiations had to be concrete, not atmospheric, and that concessions should be reciprocal. We expect to carry forward the policy of relaxation of tensions on this basis.

Yet this very success has created its own problems. There is an increasing uneasiness—all the more insidious for rarely being made explicit—that superpower diplomacy might sacrifice the interests of traditional allies and other friends. Where our allies' interests have been affected by our bilateral negotiations, as in the talks on the limitation of strategic arms, we have been scrupulous in consulting them; where our allies are directly involved, as in the negotiations on mutual balanced force reductions, our approach is to proceed jointly on the basis of agreed positions. Yet some of our friends in Europe have seemed unwilling to accord America the same trust in our motives as they received from us or to grant us the same tactical flexibility that they employed in pursuit of their own policies. The United States in now often taken to task for flexibility where we used to be criticized for rigidity.

All of this underlines the necessity to articulate a clear set of common objectives together with our allies. Once that is accomplished, it will be quite feasible, indeed desirable, for the several allies to pursue these goals with considerable tactical flexibility. If we agree on common objectives it will become a technical question whether a particular measure is pursued in a particular forum or whether to proceed bilaterally or multilaterally. Then those allies who seek reassurances of America's commitment will find it not in verbal reaffirmations of loyalty, but in an agreed framework of purpose.

We do not need to agree on all policies. In many areas of the world our approaches will differ, especially outside of Europe. But we do require an understanding of what should be done jointly and of the limits we should impose on the scope of our autonomy.

We have no intention of buying an illusory tranquillity at the expense of our friends. The United States will never knowingly sacrifice the interests of others. But the perception of common interests is not automatic; it requires constant redefinition. The relaxation of tensions to which we are committed makes allied cohesion indispensable yet more difficult. We must insure that the momentum of détente is maintained by common objectives rather than by drift, escapism, or complacency.

I believe in a world in which the United States is powerful. I think it will be a safer world and a better world if we have a strong, healthy United States, Europe, Soviet Union, China, and Japan, each balancing the other, not playing against the other, an even balance.

President Nixon, New Year address, 1972

71.

FRED R. HARRIS: Oil—Capitalism Betrayed in Its Own Camp

Fred Harris represented Oklahoma in the U.S. Senate for one term, 1967-73, after which he declined to run for re-election. Instead, he returned to Oklahoma to practice law and run a new organization, "New Populist Action," designed to foster public participation in political affairs. Coming from an oil-rich state, Harris was familiar with the oil industry and its power in the economy and in politics. The article from which this selection is taken was published in April 1973, just as the public was getting its first warnings of an impending fuel and gasoline shortage. The article was adapted from Harris' 1973 book, The New Populism.

Source: *The Progressive*, April 1973.

SOME INDIAN TRIBES once used petroleum as a medicine. And when I was young, we put kerosene—"coal oil," we called it—on cuts and scratches as a curative. We thought it had healing qualities.

Today the situation is reversed. Oil is making us sick—sick with pollution, to be sure, but also sick economically. Actually, the whole energy industry is itself sick with gluttony. It has devoured too much of the competition, too much of the market. . . .

In the beginning, there was competition in finding, refining, and selling oil and gas. "Black gold" was a fabulous bonanza for those who found it, and a gambler could hit it big. But gamblers hate odds. Improved geology reduced the risks some. But that wasn't enough for the oilmen.

Economic and political power did a much better job. The oilmen said that a busy, growing nation needed the rapid discovery of new oil reserves to fuel its continued growth, and so there ought to be special incentives for oil exploration—that was the oil industry argument. And the Congress bought it.

The oil industry was voted a special tax benefit, now worth some $2 billion a year, through the oil and gas depletion allowance. People who discover oil, and investors who buy or people who inherit interest in an existing oil well, do not have to pay any tax at all on twenty-two percent of their gross income from oil, up to a maximum of fifty percent of profits. (Until 1969 the figure was 27.5 percent.) One of the original arguments for the tax subsidy was that a part of gross income from oil production is actually a return of capital investment and is not really income. But that is just theory, because the exemption of this income from taxation is not limited to the amount of the actual capital investment. And it is not tied to the degree to which these special profits go back into new exploration, although the other argument for this loophole was that it would encourage the finding of new oil reserves. It is just a generous subsidy.

Oil companies are allowed a second lucrative tax advantage by being permitted to write off right away as expenses their intangible drilling costs, rather than have them treated as capital investment. This procedure, again, greatly reduces the part of their income that is subject to tax.

The discovery and production of crude oil, then, has become a special kind of tax-sheltered business in the United States. And the tax encourages high crude oil prices. So if an oil company is engaged in, say, both marketing and production, it is encouraged by the tax laws to charge as much of its costs and expenses as possible to its marketing arm and run up as high a rate of profit as it can in its production division.

But how can crude oil prices be kept high if there are special incentives for everybody to get into the business? That is a question the oil companies first began to ask themselves in the 1930s. They came up with a good non-competitive answer: proration—that is, limiting the production of oil by state law. One aspect of proration has a logical base in that a large underground pool of oil, when discovered, may actually belong to a number of owners. Unless restricted in some way, one owner could rapidly pump out the whole pool. Besides being greedy, this practice can also be wasteful. In the rush by one owner to get the oil out rapidly, to the exclusion of the others, the recovery potential of the pool—the possibility of extracting the maximum amount of oil discovered—can be seriously diminished.

The states set up proration procedures to protect the rights of the various owners of any discovered oil pool and to ensure that the best conservation techniques were used in production. But the procedures failed to stifle competition sufficiently to suit the oil industry. So the proration laws went a step further. The states set up procedures to determine how much crude oil could actually be sold at an established, high market price. Then they put a lid on any production above that, halting extra production that would tend to bring the price down.

But what if one state was less restrictive than another? What if competition in one place undermined the lack of competition elsewhere? The oil companies had thought about that possible loophole, and they got the Congress to plug it up. Federal laws were passed to permit the states to agree among themselves on binding limits on crude oil production. And the Congress made it illegal to sell "hot oil"—that is, oil produced any where in excess of the proration limits—in interstate commerce. . . . set the pattern for monopoly in the oil industry by driving some of his competition out of business and by buying out the rest. His career, repeated over and over, is a succinct history of the oil industry. Today the rate of concentration is faster than ever. Companies that produce their own crude oil enjoy increased control of the market and special tax advantages. So the Union Oil Company bought the Pure Oil Company and became the twelfth largest oil company in the country. The Federal Government's Antitrust Division, despite accurate warnings that this particular merger would start a new wave of similar concentration, offered no objection.

Then Getty Oil Company merged with Tidewater. Sun Oil, the thirteenth largest, and Sunray DX, the seventeenth largest oil company, combined. The fourteenth largest, Atlantic, bought the twenty-third largest, Richfield. In all, eight of America's largest oil companies disappeared after 1960. They merged with even bigger companies or were bought outright. . . .

It is a seller's market, and the sellers control it. Did you ever wonder why a filling station sells only one brand of gasoline? The system does not always have to work that way, and it did not always. Originally as independent businessman could open up a service station, buy from any one of several refiners or wholesalers, and sell the product under his own name or whatever name or brand he wished. He could compete for customers by offering a better price and better service. But he can't anymore.

There was a time when the big companies owned their own outlets. Some states, beginning with Iowa, passed laws to restrict this kind of chain operation. The companies turned the restriction to their advantage. Although they still retained ownership of some of their best stations, they began to set up "independent" dealers on a franchised basis, either through sales commission contracts or, most often, through short-term leases of filling station facilities. Now a dealer will operate a single station for a huge oil company landlord, selling its one brand alone.

In this way the company gets a sure and exclusive outlet for its product. It also gets extra lobbying power, indirectly, because politicians tend to pay more attention to the entreaties of "independent" businessmen—at least publicly—and they tend to see gas station franchises as independent. And because it is extremely difficult for the filling station employes—who are few in number in relation to the number of separate dealers they work for—to get together and organize, the oil companies are effectively protected from unionization at the marketing level.

Suppose you want to open a new filling station and sell gasoline for two or four cents cheaper than the big company outlets. The gasoline is the same. You get it from the same refinery where the national brand name companies get theirs. You put a big sign out in front of your station calling attention to your lower price. And business begins to boom.

But not for long. A lot of people tried doing this following World War II, at the end of gasoline rationing. But the major oil companies would not allow the practice then, and they will not allow it now.

First of all, if you try to beat them, they will cut off your supply of gasoline. If they own the refinery, they will refuse to sell to you until you bring your prices into line. If you are getting your wholesale gasoline from a refinery that does not control its own crude oil supply but has to buy crude oil from a major company, they will make the refinery quit selling to you. They can do this by threatening to cut off the supply of crude oil the refinery has to have in order to operate.

That is one way to stifle competition. Another way is for the company to buy you out or convert you to dealer status with them, selling their brand exclusively at their established price. And when you are a dealer who has gone through a price war with the majors, you are a lot more willing to sell out, or convert—or raise your price back up again. . . .

While dealers are being pressed to the wall, consumers are paying gasoline prices that are at least six percent higher than they would be if marketing were competitive. And the big oil companies get bloated on the profits of protected integration, of cutting out competition all the way from the oil field to the filling station.

In late 1970 some large domestic oil producers arbitrarily raised the price of crude oil by twenty-five cents a barrel. But, you may ask, what is to keep foreign produced oil from flooding into the United States and bringing down domestic prices? The oil companies thought of that question long before you did. For one thing, back in 1959, they got the President of the United States to institute oil import quotas by executive order. Backed up by no law, President Eisenhower simply *decreed* a mechanism for limiting oil imports to protect the domestic price. Its beneficiaries and their political allies sought to justify the system on the basis of national security. It was said that by restricting oil imports we would encourage the finding of more oil here at home; in wartime we would not be dependent on foreign oil. Actually, the decree did not do much for national security, but it certainly made the big oil companies more financially secure at the expense of domestic consumers.

President Nixon's Cabinet Task Force on Oil Import Control reported in 1970 that, but for these import restrictions, the U.S. domestic wellhead price for crude oil—$3 per barrel—would decline, over time, to around $2 per barrel. The President's hand-picked panel found that American consumers were paying $5 billion more each year for oil products than they would have to pay if imports were not restricted. Despite his pronouncements against inflation, President Nixon rejected the recommendations of his own task force for abandoning the oil import quota system.

Any President, by the stroke of a pen, could end the system. But the major oil companies are even prepared for that eventuality. Their trump card is a world oil cartel—they have been allowed to corner production, worldwide.

The arrangement goes back a long way. Standard of New Jersey, Royal Dutch-Shell, and Anglo-Persian (which became British Petroleum) entered into a kind of treaty back in 1928, dividing up the world market and agreeing against surplus production that might bring down the world price of oil. Since then the oil companies have become more devious in such violations of the antitrust laws, and the U.S. Government has become, if anything, more lax in enforcement. For example, seven major companies—Jersey Standard (now Exxon), Royal Dutch-Shell, British Petroleum, Mobil, Standard of California, Gulf, and Texaco—now control almost all of the production and marketing of Middle Eastern oil. . . .

The oil industry's plan is simple, and it has followed it to the letter:

—It secures Federal subsidies: by the oil and gas depletion allowance; by the write-off of intangible drilling costs; and by the foreign tax credit.

—It eliminates competition: by state proration, limiting domestic production; by exclusive dealership marketing; by merging with or buying competitors; by vertically integrating; and by international cartels and import quotas. What is left? Competition from other fuels, you say. Again, the oil companies are ahead of you. There is an increasing demand for natural gas, but most domestic gas reserves are now owned by the major oil companies, including the same ones that control international oil. And the Federal Power Commission, which is supposed to regulate gas prices, is largely dependent upon the oil industry for information about reserves and the proper level of prices. In the spring of 1972 the FPC took the oil industry's word—"crisis" is the word—about a shortage in natural gas reserves and, in effect, took the lid off all gas prices. Oil does not have to compete with gas. Both are overpriced. And both fuel sources are owned by the same companies.

In some industries, *coal* should be directly competitive with oil and gas. And in the near future that competition ought to increase—to the benefit of the consumer—because of the new processes for converting coal into synthetic gasoline through "liquefaction" and into synthetic gas through "gasification." But you guessed it, the oil companies have already moved in. Gulf Oil bought Pittsburgh and Midway Coal Company. Continental, the ninth largest oil company, purchased Consolidation, the largest coal company. In the last ten years, seven of the largest independent coal companies have been purchased by non-coal companies. Four of these purchases were made by large oil companies that are also vertically integrated in the oil and gas business.

In addition, Exxon, Kerr-McGee, Atlantic Richfield, Shell, and Sun Oil own huge coal reserves. It is supposed to be against the law to buy up the competition, but these violations continue unabated.

It is not just the oil companies that are doing it. Copper companies, steel companies, and railroads, great users of coal and other fuels, are buying up coal companies and coal reserves—controlling their own supply, reducing competition.

Demand for coal has gone up at the rate of five percent a year during the last two years. Production has gone up at the same rate. But coal prices have increased an average of seventy percent. And they have more than doubled in some places.

In uranium it is pretty much the same. Oil companies own nearly half of all known uranium reserves in the United States. New Jersey Standard and Gulf are heavily involved in uranium and atomic energy. Kerr-McGee, by itself, owns nearly one-fourth of the total uranium milling capacity in the country.

The big oil companies are moving in on *new* energy source also. They are buying up the oil shale and tar sands in the Rocky Mountains and Canada. Underground steam (hot springs) looks promising as a new power source. So a few big companies, such as Union Oil, Signal, and Getty, are rapidly gaining control of steam too, though much of it is under *public* lands in California and the other states in the West.

The main "crisis" in energy is that energy sources are monopolized. The twenty-five largest oil companies are all involved also in natural gas. Eighteen of them have invested in oil shale and uranium. Eleven are in coal. Seven are in tar sands. Six of the ten largest oil companies are involved in all four major domestic fuels—oil, gas, coal, and uranium.

The twenty largest oil companies each have more than $1 billion in assets. And seven of the twenty biggest industrial corporations in America are oil companies. You can make a chart showing competition and profits in the oil industry. The competition line falls downward, *off* the chart. The profits line zooms upward—showing an increase of thirteen percent in the first half of 1971 alone. Concentrated economic power means a redistribution of income and wealth in the wrong direction. It also translates into political power. The oil companies are trying to monopolize and dominate Government studies of how to solve the "energy crisis."...

That is a hard message to get across. The big oil companies spend millions of dollars in tax-deductible advertising to tell us what a great job they are doing toward cleaning up the environment, while they are really continuing their usual practices. They spend millions more for tax-deductible advertising to convince us that we are well served by the present system of huge subsidies and no competition. Mobil, for example, runs newspaper advertisements headed, A STAGNANT ECONOMY IS THE WORST KIND OF POLLUTION. Its message really boils down to the claim that if the energy industry has to join the free enterprise system, economic growth will be killed.

This message is nonsense, of course. Many people—from members of Congress on down—have swallowed it because the oil industry is organized, politically as well as economically.

The oil lobbyists have long flooded the country with self-serving, one-sided information, playing upon "energy crisis" fears. If the public interest forces marshal and publicize the true facts, maybe soon the people will begin to realize that the real "energy crisis" is not lack of fuel but lack of free, unsubsidized competition.

72.

DEWEY F. BARTLETT: The Energy Crisis

Beginning about the 1973 Memorial Day weekend, and continuing on through the summer, Americans were gradually made aware of an impending energy crisis when gas stations in some parts of the country ran short of gas and oil. Many independent dealers, unable to obtain supplies from the refineries, were forced out of business. The reasons for these shortages were difficult to unravel, but one of the possible causes—federal regulation of the oil industry—was dealt with in a speech by Senator Dewey Bartlett of Oklahoma on June 28, 1973. Bartlett had replaced Fred R. Harris in the Senate in January 1973.

Source: *Congressional Record*, 93 Cong., 1 Session, June 28, 1973.

THERE IS LOTS OF TALK heard about the energy crisis. There are those who question that it really exists. But I say you only need to go to the nearest filling station or go to the nearest farmer to learn that it exists. But little has been done to help solve the problems of the energy crisis.

This body and the Congress has not yet come up with solutions and in the past several years has unknowingly, I believe, added to some of those problems. We are going to address ourselves to various aspects of the energy problem, and I will discuss one approach that has been mentioned as a solution—more Federal controls.

What has been happening to the U.S. dollar abroad is alarming, even frightening when you consider the consequences.

The first quarter of this year our Nation had a balance-of-payments deficit over $10 billion. There are U.S. dollars aplenty abroad, so many in fact, that many are being cashed in hurriedly. Our domestic inflationary spiral and strangling fuel shortage add to the uneasiness of foreigners that hold U.S. dollars.

The sad, but true, fact is that in the near future we will have to spend more and more dollars abroad for crude oil and other petroleum products.

Strip mining by the Hanna Coal Company near Cadiz, Ohio

The more we spend, the less our dollars will be worth—it is a vicious cycle. We could, in a very few years, become a bankrupt nation.

Unfortunately, many cast the blame for our energy problems on the energy industry only. It is not without blame, but we should recognize that there are many reasons for our problems and certainly not the most insignificant of these has been Federal controls imposed with honorable intention, but sometimes with disastrous results.

Federal regulation of interstate natural gas prices is a classic example. It has depressed the domestic energy industry in many ways. The fuels which have had to compete with the artificially low gas prices have also been depressed to artificially low levels—all this leads to a lack of sufficient profit incentives for development of our indigenous resources.

Another offshoot of depressed prices is the premature plugging of oil and gas wells because of the unfavorable economics of maintaining production.

Controlling the price of natural gas has effectively controlled the market price of all competing fuels—providing cheap energy for the short pull, but providing shortages and inevitably higher prices for the long run. There is no telling how much this particular Federal control is costing the United States today in additional oil import requirements.

The cost to keep our environment

clean is great, too—perhaps greater than we can afford.

If the States choose to require the secondary standards of the National Environmental Policy Act, by 1975, 150 million tons of coal would be made unusable with current stack gas emission technology. That means about 1.6 million barrels per day more in imports will be required at an annual cost of about $2.5 billion more in our balance-of-payments deficit. This is assuming our dollar retains its value abroad and the price of foreign crude remains relatively constant. Both seem unlikely.

The auto emission standards that have been imposed by the Environmental Protection Agency also have a high cost. The decrease in fuel economy could cost over half a million barrels per day in imports or $900 million annually by 1975. The EPA itself recommends that the standards be reviewed.

Much needed domestic Alaskan oil has also been held up for environmental considerations and right-of-way difficulties. The 2 million barrels that we could be getting would replace imported oil—saving the country another $3 billion annually in balance-of-payments deficit.

Congress is moving like molasses in correcting the technicality in the Federal Rights-of-Way Act.

Now Congress is considering additional controls which would result in significant costs to our Nation if the architects of the language are not careful.

Tremendous coal reserves could be nullified if arbitrary surface mining limits are set. Coal must be allowed to assume a large part of the energy burden.

Other legislation that must be considered very carefully is the land use bill. . . .

The ultimate effects of such comprehensive legislation are indeterminable. The situtation is in a turmoil. Just take the National Environmental Policy Act, for example, I think I can safely say that no one at the time of its enactment realized how costly it would be in terms of dollars, energy, and delays in progress for our country.

This is not the time to take more power from the people at the state and local levels. But that is exactly what the land use bill that passed the Senate does.

In short, those who propose more Federal controls should beware. Controls have been choking the domestic energy industries for years. Energy is the basis of our Nation's strength. Now it is the "vulnerable jugular" of America's economy. New laws must be carefully drawn to assure progress, not prevent it.

The letting of blood was given up as a prescription for ills long ago. Let us quit stabbing our energy industry in the back with needless controls. We cannot afford for it to die. For those who propose, in essence if not in fact, Government ownership of the energy industry, I have a suggestion. Take a good look at the success we have had with the Federal Post Office.

I have faith in the system which has made this country great—freedom and free enterprise. They will, if given the chance, make it greater.

73.

Warren E. Burger and William O. Douglas: *Miller v. California*

In rulings handed down in 1957 and 1966, the U.S. Supreme Court had defined obscenity as material "utterly without redeeming social value." After the latter date, books, magazines, movies, and plays that would have previously been banned tended to proliferate across the nation. Many book stores and film houses catered only to a clientele ostensibly interested in "hard-core pornography." This was all occasioned by both the more relaxed social standards of the day and the fact that the rulings of the Court made it difficult to determine precisely when something was without "redeeming social value." On June 21, 1973, the Court handed down four rulings in related cases, the first of which, Miller v. California, *set forth new guidelines that would use contemporary community standards to define what was obscene. This ruling, because it attempted no definition of obscenity, seemed to many local officials to be the weapon they needed to curtail what was objectionable to them in their communities. Movies, magazines, or books that had existed unscathed for years now, in a few locations, were banned or burned. Because the new ruling left many questions unresolved, the Authors' League of America filed a brief on August 9 asking that the Court rehear arguments in the obscenity case and clarify its ruling to prevent misunderstanding by legislators, prosecutors, police departments, and judges. The League also requested the Court to adopt a First Amendment safeguard whereby no one could be prosecuted for purveying works not already judged obscene. The League hoped that the Court would adopt the view that the First Amendment prohibits restraint on distribution of books and films, regardless of content, to "willing adults." In December the Supreme Court stated that it would review its June 21 decisions in the pornography cases. The decision in* Miller v. California *was rendered by Chief Justice Warren Burger. Portions of his ruling and of the dissent by Associate Justice William O. Douglas are reprinted here.*

Source: *U.S. Supreme Court Bulletin*, 1972-1973 Term, Volume II.

Mr. Chief Justice Burger delivered the opinion of the Court.

This is one of a group of "obscenity-pornography" cases being reviewed by the Court in a re-examination of standards enunciated in earlier cases involving what Mr. Justice Harlan called "the intractable obscenity problem."...

This case involves the application of a State's criminal obscenity statute to a situation in which sexually explicit materials have been thrust by aggressive sales action upon unwilling recipients who had in no way indicated any desire to receive such materials. This Court has recognized that the States have a legitimate interest in prohibiting dissemination or exhibition of obscene material when the mode of dissemination carries with it a significant danger of offending the sensibilities of unwilling recipients or of exposure to juveniles....

Apart from the initial formulation in the *Roth* case, no majority of the Court has at any given time been able to agree on a standard to determine what constitutes obscene, pornographic material subject to regulation under the States' police power....

This much has been categorically settled by the Court, that obscene material is unprotected by the First Amendment. . . .We acknowledge, however, the inherent dangers of undertaking to regulate any form of expression. State statutes designed to regulate obscene materials must be carefully limited. As a result, we now confine the permissible scope of such regulation to works which depict or describe sexual conduct. That conduct must be specifically defined by the applicable state law, as written or authoritatively construed. A state offense must also be limited to works which, taken as a whole, appeal to the prurient interest in sex, which portray sexual conduct in a patently offensive way, and which, taken as a whole, do not have serious literary, artistic, political, or scientific value.

The basic guidelines for the trier of fact must be: (a) whether "the average person, applying contemporary community standards" would find that the work, taken as a whole, appeals to the prurient interest. . . . (b) whether the work depicts or describes, in a patently offensive way, sexual conduct specifically defined by the applicable state law, and (c) whether the work, taken as a whole, lacks serious literary, artistic, political, or scientific value. We do not adopt as a constitutional standard the "*utterly* without redeeming social value" test of *Memiors v. Massachusetts, supra,* 383 U.S., at 419 (1966); that concept has never commanded the adherence of more than three Justices at one time. If a state law that regulates obscene material is thus limited, as written or construed, the First Amendment values applicable to the States through the Fourteenth Amendment are adequately protected by the ultimate power of appellate courts to conduct an independent review of constitutional claims when necessary....

It is certainly true that the absence, since *Roth,* of a single majority view of this Court as to proper standards for testing obscenity has placed a strain on both state and federal courts. But today, for the first time since *Roth* was decided in 1957, a majority of this Court has agreed on concrete guidelines to isolate "hard core" pornography from expression protected by the First Amendment. Now we may abandon the casual practice of *Redrup v. New York, supra,* and attempt to provide positive guidance to the federal and state courts alike.

This may not be an easy road, free from difficulty. But no amount of "fatigue" should lead us to adopt a convenient "institutional" rationale—an absolutist, "anything goes" view of the First Amendment—because it will lighten our burdens. "Such an abnegation of judicial supervision in this field would be inconsistent with our duty to uphold the constitutional guarantees." *Jacobellis v. Ohio, supra,* 378 U.S., at 187-188 (1964) (opinion of Brennan, J.). Nor should we remedy "tension between state and federal courts" by arbitrarily depriving the States of a power reserved to them under the Constitution, a power which they have enjoyed and exercised continuously from before the adoption of the First Amendment to this day....

Under a national Constitution, fundamental First Amendment limitations on the powers of the States do not vary from community to community, but this does not mean that there are, or should or can be, fixed, uniform national standards of precisely what appeals to the "prurient interest" or is "patently offensive." These are essentially questions of fact, and our nation is simply too big and too diverse for this Court to reasonably expect that such standards could be articulated for all 50 States in a single formulation, even assuming the prerequisite consensus exists. When triers of fact are asked to decide whether "the average person, applying contemporary community standards" would consider certain materials "prurient," it would be unrealistic to require that the answer be based on some abstract formulation. The adversary system, with lay jurors as the usual ultimate factfinders in criminal prosecutions, has historically permitted triers-of-fact to draw on the standards of their community, guided always by limiting instructions on the law. To require a State to structure obscenity proceedings around evidence of a *national* "community standard" would be an exercise in futility.

As noted before, this case was tried on the theory that the California obscenity statute sought to incorporate the tripartite test of *Memoirs*. This, a "national" standard of First Amendment protection enumerated by a plurality of this Court, was correctly regarded at the time of trial as limiting state prosecution under the controlling case law. The jury, however, was explicitly instructed that, in determining whether the "dominant theme of the material as a whole . . . appeals to the prurient interest" and in determining whether the material "goes substantially beyond customary limits of candor and affronts contemporary community standards of decency" it was to apply "contemporary community standards of the State of California."

During the trial, both the prosecution and the defense assumed that the relevant "community standards" in making the factual determination of obscenity were those of the State of California, not some hypothetical standard of the entire United States of America. Defense counsel at trial never objected to the testimony of the State's expert on community standards or to the instructions of the trial judge on "state-wide" standards. On appeal to the Appellate Department, Superior Court of California, County of Orange, appellant for the first time contended that application of state, rather than national, standards violated the First and Fourteenth Amendments.

We conclude that neither the State's alleged failure to offer evidence of "national standards," nor the trial court's charge that the jury consider state community standards, were constitutional errors. Nothing in the First Amendment requires that a jury must consider hypothetical and unascertainable "national standards" when attempting to determine whether certain materials are obscene as a matter of fact. . . .

It is neither realistic nor constitutionally sound to read the First Amendment as requiring that the people of Maine or Mississippi accept public depiction of conduct found tolerable in Las Vegas, or New York City. . . .

People in different States vary in their tastes and attitudes, and this diversity is not to be strangled by the absolutism of imposed uniformity. As the Court made clear in *Mishkin v. New York*, 383 U.S. 502, 508-509 (1966), the primary concern with requiring a jury to apply the standard of "the average person, applying contemporary community standards" is to be certain that, so far as material is not aimed at a deviant group, it will be judged by its impact on an average person, rather than a particularly susceptible or sensitive person—or indeed a totally insensitive one. We hold the requirement that the jury evaluate the materials with reference to "contemporary standards of the State of California" serves this protective purpose and is constitutionally adequate.

The dissenting Justices sound the alarm of repression. But, in our view, to equate the free and robust exchange of ideas and political debate with commercial exploitation of obscene material demeans the grand conception of the First Amendment and its high purposes in the historic struggle for freedom. . . .

In sum we (a) reaffirm the *Roth* holding that obscene material is not protected by the First Amendment, (b) hold that such material can be regulated by the States, subject to the specific safeguards enunciated above, without a showing that the material is "*utterly* without redeeming social value," and (c) hold that obscenity is to be determined by applying "contemporary community standards," see *Kois v. Wisconsin, supra,* 408 U.S., at 230 (1972), and *Roth v. United States, supra,* 354 U.S., at 489 (1957), not "national standards." The judgment of the Appellate Department of the Superior Court, Orange County, California, is vacated and the case remanded to that court for further proceedings not inconsistent with the First Amendment standards established by this opinion.

Vacated and remanded for further proceedings.

MR. JUSTICE DOUGLAS, dissenting.

Today we leave open the way for California to send a man to prison for distributing brochures that advertise books and a movie under freshly written standards defining obscenity which until today's decision were never the part of any law. . . .

Today we would add a new three-pronged test: "(1) whether 'the average person, applying contemporary community standards' would find that the work, taken as a whole, appeal to the prurient interest, . . . (2) whether the work depicts or describes, in a patently offensive way, sexual conduct specifically defined by the applicable state law, and (3) whether the work, taken as a whole, lacks serious literary, artistic, political, or scientific value."

Those are the standards we ourselves have written into the Constitution. Yet how under these vague tests can we sustain convictions for the sale of an article prior to the time when some court has declared it to be obscene?

Today the Court retreats from the earlier formulations of the constitutional test and undertakes to make new definitions. This effort, like the earlier ones, is earnest and well-intentioned. The difficulty is that we do not deal with constitutional terms, since "obscenity" is not mentioned in the Constitution or Bill of Rights. And the First Amendment makes no such exception from "the press" which it undertakes to protect nor, as I have said on other occasions, is an exception necessarily implied, for there was no recognized exception to the free press at the time the Bill of Rights was adopted which treated "obscene" publications differently from other types of papers, magazines, and books. So there are no constitutional guidelines for deciding what is and what is not "obscene." The Court is at large because we deal with tastes and standards of literature. What shocks me may be sustenance for my neighbor. What causes one person to boil up in rage over one pamphlet or movie may reflect only his neurosis, not shared by others. We deal here with problems of censorship which, if adopted, should be done by constitutional amendment after full debate by the people.

Obscenity cases usually generate tremendous emotional outbursts. They have no business being in the courts. If a constitutional amendment authorized censorship, the censor would probably be an administrative agency. Then criminal prosecutions could follow as if and when publishers defied the censor and sold their literature. Under that regime a publisher would know when he was on dangerous ground. Under the present regime—whether the old standards or the new ones are used—the criminal law becomes a trap. A brand new test would put a publisher behind bars under a new law improvised by the courts after the publication. That was done in *Ginzburg* and has all the evils of an *ex post facto* law.

My contention is that until a civil proceeding has placed a tract beyond the pale, no criminal prosecution should be sustained. For no more vivid illustration of vague and uncertain laws could be designed than those we have fashioned. As Mr. Justice Harlan has said:

> The upshot of all this divergence in viewpoint is that anyone who undertakes to examine the Court's decisions since *Roth* which have held particular material obscene or not obscene would find himself in utter bewilderment." *Interstate Circuit v. Dallas,* 390 U.S. 676, 707. . . .

If a specific book, play, paper, or motion picture has in a civil proceeding been condemned as obscene and review of that finding has been completed, and thereafter a person publishes, shows, or displays that particular book or film, then a vague law has been made specific. There would remain the underlying question whether the First Amendment allows an implied exception in the case of obscenity. I do not think it does and my views on the issue have been stated over and again. But at least a criminal prosecution brought at that juncture would not violate the time-honored void-for-vagueness test.

No such protective procedure has been designed by California in this case. Obscenity—which even we cannot define with precision—is a hodge-podge. To send men to jail for violating standards they cannot understand, construe, and apply is a monstrous thing to do in a Nation dedicated to fair trials and due process.

While the right to know is the corollary of the right to speak or publish, no one can be forced by government to listen to disclosure that he finds offensive. That was the basis of my dissent in *Public Utilities Commission v. Pollak,* 343 U.S. 451, 467 (1952), where I protested against making a streetcar audience a "captive" audience. There is no "captive audience" problem in these obscenity cases. No one is being compelled to look or to listen. Those who enter newsstands or bookstalls may be offended by what they see. But they are not compelled by the State to frequent those places; and it is only state or governmental action against which the First Amendment, applicable to the States by virtue of the Fourteenth, raises a ban.

The idea that the First Amendment permits government to ban publications that are "offensive" to some people puts an ominous gloss on freedom of the press. That test would make it possible to ban any paper or any journal or magazine in some benighted place. The First Amendment was designed "to invite dispute," to induce "a condition of unrest," to "create dissatisfactions with conditions as they are," and even to stir "people to anger." *Terminiello v. Chicago,* 337 U.S. 1, 4. The idea that the First Amendment permits punishment for ideas that are "offensive" to the particular judge or jury sitting in judgment is astounding. No greater leveler of speech or literature has ever been designed. To give the power to the censor, as we do today, is to make a sharp and radical break with the traditions of a free society. The First Amendment was not fashioned as a vehicle for dispensing tranquilizers to the people. Its prime function was to keep debate open to "offensive" as well as to "staid" people. The tendency throughout history has been to subdue the individual and to exalt the power of government. The use of the standard "offensive" gives authority to government that cuts the very vitals out of the First Amendment. As is intimated by the Court's opinion, the materials before us may be garbage. But so is much of what is said in political campaigns, in the daily press, on TV or over the radio. By reason of the First Amendment—and solely because of it—speakers and publishers have not been threatened or subdued because their thoughts and ideas may be "offensive" to some.

The standard "offensive" is unconstitutional in yet another way. In *Coates v. Cincinnati*, 402 U.S. 611, we had before us a municipal ordinance that made it a crime for three or more persons to assemble on a street and conduct themselves "in a manner annoying to persons passing by." We struck it down, saying "If three or more people meet together on a sidewalk or street corner, they must conduct themselves so as not to annoy any police officer or other person who should happen to pass by. In our opinion this ordinance is unconstitutionally vague because it subjects the exercise of the right of assembly to an unascertainable standard, and unconstitutionally broad because it authorizes the punishment of constitutionally protected conduct.

"Conduct that annoys some people does not annoy others. Thus, the ordinance is vague, not in the sense that it requires a person to conform his conduct to an imprecise but comprehensive normative standard, but rather in the sense that no standard of conduct is specified at all." *Id.*, at 614.

How we can deny Ohio the convenience of punishing people who "annoy" others and allow California power to punish people who publish materials "offensive" to some people is difficult to square with constitutional requirements.

If there are to be restraints on what is obscene, then a constitutional amendment should be the way of achieving the end. There are societies where religion and mathematics are the only free segments. It would be a dark day for America if that were our destiny. But the people can make it such if they choose to write obscenity into the Constitution and define it.

We deal with highly emotional, not rational, questions. To many the Song of Solomon is obscene. I do not think we, the judges, were ever given the constitutional power to make definitions of obscenity. If it is to be defined, let the people debate and decide by a constitutional amendment what they want to ban as obscene and what standards they want the legislatures and the courts to apply. Perhaps the people will decide that the path towards a mature, integrated society requires that all ideas competing for acceptance must have no censor. Perhaps they will decide otherwise. Whatever the choice, the courts will have some guidelines. Now we have none except our own predilections.

74.

TERRY BLEDSOE: Black Dominance of Professional Sports

Since April 1947 when Jackie Robinson became the first black major league baseball player, black athletes have come to make up an ever larger proportion of the players in the professional sports that most people watch: basketball, football, and baseball. In the 1973 season, of 600 major league baseball players, 25 percent were blacks; the National Football League, with 1118 players, had 435 black players; and the two professional basketball leagues, with 300 players between them, counted more than 150 black players and most of the stars. Although these percentages represented a vast improvement in opportunities for black athletes, the rewards were far fewer when it came to coaching positions. There have as yet been no professional baseball managers or football head coaches. Only in pro basketball has the breakthrough been made: of the 17 teams in the National Basketball Association, four have blacks as head coaches. In the article from which this selection is taken, Milwaukee Journal *sports columnist Terry Bledsoe appraises the success of black athletes in professional sports.*

Source: *The Progressive*, June 1973: "Black Dominance of Sports: Strictly from Hunger."

THERE THEY STAND, the 1973 San Francisco Golden State Warriors of the National Basketball Association (NBA), sterling proof that racial discrimination in sports is a bygone thing. Look at this team, one of the finest in all basketball, and reflect on the evidence it offers that success in the NBA is open to anyone, regardless of race, creed, or color. Don't look at the black coach on the bench. Look at the four white guys on the starting team. *That's* the surprise.

It is a measure, too, of how swiftly black athletes have moved to dominate professional basketball. No area of athletics has been visited so heavily by black excellence, and, hearteningly, no area of athletics has responded so promptly to black involvement in management. But basketball is merely the most natural channel of a black tide that has been flooding professional sports with some of the most remarkable achievers in a hierarchy of achievers.

Professional football probably tapped black sources first and kept at it with the greatest diligence; professional baseball has been in the business of including blacks only since 1947; professional basketball has but recently achieved the national impact that made it a fair measuring ground for black achievement.

Consider, in 1972-1973, the results of black effort in American professional sports:

—The five top hitters in baseball's National League, and three of the five top hitters in the American League, are black.

—Blacks occupy three of the five

places on the NBA's first all-league team, and seven of the ten places on the first two teams.

—Blacks hold nine of the twenty-two places on the National Football League's all-pro team.

It is a black man, Hank Aaron, who is baseball's super hero, breathing hot on the heels of the game's most hidebound record of its most hidebound immortal, the 714 home runs of Babe Ruth. It is a black man, Larry Brown, who is the National Football League's reigning most valuable player. It is a black man—Wilt Chamberlain? Kareem Abdul-Jabbar?—who is the dominant force in professional basketball.

Black dominance of any pursuit would merit study, given the fact that only eleven percent of the nation's population is black. For example, black dominance of the carpenter's trade would raise eyebrows; the disproportionately high percentage of blacks on casualty lists from Vietnam became a national curiosity—although never quite the national concern it should have been.

But black dominance of sports has become a highly visible sociological phenomenon. After all, the President of the United States, who displays camaraderie with football luminaries, does not tend to call carpenters to the telephone.

Professional athletes are the dream stuff of a nation, and black dominance of sports is reshaping the hero symbols of a society. The phenomenon is easier to discern than the reasons for it. It is hardly stylish to lean upon the weary crutch of the Step 'n Fetchit days of black prominence: "You people certainly have got rhythm." That fiction provided solace to generations of white Americans attuned to the boxing grace of the Henry Armstrongs and the Joe Louises, and all the way back to the Jack Johnsons and the Peter Jacksons.

There has to be more to it than that. There must have been more to it than that all along. Perhaps, had Americans faced up to the fact in the years before bigotry had to go underground, a truer cliche could have been devised: "You people certainly have got hunger." For that may be the key to all of it, a way out of the jungle of black poverty and often the only way out.

James Baldwin, the noted black writer, provided an insight without mentioning sports. He once wrote: "Every Negro boy realizes, at once, profoundly, because he wants to live, that he stands in great peril and must find, with speed, a 'thing,' a gimmick, to lift him out, to start him on his way. And it does not matter what the gimmick is."

For many black youths, the gimmick has been sports. Pursued with the single minded dedication of desperation, sports have opened a route upward, out of the ghetto, for dozens, hundreds, even thousands of black young men. Obversely, sports have been a siren song of tragedy for hundreds and thousands of other blacks, who staked their adolescence on the hope of achieving rare excellence in a sport, fell short, and had nothing else to fall back on. . . .

It is pointed out (by whites) that black progress in the last two decades of American history has been greater than in all of American history before that, and it is pointed out (by blacks) that that does not disguise the fact that outrageous discrimination still exists and must be eradicated. Both sides are right, of course, and both sides must know the historical truth that any improvement in a bad situation can only increase impatience for further improvement.

But those in the business of sports, and

sports fans, have shown improvement in their racial attitudes; a fair analysis must conclude that the sports world has been quicker to react to wrongs than other segments of society. It should be hastily added, however, that good for goodness' sake has been no more frequent a virtue in professional sports than in, say, the huckstering of soap. Professional sports have responded to the demands of black athletes because black athletes were simply too good to be ignored—especially after Branch Rickey demonstrated in 1947 that if your favorite baseball team didn't want Jackie Robinson, his Brooklyn Dodgers did.

In the middle 1960s, when Vince Lombardi quietly changed the training camp rooming assignments of his Green Bay Packers to a strict alphabetical system, he was responding to a personal code of ethics that demanded he strike down the black and black, and white and white, sets of roommates. But Lombardi was too much of a pragmatist not to realize that by acting against segregation he also was removing a potential source of difficulty on a football team dependent on black men. In that case, good moral practice and good business took parallel paths, and Lombardi set up a system that is now widely followed. . . .

The financial rewards are fantastically high for the black athlete—just as high, in all probability, as for the white athlete of similar status. The two stars of the Milwaukee Bucks of the NBA are both black; Kareem Abdul-Jabbar makes $400,000 a season, Oscar Robertson $233,000. Baseball's Atlanta Braves pay Hank Aaron $200,000 a year.

Yet, with the exception of pro basketball, blacks have been denied the next logical step, that of progressing from an outstanding playing career to the management level. It is a galling omission. Frank Robinson of the California Angels, long recognized as one of baseball's finest players, wants badly to become Big League baseball's first black manager and has been waiting five years for the chance. Pro football, which shows exemplary progress in most other matters, has a mere sprinkling of black assistant coaches and not even a particularly likely candidate for a head job.

The National Football League commissioner, Pete Rozelle, is aware of the problem, and has talked of attacking it in a dramatic and startling way. "We're going to have to face the problem of minority ownership," he said. "Forty percent of the players in the League are black. Yet we have almost no blacks in front office positions. We will have to consider that seriously when we determine our expansion plans. It could, in effect, wind up as discrimination in reverse."

A statement like that, of course, can be counted upon to work wonders. At the moment, the only potential site for a new pro football team with a black man near the top is Orlando-Jacksonville, which lists a former NFL linebacker named Rommie Loudd as its managing general partner. But other potential as well as present franchises may be counted upon to respond quickly to the hint—which, very possibly, was precisely what Rozelle had in mind.

Basketball is different. The Golden State Warriors, with their beguiling reverse English, have the unusually high number of four white starters and one of the NBA's two black coaches, Al Attles. Wayne Embry is the Bucks' general manager, and as such he is the highest ranking black in any sports organization. Simon Gourdine is an assistant commissioner of the NBA.

Part of the reason for the remaining reticence about blacks in the other sports is undoubtedly a lingering fear on the part of the front office—it exists to some extent in basketball, too, for that matter—that what white American ticket buyers really want to see is a white American athlete, the second generation descendant of the "white hope" they kept trotting out to meet Joe Louis.

It is an unarticulated fear, and at bottom probably less a fear than an excuse. It is difficult to sustain the thesis that three black starters on a five man basketball team are all right, but four are not; that four are acceptable, but five are not; that five might be all right as long as the coach is white. The permutations are so varied that the entire thesis collapses in the face of an example such as the Bucks, who have had five black starters for two years and have posted the NBA's fourth best attendance in its smallest arena.

If history offers a lesson, though, it is that the black tide in athletics will slacken, once society gets around to opening alternate avenues to prosperity and recognition. One day, perhaps, other oppressed people will elbow their way through the door. But in the meantime, the white man's games are the black man's salvation.

75.

LEONID I. BREZHNEV: Television Address to the American People

Soviet Communist Party leader Leonid Brezhnev visited the United States from June 16 to 25, 1973, for discussions with President Nixon concerning trade, arms limitation, cultural exchange, oceanography, and other matters of importance to the two nations. The main emphasis in his effort to improve relations with the U.S. was on trade and commercial exchange. To this end he addressed a gathering of 51 American businessmen on June 22, asking for a more advantageous basis for trade and expressing the hope that Congress would grant most-favored nation status in tariff treatment. On June 24 he addressed the American public by radio and television, summing up the negotiations that had taken place between him and President Nixon over the previous few days. Portions of his speech are reprinted here.

Source: *Department of State Bulletin*, July 23, 1973.

DEAR AMERICANS: I highly appreciate this opportunity of directly addressing the people of the United States on my visit to your country.

I would like first of all to convey to all of you the greetings and friendly feelings of millions of Soviet people who are following with great interest my visit to your country and our talks with President Nixon and who are looking forward to this new Soviet-American summit meeting making a fruitful contribution to better relations between our countries and stronger universal peace.

Our discussions with President Nixon and other U.S. Government officials have been going on for several days, and they have been very intensive indeed. We came to this country anticipating that these would be responsible negotiations devoted to major questions bearing on the development of Soviet-American relations and to a search for ways in which our two nations could promote the further invigoration of the entire international atmosphere. Today I have every reason to say that those hopes were justified. We are satisfied with the way the talks went and with the results already achieved. New agreements have been signed in Washington, and in many respects they broaden the sphere of peaceful and mutually advantageous cooperation between the United States of America and the Union of Soviet Socialist Republics. Another big step has been taken along the path that we jointly mapped out a year ago during our meeting in Moscow.

Let me say frankly that personally I am also pleased that this visit has given me an opportunity to gain some firsthand impressions of America, to see some aspects of the American way of life, to meet with prominent government and public leaders of your country, and to have some contact with the life of Americans. . . .

The best possible evidence that Soviet-American relations are moving ahead, and not marking time, is provided by the important document signed the other day by President Nixon and myself, the agreement between the Soviet Union and the United States on the prevention of nuclear war. I trust I will not be accused of making an overstatement if I say that this document is one of historic significance. The Union of Soviet Socialist Republics and the United States of America have concluded an agreement to prevent the outbreak of nuclear war between themselves and to do their utmost to prevent the outbreak of nuclear war generally. It is surely clear how important this is for the peace and tranquillity of the peoples of our two countries and for the improvement of the prospects for a peaceful life for all mankind.

Even if our second meeting with the President of the United States yielded no other results, it could still be said with full grounds that it will take a fitting place in the annals of Soviet-American relations and in international affairs as a whole. The entire world can now see that, having signed last year the fundamental document entitled "Basic Principles of Relations Between the Union of Soviet Socialist Republics and the United States of America," our two nations regard it not as a mere declaration of good intent but as a program of vigorous and consistent action, a program they have already begun to implement, and one which they are determined to go on implementing.

It is also of no little significance that our countries have agreed on the main principles of further work to prepare a new agreement on strategic arms limitation, a broader one this time and of far longer duration. This means that the exceptionally important job begun in May 1972 in Moscow is continuing. It means that political détente is being backed up by military détente. And this is something from which all the peoples and the very cause of peace stand to gain.

The other day representatives of our two governments also signed new agreements on Soviet-American cooperation in several specific fields. Together with the earlier agreements concluded during the past year, they make up an impressive file of documents on cooperation between our two nations and our two great peoples in some widely ranging fields:

from the peaceful uses of atomic energy to agriculture and from outer space to the ocean depths.

Of course, the Soviet Union and the United States are countries which are, so to speak, self-sufficient. Until recently that was, in fact, how things were in our relations. However, we, as well as many Americans, realize only too well that renunciation of cooperation in the economic, scientific, technological, and cultural fields is tantamount to both sides turning down substantial extra benefits and advantages. And most important, such a renunciation would be so pointless as to defy any reasonable argument. This is particularly true of economic ties. Today, I believe, both you and we would agree that in this area it is not enough simply to overcome such an anomaly generated by the cold war as the complete freezing of Soviet-American trade. Life poses questions of far greater importance. I have in mind, above all, such forms of economic relations as stable large-scale ties in several branches of the economy and long-term scientific and technological cooperation, and in our age this is very important. The contacts we have had with American officials and businessmen confirm that it is along these lines that the main prospects for further economic cooperation between our countries can be traced.

It is alleged at times that the development of such cooperation is one-sided and only benefits the Soviet Union. But those who say so are either completely ignorant to the real state of affairs or deliberately turn a blind eye to the truth.

And the truth is that broader and deeper economic cooperation in general and the long-term and large-scale deals which are now either being negotiated or have already been successfully concluded by Soviet organizations and American firms are bound to yield real and tangible benefits to both sides. This is something that has been confirmed quite definitely by American businessmen whom I have had an opportunity to talk with both in this country and earlier in Moscow. It was in that context that we discussed the matter with President Nixon, too.

To this I would like to add that both the Soviet leadership and, as I see it, the U.S. Government attach particular importance to the fact that the development of long-term economic cooperation will also have very beneficial political consequences. It will consolidate the present trend toward better Soviet-American relations generally. . . .

We regard the improvement of Soviet-American relations not as an isolated phenomenon, but as an integral and very important part of the wider process of radically improving the international atmosphere. Mankind has outgrown the rigid cold war armor which it was once forced to wear. It wants to breathe freely and peacefully. And we will be happy if our efforts to better Soviet-American relations help draw more and more nations into the process of détente—be it in Europe or Asia, in Africa or Latin America, in the Middle or the Far East. . . .

But the main purport of all that we discussed and agreed upon with President Nixon in the field of international affairs is the firm determination of both sides to make good relations between the U.S.S.R. and the U.S.A. a permanent factor of international peace.

In our time—and I am sure you know this—there are still too many people who would rather make noise about military preparations and the arms race than discuss problems of détente and peaceful cooperation in a constructive spirit.

What can be said on that account?

The Soviet people are perhaps second to none when it comes to knowing what war means. In World War II we won a victory of world-historic significance. But in that war over 20 million Soviet citizens died. Seventy thousand of our towns and villages were devastated, and one-third of our national wealth was destroyed.

The war wounds have now been healed. Today the Soviet Union is a mightier and more prosperous country than ever before. But we remember the lessons of the war only too well, and that is why the peoples of the Soviet Union value peace so highly, that is why they strongly approve the peace policy of our party and government.

For us peace is the highest achievement to which all men should strive if they want to make their life a worthy one. We believe in reason, and we feel that this belief is shared also by the peoples of the United States and of other nations. If that belief were lost, or if it were obscured by a blind faith in strength alone, in the power of nuclear arms or some other kind of weapon, the fate of civilization—of humanity itself—would be miserable indeed.

Our path has not been an easy one. Our people are proud that in a historically short period of time, after the victory of the Socialist Revolution, backward Russia transformed itself into a major industrial power and achieved outstanding successes in science and culture. We take pride in having built a new society—a most stable and confidently developing society—which has assured all our citizens of social justice and has made the values of modern civilization the property of all the people. We are proud that dozens of previously oppressed nations and nationalities in our country have become genuinely equal and that in our close-knit family of nations they are developing their economy and culture.

We have great plans for the future. We want to raise considerably the living standards of the Soviet people. We want to make new advances in education and medicine. We want to make our villages and towns more comfortable to live in and more beautiful. We have drafted programs to develop the remote areas of Siberia, the North and the Far East, with their immense natural resources. And every Soviet individual is deeply conscious of the fact that the realization of those plans requires peace and peaceful cooperation with other nations. . . .

Dear viewers: The importance and complexity of the problems on the agenda of our talks with President Nixon, of our meeting and discussions with members of the Senate Foreign Relations Committee, headed by Senator Fulbright, and with prominent representatives of the American business community, called for a tight work schedule on this visit.

As I have already pointed out, these were fruitful discussions held in a good atmosphere. This gives us a feeling of satisfaction.

At the same time, I do personally regret that the extreme pressure of business has not given me and my colleagues who accompanied me and took part in our work a chance to see more of your country. While still in Moscow, and then here, in the United States, I received many warm letters from various American cities, organizations, companies, and private citizens kindly inviting me to visit this or that town, to see plants, farms, and universities, or to be a guest in the homes of Americans. I am taking this opportunity to express my sincere gratitude to all those who wrote such letters. I regret that, for the reasons I have just mentioned, I was unable to take up those invitations.

Of course, it would have been interesting to visit New York and Chicago and Detroit and Los Angeles, to see some of your industrial projects and farms, to talk to American working people, whose achievements are admired by Soviet people. Perhaps the future will offer such an opportunity, especially since President Nixon and I have definitely agreed that in the future our contacts will be placed on a regular footing. We are looking forward to President Nixon's visit to the Soviet Union next year.

But even though this brief visit did not give me a chance to see as much as I would like to in America, I nevertheless have every reason, when I return home, to tell my colleagues and all Soviet people both about the important political results of the visit and about the atmosphere of good will and the trend in favor of peace, of détente, and of improving relations between our two countries. It is a trend which we felt during our stay in the United States and during our contacts with government and public leaders of your country and with many American citizens. I can assure you that these feelings are fully shared by Soviet people.

I do not believe I will be divulging a major secret if I tell you that in my talks with President Nixon over the last few days we not only addressed ourselves to current political problems but also tried to look ahead and take into account the future interests of the peoples of both our countries. In so doing we proceeded from the assumption that in politics those who do not look ahead will inevitably find themselves in the rear, among the stragglers. A year ago in Moscow we laid the foundation for improving Soviet-American relations. Now this great and important objective has been successfully brought closer. It is our hope that this trend will continue, for it meets the interests of our two great peoples and of all mankind.

Though the President is elected by nationwide ballot, and is often said to represent all the people, he does not embody the nation's sovereignty. He is not above the law's commands.

Appeals Court opinion on the presidential tapes, September 1973

76.

JOHN W. DEAN III: Watergate Testimony

The 93rd Congress established a special Senate Select Committee on Presidential Campaign Activities to look into all aspects of the so-called Watergate affair. The hearings, to be in three phases, were to investigate the original break-in at Democratic National Headquarters and the subsequent White House coverup, campaign "dirty tricks" aimed at contenders for the 1972 Democratic presidential nominations, and illegal campaign financing. The committee members were Senators Sam J. Ervin, Jr., chairman; Howard H. Baker, Jr., vice-chairman; and Herman E. Talmadge, Daniel K. Inouye, Joseph M. Montoya, Edward J. Gurney, and Lowell P. Weicker, Jr. The first phase of the hearings began on May 17, 1973, and was televised daily to a national viewing audience. Of all the witnesses to come before the committee, former White House special counsel John W. Dean III presented the testimony most damaging to the President and his closest advisors. Proving or disproving Dean's allegations seemed to become the primary aim of the investigation. When it was revealed to the committee on July 16 that conversations and telephone calls in the President's office had been tape-recorded, the emphasis of the investigation immediately shifted to obtaining the tapes as a means of verifying Dean's testimony. Dean testified for five days, June 25-29, and he opened his testimony by reading a 245-page prepared statement detailing his own efforts, while on the White House staff, to cover up the Watergate conspiracy. Portions of this opening statement are reprinted here.

Source: *Presidential Campaign Activities of 1972, Hearings before the Select Committee on Campaign Activities:* Watergate and Related Activities, Phase I, Book 3, pp. 914-915; 955-956; 957-959; 995-996; 998-999; 1015-1017.

MR. DEAN. Certainly. It is a very difficult thing for me to testify about other people. It is far more easy for me to explain my own involvement in this matter, the fact that I was involved in obstructing justice, the fact that I assisted another in perjured testimony, the fact that I made personal use of funds that were in my custody. It is far easier to talk about these things myself than to talk about what others did. Some of these people I will be referring to are friends, some are men I greatly admire and respect, and particularly with reference to the President of the United States, I would like to say this. It is my honest belief that while the President was involved that he did not realize or appreciate at any time the implications of his involvement, and I think that when the facts come out I hope the President is forgiven.

Pursuant to the request of the committee I will commence with a general description of the atmosphere in the White House prior to June 1972.

To one who was in the White House and became somewhat familiar with its interworkings, the Watergate matter was an inevitable outgrowth of a climate of excessive concern over the political impact of demonstrators, excessive concern over leaks, an insatiable appetite for political intelligence, all coupled with a do-it-yourself White House staff, regardless of the law. However, the fact that many of the elements of this climate culminated with the creation of a covert intelligence operation as a part of the President's reelection committee was not by conscious designs, rather an accident of fate. . . .

The So-called Dean Investigation

It was while I was in San Clemente, at the end of August, that the President announced at a press conference the so-called "Dean Report" which cleared everybody presently employed at the White House or in the administration from any complicity in the Watergate matter. This statement was made on August 29, 1972.

I would like to recall to the committee what the White House had publicly said about this incident prior to the August 29 statement of the President.

On June 19, Ziegler reported that there was no inquiry being made by the White House into the matter. On June 20, Ziegler stated that the case is something that the President will not get into at all despite the fact that Mr. Hunt had been publicly linked to the White House.

On June 21, Ziegler stated that Colson had assured him that he was not involved, and the White House repeated the statement that the President would not get involved. On June 23, the President stated that, as Ziegler had said, the White House has had no involvement whatever in this particular incident.

On July 3, when the President was in California, he ruled out a special prosecutor and said that the FBI and other authorities will pursue the investigation thoroughly and completely. And, Ziegler further reported on that date that the President would not be getting special reports on this politically sensitive case since that would be inappropriate.

Suddenly came the August 29 statement citing the Dean investigation. I had no advance knowledge that the President was going to indicate that I had investigated the matter and found no complicity on the part of anybody at the White House or anyone presently employed in the administration. I first learned of the matter when I heard it on a television news broadcast that evening after I had departed from the compound at San Clemente. I was going to walk up to the residence and listen to the press conference that day because I had never been to a press conference on the west coast, but, at the last minute, I returned to my room and later turned on the television and heard the statement.

Had I been consulted in advance by the President, I would have strongly opposed the issuing of such a statement for several reasons which I would have told the President. First, I was aware that Gordon Strachan had close, daily, liaison with Mr. Magruder and had carried information relating to wiretapped conversations into the White House and later destroyed incriminating documents at Haldeman's direction.

Second, I had never been able to determine whether Haldeman had advance knowledge or not, and in fact, had never asked him because I didn't feel I could.

Third, I had always suspected, but never been able to completely substantiate my suspicion, that Colson was far more knowledgeable than he protested.

I was very aware of Mr. Colson's efforts to disassociate himself with Hunt and of Colson's continual production of documents that would disassociate himself with Hunt. Colson protested too much.

Finally, I was aware of the two meetings that I had attended and had reported these to both Haldeman and Ehrlichman. I reported to Haldeman, as I mentioned earlier, shortly after the meetings had occurred when I told him I thought the idea was bad and incredible and told him that I would have no connection or relationship with the matter. I had reported this to Ehrlichman in June 1972, shortly after the incident. I never understood how the Liddy plan had been approved and Magruder had indicated to me that there had been White House pressure to get the plan moving.

Accordingly, I would have been the last to say unequivocally, as the President so stated, that no one presently employed at the White House had any advance knowledge of the matter. I did believe, however, that nobody at the White House knew that there was going to be a break-in of the Democratic National Committee on June 17 because I don't believe that anyone other than those directly involved knew that that was going to happen, on that day. I don't know if the President's statement was meant to be a very literal play on carefully chosen words or whether he intended to give it the broad-brush interpretation that it later received. However, I would have certainly counseled the President against issuing the statement. And, I was very unhappy to have my name associated with the statement without being consulted whatsoever, and put out in front on the issue.

The issuing of the so-called "Dean Report" was the first time I began to think about the fact that I might be being set up in case the whole thing came crumbling down at a later time. I subsequently discussed this with other individuals—Mr. Moore, Mr. Fielding, and Mr. Mitchell—and they assured me, but not unanimously, that I need not worry because they did not believe that anyone at the White House would do that to me. . . .

Meeting with the President September 15, 1972

On September 15 the Justice Department announced the handing down of the seven indictments by the Federal grand jury investigating the Watergate. Late that afternoon I received a call requesting me to come to the President's Oval Office. When I arrived at the Oval Office I found Haldeman and the President. The President asked me to sit down. Both men appeared to be in very good spirits and my reception was very warm and cordial. The President then told me that Bob—referring to Haldeman—had kept him posted on my handling of the Watergate case. The President told me I had done a good job and he appreciated how difficult a task it had been and the President was pleased that the case had stopped with Liddy. I responded that I could not take credit because others had done much more difficult things than I had done. As the President discussed the present status of the situation I told him that all that I had been able to do was to contain the case and assist in keeping it out of the White House. I also told him that there was a long way to go before this matter would end and that I certainly could make no assurances that the day would not come when this matter would start to unravel.

Early in our conversation the President said to me that former FBI Director Hoover had told him shortly after he had assumed office in 1969 that his campaign had been bugged in 1968. The President said that at some point we should get the facts out on this and use this to counter the problems that we were encountering.

The President asked me when the criminal case would come to trial and would it start before the election. I told the President that I did not know. I said that the Justice Department had held off as long as possible the return of the indictments, but much would depend on which judge got the case. The President said that he certainly hoped that the case would not come to trial before the election.

The President then asked me about the civil cases that had been filed by the Democratic National Committee and the common cause case and about the counter suits that we had filed. I told him that the lawyers at the reelection committee were handling these cases and that they did not see the common cause suit as any real problem before the election because they thought they could keep it tied up in discovery proceedings. I then told the President that the lawyers at the reelection committee were very hopeful of slowing down the civil suit filed by the Democratic National Committee because they had been making ex parte contacts with the judge handling the case and the judge was very understanding and trying to accommodate their problems. The President was pleased to hear this and responded to the effect that, "Well, that's helpful." I also recall explaining to the President about the suits that the reelection committee lawyers had filed against the Democrats as part of their counteroffensive.

There was a brief discussion about the potential hearings before the Patman committee. The President asked me what we were doing to deal with the hearings and I reported that Dick Cook, who had once worked on Patman's committee staff, was working on the problem. The President indicated that Bill Timmons should stay on top of the hearings, that we did not need the hearings before the election.

The conversation then moved to the press coverage of the Watergate incident and how the press was really trying to make this into a major campaign issue. At one point in this conversation I recall the President telling me to keep a good list of the press people giving us trouble, because we will make life difficult for them after the election. The conversation then turned to the use of the Internal Revenue Service to attack our enemies. I recall telling the President that we had not made much use of this because the White House did not have the clout to have it done, that the Internal Revenue Service was a rather democratically oriented bureaucracy and it would be very dangerous to try any such activities. The President seemed somewhat annoyed and said that the Democratic administrations had used this tool well and after the election we would get people in these agencies who would be responsive to the White House requirements.

The conversation then turned to the President's postelection plans to replace people who were not on our team in all the agencies. It was at this point that Haldeman, I remember, started taking notes and he also told the President that he had been developing information on which people should stay and which should go after the election. I recall that several days after my meeting with the President, I was talking to Dan Kingsley, who was in charge of developing the list for Haldeman as to people who should be removed after the election. I told Kingsley that this matter had come up during my conversation with the President and he said he had wondered what had put new life into his project as he had received several calls from Higby about the status of his project within the last few days. The meeting ended with a conversation with the President about a book I was reading.

I left the meeting with the impression that the President was well aware of what had been going on regarding the success of keeping the White House out of the Watergate scandal and I also had expressed to him my concern that I was not confident that the coverup could be maintained indefinitely. . . .

Meeting of March 13

This was a rather lengthy meeting, the bulk of which was taken up by a discussion about the Gray hearings and the fact that the Senate Judiciary Committee had voted to invite me to appear in connection with Gray's nomination. It was at this time we discussed the potential of litigating the matter of executive privilege and thereby preventing anybody from going before any Senate committee until that matter was resolved. The President liked the idea very much, particularly when I mentioned to him that it might be possible that he could also claim attorney/client privilege on me so that the strongest potential case on executive privilege would probably rest on the counsel to the President. I told him that obviously, this area would have to be researched. He told me that he did not want Haldeman and Ehrlichman to go before the Ervin hearings and that if we were litigating the matter on Dean, that no one would have to appear. Toward the end of the conversation, we got into a discussion of Watergate matters specifically. I told the President about the fact that there were money demands being made by the seven convicted defendants, and that the sentencing of these individuals was not far off. It was during this conversation that Haldeman came into the office. After this brief interruption by Haldeman's coming in, but while he was still there, I told the President about the fact that there was no money to pay these individuals to meet their demands. He asked me how much it would cost. I told him that I could only make an estimate that it might be as high as $1 million or more. He told me that that was no problem, and he also looked over at Haldeman and repeated the same statement. He then asked me who was demanding this money and I told him it was principally coming from Hunt through his attorney. The President then referred to the fact that Hunt had been promised executive clemency. He said that he had discussed this matter with Ehrlichman and contrary to instructions that Ehrlichman had given Colson not to talk to the President about it, that Colson had also discussed it with him later. He expressed some annoyance at the fact that Colson had also discussed this matter with him.

The conversation then turned back to a question from the President regarding the money that was being paid to the defendants. He asked me how this was done. I told him I didn't know much about it other than the fact that the money was laundered so it could not be traced and then there were secret deliveries. I told him I was learning about things I had never known before, but the next time I would certainly be more knowledgeable. This comment got a laugh out of Haldeman. The meeting ended on this note and there was no further discussion of the matter and it was left hanging just as I have described it. . . .

Meeting of March 21

As I have indicated, my purpose in requesting this meeting particularly with the President was that I felt it necessary that I give him a full report of all the facts that I knew and explain to him what I believed to be the implication of those facts. It was my particular concern with the fact that the President did not seem to understand the implications of what was going on. For example, when I had earlier told him that I thought I was involved in an obstruction of justice situation he had argued with me to the contrary after I had explained it to him. Also, when the matter of money demands had come up previously he had very nonchalantly told me that that was no problem and I did not know if he realized that he himself could be getting involved in an obstruction of justice by having promised clemency to Hunt. What I had hoped to do in this conversation was to have the President tell me that we had to end the matter—now. Accordingly, I gave considerable thought to how I would present this situation to the President and try to make as dramatic a presentation as I could to tell him how serious I thought the situation was that the coverup continue.

I began by telling the President that there was a cancer growing on the Presidency and that if the cancer was not removed that the President himself would be killed by it. I also told him that it was important that this cancer be removed immediately because it was growing more deadly every day. I then gave him what I told him would be a broad overview of the situation and I would come back and fill in the details and answer any questions he might have about the matter.

I proceeded to tell him how the matter had commenced in late January and early February but that I did not know how the plans had finally been approved. I told him I had informed Haldeman what was occurring, and Haldeman told me I should have nothing to do with it. I told him that I had learned that there had been pressure from Colson on Magruder but I did not have all the facts as to the degree of pressure. I told him I did not know if Mitchell had approved the plans but I had been told that Mitchell had been a recipient of the wiretap information and that Haldeman had also received some information through Strachan.

I then proceeded to tell him some of the highlights that had occurred during the coverup. I told him that Kalmbach had been used to raise funds to pay these seven individuals for their silence at the instructions of Ehrlichman, Haldeman, and Mitchell and I had been the conveyor of this instruction to Kalmbach. I told him that after the decision had been made that Magruder was to remain at the reelection committee. I had assisted Magruder in preparing his false story for presentation to the grand jury. I told him that cash that had been at the White House had been funneled back to the reelection committee for the purpose of paying the seven individuals to remain silent.

I then proceeded to tell him that perjury had been committed, and for this coverup to continue it would require more perjury and more money. I told him that the demands of the convicted individuals were continually increasing and that with sentencing imminent, the demands had become specific.

I told him that on Monday the 19th, I had received a message from one of the reelection committee lawyers who had spoken directly with Hunt and that Hunt had sent a message to me demanding money. I then explained to him the message that Hunt had told Paul O'Brien the preceding Friday to be passed on to me. I told the President I'd asked O'Brien why to Dean, and O'Brien had asked Hunt the same question. But Hunt had merely said you just pass this message on to Dean. The message was that Hunt wanted $72,000 for living expenses and $50,000 for attorney's fees and if he did not get the money and get it quickly that he would have a lot of seamy things to say about what he had done for John Ehrlichman while he was at the White House. If he did not receive the money, he would have to reconsider his options.

I informed the President that I had passed this message on to both Haldeman and Ehrlichman. Ehrlichman asked me if I had discussed the matter with Mitchell. I had told Ehrlichman that I had not done so and Ehrlichman asked me to do so. I told the President I had called Mitchell pursuant to Ehrlichman's request but I had no idea of what was happening with regard to the request.

I then told the President that this was just typical of the type of blackmail that the White House would continue to be subjected to and that I didn't know how to deal with it. I also told the President that I thought that I would as a result of my name coming out during the Gray hearings be called before the grand jury and that if I was called to testify before the grand jury or the Senate committee I would have to tell the facts the way I know them. I said I did not know if executive privilege would be applicable to any appearance I might have before the grand jury. I concluded by saying that it is going to take continued perjury and continued support of these individuals to perpetuate the coverup and that I did not believe it was possible to continue it; rather I thought it was time for surgery on the cancer itself and that all those involved must stand up and account for themselves and that the President himself get out in front of this matter.

I told the President that I did not believe that all of the seven defendants would maintain their silence forever, in fact, I thought that one or more would very likely break rank.

After I finished, I realized that I had not really made the President understand because after he asked a few questions, he suggested that it would be an excellent idea if I gave some sort of briefing to the Cabinet and that he was very impressed with my knowledge of the circumstances but he did not seem particularly concerned with their implications.

It was after my presentation to the President and during our subsequent conversation the President called Haldeman into the office and the President suggested that we have a meeting with Mitchell, Haldeman, and Ehrlichman to discuss how to deal with this situation. What emerged from that discussion after Haldeman came into the office was that John Mitchell should account for himself for the pre-June 17 activities and the President did not seem concerned about the activities which had occurred after June 17.

After I departed the President's office I subsequently went to a meeting with Haldeman and Ehrlichman to discuss the matter further. The sum and substance of that discussion was that the way to handle this now was for Mitchell to step forward and if Mitchell were to step forward we might not be confronted with the activities of those involved in the White House in the coverup.

Accordingly, Haldeman, as I recall, called Mitchell and asked him to come down the next day for a meeting with the President on the Watergate matter.

In the late afternoon of March 21, Haldeman and Ehrlichman and I had a second meeting with the President. Before entering this meeting I had a brief discussion in the President's outer office of the Executive Office Building suite with Haldeman in which I told him that we had two options:

One is that this thing goes all the way and deals with both the preactivities and the postactivities, or the second alternative; if the coverup was to proceed we would have to draw the wagons in a circle around the White House and that the White House protect itself. I told Haldeman that it had been the White House's assistance to the reelection committee that had gotten us into much of this problem and now the only hope would be to protect ourselves from further involvement.

The meeting with the President that afternoon with Haldeman, Ehrlichman, and myself was a tremendous disappointment to me because it was quite clear that the coverup as far as the White House was concerned was going to continue. I recall that while Haldeman, Ehrlichman, and I were sitting at a small table in front of the President in his Executive Office Building office that I for the first time said in front of the President that I thought that Haldeman, Ehrlichman, and Dean were all indictable for obstruction of justice and that was the reason I disagreed with all that was being discussed at that point in time.

I could tell that both Haldeman, and particularly Ehrlichman, were very unhappy with my comments. I had let them very clearly know that I was not going to participate in the matter any further and that I thought it was time that everybody start thinking about telling the truth.

I again repeated to them I did not think it was possible to perpetuate the coverup and the important thing now was to get the President out in front. . . .

Meeting with the President April 15

The President was very cordial when we met. I was somewhat shaken when I went in to meet him because I knew I had taken it upon myself to end the coverup and what I had started was going to cause serious problems for the President. I shall attempt to recall the highlights of the conversation that transpired on the meeting which occurred about 9 o'clock on April 15.

I told the President that I had gone to the prosecutors. And, that I did not believe that this was an act of disloyalty but, rather in the end it would be an act of loyalty. I told him I felt this matter had to end. I informed the President that I told the prosecutors of my own involvement and the involvement of others. At one point in the conversation I recall the President asking me about Haldeman's knowledge of the Liddy plans. He asked me if I had told him earlier about the fact that I had met with Haldeman after the second meeting in Mitchell's office and told Haldeman what was going on and my reaction to what was going on. I told the President that I had reported this fact to him earlier. The President then made some reference to Henry Petersen asking about why Haldeman had not turned it off at that point and told me to testify that I had told Haldeman about the meeting in Mitchell's office. The President almost from the outset began asking me a number of leading questions, which was somewhat unlike his normal conversational relationships I had had with him, which made me think that the conversation was being taped and that a record was being made to protect himself. Although I became aware of this because of the nature of the conversation, I decided that I did not know it for a fact and that I had to believe that the President would not tape such a conversation.

Some question came up, by the President, as to whether I had immunity. As best as I can recall, I told him my lawyers had discussed this with the prosecutors but certainly I had no deal with the Government. He told me that he did not want to do anything to hurt my negotiations with the Government. I do not recall his comment on his comment regarding that. I also recall that the conversation turned to the matter of Liddy not talking. He said something about Liddy was waiting for a signal and I told him that possibly he was waiting for a signal from the President.

I discussed with him the fact that maybe if Liddy's lawyer met with him that Liddy would begin to open up because I said that I thought that that would be very helpful if Liddy did talk. It was during this part of the conversation that the President picked up the telephone and called Henry Petersen and pretended with Petersen that I was not in the room but that the matter of Liddy's coming forward and talking had arisen during our conversation. The President relayed to Petersen that if Liddy's lawyer wanted to see him to get a signal that the President was willing to do this.

The President also asked me about Petersen and I told him if any one could give him good advice Henry Petersen could. The President also asked me if I remembered what day it was in March that I had reported to him on some of the details of the Watergate matter. He said that he thought it was the 21st but was not certain. I said that I could not recall for certain without checking. . . .

Toward the end of the conversation the President recalled the fact that at one point we had discussed the difficulty in raising money and that he had said that $1 million was nothing to raise to pay to maintain the silence of the defendants. He said that he had, of course, only been joking when he made that comment. As the conversation went on, and it is impossible for me to recall anything other than the high points of it, I became more convinced that the President was seeking to elicit testimony from me and put his perspective on the record and get me to agree to it.

The most interesting thing that happened during the conversation was, very near the end, he got up out of his chair, went behind his chair to the corner of the Executive Office Building office and in a nearly inaudible tone said to me he was probably foolish to have discussed Hunt's clemency with Colson. I do not recall that I responded. The conversation ended shortly thereafter.

As I was on my way out of the office after exchanging parting pleasantries, I told the President that I hoped that my going to the prosecutors and telling the truth, would not result in the impeachment of the President. He jokingly said, "I certainly hope so also," and he said that it would be handled properly.

Antiwar demonstrators in Times Square during a November 1969 rally

POLITICS NOT AS USUAL

By 1969 the politics of upheaval had lasted long enough. Americans were ready for a reprieve from the Indochina war, from student protests, from the "new morality," from "movements," from crime in the streets, and from the mounting number of domestic problems that would not go away. If they were not demanding a return to "normalcy," Americans were at least longing for a cooling off of the rhetoric and an end to confrontations. Taking office in January 1969, the new administration of Richard M. Nixon seemed to offer hope for the return of stability, a time for consolidating gains and tackling the accumulated problems. Even the lack of fanfare by the new office holders suggested to the nation that it was time to get busy with all the tasks at hand, eschewing the spectacular and innovative approaches and slogans of the previous few years. And President Nixon, during his first term, did indeed confound his critics and occasionally dismay his friends. He did not, as many liberals had predicted, dismantle the legislative programs established by administrations of the past forty years. Many of them he sought to improve on.

(Top) President Nixon and Chou En-Lai during visit to China; (below left) Senators Edmund Muskie and George McGovern during 1972 campaign; (below right) President Nixon after renomination

(Left) U.S. Marines leave Vietnam in 1971; (right) former prisoner of war Air Force Captain Ronald Bliss arrives in the U.S. in March 1973; Bliss had been shot down in 1966.

Elected on a promise to end the Vietnam war, the Nixon Administration nevertheless carried the war on for four more years, thus perpetuating the dissent and protest that had begun in the presidency of Lyndon Johnson. But the Administration's other attainments in foreign policy were spectacular enough to overshadow, at least in the headlines, the continuing domestic crises at home. In March 1971, the ban on travel to the People's Republic of China was lifted, and a U.S. table tennis team visited Peking. In April of the same year the trade embargo was relaxed. In July presidential adviser Henry Kissinger made a secret trip to Peking to meet with Chou En-Lai and arrange for President Nixon to visit China in February 1972. Thus a 25-year breach between the two countries was bridged. This policy of Cold War détente was carried further when President Nixon visited the Soviet Union in May 1972 to confer with Premier Kosygin and Communist party leader Brezhnev. This visit was reciprocated by Brezhnev in June 1973 when he visited the United States for discussions about improving trade relations.

President Nixon confers with Henry Kissinger about the Paris peace talks.

(Above) Members and staff of the Senate Watergate Committee crowd around chairman Sam Ervin, Jr. (left) Senator Lowell Weicker, a Republican member of the committee, became a strong critic of the administration.

The lessening of domestic discord combined with the achievements of the Nixon-Kissinger foreign policy to give the President an overwhelming victory over Senator George McGovern in the 1972 election. But in 1973 the laurels of victory shriveled into ashes in the heat of the Watergate scandal. The events of Watergate—the break-in at Democratic national headquarters and the subsequent White House cover-up of involvement by administration officials—took place mostly in 1972. But they did not come under public scrutiny until 1973. As they did, the administration of Richard Nixon slowly disintegrated.

Disclosures resulting from the trial of the Watergate burglars forced the resignation of some of the President's closest advisers, including H. R. Haldeman and John Ehrlichman. Special counsel John Dean, fired by the President, testified before the Senate Watergate Committee about the cover-up of the scandal.

(Top) Convicted Watergate burglar James McCord testifies before the committee; (center) former White House special counsel John Dean and his wife, Maureen, during his week of testimony; (bottom) former presidential advisors H. R. Haldeman (1) and John Erlichman

(Above) Attorney General Elliot Richardson during a news conference shortly after he resigned; (below) Judge John Sirica presided over the Watergate grand jury and trial; (right) special prosecutor Archibald Cox was fired on October 20, 1973.

In February 1973, the U.S. Senate voted to establish a committee to investigate Watergate, the activities of the Committee to Re-elect the President, campaign practices and contributions, and any White House involvement in the whole affair. Senator Sam Ervin, Jr., Democrat of North Carolina, was named chairman of the committee, and Senator Howard Baker, Republican of Tennessee, became vice-chairman. The committee hearings began on May 17 and were televised daily throughout most of the summer. In addition, a special Watergate grand jury was convened, presided over by federal judge John Sirica, to take testimony and seek evidence of the commission of criminal offenses. A new attorney general, Elliot Richardson, was appointed by President Nixon and confirmed by the Senate upon the promise that he would appoint a special prosecutor to look into Watergate and related matters. However, the new prosecutor, Harvard Law School professor Archibald Cox, and the new attorney general remained on the job only a few months. On October 20, 1973, President Nixon fired Cox, and Richardson resigned in protest, bringing a whole new sense of crisis to the investigation. Public confidence in the President fell to a new low, and there were demands for his resignation or impeachment. On October 22 resolutions of impeachment were introduced into the House of Representatives.

Vice-President Spiro Agnew outside a Baltimore federal court house on the day he resigned

As the Watergate web unraveled throughout the summer of 1973, a whole new and unrelated scandal broke upon the administration and the country. On August 6, Vice-President Agnew called a press conference and announced that he was under investigation by a federal grand jury in Maryland for possible violations of the law concerning alleged kickbacks from architects and contractors during the years he had held various state and local offices. Agnew staunchly maintained his innocence for the next two months, but by early October a Justice Department investigation and promulgation of criminal charges led the Vice-President to resign his office on October 10, pleading "no contest" to a charge of tax evasion. Two days later the President named Gerald Ford, House minority leader, to be the new Vice-President. Although the Agnew scandal seemed quickly forgotten, the availability of a new Vice-President encouraged the pressure for the President's impeachment.

President Nixon with the new Vice-President, Gerald Ford, at Ford's swearing in ceremony

When, on July 16, 1973, former presidential aide Alexander Butterfield made the startling announcement to the Senate Watergate Committee that conversations in the President's offices had been recorded on tape since 1971, the investigation was cast in a new light. The tapes, if made available, would be the means of verifying or contradicting the damaging allegations made against the President by John Dean and others. The whole controversy began to swirl around the tapes, and it seemed likely that the firing of Archibald Cox—he was subsequently replaced by Houston attorney Leon Jaworski—had been largely the result of Cox's interest in the tapes. Toward the end of 1973, as Watergate seemed to be grinding on to resolution, the nation was beset by a new crisis: the fuel shortage. Hints of the energy crisis had appeared the previous spring, but the Mideast Arab oil boycott, announced in October, brought the reality of the shortage to the immediate attention of Americans, particularly automobile owners in the larger urban areas.

(Left) The second special prosecutor for Watergate, Leon Jaworski; (below) the 1973 gas shortage caused long lines at some service stations, like this one in Chicago.

77.

RICHARD M. NIXON: Press Conference on Watergate

Breaking five months of public silence, President Nixon held a news conference at San Clemente, California, on August 22, 1973. The main topic of the reporters' questions was that vast complex of events subsumed under the name Watergate. The intensity of concern was high at this time because a judicial decision was daily expected on the President's right to keep the White House tape recordings confidential. The portions of the news conference dealing with Watergate are reprinted here.

Source: *Weekly Compilation of Presidential Documents*, August 27, 1973.

Q.: Mr. President, on Watergate, you have said that disclosure of the tapes could jeopardize and cripple the functions of the Presidency. Question: If disclosure carries such a risk, why did you make the tapes in the first place, and what is your reaction to surveys that show three out of four Americans believe you were wrong to make the tapes?

The President: Well, with regard to the questions as to why Americans feel we were wrong to make the tapes, that is not particularly surprising. I think that most Americans do not like the idea of the taping of conversations, and frankly, it is not something that particularly appeals to me.

As a matter of fact, that is why, when I arrived in the White House and saw this rather complex situation set up where there was taping capacity, not only in the President's office, the room outside of his office, but also in the Cabinet Room, and at Camp David, and in other areas, that I had the entire system dismantled.

It was put into place again in June of 1970 (1971) because my advisers felt it was important in terms particularly of national security affairs to have a record for future years that would be an accurate one, but a record which would only be disclosed at the discretion of the President, or according to directives that he would set forth.

As you know, of course, this kind of capability not only existed during the Johnson Administration, it also existed in the Kennedy Administration, and I can see why both President Johnson and President Kennedy did have the capability because—not because they wanted to infringe upon the privacy of anybody, but because they felt that they had some obligation, particularly in the field of foreign policy and some domestic areas, to have a record that would be accurate.

As far as I am concerned, we now do not have that capability, and I am just as happy that we don't. As a matter of fact, I have a practice, whenever I am not too tired at night, of dictating my own recollections of the day. I think that perhaps will be the more accurate record of history in the end.

I think we go to the UP now, and then we will come to the television.

Q.: Mr. President, on July 6, 1972, you were warned by Patrick Gray that you were being mortally wounded by some of your top aides. Can you explain why you did not ask who they were, why, what was going on?

The President: Well, in the telephone conversation that you refer to that has been, of course, quite widely reported in the press, as well as on television, Mr. Gray said that he was concerned that as far as the investigation that he had responsibility for, that some of my top aides were not cooperating.

Whether the term was used as "mortally wounded" or not, I don't know. Some believe that it was, some believe that it was not, that is irrelevant. He could have said that.

The main point was, however, I asked him whether or not he had discussed this matter with General Walters because I knew that there had been meetings between General Walters, representing the CIA, to be sure that the CIA did not become involved in the investigation, and between the Director of the FBI.

He said that he had. He told me that General Walters agreed that the investigation should be pursued, and I told him to go forward with a full press on the investigation to which he has so testified.

It seemed to me that with that kind of a directive to Mr Gray, that that was adequate for the purpose of carrying out the responsibilities.

As far as the individuals were concerned, I assume that the individuals that he was referring to involved this operation with the CIA. That is why I asked him the Walters question. When he cleared that up, he went forward with the investigation, and he must have thought it was a very good investigation because when I sent his name down to the Senate for confirmation the next year, I asked him about his investigation. He said he was very proud of it. He said it was the most thorough investigation that had ever taken place since the assassination of President Kennedy, that he could defend it with enthusiasm, and that under the circumstances, therefore, he had carried out the directive that I had given him on July 6.

So, there was no question about Mr. Gray having direct orders from the President to carry out an investigation that was thorough.

Mr. Jarriel.

Q.: Mr. President, Assistant Attorney General Henry Petersen has testified that on April 15 of this year he met with you and warned you at that time there might be enough evidence to warrant indictments against three of your top aides, Messrs. Ehrlichman, Haldeman, and Dean. You accepted their resignations on April 30, calling Mr. Haldeman and Mr. Ehrlichman two of the finest public servants you had known. After that you permitted Mr. Haldeman, after he had left the White House, to hear confidential tapes of conversations you had had in your office with Mr. Dean. My question is, why did you permit a man who you knew might be indicted to hear those tapes which you now will not permit the American public or the Federal prosecutors handling the case to listen to?

The President: The only tape that has been referred to, that Mr. Haldeman has listened to, he listened to at my request, and he listened to that tape—that was the one on September 15, Mr. Jarriel—because he had been present and was there. I asked him to listen to it in order to be sure that as far as any allegations that had been made by Mr. Dean with regard to that conversation is concerned, I wanted to be sure that we were absolutely correct in our response. That is all he listened to. He did not listen to any tapes in which only Mr. Dean and I participated. He listened only to the tape on September 15—this is after he left office—in which he had participated in the conversation throughout.

Q.: Mr. President, one of the lingering doubts about your denial of any involvement is concerning your failure to make the tapes available either to the Senate committee or the Special Prosecutor. You have made it perfectly clear you don't intend to release those tapes.

The President: Perfectly clear?

Q.: Perfectly clear. But is there any way that you could have some group listen to tapes and give a report so that that might satisfy the public mind?

The President: I don't believe, first, it would satisfy the public mind, and it should not. The second point is that as Mr. Wright, who argued the case, I understand very well, before Judge Sirica this morning, has indicated, to have the tapes listened to—he indicated this also in his brief—either by a prosecutor or by a judge or *in camera*, or in any way, would violate the principle of confidentiality, and I believe he is correct. That is why we are standing firm on the proposition that we will not agree to the Senate committee's desire to have, for example, its chief investigator listen to the tapes, or the Special Prosecutor's desire to hear the tapes, and also why we will oppose, as Mr. Wright did in his argument this morning, any compromise of the principle of confidentiality.

Let me explain very carefully that the principle of confidentiality either exists or it does not exist. Once it is compromised, once it is known that a conversation that is held with the President can be subject to a subpoena by a Senate committee, by a grand jury, by a prosecutor, and be listened to by anyone, the principle of confidentiality is thereby irreparably damaged. Incidentally, let me say that now that tapes are no longer being made, I suppose it could be argued that, what difference does it make now, now that these tapes are also in the past. What is involved here is not only the tapes; what is involved, as you ladies and gentlemen well know, is the request on the part of the Senate committee and the Special Prosecutor, as well, that we turn over Presidential papers, in other words, the records of conversations with the President made by his associates. Those papers, and the tapes as well, cannot be turned over without breaching the principle of confidentiality. It was President Truman that made that argument very effectively in his letter to a Senate committee, or his response to a Congressional committee, a House committee it was, in 1953, when they asked him to turn over his papers. So whether it is a paper or whether it is a tape, what we have to bear in mind is that for a President to conduct the affairs of this office and conduct them effectively, he must be able to do so with the principle of confidentiality intact. Otherwise, the individuals who come to talk to him, whether it is his advisers, or whether it is a visitor in the domestic field, or whether it is someone in a foreign field, will always be speaking in a eunuch-like way, rather than laying it on the line as it has to be laid on the line if you are going to have the creative kind of dicussion that we have often had, and it has been responsible for some of our successes in the foreign policy period, particularly in the past few years.

Q.: Mr. President, could you tell us who

you personally talked to in directing that investigations be made both in June of '72, shortly after the Watergate incident, and last March 21, when you got new evidence and ordered a more intensive investigation?

The President: Certainly. In June, I, of course, talked to Mr. MacGregor first of all, who was the new chairman of the committee. He told me that he would conduct a thorough investigation as far as his entire committee staff was concerned. Apparently that investigation was very effective except for Mr. Magruder, who stayed on. But Mr. MacGregor does not have to assume responsibility for that. I say not responsibility for it because basically what happened there was that he believed Mr. Magruder, and many others have believed him, too. He proved, however, to be wrong.

In the White House, the investigation's responsibility was given to Mr. Ehrlichman at the highest level, and in turn he delegated them to Mr. Dean, the White House Counsel, something of which I was aware, and of which I approved.

Mr. Dean, as White House Counsel, therefore sat in on the FBI interrogations of the members of the White House Staff because what I wanted to know was whether any member of the White House Staff was in any way involved. If he was involved, he would be fired. And when we met on September 15, and again throughout our discussions in the month of March, Mr. Dean insisted that there was not—and I use his words—"a scintilla of evidence" indicating that anyone on the White House Staff was involved in the planning of the Watergate break-in.

Now, in terms of after March 21, Mr. Dean first was given the responsibility to write his own report, but I did not rest it there. I also had a contact made with the Attorney General himself, Attorney General Kleindienst, told him—it was on the 27th of March—to report to me directly anything that he found in this particular area, and I gave the responsibility to Mr. Ehrlichman on the 29th of March to continue the investigation that Mr. Dean was unable to conclude, having spent a week at Camp David and unable to finish the report.

Mr. Ehrlichman questioned a number of people in that period at my direction, including Mr. Mitchell, and I should also point out that as far as my own activities were concerned, I was not leaving it just to them. I met at great length with Mr. Ehrlichman, Mr. Haldeman, Mr. Dean and Mr. Mitchell on the 22nd. I discussed the whole matter with them. I kept pressing for the view that I had had throughout, that we must get this story out, get the truth out, whatever and whoever it is going to hurt, and it was there that Mr. Mitchell suggested that all the individuals involved in the White House appear in an executive session before the Ervin committee. We never got that far, but at least that is an indication of the extent of my own investigation.

Q.: Mr. President, you have said repeatedly that you tried to get all the facts, and just now you mentioned the March 22 meeting. Yet former Attorney General John Mitchell said that if you had ever asked him at any time about the Watergate matter, he would have told you the whole story, chapter and verse. Was Mr. Mitchell not speaking the truth when he said that before the committee?

The President: Now, Mr. Lisagor, I am not going to question Mr. Mitchell's veracity, and I will only say that throughout I had confidence in Mr. Mitchell. Mr. Mitchell, in a telephone call that I had with him immediately after it occurred, expressed great chagrin that he had not run a tight enough shop, and that some of the boys, as he called them, got involved in this kind of activity, which he knew to be very, very embarrassing, apart from its illegality, to the campaign. Throughout I would have expected Mr. Mitchell to tell me in the event that he was involved or that anybody else was. He did not tell me. I don't blame him for not telling me. He has given his reasons for not telling me. I regret that he did not, because he is exactly right. Had he told me, I would have blown my stack, just as I did at Ziegler the other day. [*Laughter*]

Q.: Mr. President, I wonder, sir, how much personal blame, to what degree of personal blame do you accept for the climate in the White House, and at the reelection committee, for the abuses of Watergate?

The President: I accept it all.

Q.: Mr. President, I want to state this question with due respect to your office, but also as directly as possible.

The President: That would be unusual. [*Laughter*]

Q.: I would like to think not. It concerns——

The President: You are always respectful, Mr. Rather. You know that.

Q.: Thank you, Mr. President. It concerns the events surrounding Mr. Ehrlichman's contact, and on one occasion your own contact with the judge in the Pentagon Papers case, Judge Byrne.

The President: Yes.

Q.: As I understand your own explanation of events and putting together your statement with Mr. Ehrlichman's testimony, and what Judge Byrne has said, what happened here is that sometime late in March, March 17, I believe you said, you first found out about the break-in at the psychiatrist's office of Mr. Ellsberg, that you asked to have that looked into, and that you later, I think in late April, instructed Attorney General Kleindienst to inform the judge.

Now, my question is this. If while the Pentagon Papers trial was going on, Mr. Ehrlichman secretly met once with the judge in that case, you secretly met another time the judge with Mr. Ehrlichman. Now, you are a lawyer, and given the state of the situation and what you knew, could you give us some reason why the American people should not believe that that was at least a subtle attempt to bribe the judge in that case, and it gave at least the appearance of a lack of moral leadership?

The President: Well, I would say the only part of your statement that is perhaps accurate is that I am a lawyer. Now, beyond that, Mr. Rather, let me say that with regard to the secret meeting that we had with the judge, as he said, I met with the judge briefly—after all, I had appointed him to the position—I met him for perhaps one minute outside my door here in full view of the whole White House Staff, and everybody else who wanted to see. I asked him how he liked his job, we did not discuss the case, and he went on for his meeting with Mr. Ehrlichman.

Now, why did the meeting with Mr. Ehrlichman take place? Because we had determined that Mr. Gray could not be confirmed, as you will recall. We were on a search for a Director of the FBI. Mr. Kleindienst had been here, and I asked him what he would recommend with regard to a Director, and I laid down certain qualifications.

I said I wanted a man preferably with

FBI experience, and preferably with prosecutor's experience, and preferably, if possible, a Democrat so that we would have no problem on confirmation. He said, "The man for the job is Byrne." He said, "He is the best man." I said, "Would you recommend him?" He said, "Yes."

Under those circumstances then, Mr. Ehrlichman called Mr. Byrne. He said: Under no circumstances will we talk to you—he, Ehrlichman, will talk to you—if he felt that it would in any way compromise his handling of the Ellsberg case.

Judge Byrne made the decision that he would talk to Mr. Ehrlichman, and he did talk to him privately, here. And on that occasion, he talked to him privately, the case was not discussed at all—only the question of whether or not, at the conclusion of this case, Mr. Byrne would like to be considered as Director of the FBI.

I understand, incidentally, that he told Mr. Ehrlichman that he would be interested. Of course, the way the things broke eventually, we found another name with somewhat the same qualifications, although, in this case, not a judge. In this case, a chief of police with former FBI experience.

Now, with regard to the Ellsberg break-in, let me explain that in terms of that, I discussed that on the telephone with Mr. Henry Petersen on the 18th of April. It was on the 18th of April that I learned that the grand jury was going away from some of its Watergate investigation and moving into national security areas.

I told Mr. Petersen at that time about my concern about the security areas, and particularly about the break-in as far as the Ellsberg case is concerned.

And then he asked me a very critical question, which you, as a nonlawyer will now understand, and lawyers probably will, too. He said, "Was any evidence developed out of this investigation, out of this break-in?" And I said, "No, it was a dry hole." He said, "Good."

Now, what he meant by that was that in view of the fact that no evidence was developed as a result of the break-in—which is, incidentally, illegal, unauthorized, as far as I was concerned, and completely deplorable—but since no evidence was developed, there was no requirement that it be presented to the jury that was hearing the case. That was why Mr. Petersen, a man of impeccable credentials in the law enforcement field, did not, at that time on the 18th, at a time that I told him what I had known about the Ellsberg break-in, say, "Let's present it then to the grand jury," because nothing had been accomplished, nothing had been obtained that would taint the case.

It was approximately 10 days later that Mr. Kleindienst came in and said that, after a review of the situation in the prosecutor's office in Washington, in which Mr. Petersen had also participated, that they believed that it was best that we bend over backwards in this case and send this record of the Ellsberg break-in, even though there was no evidence obtained from it that could have affected the jury one way or another, send it to the judge.

When they made that recommendation to me, I directed that it be done, instantly. It was done. Incidentally, the prosecutor argued this case just the way that I have argued it to you, and whether or not it had an effect on the eventual outcome, I do not know.

At least, as far as we know, Mr. Ellsberg went free, this being one of the factors, but that is the explanation of what happened and, obviously, you, in your commentary tonight, can attach anything you want to it.

I hope you will be just as fair and objective as I try to be in giving you the answer. . . .

Q.: Mr. President, at any time during the Watergate crisis did you ever consider resigning and would you consider resigning if you felt that your capacity to govern had been seriously weakened, and in that connection how much do you think your capacity to govern has been weakened?

The President: The answer to the first two questions is no, the answer to the third question is that it is true that as far as the capacity to govern is concerned that to be under a constant barrage—12 to 15 minutes a night on each of the three major networks for four months—tends to raise some questions in the people's mind with regard to the President, and it may raise some questions with regard to the capacity to govern. But I also know this. I was elected to do a job. Watergate is an episode that I deeply deplore, and had I been running the campaign rather than trying to run the country and particularly the foreign policy of this country at this time it would never have happened, but that is water under the bridge, it is gone now.

The point that I make now is that we are proceeding as best we know how to get all those guilty brought to justice in Watergate. But now we must move on from Watergate to the business of the people, and the business of the people is continuing with initiatives we began in the first administration. . . .

Q.: As long as we are on the subject of the American tradition and following up Mr. Rather's question, what was authorized, even if the burglary of Dr. Fielding's office was not, what was authorized was the 1970 plan which by your own description permitted illegal acts, illegal breaking and entering, mail surveillance and the like.

Now under the Constitution you swore an oath to execute the laws of the United States faithfully. If you were serving in Congress, would you not be considering impeachment proceedings and discussing impeachment possibility against an elected public official who had violated his oath of office?

The President: I would if I had violated the oath of office. I would also, however, refer you to the recent decision of the Supreme Court or at least an opinion that even last year which indicates inherent power in the Presidency to protect the national security in cases like this. I should also point out to you that in the three Kennedy years and the three Johnson years through 1966, when burglarizing of this type did take place, when it was authorized on a very large scale, there was no talk of impeachment and it was quite well known.

I shall also point out that when you ladies and gentlemen indicate your great interest in wiretaps, and I understand that, that the height of the wiretaps was when Robert Kennedy was Attorney General in 1963. I don't criticize it, however. He had over 250 in 1963, and of course the average in the Eisenhower Administration and the Nixon Administration is about 110. But if he had had ten more and as a result of wiretaps had been able to discover the Oswald plan, it would have been worth it.

So I will go to another question.

Q.: Mr. President, do you still consider Haldeman and Ehrlichman two of the finest public servants you have ever known?

The President: I certainly do. I look upon public servants as men who have got to be judged by their entire record, not by simply parts of it. Mr. Ehrlichman and Mr. Haldeman, for four and a half years, have served with great distinction, with great dedication, and like everybody in this deplorable Watergate business, at great personal sacrifice and with no personal gain.

We admit the scandalous conduct. Thank God there has been no personal gain involved. That would be going much too far, I suppose.

But the point that I make with regard to Mr. Haldeman and Mr. Ehrlichman is that I think, too, that as all the facts come out, that—and when they have an opportunity to have their case heard in court and not simply to be tried before a committee, and tried in the press, and tried in television—they will be exonerated.

Mr. Horner.

Q.: Mr. President, could you tell us your recollection of what you told John Dean on March 21 on the subject of raising funds for the Watergate defendants?

The President: Certainly. Mr. Haldeman has testified to that, and his statement is accurate. Basically, what Mr. Dean was concerned about on March 21 was not so much the raising of money for the defendants, but the raising of money for the defendants for the purpose of keeping them still—in other words, so-called hush money. The one would be legal—in other words, raising a defense fund for any group, any individual, as you know, is perfectly legal and it is done all the time. But if you raise funds for the purpose of keeping an individual from talking, that is obstruction of justice.

Mr. Dean said also on March 21 that there was an attempt, as he put it, to blackmail the White House, to blackmail the White House by one of the defendants. Incidentally, that defendant has denied it, but at least this was what Mr. Dean had claimed, and that unless certain amounts of money were paid, I think it was $120,000 for attorneys' fees and other support, that this particular defendant would make a statement, not with regard to Watergate, but with regard to some national security matters in which Mr. Ehrlichman had particular responsibility.

My reaction, very briefly, was this: I said, as you look at this, I said, "Isn't it quite obvious, first, that if it is going to have any chance to succeed, that these individuals aren't going to sit there in jail for four years? They are going to have clemency: isn't that correct?"

He said, "Yes." I said, "We can't give clemency." He agreed. Then, I went to another point. I said, "The second point is that isn't it also quite obvious, as far as this is concerned, that while we could raise the money"—and he indicated in answer to my question, it would probably take a million dollars over four years to take care of this defendant, and others, on this kind of basis—the problem was, how do you get the money to them, and also, how do you get around the problem of clemency, because they are not going to stay in jail simply because their families are being taken care of. And so, that was why I concluded, as Mr. Haldeman recalls perhaps, and did testify very effectively, one, when I said, "John, it is wrong, it won't work. We can't give clemency and we have got to get this story out. And therefore, I direct you, and I direct Haldeman, and I direct Ehrlichman, and I direct Mitchell to get together tomorrow and then meet with me as to how we get this story out."

And that is how the meeting on the 22nd took place.

Q.: Mr. President, earlier in the news

conference you said that you gave Mr. Haldeman the right to listen to one tape because you wanted to be sure that "we are correct." I think I am quoting you correctly.

Now, you have indicated that you still feel that Mr. Haldeman and Mr. Ehrlichman are two of the finest public servants that you have ever known. You have met with their lawyer at least twice that we know of. Are you and Mr. Haldeman and Mr. Ehrlichman coordinating their and your defense and, if so, why?

The President: No, no, as far as my defense is concerned, I make it myself. As far as their defense is concerned, their lawyer has demonstrated very well before the committee that he can handle it very well without any assistance from me. . . .

Q.: Sir, last week in your speech you referred to those who would exploit Watergate to keep you from doing your job. Could you specifically detail who "those" are?

The President: I would suggest that where the shoe fits, people should wear it. I would think that some political figures, some members of the press, perhaps, some members of the television, perhaps would exploit it. I don't impute, interestingly enough, motives, however, that are improper because here is what is involved. There are a great number of people in this country that would prefer that I resign. There are a great number of people in this country that didn't accept the mandate of 1972. After all, I know that most of the members of the press corps were not enthusiastic, and I understand that, about either my election in '68 or '72. That is not unusual.

Frankly, if I had always followed what the press predicted or the polls predicted, I would have never been elected President. But what I am saying is this, people who did not accept the mandate of '72, who do not want the strong America that I want to build, who do not want the foreign policy leadership that I want to give, who do not want to cut down the size of this government bureaucracy that burdens us so greatly and to give more of our government back to the people, people who do not want these things, naturally, would exploit any issue, if it weren't Watergate, anything else, in order to keep the President from doing his job.

And so I say I impute no improper motives to them, I think they would prefer that I fail. On the other hand, I am not going to fail, I am here to do a job, and I am going to do the best I can, and I am sure the fair-minded members of this press corps—and that is most of you—will report when I do well, and I am sure you will report when I do badly. . . .

Q.: Mr. President, during March and April, you received from your staff on several occasions information about criminal wrongdoing and some indication that members of your staff might have been involved. My question, sir, is why didn't you turn this information over immediately to the prosecutors instead of having your own staff continue to make these investigations?

The President: Well, for the very obvious reason that in March, for example, the man that was in constant contact with the prosecutors was my Counsel, Mr. Dean. Mr. Dean was talking to Mr. Petersen. I assumed that anything he was telling me he was telling the prosecutors. And in April, after Mr. Dean left the investigation, Mr. Ehrlichman was in charge. I would assume, and incidentally, Mr. Ehrlichman did talk to Mr. Kleindienst. That is why it was done that way. The President does not pick up the phone and call the Attorney General every time something comes up on a matter; he depends on his Counsel or whoever he has given the job to—or he has given that assignment to to do the job. And that is what I expected in this instance.

78.

JOHN J. SIRICA: The Scope of Executive Privilege

On Monday, July 16, 1973, former presidential aide Alexander P. Butterfield revealed to the Senate Watergate Committee that all conversations and meetings in the President's offices at the White House had been secretly recorded on tape for at least the two previous years. Considering the contradictory and equivocal nature of much of the testimony before the committee, access to the tapes was immediately deemed the most adequate means of learning exactly what roles President Nixon and his staff had played in some aspects of the Watergate affair. When President Nixon invoked executive privilege and refused to release the tapes, the Senate committee and the special prosecutor, Archibald Cox, both initiated suits to obtain the relevant nine tapes. On August 17, Cox and the President's lawyers both presented legal briefs on the issue before John J. Sirica, Chief Judge of the U.S. District Court for the District of Columbia. Sirica's decision, portions of which are reprinted here, ruled that the tapes were best evidence and ordered their release. The President refused, insisting that only a "definitive ruling" by the U.S. Supreme Court would cause him to release them. The case was immediately appealed to a panel of federal judges who upheld the Sirica decision. On October 23 the President's lawyers appeared in Judge Sirica's courtroom and announced that the President would comply with the order and release the tapes.

Source: 360 Fed. Supp. 1 (1973)

THE PARTIES TO THE CONTROVERSY have briefed and argued several issues including the Court's jurisdiction in the matter of compulsory process, the existence and scope of "executive privilege" generally, applicability of "executive privilege" to the tape recordings subpoenaed, and waiver of privilege. The Court has found it necessary to adjudicate but two questions for the present: (1) whether the Court has jurisdiction to decide the issue of privilege, and (2) whether the Court has authority to enforce the subpoena *duces tecum* by way of an order requiring production for inspection *in camera.* A third question, whether the materials are in fact privileged as against the grand jury, either in whole or in part, is left for subsequent adjudication. For the reasons outlined below, the Court concludes that both of the questions considered must be answered in the affirmative. . . .

Are there, then, any rights or privileges consistent with, though not mentioned in, the Constitution which are necessary to the Executive? One answer may be found in the Supreme Court decision, *United States v. Reynolds*, 345 U.S. 1. The Court recognized an executive privilege, evidentiary in nature, for military secrets. *Reynolds* held that when a court finds the privilege is properly invoked under the appropriate circumstances, it will, in a civil case at least, suppress the evidence. Thus, it must be recognized that there can be executive privileges that will bar the production of evidence. The Court is willing here to recognize and give effect to an evidentiary privilege based on the need to protect presidential privacy.

The Court, however, cannot agree with respondent that it is the Executive that finally determines whether its privilege is properly invoked. The availability of evidence including the validity and scope of privileges, is a judicial decision. . . .

The burden here then, is on the President to define exactly what it is about his office that court process commanding the production of evidence cannot reach there. To be accurate, court process in the form of a subpoena *duces tecum* has already issued to the President, and he acknowledges that pursuant to *Burr*, courts possess authority to direct such subpoenas to him. A distinction is drawn, however, between authority to issue a subpoena and authority to command obedience to it. It is this second compulsory process that the President contends may not reach him. The burden yet remains with the President, however, to explain why this must be so. What distinctive quality of the Presidency permits its incumbent to withhold evidence? To argue that the need for Presidential privacy justifies it, is not persuasive. On the occasions when such need justifies suppression, the courts will sustain a privilege. . . .

To argue that it is the constitutional separation of powers that bars compulsory court process from the White House, is also unpersuasive. Such a contention overlooks history. Although courts generally, and this Court in particular, have avoided any interference with the discretionary acts of coordinate branches, they have not hesitated to rule on nondiscretionary acts when necessary. respondent points out that these and other precedents refer to officials other than the President, and that this distinction renders the precedents inapplicable. Such an argument tends to set the White House apart as a fourth branch of government. It is true that *Mississippi v. Johnson*, 4 Wall. 475, left open the question whether the President can be required by court process to perform a purely ministerial act, but to persist in the opinion, after 1952, that he cannot would seem to exalt the form of the *Youngstown Sheet & Tube Co.* case over its substance. Though the Court's order there went to the Secretary of Commerce, it was the direct order of President Truman that was reversed.

The Special Prosecutor has correctly noted that the Framers' intention to lodge the powers of government in separate bodies also included a plan for interaction between departments. A "watertight" division of different functions was never their design. The legislative branch may organize the judiciary and dictate the procedures by which it transacts business. The judiciary may pass upon the constitutionality of legislative enactments and in some instances define the bounds of Congressional investigations. The executive may veto legislative enactments, and the legislature may override the veto. The executive appoints judges and justices and may bind judicial decisions by lawful executive orders. The judiciary may pass on the constitutionality of executive acts.

While the Constitution diffuses power the better to secure liberty, it also contemplates that practice will integrate the dispersed powers into a workable government. It enjoins upon its branches separateness but interdependence, autonomy but reciprocity.

That the Court has not the physical power to enforce its order to the President is immaterial to a resolution of the issues. Regardless of its physical power to enforce them, the Court has a duty to issue appropriate orders. The Court cannot say that the Executive's persistence in withholding the tape recordings would "tarnish its reputation," but must admit that it would tarnish the Court's reputation to fail to do what it could in pursuit of justice. In any case, the courts have always enjoyed the good faith of the Executive Branch, even in such dire circumstances as those presented by *Youngstown Sheet & Tube Co. v. Sawyer*, 343 U.S. 579, and there is no reason to suppose that the courts in this instance cannot again rely on that same good faith. Indeed, the President himself has publicly so stated. . . .

In all candor, the Court fails to perceive any reason for suspending the power of courts to get evidence and rule on questions of privilege in criminal matters simply because it is the President of the United States who holds the evidence. The *Burr* decision left for another occasion a ruling on whether compulsory process might issue to the President in situations such as this. In the words of counsel, "this is a new question," with little in the way of precedent to guide the Court. But Chief Justice Marshall clearly distinguished the amenability of the King to appear and give testimony under court process and that of this nation's chief magistrate. The conclusion reached here cannot be inconsistent with the view of that great Chief Justice nor with the spirit of the Constitution.

In deciding whether these tape recordings or portions thereof are properly the objects of a privilege, the Court must accommodate two competing policies. On the one hand, as has been noted earlier, is the need to disfavor privileges and narrow their application as far as possible. On the other hand, lies a need to favor the privacy of Presidential deliberations; to indulge a presumption in favor of the President. To the Court, respect for the President, the Presidency, and the duties of the office, gives the advantage to this second policy. This respect, however, does not decide the controversy. Such a resolution on the Court's part, as Chief Justice Marshall observed, "would deserve some other appellation than the term respect." Nevertheless, it does not hurt for the courts to remind themselves often that the authority vested in them to delimit the scope and application of privileges, particularly the privileges and immunities of government, is a trust. And as with every trust, an abuse can reap the most dire consequences. This Court, then, enters upon its present task with care and with a determination to exercise the restraint that characterizes the conduct of courts. . . .

The point is raised that, as in *Reynolds*, the sworn statements of witnesses should suffice and remove the need for access to documents deemed privileged. Though this might often be the case, here, unfortunately, the witnesses differ, sometimes completely, on the precise matters likely to be of greatest moment to the grand jury. Ironically, need for the taped evidence derives in part from the fact that witnesses *have* testified regarding the subject matter, creating important issues of fact for the grand jury to resolve. It will be noted as well in contradistinction to *Reynolds*, that this is a criminal investigation. Rather than money damages at stake, we deal here in matters of reputation and liberty. Based on this indisputably forceful showing of necessity by the grand jury, the claim of privilege cannot be accepted lightly.

In his Brief in Support, the Special Prosecutor outlines the grand jury's view regarding the validity of the respondent's claim of privilege. Its opinion is that the right of confidentiality is improperly asserted here. Principally, the Special Prosecutor cites a substantial possibility, based on the sworn testimony of participants, that the privilege is improperly invoked as a cloak for serious criminal wrongdoing.

According to the testimony of John W. Dean, many of the conversations in which he participated were part and parcel of a criminal conspiracy to obstruct justice by preventing the truth from coming out about the additional participants in the original conspiracy to break into and wiretap the offices of the Democratic National Committee. He has testified that in the presence of H. R. Haldeman he told respondent on September 15, 1972, that "all [Dean] had been able to do was to contain the case and assist in keeping it out of the White House." Dean also told respondent that he "could make no assurances that the day would not come when this matter would start to unravel." Respondent allegedly congratulated him on the "good job" he was doing on that task. Dean also has testified that on March 13, 1973, respondent told him that respondent had approved executive clemency for Hunt and that there would be no problem in raising $1 million to buy the Watergate defendants' silence. In addition, there is uncontradicted testimony that respondent was briefed on Watergate on June 20, 1972, three days after the arrests, by Haldeman, Ehrlichman and Mitchell, his closest political advisors. If these three told respondent all they allegedly knew, respondent would have been aware of details of the nascent cover-up.

It is true, of course, that other testimony indicates that the conversations did not include direct evidence of criminal misconduct. While this is not the time or place to judge credibility, Dean's testimony cannot be dismissed out of hand. In fact, Haldeman has confirmed many of the details of the meetings at which both he and Dean were present. The opposite conclusions he draws are based upon a different interpretation and different recollection of some of the details.

If the interest served by a privilege is abused or subverted, the claim of privilege fails. Such a case is well described in *Clark v. United States*, 289 U.S. 1, a decision involving the privilege of secrecy enjoyed by jurors.

The privilege takes as its postulate a genuine relation, honestly created and honestly maintained. If that condition is not satisfied, if the relation is merely a sham and a pretense, the juror may not invoke a relation dishonestly assumed as a cover and cloak for the concealment of the truth.

With the aid of this analogy [to the attorney-client privilege] we recur to the social policies competing for supremacy. A privilege surviving until the relation is abused and vanishing when abuse is shown to the satisfaction of the judge has been found to be a workable technique for the protection of the confidences of client and attorney. Is there sufficient reason to believe that it will be found to be inadequate for the protection of a juror? No doubt the need is weighty that conduct in the jury room shall be untrammeled by the fear of embarrassing publicity. The need is no less weighty that it shall be pure and undefiled. A juror of integrity and reasonable firmness will not fear to speak his mind if the confidences of debate are barred to the ears of mere impertinence or malice. He will not expect to be shielded against the disclosure of his conduct in the event that there is evidence reflecting upon his honor.

These principles are, of course, fully applicable throughout government. A court would expect that if the privacy of its deliberations, for example, were ever used to foster criminal conduct or to develop evidence of criminal wrongdoing, any privilege might be barred and privacy breached. So it is that evidentiary privileges asserted against the grand jury may be ruled inapplicable if the interest served by the privilege is subverted.

Nevertheless, without discrediting the strength of the grand jury's position, the Court cannot, as matters now stand, rule that the present claim of privilege is invalid. The President contends that the recorded conversations occurred pursuant to an exercise of his duty to "take care that the laws be faithfully executed." Although the Court is not bound by that conclusion, it is extremely reluctant to finally stand against a declaration of the President of the United States on any but the strongest possible evidence. Need for the evidence requires that a claim not be accepted lightly, but the vitality of Presidential deliberations in like manner requires that the claim not be rejected lightly. The Court is simply unable to decide the question of privilege without inspecting the tapes.

It is true that if material produced is properly the subject of privilege, even an inspection *in camera* may constitute a compromise of privilege. Nevertheless, it would be an extremely limited infraction and in this case an unavoidable one. If privileged and unprivileged evidence are intermingled, privileged portions may be excised so that only unprivileged matter goes before the grand jury (which also meets in secret proceedings). If privileged and unprivileged evidence are so inextricably connected that separation becomes impossible, the whole must be privileged and no disclosure made to the grand jury. . . .

The Court is unable to design a more cautious approach consistent with both the demonstrated critical need for the evidence and the serious questions raised concerning the applicability of the privilege asserted. The Court has attempted to walk the middle ground between a failure to decide the question of privilege at one extreme, and a wholesale delivery of tapes to the grand jury at the other. The one would be a breach of duty; the other an inexcusable course of conduct. The approach comports with precedent in this district, and honors the injunction of *Reynolds* and *Burr* to pursue fairness and protect essential privacy.

To paraphrase Chief Justice Marshall, if it be apparent that the tapes are irrelevant to the investigation, or that for state reasons they cannot be introduced into the case, the subpoena *duces tecum* would be useless. But if this be not apparent, if they *may* be important in the investigation, if they *may* be safely heard by the grand jury, if only in part, would it not be a blot on the page which records the judicial proceedings of this country, if, in a case of such serious import as this, the Court did not at least call for an inspection of the evidence in chambers?

79.

Edwin J. Holman: Self-Governing the Medical Profession

In 1972 Congress passed a Social Security measure to which was appended an amendment intended to set up a system for monitoring the competence of physicians. The amendment called for the creation of groups of doctors who would collectively review the work of colleagues to assure its professional quality. Specifically, the setting up of professional standards would determine adequacy of diagnosis and treatment and whether hospitalization was always needed when ordered. The purpose of the legislation was to exert some control over rapidly increasing costs of federal health programs. In December 1973 a convention of the American Medical Association voted to oppose this new monitoring system and to work to change it. In an article published originally in the Federation Bulletin *of the Federation of State Medical Boards, Edwin J. Holman of the office of general counsel for the AMA discussed the importance of self-governance in the medical profession if such controls as the 1972 law invoked were to be avoided. An abstract of his article appeared in the AMA* Journal.

Source: *Journal of the American Medical Association*, October 29, 1973: "Hard Cases Make Bad Law."

Medicine is largely self-governed. This is so because the public, the citizens of the state, have permitted it. Professional self-government does not result from natural or constitutional right. It is a privilege. Society believes it lacks the knowledge and expertise needed to review the quality of professional service or to evaluate professional judgments. But beliefs can and do change. The public can be stampeded into believing (1) its rights are being impinged upon (2) medicine isn't policing its own ranks (3) the privilege of self-government should be restricted or curtailed, or (4) the public should participate with the profession in administering self-government.

Medical societies appear to have been reluctant to tackle tough problems relating to questionable actions by their members. It is amazing how many excuses can be found for not conducting an investigation or for not taking action. One common excuse is that if the medical society becomes involved it will be sued, Another is that "a matter of judgment is involved and one cannot fault judgmental decisions of a fellow physician."

Neither excuse is more than that—it is merely an excuse. The profession must not rely on excuses.

If discipline is necessary, it should be adminstered. If it is properly administered, no claim or suit at law will prevail against the disciplining body. If cost of defense deters a medical society, that society should ask itself how valid it is for a patient to defer surgery because it costs money.

Patient's judgment in deferring surgery because of cost is patently wrong. Life cannot be measured in money. Neither can integrity. A physician's judgment in proceeding without consent, or in advertising to the public, may be patently wrong. Physicians need advice, help, and counsel. If judgments, in medical practice, may not be questioned, then self-government is not needed.

In the legal profession there is a saying that hard cases make bad law. This hip-pocket maxim can be applied to medicine. When cases of alleged unethical conduct are not handled within the profession and are "exposed" to the public as not handled, the ends of justice are overshadowed by the dictates of expediency and pragmatism. Hard law results. Public reaction is measured by the same degree of hardness. Reaction, overreaction, backlash—bad law is inevitable.

State medical board members are physicians. They are members of medical societies, and they are as much affected by disciplinary inertia as any other physician.

Furthermore, bad law applicable to medical society organization, management, or government will be a clear precedent for the application of the same bad law to the activities of the state board, especially when disciplinary inertia can be attributed to it as well as to medical societies.

Medical society discipline or its absence is directly related to the law. To the extent that medical society discipline is observed (and demonstrated to the public as being viable), restrictive judicial and statutory regulations will be avoided. With each example, feeling builds up, and it may manifest itself unexpectedly as the result of some trivial episode. Indeed, the warning "hard cases make bad law" is timely.

Medical societies alone and medical societies in concert with boards of medical examiners have two responsibilities today in medical discipline: (1) they must impose discipline when it is reasonably called for and (2) they must publicize their actions so the faith of the public may be restored.

The whole point of Nader—so obvious that it is often overlooked—is his single-minded dedication to making the free enterprise system work as it's supposed to—to make marketplace realities of the very virtues that businessmen ascribe to the system.

EDWARD B. RUST, President of the Chamber of Commerce of the United States, September 18, 1973

80.

RALPH NADER: The New Violence

Bess Myerson, when New York City commissioner of consumer affairs, remarked: "Mr. Nader is a remarkable man who, in the last six years, has done more as a private citizen for our country and its people than most public officials do in a lifetime." Nader, who in fact describes himself as a "public citizen," has considerably broadened the scope of his activities from his early consumer advocacy to include most of the areas of public policy with which Americans are concerned. As a lobbyist in behalf of the public, he and his co-workers have tackled a large array of private interests in testimony before Congressional committees and in countless public appearances around the country. Among the many topics he has become involved with since the early concern over auto safety have been: environmental pollution, industrial safety, the Alaska oil pipeline, the rights of American Indians, the legal professions, public responsibility, secrecy in government, the drug companies, and the food industry. The statements by Mr. Nader that comprise this selection were made to journalist Thomas Whiteside and were included in a lengthy profile of Nader in the New Yorker.

Source: *New Yorker*, October 15, 1973: "Profiles: A Countervailing Force."

"WHAT WE MUST GET ACROSS to people is that endemic forms of violence are going on daily in this country on a scale that completely dwarfs the common concept of violence as meaning primarily crimes in the street." "Air pollution alone is a devastating form of violence. It takes far more lives and maims far more victims each year than street crime, and destroys more property each year than all the bank robbers' hauls a thousand times over. According to government figures, bank robbers have gotten away with more than twenty million dollars a year in recent years—their biggest ever—but the cost of air pollution alone in one recent year ran to more than sixteen billion dollars." "The new forms of violence don't draw attention to themselves by attacking pain thresholds on contact or causing bleeding at the outset." "Their effects show up years after the initial exposure, in the statistics on lung cancer, emphysema, genetic damage, and so on."

"The problem is that our mutations occur at glacial speed and the changes in our man-made environment occur at supersonic speed." "We have to face up to the fact that we are becoming biologically obsolete, in that our senses can't smell radiation or detect these environmental damages to health and safety. The complexity and seriousness of the impact that pollutants and contaminants have on us seem to escape people's sensory abilities to comprehend. They don't respond in any active fashion. The threats that people do tend to respond to are mostly of the immediate, physical kind. People don't react to the concept of infiltration,

Ralph Nader testifying before the House-Senate Economic Subcommittee

and infiltration is an essential process of the corporate system. Industry infiltrates the whole person of the citizen. It invades his privacy as an individual. It infiltrates the bodies of millions of people in this country with its contaminants. Its violence is all-pervasive, whatever its various motivations may be."

"The fact is that those who define what is permissible and impermissible violence in our society have been responsible for committing a very large part of it. This perhaps explains why so much of the industrially caused violence that is taking place either is excluded from the embrace of the law or has had forged about it a protective system whereby the law has virtually no application. The law has to be made to develop definitions of violence that correspond to the conditions we face. In terms of the violence it is currently committing, industry is largely beyond the law. One problem is that the law in this country has not developed in such a way as to require positive duties of citizens. The law has developed to punish certain positive acts, not certain kinds of inaction. As matters stand, institutions are structured in such a way that corporations can achieve their economic objectives by inaction—for example, by reducing their costs through *not* taking steps to reduce the pollution they create. And by the same inaction they escape the law. When you couple this deficiency of the law with the new style of violence that doesn't provoke an image of a criminal act, such as a common street crime, you have a combination of the power to devastate increasingly large sections of humanity and a decreasing degree of personal accountability. That is a prescription for social suicide. The president of a chemical company knows that no matter what his company does *he* won't go to jail, as long as he *personally* does not act, or instruct his subordinates to act, in violation of the law. Our law is basically a legacy of ancient ethics in which A can harm B only by positive action against him. But increasingly, as people have become members of large organizations —for example, of the corporations that make up the automobile industry—they have arrived at a position of being able to harm people more by doing nothing."

"If you were to send ten pickpockets to New York and each of them were to do fifty jobs a day, that would, I suppose, make front-page news. But set up a system of acquisition that is derivative and obscure, like the oil-depletion allowance or the oil-import quotas, and nobody pays much attention. You can get away with it on that scale. That's the genius of the corporate system—the genius of being able to achieve the same thievery three stages removed. The genius of developing an abstraction of burglary! Again, I think we're very limited by our biological parameters; that is, we tend to react principally to biologically proximate stimuli—to see, smell, taste, feel the immediate physical blow. People tend to envision physical threats in human form. But the corporation is the antithesis of anthropomorphism. People don't know who is heading the biggest corporations in the country. They may be able to name senators enough. But the chairmen of the boards of the top four companies in the country? The machinery capable of making the names of these corporate executives universally known is there, but, as a rule, the system is directed toward the cultivation of anonymity and abstraction and physical detachment. In New York City, there are far more people angry about cabdrivers than people disturbed by the combined depredations of all the banks and finance companies in the city. 'Oh, those cheating cabdrivers!' they keep saying. But the cabdriver knows a thing or two about corporate life. He listens to those corporate executives in the back of his cab. He gets some idea of how the big boys are stealing millions. And he tells himself that if *they're* stealing millions, *he* might as well get *his* share. That's one reason New York is in an advanced stage of decomposition: the victims are becoming corrupted. And when the victims become corrupted, that's the beginning of the end. As long as the victims remain innocent, you can clean out the perpetrators, but when the victims themselves become corrupted—as in so many of the unions, for example —the perpetrators are secure. Again, that's the incredible flexible genius of the corporate system. It is not completely tyrannical. It allows the lowest levels to share a few of the crumbs in order to get the biggest possible share of the pie for itself. That's how labor has been taken over by industry. Big unions have become superb administrative devices for corporations. The corporations would rather deal with one person who is in a position to deliver, say, sixteen locals and sixteen thousand workers—and the union leadership, as part of the return for what it gets, keeps its focus narrow and doesn't trouble companies with complaints about the corruption of the political process or about the perpetration of consumer fraud. As for the union membership, can the workers in this country be aroused to spend just half as much time doing something about corruption, job hazards, or property taxes as they spend watching baseball and football on TV? There's plenty wrong with the people, and there isn't a politician around with the guts to say so. Nothing is going to work properly in this society unless there is a maximizing of those systems that give power to the victims. But it's necessary to let people know that the fact of their victimization doesn't mean that standards of performance aren't going to apply to them, too."

81.

The Resignation of Spiro T. Agnew

Vice-President Agnew announced on August 6, 1973, that he was under investigation by the U.S. Attorney for Maryland for possible law violations concerning kickbacks taken from contractors, engineers, and architects on state projects, while he was Baltimore County Executive and Governor of Maryland. Agnew asserted that he was "innocent of any wrongdoing" and expressed confidence that "my innocence will be affirmed." For the next two months, amid a flurry of news leaks to the press and much uncertainty about how serious the charges against him were, The Vice-President consistently maintained his innocence. But as the weeks went by and leaked allegations of wrongdoing became stronger, speculation arose that he would either resign or be impeached. For a time, in fact, the issue was raised whether an incumbent Vice-President could be indicted by any court without first being impeached. On September 25 Agnew wrote to Speaker Carl Albert asking the House of Representatives to begin a full inquiry into the allegations against him, but Albert decided against taking any action on the request, saying that matters were before the courts. Meanwhile, as the Justice Department contended that the evidence against Agnew was overwhelming, talks began between his lawyers, White House officials, and Justice Department lawyers to effect a settlement. The plea bargaining went on for about two weeks, and the final agreement came by the second week of October. On October 10 the Vice-President resigned and on the same day pleaded "nolo contendere"—no contest—to one charge of income tax evasion in a federal court in Baltimore. This plea was tantamount to an admission of guilt; by making it he avoided being charged with bribery, fraud, and conspiracy. The Justice Department dropped all pending charges, and Agnew was fined $10,000 and placed on three years' probation. As a condition of his plea and resignation the Justice Department released a 40-page exposition of the evidence against him. On October 12 President Nixon nominated House minority leader Gerald R. Ford to be the new Vice-President. The following selection consists of several documents relating to the resignation of the Vice-President: an exchange of letters between Agnew and President Nixon on October 10, Attorney General Elliot L. Richardson's statement in federal court, and the court statements of Mr. Agnew and Judge Walter E. Hoffman.

Exchange of Letters Between Vice-President Agnew and President Nixon

October 10, 1973

Dear Mr. President:

As you are aware, the accusations against me cannot be resolved without a long, divisive and debilitating struggle in the Congress and in the courts. I have concluded that, painful as it is to me and to my family, it is in the best interests of the nation that I relinquish the Vice-Presidency.

Accordingly, I have today resigned the office of Vice-President of the United States. A copy of the instrument of resignation is enclosed.

It has been a privilege to serve with you. May I express to the American people, through you, my deep gratitude for their confidence in twice electing me to Vice-President.

Sincerely,
Spiro T. Agnew

October 10, 1973

Dear Ted:

The most difficult decisions are often those that are the most personal, and I know your decision to resign as Vice-President has been as difficult as any facing a man in public life could be. Your departure from the Administration leaves me with a great sense of personal loss. You have been a valued associate throughout these nearly five years that we have served together. However, I respect your decision, and I also respect the concern for the national interest that led you to conclude that a resolution of the matter in this way, rather than through an extended battle in the courts and the Congress, was advisable in order to prevent a protracted period of national division and uncertainty.

As Vice-President, you have addressed the great issues of our times with courage and candor. Your strong patriotism, and your profound dedication to the welfare of the nation, have been an inspiration to all who have served with you as well as to millions of others throughout the country.

I have been deeply saddened by this whole course of events, and I hope that you and your family will be sustained in the days ahead by a well-justified pride in all that you have contributed to the nation by your years of service as Vice-President.

Sincerely,
Richard Nixon

Attorney General Richardson's Statement in Court

MAY IT PLEASE THE COURT, I am, like every other participant in these proceedings, deeply conscious of the critical national interests which surround them. The agreement between the parties now before the court is one which must be just and honorable, and which must be perceived to be just and honorable, not simply to the parties but above all to the American people.

From the outset of the negotiations which have culminated in these proceedings, the Department of Justice has regarded as an integral requirement of any agreement a full disclosure of the surrounding circumstances, for only with knowledge of these circumstances can the American people fairly judge the justice of the outcome. One critical component of these circumstances is the Government's evidence. In accordance, therefore, with the agreement of counsel, I offer for the permanent record of these proceedings an exposition of the evidence accumulated by the investigation against the defendant conducted by the office of the United States Attorney for the District of Maryland as of October 10, 1973. Because this exposition is complete and detailed, it is sufficient for present purposes simply to state that this evidence establishes a pattern of substantial cash payments to the defendant during the period when he served as Governor of Maryland in return for engineering contracts with the State of Maryland. Payments by the principal in one large engineering firm began while the defendant was County Executive of Baltimore County in the early nineteen sixties and continued into 1971. The evidence also discloses payments by another engineer up to and including December, 1972.

None of the Government's major witnesses has been promised immunity from prosecution, and each of the witnesses who would testify to having made direct payments to the Vice-President has signed a sworn statement subject to the penalties of perjury.

In the light of the serious wrongdoing shown by its evidence, the Government might have insisted, if permitted by the court to do so, on pressing forward with the return of an indictment charging bribery and extortion. To have done this, however, would have been likely to inflict upon the nation serious and permanent scars. If would have been the defendant's right to put the prosecution to its proof. The Department of Justice had conceded the power of Congress, once an indictment had been returned, to proceed by impeachment. The Congress could well have elected to exercise this constitutional power. If the Congress chose not to act, the defendant could, while retaining office, either have insisted upon his right to a trial by jury or have continued to contest the right of the Government to try an incumbent Vice-President. Whichever of these courses were followed would have consumed not simply months but years—with potentially disastrous consequences, to vital interests of the United States. Confidence in the adequacy of our fundamental institutions would itself have been put to severe trial. It is unthinkable that this nation should have been required to endure the anguish and uncertainty of a prolonged period in which the man next in line of succession to the Presidency was fighting the charges brought against him by his own Government.

On the basis of these considerations, I am satisfied that the public interest is better served by this Court's acceptance of the defendant's plea of nolo contendere to a single count: Information charging income tax evasion.

There remains the question of the Government's position toward the sentence to be imposed. One possible course would have been to avoid this difficult and painful issue by declining to make an affirmative recommendation. It became apparent, however, in the course of the negotiations that without such a recommendation no agreement could be achieved. No agreement could have been achieved, moreover, if that recommendation did not include an appeal for leniency.

I am firmly convinced that in all the circumstances leniency is justified. I am keenly aware, first, of the historic magnitude of the penalties inherent in the Vice-President's resignation from his high office and his acceptance of a judgment of conviction for a felony. To propose that a man who has suffered these penalties should, in addition, be incarcerated in a penal institution, however briefly, is more than I, as head of the Government's prosecuting arm, can recommend or wish.

Also deserving of consideration is the public service rendered by the defendant during more than four and one-half years as the nation's second highest elected official. He has been an effective spokesman for the executive branch in the councils of state and local government. He has knowledgeably and articulately represented the United States in meetings with the hads of other governments. He has participated actively and constructively in the deliberations of the Government in a diverse range of fields.

Out of compassion for the man, out of respect for the office he has held, and out of appreciation for the fact that by his resignation he has spared the nation the prolonged agony that would have attended upon his trial, I urge that the sentence imposed on the defendant by this court not include confinement.

Mr. Agnew's Statement in Court

MY DECISION TO RESIGN and enter a plea of nolo contendere rests on my firm belief that the public interest requires swift disposition of the problems which are facing me. I am advised that a full legal defense of the probable charges against me could consume several years. I am concerned that intense media interest in the case would district public attention from important national problems—to the country's detriment.

I am aware that witnesses are prepared to testify that I and my agents received payments from consulting engineers doing business with the State of Maryland during the period I was Governor. With the exception of the admission that follows, I deny the assertions of illegal acts on my part made by the Government witnesses.

I admit that I did receive payments during the year 1967 which were not expended for political purposes and that, therefore, these payments were income taxable to me in that year and that I so knew. I further acknowledge that contracts were awarded by state agencies in 1967 and other years to those who made such payments, and that I was aware of such awards. I am aware that Government witnesses are prepared to testify that preferential treatment was accorded to the paying companies pursuant to an understanding with me when I was the Governor. I stress, however, that no contracts were awarded to contractors who were not competent to perform the work and in most instances state contracts were awarded without any arrangement for the payment of money by the contractor. I deny that the payments in any way influenced my official actions. I am confident, moreover, that testimony presented in my behalf would make it clear that I at no time conducted my official duties as County Executive or Governor of Maryland in a manner harmful to the interests of the county or state, or my duties as Vice-President of the United States in a manner harmful to the nation, and, further assert that my acceptance of contributions was part of a long-established pattern of political fund-raising in the state. At no time have I enriched myself at the expense of the public trust.

In all the circumstances, I have concluded that protracted proceedings before the Grand Jury, the Congress and the courts, with the speculation and controversy surrounding them, would seriously prejudice the national interest.

These, briefly stated, are the reasons I am entering a plea of nolo contendere to the charge that I did receive payments in 1967 which I failed to report for the purposes of income taxation.

Judge Walter E. Hoffman's Ruling

FOR THE PAST TWO DAYS counsel for the defendant and the representatives of the Department of Justice have engaged in what is known as "plea bargaining," a practice which has received the judicial approval of the Supreme Court of the United States. As the judge of the court, I have refrained from making any recommendation to the parties involved as I was unaware of the facts involving the alleged charges. The agreement finally reached between the parties, and which has been fully set forth by Mr. Topkis, one of the attorneys for the defendant, and Mr. Richardson, the distinguished Attorney General of the United States, was the result of some relinquishment of rights on both sides. We are all aware of the fact that some persons will criticize the result and the sentence to be imposed but, in a case such as this, it would be impossible to satisfy everyone.

Once the agreement was reached between the parties, it had to be submitted to the judge for his approval or disapproval. It was late yesterday afternoon when I learned the final details of the negotiations. I insisted that all details would have to be submitted in open court and in the presence of the defendant before any formal approval or disapproval could be given. Such has now been accomplished and it becomes my duty to proceed.

The judge must accept the final responsibility as to any sentence, but this does not mean that he should disregard the negotiations and advices of the parties who are far more familiar with the facts, the national interest, and the consequences flowing from any sentence to be imposed.

As far as the court is involved, the defendant is on trial for willful evasion of income taxes for the calendar year 1967, which charge is a felony in the eyes of the law. He has entered a plea of nolo contendere which, so far as this criminal prosecution is concerned, is the full equivalent of a plea of guilty. Such a plea frequently is accepted in income tax evasion cases as there are generally civil consequences flowing therefrom and the criminal court is not interested in the precise amount of taxes which may be due. The plea of nolo contendere merely permits the parties to further litigate the amount due without regard to the conviction following such a plea.

A detailed statement has been filed by the Department of Justice and refuted by the defendant, all of which are wholly unrelated to the charge of income tax evasion. These statements are the part of the understanding between the parties and are submitted merely because of the charges and countercharges which have received so much advance publicity. Of course, the agreement further provides that the Federal Government will take no further action against the defendant as to any Federal criminal charge which had its inception prior to today, reserving the right to proceed against him in any appropriate civil action for moneys allegedly due. Furthermore, neither this Court nor the Department of Justice can limit the right of any state or organization to take action against the defendant. Since the Department of Justice, pursuant to its agreement, will be barred from prosecuting the defendant as to any criminal charge heretofore existing, the truth of these charges and countercharges can never be established by any judicial decision or action. It would have been my preference to omit these statements and end the verbal warfare as to this tragic event in history, but I am not inclined to reject the agreement for this reason alone.

There is a fundamental rule of law that every person accused of a crime is presumed to be innocent until such time as the guilt is established beyond a reasonable doubt. It is for this reason that I must disregard, for the purpose of imposing sentence, the charges, countercharges and denials which do not pertain to the single count of income tax evasion. I have so advised counsel for the parties and they are in agreement that this is my duty.

We come then to the charge of income tax evasion which, as I stated, is a felony and a most serious charge in itself. In approving the plea agreement between the parties, I have not overlooked my prior writings and sentences in other income tax cases. Generally speaking, where the defendant is a lawyer, a tax accountant, or a business executive, I resort to the practice of imposing a fine and a term of imprisonment, but provide that the actual period of confinement be limited to a period of from two to five months, with the defendant being placed on probation for the balance of the term. The reason for taking such action is that our method of filing income tax returns is fundamentally based upon the honor of the individual reporting his income, and a sentence of actual confinement serves as a deterrent to others who are required to file their returns.

But for the strong recommendation of the Attorney General in this case, I would be inclined to follow the same procedure. However, I am persuaded that the national interests in the present case are so great and so compelling—all as described by the chief law enforcement officer of the United States—that the ends of justice would be better served by making an exception to the general rule.

I, therefore, approve the plead agreement between the parties.

82.

MORT WEISINGER: The Biggest Business in America

"Law and order" proved a popular campaign theme and a prominent social issue for much of the 1960s and early 1970s, as the media made citizens more aware of "crime in the streets" and reported increasing rates of violent crimes such as murder, rape, assault, robbery, and arson. While the relative visibility of such crimes made them newsworthy, most crime—especially the most rewarding kind—is not in the streets. It is, rather, what has been called "white collar crime," or business-related thievery, such as embezzlement, dealing in stolen securities, extortion, tax fraud, bribery, or outright stealing of gooods or money. The selection reprinted here, in part, deals with one aspect of white collar crime: employee thievery. Since the real costs of such crime to the nation are only estimates, it may be an exaggeration to call it the biggest business in the country, but it certainly ranks among the biggest.

Source: *Parade*, December 9, 1973: Mort Weisinger, "$10 Billion a Year Employee Thievery Is Big Business."

THE BIGGEST BUSINESS in America today is not included in *Fortune* magazine's annual list of the 500 top corporations. It is the business of crime committed by the nation's work force, and it is costing U.S. companies an estimated $10 billion a year. That's more than nationwide street robberies and burglary losses combined.

According to business security experts, 70 percent of employees occasionally steal. Of this vast army, about half are the petty pilferers—the garage mechanic who pockets a spark plug; the typist who lifts a box of paper clips; the mailroom clerk who slips some personal letters through the meter machine. Although this type of miniswipery is comparable to a worker who sneaks a fistful of toothpicks out of a lumber mill, it all adds up, because the practice is so widespread.

Another hefty percentage are resident thieves who steal independently on a regular basis in department stores, supermarkets, factories, shopping centers, hotels, warehouses, hospitals and office buildings. They range from the blue-collar worker to the blue-chip executive who pads his expense account.

The lone-wolfers include the salesman who walks out of the store wearing an expensive pair of Gucci shoes after dropping his old ones in a trash can; the meat-packer who goes home with a steak tucked in the folded newspaper under his arm; the office chief who makes personal long-distance phone calls; the head of the mailroom in a gift shop who sends out merchandise addressed to himself, relatives and friends. If you're in the right spot, crime is a cinch.

But the thief who really hurts is the one worker in 12 who conducts the well-organized, systematic ripoff.

They comprise the purchasing agent who takes kickbacks, the paymaster who juggles the timecards and then credits some employees' paychecks with overtime that they split with him.

The women in a garment factory who smuggle out parts of dresses—sleeves, skirts and blouses, whatever parts they happen to be working on—in their handbags. They meet outside, swap pieces, and go home to stitch together a complete dress. They call it a buddy system. These workers don't feel they're stealing from their boss; they feel as if they're stealing from a row of machines.

The clerk at the supermarket checkout counter who rings up only every other item when a relative or friend passes through with a shopping cart.

The ring of employees in an appliance wholesale firm who conspire with the truck driver assigned to deliver deep freezers to retail outlets. All the freezers are filled with TV sets, toasters, typewriters and vacuum cleaners and then dropped off with the crooked owner of a service station, where the driver gasses up the truck.

Today, the retail industry is aghast at the fact that internal thievery is outstripping shoplifting. Recently, Norman Jaspan, president of a prominent management consulting firm, said at an executive seminar in New Orleans:

> Employee dishonesty has reached an all-time high, and there is a better than 50 percent chance of sizable dishonesty in any firm.

Reports Deputy Inspector Adam Butcher of New York City's Crime Prevention Squad: "At least 1000 retail businesses go bankrupt every year because of employee theft. In many cases, a store will lose more than twice as much of its inventory to dishonest employees as to shoplifters and burglars."

To combat this national plague of stealing by internal personnel, employers are increasingly enlisting the aid of such crime-prevention agencies as Pinkerton, Holmes Protection, Burns International Security Service, and Guardsmark. Here are just a couple of case histories from their files, made available to *Parade.* To avoid embarrassing their clients, names have been omitted.

—A jewelry shop's employees were stealing watches, rings and bracelets by taping them around their thighs. The thefts were ended by having the store attach price tags made of a specially treated material to each object. When the culprit went through the door of the shop, the tag activated an electronic scanning device which set off a secret alarm in a remote corner.

—A Texas general store discovered

that clerks came to work wearing wide cowboy boots. They would shove half-pint bottles of liquor inside the boots, two to each leg, walk out, stash the bottles in their car, and repeat the process a few times a day. To end this "bootlegging," the investigator suggested a ring of closed-circuit TV monitors be set up. But the manager balked at the prohibitive cost.

"Then make the TV sets dummies," the investigator recommended. "It's all psychological, anyway. You've got to make your employees think they're being watched." The manager agreed and installed a highly visible battery of fake cameras that not only stopped the liquor looting but cut down on shoplifting as well.

To infiltrate zones in factories, warehouses, supermarkets, department stores and offices where internal thefts are prevalent, security agencies make use of specially qualified undercover men and women who will impersonate mechanics, computer operators, electricians, and bookkeepers. "Recently, to crack a major case, we had to plant a graduate engineer on the scene," said Henry C. Neville, Pinkerton's vice-president in charge of investigation.

Ira A. Lipman, president of Guardsmark, Inc., has a knack for selecting investigators least likely of being suspected as spotters when they fraternize with workers.

A special cadre of his watchdogs includes a six-foot-seven ex-basketball player, a Marine veteran with a prosthetic hand, an egg-bald operative with a ferocious walrus mustache, and even a pair of identical twins. "So conspicuous are the physical features of these men, it quashes employees' suspicions that they might be surveillance agents," Lipman explains. "I'd hire a midget or a tattooed man of the circus," he says, "if they could help me bust a case."

According to Jerry DeRoma Jr., vice-president of Holmes Protection, Inc., pre-employment screening has become a standard procedure among security agencies. "This may involve more than a scrupulous check of the applicant's references," he says. "If a man is to be hired for a position where opportunity for theft exists, he may be required to submit to voluntary fingerprinting and lie detector tests, as permitted by unions and in certain provisions of the law. This is the ounce of crime-prevention that's really worth a ton. And we've found that honest job-seekers are happy to cooperate."

A vital phase of Pinkerton's program to discourage inside thievery calls for management to give informal briefings to new employees as to the company's security measures. These range from pocketless smocks and denims to wear on the job in plants which manufacture such small items as cigarette lighters and pocket computers; surveillance by undercover men; sophisticated electronic equipment. "And never think that your fellow workers won't squeal if they see you stealing," they are told. "They send us anonymous letters."

Given this orientation, few workers fail to get the "we-never-sleep" message.

Lipman says that most workers who steal do so because opportunity beckons, and because they "think it's coming to them. They feel they're being underpaid, so they'll just take something to even the score.

"When you caught thieves in earlier, less permissive times, they were scared. They felt guilty. They cried, offered to make restitution, and repented. Today, they're brazen. They think if they're caught—so what? Their cases won't be tried for probably two years, because we don't have enough judges. And when they finally do go to court, they're more likely to get a slap on the wrist, a fine, a suspended sentence, rather than a jail term.

"The climate of the country is so corrupt today that many employers will refuse to fire a man when he's caught stealing—if the theft isn't enormous. The attitude is: 'Hell, this man is trained and he'd be hard to replace.' "

Pinkerton's Henry C. Neville takes a harder line, however. "We urge that the employer prosecute the dishonest employee. Our experience shows that most unpunished employees sooner or later repeat their crimes. But we are compassionate and will make exceptions when we are convinced that the guilty man has a strong chance of being rehabilitated."

83.

Nairobi Draft on Monetary Reform

The International Monetary Fund was constituted in 1946 according to articles of agreement signed at Bretton Woods, New Hampshire, in July 1944. The purpose of the IMF was to stabilize exchange rates by assisting member nations to overcome difficulties with their balances of payments. Convertibility of currencies was based on either gold or the U.S. dollar. In August 1971 the Bretton Woods system collapsed when President Nixon suspended the convertibility of the dollar into gold and allowed the dollar to float in relation to other currency values. Subsequent devaluation of the dollar in relation to European and Japanese currencies helped to reverse the enormous trade deficits the U.S. had incurred in the early 1970s, but there was no longer any international monetary policy. In September 1973, 120 members of the IMF met at Nairobi, Kenya, to deal with the unresolved problems of convertibility and the flexibility of exchange rates. On September 25 a draft for monetary reform, reprinted here, set forth some agreement on general principles and established a deadline of July 31, 1974, for reaching a new monetary agreement.

Source: *IMF Survey*, Annual Meetings Issue, October 8, 1973, Issue Supplement: "First Outline of Reform."

FIRST OUTLINE OF REFORM

Introduction

1. It is generally agreed that there is need for a reformed world monetary order, based on cooperation and consultation within the framework of a strengthened International Monetary Fund, that will encourage the growth of world trade and employment, promote economic development, and help to avoid both inflation and deflation. The main features of the international monetary reform should include:

(a) an effective and symmetrical adjustment process, including better functioning of the exchange rate mechanism, with the exchange rate regime based on stable but adjustable par values and floating rates recognized as providing a useful technique in particular situations;

(b) cooperation in dealing with disequilibrating capital flows;

(c) the introduction of an appropriate degree and form of convertibility for the settlement of imbalances, with symmetrical obligations on all countries;

(d) better international management of global liquidity, with the SDR becoming the principal reserve asset and the role of gold and of reserve currencies being reduced;

(e) consistency between arrangements for adjustment, convertibility, and global liquidity;

(f) the promotion of the flow of real resources to developing countries.

2. It is recognized that the attainment of the purposes of the reform depends also upon arrangements for international trade, capital, investment, and development assistance including the access of developing countries to markets in developed countries; and it is agreed that the principles which govern the international monetary reform and arrangements in these related areas must be consistent.

Adjustment

3. There shall be a better working of the adjustment process in which adequate methods to assure timely and effective balance of payments adjustment by both surplus and deficit countries will be assisted by improved international consultation in the Fund, including the use of objective indicators. Countries will take such prompt and adequate adjustment action, domestic or external, as may be needed to avoid protracted payments imbalances. Countries should direct their policies to keeping their official reserves within limits which would be internationally agreed from time to time in the Fund and which would be consistent with the volume of global liquidity. For this purpose a reserve indicator structure should be established, subject to a more detailed study of the operational provisions involved. In choosing among different forms of adjustment action, countries should take into account repercussions on other countries as well as internal considerations.

4. In connection with adjustment it is envisaged that the Fund will introduce new procedures, involving special meetings, at regular intervals, of a Fund consultative body at an appropriate level ("the consultative body"). It has been suggested that the consultative body might be the resident Executive Board or, alternatively, a body to which constituencies could or would send representatives from capitals. In these special meetings:

(a) the world payments situation would be surveyed in relation both to the general working of the adjustment process and to developments affecting global liquidity. These surveys would allow for periodic consideration of balance of payments aims and for a review of the aggregate flow of real resources to developing countries and its financing; and

(b) particular cases of imbalance that individually or collectively have significant international repercussions, as determined by criteria to be established, would be examined.

5. A country would become subject to examination under paragraph 4(b) if either:

(a) there had been a disproportionate movement in its official reserves; or

(b) in the judgment of the Managing Director, following informal soundings among Executive Directors, there was prima facie evidence that the country was facing significant imbalance, even though this was not indicated by a disproportionate movement in the country's official reserves.

6. In the process of examination under paragraph 4(b), representatives of the country examined would be expected to comment on the country's economic prospects, including particularly its basic balance of payments position and prospects, on its external objectives, and on what domestic or external action, if any, it had taken or intended to take. An assessment by the consultative body would establish whether there was a need for adjustment. In making this assessment, the consultative body would take account of all relevant considerations, including the factors mentioned above; it would examine the consistency of the country's reserve and current account aims and policies with those of other countries, and would attach major importance to disproportionate movements of reserves. Account would be taken of the special characteristics of developing countries that make it difficult for them to achieve prompt adjustment without seriously damaging their long-term development programs. Following an assessment the consultative body would, where appropriate, call upon the country concerned to adopt or reinforce policies to correct its imbalance. A country in choosing between different forms of policy should take account of views expressed in the course of the examination on the form and size of policy action.

7. The Fund will continue to hold annual consultations with member countries. In the course of these consultations the Fund would, inter alia, assess the country's payments performance on the same basis as in paragraph 6 and taking into account all the factors mentioned there, and would, where appropriate, call upon the country concerned to adopt or reinforce policies to correct its imbalance if it had not been so called upon in a preceding special meeting.

8. It is agreed that in the revised adjustment procedures, as also in relation to convertibility, separate arrangements will need to be made for a limited number of countries with large reserves deriving from depletable resources and with small populations, e.g., certain oil-producing countries.

Pressures

9. Provision will be made for graduated pressures to be applied to both surplus and deficit countries in cases of large and persistent imbalance. Proposals have been made for both financial pressures and other pressures. Further study will be needed of these proposals. In particular, it is not agreed how financial pressures should be activated and whether or not there should be other pressures as described in paragraph 11.

10. It has been suggested that pressures would start with financial pressures of a mild form, such as penalty rates of interest on net creditor or net debtor positions in the Fund. A more severe financial pressure which has been suggested is that, if a country's reserves rise to a predetermined point, that country would lose the right to convert further accruals of currency balances, and would be required to deposit such further accruals with the Fund at progressively increasing negative interest rates. There will be further consideration of these possible forms of financial pressures, including the question of penalty or negative interest rates in the case of the more severe pressure mentioned above. There will also be further consideration of the basis on which financial pressures might be ac-

tivated. Such pressures could be activated by a positive decision of the Fund, at an appropriate level, following a finding that the country had failed to take adequate corrective measures after it had been called upon to do so. It is not agreed whether or not they could be activated on the basis of a disproportionate movement in a country's reserves, either presumptively (i.e., unless the Fund decides that pressures are unwarranted) or —in the case of the more severe pressure mentioned above—automatically.

11. It has also been suggested that, for cases of more extreme imbalance, other pressures should be available, such as the publication of a Fund report on the position of the country concerned, and trade or other current account restrictions against countries in persistent large surplus. If there were to be pressures of this sort, they would be activated by a positive decision of the Fund following a finding that the country had failed to take adequate corrective measures after it had been called upon to do so; the authority to activate these pressures would rest ultimately, either directly or upon appeal, with a Committee of Fund Governors.

The Exchange Rate Mechanism

12. In the reformed system exchange rates will continue to be a matter for international concern and consultation. Competitive depreciation or undervaluation will be avoided. The exchange rate mechanism will remain based on stable but adjustable par values, and countries should not make inappropriate par value changes. On the other hand, countries should, whether in surplus or deficit, make appropriate par value changes promptly. Changes in par values will continue to be subject to Fund approval. Further consideration will be given to whether or not there should be simplified procedures, under appropriate safeguards, for small par value changes.

13. Countries may adopt floating rates in particular situations, subject to Fund authorization, surveillance, and review. Authorization to float will relieve a country of its obligation to observe the margins mentioned in paragraph 14. There will be further study of the possibility both of defining in advance particular situations in which countries might adopt floating rates and of developing a code of conduct, to be observed both by countries with floating rates and by other countries in relation to a floating currency, which would be designed to ensure consistency with international payments equilibrium. This study will cover the question of whether Fund authorization to float should depend upon a judgment in each particular case or whether it should be readily granted to countries undertaking to observe such a code of conduct or other agreed rules.

14. Except when authorized to adopt floating rates, countries will maintain the market exchange rates for their currencies within agreed maximum margins in relation to their parities. It is agreed that it would be desirable that there should be a symmetrical system in which the maximum margins for all currencies, including intervention currencies, should be the same, and should be 2.25 percent on either side of parity. There will be further study of how symmetry can be achieved. An appropriate Fund body should be empowered to change the agreed maximum margins on a qualified majority.

Multicurrency Intervention

15. A detailed examination will be made of the practicality and desirability of establishing a system of multicurrency intervention in which countries whose

currencies are widely traded in exchange markets might participate. The object of such a system would be to promote greater symmetry among participating countries with regard to exchange rate policy and intervention and settlement obligations; and it would make possible the establishment of symmetrical margins as mentioned in paragraph 14. Attention will be paid to the implications of such a system for nonparticipating countries.

Controls

16. There will be a strong presumption against the use of controls on current account transactions or payments for balance of payments purposes. In this connection arrangements will be made for continuing close coordination between the Fund and GATT. Countries will not use controls over capital transactions for the purpose of maintaining inappropriate exchange rates or, more generally, of avoiding appropriate adjustment action.

17. Wherever possible, developing countries will be exempted from controls imposed by other countries, particularly from import controls and controls over outward long-term investment. The special circumstances of developing countries will be taken into account by the Fund in assessing controls which these countries feel it necessary to apply.

Disequilibrating Capital Flows

18. Countries will cooperate in actions designed to limit disequilibrating capital flows and in arrangements to finance and offset them. Actions that countries might choose to adopt could include a more satisfactory degree of harmonization of monetary policies, subject to the requirements of domestic demand management; prompt adjustment of inappropriate par values, use of wider margins, and the adoption of floating rates in particular situations; and the use of administrative controls, including dual exchange markets and fiscal incentives. There should be improved consultation in the Fund on actions designed to limit disequilibrating capital flows, with the following objectives: first, to increase their effectiveness and to minimize harmful effects on third countries; and secondly, to avoid unnecessary proliferation and escalation of controls and the additional flows which might be prompted by anticipation thereof.

19. Insofar as countries use controls to limit disequilibrating capital flows, they should avoid an excessive degree of administrative restriction which could damage trade and beneficial capital flows and should not retain controls longer than needed. Such controls should be applied without discrimination except as stated in paragraph 17; in this connection there will be further consideration of the special position of countries which maintain close financial ties.

Convertibility

20. It is agreed that the basic objectives to be accommodated in the reformed convertibility system should be symmetry of obligations on all countries, including those whose currencies are held in official reserves; the better management of global reserves and the avoidance of uncontrolled growth of reserve currency balances; adequate elasticity; and as much freedom for countries to choose the composition of their reserves as is consistent with the overall objectives of the reform.

21. All countries maintaining par values will settle in reserve assets those official balances of their currencies which are presented to them for conversion. It is not agreed whether, beyond this, there should be more mandatory settlement

arrangements in which countries whose currencies are held in official reserves would settle imbalances fully in reserve assets, with some accompanying limitation on other countries' accumulation of reserve currency holdings. It is, however, agreed that the amount of international liquidity and, in particular, the aggregate volume of official currency holdings should be kept under international surveillance and management, taking into account any necessary increase over time in official currency holdings in relation to the growth of international transactions.

22. There will be further consideration of the mechanism for settlements, including consideration of whether there should be direct settlement between countries or whether it should be wholly or partly centralized in the Fund. There will also be further consideration of means, including a possible substitution facility as envisaged in paragraph 31, to protect the system from any net conversion of the overhang of existing reserve currency balances.

23. It is generally recognized that there is a need for some elasticity within the settlement system, particularly to finance disequilibrating capital flows, and that provision for such elasticity should be consistent with other aspects of the reform. There will be further consideration of the appropriate degree and form of elasticity, which it has been suggested might:

(i) be limited to credit facilities, including Fund credit and official bilateral short-term credit, under international surveillance;

(ii) include, in addition to (i), a provision that the right of member countries to present currency balances for conversion into reserve assets would be suspended when their primary reserves exceeded a predetermined level and that the settlement obligation of the issuer would be correspondingly suspended; or

(iii) include, in addition to (i), provision for relaxation of the normal convertibility obligations by a collective decision in the Fund.

24. Provision could be made, if necessary, to permit the introduction of convertibility by stages. . . .

The Link and Credit Facilities In Favor of Developing Countries

34. In the light of the agreed objective to promote economic development, the reformed monetary system will contain arrangements to promote an increasing flow of real resources from the developed to developing countries. If these arrangements were to include a link between development assistance and SDR allocation, this could take one of the following forms:

(a) A link would be established between development finance and SDR allocation, the total volume of which will be determined exclusively on the basis of global liquidity needs. This link would take the form of the direct distribution to developing countries of a larger proportion of SDR allocations than they would receive on the basis of their share in Fund quotas. Link resources so allocated would be distributed to all developing countries in such a way as to be relatively favorable to the least developed countries.

(b) A link would be established between development finance and SDR allocation, the total volume of which will be determined exclusively on the basis of global liquidity needs. This link would take the form of direct allocation to international and regional development finance institutions of a predetermined share of SDR allocations. Link resources distributed to development finance institutions would be disbursed to developing countries on the basis of development need and in such a way as to be relatively favorable to the least developed countries. The use of link funds by development finance institutions, including their distribution and terms, would reflect the nature and purpose of these resources.

35. A detailed examination will be made of proposals for establishing a new facility in the Fund to provide longer-term balance of payments finance for developing countries.

84.

NICHOLAS DE B. KATZENBACH: Reworking Foreign Policy

Nicholas Katzenbach served as Under Secretary of State under President Kennedy and as Attorney General for two years under President Johnson. He was thus in public office during the years when the Vietnam War emerged as the most consuming issue in American society. And he also witnessed at first hand the devising of foreign policy as well as the decision-making processes that were part of the "Cold War" mentality of several administrations. The article, entitled "Foreign Policy, Public Opinion, and Secrecy," from which this selection is taken was published in the aftermath of several months of Watergate scandal revelations that threatened to weaken the President's role in foreign affairs.

Source: *Foreign Affairs*, October 1973.

WHAT FOREIGN POLICY will arise from the ashes of Watergate—and how it can gain that public consensus without which no foreign policy can hope to succeed—are questions we need to address now. Drift, debate, division are the inevitable aftermath of recent events; and it will take time and leadership—both in short supply—to discover, to create and to build upon a viable consensus.

The problem, of course, is not simply Watergate—though the destruction of presidential leadership and credibility and the confrontation of Executive and Congress which have accompanied that disaster would be problems enough. What adds infinitely to those difficulties is the clear connection between the sordid revelations of Watergate and the conduct of the Indochina War (at home and abroad), which in turn is related to the sometime excesses of a foreign policy too oriented to cold-war concepts of "national security." The relationship is neither accidental nor coincidental, and it is important to the future of our foreign policy to understand why this is so.

I have come to this conclusion with considerable reluctance for two reasons: First, I would feel personally more comfortable if all that is associated with Watergate could be blamed on President Nixon—if the lawless and totalitarian overtones of his administration could be seen as purely aberrational, without roots in the past. To a large degree I think they are, but unhappily they are not so rootless as I would wish.

Second, I can give no support either to Henry Kissinger, who understandably would like to segregate Watergate from the real need to consolidate and perhaps even institutionalize the Nixon administration's productive advances in moderating our relations with the Soviet Union and China; or, at the opposite extreme, to the revisionists who rewrite the history of post-World War II foreign policy in ways which adjust the past to their present and future preferences. We have to go through a difficult period if we are to build, as we must, on a solid basis of popular support for our foreign policy, and the essentials of that task are candor and honesty.

The thesis of this article is simple. Our foreign policy must be based on policy and factual premises which are accepted by the overwhelming majority of the American people. This means that this President or his successor must reestablish the credibility of that office; that there must be broad support in the Congress and in the press and public for the policy he seeks to forward, and virtually total confidence that there is no manipulation of facts to prove the wisdom of that policy or, which may often be the same thing, the honest commitment of his administration to it. Today—when confidence in the honesty and integrity of both the President and the Presidency is at rock bottom—that is a big order. We may have to modify or abandon foreign policy objectives supported by many to arrive at a satisfactory level of public confidence. But until an Administration can achieve it, we cannot hope to succeed in any foreign policy, however modest it may be by comparison with either the recent past or the somewhat lesser role which the United States might legitimately be expected to play in the future.

In foreign policy there is no substitute for presidential leadership in formulating and administering our foreign affairs. . . .

Vocal and widespread dissent may easily frustrate his policy; damage our national security as he perceives it; severely limit his capacity to lead; and encourage the view that such opposition is truly subversive, the work of our enemies, and something to fear and even seek to repress.

Yet in fact the expression of dissent, however vocally vehement, is fundamental to the functioning of our democracy. Those responsible for the creation and execution of our foreign policy must be responsive to public attitudes and cannot seek to repress dissent and disagreement, conceal the truth from the public, or violate the letter and the spirit of the Constitution. There is no "country" whose interests they serve apart from the people of the United States. There are no "interests" of that country apart from the interests of its citizens. However difficult and complex our foreign policy may be, there is no license to free it from the mandates of the Constitution or the constraints of public views, interests and wants, any more than any other difficult and complex problem can be freed from the same constraints.

All of this ought to be self-evident. That it is not—or, at least, that Presidents, and especially the present Administration, do not appear to accept it in fact—is the product of history, of the problems of a relatively open foreign policy, and finally of the rationalizations for secrecy, deception and unrestrained presidential leadership which have resulted from our conduct and national attitudes during the cold war.

First, throughout most of our history the American people have had little concern with foreign policy: there has been no continuing, everyday, costly involvement in relations with other nations. Apart from two world wars, foreign policy had little effect on our daily lives. With the notable and important exception of its negative role between those wars, Congress had little involvement and little interest.

Continuing and widespread public concern over our relations with other countries is really a phenomenon of the last 25 years. Measured in terms of even our relatively short history as a nation, we have not had much time to gain experience or adjust our political institutions to this new state of affairs.

Second, we were thrust into world affairs after World War II in an atmosphere of continuing crisis and virtually total responsibility for the future and well-being of the non-Communist world. We perceived the Soviet Union and its satellites as a major threat to our values, our national security and the continuing existence of a "free world"—and hence to our own national survival. In general, with disagreement only in degree, this view has prevailed until very recently. It may have been painting international affairs with too broad a brush, but I do not think it was essentially wrong, and I believe that the foreign policy which evolved from this thesis was by and large successful until 1965, even in cases where its stated premises were questionable. . . .

The vices of this policy—of what became a bloated concept of national security—have been that it has tended not only to overextend our national commitments but to inhibit public debate and understanding of the complex world in which foreign policy is made and executed. It has, of necessity, given a major voice in foreign affairs to our large military establishment, and for much of the past 25 years there has been a tendency to equate dissent or criticism with disloyalty, with subversion, with being a Communist "dupe." Obviously this repression of dissent reached its peak after the "loss" of China and during the era of the late Senator Joseph McCarthy. But appearing to follow the Communist line has been a political risk for critics during most of this period. And, again because of its "national security" premise, the policy has bred a host of questionable practices relating to security clearances, systems of classification of information, lists of subversive organizations, and snooping by security agents into the background, beliefs and associations of many citizens. It is not too long a step from security practices of the past to the ridiculous beliefs of the Watergate "plumbers" and their creators, and to the acts they sought to justify in the name of national security. Indeed—and I think this is a major part of the problem—very little of the protest activity associated with Vietnam would have been tolerated in the 1950s, and repressive measures might well have been accepted by the general public not so long ago.

But I think the most dangerous part of our foreign policy of containment of communism has been the extent to which it has made our Presidents prisoners of popular political passion. Any foreign policy—and certainly one as global as that of the United States—involves inevitable trade-offs among the various costs we must pay for our security and well-being. Some mix of dollar costs, lives, nuclear risks, and risks because of changing allegiances of governments and populations is the daily gruel of those who seek to decide. Dollar costs can be reduced by a policy of massive retaliation, accenting increased nuclear risks. Both costs and nuclear risks can be reduced if we are willing to tolerate the loss of various allies or of influence in countries of marginal importance to us. But costs there will be, and trade-offs will continue to be the grist of our foreign policy. Yet the public has never been made aware of this central fact—and only after the price of Vietnam became so totally unacceptable have many become aware of the costs implicit in our foreign policy as it has stretched down the years and over space from its origin in the time of the Truman Doctrine.

Thus, since China and the McCarthy aftermath, no President has been politically willing to question the basic objective of no loss of territory to Communist regimes—to admit that such an objective cannot be absolute and that it may involve excessive risks of nuclear war or unacceptable costs of limited war (as it did in the end in Vietnam and might well have done in Korea as well). Accepting that objective as all-controlling, we have promoted it by our economic and military aid programs, by our systems of alliances, and to a limited degree by covert activities. We have seen dominoes not only in Southeast Asia and in Greece and Turkey, but also in Africa and Latin America. We have hoped that we could deter and prevent loss of territory by shoring up friendly regimes, giving them the military means to prevent subversion and the economic means to claim progress and prosperity. We have not been able to be selective in the process—as we should and could have been. Our selectivity has been dictated more by crisis than by purpose or policy; wherever the danger of Communist take-over existed, there went the dollars and the arms.

Again I do not suggest that, in the reality, this fire-fighting principle was either all good or all bad. I do suggest that it was motivated as much by the fear of the domestic political consequences of any "loss of territory" to communism as it was by serious security calculations. . . .

My purpose here is not to seek to disentangle the real from the imagined. My point is that no effort to do so was politically possible. Every President felt threatened by any Communist success anywhere, and took steps—some, at least, excessive in retrospect—to insure that the blame was not his. He operated in a climate of opinion where to be "soft on communism"—to lose anywhere, any time—was a serious blow to his status at home. And Presidents acted accordingly.

I have said that Presidents became the prisoners of the cold-war view of politics, even though each also contributed to it. The general public and congressional perception of the cold war—and, incidentally, of an exaggerated American power to influence and control events—made it virtually impossible for any President to be candid about the costs and risks of our foreign policy. The "China syndrome"—the aftermath of Joe McCarthy—meant politically that it was easier to accept the premise of "no loss of territory" in the hope that his Presidency would not be called to account than to attempt to gain public and congressional acceptance that the premise might involve unacceptable risks and costs. There was no hope—perhaps no time without crisis—for a public debate in the 1960s about the premises of the 1950s. Could President Johnson have permitted a Communist take-over in the Dominican Republic or in Vietnam, stating that he did not regard "friendly regimes" as important enough to our foreign policy to warrant military intervention? Was the American public prepared for such a statement? And was it, on the other hand, prepared for the costs which Vietnam demanded?

In a sense, all of this political exposition is prelude to the major point of secrecy. But it is, I believe, tremendously important to the understanding of why we are where we are.

In our political system the President enjoys—or suffers—enormous advantages of leadership. His is an extremely difficult role to share, and to a considerable extent the advantages interact with the problems, one upon the other, to cripple the political system. His principal advantage is that the general public—even the best-informed public—views the world beyond our borders as confusing and dangerous. In the mass of information that flows to us each day, it is harder and harder to tell the players and the teams without a program. . . .

Unfortunately, Presidents are inclined to think this blind trust in their wisdom is wholly justified. Having almost sole access to the full range of classified information and expert opinion, Presidents are tempted to think that the opinions of Congressmen, academics, journalists and the public at large are, almost unavoidably, inadequately informed. It is too easy to conclude that the opinions of others lack essential knowledge and that unequal information and unequal background make their views less important. The subtle insights of specialists or classified pieces of information are often accorded a totally undeserved attention and importance in comparison to more widely shared insights and knowledge.

All this reduces the politically healthy feeling of being constrained by the disagreement of many of one's peers. But that might not be particularly serious if the President and the executive branch were bias-free and single-minded in their desire to produce results representing the long-run preferences of the American public. Unfortunately, neither of these conditions is likely to prove true.

For there are biases built into the position of the President—and the advice he receives—that are likely to lead to departures from the needs of the country as perceived by others. For one thing, the very factors which reduce the value of the opinion of others on tactical questions have a way of spreading to questions of basic values. There is a tendency to assume that such fundamentals as the amount of dollar cost the public will bear to reduce nuclear risks, or the loss of lives that we will bear to avoid a particularly offensive weapon, are technical decisions for experts—although these decisions plainly involve only value judgments, not specialized knowledge, once the choices are fairly laid out.

The problem is further complicated by the fact that Presidents in recent years have become increasingly enamored on their role on the stage of world affairs and are likely to resist a more limited role even if the public were to assign it to them. Presidents want to secure an honored place in history and feel that the scope of American power, prestige and influence is a crucial aspect of a historian's memory of their terms of office. This can be a heady business. It is compounded by the relative freedom that the President has in foreign affairs—freedom from annoying congressional restraints and freedom based on the generalized need of the public for unitary leadership in times of danger. It would be going too far to say that a President welcomes a Cuban missile crisis or a Six-Day War in the Middle East. But it would not be going too far to say that the Presidency thrives upon it, as the Nixon Presidency has thrived on his televised visits to China and Russia.

All of these pressures make a relatively retiring presidential role less likely whatever the public interest. When they lead a President to costly or risky policies with which much of the public cannot identify its interests, or which seem to exceed the discretion required by the danger, these biases can cause the President to lose that basis of popular support on which he necessarily relies.

Over the years, then, we have moved farther and farther away from the basic premises of our democratic political system to put important decisions on foreign policy in the hands of the President and, in effect, to charge him with its successful administration. Our almost total reliance on the President's leadership and accountability; the felt need to fight insurgency with counterinsurgency, often secretly; our unwillingness to test foreign policy initiatives in the ways in which we test domestic policy proposals—through debate and discussion; the appeal of "national security" as sufficient justification for a vague and extensive foreign policy; and, most of all, the fear of the President that his political popularity, his place in history and his capacity to lead all depend on not having another China, or Cuba, or other major loss to communism —all these considerations tempt a President to go it alone in the hope that the policy will succeed. The temptation to let the end justify the means is clearly present, even if the means requires dissembling or misleading the Congress and the American people. Such conduct can, in the environment of the recent past, be rationalized as necessary to maintain that secrecy on which success depends. And, after all, it is unlikely that the President's honesty and good faith will be brought effectively into question if the policy is successful. . . .

Unhappily, secrecy in foreign affairs—and particularly in the atmosphere we have lived in for the past 25 years—is easily rationalized. Yet the reasons seldom have much to do with the rationalizations. In recent years, at least, the real motive has been precisely to avoid the difficulties inherent in our political system and hopefully to present the public with triumphant *faits accomplis.* What initially stemmed largely from confrontation between a growing vocal minority in Congress and the President, as well as increasing public demonstrations, was converted into constitutional principle by Mr. Nixon. In his Administration, neither the Congress nor the public has been informed about foreign affairs except at a level of high generality, and even then without the opportunity for discussion. Indeed, not even the bureaucracy has been consulted or informed. And this in turn has led to a failure to consult with, and inform, our allies abroad, culminating in the insult to the Japanese with respect to the change in our China policy.

Thus, even without Watergate, personal diplomacy conducted in secret, without public understanding or solid institutional foundation within the government, should now be insufficient basis for a viable foreign policy. And if, as I believe, Watergate has destroyed confidence in the President's credibility, much more is now needed.

What must be done today to put our foreign policy on a viable basis is, first, to promote discussion sufficient to establish the domestic consensus necessary to gain acceptance for, and support of, our foreign initiatives. We stand as a badly divided nation and we face some very tough problems. Second, we must restore confidence in the integrity of the Presidency. The Congress and the people need to believe what the Administration says. Both of these objectives mean dramatic changes in the style of the Presidency in foreign affairs.

I would propose the following changes:

1. The President must indicate that he needs and wants the support and participation of Congress and the public in formulating his foreign policy. He must welcome public discussion and criticism of his proposals. Clearly, he must do the proposing, he must provide the leadership. But he and his principal assistants must be far more willing than in the recent past to lay out candidly the problems, the choices, the recommended actions.

To involve the Congress in this fashion is, despite congressional protestations to the contrary, as much a problem for the Congress as for the President. The unpleasant fact is that most members of Congress find little political profit with their constituents in foreign affairs and in accepting the compromises necessarily involved. The role of critic after the fact is often more politically rewarding than that of a constructive participant. It is easy for opposition—especially in the Congress—to center around short-term considerations rather than long-term policies, to make appeals to national pride, to criticize almost any negotiation on the grounds that the Administration gave away too much in the mutual bargaining. The record of Congress on many foreign policy issues, usually in the form of amendments to foreign aid bills, is far from a distinguished one; and the temptation of the Executive to interpret away crippling amendments to its foreign policy has served to create still another tear in the fabric of constitutional government.

Secrecy in foreign affairs is not, therefore, a one-way street born of presidential ambition for power. Too often it suits congressional politics quite well—particularly in the House of Representatives, with its biennial elections. The temptation in both parties is to let the President assume responsibility, and to let future events determine the length of his coattails. . . .

2. It follows that the principal makers of foreign policy decisions must be exposed to Congress, the press and the public. If presidential assistants participate in the framing and execution of foreign policy to anything like the degree that Mr. Kissinger has done, they must be exposed to public view and scrutiny, and fully available to the Congress without subterfuge or the use of devious methods.

3. We should abandon publicly all covert operations designed to influence political results in foreign countries. Specifically, there should be no secret subsidies of police or counter-insurgency forces, no efforts to influence elections, no secret monetary subsidies of groups sympathetic to the United States, whether governmental, nongovernmental or revolutionary. We should confine our covert activities overseas to the gathering of intelligence information.

I come to this conclusion with some reluctance, because in a few instances such activities have been legitimate and useful. But I believe the impossibility of controlling secret activities—and the public's apprehension about them—outweigh the losses which will be sustained. Much of this activity was phased out under Kennedy and Johnson, and I think the rest can go.

4. We must minimize the role of secret information in foreign policy.

Many Presidents have sought to tinker with the present classification and declassification system, conscious that the tendency to reclassify and to spawn classified files has been out of control for years. If public proof of that fact were necessary, the Pentagon papers and the ensuing trial provided it. All the documents involved carried high security classification, yet there was little evidence that any related importantly any longer to "national defense"—the test required by the major porvision of law under which the trial was held. On the contrary, there was at the trial much expert testimony that none did relate importantly to the "national defense," and a determined and persuasive defense argument that little of the factual information provided in the mass of documents was in fact new. What made the release newsworthy was less its content than its voyeuristic appeal—the relatively rare public exposure of governmental processes to the public eye. . . .

I do not propose that all other information be made public or even generally available. I simply suggest that it not be classified as "national defense" information, carrying such exotic labels as "Top Secret" or "Cosmic Top Secret" or the like. I have no problem with limiting distribution within the bureaucracy of information which is politically "sensitive," or with general rules concerning the confidentiality of discussions with foreign diplomats, ambassadorial or other bureaucratic recommendations as to policy, or personal or investigative records. (In the case of diplomatic exchanges, such common-sense rules long antedate the postwar expansion of classification.) Frankly, I think we can rely on the good sense of bureaucrats to keep confidential what should be confidential most of the time, without employing bloated concepts of national security to do so. I know this worked in the past within the Department of Justice and I see no reason why it should not work elsewhere.

5. Classification will not stop leaks anyhow. What minimizes these is loyalty to superiors, based not so much on agreement with policy as on respect for their fairness, integrity and openness to recommendations and ideas. A part of the new style of operation must be far greater openness within the executive branch itself. All Presidents fear becoming the prisoners of the governmental bureaucracy, and all Presidents have a healthy distrust of bureaucratic expertise. It is good that they should seek advice elsewhere and that departmental recommendations should be tested in various ways, including the competition of agencies and the interplay between full-time professional officers and those who enter government under political auspices. But to attempt to bypass the bureaucracy has heavy costs not only in the very "leaks" to which I have just referred, but above all in the failure to understand policy, to administer it effectively, to explain it to other constituencies at the appropriate time, and often to make decisions with full awareness of their consequences abroad.

In the present world situation, far greater congressional and public involvement in formulating our foreign policy seems to me not only right but nearly inevitable. There are two reasons for this:

First, problems of trade, investment, resources, development and international monetary stability promise to take on increasing importance in the future. All of these problems will require legislative solutions and therefore extensive congressional participation and action. All will involve a continuity in policy over relatively long periods of time and thus need public understanding and support.

Second, as communism has become less monolithic, as China has emerged as a competing ideological center, as the Soviet Union has become less stridently revolutionary and more concerned with China and with its own domestic progress, and as Europe and Japan have become centers for wealth and power, security considerations in the United States' foreign policy have become less consuming and less global. Mr. Nixon's approaches to both the Soviet Union and China, as well as the modest progress made in the SALT talks, are evidence of a changing security environment. Problems will remain but they will lack the felt intensity of the past 25 years.

Notwithstanding these changes in the world scene, the shift to a more open style in foreign policy will not be without its difficulties. One is the extent to which openness may in fact reduce options or be perceived as doing so. I accept the fact that it sometimes does. But I also think the extent of that reduction is exaggerated, often for improper purposes. I accept, too, that there are circumstances where the President or the Secretary cannot be totally candid without affecting the situation he is discussing. I think the press and public understand this. They know, for example, that high government officials cannot publicly discuss corruption of high South Vietnamese officials, or that high-level expressions of doubt about the viability of a foreign government may bring it down. But these inhibitions are not serious ones, because the underlying facts—if they are important to understanding policy—can be made available to the public in other ways.

The most serious problem of a more open foreign policy lies in congressional response. In Congress controversy can lead to delay, to inaction, to unworkable compromise, to missed opportunities. Minorities can obstruct; special interests can sometimes manipulate policy more easily on the Hill than in the executive branch. The accident of committee leadership and membership can skew policy away from the national interest to more parochial concerns. No one should be sanguine about these risks. The danger of getting hopelessly bogged down in a congressional quagmire is clear and present.

Nonetheless, I am prepared to take some losses in our foreign affairs if by doing so we can restore the fundamentals of representative democracy to our foreign policy. As Watergate demonstrates, democracy is too fragile to be divided into foreign and domestic affairs. We cannot give the President a free hand in the one without eroding the whole of the governmental system that all policy seeks to preserve.

Partly because so much was achieved here in America, we have tended to suppose that every problem must have a solution and that good intentions should somehow guarantee good results. Utopia was not seen as a dream but as our logical destination if only we traveled the right road. Our generation is the first to find that the road is endless, that in traveling it we will find not Utopia but ourselves. The realization of our essential loneliness accounts for so much of the frustration and rage of our time.

HENRY KISSINGER, in an address to the National Press Club, 1972

85.

Managing in a Shortage Economy

In the fall of 1973 the American people were suddenly made aware that for the first time in the nation's history the economy faced serious shortages of natural resources that would soon affect a large variety of commodities in ordinary use. The shortages were triggered in part by the oil crisis, which in turn had been aggravated when the Arab nations cut off the flow of oil exports to the United States in October because of U.S. support for Israel. Products made of paper, plastics, glass, synthetic fibers, cotton, wool, and a whole variety of things that depend on the petrochemical industry were predicted to be in short supply in the coming months, maybe even for years. In a special report published in November, Business Week *magazine analyzed the portent of impending shortages for the American standard of living.*

Source: *Business Week*, November 10, 1973.

RATHER SUDDENLY, America, the fabled land of plenty whose bountiful resources have long been the envy of the entire world, seems to be turning into a land of shortages. For some consumers, the change has thus far been no more than an annoyance. But for many businesses, the shortages have hit with shattering effects. Chrysler Corp., for example, lost $26 million in the third quarter this year largely because of new-model startup problems caused by shortages of materials and parts.

The new climate of scarcity is underscored by numerous developments: the temporary export controls imposed on scrap steel and soybeans during the past year, the government's decision to allocate supplies of fuel oil and propane gas, the sporadic shortages of gasoline and beef that many consumers experienced last summer, and other serious supply problems now plaguing a growing number of companies.

Businessmen, of course, are finding ways to survive and even thrive in the climate of scarcity. But the tide of complaints is growing, executives are beginning to count the toll in lower profits and lost sales, and a number of businesses—particularly smaller companies with little market leverage on suppliers—are hurting badly. Most of all, there is widespread concern and uncertainty about the duration of the shortages.

"This is the tightest period in the memory of current business people," declares E. F. Andrews, vice-president of materials at Allegheny Ludlum Industries, Inc., who oversees a monthly survey of purchasing agents for the National Assn. of Purchasing Management. "I've never seen so many purchasing men chasing after and failing to get materials supplies. The percent reporting slower deliveries is at a historic high, and the shortages show no signs of easing."

A *Business Week* sampling of companies around the country confirms this assessment. Executives complain about difficulties in obtaining a bewildering array of goods, ranging from basic commodities such as oil, steel, cotton, paper, and cement to such manufactured products as plumbing equipment, bearings, motors, and electronic components.

"There isn't anything not in short supply," says Edwin J. Faster, an Inland Steel Co. purchasing agent, viewing his own company's requirements. "There's nothing that's not tight after you go back to your vendor, and he goes back to his sources. It's a chain effect." George A. Harris, vice-president for materials at TRW, Inc., the Cleveland-based equipment and component manufacturer, agrees: "You can just about name a raw material, and we have a problem with long lead times and spot shortages in it."

For the Administration's economic policymakers, such tales of scarcity are a source of growing frustration. Many of the reported shortages are already breeding deep inflationary pressures within the economy. And each rise in the cost of living, each additional price hike for some basic product or commodity, stirs cries in some sector for some new form of government action.

For the present, the practitioners of Nixonomics are inclined to ignore such cries and to pin their hopes on the likelihood that the developing economic slowdown will soon temper inflation and ease the shortages. Having already resorted to a medicine-cabinet full of phases and freezes to cure the body economic, they are hardly eager to embark on a new course of treatment. "The economy," says Herbert Stein, chairman of the President's Council of Economic Advisers, "is hopefully moving away from excessive boom conditions." But while few would argue with this assertion, there is a growing belief in economic circles that—barring a steep recession—supply problems and rising materials prices are not going to disappear any time soon.

In itself, this very notion of enduring shortages is a kind of minor economic heresy, and many economists remain dubious about its validity. "A couple of years ago we were swimming in a lot of the stuff that's now in short supply." notes one man. According to the conventional wisdom, the U.S. economy is simply experiencing a severe case of the typical demand-pull inflation that develops at the peak of a business cycle. Aided by the clarity of hindsight, most economists now view the fiscal and monetary policies of recent years as far too expansionary.

Yet the undeniable fact is that the kind of explosive inflation that burst upon the U.S. early this year was anticipated by virtually no one, not even those who advocated less stimulation earlier in the game. "This inflation is very disconcerting . . . it took us by surprise," admits Arthur M. Okun, who was chief economic adviser to President Johnson.

The reasons for this rather astonishing lapse are somewhat complex, but one answer is obviously the inability of economists to assess correctly the degree of slack in the economy. As long as there is a significant distance between what the nation can produce efficiently and what it is actually producing, the reasoning goes, you can speed up economic growth without generating excessive inflationary pressures.

Since the 1960s economists have leaned heavily upon a concept known as potential gross national product to calculate the non-inflationary limits of economic activity. And according to this measure, there was still a comfortable $27-billion gap between actual and potential GNP in the first quarter of 1973. Indeed, the GNP gap was even larger in the third quarter of this year, even while inflation was galloping ahead.

The trouble with the GNP gap notion, however, is that it is little more than an unemployment measure. Its upper limit, potential GNP, is calculated simply by multiplying the number of people that would be employed at full employment by their expected average individual output. In other words, an underlying assumption is that the available supply of labor is the main limiting factor that comes into play when the economy reaches a cyclical peak. But while this was largely true in the 1960s, a shortage of labor was plainly not the main culprit in today's inflationary drama.

"It's a different story," concedes Okun, who helped develop the potential GNP concept. "While we all looked at labor, that isn't where the problem was." Paul W. McCracken, former head of President Nixon's economic team, concurs: "We're dealing with an explosive commodities inflation. In the current expansion, we obviously have run out of plant capacity before we have run out of employable labor."

Why then weren't economists warned by the various capacity utilization measures that focus on industry's use of plant and equipment? For one thing, the two most widely used indexes—those of the Federal Reserve Board and of the McGraw-Hill Economics Dept.—have been running only a bit over 80 percent for U.S. industry as a whole. For another, both measures use different methods (McGraw-Hill's is based entirely on a survey), and some economists are leery about the indexes' reliability. "There are a lot of problems with capacity measurement," says University of Chicago professor Victor Zarnowitz, who notes that a lot of obsolete plant may be counted as capacity when it really is not usable.

Nonetheless, Otto Eckstein, president of Data Resources, Inc., a consulting firm, believes economists could have gotten a clue from the indexes if they had looked at specific sectors instead of over-all operating rates. "Our capacity problems," he says, "are not economy-wide, but are focused in the primary processing and materials industries. The disparity between the operating rates for over-all manufacturing and for primary processing industries is greater than it has ever been." Eckstein's assessment is confirmed by the Fed's recently released index of 12 major materials industries, a revised series showing that such industries as paper, oil refining, steel, and cement ran at a record rate of 96.3 percent of capacity during the third quarter, virtually at their operating ceilings.

The implications of this are obvious. When a basic materials industry is running flat out, other industries dependent on it cannot expand their production even if they have idle men and machines. "If steel is in short supply, then the effective capacity of steel-using industries drops below their rated capacity," explains Alan Greenspan, president of Townsend-Greenspan & Co., economic consultants.

What makes the present situation even more troublesome, of course, is that a number of materials industries are all pressed up against capacity together. When this happens, the impact spreads through the economy causing a series of reverberating bottlenecks. Some steel mills, for example, are reportedly cutting back production because of a lack of fuel at the same time that the oil industry is crying for steel to build the refinery capacity that would ease the steel industry's fuel needs.

Viewing such interrelationships, Greenspan says: "We're experiencing something out of all dimension to what we experienced in the past." Tilford C. Gaines, senior vice-president and economist of Manufacturers Hanover Trust, labels the present deceleration of economic activity "a supply slowdown" because he feels that it has been largely caused by the physical inability of the economy to grow faster in the face of serious materials shortages.

There is little doubt that such shortages will ease as recent tight monetary policy reinforces the economic slowdown, and most would undoubtedly disappear in a fullfledged recession. But economists are uncertain about the longer-term outlook. "Whether we face continuing materials inflation over the next few years is the big unanswered question," says Okun.

In essence, the question boils down to whether the U.S. and world economies are entering the upward phase of what economic theorists call a "long cycle," a prolonged period of rising commodity prices. Though they have been the subject of much speculation, not much is known about such periods beyond the fact that they are usually associated with the economic activity generated by wars and the pressures of population growth on existing agricultural capacity. The last such period began in the mid-1930s and ended in the early 1950s.

Economic historian Walt W. Rostow, for one, spots similar long-term factors at work today: excessive population growth in many areas, growing demand for "grain-expensive" proteins in the more affluent nations, fast-paced economic growth in the developing world, and the energy crisis. "When you add to these the cost of cleaning up the environment," says Rostow, "it appears likely that we are in for a lengthy period of relatively rising wholesale prices."

Skeptics point to a number of temporary factors that have exacerbated the present inflation and are likely to fade away. Perhaps the most significant is the fact that this year and last mark the first time wince World War II that all of the world economies have been accelerating together. "This has placed tremendous pressure on world resources," says Brookings Institution economist Barry Bosworth, "but such a coincidence of demand pressures is unlikely to be repeated." Indeed, with many of the major economies showing signs of slowing, some observers fear a worldwide recession next year with a devastating impact on commodity prices.

Given the commitment of governments to high employment and growth, however, such a pause—if it does occur—is likely to be short-lived. A more likely scenario is an over-all slowing of the world economy during the next few years, with individual countries moving out of phase as some slow rather quickly and others maintain their pace for a while.

Raw materials prices have also been affected by the collapse of the international monetary system as foreign holders of dollars, seeking to protect themselves against currency shifts, pushed up prices in world commodity markets. But with the dollar now widely regarded as undervalued, this rash of speculative fever has probably run its course.

And the government's price controls program has undoubtedly intensified shortages of a number of products. For one thing, prices have not been allowed to rise freely in this expansion to allocate scarce resources and encourage new production. Some companies have simply reduced or discontinued production of their least profitable items. For another, the tight lid on domestic prices of such materials as copper, zinc, fertilizer, petrochemicals, and steel has led many U.S. producers to quietly divert some of their output to the more lucrative export market where prices have run as much as 25 percent to 100 percent higher. Some U.S. companies have been unable to pay the higher foreign tab because it would put them at a great price disadvantage *vis-à-vis* competitors able to obtain the cheaper domestic product. "This has been particularly true for the smaller independent fuel distributors," says Greenspan. . . .

No one doubts, of course, that supply will eventually adjust to demand. "Prices will rise and companies will expand, with or without controls," asserts Argus Research economist William Wolman. But the question is whether the expansion will be smooth and orderly, or whether it will proceed in fits and starts with chronic shortages and wildly fluctuating prices. With two or three years lead time needed to bring new facilities on stream, CLC Director John Dunlop himself concedes that "we are dealing with some fairly long-term problems here in terms of having adequate investments in new capacity."

These long-term problems are not due simply to America's new trading position. Wolman points to a big shift in the nation's population mix. The 25-to-39 age group, which grew by only 1.2 million during the 1950s and 1960s, he says, will soar by nearly 15 million in the seventies, "generating enormous demand for consumer durables."

These children of the postwar baby boom have already helped push the annual growth rate of the labor force to 2.2 percent since 1965, compared with 1.3 percent in the previous 15 years. James Cooper, a vice-president of Irving Trust Co., notes that the growth rate of real capital spending (adjusted for inflation) has dropped significantly in the same period. "It's clear that we face a deficit in the capital stock needed to employ these young people productively," he says.

Another long-term factor affecting the economy is growing U.S. dependence on imports for many key fuel and non-fuel minerals. In the past two decades, the U.S. has lost basic self-sufficiency in such minerals as iron ore, zinc, and tungsten. Spurred by the burdens of environmental costs and declining domestic ore grades, the trend will accelerate in the decades ahead. Devaluation has already made such foreign resources more expensive, but shipping costs, greater bargaining leverage exercised by exporting nations, political instability in resource-rich areas, and increased competition among consuming nations will add to the tab. Sums up Gaines: "We are at a watershed in our history. We have simply run out of cheap and easily available energy and raw materials."

All of this suggests that the U.S. economy is indeed riding the crest of a long-run upward adjustment in materials prices, and economists are already theorizing about the era that lies ahead. Rostow notes that such periods in the past have been characterized by "high interest rates and profits and a slowing in the growth of real wages as capital is mobilized to bring new supplies into the market."

Wolman of Argus sees a similar scenario: "We have to recognize that the overvalued dollar allowed us to live beyond our means. Now we are in for a relatively long period of inflation with the pressure coming from goods rather than services. But we can also expect faster real growth and bigger profits."

Greenspan foresees greater stress on research and development to reduce energy costs and materials usage and spur substitution. "The focus will shift," he says, "from labor productivity to materials and energy productivity."

Economists also believe that the new era of scarcity will require some changes in economic strategy. Most believe that price controls in shortage-plagued sectors are self-defeating, and the prices should be allowed to rise to stimulate new production. "We have to swallow our past mistakes on the price front," says Greenspan.

There is also general agreement that macroeconomic policy must tread a narrower line between stimulation and restraint. "Putting the economy into a recession to cure a materials inflation is counterproductive," says Brookings' Bosworth. "The prospect of steady growth is the best encouragement we can offer basic industry to invest in capacity." At the same time, however, banker Gaines warns that expansitionary policy must be guided by materials and energy availability. "We cannot pump up the money supply in a futile effort to achieve impossible growth," he says.

The experts have specific recommendations, as well. While opposing new general tax incentives for capital investment, Bosworth thinks that specific industries facing high environmental costs might be granted a temporary credit to be phased out over several years. Some government economists are playing with the idea of using economic data to set up an early warning system for industries whose capacity growth appears to be lagging behind demand trends. And many mining executives argue for greater government guarantees for overseas investment.

But the simple fact, says Gaines, is that modern economic theory is not really tuned in to the problems of scarcity that are emerging today. Says he: "The underlying assumption of economic thinking since the depression has been that the supply of goods is unlimited and that demand can be manipulated to insure full employment. Now we must shift the focus of economic analysis to the supply side, to bringing forth the raw materials required to sustain demand."

We can say with some confidence that, under the assumption of no major change in the present system, population and industrial growth will certainly stop within the next century, at the latest.

The Limits to Growth: A Report for the Club of Rome's Project on the Predicament of Mankind (1972)

86.

BARRY COMMONER: Is the Fuel Crisis Real?

The energy crisis seemed to come upon Americans so suddenly late in 1973 that many of them wondered how it could have happened so swiftly. The situation had actually been building up toward a crisis for several years, as some persons in the government and the oil industry knew. What bothered many public officials, journalists, and particularly the environmentalists was not so much the current existence of a shortage, but the nagging doubt whether the crisis had been contrived by the oil industry with the federal government standing by doing nothing. The environmentalists were especially fearful that the crisis might be used as an excuse by industry to roll back the ecological gains of the previous few years. In an interview published on November 19, 1973, the noted ecologist, Barry Commoner, assessed the seriousness of the fuel shortage and its effect on environmental goals.

Source: *Chicago Tribune*, November 19, 1973.

Q.: In view of what you have written about the role of petroleum and petroleum products in creating the environmental crisis, do you see the energy crisis as an opportunity to save the environment?

A.: I've felt for a long time that the energy crisis is the cutting edge of the environmental crisis for the reason that—well, it has two edges. One is that it involves a counter-ecological step in that we're using nonrenewable resources, and that's a fundamental violation of a basic principle of ecology.

The other reason is that in using fuel we inevitably pollute the environment with heat, with waste products and so on. So that for those reasons and also because energy—power—has become increasingly important in the design of new technology, which is the main source of the environmental crisis, the role of energy in industry and agriculture becomes a sort of red thread through the environmental crisis.

Q.: Are you surprised that the crisis—or at least our awareness of it—has come so fast?

A.: Let me put it this way: I have a feeling that there is some hidden explanation for the fact that—I don't even know it's a fact—for the claim that we are confronted with shortages between supply and demand of fuel, and it's very puzzling.

Q.: Do you have any guesses?

A.: Well, there are various ways of guessing at it. First, let me put it as simply as I can. In terms of the present situation—let's say the situation in a three-year period—there is no material reason why there should be a shortage of fuel in the United States. We have proven reserves that would last 10, 15, 20 years.

Q.: And the technology to get it?

A.: And the technology to get it. And no one has claimed that we shouldn't be using so much of, let's say, a 15-year supply of oil and gas. No one has said we should be saving it. So we clearly have enough fuel accessible to us in the United States to take care of our immediate needs.

So the only possible explanations of the shortage are that the rate of production from the ground, which means mining and refining, has fallen behind the demand, or, that confusion and inequities in distribution have resulted or will result in local shortages.

So then you come to the question of how such failures could have come about. And there is one fundamental fact that I've found of growing importance in the last couple of days of thinking—and that is that, literally, we don't know what's going on, "we" being the public and, I think, the government.

That is because the statistics on production and distribution of petroleum products are totally in the hands of the industry.

We know what the industry tells us, and I think that at this point I would like to see full disclosure of what the oil industry has on its books with reference to the rate of exploration, the rate of drilling, the pattern of distribution of oil and gas.

Q.: Is anyone making a serious attempt to get the companies to disclose this information?

A.: No. In fact, I want to make the serious attempt right now. It seems to me there's no way of responding rationally to the claim that there's a shortage of fuel until and unless the oil industry makes a full disclosure of the recent pattern in exploration, drilling, distribution, and uses of petroleum products.

We're being asked to take on faith that there isn't enough fuel available and, as far as I'm concerned, it's a little bit like Watergate. What we need, I think, is a congressional investigation that will get all the facts out. We need their tapes—the computer tapes.

Q.: You seem skeptical, though. Is there any real reason to be suspicious that this crisis is contrived?

A.: There are reasons to worry about it. One is—well, just the other day there was a report from the Petroleum Institute meeting in Houston where some of the people who were interviewed referred to what they called "press release refineries." A few months ago many of the oil companies announced plans to build refineries because the demand was increasing and their capacity was inadequate. The story reported now is that they're having second thoughts and that it was suspected that some of those announcements were just announcements and not real, hard-nosed plans to build the refineries.

Another reason to worry about the reality of the crisis is that the Nixon administration is making certain proposals which would waste fuel. In particular, I refer to the Penn Central Railroad. The administration's proposals would increase fuel consumption used for transportation by 3.5 percent because they're proposing to get rid of half the trackage of the railroad and shift the freight to trucks. Trucks use six times as much fuel to carry a ton-mile as a railroad.

In fact, if the government were serious about saving fuel, the biggest area in which we could save it is where it's most used: transportation. And the railroads are far more efficient than any other means of transportation for carrying people or freight. Clearly the sensible step would be not only to keep railroads from deteriorating but to rebuild enormously the railroad system of the United States.

Q.: Now we get into priorities, and isn't that what the energy crisis—the environmental crisis —is all about?

A.: Yeah, and incidentally, let me make one point there. We're being told, almost as a form of blackmail, that we have to give up on environmental quality in order to deal with the fuel crisis—and that's simply not true. We don't have to. There are direct ways of improving both the fuel situation and the environmental situations—and the way to do that is to cut out the waste of fuel.

So, for example, if we were to get the railroads organized to the point where they could recover the freight they've lost to trucks, we would be saving fuel and improving air quality. In the same way, if we develop mass transit in cities, we would be saving fuel and improving air pollution.

One of the most immediate things that could be done, in my opinion, to save fuel and improve the environment would be to develop in each city a really efficient, rapid, free bus system—free. This is being done in a number of Italian cities and in some of the cities, such as Bologna, they've been able to ban the use of cars completely. Buses are far more efficient in terms of fuel used per passenger carried. In fact, they're even slightly more efficient than railroads. So the obvious thing is to get, ideally, all of the people in cities into buses and get cars out entirely.

Q.: But what about costs? And where do we get the buses?

A.: Experiences are that cost is a very important part of public transportation. The fastest-growing consumer cost is that of public transportation, and I think one simple way of accomplishing this would be to operate transportation publicly and absorb the cost in taxes. We might have to force Detroit to build the buses.

The way it is now, people who live in the city drive to work. If they work in the suburbs they have to drive—their livelihood depends on it—so as the price of gasoline rises, we're putting a tax on the poor.

In other words, the fuel crisis, real or not, has made fuel essential to the livelihood and well-being of people and less and less accessible to them because of prices.

Q.: Why does the Nixon administration, as I think you suggested earlier, fail to understand this?

A.: Well, maybe they do understand it. But you have to ask yourself, who benefits from the fuel crisis? And somebody does. The oil industry has reported on the average a 50 percent increase in profits last year. The increase was so sharp that oil officials were said to be embarrassed about it. It turns out that in time of shortage, they somehow manage to make record profits!

They don't mind that the price is going up because that will not only maintain their income but even improve it.

Q.: And if they are diverting it, say, to the petrochemical industry, they are also getting more profits for more sales there.

A.: Since we don't know what they're doing with the fuel, they have opportunities for even greater income by diverting it toward petrochemicals and possibly even by diverting it to foreign markets, because the price of fuel is higher abroad than it is in the United States. And that's another reason why we need to have their tapes.

Q.: In your book, you make clear that the economy has been redesigned since World War II on the assumption that petroleum is easy to get, cheap, and almost totally useable for profit-making in byproducts—as well as the major source of pollution. What happens to the economy if the fuel crisis is real?

A.: I think that, real or not, if it goes on very long we're going to see severe disruption in the stability of the entire productive system.

If it turns out on investigation that this thing was a big ploy to restore the balance of trade, the administration may restore it at the expense of a depression the likes of which they've never seen.

Q.: Are we discovering that the profit motive is not the answer to all our troubles, but—

A.: But the cause of all our troubles? I think it is possible.

87.

The Crisis of Public Confidence

In August 1973, the Subcommittee on Intergovernmental Relations of the U. S. Senate hired Louis Harris and Associates, the public opinion research firm, to survey popular attitudes toward all levels of government. The survey was to gauge how responsive Americans felt their governmental bodies were to public standards and expectations. Secondarily the survey sought to learn how public officials, elected or appointed, felt they were coping with the needs of society. The results of this investigation of the national mood were published on December 3 under the title, Confidence and Concern: Citizens View American Government. *The foreward to the report notes that the survey was conducted during September when much of the public's attention was riveted on the Watergate affair. Therefore answers to questions were bound to reflect this overriding national concern. Exclusive of tables and charts, this selection reprints the first chapter of the report, "Crisis of Confidence."*

Source: *Confidence and Concern: Citizens View American Government*, A Survey of Public Attitudes by the Subcommittee on Intergovernmental Relations of the Committee on Government Operations, United States Senate, Part I; Washington, D.C., 1973.

IN THE FALL OF 1973, for the first time since the 1968 assassinations of Martin Luther King and Robert Kennedy, a majority of the American people (by 53-37 percent) felt "there is something deeply wrong in America" today, that these are no ordinary times of crisis.

The new, profound concern for the country permeates all segments of the public. No group has been unmoved.

Majorities of lower middle-income (55 percent) and upper middle-income (52 percent) Americans, of skilled laborers (54 percent) and white-collar workers (55 percent), of rural citizens (58 percent), residents of small towns (52 percent) and city dwellers (55 percent) and of grade-school (67 percent) and high-school (56 percent) graduates reflect this grave unease. Additionally, more people in the South (55 percent) than in the East (49 percent) feel "there is something deeply wrong" and those 50 years of age and over (62 percent) feel more alarm than those under 30 (44 percent). And while 57 percent of Democrats nationwide are deeply concerned, 50 percent of all Republicans share these sentiments.

Much of this shift in attitude originates in disillusionment about government. For example, when asked to explain their concern, one quarter of those sampled—the largest segment—volunteered the belief that "government leaders are corrupt and immoral." As a tobacco farmer in eastern North Carolina put it, "The whole moral character of the country is going downhill or we wouldn't have had a Watergate crisis. People in the top of government are power hungry and they will do almost anything to get and keep their power. They want nothing but raw power. And that's just downright corrupting."

Another 14 percent cited "inflation and the high cost of living" as reasons for their disaffection, while 10 percent mentioned "Watergate" specifically, and 8 percent said "the country is going through too many problems all at the same time."

For the first time in over a decade of opinion sampling, a new majority of disaffected Americans has been found in this country. On a scale of alienation, powerlessness, and cynicism used by the Harris firm since 1966, an average of 55 percent on a four-question scale expressed disenchantment, compared with no more than 29 percent who felt the same way back in 1966. . . .

While blacks have been most alienated (an average 68 percent nationwide), many other groups now express their discontents: residents of big cities (62 percent), people 50 and over (54 percent), residents of the South (54 percent), skilled labor (59 percent), and rural residents (59 percent). In the past year, the most sizable shifts upward were recorded among rural people (up from 45 to 59 percent) and among people who live in the West (up from 45 to 59 percent).

Nor were the four usual statements which made up the scale of alienation the only signs of public disenchantment:

—The proposition that "most people with power try to take advantage of people like yourself" was accepted by 33 percent of the adult public in 1971, rose to 38 percent by mid-1972, but climbed to 55 percent by the fall of 1973.

—The claim that "the tax laws are written to help the rich, not the average man" was believed by 74 percent of the public in 1972 and by precisely the same 74 percent in 1973.

In addition, new sources of alienation and concern were recorded in responses to new questions designed for this study:

—Three in every four people, 75 percent, felt that "wire-tapping and spying under the excuse of national security is a serious threat to people's privacy."

—Almost as many, 74 percent, believed that "special interests get more from the government than the people do."

—A majority of 60 percent agreed with the proposition that "most elective officials are in politics for all they personally can get out of it for themselves."

—A substantial 59 percent felt "the federal government in Washington has been trying to dictate too much what people locally can and cannot do."

—Almost half the public, 49 percent, agreed with the statement that "local government is so disorganized, it's hard to know where to go for help."

CONFIDENCE IN PUBLIC AND PRIVATE INSTITUTIONS

To determine how much of this underlying disaffection is related to discontent with government—as contrasted with other traditional aspects of society—the survey sought to measure levels of confidence in the institutions of government and compare them to levels of trust and respect for the leadership of private activities and institutions.

In only two cases has the standing of any of the key institutions improved since 1966: television news, which has risen in acceptance from 25 percent to 41 percent who expressed "a great deal of confidence in the people running it," and the press, up marginally from 29 to 30 percent. In every other case, confidence in these key institutions has fallen off rather sharply in the past seven years.

However, for most institutions, the low point apparently was reached in 1972. This year gains in confidence have been registered for a number of institutional leaders: medicine has risen from a low of 48 percent to 57 percent; those in charge of running higher education, given the relative calm on college campuses, have gone up from a low of 33 to 44 percent; with the end of the Vietnam conflict, the military has risen in prestige from 35 to 40 percent; religion is up from 30 to 36 percent; the heads of major companies have gone up slightly in respect from 27 to 29 percent; and the heads of organized labor from 15 to 20 percent, in the past year.

Within the federal government establishment, the trend has been mixed. The U.S. Supreme Court has come back from its 1972 low of 28 percent to 33 percent, but still scores well below the 51 percent who expressed a "great deal of confidence" in 1966. The U.S. Senate has risen from 21 to 30 percent just in the past year, but is still below the 42 percent mark recorded in 1966. The House of Representatives has gone up from 21 to 29 percent, but again is under its high water mark of 42 percent of seven years ago.

The one area of government—and, indeed, the only one of all major institutions—which did not show any rise in confidence was the "executive branch of the federal government," which fell from 41 percent in 1966, to 27 percent in 1972, and in 1973 had sunk to a new low of 19 percent who expressed a "great deal of confidence" in it.

OFFICIALS DISCLAIM THE CRISIS

State and local government officials tend to sharply disagree with the public's sense of unusual crisis. By 63-34 percent, state leaders deny there is "something deeply wrong" in the country. Local government officials are less certain, although by 48-45 percent, they, too, tend to dispute the claim that "something is deeply wrong."

Accustomed themselves to urgency, the leaders tend to regard crisis as endemic to democracy, traditional in American history. Asked to explain their reasoning, a significant number of the public officials called crises "inherent" or said that "we always have a crisis." One county official with more than 20 years of service in a major California city views crises as permanent and diagnoses: "The American public is better educated, more aware and interested in the major issues . . . Important issues are quickly and accurately reported . . . (and) this process identifies many problems and negative factors. . . ."

The perception of aroused public awareness, however, contrasts with the assessment of those officials who felt "something was deeply wrong" and who listed "the apathy of the public" as a major contributing factor, along with the immorality of politicians and a loss of respect for authority.

The charge of public apathy runs quite deep among state and local leaders. When asked to name those elements which impede their doing a better job, the second highest impediment on the state leaders' list and the third on the local leaders' list was "an apathetic public," cited by 43 percent of the state officials and 41 percent of their local counterparts.

COMPARATIVE TRUST IN INSTITUTIONS

THE LEADERS AND THE PUBLIC also have somewhat different perceptions of the degree of confidence they have in key institutions in the country. . . .

The leaders and the public tend to agree in their relatively positive assessment of these institutions: local trash collection, medicine, and local police department. They also share these low estimates: law firms, the White House, and the executive branch of the federal government. The officials also agree with the public in their estimate of the Houses of Congress. The leaders tend to show considerably higher esteem for local public schools, and local united fund, state highway systems, the U.S. Supreme Court, major companies, and local tax assessment, and, above all, for local government leaders.

Viewing local government services as a separate category—one for which no comparative trends are available—it is significant that both the leaders and their constituents share a relatively high regard for the work done in education, sanitation and law enforcement, and for state highway construction and maintenance. The one local government function that earns the leaders' confidence but the public's disdain is tax assessment.

The leaders have less respect for a number of institutions than the general public: higher educational institutions, the military, organized religion, and organized labor. However, most striking is the wide disparity between the confidence levels of state and local leadership in television news and the press and those held by the public. A rather high 41 percent of the public expresses a "great deal" of confidence in TV news, but no more than 17 percent of the leaders share this feeling. In the case of the press, 30 percent of the public holds that medium in high regard, compared with no more than 19 percent of the leaders.

CONFIDENCE IN LOCAL, STATE, AND FEDERAL GOVERNMENT

THE PUBLIC AND PUBLIC OFFICIALS in the survey are at real odds in their estimate about what has happened to public confidence in local, state, and federal government. . . .

A majority of the public tends to feel that both state and local government have remained static in their esteem, although in both cases approximately twice as many feel less confidence in these levels of government as feel more confidence. State officials sharply disagree with the public estimate and credit their type of government with a substantial rise in confidence. Local officials also disagree with the public and believe local government has earned more confidence.

CONFIDENCE IN LOCAL GOVERNMENT

THE REASONS for these differences emerged when all those interviewed were asked to say why they felt confidence had risen, diminished, or stayed the same. The public tends to see local leaders as promising action they never deliver, and 10 percent of the people view local government as being "inefficient and inept" in the way it is run. As a 47-year-old worker in Cleveland put it: "Sure, around election time, the politicians promise us a city like we've never seen. But after the election, all the promises are empty, and we go into four more years of decay." A doctor in Winnetka, Illinois said: "You can bet on one thing: local government will attract people who are not well trained, are political hangers-on, and are more interested in collecting their pay than in doing a job for local government."

Local government leaders disagree. They tend to feel that their level of government has become more responsive in recent years and that the excellence of performance has sharply risen. As the mayor of a medium-sized southwestern city said, "In the past five years, for the first time we have had real professionals on the payroll to do the job. They know modern budgeting, capital outlay management, and long range planning. Elected officials know they will be held accountable, not for what they promise, but what they do." This kind of recognition simply was not forthcoming from the public in any numbers approximating the general commendation leaders feel they deserve.

CONFIDENCE IN STATE GOVERNMENT

AT THE STATE LEVEL, the public tends to be critical of "politicians out for themselves" and complains that "we have Watergates of our own right here in this state." As a housewife in a large eastern state put it: "The governor here seems more intent on reaching a higher place in political life than in helping the people. He just wants to feather his own nest, and couldn't care less about what kind of nests we live in." A resident of Boston added: "The older I get the more I know, and the more I know, the more I know that state government is made up of politicians who are on the take and willing to make a deal for themselves any time at the expense of the public."

Again, state officials vehemently disagree. They believe they have recruited a much higher caliber of officials in the past five years and that the public has kept them on their toes much more than before. As the governor of a Deep South state said: "State government is where the better talent is gravitating to these days. In my own experience, we are finding young people better trained and more motivated than ever before who will not go to work for the federal government, but will come to work for state government. It is almost as though many talented people want to rediscover government at the state level these days." Again, if this governor is correct, then the American people by and large simply have not heard about it.

CONFIDENCE IN THE FEDERAL GOVERNMENT

IN ONE RESPECT, the public and public officials do agree: confidence in the federal government has dropped. And they tend to agree on the basic reasons for this decline: Watergate, inflation, and lack of openness and candor from governmental leaders. Officials also list federal remoteness and inefficiency as contributing factors, while the people cite a general distrust of the executive branch as well.

As a secretary in Grand Rapids, Michigan put it: "Every day when I wake up I feel something new in the way of trouble is coming out of Washington. Another rise in the cost of living, the government selling food and then we have shortages, another terrible scandal with Watergate. It's all too discouraging for words." In Ashland, Kentucky, a store owner said: "People now want some changes made, but nothing good comes out. The laws are all written for the rich and the people who know the right people." The lieutenant governor of a border state added: "What a mess. We have had extortionist campaign collections and a Congress that is more political than statesmanlike and an executive branch that's covert, secretive, and dishonest."

Leaders, when asked at the beginning of each questionnaire to list the "main reasons" for the loss of confidence in public officials, overwhelmingly volunteered "corruption, use of office and public funds for personal gain" (49 percent of the mentions) and "Watergate" (28 percent). Even though their responses to other, later queries revealed a tendency to play down these considerations, in their first answer the leaders showed their clear bias toward blaming the federal government for many of the nation's ills.

Observation: The American people tend to feel that much work is needed to restore confidence in government at all levels. One of the marks of state and local leadership is the conviction that the crisis in responsiveness in government is essentially a federal problem. They tend to believe that federal actions have cast a cloud over politics and politicians generally, but they also tend to believe that their own levels of government are exceptions to the rule.

The public would suggest in turn that state and local officials have much to correct close to home before putting the bulk of blame on the federal government. But there is also no doubt that the public shares the state and local leaders' concern that the federal establishment has fallen precipitously from grace. And, together, both would agree that restoration of confidence in the federal government would be a major and significant step forward in enhancing confidence in government at all levels.

WHAT SIGNIFICANT PROBLEMS FACE AMERICA?

In the last eighteen months, America's preoccupations have changed dramatically. From a high level of concern with the Vietnam War in May 1972, public attention has shifted to alarm at corruption in government. That issue now ranks second only to the traditional worry over economic problems and inflation. . . .

In general, the responses of state and local officials paralleled those of the public in reading national concerns, if not their causes. Leaders gave integrity in government first place in their mentions (58 percent), followed closely by inflation (55 percent), and then the energy shortage (21 percent), crime (19 percent), pollution (15 percent), welfare reform (11 percent), and taxes (10 percent).

The leaders and the public agree on what the real problems are for most Americans: the high price of meat and other food, the lack of trust and confidence in government (mainly federal, however, in the eyes of state and local officials), people's troubles in making ends meet, breathing polluted air, the pressures of day-to-day living, and too much overcrowding and noise. Officials also agree with the public that local government, police and fire protection, trash collection and keeping the streets clean do not present major personal problems for the majority of Americans.

But there are also real gaps between the public and the leadership. While 70 percent of the public feels that "corrupt politicians" are a real problem for most citizens, no more than 48 percent of the local and state public officials share this view. Compared with 61 percent of the public which feels that the "inability of government to solve problems" is a high priority matter, no more than 37 percent of government leadership feels that way. A majority of 58 percent of the public believes a real problem is "getting people to trust each other," but only a plurality of 47 percent of the leaders share that view. A majority of 56 percent of the people feel "there are too many national crises all the time," but no more than 40 percent of the leaders feel that way. A majority of 54 percent of the public sees as a serious matter "the lack of response by government to problems facing the people," while a minority of 43 percent of the leaders feel the same way.

The leaders tend to believe that today's lack of public trust is almost wholly due to the Watergate disclosures and the charges of corruption against a relatively few highly placed public officials at the federal levels. They believe that this situation can be rectified by passing laws which provide a more stringent code of ethics for men in public life, by electing public officials more responsive to public needs, finding leaders with more integrity, reforming campaign financing laws, educating the public to the real issues facing the country, and getting the news media to report more fairly. In other words, the state and local leaders feel that if the federal government responds to the specific wrongs which have been disclosed in the Watergate investigation, then much of the current malaise could be cleared up rapidly.

The public also wants a prompt and drastic response to the Watergate disclosures, but feels that government at all levels has a credibility problem, must adopt methods of far more openness and an end to secrecy, and, above all, must learn to deliver on promises much more fully. And the people are not quite as sanguine as the leaders that men of integrity can be readily found to serve in high public office, although neither the public nor the leadership has lost faith that government can be conducted with efficiency and effectiveness.

LEADERS FOR A DAY: IF PEOPLE MET POWER

Given a chance to express themselves and their concern directly to the top executive officials in their community, their state and their country, Americans overwhelmingly would choose Watergate as the issue they would raise in the White House, but picked taxes and school funds as the first gripes to hand their governors, and street repair, traffic congestion and police performance as the major problems to lay before their mayors. As measurements of confidence in the different levels of government, these responses are somewhat deficient. They only dramatize the immediate, personal credibility problems of the President, without giving clear guidance to the public's view of the responsiveness of the whole federal establishment.

A little more than halfway through each interview, people were asked, "If you could sit down and talk to the President (the governor of your state, the top local official around here), what two or three things would you like to tell him?"

Their responses, if only a measurement of confidence in the case of the President, provide a forthright look at Americans' daily concerns with their government and impressions of their leaders.

In the case of their top local official, at the head of the diffuse list of orders they would give him was street and road repair along with clearing up traffic problems. As a farmer in Wisconsin put it: "These county roads are running down, and he ought to get them paved more often, especially before the winter comes so they don't wash out on us." In a major Eastern city, a lathe operator said: "If the Mayor would pay less attention to going on TV and did something to untangle the traffic mess we have in this town, then maybe we could get this city moving again."

Right up with streets and traffic was the matter of better law enforcement and police protection at the local level. As a housewife in Macon, Georgia, said: "I do wish the police would crack down on the hot-rodders around here and give us all more protection." In Milwaukee, a salesman added: "The local police could do a much better job of patrolling the streets where crime takes place, instead of hanging around the station house."

The public would also like to praise some of their top local officials. As a businessman in Yonkers, New York put it: "I'd like to tell him he's done a good job, the first time in my memory when a mayor has done a real job." But others would also like to see constituent needs better met, particularly in school problems. As the mother of three grade children said in Modesto, California: "Somehow, we always have to take the initiative in getting things done for education. I'd like to know why he won't speak out and lead on some of these pressing school problems."

Taxes are another absorbing issue the public would like to talk to their local authorities about. As a white collar worker in Fort Wayne, Indiana put it: "All I know is that the Mayor keeps asking for more and more taxes and I don't see much coming back for my money. I'd like to ask him where it all goes." Tax inequities, especially on real estate, are another sore issue. As a homeowner in Des Moines, Iowa, said: "I'd like to know how the tax assessment works and why we seem to pay more than other people with better houses and more land."

The issue of honesty and corruption also cropped up at the local level, although not as much as in the case of state and federal governments. A taxpayer in a large midwestern city said: "I'd remind him about how councilmen in this city can buy their way into office and ask him to check this and cut it out once and for all. I'd like to see his answer to that one."

At the state level, the nation's governors would be confronted with a somewhat different roster of comments and queries. At the top of the list of things people would like to talk to their governors about is taxes. As important as "high taxes" are, the variety of state taxes worries people even more. As a department clerk in Delaware put it: "I'd ask the Governor why there is always another kind of tax on everything you buy and for everything you do. It's just one tax after another. Too much for me to take."

But a substantial number would also like to praise their governor. As a young lawyer in a southern state put it: "I'd like to give him some encouragement, tell him he's doing 'A-OK' on the job and that's why we reelected him and would do it again. You know, there aren't many in office you can say that to these days."

On the other hand, almost as many citizens would like to urge their own governor to be more active, to get more done. As a New England store owner put it: "I'd tell him to get more life into himself, not to be so dull, have more spirit, take the leadership bit in his teeth more. He's too passive for my tastes."

The two specific problem areas the public would present to their governor above any others are education and roads. On education, a housewife in Tulare, California, put it this way: "We're always patting ourselves on the back in California about our quality education. But I'd like to ask the Governor to stop taking the praise and take a hard look at just where all the quality has disappeared to in our public schools." On highways, people tended to have specific complaints about the state of particular roads. One small-town resident outside of Wilkes-Barre, Pennsylvania, said: "We've had a lot of our roads gutted from the floods back a spell. I'd like to ask the Governor when he's going to get it all cleaned up and repaired and back in good order."

Governors would also have to handle some complaints about the welfare system. As an engineer in Arizona said: "I feel more and more of my taxes are going for welfare payments every year and it's like a spigot that can't be turned off. Isn't there some way to get those people off the rolls and get them to earn an honest living."

If people had the chance to sit down and talk with the President of the United States, the central thrust of their message would be considerably different from those they would give their top local and state officials. Most people would have more than one thing they would like to get off their chests in talking to the President.

Easily at the top of the list, with a 74 percent voluntary response, were messages from the people concerning honesty and integrity in office at the federal level. At the top of the list was "tell the truth about Watergate," followed by "be honest," "resign," "don't be crooked," "listen to the people more," "release all the Watergate tapes," "stop wrecking government," "get better advisors," "I wouldn't talk to him," "don't be so secretive," "stop using government money for personal use," "cooperate more with Congress," "become more moral and religious," and "restore individual freedom in the country."

After the firing of Special Prosecutor Archibald Cox, the Harris Survey rechecked this question among 1008 respondents in a nationwide telephone recheck survey and found no substantive change in the magnitude of the number of the people who would want to raise with President Nixon questions concerning Watergate and integrity. In fact, the total number of responses indicating a desire to raise questions of this type with the President came to precisely the same 74 percent as in the first survey.

A second area people would like to talk to the President about concerned economic matters, volunteered by an aggregate 51 percent. People would like to express their worry over inflation, urge the President not to raise taxes, and would like to see more security for the elderly. A third major area centers on foreign policy, volunteered by 21 percent: keep the country out of war, handle Russia and China warily but also keep the door open to making peace with them. Also several would like to praise the President for his role in ending U. S. involvement in the war in Vietnam.

Two other areas of importance also emerged in the hypothetical conversation people would like to have with President Nixon. Some 20 percent volunteered comments in the social area: the need to help the poor more, turning more to our problems here at home, helping solve the energy shortage on an equitable basis, and help in cleaning up the environment. Finally, with a 14 percent response, the people said they would talk with the President about personal matters, concerning his own record and life: tell him how much they admire his courage, that he should stick in there and do his job, that he ought to stay in Washington more, ask him why he wants to be President, and talk about his wife and daughters. Most of these personal comments were largely favorable to Mr. Nixon.

THE QUALITY OF LIFE

AS A FINAL MEASURE of levels of confidence, the survey put two broad questions to leaders and officials, asking them to assess the "quality of life" in America now in comparison to ten years ago and to indicate the positive or negative impact of all levels of government on that quality.

Once again, sharp differences between the public and the leadership emerged. By 45-35 percent, the public tends to believe that the quality of life in the country has deteriorated. However, by a thumping 84-6 percent, state leaders believe the quality of life has improved and local leaders share this optimism by 55-24 percent. The leaders believe that the standard of living in the country has increased, that people have much more free time to enjoy themselves, and that housing has improved. The public, citing worries that range from money to morality, disputes the leaders' cheerful outlook.

The public, for example, is much more disturbed than the officials about what inflation has done to them. As a young medical engineer in Del Ray, Florida, put it: "I feel I have a permanent hand in my pocket, picking my money out every couple of hours. That isn't comfortable." A retired man in Sarasota added: "I thought I had worked all my life to retire comfortably. Now inflation is out of control, and I feel poor all the time."

Still another public complaint about the quality of life is that crime has not been checked. As a 44-year-old processing worker in Texarkana, Texas, put it: "We get a lot of talk about law and order and nobody seems to do much or care much if we actually have it. That makes the quality of life worse, as far as I'm concerned." Others talked about drug abuse, Watergate, loss of confidence in government, erosion of moral standards, shortages of food and gasoline, unrest, and high taxes.

In believing that the quality of life has improved, state and local leaders were inclined to give government at all levels credit for the improvement. State leaders, for example, believe by 78-1 percent that state government has made a real contribution toward improving the quality of life. Local leaders, by 62-5 percent, believe local government has helped improve the quality of life. In addition, by 61-9 percent, state leaders think the federal government has helped contribute to the improvement of the quality of life in the country, and local leaders agree with them by 43-25 percent. The public disagrees by 37-23 percent, with 34 percent seeing no change from the federal input into a better life in the United States.

Index

Note: An asterisk (*) following a proper name indicates that the person is the author of one or more of the selections in this volume. In the case of multiple references, the more important ones are listed first.